World's Largest Stamp Firm — founded in 1916

Dear Collector:

FOREWORD

This new 1988 edition of the Harris Postage Stamp Catalog has been substantially revised to represent today's stamp market. There were thousands of price changes — mainly up, some down — that reflect the increasing activity in the stamp world generated by the return of the true collector to the hobby.

The Harris Postage Stamp Catalog remains the most comprehensive and affordable U.S. price reference guide available. Although we no longer find it practical to maintain an inventory of all the items listed in this catalog, we have kept the catalog fairly complete in order to retain its value as a reference guide. If you are unable to obtain your needs through your local stamp dealer or hobby center, please write to us and ask for our latest Direct Mail Catalog which lists our basic stamp line and numerous special offers.

In addition to our basic catalog, we are pleased to include two valuable aids: a handy Stamp Identifier (pages 298-308) and a Grading Guide (pages 295-297), both of which have been designed to help beginning collectors as well as more advanced philatelists improve their understanding of our hobby. We also list a comprehensive selection of stamp collecting supplies.

Before you place your order, please read the Terms and General Information on page ii. You may also want to consider other Harris collector services as outlined on page v and vi.

Although we make every effort to come up with the best possible Stamp Catalog, we realize that not everyone will always agree with our pricing decisions, etc. This catalog is meant to be your catalog and I hope you will contact me whenever you have any suggestions as to how we can improve its value to the stamp collector.

Sincerely yours,

David S. Macdonald
Editor

STREET ADDRESS	**MAILING ADDRESS**
H.E. Harris & Co., Inc.	(For fastest service)
Lafayette West Industrial Park	H.E. Harris & Co., Inc.
170 West Road	Box 7082
Portsmouth, NH 03801	Portsmouth, NH 03801

TERMS AND GENERAL INFORMATION

1988 EDITION

Prices in this edition will generally be effective until August 31, 1988, subject to conditions mentioned under 'Our Prices Are Net,' below.

Our guarantee protects you. All stamps are guaranteed genuine; and in addition, any purchases which for any reason whatsoever should prove unsatisfactory upon receipt and examination may be returned for prompt and cheerful exchange, credit or cash refund. Our only stipulation is that returns should be made within thirty days, **in the original envelope or container, and accompanied by the original order form.**

Each cash order must total at least $5.00, charge orders $15.00. Due to present day handling costs, and because of our continuing desire to keep prices as low as possible, it is necessary to require that individual cash orders must total at least $5.00, and charge orders $15.00. Also, please see "How To Write Your Order.'

Payment should be enclosed with your order (unless you now have or wish to open a charge account with us) in any form that is most convenient for you: check, money order, or — by registered mail only — currency. Add 40% for Canadian Funds. **MasterCard and VISA** are accepted.

Canada customs duties are extra and must be paid by the customer.

Our prices are net. It will be our policy, during the life of this catalog edition, to try to maintain the quotations published herein — even though the market (over which we have no control) has been volatile for a number of years. Occasional price increases during the life of this edition may be absolutely unavoidable, but you are always fully protected by our guarantee that anything you order may be returned — because of price or any other reason. We also reserve the right to limit quantities on certain items if necessary.

Inquiries or remarks should be made on a separate sheet of paper, addressed to Customer Service Department. This will help us; more importantly, it will insure prompt attention to your orders and inquiries.

This list supersedes all previous lists.

INTERNATIONAL AWARD WINNING
HARRIS REFERENCE
CATALOG
1988 Edition

POSTAGE
STAMP
PRICES
of the
UNITED STATES
UNITED NATIONS
CANADA & PROVINCES

Plus: Confederate States, U.S. Possessions,
U.S. Trust Territories,
Albums and Accessories,
Comprehensive U.S. Stamp Identifier
Quality and Condition Guide

H.E. HARRIS & CO., INC.

The World's Largest Stamp Firm. Founded in 1916.
170 West Road
Lafayette West Industrial Park
Portsmouth, NH 03801

Stock No. 28600
ISBN 0-937458-43-0
Copyright ©1987 by H.E. Harris & Co., Inc.
All Rights Reserved. Printed in U.S.A.

Scott catalog numbers are used within this publication with the
permission of Scott Publishing Co.

INTRODUCTION TO THE HARRIS CATALOG

Published for over 55 years, the Harris "US/BNA Catalog" as it is often called, lists (with the exception of the great rarities) all stamps of the United States, United Nations and British North America — that is, Canada and Provinces — and shows current retail prices for each, for ordering and for reference purposes. Our stamp listings use, with permission, the numbering system according to the Scott Standard Postage Stamp Catalog, the most widely-used stamp cataloguing system in North America.

Underneath each illustration is the Scott Catalog number of the one or more stamps having that particular design. When more than one issue features the same design, exact identification may be determined by referring to the descriptive text of each number or to the Stamp Identifier section near the back of this catalog.

ABOUT OUR PRICES

We reasonably expect the prices in this catalog to be valid for the entire life of this edition, but once in a while, an unusually active market may force us to increase a few prices. In all such instances, however, you are fully protected by our Harris guarantee of satisfaction, and you may return within thirty days any item that is not fully satisfactory at the price charged. Original order blank must be included.

Whether you use the catalog for ordering or for reference, condition is an important consideration. Our catalog gives prices for unused gum (o.g.); unused, and used stamps.

"Unused" and "used" stamps are just what their names imply. "Mint" stamps are unused stamps that have never been hinged; they are in mint condition, just as they came from the printer. If you require stamps in this condition, please specify "NH". Never Hinged stamps generally command premium prices and are priced accordingly. From 1964 to date, our unused prices are for Fine, Never Hinged quality.

Condition is relative. In the case of certain issues, especially older stamps printed before the days of electronic centering, the very best obtainable copies (which command premium prices) may appear poor by today's centering standards, and yet be very desirable to knowledgeable collectors. Centering on most recent issues is excellent.

THE HARRIS GUARANTEE

All our stamps are guaranteed genuine, and we also stand behind every product that we sell. We are members in good standing with the Better Business Bureau, American Stamp Dealer's Association, International Federation of Stamp Dealers and other business and professional organizations. Our staff of employees includes many qualified philatelists as well as experts in other fields, accounting, data processing, customer service and the like. It is our collective desire to serve you in any way that we can, and to help you get the maximum pleasure out of the world's greatest hobby, stamp collecting.

WHAT IS "H.E. HARRIS & CO., INC."?

H.E. Harris was founded in 1916 by Henry Harris. Starting as a boy, Mr. Harris branched into all areas of stamp collecting, always providing a quality product at fair prices to his growing clientele. Today, over 70 years later, H.E. Harris & Co., Inc. continues to follow his example and backs up every sale with a full 30-day, no-hassle, money-back guarantee. Some of the services provided at Harris are described in the following:

HARRIS MAIL ORDER SALES:

Harris operates one of the largest mail order sales programs in the nation. The Harris Catalog; a 48-page sales brochure published eight times a year, lists our comprehensive line of United States stamps, plate blocks, sheets, first day covers and more, plus Canal Zone, Ryukyu Islands, Marshall Is., Micronesia, Palau, United Nations and Canada. In addition, it contains a broad line of accessories manufactured by Harris and other suppliers.

BARGAIN BULLETINS: Every 6-7 weeks, Harris issues a special 16-page Bargain Bulletin offering U.S., Canada, British and Worldwide stamps, sets, covers and packets at substantial savings from their normal retail price.

WORLDWIDE CATALOG: Harris periodically publishes 32-page catalogs listing thousands of Mint, Never Hinged sets from around the world plus a very broad offering of country, topical and specialty packets.

HARRIS FIRST DAY COVER CLUB:

Through the Harris First Day Cover Club, members are supplied with each newly-issued U.S. stamp on a beautifully cacheted cover bearing the official First Day of Issue Cancellation applied by the post office. Two forms of cachet are available — "Engraved" and "silk" — and club members can choose to receive either or both. A **FREE** Album is provided to new members and periodic special offers add to the value and enjoyment of belonging to the Harris Cover Club.

SCOTT NO.	DESCRIPTION	UNUSED O.G. F	AVG	UNUSED F	AVG	USED F	AVG

GENERAL ISSUES

1,3,948a
Franklin

2,4,948b
Washington

1847. Imperforate

1	5¢ red brown	....	....	....	....	900.00	600.00
1	— Pen cancel	....	....	....	....	525.00	350.00
2	10¢ black	....	....	....	....	2900.00	1950.00
2	— Pen cancel	....	....	....	....	1700.00	1150.00

1875. Reprints of 1847 Issues, without gum

3	5¢ red brown	....	....	2200.00	1500.00	....	....
4	10¢ black	....	....	2350.00	1600.00	....	....

5-9,18-24,40
Franklin

10,11,25,26,41
Washington

12,27-30A,42
Jefferson

13-16,31-35,43

17,36,44
Washington

1851-56. Imperforate

5A	1¢ blue (Ib)	....	....	....	....	5000.00	3350.00
6	1¢ blue(Ia)	....	....	....	....	6000.00	4000.00
7	1¢ blue (II)	775.00	500.00	525.00	350.00	125.00	85.00
8	1¢ blue (III)	....	....	5500.00	3650.00	1650.00	1100.00
8A	1¢ blue (IIIa)	....	....	1900.00	1250.00	700.00	475.00
9	1¢ blue (IV)	500.00	335.00	350.00	225.00	115.00	75.00
10	3¢ orange brown (I)	....	....	1450.00	975.00	75.00	50.00
11	3¢ dull red (I)	230.00	150.00	160.00	105.00	10.00	5.75
12	5¢ red brown (I)	....	....	11000.00	7250.00	1650.00	1100.00
13	10¢ green (I)	....	....	9500.00	6350.00	850.00	575.00
14	10¢ green (II)	....	....	1850.00	1250.00	350.00	225.00
15	10¢ green (III)	....	....	1950.00	1300.00	360.00	240.00
16	10¢ green (IV)	....	....	12000.00	8000.00	1700.00	1150.00
17	12¢ black	....	....	2175.00	1450.00	300.00	200.00

1857-61. Same design as prededing Issue, Perf. 15(†)

18	1¢ blue (I)	1100.00	725.00	775.00	475.00	400.00	240.00
19	1¢ blue (Ia)	....	....	10000.00	6000.00	2600.00	1550.00
20	1¢ blue (II)	700.00	425.00	500.00	300.00	190.00	120.00
21	1¢ blue (III)	....	....	4750.00	2800.00	1300.00	775.00
22	1¢ blue (IIIa)	....	625.00	700.00	425.00	250.00	150.00
23	1¢ blue (IV)	....	....	2000.00	1200.00	325.00	195.00
24	1¢ blue (V)	200.00	120.00	140.00	85.00	40.00	24.00
25	3¢ rose (I)	1050.00	625.00	750.00	450.00	40.00	24.00
26	3¢ dull red (II)	110.00	67.50	80.00	47.50	4.75	2.85
26a	3¢ dull red (IIa)	175.00	105.00	125.00	75.00	25.00	15.00

VERY FINE QUALITY: To determine the Very Fine price, add the difference between the Fine and Average prices to the Fine quality price. For example: if the Fine price is $10.00 and the Average price is $6.00, the Very Fine price would be $14.00. From 1935 to date, add 20% to the Fine price to arrive at the Very Fine price.

SCOTT NO.	DESCRIPTION	UNUSED O.G. F	UNUSED O.G. AVG	UNUSED F	UNUSED AVG	USED F	USED AVG
27	5¢ brick red (I)	....	....	8500.00	5150.00	1150.00	685.00
28	5¢ red brown (I)	....	....	1700.00	1000.00	325.00	195.00
28A	5¢ Indian red (I)	....	....	10000.00	6000.00	1650.00	1000.00
29	5¢ brown (I)	1250.00	750.00	875.00	525.00	290.00	175.00
30	5¢ orange brown (II)	1200.00	725.00	875.00	525.00	1000.00	600.00
30A	5¢ brown (II)	700.00	425.00	500.00	a300.00	250.00	150.00
31	10¢ green (I)	....	....	5475.00	3300.00	600.00	365.00
32	10¢ green (II)	....	....	1875.00	1100.00	215.00	125.00
33	10¢ green (III)	....	....	2000.00	1185.00	225.00	135.00
34	10¢ green (IV)	....	....	16000.00	10000.00	1750.00	1050.00
35	10¢ green (V)	295.00	175.00	210.00	125.00	87.50	52.50

37,45
Washington

38,46
Franklin

39,47
Washington

36	12¢ black, Plate I	515.00	315.00	375.00	225.00	110.00	67.50
36b	12¢ black, Plate III	400.00	250.00	285.00	175.00	120.00	72.50
37	24¢ gray lilac	1050.00	625.00	750.00	450.00	235.00	140.00
38	30¢ orange	1275.00	775.00	900.00	550.00	325.00	195.00
39	90¢ blue	....	....	1650.00	1000.00	3350.00	2000.00

1875. Reprints of 1857-61 Issue. Perf. 12 Without Gum

40	1¢ bright blue	....	....	625.00	415.00	....	....
41	3¢ scarlet	....	....	3250.00	2150.00	....	....
42	5¢ orange brown	....	....	1100.00	700.00	....	....
43	10¢ blue green	....	....	2500.00	1600.00	....	....
44	12¢ greenish black	....	....	3000.00	2000.00	....	....
45	24¢ blackish violet	....	....	3250.00	2150.00	....	....
46	30¢ yellow orange	....	....	3150.00	2100.00	....	....
47	90¢ deep blue	....	....	4750.00	3200.00	....	....

**55,63,85A
86,92,102**
Franklin

**56,64-66,74,79,82,
83,85,85C,88,94,104**
Washington

**57,67,75,76,
80,95,105**
Jefferson

**58,62B,68
85D,89,96,10S**
Washington

59,69,85E,90,97,107
Washington

60,70,78,99,109
Washington

61,71,81,100,110
Franklin

62,72,101,111
Washington

1861. First Designs (†) Perf. 12

56	3¢ brown red	1200.00	725.00	825.00	500.00	....	....
62B	10¢ dark green	....	....	5500.00	3500.00	550.00	325.00

1861-62. Second Design (†) Perf. 12

63	1¢ blue	170.00	100.00	120.00	72.50	27.50	16.50
64	3¢ pink	....	....	3975.00	2500.00	295.00	180.00
64b	3¢ rose pink	425.00	250.00	300.00	180.00	67.50	40.00
65	3¢ rose	95.00	57.50	67.50	40.00	2.25	1.35
66	3¢ lake	....	....	1900.00	1175.00	....	....
67	5¢ buff	....	....	4350.00	2650.00	425.00	260.00

SCOTT NO.	DESCRIPTION	UNUSED O.G. F	AVG	UNUSED F	AVG	USED F	AVG
68	10¢ yellow green	375.00	225.00	265.00	160.00	37.50	22.50
69	12¢ black	650.00	395.00	485.00	295.00	75.00	45.00
70	24¢ red lilac	825.00	500.00	600.00	365.00	100.00	60.00
71	30¢ orange	725.00	450.00	525.00	325.00	85.00	50.00
72	90¢ blue	1875.00	1100.00	1400.00	850.00	300.00	180.00

73,84,85B,87,93,103
Jackson

77,85F,91,98,108
Lincoln

1861-66 (†)

73	2¢ black	195.00	115.00	140.00	80.00	33.50	20.00
74	3¢ scarlet	....	....	4000.00	2500.00	2000.00	1200.00
75	5¢ red brown	....	....	1400.00	850.00	250.00	150.00
76	5¢ brown	460.00	290.00	335.00	200.00	60.00	36.50
77	15¢ black	725.00	450.00	525.00	325.00	85.00	51.50
78	24¢ lilac	375.00	225.00	275.00	165.00	65.00	38.50

1867. Grill with Points Up
A. Grill Covering Entire Stamp (†)

79	3¢ rose	....	....	1850.00	1100.00	500.00	300.00

C. Grill About 13x16 mm. (†)

83	3¢ rose	....	....	1800.00	1075.00	425.00	250.00

1867. Grill with Points Down
D. Grill About 12x14 mm. (†)

84	2¢ black	....	....	3250.00	1900.00	1000.00	600.00
85	3¢ rose	....	....	1500.00	900.00	475.00	285.00

Z. Grill About 11x14 mm. (†)

85B	2¢ black	1450.00	875.00	1200.00	675.00	375.00	225.00
85C	3¢ rose	....	....	3500.00	2100.00	1000.00	600.00
85E	12¢ black	....	....	1600.00	975.00	570.00	350.00

E. Grill About 11x13 mm. (†)

86	1¢ blue	1075.00	650.00	800.00	485.00	265.00	160.00
87	2¢ black	535.00	325.00	385.00	230.00	75.00	42.50
88	3¢ rose	350.00	215.00	260.00	155.00	13.50	8.00
89	10¢ green	1700.00	1000.00	1250.00	750.00	200.00	120.00
90	12¢ black	2000.00	1200.00	1500.00	900.00	200.00	120.00
91	15¢ black	....	....	3150.00	1850.00	500.00	300.00

F. Grill About 9x13 mm. (†)

92	1¢ blue	435.00	260.00	325.00	195.00	110.00	65.00
93	2¢ black	195.00	110.00	140.00	80.00	37.50	20.00
94	3¢ red	125.00	75.00	90.00	55.00	5.50	3.25
95	5¢ brown	1300.00	775.00	950.00	575.00	240.00	145.00
96	10¢ yellow green	900.00	535.00	675.00	400.00	110.00	65.00
97	12¢ black	925.00	550.00	675.00	400.00	125.00	75.00
98	15¢ black	925.00	550.00	675.00	400.00	130.00	80.00
99	24¢ gray lilac	1750.00	1050.00	1250.00	750.00	500.00	300.00
100	30¢ orange	2100.00	1275.00	1500.00	900.00	400.00	240.00
101	90¢ blue	....	....	4500.00	2700.00	1000.00	600.00

Below each illustration we list all catalog numbers of stamps that resemble it. If a particular number under an illustration is not listed with a quotation it is a very scarce variety; reference to a Scott Catalog will give you further information.

ORIGINAL GUM: Prior to 1893, the Unused price is for stamps either without gum or with partial gum. If you require full original gum, use the Unused OG column. Never Hinged quality is scarce on these issues — please write for specific quotations if NH is required.

SCOTT NO.	DESCRIPTION	UNUSED O.G. F	AVG	UNUSED F	AVG	USED F	AVG
	1875. Re-issue of 1861-66 Issue. Hard White Paper						
102	1¢ blue..........................	775.00	515.00	575.00	385.00	900.00	600.00
103	2¢ black..........................	....	....	2850.00	1900.00	4250.00	2850.00
104	3¢ brown red	....	....	3750.00	2500.00	4850.00	3250.00
105	5¢ light brown	....	....	2000.00	1300.00	2500.00	1700.00
106	10¢ green.......................	....	....	2350.00	1500.00	4000.00	2700.00
107	12¢ black.......................	....	....	3250.00	2150.00	4500.00	2950.00
108	15¢ black.......................	....	....	3250.00	2150.00	5000.00	3350.00
109	24¢ deep violet	....	....	4500.00	3000.00	6000.00	4000.00
110	30¢ brownish orange	....	....	4650.00	3100.00	7000.00	4500.00
111	90¢ blue	....	....	6250.00	4150.00	20000.00	12000.00

112,123,133
Franklin

113,124
Pony Express Rider

114,125
Locomotive

115,126
Washington

116,127
Shield and Eagle

117,128
S.S. Adriatic

118,119,129
Landing of Columbus

120,130
Signing of Declaration

121,131
Shield, Eagle & Flags

122,132
Lincoln

SCOTT NO.	DESCRIPTION	UNUSED O.G. F	AVG	UNUSED F	AVG	USED F	AVG
	1869. Grill measuring 9-1/2x9-1/2 mm. (†)						
112	1¢ buff..........................	335.00	200.00	250.00	150.00	87.50	52.50
113	2¢ brown.......................	250.00	150.00	185.00	110.00	35.00	21.50
114	3¢ ultramarine	215.00	130.00	160.00	95.00	7.75	4.65
115	6¢ ultramarine	1150.00	685.00	850.00	515.00	110.00	67.50
116	10¢ yellow	1275.00	775.00	950.00	575.00	110.00	67.50
117	12¢ green.......................	1075.00	650.00	800.00	475.00	115.00	70.00
118	15¢ brown & blue(I)	2500.00	1500.00	1900.00	1150.00	275.00	165.00
119	15¢ brown & blue (II) ...	1275.00	765.00	950.00	575.00	145.00	90.00
120	24¢ green & violet	....	....	2650.00	1600.00	550.00	335.00
121	30¢ blue & carmine	....	....	2400.00	1450.00	285.00	175.00
122	90¢ carmine & black ...	....	....	8500.00	5250.00	1375.00	825.00
	1875. Re-issue of 1869 Issue. Hard White Paper. Without Grill						
123	1¢ buff..........................	475.00	315.00	375.00	250.00	250.00	165.00
124	2¢ brown.......................	550.00	365.00	425.00	285.00	350.00	235.00
125	3¢ blue..........................	....	....	3250.00	2150.00	1500.00	1000.00
126	6¢ blue..........................	1200.00	800.00	950.00	625.00	625.00	425.00
127	10¢ yellow	1950.00	1300.00	1550.00	1050.00	1300.00	875.00
128	12¢ green.......................	2100.00	1400.00	1650.00	1100.00	1300.00	875.00
129	15¢ brown & white (III)	1900.00	1250.00	1500.00	1000.00	600.00	400.00
130	24¢ green & violet	1750.00	1150.00	1400.00	950.00	600.00	400.00
131	30¢ blue & carmine	2500.00	1650.00	1950.00	1300.00	1100.00	750.00
132	90¢ carmine & black ...	....	....	6250.00	4250.00	8500.00	5750.00
	1880. Same as above. Soft Porous Paper						
133	1¢ buff..........................	295.00	200.00	235.00	160.00	160.00	110.00
133a	1¢ brown orange (w/o gum)	....	....	200.00	135.00	150.00	100.00

(†) means issue is usually very poorly centered.
Perforations may touch the design on "Fine" quality.

NOTE: For further detail on the various types of similar appearing stamps, please refer to our U.S. Stamp Identifier.

SCOTT NO.	DESCRIPTION	UNUSED O.G. F	AVG	UNUSED F	AVG	USED F	AVG

134,145,156,167 182,192,206 — *Franklin*

135,146,157,168,178 180,183,193,203 — *Jackson*

136,147,158,169 184,194,207,214 — *Washington*

137,148,159,170, 186,195,208 — *Lincoln*

138,149,160, 171,196 — *Stanton*

139,150,161,172, 187,188,197,209 — *Jefferson*

140,151,162, 173,198 — *Clay*

141,152,163 174,189,199 — *Webster*

142,153,164 175,200 — *Scott*

143,154,165,176, 190,201,217 — *Hamilton*

144,155,166,177, 191,202,218 — *Perry*

1870-71. Printed by National Bank Note Co. with Grill (†)

134	1¢ ultramarine	610.00	365.00	485.00	295.00	60.00	36.50
135	2¢ red brown	435.00	260.00	350.00	215.00	40.00	25.00
136	3¢ green	325.00	195.00	260.00	160.00	12.50	7.50
137	6¢ carmine	1875.00	1100.00	1500.00	900.00	295.00	180.00
138	7¢ vermilion	1400.00	850.00	1100.00	675.00	250.00	150.00
139	10¢ brown	1750.00	1050.00	1400.00	850.00	425.00	250.00
141	15¢ orange	....	....	1800.00	1100.00	750.00	450.00
143	30¢ black	....	....	4500.00	2750.00	900.00	550.00
144	90¢ carmine	....	....	6250.00	3750.00	825.00	500.00

1870-71. Same as above, without Grill (†)

145	1¢ ultramarine	200.00	120.00	160.00	100.00	10.00	6.00
146	2¢ red brown	95.00	55.00	75.00	45.00	7.00	4.25
147	3¢ green	150.00	90.00	125.00	75.00	.90	.55
148	6¢ carmine	285.00	175.00	225.00	135.00	14.75	8.75
149	7¢ vermilion	435.00	265.00	350.00	215.00	62.50	37.50
150	10¢ brown	285.00	175.00	225.00	135.00	15.00	9.00
151	12¢ dull violet	650.00	400.00	525.00	325.00	70.00	42.50
152	15¢ bright orange	625.00	375.00	500.00	300.00	65.00	40.00
153	24¢ purple	700.00	425.00	575.00	350.00	90.00	55.00
154	30¢ black	1250.00	750.00	1000.00	600.00	95.00	57.50
155	90¢ carmine	1500.00	900.00	1200.00	725.00	185.00	110.00

1873. Same designs as 1870-71 with Secret Marks (†)
Printed by Continental Bank Note Co. Thin hard grayish white paper.

156	1¢ ultramarine	68.50	42.50	55.00	33.50	2.75	1.65
157	2¢ brown	185.00	110.00	150.00	90.00	9.75	5.75
158	3¢ green	52.50	31.50	42.50	25.00	.25	.15
159	6¢ dull pink	235.00	140.00	190.00	115.00	12.50	7.50
160	7¢ orange vermilion	550.00	335.00	425.00	265.00	65.00	40.00
161	10¢ brown	240.00	140.00	195.00	115.00	11.75	7.00
162	12¢ black violet	765.00	465.00	625.00	375.00	77.50	46.50
163	15¢ yellow orange	675.00	425.00	550.00	335.00	62.50	37.50
165	30¢ gray black	675.00	425.00	550.00	335.00	62.50	37.50
166	90¢ rose carmine	1450.00	975.00	1175.00	700.00	210.00	125.00

NOTE: 167-77, 180-81, 192-204, 205C, 211B, 211D, are rare special printings.

ORIGINAL GUM: Prior to 1893, the Unused price is for stamps either without gum or with partial gum. If you require full original gum, use the Unused OG column. Never Hinged quality is scarce on these issues — please write for specific quotations if NH is required.

SCOTT NO.	DESCRIPTION	UNUSED O.G. F	AVG	UNUSED F	AVG	USED F	AVG

179,181,185,204
Taylor

205,205C,216
Garfield

210,211B,213
Washington

211,211D,215
Jackson

212
Franklin

1875. Yellowish Hard paper (†)

| 178 | 2¢ vermilion | 180.00 | 110.00 | 145.00 | 87.50 | 6.00 | 3.65 |
| 179 | 5¢ blue | 200.00 | 120.00 | 160.00 | 95.00 | 10.50 | 6.35 |

1879. Same Type as 1870-75 Issues.
Printed by the American Bank Note Co. soft porous yellowish paper. (†)

182	1¢ dark ultramarine	150.00	90.00	120.00	75.00	1.75	1.05
183	2¢ vermilion	70.00	42.50	57.50	35.00	1.75	1.05
184	3¢ green	57.50	35.00	47.50	28.50	.25	.15
185	5¢ blue	235.00	140.00	195.00	115.00	10.00	6.00
186	6¢ pink	535.00	325.00	450.00	275.00	15.00	9.00
187	10¢ brn. (no secret mark)	850.00	515.00	700.00	425.00	16.00	9.75
188	10¢ brn. (secret mark)	525.00	315.00	435.00	260.00	20.00	12.00
189	15¢ red orange	200.00	120.00	170.00	100.00	18.75	11.00
190	30¢ full black	600.00	365.00	500.00	300.00	35.00	21.50
191	90¢ carmine	1350.00	800.00	1100.00	675.00	175.00	105.00

1882. (NH = OG + 60%)

| 205 | 5¢ yellow brown | 130.00 | 80.00 | 110.00 | 65.00 | 5.85 | 3.50 |

1881-82. Designs of 1873 Issue, Re-engraved. (NH = OG + 60%)

206	1¢ gray blue	45.00	26.75	37.50	22.50	.90	.55
207	3¢ blue green	46.50	28.00	40.00	24.50	.25	.15
208	6¢ rose	265.00	150.00	225.00	135.00	62.50	37.50
208a	6¢ brown red	240.00	145.00	200.00	120.00	75.00	45.00
209	10¢ brown	100.00	60.00	85.00	52.50	2.75	1.65
209b	10¢ black brown	130.00	77.50	110.00	65.00	10.00	6.00

1883 (NH = OG + 60%)

| 210 | 2¢ red brown | 37.50 | 22.50 | 31.50 | 19.00 | .18 | .11 |
| 211 | 4¢ blue green | 175.00 | 100.00 | 150.00 | 90.00 | 9.00 | 5.35 |

1887 (NH = OG + 50%)

212	1¢ ultramarine	75.00	43.50	62.50	37.50	1.00	.60
213	2¢ green	27.50	16.50	23.75	14.00	.16	.10
214	3¢ vermilion	53.75	32.50	46.50	28.00	50.00	30.00

1888 (NH = OG + 50%)

215	4¢ carmine	175.00	105.00	155.00	95.00	13.50	8.25
216	5¢ indigo	150.00	88.50	130.00	80.00	7.95	5.00
217	30¢ orange brown	465.00	280.00	400.00	240.00	90.00	55.00
218	90¢ purple	925.00	565.00	800.00	485.00	185.00	110.00

219
Franklin

219D,220
Washington

221
Jackson

222
Lincoln

223
Grant

224
Garfield

225
Sherman

226
Webster

227
Clay

228
Jefferson

229
Perry

SCOTT NO.	DESCRIPTION	UNUSED O.G.		UNUSED		USED	
		F	AVG	F	AVG	F	AVG

1890-93 (†) (NH = OG + 50%)

SCOTT NO.	DESCRIPTION	F	AVG	F	AVG	F	AVG
219	1¢ dull blue	26.00	15.00	22.50	13.50	.17	.10
219D	2¢ lake	190.00	115.00	165.00	100.00	.70	.40
220	2¢ carmine	22.00	13.00	18.00	11.50	.10	.06
220a	"Cap on left 2"	60.00	35.00	47.50	28.75	1.35	.80
220c	"Cap on both 2's"	150.00	90.00	130.00	80.00	9.50	5.75
221	3¢ purple	78.50	47.50	67.50	40.00	7.50	4.50
222	4¢ dark brown	70.00	42.50	60.00	36.50	2.10	1.25
223	5¢ chocolate	75.00	45.00	65.00	39.50	2.10	1.25
224	6¢ brown red	78.50	47.50	67.50	40.00	21.75	13.00
225	8¢ lilac	47.50	27.50	40.00	24.50	10.50	6.25
226	10¢ green	130.00	72.50	110.00	65.00	2.50	1.50
227	15¢ indigo	190.00	105.00	165.00	95.00	23.50	14.00
228	30¢ black	275.00	160.00	240.00	145.00	25.00	15.50
229	90¢ orange	465.00	265.00	400.00	240.00	125.00	75.00

230
In Sight of Land

231
Landing of Columbus

232
Flagship

233
Fleet of Columbus

234
Soliciting Aid

235
At Barcelona

236
Restored To Favor

237
Presenting Natives

238
Discovery

239
At La Rabida

240
Recall of Columbus

241
Pledging Jewels

242
Columbus in Chains

243
Describing 3rd Voyage

244
Isabella & Columbus

245
Portrait of Columbus

VERY FINE QUALITY: To determine the Very Fine price, add the difference between the Fine and Average prices to the Fine quality price. For example: if the Fine price is $10.00 and the Average price is $6.00, the Very Fine price would be $14.00. From 1935 to date, add 20% to the Fine price to arrive at the Very Fine price.

SCOTT NO.	DESCRIPTION	UNUSED N.H. F	AVG	UNUSED O.G F	AVG	USED F	AVG

1893. COLUMBIAN ISSUE

SCOTT NO.	DESCRIPTION	UNUSED N.H. F	AVG	UNUSED O.G F	AVG	USED F	AVG
230-45	1¢-$5, 16 vars., cpl.	22500.00	12700.00	15000.00	9000.00	6650.00	3950.00
230-37	1¢-10¢, 8 varieties	860.00	475.00	575.00	340.00	93.50	55.00
230	1¢ blue	45.00	25.00	29.50	17.50	.50	.30
231	2¢ violet	42.50	24.00	28.50	17.00	.12	.07
231c	2¢ "broken hat"	125.00	72.50	85.00	52.50	.60	.35
232	3¢ green	90.00	50.00	60.00	36.50	22.50	13.50
233	4¢ ultramarine	120.00	66.50	80.00	47.50	8.75	5.25
234	5¢ chocolate	145.00	82.50	95.00	57.50	10.75	6.50
235	6¢ purple	120.00	66.50	80.00	47.50	31.50	18.75
236	8¢ magenta	100.00	55.00	67.50	40.00	11.00	6.50
237	10¢ black brown	200.00	110.00	135.00	80.00	9.00	5.50
238	15¢ dark green	375.00	210.00	250.00	150.00	95.00	57.50
239	30¢ orange brown	550.00	310.00	365.00	220.00	105.00	62.50
240	50¢ slate blue	625.00	350.00	415.00	250.00	155.00	95.00
241	$1 salmon	1950.00	1100.00	1275.00	765.00	675.00	400.00
242	$2 brown red	2150.00	1200.00	1400.00	850.00	600.00	365.00
243	$3 yellow green	4350.00	2500.00	2850.00	1750.00	1300.00	775.00
244	$4 crimson lake	5850.00	3250.00	3875.00	2300.00	1650.00	975.00
245	$5 black	6150.00	3400.00	4000.00	2400.00	2000.00	1200.00

246,247, 264,279 — Franklin   **248-252,265-267,279B** — Washington   **253,268** — Jackson   **254,269,280** — Lincoln   **255,270,281** — Grant   **256,271,282** — Garfield

257,272 — Sherman   **258,273,282C,283** — Webster   **259,274,284** — Clay   **260,275,** — Jefferson

261,261A,276,276A — Perry   **262,277** — Madison   **263,278** — Marshall

1894. Unwatermarked (†)

SCOTT NO.	DESCRIPTION	UNUSED N.H. F	AVG	UNUSED O.G F	AVG	USED F	AVG
246	1¢ ultramarine	35.00	21.00	23.75	14.50	4.50	2.75
247	1¢ blue	87.50	50.00	58.50	35.00	2.00	1.20
248	2¢ pink, Type I	29.50	16.50	19.50	11.50	2.50	1.50
249	2¢ carmine lake, Type I	215.00	120.00	140.00	85.00	1.95	1.15
250	2¢ carmine, Type I	37.50	21.00	25.00	15.00	.35	.22
251	2¢ carmine, Type II	275.00	160.00	185.00	110.00	3.15	1.90
252	2¢ carmine, Type III	145.00	85.00	95.00	56.50	4.75	2.85
253	3¢ purple	135.00	75.00	90.00	53.50	8.75	5.25
254	4¢ dark brown	165.00	90.00	110.00	67.50	3.25	1.95
255	5¢ chocolate	135.00	76.50	90.00	55.00	4.75	2.85
256	6¢ dull brown	250.00	137.50	165.00	97.50	18.50	11.75
257	8¢ violet brown	175.00	95.00	115.00	67.50	13.50	8.00
258	10¢ dark green	300.00	170.00	200.00	120.00	9.00	5.65
259	15¢ dark blue	450.00	250.00	300.00	180.00	62.50	37.50
260	50¢ orange	600.00	335.00	400.00	240.00	100.00	60.00
261	$1 black (I)	1600.00	875.00	1050.00	625.00	285.00	175.00
261A	$1 black (II)	3100.00	1700.00	2050.00	1200.00	550.00	335.00
262	$2 blue	3900.00	2100.00	2550.00	1500.00	675.00	400.00
263	$5 dark green	6000.00	3300.00	3900.00	2350.00	1200.00	725.00

SCOTT NO.	DESCRIPTION	UNUSED NH F	AVG	UNUSED OG F	AVG	USED F	AVG
	1985 Double Line Watermark "USPS" (†)						
264	1¢ blue	11.50	6.50	7.50	4.50	.15	.09
265	2¢ carmine, Type I	45.00	25.00	30.00	18.00	.90	.55
266	2¢ carmine, Type II	41.50	22.00	27.50	16.50	3.00	1.80
267	2¢ carmine, Type III	8.25	4.75	5.50	3.35	.11	.07
268	3¢ purple	60.00	35.00	40.00	24.00	1.30	.80
269	4¢ dark brown	60.00	35.00	40.00	24.00	1.60	1.00
270	5¢ chocolate	60.00	33.75	40.00	24.00	2.25	1.35
271	6¢ dull brown	120.00	65.00	77.50	46.50	4.75	2.85
272	8¢ violet	72.50	39.50	47.50	28.50	1.50	.95
273	10¢ dark green	95.00	52.50	62.50	37.50	1.95	1.20
274	15¢ dark blue	300.00	170.00	200.00	120.00	11.75	7.00
275	50¢ dull orange	475.00	270.00	315.00	190.00	27.50	16.50
276	$1 black (I)	1100.00	600.00	700.00	425.00	90.00	55.00
276A	$1 black (III)	2300.00	1300.00	1500.00	900.00	140.00	85.00
277	$2 blue	1700.00	925.00	1100.00	650.00	325.00	195.00
278	$5 dark green	3500.00	2000.00	2300.00	1400.00	465.00	280.00
	1898 New Colors (†)						
279	1¢ deep green	19.50	10.75	12.75	7.65	.13	.08
279B	2¢ red	19.00	10.50	12.50	7.50	.13	.08
279c	2¢ rose carmine	250.00	140.00	165.00	100.00	37.50	22.50
279d	2¢ orange red	20.00	11.00	13.50	8.00	.17	.11
280	4¢ rose brown	52.50	30.00	35.00	21.00	1.10	.65
281	5¢ dark blue	62.50	35.00	41.50	25.00	1.00	.60
282	6¢ lake	82.50	47.50	55.00	33.50	2.95	1.75
282C	10¢ brown (I)	275.00	150.00	180.00	110.00	2.75	1.70
283	10¢ orange brown (II)	175.00	100.00	115.00	70.00	2.50	1.50
284	15¢ olive green	215.00	120.00	140.00	85.00	9.50	5.95

285
Marquette on the Mississippi

286
Farming in the West

287
Indian Hunting Buffalo

288
Fremont on the Rocky Mountains

289
Troops Guarding Train

290
Hardships of Emigration

291
Western Mining Prospector

292
Western Cattle in Storm

293
Eads Bridge over Mississippi River

1898 TRANS-MISSISSIPPI EXPOSITION ISSUE

SCOTT NO.	DESCRIPTION	UNUSED NH F	AVG	UNUSED OG F	AVG	USED F	AVG
285-93	1¢-$2, 9 vars., cpl.	11,000.00	6450.00	6900.00	4500.00	2000.00	1225.00
285-90	1¢-10¢, 6 varieties	1190.00	715.00	785.00	500.00	148.50	88.75
285	1¢ yellow green	55.00	33.50	36.50	23.00	7.00	4.25
286	2¢ copper red	50.00	30.00	33.75	21.50	1.85	1.10
287	4¢ orange	250.00	150.00	165.00	105.00	33.50	19.75
288	5¢ dull blue	200.00	120.00	135.00	85.00	30.00	18.00
289	8¢ violet brown	295.00	175.00	195.00	125.00	50.00	30.00
290	10¢ gray violet	350.00	210.00	225.00	145.00	27.50	16.50
291	50¢ sage green	1300.00	775.00	850.00	550.00	190.00	120.00
292	$1 black	3400.00	2000.00	2200.00	1400.00	725.00	435.00
293	$2 orange brown	5150.00	3000.00	3350.00	2100.00	975.00	600.00

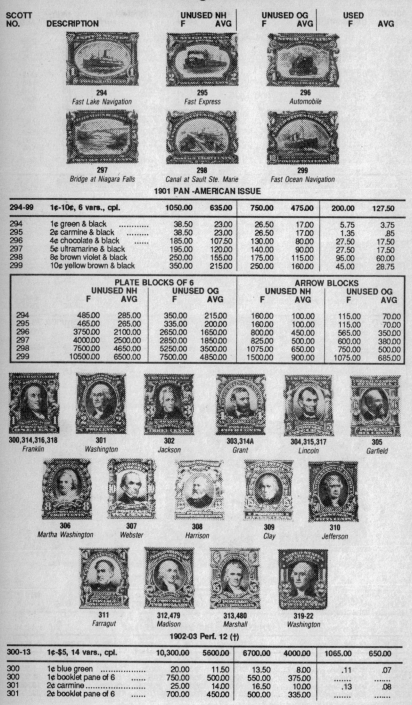

SCOTT NO.	DESCRIPTION	UNUSED NH		UNUSED OG		USED	
		F	AVG	F	AVG	F	AVG

294 — Fast Lake Navigation
295 — Fast Express
296 — Automobile
297 — Bridge at Niagara Falls
298 — Canal at Sault Ste. Marie
299 — Fast Ocean Navigation

1901 PAN-AMERICAN ISSUE

SCOTT NO.	DESCRIPTION	F	AVG	F	AVG	F	AVG
294-99	1¢-10¢, 6 vars., cpl.	1050.00	635.00	750.00	475.00	200.00	127.50
294	1¢ green & black	38.50	23.00	26.50	17.00	5.75	3.75
295	2¢ carmine & black	38.50	23.00	26.50	17.00	1.35	.85
296	4¢ chocolate & black	185.00	107.50	130.00	80.00	27.50	17.50
297	5¢ ultramarine & black	195.00	120.00	140.00	90.00	27.50	17.50
298	8¢ brown violet & black	250.00	155.00	175.00	115.00	95.00	60.00
299	10¢ yellow brown & black	350.00	215.00	250.00	160.00	45.00	28.75

	PLATE BLOCKS OF 6				ARROW BLOCKS			
	UNUSED NH		UNUSED OG		UNUSED NH		UNUSED OG	
	F	AVG	F	AVG	F	AVG	F	AVG
294	485.00	285.00	350.00	215.00	160.00	100.00	115.00	70.00
295	465.00	265.00	335.00	200.00	160.00	100.00	115.00	70.00
296	3750.00	2100.00	2650.00	1650.00	800.00	450.00	565.00	350.00
297	4000.00	2500.00	2850.00	1850.00	825.00	500.00	600.00	380.00
298	7500.00	4650.00	5250.00	3500.00	1075.00	650.00	750.00	500.00
299	10500.00	6500.00	7500.00	4850.00	1500.00	900.00	1075.00	685.00

300,314,316,318 — Franklin
301 — Washington
302 — Jackson
303,314A — Grant
304,315,317 — Lincoln
305 — Garfield
306 — Martha Washington
307 — Webster
308 — Harrison
309 — Clay
310 — Jefferson
311 — Farragut
312,479 — Madison
313,480 — Marshall
319-22 — Washington

1902-03 Perf. 12 (†)

SCOTT NO.	DESCRIPTION	F	AVG	F	AVG	F	AVG
300-13	1¢-$5, 14 vars., cpl.	10,300.00	5600.00	6700.00	4000.00	1065.00	650.00
300	1¢ blue green	20.00	11.50	13.50	8.00	.11	.07
300	1¢ booklet pane of 6	750.00	500.00	550.00	375.00	....	....
301	2¢ carmine	25.00	14.00	16.50	10.00	.13	.08
301	2¢ booklet pane of 6	700.00	450.00	500.00	335.00	....	....

SCOTT NO.	DESCRIPTION	UNUSED NH F	AVG	UNUSED OG F	AVG	USED F	AVG
302	3¢ violet	87.50	50.00	57.50	35.00	4.00	2.40
303	4¢ brown	87.50	50.00	57.50	35.00	1.30	.80
304	5¢ blue	105.00	57.50	67.50	40.00	1.20	.75
305	6¢ claret	110.00	61.50	72.50	43.50	3.75	2.25
306	8¢ violet black	65.00	36.50	43.50	26.00	2.75	1.65
307	10¢ red brown	125.00	68.50	80.00	48.50	1.85	1.10
308	13¢ purple black	65.00	36.50	43.50	26.00	11.00	6.65
309	15¢ olive green	250.00	140.00	165.00	100.00	9.50	5.65
310	50¢ orange	875.00	500.00	575.00	350.00	29.00	17.50
311	$1 black	1475.00	775.00	975.00	575.00	90.00	55.00
312	$2 dark blue	1875.00	1000.00	1250.00	750.00	225.00	135.00
313	$2 dark green	5150.00	2850.00	3350.00	2000.00	700.00	425.00

1906 Imperforate

This and all subsequent imperforate issues can usually be supplied in unused pairs at double the single price.

314	1¢ blue green	52.50	33.50	38.75	26.50	30.00	20.00
315	5¢ blue	950.00	600.00	675.00	450.00	350.00	225.00

1903 Perf. 12 (†)

319	2¢ carmine, Die I	13.75	7.75	9.75	5.75	.13	.08
319g	2¢ booklet pane of 6	175.00	100.00	125.00	75.00	....	....
319f	2¢ lake, Die II	14.75	8.50	10.50	6.25	.25	.15

1906 Imperforate

320	2¢ carmine, Die I	50.00	31.75	37.50	25.00	30.00	20.00
320a	2¢ lake, Die II	150.00	90.00	110.00	70.00	45.00	30.00

SCOTT NO.	UNUSED NH F	AVG	UNUSED OG F	AVG	SCOTT NO.	UNUSED NH F	AVG	UNUSED OG F	AVG
	PLATE BLOCKS OF 6					**CENTER LINE BLOCKS**			
300	350.00	195.00	230.00	135.00	314	350.00	225.00	250.00	165.00
301	375.00	210.00	250.00	150.00	320	365.00	235.00	260.00	175.00
314	465.00	285.00	335.00	225.00		**ARROW BLOCKS**			
319	195.00	110.00	130.00	77.50	314	220.00	140.00	160.00	110.00
320	525.00	325.00	375.00	250.00	320	220.00	140.00	160.00	110.00

323
Robert R. Livingston

324
Jefferson

325
Monroe

326
McKinley

327
Map of Louisiana Purchase

SCOTT NO.	DESCRIPTION	UNUSED NH F	AVG	UNUSED OG F	AVG	USED F	AVG
	1904 LOUISIANA PURCHASE ISSUE						
323-27	1¢-10¢, 5 vars., cpl.	790.00	475.00	550.00	350.00	130.00	85.00
323	1¢ green	57.50	33.50	38.75	25.75	6.75	4.50
324	2¢ carmine	47.50	28.50	33.75	21.50	2.25	1.50
325	3¢ violet	160.00	100.00	110.00	72.50	45.00	30.00
326	5¢ dark blue	195.00	115.00	135.00	85.00	30.00	19.50
327	10¢ red brown	335.00	200.00	240.00	150.00	50.00	32.50

SCOTT NO.	DESCRIPTION	UNUSED NH F	AVG	UNUSED OG F	AVG	USED F	AVG

328
Capt. John Smith

329
Founding of Jamestown

330
Pocahontas

1907 JAMESTOWN EXPOSITION ISSUE (†)

SCOTT NO.	DESCRIPTION	UNUSED NH F	AVG	UNUSED OG F	AVG	USED F	AVG
328-30	1¢-5¢, 3 vars., cpl.	310.00	165.00	220.00	120.00	57.50	32.50
328	1¢ green	37.50	19.50	26.50	14.50	6.75	3.85
329	2¢ carmine	50.00	27.00	35.00	20.00	4.35	2.40
330	5¢ blue	225.00	120.00	160.00	90.00	47.50	26.50

	PLATE BLOCKS OF 6				ARROW BLOCKS			
SCOTT NO.	UNUSED NH F	AVG	UNUSED OG F	AVG	UNUSED NH F	AVG	UNUSED OG F	AVG
323	575.00	330.00	385.00	250.00	250.00	145.00	165.00	110.00
324	495.00	300.00	350.00	225.00	200.00	120.00	140.00	92.50
325	1550.00	950.00	1100.00	715.00	675.00	435.00	475.00	310.00
326	1875.00	1150.00	1350.00	850.00	825.00	480.00	575.00	365.00
327	3750.00	2350.00	2650.00	1750.00	1400.00	835.00	1000.00	635.00
328	550.00	290.00	395.00	215.00	157.50	85.00	110.00	60.00
329	735.00	400.00	525.00	300.00	210.00	115.00	150.00	85.00
330	4500.00	2400.00	3250.00	1850.00	965.00	515.00	675.00	385.00

331-392
Franklin

332-393,519
Washington

333-541

SCOTT NO.	DESCRIPTION	UNUSED NH F	AVG	UNUSED OG F	AVG	USED F	AVG

1908-09 Double Line Watermark "USPS" Perf. 12

SCOTT NO.	DESCRIPTION	UNUSED NH F	AVG	UNUSED OG F	AVG	USED F	AVG
331-42	1¢-$1, 12 vars., cpl.	2000.00	1150.00	1400.00	850.00	190.00	112.50
331	1¢ green	13.50	7.75	9.50	5.75	.11	.07
331a	1¢ booklet pane of 6	250.00	140.00	175.00	105.00	....	....
332	2¢ carmine	11.50	7.00	8.75	5.25	.11	.07
332a	2¢ booklet pane of 6	200.00	110.00	140.00	85.00	....	....
333	3¢ violet	55.00	31.00	38.75	23.00	4.25	2.50
334	4¢ orange brown	55.00	31.00	38.75	23.50	1.50	.90
335	5¢ blue	75.00	45.00	55.00	32.50	2.65	1.60
336	6¢ red orange	85.00	48.75	60.00	36.50	6.25	3.75
337	8¢ olive green	62.50	36.50	45.00	27.50	3.50	2.10
338	10¢ yellow	105.00	60.00	75.00	45.00	1.85	1.10
339	13¢ blue green	58.50	33.75	41.50	25.00	36.50	22.00
340	15¢ pale ultramarine	97.50	56.50	70.00	42.50	8.00	4.75
341	50¢ violet	565.00	325.00	395.00	240.00	17.50	10.75
342	$1 violet black	825.00	475.00	575.00	350.00	110.00	65.00

1908-09 Imperforate

SCOTT NO.	DESCRIPTION	UNUSED NH F	AVG	UNUSED OG F	AVG	USED F	AVG
343-47	1¢-5¢, 5 vars., cpl.	240.00	150.00	180.00	120.00	105.00	70.00
343	1¢ green	16.75	10.50	12.50	8.25	5.00	3.35
344	2¢ carmine	23.50	14.75	17.50	11.75	5.00	3.35
345	3¢ deep violet	37.50	23.50	27.50	18.50	22.50	15.00
346	4¢ orange brown	70.00	43.75	52.50	35.00	27.50	18.50
347	5¢ blue	97.50	61.50	72.50	48.50	47.50	31.75

1908-10 Coil Stamps Perf. 12 Horizontally (†)

SCOTT NO.	DESCRIPTION	UNUSED NH F	AVG	UNUSED OG F	AVG	USED F	AVG
348	1¢ green	37.50	21.50	26.50	16.00	18.50	11.50
349	2¢ carmine	72.50	43.50	52.50	32.50	7.75	4.65
350	4¢ orange brown	170.00	97.50	120.00	72.50	80.00	48.50
351	5¢ blue	210.00	117.50	145.00	87.50	100.00	60.00

NOTE: Counterfeits are common on #348-56 and #385-89.

SCOTT NO.	DESCRIPTION	UNUSED NH F	AVG	UNUSED OG F	AVG	USED F	AVG

1909 Coil Stamps Perf. 12 Vertically (†)

SCOTT NO.	DESCRIPTION	UNUSED NH F	AVG	UNUSED OG F	AVG	USED F	AVG
352	1¢ green	95.00	53.50	67.50	40.00	25.00	15.00
353	2¢ carmine	77.50	43.50	55.00	32.50	7.50	4.50
354	4¢ orange brown	210.00	117.50	145.00	87.50	62.50	37.50
355	5¢ blue	225.00	135.00	160.00	100.00	90.00	55.00
356	10¢ yellow	2100.00	1175.00	1450.00	875.00	450.00	275.00

SCOTT NO.	UNUSED NH F	AVG	UNUSED OG F	AVG	SCOTT NO.	UNUSED NH F	AVG	UNUSED OG F	AVG
	PLATE BLOCKS OF 6					**CENTER LINE BLOCKS**			
331	135.00	75.00	95.00	55.00	343	100.00	62.50	75.00	48.50
332	130.00	70.00	90.00	52.50	344	140.00	90.00	105.00	70.00
333	550.00	325.00	400.00	240.00	345	215.00	140.00	160.00	105.00
334	595.00	340.00	425.00	255.00	346	385.00	250.00	285.00	185.00
335	1075.00	635.00	775.00	465.00	347	550.00	350.00	415.00	275.00
337	850.00	495.00	600.00	370.00					
338	415.00	240.00	300.00	180.00		**ARROW BLOCKS**			
339	775.00	450.00	550.00	335.00					
343	165.00	105.00	125.00	82.50	343	72.50	46.50	55.00	36.00
344	275.00	170.00	210.00	140.00	344	105.00	67.50	77.50	51.75
345	450.00	270.00	325.00	215.00	345	160.00	100.00	120.00	80.00
346	775.00	475.00	575.00	385.00	346	295.00	185.00	220.00	145.00
347	1125.00	700.00	835.00	550.00	347	415.00	275.00	310.00	210.00

	COIL LINE PAIRS					COIL PAIRS			
	UNUSED NH F	AVG	UNUSED OG F	AVG		UNUSED NH F	AVG	UNUSED OG F	AVG
348	300.00	165.00	215.00	130.00		90.00	51.50	65.00	38.50
349	350.00	200.00	250.00	150.00		165.00	100.00	120.00	75.00
350	1250.00	700.00	875.00	525.00		375.00	215.00	265.00	160.00
351	1300.00	750.00	925.00	565.00		465.00	260.00	325.00	195.00
352	465.00	260.00	325.00	195.00		220.00	125.00	157.50	92.50
353	465.00	260.00	325.00	195.00		175.00	100.00	125.00	75.00
354	1250.00	700.00	875.00	525.00		475.00	265.00	325.00	200.00
355	1350.00	750.00	90.00	550.00		500.00	300.00	360.00	225.00

SCOTT NO.	DESCRIPTION	UNUSED NH F	AVG	UNUSED OG F	AVG	USED F	AVG

1909 Bluish Gray paper Perf. 12

SCOTT NO.	DESCRIPTION	UNUSED NH F	AVG	UNUSED OG F	AVG	USED F	AVG
357	1¢ green	190.00	110.00	135.00	82.50	125.00	75.00
358	2¢ carmine	160.00	95.00	115.00	70.00	85.00	52.50
359	3¢ violet	2550.00	1435.00	1750.00	1075.00	1350.00	800.00
360	4¢ orange brown	....	....	16,000.00	11,000.00	....	....
361	5¢ blue	....	....	4000.00	2500.00	4500.00	2750.00
362	6¢ orange	1500.00	875.00	1075.00	650.00	775.00	465.00
363	8¢ olive green	....	....	16,500.00	11,500.00	....	....
364	10¢ yellow	1600.00	925.00	1150.00	675.00	800.00	485.00
365	13¢ blue green	3375.00	1900.00	2300.00	1400.00	1250.00	750.00
366	15¢ pale ultramarine	1500.00	875.00	1075.00	650.00	800.00	485.00

367-369
Lincoln

370,371
William H. Seward

372,373
S.S. Clermont

1909 LINCOLN MEMORIAL ISSUE

SCOTT NO.	DESCRIPTION	UNUSED NH F	AVG	UNUSED OG F	AVG	USED F	AVG
367	2¢ carmine, perf.	11.50	7.00	8.50	5.25	3.95	2.35
368	2¢ carmine imperf.	73.50	45.00	55.00	36.50	45.00	30.00
369	2¢ carmine (blue gray pr.)	435.00	265.00	315.00	195.00	250.00	155.00

1909 ALASKA-YUKON ISSUE

| 370 | 2¢ carmine, perf. | 21.00 | 12.00 | 15.00 | 9.00 | 3.25 | 1.95 |
| 371 | 2¢ carmine, imperf. | 100.00 | 62.50 | 75.00 | 50.00 | 50.00 | 33.50 |

1909 HUDSON-FULTON ISSUE

| 372 | 2¢ carmine, perf. | 26.00 | 15.00 | 18.75 | 11.50 | 6.50 | 3.95 |
| 373 | 2¢ carmine, imperf. | 105.00 | 65.00 | 80.00 | 53.50 | 50.00 | 33.50 |

SCOTT NO.	DESCRIPTION	UNUSED NH F	AVG	UNUSED OG F	AVG	USED F	AVG
	1910-11 Single Line Watermark "USPS" Perf. 12						
374-82	1¢-15¢, 9 vars., cpl.	975.00	550.00	685.00	410.00	47.50	28.50
374	1¢ green....................	13.00	7.65	9.50	5.75	.12	.07
374a	1¢ booklet pane of 6	225.00	125.00	160.00	95.00	....	....
375	2¢ carmine..................	12.50	7.00	9.00	5.35	.11	.06
375a	2¢ booklet pane of 6	190.00	105.00	135.00	82.50	....	....
376	3¢ deep violet	27.50	16.00	20.00	12.00	2.50	1.50
377	4¢ brown....................	42.50	24.00	30.00	18.00	.65	.40
378	5¢ blue.....................	42.50	24.00	30.00	18.00	.75	.45
379	6¢ red orange	60.00	33.75	42.50	25.00	1.10	.65
380	8¢ olive green	185.00	110.00	130.00	80.00	18.00	11.00
381	10¢ yellow	185.00	110.00	130.00	80.00	4.75	2.85
382	15¢ ultramarine	425.00	235.00	295.00	175.00	20.00	12.00
	1911 Imperforate						
383	1¢ green....................	8.75	5.50	6.50	4.35	4.25	2.85
384	2¢ carmine..................	13.75	8.15	10.00	6.50	3.50	2.35

SCOTT NO.	UNUSED NH F	AVG	UNUSED OG F	AVG	SCOTT NO.	UNUSED NH F	AVG	UNUSED OG F	AVG
	PLATE BLOCKS OF 6					**CENTER LINE BLOCKS**			
367	265.00	150.00	190.00	120.00	368	435.00	270.00	335.00	215.00
368	575.00	360.00	450.00	290.00	371	595.00	375.00	450.00	300.00
370	450.00	270.00	335.00	210.00	373	650.00	410.00	500.00	335.00
371	800.00	500.00	600.00	400.00	383	70.00	45.00	52.50	35.00
372	475.00	290.00	350.00	225.00	384	135.00	80.00	97.50	62.50
373	850.00	535.00	635.00	425.00					
374	150.00	86.50	110.00	65.00		**ARROW BLOCKS**			
375	140.00	80.00	100.00	60.00					
376	275.00	160.00	200.00	120.00	368	335.00	210.00	250.00	165.00
377	385.00	220.00	275.00	165.00	371	465.00	290.00	345.00	230.00
378	415.00	240.00	300.00	180.00	373	485.00	300.00	365.00	245.00
383	135.00	82.50	97.50	65.00	383	38.50	24.50	28.75	18.75
384	350.00	220.00	265.00	175.00	384	82.50	49.50	60.00	38.75

SCOTT NO.	DESCRIPTION	UNUSED NH F	AVG	UNUSED OG F	AVG	USED F	AVG
	COIL STAMPS						
	1910 Perf. 12 Horizontally (†)						
385	1¢ green...............	41.50	23.50	28.75	17.50	15.75	9.50
386	2¢ carmine.............	58.50	33.50	41.50	25.00	13.75	8.25
	1910-11 Perf. 12 Vertically (†)						
387	1¢ green...............	120.00	70.00	85.00	52.50	27.50	16.50
388	2¢ carmine.............	850.00	495.00	600.00	365.00	87.50	52.50
	1910 Perf. 8-1/2 Horizontally						
390	1¢ green...............	9.00	5.35	6.75	4.00	4.25	2.50
391	2¢ carmine.............	60.00	35.00	42.50	26.50	11.75	7.00
	1910-13 Perf. 8-1/2 Vertically						
392	1¢ green...............	39.75	22.50	28.75	17.00	22.50	13.50
393	2¢ carmine.............	72.50	43.50	52.50	32.50	7.00	4.25
394	3¢ violet	80.00	46.50	57.50	35.00	39.50	24.00
395	4¢ brown...............	80.00	46.50	57.50	35.00	39.50	24.00
396	5¢ blue................	80.00	46.50	57.50	35.00	39.50	24.00

	COIL LINE PAIRS				COIL PAIRS			
	UNUSED NH F	AVG	UNUSED OG F	AVG	UNUSED NH F	AVG	UNUSED OG F	AVG
385	280.00	160.00	200.00	120.00	100.00	57.50	71.50	43.50
386	405.00	260.00	325.00	195.00	140.00	82.50	100.00	60.00
387	485.00	280.00	350.00	210.00	300.00	175.00	210.00	130.00
390	47.50	26.75	33.75	20.00	19.50	11.75	14.75	8.75
391	325.00	190.00	235.00	140.00	135.00	80.00	97.50	60.00
392	175.00	100.00	125.00	75.00	87.50	50.00	65.00	37.50
393	315.00	180.00	225.00	135.00	160.00	95.00	115.00	72.50
394	495.00	285.00	365.00	215.00	175.00	105.00	125.00	77.50
395	495.00	285.00	365.00	215.00	175.00	105.00	125.00	77.50
396	495.00	285.00	365.00	215.00	175.00	105.00	125.00	77.50

SCOTT NO.	DESCRIPTION	UNUSED NH F	AVG	UNUSED OG F	AVG	USED F	AVG

397,401
Balboa

398,402
Panama Canal

399,403
Golden Gate

400,400A,404
Discovery of San Francisco Bay

PANAMA-PACIFIC ISSUE
1913 Perf. 12

SCOTT NO.	DESCRIPTION	UNUSED NH F	AVG	UNUSED OG F	AVG	USED F	AVG
397-400A	1¢-10¢, 5 vas., cpl.	875.00	535.00	625.00	400.00	78.50	46.50
397	1¢ green	32.50	19.50	22.50	14.50	2.10	1.25
398	2¢ carmine	35.00	21.00	25.00	16.00	.90	.55
399	5¢ blue	145.00	90.00	105.00	67.50	16.50	10.00
400	10¢ orange yellow	250.00	155.00	180.00	115.00	32.50	19.50
400A	10¢ orange	425.00	260.00	300.00	195.00	27.50	16.50

1914-15 Perf. 10

SCOTT NO.	DESCRIPTION	UNUSED NH F	AVG	UNUSED OG F	AVG	USED F	AVG
401-04	1¢-10¢, 4 vars., cpl.	2850.00	1735.00	2025.00	1285.00	133.50	80.00
401	1¢ green	60.00	33.75	42.50	25.75	8.00	5.00
402	2¢ carmine	160.00	105.00	110.00	70.00	2.75	1.65
403	5¢ blue	335.00	210.00	240.00	155.00	25.00	15.00
404	10¢ orange	2300.00	1400.00	1650.00	1050.00	100.00	60.00

405-545   **406-546**   **414-518**

1912-14 Single Line Watermark Perf. 12

SCOTT NO.	DESCRIPTION	UNUSED NH F	AVG	UNUSED OG F	AVG	USED F	AVG
405	1¢ green	12.75	7.25	9.00	5.35	.11	.07
405b	1¢ booklet pane of 6	100.00	58.50	72.50	43.50	....	....
406	2¢ carmine	12.00	6.85	8.50	5.15	.11	.07
406a	2¢ booklet pane of 6	110.00	62.50	77.50	46.50	....	....
407	7¢ black	175.00	105.00	125.00	76.50	10.00	6.00

1912 Imperforate

SCOTT NO.	DESCRIPTION	UNUSED NH F	AVG	UNUSED OG F	AVG	USED F	AVG
408	1¢ green	3.00	1.85	2.25	1.50	.90	.60
409	2¢ carmine	3.25	2.00	2.40	1.60	.90	.60

SCOTT NO.	UNUSED NH F	AVG	UNUSED OG F	AVG	SCOTT NO.	UNUSED NH F	AVG	UNUSED OG F	AVG
		PLATE BLOCKS OF 6					**CENTER LINE BLOCKS**		
397	290.00	170.00	215.00	135.00	408	21.50	12.75	15.75	10.50
398	535.00	335.00	395.00	250.00	409	22.50	14.00	17.00	11.50
401	625.00	400.00	485.00	295.00					
405	195.00	105.00	135.00	80.00			**ARROW BLOCKS**		
406	240.00	150.00	180.00	120.00					
408	48.75	31.00	36.50	24.50	408	13.00	8.00	9.50	6.50
409	80.00	50.00	60.00	40.00	409	14.00	9.00	10.50	7.00

SCOTT NO.	DESCRIPTION	UNUSED NH F	AVG	UNUSED OG F	AVG	USED F	AVG

COIL STAMPS
1912 Perf. 8-1/2 Horizontally

SCOTT NO.	DESCRIPTION	UNUSED NH F	AVG	UNUSED OG F	AVG	USED F	AVG
410	1¢ green	10.25	6.35	7.35	4.75	5.25	3.15
411	2¢ carmine	13.00	7.65	9.25	5.75	5.50	3.35

1912 Perf. 8-1/2 Vertically

SCOTT NO.	DESCRIPTION	UNUSED NH F	AVG	UNUSED OG F	AVG	USED F	AVG
412	1¢ green	35.00	21.00	25.00	15.50	6.75	4.00
413	2¢ carmine	66.50	38.50	47.50	28.50	.85	.50

SCOTT NO.	COIL LINE PAIRS				COIL PAIRS			
	UNUSED NH		UNUSED OG		UNUSED NH		UNUSED OG	
	F	AVG	F	AVG	F	AVG	F	AVG
410	59.50	35.00	42.50	26.00	22.50	13.50	15.50	10.00
411	70.00	40.00	50.00	30.00	28.00	16.50	19.50	12.50
412	160.00	95.00	115.00	70.00	75.00	45.00	53.50	33.50
413	295.00	170.00	210.00	125.00	145.00	83.50	100.00	62.50

SCOTT NO.	DESCRIPTION	UNUSED NH		UNUSED OG		USED	
		F	AVG	F	AVG	F	AVG

1912-14 Perf. 12 Single Line Watermark

414-21	8¢-50¢, 8 vars., cpl.	1700.00	975.00	1200.00	735.00	95.00	58.50
414	8¢ olive green	60.00	35.00	42.50	26.00	2.00	1.20
415	9¢ salmon red	75.00	45.00	55.00	32.50	19.75	11.75
416	10¢ orange yellow	55.00	32.50	40.00	24.00	.40	.25
417	12¢ claret brown	66.50	37.50	47.50	28.50	5.25	3.25
418	15¢ gray	120.00	70.00	87.50	52.50	5.00	3.00
419	20¢ ultramarine	275.00	160.00	200.00	120.00	21.50	13.50
420	30¢ orange red	210.00	117.50	145.00	87.50	21.50	13.50
421	50¢ violet	875.00	500.00	625.00	375.00	21.50	13.50

1912 Double Line Watermark "USPS"

422	50¢ violet	465.00	260.00	325.00	195.00	21.50	13.50
423	$1 violet black	975.00	575.00	700.00	425.00	85.00	52.50

1914-15 Single Line Watermark, "USPS" Perf. 10

424-40	1¢-50¢, 16 vars., cpl.	2850.00	1650.00	2050.00	1250.00	100.00	62.50
424	1¢ green	5.00	2.85	3.75	2.25	.12	.07
424d	1¢ booklet pane of 6	12.00	6.85	9.00	5.50	....	....
425	2¢ carmine	5.00	2.85	3.75	2.25	.11	.06
425e	2¢ booklet pane of 6	32.50	18.50	24.50	14.75	....	....
426	3¢ deep violet	23.50	13.00	17.50	10.50	2.25	1.35
427	4¢ brown.............................	55.00	30.00	38.50	22.75	.65	.40
428	5¢ blue................................	45.00	26.00	32.50	19.50	.65	.40
429	6¢ orange	60.00	35.00	43.50	26.50	1.75	1.05
430	7¢ black..............................	150.00	87.50	105.00	65.00	7.00	4.25
431	8¢ olive green	60.00	35.00	43.50	26.50	1.95	1.20
432	9¢ salmon red	80.00	46.50	57.50	33.50	10.00	6.00
433	10¢ orange yellow	75.00	43.75	55.00	33.50	.35	.20
434	11¢ dark green	38.50	21.00	27.50	16.50	10.50	6.35
435	12¢ claret brown	42.50	24.00	30.00	18.00	6.25	3.75
437	15¢ gray	190.00	110.00	135.00	80.00	9.50	5.65
438	20¢ ultramarine	350.00	200.00	250.00	150.00	5.75	3.50
439	30¢ orange red	465.00	260.00	325.00	195.00	22.50	13.75
440	50¢ violet	1250.00	735.00	900.00	550.00	25.00	15.00

PLATE BLOCKS OF 6									
SCOTT NO.	UNUSED NH		UNUSED OG		SCOTT NO.	UNUSED NH		UNUSED OG	
	F	AVG	F	AVG		F	AVG	F	AVG
414	875.00	500.00	625.00	375.00	427	600.00	350.00	435.00	260.00
415	1250.00	735.00	900.00	550.00	428	495.00	280.00	350.00	210.00
416	950.00	535.00	675.00	400.00	429	535.00	300.00	385.00	230.00
417	835.00	485.00	600.00	365.00	430	1500.00	900.00	1100.00	675.00
418	1300.00	750.00	950.00	565.00	431	650.00	375.00	465.00	280.00
424(6)	95.00	55.00	70.00	42.50	432	900.00	525.00	650.00	395.00
424(10)	265.00	150.00	195.00	115.00	433	875.00	500.00	625.00	375.00
425(6)	67.50	38.75	47.50	29.50	434	335.00	195.00	240.00	145.00
425(10)	265.00	150.00	195.00	115.00	435	425.00	240.00	300.00	180.00
426	240.00	140.00	175.00	105.00	437	1400.00	800.00	1000.00	600.00

SCOTT NO.	DESCRIPTION	UNUSED NH		UNUSED OG		USED	
		F	AVG	F	AVG	F	AVG

COILSTAMPS
1914 Perf. 10 Horizontally

441	1¢ green.............................	2.10	1.20	1.60	.95	1.10	.65
442	2¢ carmine	17.00	9.75	12.50	7.50	10.75	6.50

SCOTT NO.	DESCRIPTION	UNUSED NH F	UNUSED NH AVG	UNUSED OG F	UNUSED OG AVG	USED F	USED AVG
		1914 Perf.10 Vertically					
443	1¢ green	38.50	22.50	28.50	17.50	7.50	4.50
444	2¢ carmine	62.50	35.75	45.00	27.00	1.75	1.05
445	3¢ violet	375.00	210.00	265.00	160.00	135.00	80.00
446	4¢ brown	225.00	130.00	165.00	100.00	50.00	30.00
447	5¢ blue	75.00	43.50	55.00	32.50	27.50	16.50
		ROTARY PRESS COIL STAMPS **1915-16 Perf. 10 Horizontally**					
448	1¢ green	10.00	5.75	7.50	4.50	3.50	2.15
449	2¢ red(I)	....	....	1750.00	1075.00	185.00	110.00
450	2¢ carmine (III)	19.50	12.50	14.50	9.75	3.50	2.15
		1914-16 Perf. 10 Vertically					
452	1¢ green	20.00	11.50	15.00	9.00	2.25	1.35
453	2¢ carmine rose (I)	200.00	115.00	145.00	87.50	5.25	3.15
454	2¢ red (II)	210.00	120.00	150.00	90.00	16.50	10.00
455	2¢ carmine (III)	18.00	10.50	13.50	8.25	1.50	.90
456	3¢ violet	485.00	285.00	350.00	215.00	135.00	80.00
457	4¢ brown	55.00	32.75	39.50	23.75	21.50	13.00
458	5¢ blue	55.00	32.75	39.50	23.75	21.50	13.00
		1914 Imperforate Coil					
459	2¢ carmine	750.00	465.00	550.00	365.00	....	....

	COIL LINE PAIRS				COIL PAIRS			
SCOTT NO.	UNUSED NH F	UNUSED NH AVG	UNUSED OG F	UNUSED OG AVG	UNUSED NH F	UNUSED NH AVG	UNUSED OG F	UNUSED OG AVG
441	15.00	8.50	11.50	6.85	4.65	2.60	3.50	2.10
442	90.00	55.00	65.00	41.50	36.50	21.00	26.50	16.00
443	165.00	92.50	120.00	72.50	87.50	52.50	67.50	40.00
444	265.00	145.00	195.00	115.00	145.00	80.00	105.00	65.00
445	1600.00	900.00	1200.00	725.00	825.00	465.00	585.00	350.00
446	1000.00	575.00	750.00	450.00	495.00	285.00	360.00	220.00
447	360.00	200.00	265.00	160.00	165.00	95.00	120.00	72.50
448	75.00	41.50	55.00	33.50	22.00	12.50	16.50	10.00
450	135.00	76.50	100.00	62.50	41.50	26.50	31.00	21.00
452	135.00	76.50	100.00	62.50	45.00	25.00	32.50	20.00
453	1100.00	625.00	785.00	465.00	425.00	250.00	315.00	195.00
454	1185.00	700.00	850.00	525.00	450.00	260.00	325.00	200.00
455	130.00	70.00	95.00	55.00	38.75	22.75	28.50	17.50
456	975.00	575.00	700.00	425.00	1050.00	625.00	750.00	465.00
457	315.00	180.00	225.00	135.00	120.00	70.00	87.50	51.50
458	315.00	180.00	225.00	135.00	120.00	70.00	87.50	51.50
459	3250.00	2050.00	2400.00	1600.00	1600.00	1000.00	1175.00	785.00

SCOTT NO.	DESCRIPTION	UNUSED NH F	UNUSED NH AVG	UNUSED OG F	UNUSED OG AVG	USED F	USED AVG
		1915 Flat Plate Printing Double Line Watermark Perf. 10					
460	$1 violet black	1500.00	885.00	1100.00	665.00	130.00	80.00
		1915 Single Line Watermark "USPS" Perf. 11					
461	2¢ pale carmine red	185.00	105.00	135.00	80.00	125.00	75.00
		1916-17 Unwatermarked Perf. 10					
462	1¢ green	14.00	8.00	8.75	6.00	.40	.24
462a	1¢ booklet pane of 6	19.50	11.00	14.50	8.75	....	....
463	2¢ carmine	7.50	4.35	5.50	3.35	.18	.11
463a	2¢ booklet pane of 6	160.00	90.00	120.00	72.50	....	....
464	3¢ violet	145.00	82.50	105.00	62.50	15.00	9.00
465	4¢ orange brown	77.50	45.00	55.00	33.50	2.25	1.35
466	5¢ blue	135.00	75.00	95.00	55.00	2.25	1.35
467	5¢ carmine (error)	1250.00	735.00	900.00	550.00	650.00	395.00
468	6¢ red orange	150.00	88.75	110.00	66.50	9.75	5.75
469	7¢ black	195.00	115.00	140.00	85.00	16.50	10.00
470	8¢ olive green	80.00	46.75	57.50	35.00	8.75	5.25
471	9¢ salmon red	95.00	53.50	67.50	40.00	23.50	14.00
472	10¢ orange yellow	175.00	100.00	125.00	75.00	1.35	.80
473	11¢ dark green	48.50	26.50	33.50	20.00	21.00	12.75
474	12¢ claret brown	85.00	48.50	60.00	36.50	7.75	4.65
475	15¢ gray	275.00	160.00	200.00	120.00	17.50	10.50
476	20¢ ultramarine	440.00	250.00	315.00	190.00	16.50	10.00
477	50¢ light violet	2300.00	1350.00	1650.00	1000.00	95.00	57.50
478	$1 violet black	1485.00	850.00	1050.00	625.00	23.50	14.00

SCOTT NO.	DESCRIPTION	UNUSED NH F	AVG	UNUSED OG F	AVG	USED F	AVG

Design of 1902-03

SCOTT NO.	DESCRIPTION	UNUSED NH F	AVG	UNUSED OG F	AVG	USED F	AVG
479	$2 dark blue	875.00	500.00	625.00	375.00	65.00	38.75
480	$5 light green	735.00	425.00	525.00	315.00	67.50	40.00

1916-17 Imperforate

481	1¢ green	1.75	1.10	1.30	.85	1.10	.75
482	2¢ carmine	2.75	1.70	2.10	1.40	2.35	1.55
483	3¢ violet (I)	37.50	24.00	28.75	19.50	11.50	7.65
484	3¢ violet (II)	23.50	14.50	17.50	11.50	5.00	3.35

SCOTT NO.	UNUSED NH F	AVG	UNUSED OG F	AVG	SCOTT NO.	UNUSED NH F	AVG	UNUSED OG F	AVG
	PLATE BLOCKS OF 6					PLATE BLOCKS OF 6			
462	235.00	130.00	170.00	100.00	472	2300.00	1350.00	1675.00	1000.00
463	155.00	90.00	115.00	70.00	473	485.00	280.00	350.00	210.00
464	2250.00	1200.00	1600.00	975.00	474	875.00	500.00	625.00	375.00
465	1100.00	700.00	875.00	525.00	481	27.50	17.00	20.00	13.50
466	1600.00	925.00	1150.00	685.00	482	58.75	35.00	43.50	28.50
470	950.00	535.00	675.00	400.00	483	385.00	250.00	295.00	200.00
471	1000.00	585.00	725.00	435.00	484	265.00	165.00	185.00	125.00
	CENTER LINE BLOCKS					ARROW BLOCKS			
481	17.50	11.00	13.00	8.50	481	7.75	4.85	5.75	3.75
482	18.75	12.00	14.75	9.75	482	12.50	7.50	9.35	6.25
483	225.00	145.00	170.00	115.00	483	160.00	100.00	120.00	82.50
484	140.00	87.50	105.00	68.75	484	100.00	62.50	75.00	50.00

SCOTT NO.	DESCRIPTION	UNUSED NH F	AVG	UNUSED OG F	AVG	USED F	AVG

ROTARY PRESS COIL STAMPS

| 486/497 | (486-90,492-97) 11 vars. | 210.00 | 120.00 | 155.00 | 95.00 | 32.50 | 19.25 |

1916-19 Perf. 10 Horizontally

486	1¢ green	1.95	1.15	1.45	.85	.30	.18
487	2¢ carmine (II)	30.00	17.00	22.50	13.50	3.65	2.15
488	2¢ carmine (III)	5.85	3.25	4.35	2.60	2.10	1.25
489	3¢ violet	8.75	5.00	6.50	4.00	1.75	1.05

1916-22 Perf. 10 Vertically

490	1¢ green	1.50	.90	1.15	.70	.25	.15
491	2¢ carmine (III)	....	....	1650.00	975.00	250.00	150.00
492	2¢ carmine (III)	19.75	12.50	14.75	8.75	.20	.12
493	3¢ violet (I)	40.00	23.00	29.50	17.50	3.50	2.10
494	3¢ violet (II)	21.50	12.00	16.00	9.75	1.00	.60
495	4¢ orange brown	25.00	13.75	18.75	11.00	5.25	3.15
496	5¢ blue	8.50	4.85	6.35	3.85	1.15	.70
497	10¢ orange yellow	50.00	28.00	37.50	22.50	13.50	8.00

SCOTT NO.	COIL LINE PAIRS UNUSED NH F	AVG	UNUSED OG F	AVG	COIL PAIRS UNUSED NH F	AVG	UNUSED OG F	AVG
486	10.75	6.15	8.00	4.85	4.35	2.50	3.10	1.85
487	250.00	140.00	185.00	110.00	65.00	37.00	48.50	29.00
488	50.00	28.50	37.50	22.50	12.50	7.00	9.50	5.65
489	70.00	39.75	52.50	31.75	18.50	10.75	13.75	8.50
490	8.75	4.95	6.50	3.95	3.25	1.95	2.50	1.50
492	98.50	55.00	73.50	44.00	42.50	26.75	31.00	18.50
493	265.00	150.00	200.00	120.00	85.00	48.75	62.50	37.50
494	150.00	85.00	110.00	67.50	46.50	25.00	33.50	20.00
495	170.00	95.00	125.00	75.00	52.50	28.50	40.00	23.00
496	49.50	27.50	36.50	21.75	18.00	10.00	13.50	8.00
497	240.00	137.50	180.00	110.00	105.00	58.75	80.00	47.50

VERY FINE QUALITY: To determine the Very Fine price, add the difference between the Fine and Average prices to the Fine quality price. For example: if the Fine price is $10.00 and the Average price is $6.00, the Very Fine price would be $14.00. From 1935 to date, add 20% to the Fine price to arrive at the Very Fine price.

SCOTT NO.	DESCRIPTION	UNUSED NH F	AVG	UNUSED OG F	AVG	USED F	AVG

1917-19 Flat Plate Printing Perf. 11

SCOTT NO.	DESCRIPTION	UNUSED NH F	AVG	UNUSED OG F	AVG	USED F	AVG
498/518	(498-99,501-04,506-18) 19 var.	885.00	510.00	665.00	400.00	33.50	20.00
498	1¢ green	.90	.50	.65	.40	.12	.07
498e	1¢ booklet pane of 6	4.75	2.60	3.60	2.15	....	....
498f	1¢ booklet pane of 30	775.00	475.00	575.00	375.00	....	....
499	2¢ rose (I)	1.00	.55	.75	.45	.12	.07
499e	2¢ booklet pane of 6	7.50	4.35	5.75	3.50	....	....
500	2¢ deep rose (1a)	465.00	260.00	325.00	195.00	150.00	90.00
501	3¢ violet (I)	30.00	16.75	22.50	13.50	.20	.12
501b	3¢ booklet pane of 6	200.00	115.00	150.00	90.00	....	....
502	3¢ violet (II)	31.50	17.50	23.50	14.00	.45	.27
502b	3¢ booklet pane of 6	130.00	72.50	97.50	57.50	....	....
503	4¢ brown	25.00	13.75	18.75	11.00	.25	.15
504	5¢ blue	15.75	8.75	11.75	7.00	.17	.10
505	5¢ rose (error)	835.00	475.00	595.00	360.00	475.00	275.00
506	6¢ red orange	28.50	16.00	21.50	12.75	.40	.25
507	7¢ black	48.75	28.00	36.50	22.50	1.75	1.05
508	8¢ olive bistre	25.00	13.75	18.75	11.00	1.30	.80
509	9¢ salmon red	31.50	17.50	22.75	13.75	3.25	1.95
510	10¢ orange	42.50	24.50	31.75	19.50	.20	.12
511	11¢ light green	17.00	9.50	12.50	7.50	5.00	3.00
512	12¢ claret brown	18.75	10.50	14.00	8.35	.85	.50
513	13¢ apple green	22.75	12.50	17.00	10.00	12.75	7.85
514	15¢ gray	77.50	43.50	57.50	35.00	1.35	.85
515	20¢ ultramarine	110.00	62.50	80.00	48.50	.40	.25
516	30¢ orange red	77.50	43.75	57.50	35.00	1.35	.85
517	50¢ red violet	155.00	90.00	115.00	70.00	1.15	.70
518	$1 violet black	140.00	82.50	110.00	65.00	3.00	1.80

1917 Design of 1908-09
Double Line Watermark Perf. 11

SCOTT NO.	DESCRIPTION	UNUSED NH F	AVG	UNUSED OG F	AVG	USED F	AVG
519	2¢ carmine	385.00	220.00	275.00	165.00	300.00	180.00

523, 524, 547
Franklin

537
"Victory" and Flags

1918 Unwatermarked

SCOTT NO.	DESCRIPTION	UNUSED NH F	AVG	UNUSED OG F	AVG	USED F	AVG
523	$2 orange red & black	1750.00	1025.00	1250.00	775.00	275.00	165.00
524	$5 deep green & black	725.00	425.00	525.00	315.00	47.50	28.50

SCOTT NO.	UNUSED NH F	AVG	UNUSED OG F	AVG	SCOTT NO.	UNUSED NH F	AVG	UNUSED OG F	AVG
	PLATE BLOCKS OF 6					PLATE BLOCKS OF 6			
498	33.50	18.75	25.00	15.00	511	250.00	140.00	185.00	110.00
499	29.50	16.75	22.50	13.50	512	215.00	125.00	160.00	97.50
501	280.00	160.00	210.00	125.00	513	235.00	132.50	175.00	105.00
502	360.00	200.00	265.00	160.00	514	1035.00	585.00	775.00	465.00
503	325.00	180.00	240.00	145.00	515	1175.00	665.00	875.00	525.00
504	230.00	125.00	170.00	100.00	516	950.00	540.00	715.00	430.00
506	350.00	195.00	260.00	155.00	517	2275.00	1250.00	1700.00	1000.00
507	575.00	325.00	425.00	260.00	518	1800.00	1025.00	1350.00	815.00
508	335.00	190.00	250.00	150.00					
509	335.00	190.00	250.00	150.00		ARROW BLOCK			
510	475.00	265.00	350.00	210.00	518	600.00	350.00	465.00	280.00

SCOTT NO.	DESCRIPTION	UNUSED NH F	AVG	UNUSED OG F	AVG	USED F	AVG

1918-20 Offset Printing Perf. 11

SCOTT NO.	DESCRIPTION	UNUSED NH F	AVG	UNUSED OG F	AVG	USED F	AVG
525-30	1¢-3¢, 8 vars.	240.00	135.00	180.00	110.00	8.25	5.50
525	1¢ gray green	4.00	2.25	3.00	1.80	.85	.50
526	2¢ carmine (IV)	60.00	33.75	45.00	27.50	5.25	3.15
527	2¢ carmine (V)	32.50	18.75	25.00	15.00	1.15	.70
528	2¢ carmine (Va)	18.50	10.75	14.00	8.50	.22	.13

SCOTT NO.	DESCRIPTION	UNUSED NH F	AVG	UNUSED OG F	AVG	USED F	AVG
528A	2¢ carmine (VI)	80.00	45.00	60.00	36.50	1.30	.80
528B	2¢ carmine (VII)	37.50	21.50	28.50	17.00	.17	.10
529	3¢ violet (III)	6.50	3.75	4.85	2.95	.20	.12
530	3¢ purple (IV)	1.65	.95	1.25	.75	.13	.08

1918-20 Offset Printing Imperforate

531	1¢ gray green	30.00	18.75	22.50	15.00	12.50	8.25
532	2¢ carmine (IV)	100.00	62.50	75.00	50.00	45.00	30.00
533	2¢ carmine (V)	435.00	265.00	315.00	210.00	90.00	60.00
534	2¢ carmine (Va)	32.50	21.00	24.50	16.50	13.50	9.00
534A	2¢ carmine (VI)	80.00	50.00	60.00	40.00	40.00	26.50
534B	2¢ carmine (VII)	2650.00	1650.00	1950.00	1300.00	525.00	350.00
535	3¢ violet	22.50	14.00	17.00	11.50	10.00	6.65

1919 Offset Printing Perf. 12-1/2

536	1¢ gray green	29.50	16.75	22.50	13.50	21.50	13.00

1919 VICTORY ISSUE

537	3¢ violet	17.50	10.00	13.00	8.00	5.75	3.50

1919-21 (†)
Rotary Press Printings - Perf. 11 x 10

538	1¢ green	18.75	9.75	14.00	7.75	11.75	6.75
538a	Same, imperf. horizontally	100.00	52.50	75.00	41.75	....	....
539	2¢ carmine rose (II)	....	....	2750.00	1500.00	950.00	525.00
540	2¢ carmine rose (III)	25.00	13.00	18.75	10.50	15.00	8.25
540a	Same, imperf. horizontally	100.00	52.50	75.00	41.75	....	....
541	3¢ violet	65.00	33.75	48.75	27.50	47.50	26.50

Perf. 10 x 11

542	1¢ green	15.00	8.15	11.50	6.50	1.25	.70

Perf. 10

543	1¢ green	1.30	.70	1.00	.55	.15	.09

Perf. 11

544	1¢ green (19 x 22-1/2mm)	....	....	....	....	1850.00	1100.00
545	1¢ green (19-1/2 x 22mm)	250.00	130.00	180.00	100.00	125.00	70.00
546	2¢ carmine rose	170.00	95.00	125.00	70.00	110.00	62.50

1920 Flat Plate Printing Perf. 11

547	$2 carmine & black	650.00	385.00	475.00	295.00	57.50	35.00

SCOTT NO.	UNUSED NH F	AVG	UNUSED OG F	AVG	SCOTT NO.	UNUSED NH F	AVG	UNUSED OG F	AVG
	PLATE BLOCKS OF 6					PLATE BLOCKS OF 6			
525(6)	52.50	29.75	39.50	23.75	535(6)	180.00	110.00	135.00	95.00
526(6)	425.00	250.00	315.00	200.00	536(6)	350.00	195.00	265.00	165.00
527(6)	230.00	125.00	170.00	100.00	537(6)	290.00	165.00	215.00	130.00
528(6)	115.00	65.00	85.00	51.50	538(4)	185.00	95.00	135.00	75.00
528A(6)	650.00	360.00	485.00	285.00	540(4)	250.00	130.00	185.00	105.00
528B(6)	300.00	175.00	225.00	135.00	541(4)	685.00	375.00	515.00	300.00
529(6)	100.00	56.50	75.00	45.00	542(6)	235.00	122.50	175.00	97.50
530(6)	27.50	15.00	20.00	12.00	543(4)	30.00	16.00	22.50	12.75
531(6)	285.00	180.00	210.00	140.00	543(6)	60.00	31.50	45.00	25.00
532(6)	800.00	500.00	600.00	400.00	545(4)	1800.00	950.00	350.00	750.00
534(6)	295.00	190.00	220.00	150.00	546(4)	1350.00	725.00	1000.00	565.00
534A(6)	700.00	425.00	535.00	350.00					
	CENTER LINE BLOCKS					ARROW BLOCKS			
531	210.00	130.00	157.50	105.00	531	130.00	80.00	95.00	63.50
532	500.00	310.00	375.00	250.00	532	425.00	265.00	315.00	210.00
533	2000.00	1200.00	1450.00	975.00	533	1800.00	1100.00	1300.00	875.00
534	170.00	110.00	125.00	82.50	534	135.00	87.50	102.50	70.00
534A	400.00	250.00	300.00	200.00	534A	335.00	210.00	250.00	170.00
535	135.00	85.00	100.00	67.50	535	95.00	60.00	72.50	47.50
547	3150.00	1700.00	2250.00	1375.00	547	2650.00	1600.00	1950.00	1200.00

PLATE BLOCKS: are portions of a sheet of stamps adjacent to the number(s) indicating the printing plate number used to produce that sheet. Flat plate issues are usually collected in plate blocks of six (number opposite middle stamp) while rotary issues are normally corner blocks of four.

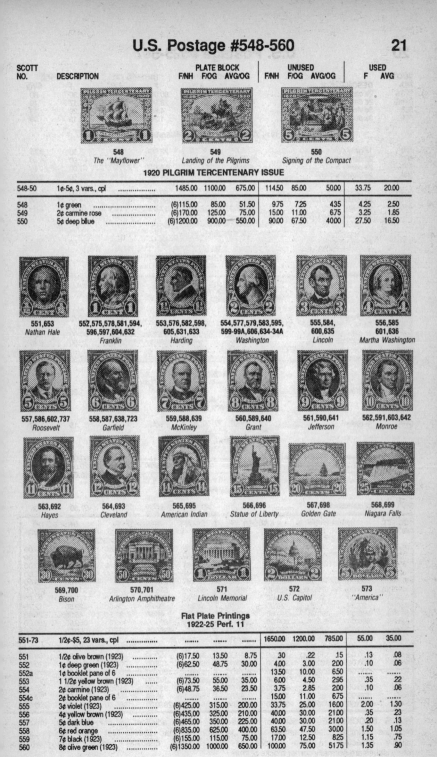

SCOTT NO.	DESCRIPTION	PLATE BLOCK F/NH	F/OG	AVG/OG	UNUSED F/NH	F/OG	AVG/OG	USED F	AVG

548
The "Mayflower"

549
Landing of the Pilgrims

550
Signing of the Compact

1920 PILGRIM TERCENTENARY ISSUE

SCOTT NO.	DESCRIPTION	PLATE BLOCK F/NH	F/OG	AVG/OG	UNUSED F/NH	F/OG	AVG/OG	USED F	AVG
548-50	1¢-5¢, 3 vars., cpl	1485.00	1100.00	675.00	114.50	85.00	50.00	33.75	20.00
548	1¢ green	(6)115.00	85.00	51.50	9.75	7.25	4.35	4.25	2.50
549	2¢ carmine rose	(6)170.00	125.00	75.00	15.00	11.00	6.75	3.25	1.85
550	5¢ deep blue	(6)1200.00	900.00	550.00	90.00	67.50	40.00	27.50	16.50

551,653
Nathan Hale

552,575,578,581,594, 596,597,604,632
Franklin

553,576,582,598, 605,631,633
Harding

554,577,579,583,595, 599-99A,606,634-34A
Washington

555,584, 600,635
Lincoln

556,585 601,636
Martha Washington

557,586,602,737
Roosevelt

558,587,638,723
Garfield

559,588,639
McKinley

560,589,640
Grant

561,590,641
Jefferson

562,591,603,642
Monroe

563,692
Hayes

564,693
Cleveland

565,695
American Indian

566,696
Statue of Liberty

567,698
Golden Gate

568,699
Niagara Falls

569,700
Bison

570,701
Arlington Amphitheatre

571
Lincoln Memorial

572
U.S. Capitol

573
"America"

Flat Plate Printings
1922-25 Perf. 11

SCOTT NO.	DESCRIPTION	PLATE BLOCK F/NH	F/OG	AVG/OG	UNUSED F/NH	F/OG	AVG/OG	USED F	AVG
551-73	1/2¢-$5, 23 vars., cpl	......	......	......	1650.00	1200.00	785.00	55.00	35.00
551	1/2¢ olive brown (1923)	(6)17.50	13.50	8.75	.30	.22	.15	.13	.08
552	1¢ deep green (1923)	(6)62.50	48.75	30.00	4.00	3.00	2.00	.10	.06
552a	1¢ booklet pane of 6	......	......	......	13.50	10.00	6.50	......	......
553	1 1/2¢ yellow brown (1923)	(6)73.50	55.00	35.00	6.00	4.50	2.95	.35	.22
554	2¢ carmine (1923)	(6)48.75	36.50	23.50	3.75	2.85	2.00	.10	.06
554c	2¢ booklet pane of 6	......	......	......	15.00	11.00	6.75	......	......
555	3¢ violet (1923)	(6)425.00	315.00	200.00	33.75	25.00	16.00	2.00	1.30
556	4¢ yellow brown (1923)	(6)435.00	325.00	210.00	40.00	30.00	21.00	.35	.23
557	5¢ dark blue	(6)465.00	350.00	225.00	40.00	30.00	21.00	.20	.13
558	6¢ red orange	(6)835.00	625.00	400.00	63.50	47.50	30.00	1.50	1.05
559	7¢ black (1923)	(6)155.00	115.00	75.00	17.00	12.50	8.25	1.15	.75
560	8¢ olive green (1923)	(6)1350.00	1000.00	650.00	100.00	75.00	51.75	1.35	.90

SCOTT NO.	DESCRIPTION	PLATE BLOCK F/NH	F/OG	AVG/OG	UNUSED F/NH	F/OG	AVG/OG	USED F	AVG
561	9¢ rose (1923)	(6)335.00	250.00	160.00	27.50	20.75	14.00	2.00	1.35
562	10¢ orange (1923)	(6)565.00	425.00	275.00	45.00	33.50	22.50	.21	.14
563	11¢ blue	(6)70.00	52.50	33.75	3.35	2.50	1.60	.45	.30
564	12¢ brown violet (1923)	(6)170.00	135.00	85.00	16.50	12.50	8.25	.20	.13
565	14¢ dark blue (1923)	(6)120.00	90.00	57.50	11.50	8.50	5.75	1.10	.70
566	15¢ gray	(6)500.00	365.00	235.00	45.00	33.50	21.50	.13	.08
567	20¢ carmine rose (1923)	(6)480.00	360.00	235.00	45.00	32.50	21.00	.13	.08
568	25¢ green	(6)550.00	400.00	265.00	50.00	37.50	25.00	.80	.50
569	30¢ olive brown (1923)	(6)750.00	575.00	375.00	68.75	51.50	33.50	.65	.40
570	50¢ lilac	(6)1850.00	1400.00	900.00	135.00	100.00	65.00	.25	.16
571	$1 violet black (1923)	(6)1000.00	765.00	500.00	115.00	85.00	55.00	.80	.50
572	$2 deep blue (1923)	(6)2975.00	2250.00	1450.00	235.00	175.00	110.00	16.50	10.75
573	$5 carmine & blue (1923)	....	....	....	550.00	410.00	260.00	25.00	16.00

1923-25 Imperforate

SCOTT NO.	DESCRIPTION	PLATE BLOCK F/NH	F/OG	AVG/OG	UNUSED F/NH	F/OG	AVG/OG	USED F	AVG
575	1¢ green	(6)210.00	165.00	110.00	22.50	17.00	11.50	5.25	3.50
576	1 1/2¢ yellow brown (1925)	(6)52.50	41.50	27.50	4.35	3.50	2.35	3.25	2.15
577	2¢ carmine	(6)50.00	40.00	26.50	4.35	3.50	2.35	3.25	2.15

SCOTT NO.		CENTER LINE BLOCKS F/NH	F/OG	AVG/OG	ARROW BLOCKS F/NH	F/OG	AVG/OG
571	$1 violet black	....	....	....	500.00	360.00	230.00
572	$2 deep blue	....	....	....	990.00	725.00	475.00
573	$5 carmine & blue	2350.00	1750.00	1125.00	2250.00	1675.00	1075.00
575	1¢ imperforate	110.00	85.00	57.50	95.00	72.50	50.00
576	1 1/2¢ imperforate	25.00	20.00	13.50	14.50	12.00	8.00
577	2¢ imperforate	27.50	22.50	15.00	18.50	15.00	10.00

SCOTT NO.	DESCRIPTION	PLATE BLOCK F/NH	F	AVG	UNUSED F/NH	F	AVG	USED F	AVG
		Rotary Press Printings 1923 Perf. 11 x 10 (†)							
578	1¢ green	1200.00	875.00	485.00	130.00	95.00	53.50	82.50	46.50
579	2¢ carmine	725.00	525.00	285.00	90.00	65.00	36.50	62.50	36.50
		1923-26 Perf. 10 (†)							
581-91	1¢-10¢, 11 vars. cpl	....	....	....	315.00	240.00	145.00	22.75	13.75
581	1¢ green	177.50	135.00	81.50	15.00	11.50	6.75	1.00	.60
582	1 1/2¢ brown (1925)	65.00	50.00	30.00	7.00	5.50	3.35	1.00	.60
583	2¢ carmine (1924)	55.00	41.50	25.00	5.00	3.75	2.25	.12	.07
583a	2¢ booklet pane of 6 (1926)	....	....	....	160.00	120.00	75.00	....	....
584	3¢ violet (1925)	435.00	335.00	200.00	42.50	32.50	19.50	2.50	1.50
585	4¢ yellow brown (1925)	300.00	230.00	140.00	30.00	22.50	13.50	.65	.40
586	5¢ blue (1925)	325.00	235.00	145.00	32.50	23.75	14.50	.33	.20
587	6¢ red orange (1925)	120.00	90.00	55.00	13.75	10.50	6.25	.80	.50
588	7¢ black (1926)	200.00	150.00	90.00	20.00	15.00	9.00	8.50	5.15
589	8¢ olive green (1926)	475.00	360.00	215.00	48.50	36.50	22.00	4.25	2.50
590	9¢ rose (1926)	82.50	62.50	37.50	9.50	7.00	4.25	3.75	2.25
591	10¢ orange (1925)	1085.00	825.00	500.00	100.00	77.50	46.50	.16	.10
		Perf. 11(†)							
595	2¢ carmine	....	....	....	315.00	225.00	125.00	200.00	110.00

1923-29 Rotary Press Coil Stamps

SCOTT NO.	DESCRIPTION	LINE PAIRS F/NH	F	AVG	UNUSED F/NH	F	AVG	USED F	AVG
597/606	(597-99, 600-06) 10 vars	240.0	190.00	120.00	33.75	27.00	17.00	2.45	1.50
		Perf. 10 Vertically							
597	1¢ green	4.75	3.85	2.50	.70	.55	.35	.12	.07
598	1 1/2¢ deep brown (1923)	11.75	9.50	6.00	1.35	1.10	.65	.20	.13
599	2¢ carmine (I)	3.50	2.75	1.75	.65	.50	.32	.12	.07
599A	2¢ carmine (II) (1929)	1200.00	850.00	475.00	210.00	150.00	85.00	16.50	9.25
600	3¢ deep violet (1924)	69.50	53.50	32.50	15.00	12.00	7.50	.12	.07
601	4¢ yellow brown	70.00	55.00	35.00	6.50	5.25	3.25	.75	.45
602	5¢ dark blue (1924)	19.75	15.75	10.00	2.65	2.10	1.30	.30	.20
603	10¢ orange (1924)	50.00	40.00	25.00	6.35	5.00	3.25	.25	.16

SCOTT NO.	DESCRIPTION	PLATE BLOCK F/NH	F	AVG	UNUSED F/NH	F	AVG	USED F	AVG
		Perf. 10 Horizontally							
605	1¢ green (1924)	6.25	5.00	3.25	.40	.33	22	.15	.10
605	1 1/2¢ yellow brown (1925)	4.75	3.75	2.35	.40	.33	22	.30	20
606	2¢ carmine	3.50	2.75	1.75	.45	.35	23	.20	.14

NOTE: Pairs of the above can be supplied at two times the single price.

610-613
Harding

614
Ship ''New Netherlands''

615
Landing at Fort Orange

616
Monument at Maypor' Fla.

1923 HARDING MEMORIAL ISSUE
PLATE BLOCK

610	2¢ black, pf. 11 flat	(6)60.00	48.50	31.50	1.75	1.30	85	.16	.10
611	2¢ black, imperf.	(6)260.00	215.00	145.00	19.50	16.00	1050	10.00	6.65
611	2¢ center line block	135.00	110.00	72.50	....	....	....	....	....
611	2¢ arrow block	85.00	67.50	45.00	....	....	....	....	....
612	2¢ black, pf. 10 rotary	650.00	500.00	300.00	40.00	32.50	1950	3.75	2.25

1924 HUGUENOT-WALLOON ISSUE

614-16	1¢-5¢, 3 vars., cpl.	985.00	785.00	515.00	98.50	79.50	5350	42.50	28.75
614	1¢ green	(6)105.00	82.50	55.00	8.75	7.00	4.75	6.75	4.50
615	2¢ carmine rose	(6)175.00	140.00	90.00	15.00	12.00	8.00	4.75	3.15
616	5¢ dark blue	(6)715.00	575.00	375.00	77.50	61.50	4150	32.50	21.50

617
Washington at Cambridge

618
Birth of Liberty

619
The Minute Man

1925 LEXINGTON-CONCORD SESQUICENTENNIAL

617-19	1¢-5¢, 3 vars., cpl.	925.00	735.00	485.00	89.95	70.00	4750	50.00	33.50
617	1¢ green	(6)105.00	82.50	55.00	8.50	6.75	4.50	8.25	5.50
618	2¢ carmine rose	(6)165.00	135.00	87.50	13.50	11.00	735	10.75	7.25
619	5¢ dark blue	(6)665.00	525.00	350.00	68.75	55.00	3650	32.50	21.50

620
Sloop ''Restaurationen''

621
Viking Ship

622,694
Harrison

623,697
Wilson

1925 NORSE-AMERICAN ISSUE

620	2¢ carmine & black	(8)450.00	365.00	240.00	12.50	10.00	6.50	8.75	5.85
620	2¢ center line block	60.00	48.75	31.50	....	....	....	....	....
620	2¢ arrow block	52.50	41.50	27.00	....	....	....	....	....
621	5¢ dk. blue & black	(8)1575.00	1250.00	825.00	40.00	32.50	2150	37.50	25.00
621	5¢ center line block	190.00	160.00	100.00	....	....	....	....	....
621	5¢ arrow block	165.00	135.00	90.00	....	....	....	....	....

1925-26 Flat Plate Printings, Perf. 11

622	13¢ green (1926)	(6)345.00	260.00	160.00	30.00	23.00	1400	1.25	.80
623	17¢ black	(6)400.00	300.00	180.00	42.50	32.50	2000	.45	.30

SCOTT NO.	DESCRIPTION	PLATE BLOCK F/NH	F	AVG	UNUSED F/NH	F	AVG	USED F	AVG

627
Liberty Bell

628
John Ericsson Statue

629
Hamilton's Battery

1926-27 COMMEMORATIVES

Scott No.	Description	P.B. F/NH	F	AVG	Unused F/NH	F	AVG	Used F	AVG
627/644	(627-29, 43-44) 5 vars., cpl.				40.00	32.50	20.75	19.75	12.75

1926 Commemoratives

Scott No.	Description	P.B. F/NH	F	AVG	Unused F/NH	F	AVG	Used F	AVG
627	2¢ Sesquicentennial	(6)90.00	72.50	47.50	6.50	5.25	3.50	.90	.60
628	5¢ Ericsson Memorial	(6)195.00	157.50	105.00	18.50	14.75	9.50	6.50	4.35
629	2¢ White Plains	(6)110.00	90.00	60.00	5.25	4.15	2.75	3.25	2.15
630	White Plains Souv. Sht. of 25				725.00	600.00	400.00		
630V	2¢ "Dot over S" var.				775.00	635.00	425.00		

Rotary Press Printings Designs of 1922-25 1926 Imperforate

Scott No.	Description	P.B. F/NH	F	AVG	Unused F/NH	F	AVG	Used F	AVG
631	1 1/2¢ brown	115.00	95.00	62.50	5.00	4.15	2.75	4.00	2.60
631	1 1/2¢ center line block	50.00	41.50	27.50					
631	1 1/2¢ arrow block	25.00	20.00	13.50					

1926-28 Perf. 11 x 10 1/2

Scott No.	Description	P.B. F/NH	F	AVG	Unused F/NH	F	AVG	Used F	AVG
632/42	1¢-10¢ (632-34, 35-42) 11 vars.	635.00	510.00	310.00	47.50	38.50	23.50	1.25	.80
632	1¢ green (1927)	4.15	3.35	2.00	.25	.20	.13	.10	.06
632a	1¢ booklet pane of 6				8.75	7.00	4.75		
633	1 1/2¢ yellow brown (1927)	155.00	125.00	75.00	5.25	4.25	2.60	.18	.11
634	2¢ carmine (I)	3.50	2.85	1.90	.25	.20	.13	.10	.06
634	Electric Eye Plate	(10)10.00	8.25	5.50					
634d	2¢ booklet pane of 6				3.75	3.00	1.80		
634A	2¢ carmine (II) (1928)				575.00	425.00	235.00	16.50	9.25
635	3¢ violet shades (1927)	9.75	7.85	5.25	.75	.60	.40	.11	.07
636	4¢ yellow brown (1927)	185.00	150.00	90.00	5.50	4.50	2.75	.16	.11
637	5¢ dark blue (1927)	40.00	32.50	19.50	5.50	4.50	2.75	.11	.07
638	6¢ red orange (1927)	42.75	33.75	21.00	5.50	4.50	2.75	.11	.07
639	7¢ black (1927)	42.75	33.75	21.00	5.50	4.50	2.75	.12	.08
640	8¢ olive green (1927)	42.75	33.75	21.00	5.50	4.50	2.75	.11	.07
641	9¢ orange red (1927)	42.75	33.75	21.00	5.50	4.50	2.75	.11	.07
642	10¢ orange (1927)	68.50	55.00	33.50	8.75	7.00	4.65	.11	.07

643	644	645	646	647	648

1927 Commemoratives

Scott No.	Description	P.B. F/NH	F	AVG	Unused F/NH	F	AVG	Used F	AVG
643	2¢ Vermont	(6)110.00	92.50	62.50	3.25	2.65	1.70	3.25	2.15
644	2¢ Burgoyne	(6)105.00	85.00	56.50	8.00	6.75	4.50	6.75	4.50

1928 COMMEMORATIVES

Scott No.	Description	P.B. F/NH	F	AVG	Unused F/NH	F	AVG	Used F	AVG
645-50	6 varieties, cpl.				55.00	46.50	27.50	48.75	29.50
645	2¢ Valley Forge	(6)80.00	67.50	45.00	2.25	1.80	1.20	1.15	.75
646	2¢ Monmouth	125.00	100.00	60.00	2.35	1.95	1.15	1.85	1.10
647	2¢ Hawaii	335.00	265.00	160.00	9.35	7.75	4.65	9.75	5.85
648	5¢ Hawaii	750.00	625.00	375.00	28.50	23.50	14.00	29.50	17.50

SCOTT NO.	DESCRIPTION	PLATE BLOCK F/NH	F	AVG	UNUSED F/NH	F	AVG	USED F	AVG

| | 649 | | 650 | | | 651 | | 654-656 | | 657 |

| 649 | 2¢ Aeronautics. | (6)38.50 | 31.50 | 21.00 | 225 | 1.85 | 120 | 1.95 | 1.30 |
| 650 | 5¢ Aeronautics | (6)160.00 | 130.00 | 85.00 | 12.75 | 10.65 | 7.00 | 6.25 | 4.15 |

1929 COMMEMORATIVES

| 651/81 | (651, 654-55, 657, 680-81) 6 varieties | | | | 9.25 | 7.50 | 5.00 | 7.50 | 5.00 |

| 651 | 2¢ George R. Clark | (6)26.00 | 21.75 | 14.50 | 1.70 | 1.35 | 90 | 1.65 | 1.10 |
| 651 | Same, arrow block of 4 | 7.50 | 6.00 | 4.00 | | | | | |

1929 Design of 1922-25
Rotary Press Printing Perf. 11 x 10 1/2

| 653 | 1/2¢ olive brown | 2.75 | 2.25 | 1.35 | .16 | .13 | .08 | .10 | .06 |

1929 Commemoratives

| 654 | 2¢ Edison, Flat, Perf. 11 | (6)80.00 | 67.50 | 45.00 | 1.60 | 1.25 | 85 | 1.60 | 1.10 |
| 655 | 2¢ Edison, Rotary, 11x10 1/2 | 135.00 | 110.00 | 67.50 | 1.50 | 1.20 | 80 | .40 | .25 |

LINE PAIR

| 656 | 2¢ Edison, Rotary Press Coil, Perf. Perf. 10 Vertically | 135.00 | 110.00 | 73.50 | 27.00 | 22.50 | 13.75 | 2.50 | 1.50 |

PLATE BLOCK

| 657 | 2¢ Sullivan Expedition | (6)72.50 | 60.00 | 40.00 | 1.60 | 1.30 | 85 | 1.30 | .85 |

1929 632-42 Overprinted Kansas

| 658-68 | 1¢-10¢ 11 Vars., cpl. | | | | 400.00 | 300.00 | 170.00 | 260.00 | 145.00 |

658	1¢ green	65.00	50.00	27.50	4.15	3.15	175	3.25	1.85
659	1 1/2¢ brown	75.00	57.50	31.50	7.00	5.50	3.00	4.50	2.50
660	2¢ carmine	75.00	57.50	31.50	6.50	5.00	275	1.10	.60
661	3¢ violet	295.00	225.00	125.00	3250	25.00	1375	22.50	12.50
662	4¢ yellow brown	295.00	225.00	125.00	3250	25.00	1375	12.75	7.25
663	5¢ deep blue	280.00	215.00	115.00	25.75	19.75	1100	15.00	8.25
664	6¢ red orange	735.00	565.00	310.00	50.00	38.75	2150	25.00	13.75
665	7¢ black	615.00	475.00	265.00	5250	40.00	2250	40.00	22.50
666	8¢ olive green	1250.00	965.00	525.00	145.00	110.00	6000	110.00	60.00
667	9¢ light rose	325.00	250.00	140.00	24.75	18.75	1050	17.50	9.75
668	10¢ orange yellow	615.00	465.00	265.00	45.00	33.50	1800	17.50	9.75

1929. 632-42 Overprinted Nebraska

| 669-79 | 1¢-10¢, 11 Vars., cpl | | | | 500.00 | 385.00 | 215.00 | 245.00 | 133.50 |

669	1¢ green	54.50	41.75	23.50	4.50	3.35	185	3.00	1.65
670	1 1/2¢ brown	88.50	67.50	37.50	5.35	4.15	235	3.75	2.10
671	2¢ carmine	71.50	55.00	30.00	4.50	3.35	185	1.50	.85
672	3¢ violet	315.00	240.00	135.00	25.00	18.75	1050	15.75	8.75
673	4¢ brown	400.00	310.00	170.00	45.00	33.75	1850	21.50	11.75
674	5¢ blue	415.00	315.00	175.00	3250	25.00	1375	21.50	11.75
675	6¢ orange	835.00	650.00	365.00	71.50	55.00	3000	37.50	20.75
676	7¢ black	415.00	315.00	175.00	3950	30.00	1650	30.00	16.50
677	8¢ olive green	525.00	400.00	225.00	55.00	42.50	2375	37.50	20.75
678	9¢ rose	625.00	485.00	265.00	71.50	55.00	3000	42.75	23.75
679	10¢ orange yellow	1450.00	1100.00	600.00	185.00	140.00	7750	32.75	18.00

AVERAGE, NH: To determine the price for a Never Hinged stamp in Average condition, add 50% of the difference between the Fine, NH and Fine prices to the Average price. Average prices are for hinged stamps.

680   681   682   683

1929 Commemoratives

SCOTT NO.	DESCRIPTION	PLATE BLOCK F/NH	F	AVG	UNUSED F/NH	F	AVG	USED F	AVG
680	2¢ Fallen Timbers	(6)67.50	55.00	36.50	1.95	1.55	1.10	1.60	1.10
681	2¢ Ohio River Canal	(6)55.00	45.00	30.00	1.15	.95	.65	1.20	.80

1930-31 COMMEMORATIVES

682/703	(682-83, 688-90, 702-03) 7 Vars., cpl.	....	....	....	8.00	6.65	4.50	7.65	5.15

1930 COMMEMORATIVES

682	2¢ Massachusetts Bay	(6)75.00	62.50	41.75	1.30	1.05	.70	1.10	.75
683	2¢ Carolina-Charleston	(6)120.00	100.00	66.50	2.65	2.15	1.45	2.50	1.65

684,686   685, 687   688   689   690

1930 Rotary Press Printing Perf. 11 x 10 1/2

684	1 1/2¢ Harding		6.50	5.50	3.35	.65	.55	.35	.10	.06
685	4¢ Taft		25.00	21.00	14.00	1.85	1.55	1.05	.11	.07

1930 Rotary Press Coil Stamps Perf. 10 Vertically
LINE PAIR

686	1 1/2¢ Harding	16.50	13.00	8.00	3.00	2.50	1.50	.11	.07
687	4¢ Taft	26.50	21.75	14.00	6.50	5.25	3.25	.95	.60

1930 COMMEMORATIVES
PLATE BLOCK

688	2¢ Braddock's Field	(6)90.00	75.00	50.00	1.80	1.50	1.00	2.25	1.50
689	2¢ Von Steuben	(6)57.50	47.50	31.75	1.25	1.05	.70	.95	.65

1931 COMMEMORATIVES

690	2¢ Pulaski	(6)45.00	37.50	25.00	.50	.40	.27	.35	.23

1931 Designs of 1922-26. Rotary Press Ptg.

692-701	11¢ to 50¢, 10 Vars., cpl	....	....	....	250.00	205.00	125.00	2.35	1.40

Perf. 11 x 10 1/2

692	11¢ light blue	36.50	30.00	18.50	5.35	4.50	2.75	.18	.11
693	12¢ brown violet	60.00	50.00	30.00	10.25	8.50	5.25	.12	.07
694	13¢ yellow green	36.50	30.00	18.50	3.95	3.25	1.95	.30	.18
695	14¢ dark blue	51.50	42.50	25.00	7.00	5.85	3.50	.70	.45
696	15¢ gray	120.00	95.00	60.00	22.50	18.75	11.50	.11	.07

Perf. 10 1/2 x 11

697	17¢ black	72.50	60.00	36.50	11.00	8.75	5.25	.45	.27
698	20¢ carmine rose	150.00	125.00	75.00	23.50	19.50	11.75	.11	.07
699	25¢ blue green	135.00	110.00	67.50	22.50	18.75	11.50	.18	.11
700	30¢ brown	195.00	160.00	97.50	35.00	28.50	17.00	.13	.08
701	50¢ lilac	525.00	425.00	250.00	115.00	95.00	57.50	.13	.08

VERY FINE QUALITY: To determine the Very Fine price, add the difference between the Fine and Average prices to the Fine quality price. For example: if the Fine price is $10.00 and the Average price is $6.00, the Very Fine price would be $14.00. From 1935 to date, add 20% to the Fine price to arrive at the Very Fine price.

SCOTT NO.	DESCRIPTION	PLATE BLOCK F/NH	F	AVG	UNUSED F/NH	F	AVG	USED F	AVG

702

703

1931 COMMEMORATIVES

SCOTT NO.	DESCRIPTION	F/NH	F	AVG	F/NH	F	AVG	F	AVG
702	2¢ Red Cross	5.25	4.25	2.85	.25	.20	.13	.23	.15
702	2¢ arrow block	1.20	.95	.65	......	......	......	......	......
703	2¢ Yorktown	6.00	5.00	3.35	.75	.60	.40	.65	.45
703	2¢ center line block	3.50	2.80	1.90	......	......	......	......	......
703	2¢ arrow block	3.25	2.60	1.75	......	......	......	......	......

704   705   706   707   708   709

710   711   712   713   714   715

1932 WASHINGTON BICENTENNIAL

SCOTT NO.	DESCRIPTION	F/NH	F	AVG	F/NH	F	AVG	F	AVG
704-15	1/2¢ to 10¢ 12 Vars., cpl	850.00	695.00	415.00	55.00	46.50	27.50	3.65	2.15
704	1/2¢ olive brown	9.75	7.85	4.75	.17	.13	.08	.12	.08
705	1¢ green	9.00	7.50	4.50	.27	.23	.14	.10	.06
706	1 1/2¢ brown	42.50	35.00	21.50	.95	.80	.50	.18	.11
707	2¢ carmine	4.75	3.95	2.60	.18	.15	.09	.10	.06
708	3¢ purple	36.00	30.00	18.00	1.35	1.15	.70	.12	.08
709	4¢ light brown	15.00	12.50	7.50	.65	.55	.35	.16	.10
710	5¢ blue	47.50	39.50	23.75	3.85	3.15	1.95	.20	.13
711	6¢ orange	150.00	125.00	75.00	7.50	6.25	3.75	.16	.10
712	7¢ black	16.50	13.50	8.25	.85	.70	.45	.35	.22
713	8¢ olive bistre	160.00	130.00	77.50	7.50	6.25	3.75	1.75	1.05
714	9¢ pale red	115.00	95.00	57.50	6.75	5.50	3.35	.35	.22
715	10¢ orange yellow	275.00	225.00	135.00	30.00	25.00	15.00	.18	.12

716   717   718   719   720-722   724

1932 COMMEMORATIVES

SCOTT NO.	DESCRIPTION	F/NH	F	AVG	F/NH	F	AVG	F	AVG
716-25	(716-19, 724-25) 6 Vars.	......	......	......	12.50	10.50	6.75	2.10	1.35
716	2¢ Winter Olympics	(6)26.00	21.50	14.00	1.10	.90	.60	.45	.30
717	2¢ Arbor Day	18.00	15.00	10.00	.30	.25	.16	.18	.12
718	3¢ Summer Olympics	50.00	42.50	27.50	3.75	3.15	2.00	.16	.10
719	5¢ Summer Olympics	60.00	50.00	31.50	6.25	5.25	3.35	.45	.28

1932 Rotary Press

SCOTT NO.	DESCRIPTION	F/NH	F	AVG	F/NH	F	AVG	F	AVG
720	3¢ deep violet	4.00	3.35	2.10	.40	.35	.22	.09	.06
720b	2¢ booklet pane of 6	......	......	......	75.00	60.00	36.50	......	......

SCOTT NO.	DESCRIPTION	LINE PAIR F/NH	F	AVG	UNUSED F/NH	F	AVG	USED F	AVG
721	3¢ deep violet coil perf. 10 vertically	14.00	11.75	7.00	5.95	4.85	3.15	.13	.08
722	3¢ deep violet coil perf. 10 horizontally	11.00	9.25	5.75	2.75	2.25	1.40	.85	.55
723	6¢ Garfield, coil perf. 10 vertically	105.00	87.50	55.00	26.75	21.75	13.75	.30	.18

1932 COMMEMORATIVES
PLATE BLOCK

| 724 | 3¢ Penn | (6)27.50 | 22.50 | 15.00 | .65 | .55 | .35 | .40 | .26 |

725   726   727,752   728,730,766   729,731,767   732

| 725 | 3¢ Webster | (6)55.00 | 45.00 | 30.00 | .90 | .75 | .50 | .55 | .35 |

1933 COMMEMORATIVES

726/34	(726-29, 732-34) 7 Vars	......	......	......	3.85	3.15	2.00	2.50	1.65
726	3¢ Oglethorpe	(6)33.50	27.50	18.00	.65	.55	.36	.33	.22
726	Plate Block with "cs"	(10)42.50	33.50	22.50	......	......	......	......	......
727	3¢ Washington Hdqrs	13.50	11.00	7.00	.24	.20	.13	.17	.11
728	1¢ Fort Dearborn	5.75	4.75	3.15	.22	.18	.12	.11	.07
729	3¢ Federal Building	8.00	8.00	5.00	.30	.25	.16	.11	.07

Special Printing for A.P.S. Convention
Imperforate: without Gum

730	1¢ yellow green, Sheet of 25	......	......	......	......	60.00	......	65.00	60.00
730a	1¢ yellow green single	......	......	......	......	1.25	.95	.75	.50
731	3¢ violet, Sheet of 25	......	......	......	......	57.50	......	62.50	57.50
731a	3¢ violet, single	......	......	......	......	1.25	.95	.75	.50
732	3¢ N.R.A.	5.00	4.00	2.65	.22	.18	.12	.09	.06

733,735,753,768   734   736   737,738,754   739,755

| 733 | 3¢ Byrd | (6)50.00 | 40.00 | 26.75 | 1.20 | 1.00 | .65 | 1.35 | .85 |
| 734 | 5¢ Kosciuszko | (6)95.00 | 80.00 | 53.50 | 1.15 | .95 | .60 | .50 | .35 |

1934 NATIONAL PHILATELIC EXHIBITION
Imperf. Without Gum

| 735 | 3¢ dark blue, Sheet of 6 | ...... | ...... | ...... | ...... | 35.00 | ...... | 37.50 | 32.50 |
| 735a | 3¢ dark blue, single | ...... | ...... | ...... | ...... | 4.50 | 3.50 | 4.00 | 3.00 |

1934 COMMEMORATIVES

736-39	4 Varieties	......	......	......	1.15	.95	.60	.95	.65
736	3¢ Maryland	(6)27.50	22.50	15.00	.30	.25	.16	.25	.16
737	3¢ Mother's Day, rotary, perf. 11 x 10 1/2	3.75	3.00	2.00	.22	.18	.12	.11	.07
738	3¢ Mother's Day, flat, perf. 11	(6)12.65	10.50	7.00	.37	.30	.20	.45	.30
739	3¢ Wisconsin	(6)11.50	9.50	6.25	.30	.25	.16	.20	.13

AVERAGE, NH: To determine the price for a Never Hinged stamp in Average condition, add 50% of the difference between the Fine, NH and Fine prices to the Average price. Average prices are for hinged stamps.

SCOTT NO.	DESCRIPTION	PLATE BLOCK F/NH	F	AVG	UNUSED F/NH	F	AVG	USED F	AVG

741,757

742,750,758,770

740,751,756,769

744,760

743,759

745,761

747,763

746,762

748,764

749,765,797

1934 NATIONAL PARKS ISSUE

SCOTT NO.	DESCRIPTION	PLATE BLOCK F/NH	F	AVG	UNUSED F/NH	F	AVG	USED F	AVG
740-49	1¢-10¢ Vars., cpl	285.00	240.00	160.00	23.50	19.50	12.75	13.50	9.00
740	1¢ Yosemite	(6)3.00	2.50	1.65	.16	.14	.09	.14	.09
741	2¢ Grand Canyon	(6)3.35	2.75	1.85	.25	.22	.14	.17	.11
742	3¢ Mt. Rainier	(6)5.25	4.25	2.85	.33	.27	.18	.17	.11
743	4¢ Mesa Verde	(6)21.75	18.00	12.00	.95	.80	.50	.85	.55
744	5¢ Yellowstone	(6)26.00	21.50	14.00	1.80	1.50	1.00	1.50	1.00
745	6¢ Crater Lake	(6)43.75	36.50	24.50	2.85	2.35	1.60	2.35	1.60
746	7¢ Acadia	(6)29.75	24.50	16.50	1.65	1.35	.90	1.75	1.15
747	8¢ Zion	(6)46.75	38.75	26.00	4.50	3.75	2.50	3.95	2.65
748	9¢ Glacier	(6)46.75	38.75	26.00	4.35	3.65	2.40	1.30	.85
749	10¢ Great Smoky Mts.	(6)81.50	67.50	45.00	7.50	6.25	4.15	1.95	1.30

Special Printing for the A.P.S. Convention & Exhibition of Atlantic City
Imperforate Souvenir Sheet

750	3¢ deep violet, Sheet of 6	....	....	....	75.00	60.00	......	75.00	55.00
750a	3¢ deep violet, single	....	....	....	7.75	6.35	4.75	6.00	4.25

Special Printing for TransMississippi Philatelic Exposition and Convention at Omaha
Imperforate Souvenir Sheet

751	1¢ green, Sheet of 6	....	....	....	28.75	25.00	......	28.50	20.00
751a	1¢ green, single	....	....	....	3.50	3.00	2.25	2.50	1.70

SELECTED U.S. COMMEMORATIVE MINT SHEETS

Scott No.	F/NH SHEET	Scott No.	F/NH SHEET	Scott No.	F/NH SHEET	Scott No.	F/NH SHEET
610(100)	225.00	651(50)	115.00	708(100)	160.00	732(100)	32.50
614(50)	450.00	654(100)	275.00	709(100)	75.00	733(50)	97.50
615(50)	800.00	655(100)	275.00	710(100)	415.00	734(100)	200.00
617(50)	500.00	657(100)	260.00	711(100)	850.00	736(100)	53.50
618(50)	750.00	680(100)	300.00	712(100)	97.50	737(50)	14.50
620(100)	1500.00	681(100)	195.00	713(100)	895.00	738(50)	27.50
627(50)	395.00	682(100)	190.00	714(100)	750.00	739(50)	23.50
628(50)	1050.00	683(100)	350.00	715(100)	3100.00	740-49 set	1150.00
629(100)	650.00	688(100)	250.00	716(100)	125.00	740(50)	9.50
643(100)	475.00	689(100)	170.00	717(100)	46.50	741(50)	13.50
644(50)	465.00	690(100)	87.50	718(100)	400.00	742(50)	18.50
645(100)	335.00	702(100)	35.00	719(100)	650.00	743(50)	55.00
646(100)	315.00	703(50)	45.00	724(100)	85.00	744(50)	97.50
647(100)	1150.00	704-15 set	6250.00	725(100)	135.00	745(50)	150.00
648(100)	3250.00	704(100)	25.00	726(100)	85.00	746(50)	95.00
649(50)	150.00	705(100)	32.50	727(100)	37.50	747(50)	225.00
650(50)	750.00	706(100)	130.00	728(100)	26.50	748(50)	200.00
		707(100)	21.50	729(100)	38.75	749(50)	350.00

SCOTT NO.		PLATE BLOCK	CENTER LINE BLOCK	T OR B ARROW BLOCK	L OR R ARROW BLOCK	PAIR WITH V. LINE	PAIR WITH H. LINE	FINE UNUSED	FINE USED
	1935 "FARLEY SPECIAL PRINTINGS" Designs of 1933-34 Imperforate (#752, 753 Perf.) Ungummed								
752-71	20 Vars., cpl	....	875.00	....	....	250.00	172.50	50.00	52.50
752	3¢ Newburgh	27.75	85.00	32.50	13.75	15.00	6.25	.25	.25
753	3¢ Byrd	(6)37.50	175.00	160.00	6.50	75.00	3.00	.90	.95
754	3¢ Mother's Day	(6)37.50	17.50	6.50	7.00	2.95	3.25	1.10	1.20
755	3¢ Wisconsin	(6)37.50	17.50	6.50	7.00	2.95	3.25	1.10	1.20
756-65	1¢-10¢ Parks 10 Vars., cpl.	575.00	300.00	175.00	175.00	78.50	79.50	30.00	31.50
756	1¢ Yosemite	(6)9.75	7.50	2.75	2.00	1.25	.95	.35	.37
757	2¢ Grand Canyon	(6)12.50	10.75	3.25	3.50	1.50	1.60	.50	.55
758	3¢ Mt. Rainier	(6)32.50	12.50	6.50	7.00	3.00	3.25	1.00	1.10
759	4¢ Mesa Verde	(6)45.00	22.50	12.75	14.75	5.50	6.25	2.00	2.25
760	5¢ Yellowstone	(6)55.00	35.00	21.50	19.00	9.50	8.25	3.75	3.75
761	6¢ Crater Lake	(6)82.50	45.00	25.00	26.50	11.50	12.50	5.00	4.50
762	7¢ Acadia	(6)70.00	37.50	19.50	21.50	8.50	9.50	3.50	3.75
763	8¢ Zion	(6)85.00	40.00	23.00	20.75	10.00	9.00	3.85	4.00
764	9¢ Glacier	(6)100.00	42.50	23.50	24.50	10.50	10.75	4.50	4.50
765	10¢ Gt. Smoky Mts.	(6)110.00	65.00	47.50	45.00	21.50	20.00	7.50	8.00
766a-70a	5 Vars., cpl.		165.00	....	....	72.50	68.50	15.00	14.75
766a	1¢ Ft. Dearborn	....	31.50	....	....	14.00	13.00	1.35	.95
767a	3¢ Federal Building	....	31.50	....	....	14.00	13.00	1.35	.95
768a	3¢ Byrd	....	38.75	....	....	17.50	15.00	5.75	5.25
769a	1¢ Yosemite	....	21.50	....	....	10.00	9.00	2.25	2.40
770a	3¢ Mt. Rainier	....	50.00	....	....	21.50	22.50	5.50	6.00
771	16¢ Airmail Spec. Deliv.	(6)145.00	150.00	26.50	28.50	12.00	13.00	5.00	5.25

U.S. FARLEY ISSUE COMPLETE MINT SHEETS

Scott No.	F/WG SHEET	Scott No.	F/WG SHEET	Scott No.	F/WG SHEET	Scott No.	F/WG SHEET
752-71 set	15000.00	756-65 set	7750.00	761(200)	1150.00	767(225)	850.00
752(400)	575.00	756(200)	115.00	762(200)	900.00	768(150)	1100.00
753(200)	1150.00	757(200)	140.00	763(200)	1075.00	769(120)	500.00
754(200)	350.00	758(200)	315.00	764(200)	1150.00	770(120)	1200.00
755(200)	350.00	759(200)	565.00	765(200)	1800.00	771(200)	1500.00
		760(200)	825.00	766(225)	850.00		

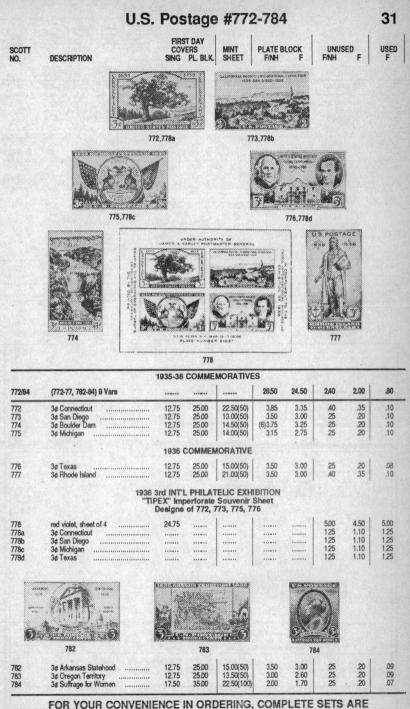

772,778a

773,778b

775,778c

776,778d

774

778

777

1935-36 COMMEMORATIVES

772/84	(772-77, 782-84) 9 Vars	....	....	....	28.50	24.50	2.40	2.00	.80
772	3¢ Connecticut	12.75	25.00	22.50(50)	3.85	3.35	.40	.35	.10
773	3¢ San Diego	12.75	25.00	13.00(50)	3.50	3.00	.25	.20	.10
774	3¢ Boulder Dam	12.75	25.00	14.50(50)	(6)3.75	3.25	.25	.20	.10
775	3¢ Michigan	12.75	25.00	14.00(50)	3.15	2.75	.25	.20	.10

1936 COMMEMORATIVE

776	3¢ Texas	12.75	25.00	15.00(50)	3.50	3.00	.25	.20	.08
777	3¢ Rhode Island	12.75	25.00	21.00(50)	3.50	3.00	.40	.35	.10

1936 3rd INT'L PHILATELIC EXHIBITION
"TIPEX" Imperforate Souvenir Sheet
Designs of 772, 773, 775, 776

778	red violet, sheet of 4	24.75	....	....	....	....	5.00	4.50	5.00
778a	3¢ Connecticut	....	....	....	....	....	1.25	1.10	1.25
778b	3¢ San Diego	....	....	....	....	....	1.25	1.10	1.25
778c	3¢ Michigan	....	....	....	....	....	1.25	1.10	1.25
778d	3¢ Texas	....	....	....	....	....	1.25	1.10	1.25

782

783

784

782	3¢ Arkansas Statehood	12.75	25.00	15.00(50)	3.50	3.00	.25	.20	.09
783	3¢ Oregon Territory	12.75	25.00	13.50(50)	3.00	2.60	.25	.20	.09
784	3¢ Suffrage for Women	17.50	35.00	22.50(100)	2.00	1.70	.25	.20	.07

**FOR YOUR CONVENIENCE IN ORDERING, COMPLETE SETS ARE
LISTED BEFORE SINGLE STAMP LISTINGS**

SCOTT NO.	DESCRIPTION	FIRST DAY COVERS SING PL. BLK.		MINT SHEET	PLATE BLOCK F/NH F		UNUSED F/NH F		USED F

785

786

787

788

789

790

791

792

793

794

1936-37 ARMY AND NAVY ISSUE

SCOTT NO.	DESCRIPTION	SING	PL. BLK.	MINT SHEET	F/NH	F	F/NH	F	USED F
785-94	10 Vars., cpl.	70.00	150.00	375.00	100.00	85.00	6.25	5.50	2.50

ARMY COMMEMORATIVES

785	1¢ green	7.50	15.00	8.75(50)	2.50	2.20	.14	.12	.10
786	2¢ carmine	7.50	15.00	10.75(50)	2.25	1.95	.18	.16	.10
787	3¢ purple	7.50	15.00	22.50(50)	3.00	2.50	.45	.40	.10
788	4¢ gray	7.50	17.50	65.00(50)	22.00	19.00	.90	.75	.50
789	5¢ ultramarine	7.50	17.50	90.00(50)	22.50	19.50	1.70	1.50	.50

NAVY COMMEMORATIVES

790	1¢ green	7.50	15.00	8.75(50)	2.50	2.20	.14	.12	.10
791	2¢ carmine	7.50	15.00	10.75(50)	2.25	1.95	.18	.16	.10
792	3¢ purple	7.50	15.00	17.50(50)	3.00	2.50	.33	.28	.10
793	4¢ gray	7.50	17.50	65.00(50)	22.00	19.00	.90	.75	.50
794	5¢ ultramarine	7.50	17.50	90.00(50)	22.50	19.50	1.70	1.50	.50

795

796

797

1937 COMMEMORATIVES

795/802	(795-96, 798-802) 7 vars.				33.50	27.50	1.70	1.50	.90
795	3¢ N.W. Ordinance	11.00	21.50	12.50(50)	3.00	2.65	.23	.20	.08
796	5¢ Virginia Dare	13.75	27.50	32.50(48)	(6)16.50	14.00	.35	.32	.35

1937 S.P.A. CONVENTION ISSUE
Design of 749 Imperforate Souvenir Sheet

797	10¢ blue green	12.50					1.60	1.40	1.35

SCOTT NO.	DESCRIPTION	FIRST DAY COVERS SING	PL. BLK.	MINT SHEET	PLATE BLOCK F/NH	F	UNUSED F/NH	F	USED F

798

799

800

801

802

798	3¢ Constitution	9.50	18.75	13.75(50)	3.00	2.85	25	.22	.09
799	3¢ Hawaii	11.75	23.50	13.50(50)	3.15	2.75	23	.20	.11
800	3¢ Alaska	11.75	23.50	15.00(50)	3.15	2.75	23	.20	.11
801	3¢ Puerto Rico	11.75	28.50	13.50(50)	3.15	2.75	23	.20	.11
802	3¢ Virgin Islands	11.75	23.50	13.50(50)	3.15	2.75	23	.20	.11

803   804,839,848   805,840,849   806,841,850   807,842,851   808,843   809,844

810,845   811,846   812   813   814   815,847   816

817   818   819   820   821   822   823

824   825   826   827   828   829   830

831   832   833   834

1938 PRESIDENTIAL SERIES

803-34	1/2¢-$5, 32 Vars., cpl.	550.00	....	....	1725.00	1475.00	360.00	310.00	24.50
803-31	1/2¢-50¢, 29 Vars.	140.00	....	....	385.00	325.00	78.50	67.50	5.50
803	1/2¢ Franklin	2.50	5.00	7.50(100)	.70	.60	.07	.06	.06
804	1¢ G. Washington	3.00	6.00	10.00(100)	.45	.40	.10	.09	.06
804b	1¢ booklet pane of 6	18.75	....	....	....	....	3.75	3.15	....
805	1 1/2¢ M. Washington	3.00	6.00	9.00(100)	.40	.35	.09	.08	.06

SCOTT NO.	DESRIPTION	FIRST DAY COVERS SING	PL. BLK.	MINT SHEET	PLATE BLOCK F/NH	F	UNUSED F/NH	F	USED F
806	2¢ J. Adams	3.00	6.00	22.50(100)	1.00	.90	22	.20	.06
806	E.E. Plate Block of 10	......	......	......	9.75	8.75	......	......	......
806b	2¢ booklet pane of 6	18.75	......	......	......	......	8.75	7.75	......
807	3¢ Jefferson	3.00	6.00	13.50(100)	.70	.60	.15	.13	.06
807	E.E. Plate Block of 10	......	......	......	37.50	33.50	......	......	......
807a	3¢ booklet pane of 6	22.50	......	......	......	......	1500	13.50	......
808	4¢ Madison	3.35	6.75	92.50(100)	4.00	3.50	.95	.85	.06
809	4 1/2¢ White House	3.75	7.50	27.50(100)	3.00	2.70	.30	.27	.12
810	5¢ J. Monroe	3.75	7.50	55.00(100)	2.40	2.00	.55	.48	.06
811	6¢ J.Q. Adams	3.75	7.50	55.00(100)	2.65	2.25	.55	.48	.06
812	7¢ A. Jackson	3.75	7.50	58.75(100)	3.25	2.75	.65	.55	.07
813	8¢ Van Buren	3.75	7.50	100.00(100)	4.85	4.25	1.10	.95	.07
814	9¢ Harrison	3.75	7.50	100.00(100)	4.50	3.85	1.00	.85	.07
815	10¢ Tyler	3.75	7.50	60.00(100)	3.00	2.50	.65	.55	.06
816	11¢ Polk	4.75	9.50	130.00(100)	7.25	6.25	1.35	1.20	.09
817	12¢ Taylor	4.75	9.50	275.00(100)	12.00	10.50	2.75	2.35	.07
818	13¢ Fillmore	4.75	9.50	365.00(100)	18.75	16.50	4.00	3.50	.20
819	14¢ Pierce	4.75	9.50	215.00(100)	11.00	9.25	235	2.00	.20
820	15¢ Buchanan	4.75	9.50	110.00(100)	5.00	4.35	1.10	1.00	.06
821	16¢ Lincoln	5.50	10.75	225.00(100)	13.50	11.50	250	2.15	.85
822	17¢ Johnson	5.50	10.75	210.00(100)	10.50	9.00	235	2.00	.17
823	18¢ Grant	5.50	10.75	425.00(100)	21.75	18.75	4.50	3.85	.17
824	19¢ Hayes	5.50	10.75	350.00(100)	16.75	14.50	3.75	3.25	1.15
825	20¢ Garfield	6.25	12.00	235.00(100)	10.50	9.00	225	1.95	.06
826	21¢ Arthur	6.25	12.00	475.00(100)	23.50	20.00	5.00	4.35	.22
827	22¢ Cleveland	6.25	12.00	260.00(100)	22.50	19.50	2.75	2.35	1.10
828	24¢ B. Harrison	6.25	12.00	825.00(100)	45.00	38.75	8.75	7.50	.35
829	25¢ McKinley	7.50	15.00	175.00(100)	8.50	7.25	1.75	1.50	.06
830	30¢ T. Roosevelt	9.50	18.50	1175.00(100)	60.00	50.00	12.50	10.75	.07
831	50¢ Taft	18.75	35.00	1650.00(100)	85.00	72.50	17.50	15.00	.08

Flat Plate Printing Perf. 11

SCOTT NO.	DESRIPTION	FIRST DAY COVERS SING	PL. BLK.	MINT SHEET	PLATE BLOCK F/NH	F	UNUSED F/NH	F	USED F
832	$1 Wilson	70.00	135.00	2100.00(100)	97.50	83.50	21.75	18.75	.13
832	$1 center line block	......	......	......	95.00	82.50	......	......	......
832	$1 arrow block	......	......	......	90.00	78.50	......	......	......
832b	$1 Watermarked "USIR"	......	......	......	......	......	425.00	365.00	90.00
832c	$1 dry print thick paper (1954)	45.00	85.00	1500.00(100)	85.00	72.50	16.50	14.50	.25
833	$2 Harding	125.00	250.00	......	315.00	265.00	49.50	42.50	10.00
833	$2 center line block	......	......	......	220.00	190.00	......	......	......
833	$2 arrow block	......	......	......	210.00	180.00	......	......	......
834	$5 Coolidge	225.00	450.00	......	975.00	850.00	225.00	190.00	9.50
834	$5 center line block	......	......	......	1025.00	875.00	......	......	......
834	$5 arrow block	......	......	......	925.00	800.00	......	......	......

835	836	837	838

1938-39 COMMEMORATIVES

835/58	(835-38, 852-58) 11 Vars., cpl	......	......	......	80.00	70.00	4.50	3.75	1.10
835	3¢ Ratification	9.00	18.50	25.00(50)	8.75	7.50	.40	.35	.10
836	3¢ Swedes-Finns	9.00	18.50	16.50(48)	(6)8.00	6.85	.27	.23	.12
837	3¢ North West Territory	9.00	18.50	47.50(100)	20.00	17.50	.35	.30	.10
838	3¢ Iowa Territory	9.00	18.50	30.00(50)	13.50	12.00	.45	.40	.14

FIRST DAY COVERS: First Day Covers are envelopes cancelled on the "First Day of Issue" of the stamp used on the envelope. Usually they also contain a picture (cachet) on the left side designed to go with the theme of the stamp. From 1935 to 1944, prices listed are for cacheted, addressed covers. From 1945 to date, prices are for cacheted, unaddressed covers.

SCOTT NO.	DESRIPTION	FIRST DAY COVERS SING PL. BLK.		MINT SHEET	PLATE BLOCK F/NH F		UNUSED F/NH F		USED F

1939 Presidentials Rotary Press Coil

			L. PR.		LINE PAIR				
839-51	13 Vars., cpl.	87.50	145.00	......	260.00	225.00	61.50	52.75	6.75

Perforated 10 Vertically

839	1¢ G. Washington	6.25	10.50	......	2.25	1.95	.55	.48	.07
840	1 1/2¢ M. Washington	6.25	10.50	......	2.75	2.35	.60	.50	.10
841	2¢ J. Adams	6.25	10.50	......	3.00	2.60	.60	.50	.06
842	3¢ T. Jefferson	6.25	10.50	......	3.15	2.70	.90	.80	.06
843	4¢ J. Madison	7.50	12.50	......	55.00	47.50	12.75	10.85	.80
844	4 1/2¢ White House	7.50	12.50	......	10.75	9.50	1.00	.90	.95
845	5¢ J. Monroe	8.00	13.00	......	55.00	47.50	10.75	9.25	.65
846	6¢ J.Q. Adams	8.00	13.00	......	13.75	11.75	2.00	1.70	.15
847	10¢ J. Tyler	12.00	20.00	......	95.00	82.50	21.75	18.50	1.10

Perforated 10 Horizontally

848	1¢ G. Washington	6.25	10.50	......	3.75	3.25	1.50	1.30	.16
849	1 1/2¢ M. Washington	6.25	10.50	......	7.50	6.50	3.00	2.50	.80
850	2¢ Adams	6.25	10.50	......	11.75	10.00	5.25	4.50	1.20
851	3¢ T. Jefferson	6.25	10.50	......	11.75	10.00	4.50	3.85	.85

852

853

854

857

855

856

858

1939 COMMEMORATIVES

852	3¢ Golden Gate	9.00	17.50	12.50(50)	3.50	3.00	.22	.18	.08
853	3¢ World's Fair	10.75	21.50	16.50(50)	4.25	3.65	.30	.25	.08
854	3¢ Inauguration	9.00	17.50	40.00(50)	(6)7.50	6.50	.75	.65	.11
855	3¢ Baseball	37.50	57.50	52.50(50)	6.50	5.50	1.05	.90	.11
856	3¢ Panama Canal	9.00	17.50	24.00(50)	(6)7.50	6.50	.45	.40	.11
857	3¢ Printing	9.00	17.50	12.00(50)	2.25	1.90	.25	.20	.11
858	3¢ Four States	7.75	15.00	13.50(50)	3.25	2.75	.25	.20	.11

859

860

861

862

863

1940 FAMOUS AMERICANS ISSUES

859-93	35 Vars., cpl.	120.00	......	4250.00	850.00	725.00	60.00	52.50	31.50
859/91	All 1¢, 2¢, 3¢ values, 21 Vars ...	......	......	......	65.00	55.00	3.50	2.95	2.25

American Authors

859	1¢ Washington Irving	2.35	4.65	10.75(70)	2.50	2.15	.13	.11	.11
860	2¢ James F. Cooper	2.35	4.65	11.50(70)	2.65	2.25	.15	.13	.12
861	3¢ Ralph W. Emerson	3.15	6.25	12.50(70)	2.80	2.40	.15	.13	.10
682	5¢ Louisa May Alcott	3.75	7.50	55.00(70)	25.00	21.50	.70	.60	.40
863	10¢ Samuel L. Clemens	8.50	25.00	275.00(70)	100.00	85.00	3.25	2.75	3.75

| SCOTT NO. | DESCRIPTION | FIRST DAY COVERS | | MINT SHEET | PLATE BLOCK | | UNUSED | | USED |
| | | SING | PL. BLK. | | F/NH | F | F/NH | F | F |

864   865   866   867   868

American Poets

SCOTT NO.	DESCRIPTION	SING	PL. BLK.	MINT SHEET	F/NH	F	F/NH	F	USED F
864	1¢ Henry W. Longfellow	2.25	4.50	14.50(70)	4.75	4.25	.15	.13	.15
865	2¢ John Whittier	2.25	4.50	14.50(70)	3.85	3.35	.15	.13	.12
866	3¢ James Lowell	3.15	6.25	16.50(70)	5.95	5.15	.20	.17	.10
867	5¢ Walt Whitman	3.75	7.50	67.50(70)	25.00	21.50	.65	.55	.55
868	10¢ James Riley	6.00	22.50	350.00(70)	87.50	75.00	4.25	3.60	4.50

869   870   871   872   873

American Educators

SCOTT NO.	DESCRIPTION	SING	PL. BLK.	MINT SHEET	F/NH	F	F/NH	F	USED F
869	1¢ Horace Mann	2.25	4.50	12.75(70)	4.00	3.50	.15	.13	.12
870	2¢ Mark Hopkins	2.25	4.50	11.50(70)	2.95	2.50	.14	.11	.12
871	3¢ Charles W. Eliot	3.00	6.00	28.75(70)	6.00	5.00	.35	.40	.10
872	5¢ Frances Willard	3.75	7.50	77.50(70)	26.50	22.50	.80	.70	.50
873	10¢ Booker T. Washington	6.00	16.75	260.00(70)	65.00	56.50	3.35	2.85	3.25

874   875   876   877   878

American Scientists

SCOTT NO.	DESCRIPTION	SING	PL. BLK.	MINT SHEET	F/NH	F	F/NH	F	USED F
874	1¢ John J. Audubon	2.25	4.50	10.50(70)	2.65	2.25	.12	.10	.10
875	2¢ Dr. Crawford Long	3.75	7.50	11.00(70)	2.15	1.80	.15	.13	.12
876	3¢ Luther Burbank	3.00	6.00	13.00(70)	2.50	2.15	.15	.13	.09
877	5¢ Dr. Walter Reed	3.75	7.50	45.00(70)	18.50	16.00	.40	.35	.35
878	10¢ Jane Addams	6.00	14.75	195.00(70)	55.00	47.50	2.50	2.15	2.65

879   880   881   882   883

American Composers

SCOTT NO.	DESCRIPTION	SING	PL. BLK.	MINT SHEET	F/NH	F	F/NH	F	USED F
879	1¢ Stephen Foster	2.25	4.50	8.95(70)	2.50	2.15	.11	.10	.10
880	2¢ John Philip Sousa	2.25	4.50	16.50(70)	2.50	2.15	.20	.18	.11
881	3¢ Victor Herbert	3.00	6.00	16.00(70)	2.75	2.35	.23	.20	.10
882	5¢ Edward A. MacDowell	3.75	7.50	78.50(70)	26.50	22.50	.90	.80	.60
883	10¢ Ethelbert Nevin	6.00	21.50	650.00(70)	85.00	72.50	10.00	8.50	3.50

MINT SHEETS: From 1935 to date, we list prices for our standard size Mint Sheets in Fine, Never Hinged condition. The number off stamps in each sheet is noted in ( ).

FAMOUS AMERICANS: Later additions to the Famous American series include #945 Edison, #953 Carver, #960 White, #965 Stone, #975 Rogers, #980 Harris, #986 Poe, and #988 Gompers.

SCOTT NO.	DESRIPTION	FIRST DAY COVERS SING	PL. BLK.	MINT SHEET	PLATE BLOCK F/NH	F	UNUSED F/NH	F	USED F

884   885   886   887   888

American Artists

Scott	Description	Sing	Pl.Blk	Mint Sheet	PB F/NH	PB F	Unused F/NH	Unused F	Used F
884	1¢ Gilbert Stuart	2.25	4.50	8.00(70)	2.25	1.90	.10	.09	.11
885	2¢ James Whistler	2.25	4.50	9.75(70)	2.25	1.90	.13	.11	.11
886	3¢ A. Saint-Gaudens	3.15	6.25	11.00(70)	2.25	1.90	.15	.13	.10
887	5¢ Daniel C. French	3.85	7.65	80.00(70)	23.50	20.00	1.25	1.10	.40
888	10¢ Fredric Remington	6.00	21.50	325.00(70)	82.50	72.50	4.00	3.40	3.35

889   890   891   892   893

American Inventors

Scott	Description	Sing	Pl.Blk	Mint Sheet	PB F/NH	PB F	Unused F/NH	Unused F	Used F
889	1¢ Eli Whitney	2.25	4.50	15.50(70)	5.00	4.35	.18	.15	.12
890	2¢ Samuel Morse	2.25	4.50	13.50(70)	2.75	2.40	.20	.17	.12
891	3¢ Cyrus McCormick	3.00	6.00	27.50(70)	3.75	3.25	.35	.30	.10
892	5¢ Elias Howe	3.75	7.50	175.00(70)	37.50	32.50	2.25	1.95	.80
893	10¢ Alexander G. Bell	9.00	40.00	1650.00(70)	175.00	150.00	26.50	23.00	4.75

894   896   898

895   897   902

899   900   901

1940 COMMEMORATIVES

Scott	Description	Sing	Pl.Blk	Mint Sheet	PB F/NH	PB F	Unused F/NH	Unused F	Used F
894-902	9 Vars., cpl.	....	....	....	42.75	38.75	2.85	2.55	1.05
894	3¢ Pony Express	6.50	12.50	36.50(50)	8.75	7.95	.60	.55	.17
895	3¢ Pan-Am Union	6.50	12.50	33.00(50)	8.50	7.75	.60	.55	.14
896	3¢ Idaho Statehood	6.50	12.50	18.75(50)	5.75	5.15	.30	.27	.12
897	3¢ Wyoming Statehood	6.50	12.50	17.50(50)	4.50	4.00	.33	.30	.12
898	3¢ Coronado Expedition	6.50	12.50	18.75(50)	3.75	3.35	.30	.27	.12

SCOTT NO.	DESRIPTION	FIRST DAY COVERS SING PL. BLK.		MINT SHEET	PLATE BLOCK F/NH	F	UNUSED F/NH	F	USED F

NATIONAL DEFENSE ISSUE

899	1¢ Liberty	4.75	9.50	13.00(100)	1.25	1.10	.15	.13	.06
900	2¢ Gun	4.75	9.50	14.00(100)	1.25	1.10	.15	.13	.06
901	3¢ Torch	4.75	9.50	18.75(100)	1.75	1.55	.20	.18	.06
902	3¢ Emancipation	6.25	12.50	27.50(50)	9.00	8.15	.37	.33	.25

903

904

905

906

907

908

1941-43 COMMEMORATIVES

| 903-08 | 6 Varieties | .... | .... | .... | 36.75 | 33.50 | 1.40 | 1.25 | .85 |

1941 COMMEMORATIVES

| 903 | 3¢ Vermont | 6.25 | 12.75 | 17.50(60) | 5.00 | 4.50 | .33 | .30 | .16 |

1942 COMMEMORATIVES

904	3¢ Kentucky	6.00	12.00	14.50(50)	3.00	2.70	.25	.22	.16
905	3¢ Win The War	4.75	9.50	15.00(100)	.95	.85	.17	.15	.06
906	5¢ China Resistance	6.25	14.75	42.75(50)	27.50	25.00	.50	.45	.40

1943 COMMEMORATIVES

| 907 | 2¢ Allied Nations | 4.75 | 9.50 | 10.65(100) | .80 | .70 | .11 | .10 | .07 |
| 908 | 1¢ Four Freedoms | 6.25 | 12.50 | 9.00(100) | 1.50 | 1.35 | .09 | .08 | .07 |

909

910

911

912

913

914

915

916

917

918

919

920

921

SCOTT NO.	DESCRIPTION	FIRST DAY COVERS SING PL. BLK.		MINT SHEET	PLATE BLOCK F/NH	F	UNUSED F/NH	F	USED F
				1943-44 OVERRUN COUNTRIES SERIES					
909-21	13 Vars., cpl.	57.50	145.00	360.00	140.00	125.00	5.25	4.75	4.85
909	5¢ Poland	6.50	13.75	28.50(50)	16.50	15.00	.30	.27	.35
910	5¢ Czechoslovakia	4.50	11.00	25.00(50)	7.75	7.00	.40	.35	.22
911	5¢ Norway	4.50	11.00	13.50(50)	3.35	3.00	.25	.22	.22
912	5¢ Luxembourg	4.50	11.00	13.50(50)	2.95	2.65	.25	.22	.22
913	5¢ Netherlands	4.50	11.00	13.50(50)	2.95	2.65	.25	.22	.20
914	5¢ Belgium	4.50	11.00	13.50(50)	3.25	2.95	.25	.22	.22
915	5¢ France	4.50	11.00	13.50(50)	3.35	3.00	.25	.22	.22
916	5¢ Greece	4.50	11.00	75.00(50)	35.00	31.50	.95	.85	.85
917	5¢ Jugoslavia	4.50	11.00	47.50(50)	16.50	15.00	.70	.65	.55
918	5¢ Albania	4.50	11.00	41.50(50)	16.50	15.00	.55	.50	.60
919	5¢ Austria	4.50	11.00	31.50(50)	10.75	9.75	.50	.45	.50
920	5¢ Denmark	4.50	11.00	41.50(50)	15.00	13.75	.65	.60	.65
921	5¢ Korea (1944)	5.00	15.00	25.00(50)	13.50	12.00	.28	.25	.30

922   923   924   925

				1944 COMMEMORATIVES					
922-26	5 Varieties	....	....	....	14.00	12.50	1.35	1.10	.85
922	3¢ Railroad	4.75	9.50	30.00(50)	3.75	3.40	.60	.50	.18
923	3¢ Steamship	3.75	7.50	14.00(50)	3.65	3.30	.25	.20	.18
924	3¢ Telegraph	3.75	7.50	11.00(50)	2.25	2.00	.20	.16	.18
925	3¢ Corregidor	3.75	7.50	11.50(50)	2.65	2.35	.20	.17	.20

926   927   928   929

| 926 | 3¢ Motion Picture | 3.85 | 7.75 | 11.00(50) | 2.25 | 2.00 | .20 | .16 | .15 |

				1945 COMMEMORATIVES					
927-38	12 Varieties, cpl.	....	....	....	9.65	8.80	1.90	1.65	.95
927	3¢ Florida	3.75	7.50	9.25(50)	1.50	1.35	.18	.15	.15
928	5¢ Peace Conference	3.75	7.50	11.50(50)	1.20	1.10	.23	.21	.09
929	3¢ Iwo Jima	3.75	7.50	9.00(50)	.85	.75	.18	.15	.09

930   931   932   933

930	1¢ FDR & Hyde Park	3.75	7.50	3.95(50)	.35	.32	.08	.07	.07
931	2¢ FDR & "Little White House"	3.75	7.50	5.75(50)	.60	.55	.11	.10	.09
932	3¢ FDR & White House	3.75	7.50	8.75(50)	.90	.75	.18	.15	.09
933	5¢ FDR & Globe (1946)	3.75	7.50	11.00(50)	1.15	1.05	.24	.22	.10

NEVER HINGED: From 1893 to 1965, Unused OG or Unused prices are for stamps with original gum that have been hinged. If you desire Never Hinged stamps, order from the NH listings.

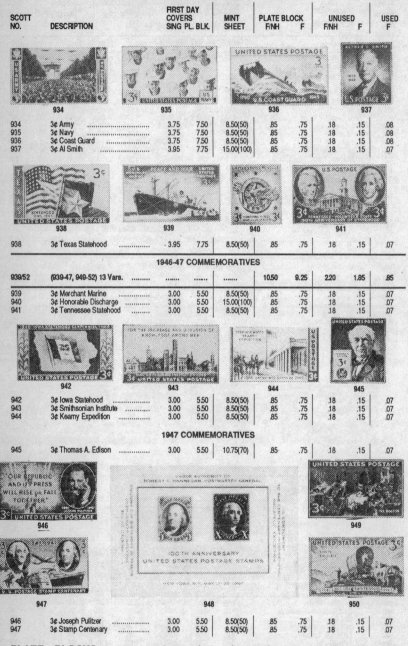

SCOTT NO.	DESCRIPTION	FIRST DAY COVERS SING PL. BLK.		MINT SHEET	PLATE BLOCK F/NH	F	UNUSED F/NH	F	USED F

934   **935**   **936**   **937**

934	3¢ Army	3.75	7.50	8.50(50)	.85	.75	.18	.15	.08
935	3¢ Navy	3.75	7.50	8.50(50)	.85	.75	.18	.15	.08
936	3¢ Coast Guard	3.75	7.50	8.50(50)	.85	.75	.18	.15	.08
937	3¢ Al Smith	3.95	7.75	15.00(100)	.85	.75	.18	.15	.07

938   **939**   **940**   **941**

| 938 | 3¢ Texas Statehood | 3.95 | 7.75 | 8.50(50) | .85 | .75 | .18 | .15 | .07 |

1946-47 COMMEMORATIVES

| 939/52 | (939-47, 949-52) 13 Vars. | | | | 10.50 | 9.25 | 2.20 | 1.85 | .85 |

939	3¢ Merchant Marine	3.00	5.50	8.50(50)	.85	.75	.18	.15	.07
940	3¢ Honorable Discharge	3.00	5.50	15.00(100)	.85	.75	.18	.15	.07
941	3¢ Tennessee Statehood	3.00	5.50	8.50(50)	.85	.75	.18	.15	.07

942   **943**   **944**   **945**

942	3¢ Iowa Statehood	3.00	5.50	8.50(50)	.85	.75	.18	.15	.07
943	3¢ Smithsonian Institute	3.00	5.50	8.50(50)	.85	.75	.18	.15	.07
944	3¢ Kearny Expedition	3.00	5.50	8.50(50)	.85	.75	.18	.15	.07

1947 COMMEMORATIVES

| 945 | 3¢ Thomas A. Edison | 3.00 | 5.50 | 10.75(70) | .85 | .75 | .18 | .15 | .07 |

946   **949**

947   **948**   **950**

| 946 | 3¢ Joseph Pulitzer | 3.00 | 5.50 | 8.50(50) | .85 | .75 | .18 | .15 | .07 |
| 947 | 3¢ Stamp Centenary | 3.00 | 5.50 | 8.50(50) | .85 | .75 | .18 | .15 | .07 |

PLATE BLOCKS: are portions of a sheet of stamps adjacent to the number(s) indicating the printing plate number used to produce that sheet. Flat plate issues are usually collected in plate blocks of six (number opposite middle stamp) while rotary issues are normally corner blocks of four.

SCOTT NO.	DESCRIPTION	FIRST DAY COVERS SING PL.BLK.		MINT SHEET	PLATE BLOCK F/NH	F	UNUSED F/NH	F	USED F

"CIPEX" SOUVENIR SHEET

948	5¢ & 10¢ Sheet of 2	4.50	......	......	......	......	1.65	1.50	1.50
948a	5¢ blue, single stamp	......	......	......	......	......	.65	.60	.50
948b	10¢ brown orange, single stamp	......	......	......	......	......	.90	.80	.50
949	3¢ Doctors	3.00	5.50	8.50(50)	.85	.75	.18	.15	.07
950	3¢ Utah Centennial	3.00	5.50	8.50(50)	.85	.75	.18	.15	.07

951   952   953   954

| 951 | 3¢ *Constitution | 3.00 | 5.50 | 8.50(50) | .85 | .75 | .18 | .15 | .07 |
| 952 | 3¢ Everglades Nt'l. Park | 3.00 | 5.50 | 8.50(50) | .85 | .75 | .18 | .15 | .07 |

1948 COMMEMORATIVES

953-80	28 Vars., cpl.	......	......	......	28.50	26.00	4.00	3.50	2.65
953	3¢ George Washington Carver...	3.00	5.50	9.50(70)	.70	.65	.15	.13	.07
954	3¢ Gold Rush	3.00	5.50	7.25(50)	.70	.65	.15	.13	.07

955   956   957   958

955	3¢ Mississippi Territory	3.00	5.50	7.25(50)	.70	.65	.15	.13	.07
956	3¢ Chaplains	3.00	5.50	7.25(50)	.70	.65	.15	.13	.07
957	3¢ Wisconsin Statehood	3.00	5.50	7.25(50)	.70	.65	.15	.13	.07
958	5¢ Swedish Pioneers	3.00	6.50	11.50(50)	1.35	1.25	.23	.21	.13

959   960   961   962

963   964   965   966

959	3¢ Women's Progress	3.00	5.50	7.25(50)	.70	.65	.15	.13	.07
960	3¢ William White	3.00	5.50	9.75(70)	1.30	1.20	.15	.13	.08
961	3¢ U.S. Canada Friendship	3.00	5.50	7.25(50)	.70	.65	.15	.13	.08
962	3¢ Francis S. Key	3.00	5.50	7.25(50)	.70	.65	.15	.13	.08
963	3¢ Salute to Youth	3.00	5.50	7.25(50)	.70	.65	.15	.13	.08
964	3¢ Oregon Territory	3.00	5.50	7.35(50)	.85	.75	.15	.13	.11
965	3¢ Harlan Stone	3.00	5.50	10.50(70)	2.00	1.80	.15	.13	.11
966	3¢ Mt. Palomar	3.25	6.00	11.75(70)	3.50	3.15	.15	.13	.12

AVERAGE QUALITY: From 1935 to date, deduct 20% from the Fine price to determine the price for an Average quality stamp.

SCOTT NO.	DESCRIPTION	FIRST DAY COVERS SING PL.BLK.		MINT SHEET	PLATE BLOCK F/NH F		UNUSED F/NH F		USED F

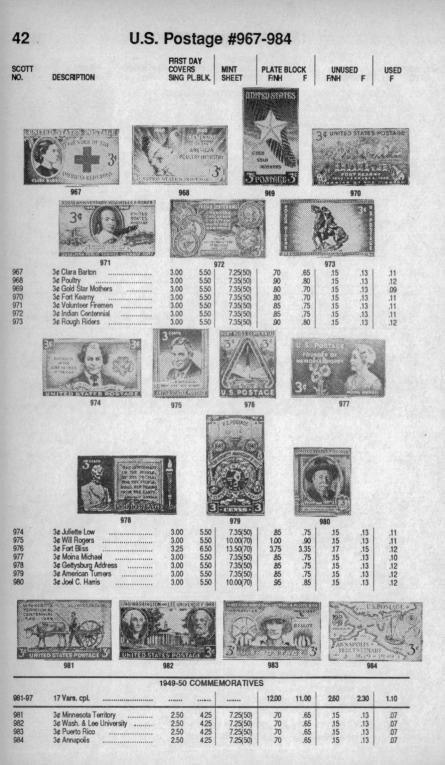

967   968   969   970
971   972   973

967	3¢ Clara Barton	3.00	5.50	7.25(50)	.70	.65	.15	.13	.11
968	3¢ Poultry	3.00	5.50	7.35(50)	.90	.80	.15	.13	.12
969	3¢ Gold Star Mothers	3.00	5.50	7.35(50)	.80	.70	.15	.13	.09
970	3¢ Fort Kearny	3.00	5.50	7.35(50)	.80	.70	.15	.13	.11
971	3¢ Volunteer Firemen	3.00	5.50	7.35(50)	.85	.75	.15	.13	.11
972	3¢ Indian Centennial	3.00	5.50	7.35(50)	.85	.75	.15	.13	.11
973	3¢ Rough Riders	3.00	5.50	7.35(50)	.90	.80	.15	.13	.12

974   975   976   977
978   979   980

974	3¢ Juliette Low	3.00	5.50	7.35(50)	.85	.75	.15	.13	.11
975	3¢ Will Rogers	3.00	5.50	10.00(70)	1.00	.90	.15	.13	.11
976	3¢ Fort Bliss	3.25	6.50	13.50(70)	3.75	3.35	.17	.15	.12
977	3¢ Moina Michael	3.00	5.50	7.35(50)	.85	.75	.15	.13	.10
978	3¢ Gettysburg Address	3.00	5.50	7.35(50)	.85	.75	.15	.13	.12
979	3¢ American Turners	3.00	5.50	7.35(50)	.85	.75	.15	.13	.12
980	3¢ Joel C. Harris	3.00	5.50	10.00(70)	.95	.85	.15	.13	.12

981   982   983   984

1949-50 COMMEMORATIVES

981-97	17 Vars. cpl.				12.00	11.00	2.60	2.30	1.10
981	3¢ Minnesota Territory	2.50	4.25	7.25(50)	.70	.65	.15	.13	.07
982	3¢ Wash. & Lee University	2.50	4.25	7.25(50)	.70	.65	.15	.13	.07
983	3¢ Puerto Rico	2.50	4.25	7.25(50)	.70	.65	.15	.13	.07
984	3¢ Annapolis	2.50	4.25	7.25(50)	.70	.65	.15	.13	.07

SCOTT NO.	DESCRIPTION	FIRST DAY COVERS SING	PL.BLK.	MINT SHEET	PLATE BLOCK F/NH	F	UNUSED F/NH	F	USED F
985	3¢ G.A.R.	2.50	4.25	7.25(50)	.70	.65	.15	.13	.07
986	3¢ Edgar A. Poe	2.50	4.25	9.50(70)	.70	.65	.15	.13	.07

1950 COMMEMORATIVES

987	3¢ Bankers Association	2.50	4.25	7.25(50)	.70	.65	.15	.13	.07
988	3¢ Samuel Gompers	2.50	4.25	9.50(70)	.70	.65	.15	.13	.07
989	3¢ Statue of Freedom	2.50	4.75	8.75(50)	.85	.75	.18	.16	.07
990	3¢ Executive Mansion	2.50	4.75	8.75(50)	.85	.75	.18	.16	.07
991	3¢ Supreme Court	2.50	4.75	8.75(50)	.85	.75	.18	.16	.07
992	3¢ United States Capitol	2.50	4.75	8.75(50)	.85	.75	.18	.16	.07
993	3¢ Railroad	2.50	4.75	8.50(50)	.80	.70	.17	.15	.07
994	3¢ Kansas City	2.50	4.75	7.25(50)	.70	.65	.15	.13	.07
995	3¢ Boy Scouts	3.00	5.50	8.50(50)	.80	.70	.17	.15	.07
996	3¢ Indiana Territory	2.50	4.75	7.25(50)	.70	.65	.15	.13	.07
997	3¢ California Statehood	2.50	4.75	8.25(50)	.80	.70	.17	.15	.07

1951-52 COMMEMORATIVES

996-1016	19 Vars., cpl.	......	......	......	13.65	12.50	3.00	2.65	1.25
998	3¢ Confederate Veterans	2.50	4.75	8.25(50)	.80	.70	.17	.15	.07
999	3¢ Nevada Settlement	2.50	4.75	7.25(50)	.70	.65	.15	.13	.07
1000	3¢ Landing of Cadillac	2.50	4.75	7.25(50)	.70	.65	.15	.13	.07
1001	3¢ Colorado Statehood	2.50	4.75	8.25(50)	.80	.70	.17	.15	.07

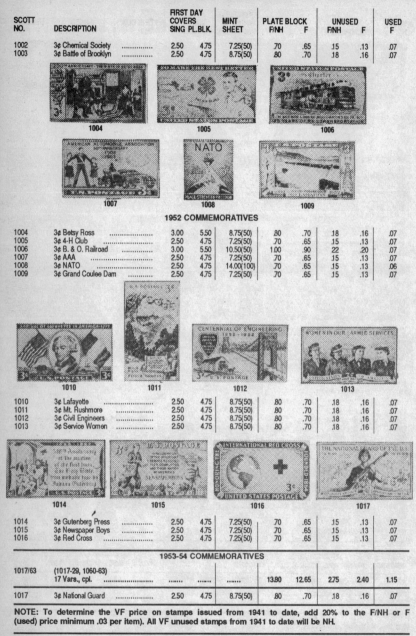

SCOTT NO.	DESCRIPTION	FIRST DAY COVERS SING	PL.BLK.	MINT SHEET	PLATE BLOCK F/NH	F	UNUSED F/NH	F	USED F
1002	3¢ Chemical Society	2.50	4.75	7.25(50)	.70	.65	.15	.13	.07
1003	3¢ Battle of Brooklyn	2.50	4.75	8.75(50)	.80	.70	.18	.16	.07

1004   **1005**   **1006**

1007   **1008**   **1009**

1952 COMMEMORATIVES

SCOTT NO.	DESCRIPTION	FIRST DAY COVERS SING	PL.BLK.	MINT SHEET	PLATE BLOCK F/NH	F	UNUSED F/NH	F	USED F
1004	3¢ Betsy Ross	3.00	5.50	8.75(50)	.80	.70	.18	.16	.07
1005	3¢ 4-H Club	2.50	4.75	7.25(50)	.70	.65	.15	.13	.07
1006	3¢ B. & O. Railroad	3.00	5.50	10.50(50)	1.00	.90	22	.20	.07
1007	3¢ AAA	2.50	4.75	7.25(50)	.70	.65	.15	.13	.07
1008	3¢ NATO	2.50	4.75	14.00(100)	.70	.65	.15	.13	.06
1009	3¢ Grand Coulee Dam	2.50	4.75	7.25(50)	.70	.65	.15	.13	.07

1010   **1011**   **1012**   **1013**

SCOTT NO.	DESCRIPTION	FIRST DAY COVERS SING	PL.BLK.	MINT SHEET	PLATE BLOCK F/NH	F	UNUSED F/NH	F	USED F
1010	3¢ Lafayette	2.50	4.75	8.75(50)	.80	.70	.18	.16	.07
1011	3¢ Mt. Rushmore	2.50	4.75	8.75(50)	.80	.70	.18	.16	.07
1012	3¢ Civil Engineers	2.50	4.75	8.75(50)	.80	.70	.18	.16	.07
1013	3¢ Service Women	2.50	4.75	8.75(50)	.80	.70	.18	.16	.07

1014   **1015**   **1016**   **1017**

SCOTT NO.	DESCRIPTION	FIRST DAY COVERS SING	PL.BLK.	MINT SHEET	PLATE BLOCK F/NH	F	UNUSED F/NH	F	USED F
1014	3¢ Gutenberg Press	2.50	4.75	7.25(50)	.70	.65	.15	.13	.07
1015	3¢ Newspaper Boys	2.50	4.75	7.25(50)	.70	.65	.15	.13	.07
1016	3¢ Red Cross	2.50	4.75	7.25(50)	.70	.65	.15	.13	.07

1953-54 COMMEMORATIVES

SCOTT NO.	DESCRIPTION	FIRST DAY COVERS SING	PL.BLK.	MINT SHEET	PLATE BLOCK F/NH	F	UNUSED F/NH	F	USED F
1017/63	(1017-29, 1060-63) 17 Vars., cpl.	....	....	....	13.80	12.65	2.75	2.40	1.15
1017	3¢ National Guard	2.50	4.75	8.75(50)	.80	.70	.18	.16	.07

NOTE: To determine the VF price on stamps issued from 1941 to date, add 20% to the F/NH or F (used) price minimum .03 per item). All VF unused stamps from 1941 to date will be NH.

FIRST DAY COVERS: First Day Covers are envelopes cancelled on the "First Day of Issue" of the stamp used on the envelope. Usually they also contain a picture (cachet) on the left side designed to go with the theme of the stamp. From 1935 to 1944, prices listed are for cacheted, addressed covers. From 1945 to date, prices are for cacheted, unaddressed covers.

SCOTT NO.	DESCRIPTION	FIRST DAY COVERS SING	PL.BLK.	MINT SHEET	PLATE BLOCK F/NH	F	UNUSED F/NH	F	USED F
1018	3¢ Ohio Statehood	2.50	4.75	9.50(70)	.70	.65	.15	.13	.07
1019	3¢ Washington Territory	2.50	4.75	7.25(50)	.70	.65	.15	.13	.07
1020	3¢ Louisiana Purchase	2.50	4.75	7.25(50)	.70	.65	.15	.13	.07
1021	5¢ Opening of Japan	2.50	4.75	12.00(50)	2.25	2.00	.25	.20	.09
1022	3¢ American Bar Assoc.	2.50	4.75	7.25(50)	.70	.65	.15	.13	.07
1023	3¢ Sagamore Hill	2.50	4.75	7.25(50)	.70	.65	.15	.13	.07
1024	3¢ Future Farmers	2.50	4.75	7.25(50)	.70	.65	.15	.13	.07
1025	3¢ Trucking Industry	2.50	4.75	7.25(50)	.70	.65	.15	.13	.07
1026	3¢ Gen. George S. Patton	2.50	4.75	11.50(50)	1.10	1.00	.24	.22	.07
1027	3¢ New York City	2.50	4.75	8.75(50)	.80	.70	.18	.16	.07
1028	3¢ Gadsden Purchase	2.50	4.75	8.75(50)	.80	.70	.18	.16	.07

1954 COMMEMORATIVE

1029	3¢ Columbia University	2.50	4.75	7.25(50)	.70	.65	.15	.13	.07

1954-61 LIBERTY SERIES

SCOTT NO.	DESCRIPTION	FDC SING	PL.BLK.	MINT SHEET	PLATE BLOCK F/NH	F	UNUSED F/NH	F	USED F
1030-53	1/2¢-$5, 27 Vars., cpl.	155.00	335.00	....	1000.00	925.00	210.00	195.00	16.00
1030-51	1/2¢-50¢, 25 Vars.	70.00	125.00	....	115.00	105.00	23.75	21.50	1.55
1030	1/2¢ Benjamin Franklin (1955)	2.50	4.50	6.35(100)	.45	.40	.07	.06	.06
1031	1¢ George Washington	2.50	4.50	5.75(100)	.33	.28	.07	.06	.06
1031A	1 1/4¢ Palace of Gov. (1960)	2.50	4.50	6.75(100)	1.00	.90	.07	.06	.06
1032	1 1/2¢ Mt. Vernon	2.50	4.50	13.50(100)	6.50	5.85	.09	.08	.07
1033	2¢ Thomas Jefferson	2.50	4.50	8.50(100)	.45	.40	.09	.08	.07
1034	2 1/2¢ Bunker Hill (1959)	2.50	4.50	13.50(100)	1.15	1.05	.14	.12	.07
1035	3¢ Statue of Liberty	2.50	4.50	13.50(100)	.70	.60	.15	.13	.06
1035a	3¢ booklet pane of 6	4.00		....	....	....	6.50	5.85	

SCOTT NO.	DESCRIPTION	FIRST DAY COVERS SING PL.BLK.		MINT SHEET	PLATE BLOCK F/NH	F	UNUSED F/NH	F	USED F
1036	4¢ Abraham Lincoln	2.50	4.50	18.50(100)	.90	.80	20	.18	.06
1036a	4¢ booklet pane of 6	4.00	....	....	....	....	6.00	5.50	
1037	4 1/2¢ Hermitage (1959)	2.50	4.50	21.00(100)	1.25	1.15	23	.21	.07
1038	5¢ James Monroe	2.50	4.50	25.00(100)	1.15	1.05	25	.23	.06
1039	6¢ T. Roosevelt (1955)	2.50	4.50	70.00(100)	3.25	3.00	70	.65	.06
1040	7¢ Woodrow Wilson (1956)	2.50	4.50	42.75(100)	2.95	2.65	45	.40	.07

1041,1075b

1042 (re-engraved)

1042A

1043

1044

1044A

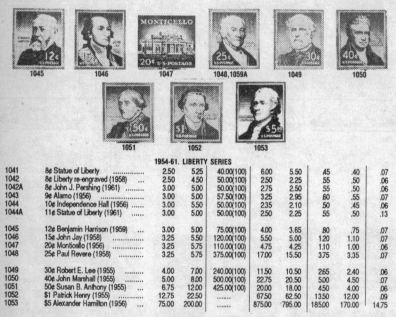

1045   1046   1047   1048,1059A   1049   1050

1051   1052   1053

1954-61. LIBERTY SERIES

1041	8¢ Statue of Liberty	2.50	5.25	40.00(100)	6.00	5.50	45	.40	.07
1042	8¢ Liberty re-engraved (1958)	2.50	4.50	50.00(100)	2.50	2.25	55	.50	.06
1042A	8¢ John J. Pershing (1961)	3.00	5.00	50.00(100)	2.75	2.50	55	.50	.06
1043	9¢ Alamo (1956)	3.00	5.00	57.50(100)	3.25	2.95	60	.55	.07
1044	10¢ Independence Hall (1956)	3.00	5.50	50.00(100)	2.35	2.10	50	.45	.06
1044A	11¢ Statue of Liberty (1961)	3.00	5.00	50.00(100)	2.50	2.25	55	.50	.13
1045	12¢ Benjamin Harrison (1959)	3.00	5.00	75.00(100)	4.00	3.65	80	.75	.07
1046	15¢ John Jay (1958)	3.25	5.50	120.00(100)	5.50	5.00	1.20	1.10	.07
1047	20¢ Monticello (1956)	3.25	5.75	110.00(100)	4.75	4.25	1.10	1.00	.06
1048	25¢ Paul Revere (1958)	3.25	5.75	375.00(100)	17.00	15.50	3.75	3.35	.07
1049	30¢ Robert E. Lee (1955)	4.00	7.00	240.00(100)	11.50	10.50	2.65	2.40	.06
1050	40¢ John Marshall (1955)	5.00	8.00	500.00(100)	22.75	20.50	5.00	4.50	.07
1051	50¢ Susan B. Anthony (1955)	6.75	12.00	425.00(100)	20.00	18.00	4.50	4.00	.06
1052	$1 Patrick Henry (1955)	12.75	22.50	....	67.50	62.50	13.50	12.00	.09
1053	$5 Alexander Hamilton (1956)	75.00	200.00	....	875.00	795.00	185.00	170.00	14.75

1954-65 COIL STAMPS
Perf. 10 Vertically or Horizontally

		L.PAIR			LINE PAIR				
1054-59A	1¢-25¢ Vars., cpl.	19.75	29.75	....	56.50	51.50	6.15	5.35	3.65
1054	1¢ George Washington	2.50	3.75	....	2.25	2.00	50	.45	.07
1054A	1 1/4¢ Palace of Gov. (1960)	2.50	3.75	....	6.25	5.75	30	.27	.35
1055	2¢ Thomas Jefferson	2.50	3.75	....	.75	.65	.12	.11	.06
1056	2 1/2¢ Bunker Hill Mon. (1959)	2.50	3.75	....	11.75	10.75	55	.50	.60
1057	3¢ Statue of Liberty	2.50	3.75	....	1.30	1.20	.18	.15	.06
1058	4¢ Abraham Lincoln (1958)	2.50	3.75	....	1.40	1.30	22	.20	.06
1059	4 1/2¢ Hermitage (1959)	2.50	3.75	....	31.50	28.75	3.50	2.95	2.35
1059A	25¢ Paul Revere (1965)	3.25	5.00	....	4.00	3.75	1.10	1.00	.27

NOTE: Pairs of the above can be supplied at two times the single price.

COIL LINE PAIRS: are two connected coil stamps with a line the same color as the stamps printed between the two stamps. This line usually appears every twenty to thirty stamps on a roll depending on the issue.

SCOTT NO.	DESCRIPTION	FIRST DAY COVERS SING PL.BLK.		MINT SHEET	PLATE BLOCK F/NH	F	UNUSED F/NH	F	USED F

1060 1061 1062 1063

1060	3¢ Nebraska Territory	....	2.50	4.50	7.25(50)	.70	.65	.15	.13	.07
1061	3¢ Kansas Territory	....	2.50	4.50	7.25(50)	.70	.65	.15	.13	.07
1062	3¢ George Eastman	....	2.50	4.50	11.50(70)	.80	.70	.18	.16	.07
1063	3¢ Lewis & Clark	....	2.50	4.50	8.75(50)	.80	.70	.18	.16	.07

1064 1065 1066 1067 1068

1955 COMMEMORATIVES

1064-72	9 Vars., cpl.	....	....	....	....	8.35	7.50	1.65	1.40	.60
1064	3¢ Pennsylvania Academy	....	2.50	4.25	7.25(50)	.70	.65	.15	.13	.07
1065	3¢ Land Grant Colleges	....	2.50	4.25	8.75(50)	.80	.70	.18	.16	.07
1066	8¢ Rotary International	....	2.50	4.25	19.50(50)	2.50	2.25	.40	.35	.10
1067	3¢ Armed Forces Reserves	....	2.50	4.25	7.25(50)	.75	.70	.15	.13	.07
1068	3¢ Great Stone Face	....	2.50	4.25	10.50(50)	1.00	.90	.20	.18	.07

1069 1070 1071 1072

1069	3¢ Soo Locks	....	2.50	4.25	7.25(50)	.70	.65	.15	.13	.07
1070	3¢ Atoms for Peace	....	2.50	4.25	8.00(50)	.80	.70	.15	.13	.07
1071	3¢ Ft. Ticonderoga	....	2.50	4.25	8.75(50)	.80	.70	.18	.16	.07
1072	3¢ Andrew Mellon	....	2.50	4.25	9.50(70)	.70	.65	.15	.13	.07

1073 1074 1075

1956 COMMEMORATIVES

1073/85	(1073-74, 76-85) 12 Vars.	....	....	....	....	9.00	8.15	1.90	1.70	.75
1073	3¢ Benjamin Franklin	....	2.50	4.25	8.75(50)	.80	.70	.18	.16	.07
1074	3¢ Booker T. Washington	....	2.50	4.25	8.75(50)	.80	.70	.18	.16	.07

Plate blocks will be blocks of 4 stamps unless otherwise noted.

SCOTT NO.	DESCRIPTION	FIRST DAY COVERS SING	FIRST DAY COVERS PL.BLK.	MINT SHEET	PLATE BLOCK F/NH	PLATE BLOCK F	UNUSED F/NH	UNUSED F	USED F
1075	3¢ & 8¢ FIPEX Sh. of 2	10.95	....	....	....	....	5.75	5.25	5.75
1075a	3¢ deep violet, single	....	....	....	....	....	2.50	2.25	2.50
1075b	8¢ violet blue & car., single	....	....	....	....	....	3.00	2.75	3.00

1076	3¢ FIPEX	2.50	4.25	7.25(50)	.70	.65	.15	.13	.07
1077	3¢ Wild Turkey	2.50	4.25	8.75(50)	.90	.80	.18	.16	.07
1078	3¢ Antelope	2.50	4.25	8.75(50)	.90	.80	.18	.16	.07
1079	3¢ Salmon	2.50	4.25	8.75(50)	.90	.80	.18	.16	.07

1080	3¢ Pure Food & Drug Act	2.50	4.25	7.25(50)	.70	.65	.15	.13	.07
1081	3¢ "Wheatland"	2.50	4.25	7.25(50)	.70	.65	.15	.13	.07
1082	3¢ Labor Day	2.50	4.25	7.25(50)	.70	.65	.15	.13	.07
1083	3¢ Nassau Hall	2.50	4.25	8.75(50)	.85	.75	.18	.16	.07
1084	3¢ Devil's Tower	2.50	4.25	8.75(50)	.85	.75	.18	.16	.07

1085	3¢ Children of the World	2.50	4.25	7.25(50)	.70	.65	.15	.13	.07

1957 COMMEMORATIVES

1086-99	14 Vars., cpl.	....	....	....	12.00	10.75	2.50	2.20	1.00
1086	3¢ Alexander Hamilton	2.50	4.25	8.75(50)	.85	.75	.18	.16	.07
1087	3¢ Polio	2.50	4.25	7.25(50)	.70	.65	.15	.13	.07
1088	3¢ Coast and Geodetic Sur	2.50	4.25	7.25(50)	.70	.65	.15	.13	.07
1089	3¢ Architects	2.50	4.25	7.25(50)	.70	.65	.15	.13	.07
1090	3¢ Steel Industry	2.50	4.25	8.75(50)	.85	.75	.18	.16	.07
1091	3¢ Int'l. Naval Review	2.50	4.25	8.75(50)	.85	.75	.18	.16	.07
1092	3¢ Oklahoma Statehood	2.50	4.25	8.75(50)	.85	.75	.18	.16	.07

FIRST DAY COVERS: First Day Covers are envelopes cancelled on the "First Day of Issue" of the stamp used on the envelope. Usually they also contain a picture (cachet) on the left side designed to go with the theme of the stamp. From 1935 to 1944, prices listed are for cacheted, addressed covers. From 1945 to date, prices are for cacheted, unaddressed covers.

SCOTT NO.	DESCRIPTION	FIRST DAY COVERS SING PL.BLK.		MINT SHEET	PLATE BLOCK F/NH F		UNUSED F/NH F		USED F

1093　**1094**　**1095**　**1096**　**1097**

1093	3¢ School Teachers	2.50	4.25	8.75(50)	.85	.75	.18	.16	.07
1094	4¢ 48-Star Flag	2.50	4.25	9.50(50)	.90	.80	.20	.18	.07
1095	3¢ Shipbuilding Anniv.	2.50	4.25	9.50(70)	.70	.65	.15	.13	.07
1096	8¢ Ramon Magsaysay	2.50	4.50	18.50(48)	2.25	2.00	.40	.35	.15
1097	3¢ Birth of Lafayette	2.50	4.25	8.75(50)	.85	.75	.18	.15	.07

1098　**1099**　**1100**　**1104**　**1105**

| 1098 | 3¢ Whooping Cranes | 2.50 | 4.25 | 7.25(50) | .70 | .65 | .15 | .13 | .07 |
| 1099 | 3¢ Religious Freedom | 2.50 | 4.25 | 8.75(50) | .85 | .75 | .18 | .16 | .07 |

1958 COMMEMORATIVES

1100-23	21 Vars., cpl.				24.00	21.50	4.10	3.60	1.60
1100	3¢ Gardening & Horticulture	2.50	4.25	7.25(50)	.70	.65	.15	.13	.07
1104	3¢ Brussels Exhibition	2.50	4.25	7.25(50)	.70	.65	.15	.13	.07
1105	3¢ James Monroe	2.00	4.25	11.00(70)	.85	.75	.18	.16	.07

1106　**1107**　**1108**　**1109**

1106	3¢ Minnesota Statehood	2.50	4.25	7.25(50)	.70	.65	.15	.13	.07
1107	3¢ Int'l. Geophysical Year	2.50	4.25	7.25(50)	.70	.65	.15	.13	.07
1108	3¢ Gunston Hall	2.50	4.25	7.25(50)	.70	.65	.15	.13	.07
1109	3¢ Mackinac Bridge	2.50	4.25	7.25(50)	.70	.65	.15	.13	.07

PLATE BLOCKS: are portions of a sheet of stamps adjacent to the number(s) indicating the printing plate number used to produce that sheet. Flat plate issues are usually collected in plate blocks of six (number opposite middle stamp) while rotary issues are normally corner blocks of four.

SCOTT NO.	DESCRIPTION	FIRST DAY COVERS SING PL.BLK.		MINT SHEET	PLATE BLOCK F/NH	F	UNUSED F/NH	F	USED F

1110,1111

1113

1114

1117,1118

1112

1115

1116

1110	4¢ Simon Bolivar	2.50	4.25	13.00(70)	.90	.80	20	.18	.07
1111	8¢ Simon Bolivar	2.50	4.50	29.50(72)	4.95	4.50	40	.35	.17
1112	4¢ Atlantic Cable Centenary	2.50	4.25	9.50(50)	.90	.80	20	.18	.07
1113	1¢ Abraham Lincoln (1959)	2.50	4.25	3.35(50)	.33	.30	.07	.06	.06
1114	3¢ Bust of Lincoln (1959)	2.50	4.25	8.75(50)	.85	.75	.18	.16	.10
1115	4¢ Lincoln-Douglas Debates	2.50	4.25	11.50(50)	1.10	1.00	24	.22	.07
1116	4¢ Statue of Lincoln (1959)	2.50	4.25	12.00(50)	1.15	1.05	25	.20	.07
1117	4¢ Lajos Kossuth	2.50	4.25	13.00(70)	.90	.80	20	.18	.07
1118	8¢ Lajos Kossuth	2.50	4.50	30.00(72)	4.50	4.00	45	.40	.17

1119

1120

1121

1122

1123

1119	4¢ Freedom of Press	2.50	4.25	10.75(50)	1.00	.90	22	.20	.07
1120	4¢ Overland Mail	2.50	4.25	9.50(50)	.90	.80	20	.18	.07
1121	4¢ Noah Webster	2.50	4.25	12.75(70)	.90	.80	20	.18	.07
1122	4¢ Forest Conservation	2.50	4.25	9.50(50)	.90	.80	20	.18	.07
1123	4¢ Ft. Duquesne	2.50	4.25	9.50(50)	.90	.80	20	.18	.07

1124

1125,1126

1127

1128

1959 COMMEMORATIVES									
1124-38	15 Vars.	......	......	......	16.95	15.00	3.45	3.00	1.20
1124	4¢ Oregon Statehood	2.50	4.25	9.50(50)	.90	.80	20	.18	.07
1125	4¢ Jose de San Martin	2.50	4.25	12.75(70)	.90	.80	20	.18	.07
1126	8¢ Jose de San Martin	2.50	4.50	27.50(72)	2.25	2.00	40	.35	.17
1127	4¢ NATO	2.50	4.25	12.75(70)	.90	.80	20	.18	.07
1128	4¢ Arctic Exploration	2.50	4.25	9.50(50)	.90	.80	20	.18	.07

SCOTT NO.	DESCRIPTION	FIRST DAY COVERS SING PL.BLK.		MINT SHEET	PLATE BLOCK F/NH F		UNUSED F/NH F		USED F
1129	8¢ World Peace & Trade	2.50	4.50	19.50(50)	225	2.00	40	.35	.10
1130	4¢ Silver Centennial	2.50	4.25	9.50(50)	.90	.80	20	.18	.07
1131	4¢ St. Lawrence Seway	2.50	4.25	9.50(50)	.90	.80	20	.18	.07
1132	4¢ 49-Star Flag	2.50	4.25	9.50(50)	.90	.80	20	.18	.07
1133	4¢ Soil Conservation	2.50	4.25	9.50(50)	.90	.80	20	.18	.07
1134	4¢ Petroleum	2.50	4.25	9.50(50)	.90	.80	20	.18	.07
1135	4¢ Dental Health	2.50	4.25	9.50(50)	.90	.80	22	.20	.07
1136	4¢ Ernst Reuter	2.50	4.25	9.50(50)	.90	.80	20	.18	.07
1137	8¢ Ernst Reuter	2.50	4.50	28.50(72)	250	2.25	40	.35	.16
1138	4¢ Dr. Ephraim McDowell	2.50	4.25	12.75(70)	.90	.80	20	.18	.07

1960-61 CREDO OF AMERICA SERIES

1139-44	4¢ cpl., 6 vars.				6.75	5.95	1.45	1.30	.40
1139	4¢ Credo-Washington	2.50	4.25	9.75(50)	.90	.80	20	.18	.07
1140	4¢ Credo-Franklin	2.50	4.25	9.75(50)	.90	.80	20	.18	.07
1141	4¢ Credo-Jefferson	2.50	4.25	12.00(50)	1.15	1.00	25	.23	.07
1142	4¢ Credo-Key	2.50	4.25	12.00(50)	1.15	1.00	25	.23	.07
1143	4¢ Credo-Lincoln	2.50	4.25	15.00(50)	1.50	1.30	30	.27	.07
1144	4¢ Credo-Henry (1961)	2.50	4.25	15.00(50)	1.50	1.30	30	.27	.07

CHAMPIONS OF LIBERTY: From 1957 to 1961, the U.S. issued a series of commemoratives honoring famous people from other countries that have striven for liberty. This series includes numbers: 1096, 1110-11, 1117-18, 1125-26, 1136-37, 1147-48, 1159-60, 1165-66, 1168-69 and 1174-75.

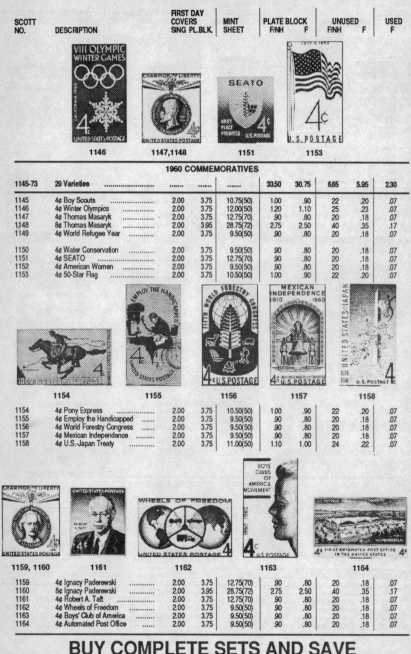

SCOTT NO.	DESCRIPTION	FIRST DAY COVERS SING PL.BLK.		MINT SHEET	PLATE BLOCK F/NH	F	UNUSED F/NH	F	USED F

1146   **1147,1148**   **1151**   **1153**

1960 COMMEMORATIVES

SCOTT NO.	DESCRIPTION	SING	PL.BLK.	MINT SHEET	PL.BLK F/NH	F	F/NH	F	USED F
1145-73	29 Varieties	......	......	......	33.50	30.75	6.65	5.95	2.30
1145	4¢ Boy Scouts	2.00	3.75	10.75(50)	1.00	.90	22	.20	.07
1146	4¢ Winter Olympics	2.00	3.75	12.00(50)	120	1.10	25	.23	.07
1147	4¢ Thomas Masaryk	2.00	3.75	12.75(70)	.90	.80	20	.18	.07
1148	8¢ Thomas Masaryk	2.00	3.95	28.75(72)	2.75	2.50	40	.35	.17
1149	4¢ World Refugee Year	2.00	3.75	9.50(50)	.90	.80	20	.18	.07
1150	4¢ Water Conservation	2.00	3.75	9.50(50)	.90	.80	20	.18	.07
1151	4¢ SEATO	2.00	3.75	12.75(70)	.90	.80	20	.18	.07
1152	4¢ American Women	2.00	3.75	9.50(50)	.90	.80	20	.18	.07
1153	4¢ 50-Star Flag	2.00	3.75	10.50(50)	1.00	.90	22	.20	.07

1154   **1155**   **1156**   **1157**   **1158**

1154	4¢ Pony Express	2.00	3.75	10.50(50)	1.00	.90	22	.20	.07
1155	4¢ Employ the Handicapped	2.00	3.75	9.50(50)	.90	.80	20	.18	.07
1156	4¢ World Forestry Congress	2.00	3.75	9.50(50)	.90	.80	20	.18	.07
1157	4¢ Mexican Independence	2.00	3.75	9.50(50)	.90	.80	20	.18	.07
1158	4¢ U.S.-Japan Treaty	2.00	3.75	11.00(50)	1.10	1.00	24	.22	.07

1159, 1160   **1161**   **1162**   **1163**   **1164**

1159	4¢ Ignacy Paderewski	2.00	3.75	12.75(70)	.90	.80	20	.18	.07
1160	8¢ Ignacy Paderewski	2.00	3.95	28.75(72)	2.75	2.50	40	.35	.17
1161	4¢ Robert A. Taft	2.00	3.75	12.75(70)	.90	.80	20	.18	.07
1162	4¢ Wheels of Freedom	2.00	3.75	9.50(50)	.90	.80	20	.18	.07
1163	4¢ Boys' Club of America	2.00	3.75	9.50(50)	.90	.80	20	.18	.07
1164	4¢ Automated Post Office	2.00	3.75	9.50(50)	.90	.80	20	.18	.07

BUY COMPLETE SETS AND SAVE

NEVER HINGED: From 1893 to 1965, Unused OG or Unused prices are for stamps with original gum that have been hinged. If you desire Never Hinged stamps, order from the NH listings.

SCOTT NO.	DESCRIPTION	FIRST DAY COVERS SING	PL.BLK.	MINT SHEET	PLATE BLOCK F/NH	F	UNUSED F/NH	F	USED F
1165	4¢ Gustaf Mannerheim	2.00	3.75	12.75(70)	.90	.80	.20	.18	.07
1166	8¢ Gustaf Mannerheim	2.00	3.95	28.75(72)	2.50	2.25	.40	.35	.17
1167	4¢ Camp Fire Girls	2.00	3.75	9.50(50)	.90	.80	.20	.18	.07
1168	4¢ Giuseppe Garibaldi	2.00	3.75	12.75(70)	.90	.80	.20	.18	.07
1169	8¢ Giuseppe Garibaldi	2.00	3.95	28.75(72)	2.50	2.25	.40	.35	.17
1170	4¢ Walter George	2.00	3.75	12.75(70)	.90	.80	.20	.18	.07
1171	4¢ Andrew Carnegie	2.00	3.75	12.75(70)	.90	.80	.20	.18	.07
1172	4¢ John Foster Dulles	2.00	3.75	12.75(70)	.90	.80	.20	.18	.07
1173	4¢ "ECHO 1" Satellite	3.75	7.75	25.00(50)	2.10	1.90	.45	.40	.08

1961 COMMEMORATIVES

SCOTT NO.	DESCRIPTION	FIRST DAY COVERS SING	PL.BLK.	MINT SHEET	PLATE BLOCK F/NH	F	UNUSED F/NH	F	USED F
1174/90	(1174-77, 83-90) 12 Vars.	....	....	....	11.75	10.25	2.40	2.10	.90
1174	4¢ Mahatma Gandhi	2.00	3.75	12.75(70)	.90	.80	.20	.18	.07
1175	8¢ Mahatma Gandhi	2.00	3.95	29.50(72)	2.75	2.50	.40	.35	.17
1176	4¢ Range Conservation	2.00	3.75	10.50(50)	1.00	.90	.22	.20	.07
1177	4¢ Horace Greeley	2.00	3.75	12.75(70)	.90	.80	.20	.18	.07

1961-65 CIVIL WAR CENTENNIAL SERIES

SCOTT NO.	DESCRIPTION	FIRST DAY COVERS SING	PL.BLK.	MINT SHEET	PLATE BLOCK F/NH	F	UNUSED F/NH	F	USED F
1178-82	5 Vars., cpl.	....	....	....	7.00	6.35	1.50	1.35	.32
1178	4¢ Fort Sumter	2.75	4.75	16.50(50)	1.60	1.35	.33	.30	.07
1179	4¢ Shiloh (1962)	2.75	4.75	11.50(50)	1.20	1.10	.25	.23	.07
1180	5¢ Gettysburg (1963)	2.75	4.75	13.50(50)	1.25	1.15	.28	.25	.07
1181	5¢ Wilderness (1964)	2.75	4.75	13.50(50)	1.25	1.15	.28	.25	.07
1181	Zip Code Block	....	....	....	1.20	....	....	....	....
1182	5¢ Appomattox (1965)	2.75	4.75	22.50(50)	2.10	1.90	.45	.40	.07
1182	Zip Code Block	....	....	....	2.00	....	....	....	....

1961 COMMEMORATIVES

SCOTT NO.	DESCRIPTION	FIRST DAY COVERS SING	PL.BLK.	MINT SHEET	PLATE BLOCK F/NH	F	UNUSED F/NH	F	USED F
1183	4¢ Kansas Statehood	2.00	3.75	9.50(50)	.90	.80	.20	.18	.07
1184	4¢ George W. Norris	2.00	3.75	9.50(50)	.90	.80	.20	.18	.07

SCOTT NO.	DESCRIPTION	FIRST DAY COVERS SING PL.BLK.		MINT SHEET	PLATE BLOCK F/NH	F	UNUSED F/NH	F	USED F
1185	4¢ Naval Aviation	2.00	3.75	11.50(50)	1.10	1.00	24	.22	.07
1186	4¢ Workmen's Compensation	2.00	3.75	9.50(50)	.90	.80	20	.18	.07
1187	4¢ Frederic Remington	2.00	4.25	11.75(50)	1.15	1.05	25	.23	.07
1188	4¢ Sun Yat-sen	2.00	3.75	10.50(50)	1.00	.85	22	.18	.07
1189	4¢ Basketball	2.25	4.00	12.50(50)	1.15	1.05	25	.23	.07
1190	4¢ Nursing	2.00	3.75	10.50(50)	.90	.80	20	.18	.07

1962 COMMEMORATIVES'

1191-1207	17 Vars.	....	....	....	17.50	15.75	330	3.00	1.25
1191	4¢ New Mexico Statehood	2.00	3.75	9.50(50)	.90	.80	20	.18	.07
1192	4¢ Arizona Statehood	2.00	3.75	9.50(50)	.90	.80	20	.18	.07
1193	4¢ Project Mercury	3.00	5.25	9.75(50)	.90	.80	20	.18	.07
1194	4¢ Malaria Eradication	2.00	3.75	9.50(50)	.90	.80	20	.18	.07

1195	4¢ Charles Evans Hughes	2.00	3.75	9.50(50)	.90	.80	20	.18	.07
1196	4¢ Seattle World's Fair	2.00	3.75	9.50(50)	.90	.80	20	.18	.07
1197	4¢ Louisiana Statehood	2.00	3.75	9.50(50)	.90	.80	20	.18	.07
1198	4¢ Homestead Act	2.00	3.75	9.50(50)	.90	.80	20	.18	.07
1199	4¢ Girl Scouts	2.00	3.75	9.50(50)	.90	.80	20	.18	.07
1200	4¢ Brien McMahon	2.00	3.75	9.50(50)	.90	.80	20	.18	.07
1201	4¢ Apprenticeship	2.00	3.75	9.50(50)	.90	.80	20	.18	.07
1202	4¢ Sam Rayburn	2.00	3.75	9.50(50)	.90	.80	20	.18	.07

NOTE: To determine the VF price on stamps issued from 1941 to date, add 20% to the F/NH or F (used) price (minimum .03 per item). All VF unused stamps from 1941 date will be NH.

SCOTT NO.	DESCRIPTION	FIRST DAY COVERS SING PL.BLK.		MINT SHEET	PLATE BLOCK F/NH	F	UNUSED F/NH	F	USED F

| | 1203 | | 1204 | | 1205 | | | 1206 | |

1203	4¢ Dag Hammarskjold	2.00	3.75	9.50(50)	.90	.80	20	.18	.07
1204	4¢ Hammarskjold Inverted	6.50	12.00	13.50(50)	3.75	3.35	22	.20	.22
1205	4¢ Christmas '62	2.00	3.75	18.50(100)	.90	.80	20	.18	.06
1206	4¢ Higher Education	2.00	3.75	10.75(50)	1.10	1.00	22	.20	.07

| | 1207 | | 1208 | | 1209, 1225 | | | 1213, 1229 | |

| 1207 | 4¢ Winslow Homer | 2.00 | 3.75 | 11.00(50) | 1.10 | 1.00 | 24 | .22 | .07 |

1962-63 REGULAR ISSUE

1208	5¢ Flag & White House	2.00	3.50	22.50(100)	1.10	1.00	24	.22	.06
1209	1¢ Andrew Jackson	1.75	3.00	6.25(100)	.35	.30	.07	.06	.06
1213	5¢ Washington	2.00	3.50	22.50(100)	1.10	1.00	24	.22	.06
1213a	5¢ b. pane of 5 - Slog. I	3.50					10.75	9.75	
1213a	5¢ b. pane of 5 - Slog. II(1963)						27.50	25.00	
1213a	5¢ b. pane of 5 - Slog. III(1964)						4.00	3.65	
1213c	5¢ Tagged pane of 5 Slogan II (1963)	19.50					130.00	120.00	
1213c	5¢ b. p. of 5 - Slog. III (1964)						2.50	2.25	

Slogan I - Your Mailman Deserves Your Help • Keep Harmful Objects Out of...
Slogan II - Add Zip to Your Mail • Use Zone Numbers for Zip Code.
Slogan III - Add Zip to Your Mail • Always Use Zip Code.

1962-63 COIL STAMPS Perf. 10 Vertically

			L.PR.		LINE PAIRS				
1225	1¢ Andrew Jackson	1.75	2.75		1.50	1.35	.15	.13	.07
1229	5¢ George Washington	2.00	3.50		5.75	5.25	2.25	2.00	.06

| | 1230 | 1231 | 1232 | 1233 |

1963 COMMEMORATIVES

1230-41	12 Varieties				PLATE BLOCK 11.50	10.25	2.50	2.25	.80
1230	5¢ Carolina Charter	1.75	3.25	11.50(50)	1.10	1.00	24	.22	.07
1231	5¢ Food for Peace	1.75	3.25	11.50(50)	1.10	1.00	24	.22	.07
1232	5¢ West Virginia Statehood	1.75	3.25	11.50(50)	1.10	1.00	24	.22	.07
1233	5¢ Emancipation Proclamation	1.75	3.25	11.50(50)	1.10	1.00	24	.22	.07

PLATE BLOCKS: are portions of a sheet of stamps adjacent to the number(s) indicating the printing plate number used to produce that sheet. Flat plate issues are usually collected in plate blocks of six (number opposite middle stamp) while rotary issues are normally corner blocks of four.

SCOTT NO.	DESCRIPTION	FIRST DAY COVERS SING PL.BLK.	MINT SHEET	PLATE BLOCK F/NH F	UNUSED F/NH F	USED F

1234

1235

1236

1237

1238

1239

1240

1241

1242

Scott No.	Description	FDC Sing	FDC PlBlk	Mint Sheet	PB F/NH	PB F	Un F/NH	Un F	Used F
1234	5¢ Alliance for Progress	1.75	3.25	11.50(50)	1.10	1.00	24	.22	.07
1235	5¢ Cordell Hull	1.75	3.25	11.50(50)	1.10	1.00	24	.22	.07
1236	5¢ Eleanor Roosevelt	1.75	3.25	11.50(50)	1.10	1.00	24	.22	.07
1237	5¢ The Sciences	1.75	3.25	11.50(50)	1.10	1.00	24	.22	.07
1238	5¢ City Mail Delivery	1.75	3.25	11.50(50)	1.10	1.00	24	.22	.07
1239	5¢ Int'l Red Cross	1.75	3.25	11.50(50)	1.10	1.00	24	.22	.07
1240	5¢ Christmas '63	1.75	3.25	22.50(100)	1.10	1.00	24	.22	.06
1241	5¢ John J. Audubon	1.75	3.25	11.50(50)	1.10	1.00	24	.22	.07

1243

1244

1246

1248

1245

1247

1249

1250

1251

NOTE: From 1964 onward we only list F/NH quality on unused stamps.

SCOTT NO.	DESCRIPTION	FIRST DAY COVERS SING. PL.BLK.	MINT SHEET	ZIP	PLATE BLOCK	UN-USED	USED

1964 COMMEMORATIVES

Scott No.	Description	FDC Sing	FDC PlBlk	Mint Sheet	Zip	Plate Block	Unused	Used
1242-60	19 Varieties	....	....	....	....	20.00(16)	7.00	1.25
1242	5¢ Sam Houston	1.75	3.25	11.50(50)	1.10	1.10	.24	.07
1243	5¢ Charles M. Russell	1.75	3.25	12.50(50)	1.10	1.10	.24	.07
1244	5¢ New York World's Fair	1.75	3.25	11.50(50)	1.10	1.10	.24	.07
1245	5¢ John Muir	1.75	3.25	11.50(50)	....	1.10	.24	.07
1246	5¢ John F. Kennedy	2.00	3.75	11.50(50)	1.10	1.10	.24	.07
1247	5¢ New Jersey Tercenten.	1.75	3.25	16.00(50)	1.60	1.60	.35	.07
1248	5¢ Nevada Statehood	1.75	3.25	11.50(50)	1.10	1.10	.24	.07
1249	5¢ Register and Vote	1.75	3.25	11.50(50)	1.10	1.10	.24	.07
1250	5¢ Shakespeare	1.75	3.25	11.50(50)	1.10	1.10	.24	.07
1251	5¢ Mayo Brothers	1.75	3.25	11.50(50)	1.10	1.10	.24	.07

COMMEMORATIVES: Commemorative stamps are special issues released to honor or recognize persons, organizations, historical events or landmarks. They are usually issued in the current first class denomination to supplement regular issues.

SCOTT NO.	DESCRIPTION	FIRST DAY COVERS SING.	PL.BLK.	MINT SHEET	ZIP	PLATE BLOCK	UN-USED	USED

1252	5¢ American Music	1.75	3.25	11.50(50)	1.10	1.10	.24	.07
1253	5¢ Homemakers	1.75	3.25	11.50(50)	1.10	1.10	.24	.07
1254-57	5¢ Xmas, 4 vars., attd.	6.25	11.75	82.50(100)	4.25	4.35	3.75	3.25
1254	5¢ Holly	3.00					.70	.07
1255	5¢ Mistletoe	3.00					.70	.07
1256	5¢ Poinsettia	3.00					.70	.07
1257	5¢ Pine Cone	3.00					.70	.07

1258	5¢ Verraz.-Nar. Bridge	1.75	3.25	11.50(50)	1.10	1.10	.24	.07
1259	5¢ Modern Art	1.75	3.25	11.50(50)	1.10	1.10	.24	.07
1260	5¢ Radio Amateurs	1.75	3.25	11.50(50)	1.10	1.10	.24	.07

1965 COMMEMORATIVES

1261-76	16 Varieties				18.95	33.50	4.25	1.35
1261	5¢ Battle of New Orleans	1.75	3.25	11.50(50)	1.10	1.10	.24	.07
1262	5¢ Physical Fitness	1.75	3.25	11.50(50)	1.10	1.10	.24	.07
1263	5¢ Crusade Against Cancer	1.75	3.25	11.50(50)	1.10	1.10	.24	.07
1264	5¢ Winston Churchill	1.75	3.25	11.50(50)	1.10	1.10	.24	.07
1265	5¢ Magna Carta	1.75	3.25	11.50(50)	1.10	1.10	.24	.07
1266	5¢ Int'l Cooperation Year	1.75	3.25	11.50(50)	1.10	1.10	.24	.07

SCOTT NO.	DESCRIPTION	FIRST DAY COVERS SING.	FIRST DAY COVERS PL.BLK.	MINT SHEET	ZIP	PLATE BLOCK	UN-USED	USED
1267	5¢ Salvation Army	1.75	3.25	11.50(50)	1.10	1.10	.24	.07
1268	5¢ Dante Alighieri	1.75	3.25	11.50(50)	1.10	1.10	.24	.07
1269	5¢ Herbert Hoover	1.75	3.25	11.50(50)	1.10	1.10	.24	.07
1270	5¢ Robert Fulton	1.75	3.25	11.50(50)	1.10	1.10	.24	.07
1271	5¢ Florida Settlement	1.75	3.25	11.50(50)	1.10	1.10	.24	.07
1272	5¢ Traffic Safety	1.75	3.25	11.50(50)	1.10	1.10	.24	.07
1273	5¢ John S. Copley	1.75	3.25	12.00(50)	1.15	1.15	.25	.07
1274	11¢ Telecommunication	1.75	3.25	57.50(50)	4.50	19.75	.85	.40
1275	5¢ Adlai Stevenson	1.75	3.25	11.50(50)	....	1.10	.24	.07
1276	5¢ Christmas '65	1.75	3.25	22.50(50)	1.10	1.10	.24	.06

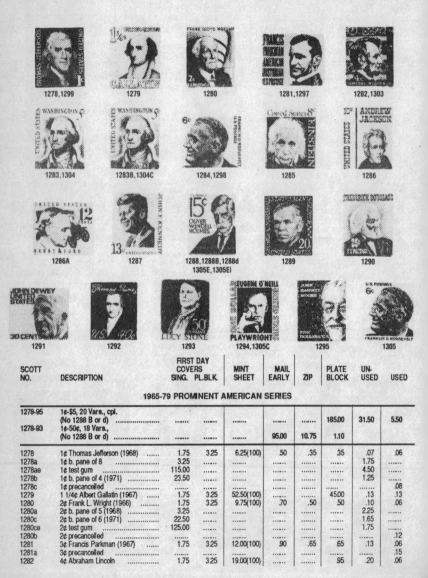

1278,1299   1279   1280   1281,1297   1282,1303

1283,1304   1283B,1304C   1284,1298   1285   1286

1286A   1287   1288,1288B,1288d 1305E,1305EI   1289   1290

1291   1292   1293   1294,1305C   1295   1305

SCOTT NO.	DESCRIPTION	FIRST DAY COVERS SING.	FIRST DAY COVERS PL.BLK.	MINT SHEET	MAIL EARLY	ZIP	PLATE BLOCK	UN-USED	USED
				1965-79 PROMINENT AMERICAN SERIES					
1278-95	1¢-$5, 20 Vars., cpl. (No 1288 B or d)	....	....	....	....	....	185.00	31.50	5.50
1278-93	1¢-50¢, 18 Vars., (No 1288 B or d)	....	....	....	95.00	10.75	1.10		
1278	1¢ Thomas Jefferson (1968)	1.75	3.25	6.25(100)	.50	.35	.35	.07	.06
1278a	1¢ b. pane of 8	3.25	....	....	....	....	....	1.75	....
1278ae	1¢ test gum	115.00	....	....	....	....	....	4.50	....
1278b	1¢ b. pane of 4 (1971)	23.50	....	....	....	....	....	1.25	....
1278c	1¢ precancelled	....	....	....	....	....	....	....	.08
1279	1 1/4¢ Albert Gallatin (1967)	1.75	3.25	52.50(100)	....	....	45.00	.13	.13
1280	2¢ Frank L. Wright (1966)	1.75	3.25	9.75(100)	.70	.50	.50	.10	.06
1280a	2¢ b. pane of 5 (1968)	3.25	....	....	....	....	....	2.25	....
1280c	2¢ b. pane of 6 (1971)	22.50	....	....	....	....	....	1.65	....
1280ce	2¢ test gum	125.00	....	....	....	....	....	1.75	....
1280b	2¢ precancelled	....	....	....	....	....	....	....	.12
1281	3¢ Francis Parkman (1967)	1.75	3.25	12.00(100)	.90	.65	.65	.13	.06
1281a	3¢ precancelled	....	....	....	....	....	....	....	.15
1282	4¢ Abraham Lincoln	1.75	3.25	19.00(100)	....	....	.95	.20	.06

SCOTT NO.	DESCRIPTION	FIRST DAY COVERS SING.	PL.BLK.	MINT SHEET	MAIL EARLY	ZIP	PLATE BLOCK	UN-USED	USED
1283	5¢ G. Washington (1966)	1.75	3.25	27.50(100)	......	....	1.50	.30	.06
1283B	5¢ Wash., redrawn (1967)	1.75	3.25	22.50(100)	......	....	1.25	.25	.06
1283Bd	5¢ precancelled	....	....	....	......	....	....	....	.30
1284	6¢ F.D. Roosevelt (1966)	2.00	3.50	31.50(100)	5.25	4.50	1.75	.35	.06
1284b	6¢ b. pane of 8 (1967)	3.75	....	....	......	....	....	2.95	......
1284c	6¢ b. pane of 5 (1968)	185.00	....	....	......	....	....	2.75	......
1285	8¢ Albert Einstein (1966)	2.00	3.75	35.00(100)	2.90	1.95	2.25	.40	.06
1286	10¢ Andrew Jackson (1967)	2.00	3.75	42.50(100)	3.00	2.10	2.10	.45	.06
1286b	10¢ precancelled	....	....	....	......	....	....	....	.45
1286A	12¢ Henry Ford (1968)	2.00	3.75	47.50(100)	3.25	2.25	2.50	.50	.07
1286Ac	12¢ precancelled	....	....	....	......	....	....	....	.50
1287	13¢ John F. Kennedy (1967)	2.50	4.50	55.00(100)	......	....	2.85	.60	.06
1287a	13¢ precancelled	....	....	....	......	....	....	....	.60
1288	15¢ Oliver W. Holmes, die I (1968)	2.50	4.50	55.00(100)	4.00	2.85	3.25	.60	.06
1288a	15¢ precancelled	....	....	....	......	....	....	....	.75
1288d	15¢ Holmes, die II (1979)	....	....	65.00(100)	......	3.00	5.75	.65	.06
1288B	Same, from B. Pane (1978)	2.50	....	....	......	....	....	.70	.06
1288Bc	15¢ b. pane of 8	4.50	....	....	......	....	....	5.75	......
1289	20¢ G.C. Marshall (1967)	2.50	4.50	85.00(100)	5.75	4.00	4.25	.90	.06
1290	25¢ Frederick Douglass (1967)	3.00	5.00	100.00(100)	6.85	4.75	5.00	1.05	.06
1291	30¢ John Dewey (1968)	3.00	5.00	120.00(100)	8.50	5.75	5.75	1.25	.06
1292	40¢ Thomas Paine (1968)	3.75	6.00	160.00(100)	11.00	7.50	8.00	1.75	.08
1293	50¢ Lucy Stone (1968)	4.75	7.25	220.00(100)	14.50	10.00	10.00	2.25	.07
1294	$1 E. O'Neill (1967)	7.75	16.50	400.00(100)	28.50	19.00	19.75	4.50	.15
1295	$5 John Bassett Moore (1966)	65.00	115.00		......	....	80.00	17.50	4.50

BOOKLET PANE SLOGANS

Slogan IV: Mail Early in the Day
Slogan V: Use Zip Code

#1278b - Slogans IV and V.
#1280a, 1284c - Slogans IV or V.

1966-81 COIL STAMPS

		LINE PAIR					LINE PAIR		
1297-1305Ei	1¢-$1, 9 Vars., (No 1305E)	......	....	....	....	......	18.95	4.65	1.75

Perf. 10 Horizontally

1297	3¢ Francis Parkman (1975)	1.75	2.75				1.10	.15	.06
1297b	3¢ precancelled	....	....				....	....	.18
1298	6¢ F.D. Roosevelt (1967)	1.75	2.75				2.65	.30	.06

Perf. 10 Vertically

1299	1¢ T. Jefferson (1968)	1.75	2.50				.35	.09	.06
1299a	1¢ precancelled	....	....				....	....	.10
1303	4¢ Abraham Lincoln	1.75	2.75				1.10	.20	.14
1303a	4¢ precancelled	....	....				....	....	.35
1304	5¢ George Washington	1.75	2.75				.75	.25	.06
1304a	5¢ precancelled	....	....				....	....	.30
1304C	5¢ Wash., redrawn (1981)	1.75	2.75				1.80	.25	.06
1305	6¢ F.D. Roosevelt (1968)	1.75	2.75				1.10	.40	.06
1305b	6¢ precancelled	....	....				....	....	.45
1305E	15¢ O.W. Holmes, die I (1978)	2.50	4.50				1.95	.75	.06
1305Ef	15¢ precancelled	....	....				....	....	.75
1305Ei	15¢ O.W. Holmes, die II (1979)	....	....				1.95	.75	.06
1305C	$1 E. O'Neill (1973)	6.50	10.75				9.25	2.50	1.30

ZIP BLOCKS: are generally corner Blocks of Four that contain a drawing of "Mr. Zip" and the legend "USE ZIP CODE" or a similar design. They were introduced in 1964 and are still in use today.

SCOTT NO.	DESCRIPTION	FIRST DAY COVERS SING.	PL.BLK.	MINT SHEET	ZIP	PLATE BLOCK	UN-USED	USED

1306   1307   1310,1311   1314

1308   1309   1312   1313   1315

1966 COMMEMORATIVES

1306/22	(1306-10, 1312-22) 16 Vars.	....	....	....	16.75	17.00	3.75	1.00
1306	5¢ Migratory Bird Treaty	1.75	3.25	11.50(50)	1.10	1.10	.24	.07
1307	5¢ A.S.P.C.A.	1.75	3.25	11.50(50)	1.10	1.10	.24	.07
1308	5¢ Indiana Statehood	1.75	3.25	11.50(50)	1.10	1.10	.24	.07
1309	5¢ American Circus	1.75	3.25	12.00(50)	1.20	1.20	.25	.07
1310	5¢ SIPEX, (single)	1.75	3.25	11.50(50)	1.10	1.10	.24	.07

Imperforate Souvenir Sheet

1311	5¢ SIPEX	1.75	....	....	....	....	.32	.40
1312	5¢ Bill of Rights	1.75	3.25	11.50(50)	1.10	1.10	.24	.07
1313	5¢ Polish Millenium	1.75	3.25	11.50(50)	1.10	1.10	.24	.07
1314	5¢ Nat'l. Park Service	1.75	3.25	11.50(50)	1.10	1.10	.24	.07
1315	5¢ Marine Corps Res.	1.75	3.25	11.50(50)	1.10	1.10	.24	.07

1316   1318   1321   1322

1317   1319   1320   1323

1316	5¢ Womens' clubs	1.75	3.25	11.50(50)	1.10	1.10	.24	.07
1317	5¢ Johnny Appleseed	1.75	3.25	11.50(50)	1.10	1.10	.24	.07
1318	5¢ Beautification	1.75	3.25	11.50(50)	1.10	1.10	.24	.07
1319	5¢ Great River Road	1.75	3.25	11.50(50)	1.10	1.10	.24	.07
1320	5¢ Servicemen-Bonds	1.75	3.25	11.50(50)	1.10	1.10	.24	.07
1321	5¢ Christmas '66	1.75	3.25	22.50(50)	1.10	1.10	.24	.06
1322	5¢ Mary Cassatt	1.75	3.25	15.00(50)	1.60	1.65	.35	.07

NOTE: All stamps from #1242 to date are priced for F/NH condition. For VF/NH price, add 20% (minimum .03 per item) to listed price.

MINT SHEETS: From 1935 to date, we list prices for our standard size Mint Sheets in Fine, Never Hinged condition. The number of stamps in each sheet is noted in ( ).

SCOTT NO.	DESCRIPTION	FIRST DAY COVERS		MINT SHEET	ZIP	PLATE BLOCK	UN-USED	USED
		SING.	PL.BLK.					
	1967 COMMEMORATIVES							
1323-37	15 Vars., cpl.	....	....	....	23.50(13)	26.00(14)	6.65	1.40
1323	5¢ National Grange	1.75	3.25	11.50(50)	1.10	1.10	.24	.07

1324   1325   1326

1324	5¢ Canada Centennial	1.75	3.25	11.50(50)	1.10	1.10	.24	.07
1325	5¢ Erie Canal.....................	1.75	3.25	11.50(50)	1.10	1.10	.24	.07
1326	5¢ Search for Peace	1.75	3.25	11.50(50)	1.10	1.10	.24	.07

1327   1328   1329   1330

1327	5¢ Henry D. Thoreau	1.75	3.25	12.00(50)	1.15	1.15	.25	.07
1328	5¢ Nebraska Statehood ...	1.75	3.25	12.00(50)	1.15	1.15	.25	.07
1329	5¢ Voice of America	1.75	3.25	11.50(50)	1.10	1.10	.24	.07
1330	5¢ Davy Crockett	2.75	4.25	11.50(50)	1.10	1.10	.24	.07

1331   1332

1331-32	Space, att'd., 2 vars.	15.00	25.00	85.00(50)	11.00	11.50	3.75	2.75
1331	5¢ Astronaut	3.75	....	....	....	....	.90	.30
1332	5¢ Gemini 4 Capsule	3.75	....	....	....	....	.90	.30

1333   1334

1333	5¢ Urban Planning	1.75	3.25	13.00(50)	1.35	1.50	.27	.07
1334	5¢ Finnish Independence ...	1.75	3.25	13.00(50)	1.35	1.50	.27	.07

FOR YOUR CONVENIENCE IN ORDERING, COMPLETE SETS ARE LISTED BEFORE SINGLE STAMP LISTINGS!

SCOTT NO.	DESCRIPTION	FIRST DAY COVERS SING.	PL.BLK.	MINT SHEET	MAIL EARLY	ZIP	PLATE BLOCK	UN-USED	USED

1335

1336

1337

1335	5¢ Thomas Eakins	1.75	3.25	12.50(50)	....	....	1.60	.27	.07
1336	5¢ Christmas '67	1.75	3.25	11.50(50)	....	1.10	1.10	.24	.06
1337	5¢ Mississippi Statehood	1.75	3.25	13.00(50)	....	1.40	1.50	.30	.07

1338,1338A-G

1339

1340

GIORI PRESS
1968 Design size: 18-1/2 x 22mm Perf. 11

| 1338 | 6¢ Flag & White House .... | 1.75 | 3.25 | 27.50(100) | 1.95 | 1.35 | 1.40 | .30 | .06 |

HUCK PRESS Design size: 18 x 21mm
1969 Coil Stamp Perf. 10 Vertically

| 1338A | 6¢ Flag & White House .... | 1.75 | .... | .... | .... | .... | .... | .30 | .06 |

1970 Perf. 11 x 10-1/2

| 1338D | 6¢ Flag & White House .... | 2.25 | 3.75 | 26.95(100) | .... | .... | 6.50(20) | .30 | .06 |

1971 Perf. 11 x 10-1/2

| 1338F | 8¢ Flag & White House .... | 2.50 | 4.25 | 32.50(100) | .... | .... | 7.75(20) | .35 | .06 |

Coil Stamp Perf. 10 Vertically

| 1338G | 8¢ Flag & White House .... | 2.50 | .... | .... | .... | .... | .... | .45 | .06 |

1968 COMMEMORATIVES

1339/64	(1339-40, 42-44, 55-64) 15 Vars.	....	....	....	26.75(13)	19.75(14)	25.00	4.95	1.00
1339	6¢ Illinois Statehood	1.75	3.25	14.00(50)	....	1.40	1.50	.30	.07
1340	6¢ Hemisfair '68	1.75	3.25	14.00(50)	2.00	1.40	1.50	.30	.07

1341

1342

1343

1344

SCOTT NO.	DESCRIPTION	FIRST DAY COVERS SING.	FIRST DAY COVERS PL.BLK.	MINT SHEET	MAIL EARLY	ZIP	PLATE BLOCK	UN-USED	USED
1341	$1 Airlift to Servicemen	10.75	22.50	425.00(50)	60.00	41.50	4250	8.95	4.75
1342	6¢ Support our Youth	1.75	3.25	14.00(50)	2.00	1.35	150	.30	.07
1343	6¢ Law and Order	1.75	3.25	14.00(50)	2.00	1.35	150	.30	.07
1344	6¢ Register and Vote	1.75	3.25	14.00(50)	2.00	1.35	150	.30	.07

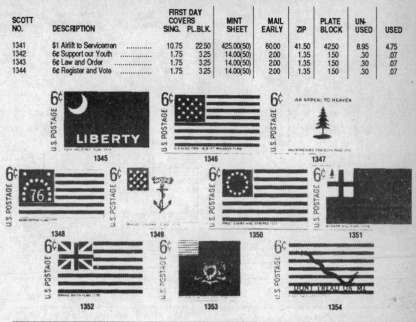

1345 · 1346 · 1347 · 1348 · 1349 · 1350 · 1351 · 1352 · 1353 · 1354

1968 HISTORIC AMERICAN FLAGS

1345-54	10 Vars., cpl., att'd	15.00		35.00(50)			1875	8.50	
1345-54	Same, set of singles	62.50						7.50	6.85
1345/54	Inscr. blks.				4.00	3.50	6.50		
1345	6¢ Fort Moultrie Flag	6.50						1.95	.90
1346	6¢ Fort McHenry Flag	6.50						1.35	.90
1347	6¢ Washington's Cruisers	6.50						.60	.90
1348	6¢ Bennington Flag	6.50						.60	.65
1349	6¢ Rhode Island Flag	6.50						.60	.65
1350	6¢ 1st Stars & Stripes	6.50						.75	.65
1351	6¢ Bunker Hill Flag	6.50						.75	.65
1352	6¢ Grand Union Flag	6.50						.80	.65
1353	6¢ Philadelphia Light Horse	6.50						.80	.65
1354	6¢ First Navy Jack	6.50						.80	.65

NOTE: All 10 varieties of 1345-54 were printed on the same sheet; therefore, plate and regular blocks are not available for each variety separately. Plate blocks of 4 will contain two each of #1346, with number adjacent to #1345 only; Zip blocks will contain two each of #1353 and #1354, with inscription adjacent to #1354 only; Mail Early blocks will contain two each of #1347-49 with inscription adjacent to #1348 only. A plate strip of 20 stamps, with two of each variety will be required to have all stamps in plate block form and will contain all marginal inscription.

1355 · 1356 · 1357 · 1358 · 1359

1355	6¢ Walt Disney	3.75	7.00	18.50(50)	2.65	1.80	2.00	.40	.07
1356	6¢ Father Marquette	1.75	3.25	14.00(50)	2.00	1.35	150	.30	.07
1357	6¢ Daniel Boone	1.75	3.25	14.00(50)	2.00	1.35	150	.30	.07
1358	6¢ Arkansas River	1.75	3.25	14.00(50)	2.00	1.35	150	.30	.07
1359	6¢ Leif Erikson	1.75	3.25	14.00(50)	2.00	1.35	150	.30	.07

SCOTT NO.	DESCRIPTION	FIRST DAY COVERS SING.	PL.BLK.	MINT SHEET	MAIL EARLY	ZIP	PLATE BLOCK	UN-USED	USED

1360   **1361**   **1363**   **1364**   **1362**

1360	6¢ Cherokee Strip	1.75	3.25	15.00(50)	1.95	1.35	1.50	.30	.07
1361	6¢ Trumbull Art	1.75	3.25	17.00(50)	2.35	1.65	1.75	.35	.07
1362	6¢ Wildlife Conservation	1.75	3.25	18.75(50)	2.65	1.85	2.25	.40	.07
1363	6¢ Christmas '68	1.75	3.25	14.00(50)	......	......	3.25(10)	.30	.06
1364	6¢ Chief Joseph	1.75	3.25	18.00(50)	2.65	1.85	2.25	.40	.07

1365   **1366**   **1367**   **1368**

1969 COMMEMORATIVES

1365-86	22 Vars., cpl.	......	......	......	52.50(15)	38.75(15)	43.50(16)	20.75	1.90
1365-68	Beautification, 4 Vars., attd	7.50	9.50	59.75(50)	8.50	6.75	7.00	5.25	6.50
1365	6¢ Azaleas & Tulips	3.75	......	......	......	......	......	.95	.11
1366	6¢ Daffodils	3.75	......	......	......	......	......	.95	.11
1367	6¢ Poppies	3.75	......	......	......	......	......	.95	.11
1368	6¢ Crabapple Trees	3.75	......	......	......	......	......	.95	.11

1369   **1370**   **1371**   **1372**

1369	6¢ American Legion	1.75	3.25	14.00(50)	1.95	1.35	1.40	.30	.07
1370	6¢ Grandma Moses	1.75	3.25	14.00(50)	1.95	1.35	1.40	.30	.07
1371	6¢ Apollo 8 Moon Orbit	1.75	3.25	18.75(50)	2.75	1.95	1.95	.40	.07
1372	6¢ W.C. Handy-Musician	1.75	3.25	14.00(50)	1.95	1.35	1.40	.30	.07

1373   **1374**   **1375**

1373	6¢ California Settlement	1.75	3.25	14.00(50)	1.95	1.35	1.40	.30	.07
1374	6¢ Major John W. Powell	1.75	3.25	14.00(50)	1.95	1.35	1.40	.30	.07
1375	6¢ Alabama Statehood	1.75	3.25	14.00(50)	1.95	1.35	1.40	.30	.07

AVERAGE QUALITY: From 1935 to date, deduct 20% from the Fine price to determine the price for an Average quality stamp.

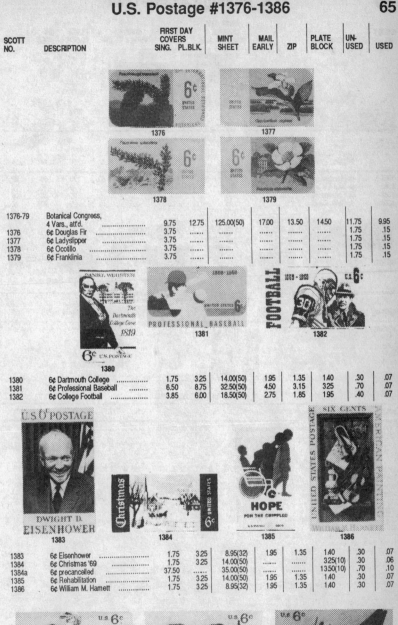

SCOTT NO.	DESCRIPTION	FIRST DAY COVERS SING.	FIRST DAY COVERS PL.BLK.	MINT SHEET	MAIL EARLY	ZIP	PLATE BLOCK	UN-USED	USED
1376-79	Botanical Congress, 4 Vars., att'd.	9.75	12.75	125.00(50)	17.00	13.50	14.50	11.75	9.95
1376	6¢ Douglas Fir	3.75	....	....	....	....	....	1.75	.15
1377	6¢ Ladyslipper	3.75	....	....	....	....	....	1.75	.15
1378	6¢ Ocotillo	3.75	....	....	....	....	....	1.75	.15
1379	6¢ Franklinia	3.75	....	....	....	....	....	1.75	.15
1380	6¢ Dartmouth College	1.75	3.25	14.00(50)	1.95	1.35	1.40	.30	.07
1381	6¢ Professional Baseball	6.50	8.75	32.50(50)	4.50	3.15	3.25	.70	.07
1382	6¢ College Football	3.85	6.00	18.50(50)	2.75	1.85	1.95	.40	.07
1383	6¢ Eisenhower	1.75	3.25	8.95(32)	1.95	1.35	1.40	.30	.07
1384	6¢ Christmas '69	1.75	3.25	14.00(50)	....	....	3.25(10)	.30	.06
1384a	6¢ precancelled	37.50	....	35.00(50)	....	....	13.50(10)	.70	.10
1385	6¢ Rehabilitation	1.75	3.25	14.00(50)	1.95	1.35	1.40	.30	.07
1386	6¢ William M. Harnett	1.75	3.25	8.95(32)	1.95	1.35	1.40	.30	.07

AMERICAN BALD EAGLE
1387

AFRICAN ELEPHANT HERD
1388

HAIDA CEREMONIAL CANOE
1389

MINT SHEETS: From 1935 to date, we list prices for our standard size Mint Sheets in Fine, Never Hinged condition. The number of stamps in each sheet is noted in ( ).

1391

THE AGE OF REPTILES
1390

1392

1970 COMMEMORATIVES

SCOTT NO.	DESCRIPTION	FIRST DAY COVERS SING.	PL.BLK.	MINT SHEET	MAIL EARLY	ZIP	PLATE BLOCK	UN-USED	USED
1387/1422	(1387-92, 1405-22) 24 Vars., (No precancels	....	....	....	33.95	24.00	37.50	12.00	2.35
1387-90	Natural History, 4 vars., attd	6.50	8.50	9.95(32)	2.25	1.50	1.70	1.30	1.50
1387	6¢ Bald Eagle	3.25	....	....	....	....	....	.33	.12
1388	6¢ Elephant Herd	3.25	....	....	....	....	....	.33	.12
1389	6¢ Haida Canoe	3.25	....	....	....	....	....	.33	.12
1390	6¢ Reptiles	3.25	....	....	....	....	....	.33	.12
1391	6¢ Maine Statehood	1.75	3.25	14.00(50)	1.95	1.35	1.40	.30	.07
1392	6¢ Wildlife-Buffalo	1.75	3.25	14.00(50)	1.95	1.35	1.40	.30	.07

1393,1401

1393D

1394

1395,1402

1396

1397

Ernie Pyle
Journalist
1398

1399

GIANNINI
1400

1970 -74 REGULAR ISSUE

SCOTT NO.	DESCRIPTION	FIRST DAY COVERS SING.	PL.BLK.	MINT SHEET	MAIL EARLY	ZIP	PLATE BLOCK	UN-USED	USED
1393-1400	6¢-21¢ cpl. 8 vars., (No 1395)	....	....	....	25.00	17.75	21.50	3.85	.75
1393	6¢ Dwight Eisenhower	1.75	3.25	27.50(100)	1.95	1.35	1.35	.30	.06
1393c	6¢ precancelled	....	....	....	....	....	....	....	.30
1393a	6¢ b. pane of 8	3.25	....	....	....	....	....	2.75	....
1393ae	6¢ test gum	115.00	....	....	....	....	....	3.75	....
1393b	6¢ b. pane of 5-Slo. IV or V	4.75	....	....	....	....	....	2.25	....
1393D	7¢ Benjamin Franklin (1972)	1.50	2.75	28.00(100)	1.95	1.35	1.40	.30	.07
1393De	7¢ precancelled	....	....	....	....	....	....	....	.30
1394	8¢ Ike-black, blue, red (1971)	1.50	2.75	30.00(100)	2.30	1.60	1.70	.35	.06
1395	Same, rose violet bklt.sgl. (1971)	2.50	....	....	....	....	....	.45	.06
1395a	8¢ booklet pane of 8	3.25	....	....	....	....	....	3.75	....
1395b	8¢ booklet pane of 6	3.25	....	....	....	....	....	3.00	....
1395c	8¢ b. pane of 4, VI & VII (1972)	2.75	....	....	....	....	....	2.50	....
1395d	8¢ b. pane of 7, II or V (1972)	3.25	....	....	....	....	....	3.75	....
1396	8¢ Postal Service Emblem (1971)	1.50	2.75	31.75(100)	1.60	1.60	4.95(12)	.35	.06
1397	14¢ Fiorello LaGuardia (1972)	1.75	3.25	55.00(100)	3.90	2.70	2.75	.60	.11
1397a	14¢ precancelled	....	....	....	....	....	....	....	.60
1398	16¢ Ernie Pyle (1971)	2.50	4.25	60.00(100)	4.25	2.90	2.95	.65	.07
1398a	16¢ precancelled	....	....	....	....	....	....	....	.65
1399	18¢ Elizabeth Blackwell (1974)	2.00	3.75	70.00(100)	5.00	3.50	3.65	.75	.07
1400	21¢ Amadeo P. Giannini (1973)	2.50	4.25	75.00(100)	5.35	3.75	3.85	.80	.30

1970-71 COIL STAMPS - Perf. 10 Vertically

SCOTT NO.	DESCRIPTION	L. PR. SING.	PL.BLK.				LINE PAIR	UN-USED	USED
1401	6¢ Dwight Eisenhower	1.75	2.75	....	....	....	.75	.30	.06
1401a	6¢ precancelled	....	....	....	....	....	....	....	.45
1402	8¢ Eisenhower, rose violet (1971)	1.75	2.75	....	....	....	.85	.35	.06
1402b	8¢ precancelled	....	....	....	....	....	....	....	1.25

SCOTT NO.	DESCRIPTION	FIRST DAY COVERS SING.	PL.BLK.	MINT SHEET	MAIL EARLY	ZIP	PLATE BLOCK	UN-USED	USED

1405

1406

1407

1408

1409

1970 COMMEMORATIVES

SCOTT NO.	DESCRIPTION	SING.	PL.BLK.	MINT SHEET	MAIL EARLY	ZIP	PLATE BLOCK	UN-USED	USED
1405	6¢ Edgar L. Masters-Poet	1.75	3.25	14.00(50)	1.95	1.35	1.40	.30	.07
1406	6¢ Woman Suffrage	1.75	3.25	14.00(50)	1.95	1.35	1.40	.30	.07
1407	6¢ South Carolina Terc.	1.75	3.25	14.00(50)	1.95	1.35	1.40	.30	.07
1408	6¢ Stone Mt. Memorial	1.75	3.25	14.00(50)	1.95	1.35	1.40	.30	.07
1409	6¢ Fort Snelling	1.75	3.25	14.00(50)	1.95	1.35	1.40	.30	.07

1410

1411

1412

1413

1410-13	Anti-Pollution, 4 Vars., att'd	6.50	9.00	28.50(50)	4.25	3.25	7.50(10)	2.75	3.75
1410	6¢ Globe & Wheat	3.25						.40	.18
1411	6¢ Globe & City	3.25						.40	.18
1412	6¢ Globe & Bluegill	3.25						.40	.18
1413	6¢ Globe & Seagull	3.25						.40	.18

1415

1416

1417

1414

1418

1414	6¢ Nativity	1.75	3.25	14.00(50)	1.95	1.30	2.75(8)	.30	.06
1415-18	Christmas Toys, 4 Vars. att'd	6.75	9.50	52.50(50)	7.50	5.75	11.50(8)	5.00	4.50
1415	6¢ Locomotive	3.75						.80	.09
1416	6¢ Horse	3.75						.80	.09
1417	6¢ Tricycle	3.75						.80	.09
1418	6¢ Doll Carriage	3.75						.80	.09

Precancelled

1414a	6¢ Nativity (precancelled)	15.00		15.00(50)	1.95	1.30	5.50(8)	.30	.06
1415a-18a	Xmas Toys, precan. 4 vars. att'd	32.50		127.50(50)	17.75	13.75	28.75(8)	11.75	11.50
1415a	6¢ Locomotive	16.50						2.40	.13
1416a	6¢ Horse	16.50						2.40	.13
1417a	6¢ Tricycle	16.50						2.40	.13
1418a	6¢ Doll Carriage	16.50						2.40	.13

NOTE: Unused precancels are with original gum while used are without gum.

SCOTT NO.	DESCRIPTION	FIRST DAY COVERS SING.	PL.BLK.	MINT SHEET	MAIL EARLY	ZIP	PLATE BLOCK	UN-USED	USED

| | | 1419 | | 1420 | | 1421 | 1422 | 1423 | 1424 |

1419	6¢ U.N. 25th Anniv.	....	1.75	3.25	14.00(50)	1.95	1.35	1.40	.30	.07
1420	6¢ Pilgrim Landing	....	1.75	3.25	14.00(50)	1.95	1.35	1.40	.30	.07
1421-22	D.A.V. Servicemen, 2 Vars., att'd.	....	2.50	3.75	14.50(50)	2.25	1.50	3.25	.60	.70
1421	6¢ Disabled Vets	....	1.75	....	....	....	....	....	.30	.10
1422	6¢ Prisoners of War	....	1.75	....	....	....	....	....	.30	.10

1971 COMMEMORATIVES

1423-45	23 Vars., cpl.	....	....	....	....	36.50(16)	27.50(16)	40.50(16)	8.50	1.95
1423	6¢ Sheep	....	1.75	3.25	14.00(50)	1.95	1.35	1.40	.30	.07
1424	6¢ General D. MacArthur	....	1.75	3.25	14.00(50)	1.95	1.35	1.40	.30	.07

| 1425 | | 1427 | 1426 |
| 1428 | | 1429 | 1430 |

1425	6¢ Blood Donors	....	1.75	3.25	14.00(50)	1.95	1.35	1.40	.30	.07
1426	8¢ Missouri Statehood	....	1.75	3.25	18.00(50)	1.85(4)	1.85	5.25(12)	.40	.07
1427-30	Wildlife Conserv. 4 Vars. attd	...	4.75	7.50	11.50(32)	2.75	1.85	2.00	1.60	1.50
1427	8¢ Trout	....	3.25	....	....	....	....	....	.40	.12
1428	8¢ Alligator	....	3.25	....	....	....	....	....	.40	.12
1429	8¢ Polar Bear	....	3.25	....	....	....	....	....	.40	.12
1430	8¢ Condor	....	3.25	....	....	....	....	....	.40	.12

| 1431 | 1433 | 1434 | 1435 |

FIRST DAY COVERS: First Day Covers are envelopes cancelled on the "First Day of Issue" of the stamp used on the envelope. Usually they also contain a picture (cachet) on the left side designed to go with the theme of the stamp. From 1935 to 1944, prices listed are for cacheted, addressed covers. From 1945 to date, prices are for cacheted, unaddressed covers.

SCOTT NO.	DESCRIPTION	FIRST DAY COVERS SING.	PL.BLK.	MINT SHEET	MAIL EARLY	ZIP	PLATE BLOCK	UN-USED	USED

1432 · 1436 · 1437 · 1438 · 1439

1431	8¢ Antarctic Treaty	1.75	3.25	18.00(50)	2.65	1.85	1.90	.40	.07
1432	8¢ American Revolution	1.75	3.25	20.00(50)	2.65	1.85	2.75	.40	.07
1433	8¢ J. Sloan-Artist	1.75	3.25	18.00(50)	2.65	1.85	1.90	.40	.07
1434-35	Space Achievements, 2 Vars., att'd.	3.00	5.25	18.00(50)	2.65	1.85	1.90	.80	.65
1434	8¢ Moon, Earth , Sun & Landing Craft	1.75	......	......	......	......	......	.40	.11
1435	8¢ Lunar Rover	1.75	......	......	......	......	......	.40	.11
1436	8¢ Emily Dickinson	1.75	3.25	18.00(50)	2.65	1.85	1.90	.40	.11
1437	8¢ San Juan	1.75	3.25	18.00(50)	2.65	1.85	1.90	.40	.07
1438	8¢ Drug Addiction	1.75	3.25	18.00(50)	2.65	1.85	2.75(6)	.40	.07
1439	8¢ CARE	1.75	3.25	18.00(50)	2.65	1.85	3.75(8)	.40	.07

1440 · 1441 · 1442

1444 · 1445 · 1443 · 1446 · 1447

1440-43	Historic Preservation, 4 Vars. att'd.	4.75	7.50	12.00(32)	2.65	1.85	1.90	1.60	1.75
1440	8¢ Decatur House	3.25	......	......	......	......	......	.40	.11
1441	8¢ Whaling Ship	3.25	......	......	......	......	......	.40	.11
1442	8¢ Cable Car	3.25	......	......	......	......	......	.40	.11
1443	8¢ Mission	3.25	......	......	......	......	......	.40	.11
1444	8¢ Christmas Nativity	1.75	3.25	18.00(50)	1.85(4)	1.85	5.25(12)	.40	.06
1445	8¢ Christmas Partridge	1.75	3.25	18.00(50)	1.85(4)	1.85	5.25(12)	.40	.06

1972 COMMEMORATIVES

1446/74	(1446-47, 55-74) 22 Vars.	......	......	......	37.50(15)	29.50(16)	52.50(16)	8.50	2.60
1446	8¢ Sidney Lanier-Poet	1.75	3.25	18.00(50)	2.65	1.85	1.90	.40	.07
1447	8¢ Peace Corps	1.75	3.25	18.00(50)	2.65	1.85	2.85(6)	.40	.07

SE-TENANTS: Beginning with the 1964 Christmas issue (#1254-57), the United States has issued numerous Se-Tenant stamps covering a wide variety of subjects. Se-Tenants are issues where two or more different stamp designs are produced on the same sheet in pair, strip or block form. Mint stamps are usually collected in attached blocks, etc.; used are generally saved as single stamps. Our Se-Tenant sets follow in this collecting pattern.

SCOTT NO.	DESCRIPTION	FIRST DAY COVERS SING.	PL.BLK.	MINT SHEET	MAIL EARLY	ZIP	PLATE BLOCK	UN-USED	USED

1452

1448-51

1454

1453

Family Planning 1455

1972 NATIONAL PARKS CENTENNIAL

SCOTT NO.	DESCRIPTION	SING.	PL.BLK.	MINT SHEET	MAIL EARLY	ZIP	PLATE BLOCK	UN-USED	USED
1448-54	cpl. 7 Vars.	....	....	....	9.50(4)	6.50(4)	7.50(4)	1.70	1.20
1448-51	Cape Hatteras, 4 Vars., attd	2.50	3.75	7.75(100)	1.10(8)	.60	1.35	.40	.45
1448	2¢ Ship's Hull	....	....	....	....	....	....	.10	.10
1449	2¢ Lighthouse	....	....	....	....	....	....	.10	.10
1450	2¢ Three Seagulls	....	....	....	....	....	....	.10	.10
1451	2¢ Two Seagulls	....	....	....	....	....	....	.10	.10
1452	6¢ Wolf Trap Farm Park	2.50	4.25	14.00(50)	1.95	1.35	1.40	.30	.15
1453	8¢ Yellowstone Park	2.50	4.25	12.00(32)	2.65	1.85	1.90	.40	.07
1454	15¢ Mt. Mckinley	2.50	4.25	32.50(50)	4.45	2.95	3.25	.70	.65

1972 COMMEMORATIVES

1455	8¢ Family Planning	1.75	3.25	18.00(50)	2.65	1.85	1.90	.40	.07

1456

1457

1458

1459

SCOTT NO.	DESCRIPTION	SING.	PL.BLK.	MINT SHEET	MAIL EARLY	ZIP	PLATE BLOCK	UN-USED	USED
1456-59	Colonial Craftsmen, 4 Vars., attd.	4.75	6.50	18.00(50)	....	1.85	1.90	1.60	1.75
1456-59	Bicent. Emblem block	....	....	....	2.75	....	....	....	....
1456	8¢ Glassmaker	3.25	....	....	....	....	....	.40	.11
1457	8¢ Silversmith	3.25	....	....	....	....	....	.40	.11
1458	8¢ Wigmaker	3.25	....	....	....	....	....	.40	.11
1459	8¢ Hatter	3.25	....	....	....	....	....	.40	.11

1460

1461

1462

1463

SCOTT NO.	DESCRIPTION	SING.	PL.BLK.	MINT SHEET	MAIL EARLY	ZIP	PLATE BLOCK	UN-USED	USED
1460	6¢ Olympics-Cycling	3.00	5.25	14.75(50)	2.15	1.50	3.50(10)	.32	.18
1461	8¢ Olympics-Bob Sled Rcg.	2.75	4.75	18.00(50)	2.65	1.85	5.00(10)	.40	.07
1462	15¢ Olympics-Foot Racing	3.00	5.25	33.75(50)	5.00	3.50	8.25(10)	.75	.90
1463	8¢ Parents-Teachers Assoc.	2.00	3.75	18.00(50)	2.65	1.85	1.90	.40	.07
1463a	Same, Reversed Plate No.	....	....	19.00(50)	....	....	2.15	....	....

1464

1465

1466

SCOTT NO.	DESCRIPTION	FIRST DAY COVERS SING.	FIRST DAY COVERS PL.BLK.	MINT SHEET	MAIL EARLY	ZIP	PLATE BLOCK	UN-USED	USED

1467

100th Anniversary of Mail Order
1468

SCOTT NO.	DESCRIPTION	SING.	PL.BLK.	MINT SHEET	MAIL EARLY	ZIP	PLATE BLOCK	UN-USED	USED
1464-67	Wildlife conserv., 4 Vars., att'd.	3.25	4.75	12.00(32)	2.65	1.85	1.90	1.60	1.40
1464	8¢ Fur Seal	2.00	......	......	......	......	......	.40	.10
1465	8¢ Cardinal	2.00	......	......	......	......	......	.40	.10
1466	8¢ Brown Pelican	2.00	......	......	......	......	......	.40	.10
1467	8¢ Bighorn Sheep	2.00	......	......	......	......	......	.40	.10
1468	8¢ Mail Order Business	1.75	3.25	18.00(50)	1.85(4)	1.85	5.25(12)	.40	.07

1469

Tom Sawyer / United States 8¢
1470

Christmas
1471

U.S. POSTAGE 8¢
1472

SCOTT NO.	DESCRIPTION	SING.	PL.BLK.	MINT SHEET	MAIL EARLY	ZIP	PLATE BLOCK	UN-USED	USED
1469	8¢ Osteopathic Medicine	1.75	3.25	18.00(50)	2.65	1.85	2.85(6)	.40	.07
1470	8¢ Tom Sawyer-Folklore	1.75	3.25	18.00(50)	2.65	1.85	1.90	.40	.07
1471	8¢ Xmas-Virgin Mother	1.75	3.25	18.00(50)	1.85(4)	1.85	5.25(12)	.40	.06
1472	8¢ Xmas-Santa Claus	1.75	3.25	18.00(50)	1.85(4)	1.85	5.25(12)	.40	.06

PHARMACY / UNITED STATES POSTAGE 8¢
1473

Stamp Collecting U.S. 8¢
1474

LOVE US 8¢
1475

SCOTT NO.	DESCRIPTION	SING.	PL.BLK.	MINT SHEET	MAIL EARLY	ZIP	PLATE BLOCK	UN-USED	USED
1473	8¢ Pharmacy	1.75	3.25	18.00(50)	2.65	1.85	1.90	.40	.07
1474	8¢ Stamp Collecting	2.00	3.50	14.50(40)	2.65	1.85	1.90	.40	.07

1973 COMMEMORATIVES

SCOTT NO.	DESCRIPTION	SING.	PL.BLK.	MINT SHEET	MAIL EARLY	ZIP	PLATE BLOCK	UN-USED	USED
1475/1508	(1475-88, 1499-1504, 1507-08) 22 Vars.	......	......	......	32.50(13)	30.00(17)	58.50(19)	8.50	2.40
1475	8¢ "Love"	2.75	4.25	18.00(50)	2.65	1.85	2.85(6)	.40	.07

Rise of the Spirit of Independence
1476

Rise of the Spirit of Independence
1477

Rise of the Spirit of Independence
1478

Rise of the Spirit of Independence
1479

THE BOSTON TEA PARTY
1480-83

SCOTT NO.	DESCRIPTION	FIRST DAY COVERS SING.	PL.BLK.	MINT SHEET	MAIL EARLY	ZIP	PLATE BLOCK	UN-USED	USED
	COLONIAL COMMUNICATIONS								
1476	8¢ Pamphlet Printing	2.00	3.75	18.00(50)	2.65	1.85	190	.40	.07
1477	8¢ Posting Broadside	2.00	3.75	18.00(50)	2.65	1.85	190	.40	.07
1477	8¢ Bicent. Emblem block	....	....	....	2.65	....	....	....	....
1478	8¢ Colonial Post Rider	2.00	3.75	18.00(50)	2.65	1.85	190	.40	.07
1478	8¢ Bicent. Emblem block	....	....	....	2.65	....	....	....	....
1479	8¢ Drummer & Soldiers	2.00	3.75	18.00(50)	2.65	1.85	190	.40	.07
1479	8¢ Bicent. Emblem block	....	....	....	2.65	....	....		
1480-83	Boston Tea Party, 4 Vars., att'd.	5.50	8.25	18.00(50)	2.65	1.85	190	1.60	1.50
1480-83	8¢ Bicent. Emblem block	....	....	....	2.65	1.85			
1480	8¢ Throwing Tea	3.25	....	....	....	....	....	.40	.11
1481	8¢ Ship	3.25	....	....	....	....	....	.40	.11
1482	8¢ Rowboats	3.25	....	....	....	....	....	.40	.11
1483	8¢ Rowboats & Dock	3.25	....	....	....	....	....	.40	.11

1484 GEORGE GERSHWIN

1485 ROBINSON JEFFERS

1488 Copernicus 1473 - 1973 8¢ls

1486 HENRY O. TANNER

1487 WILLA CATHER

AMERICAN ARTS

1484	8¢ George Gershwin-Composer	1.75	3.25	14.50(40)	(combo)	1.85	5.25(12)	.40	.07
1485	8¢ Robinson Jeffers-Poet	1.75	3.25	14.50(40)	(combo)	1.85	5.25(12)	.40	.07
1486	8¢ Henry O. Tanner-Artist	1.75	3.25	14.50(40)	(combo)	1.85	5.25(12)	.40	.07
1487	8¢ Willa Cather-Novelist	1.75	3.25	14.50(40)	(combo)	1.85	5.25(12)	.40	.07
1488	8¢ Nicolaus Copernicus	1.75	3.25	18.00(50)	2.65	1.85	190	.40	.07

U.S. POSTAL SERVICE 8

1489

1490

1491

1492

1493

1494

1495

1496

1497

1498

U.S. Postage #1489-1508

73

SCOTT NO.	DESCRIPTION	FIRST DAY COVERS SING.	PL.BLK.	MINT SHEET	MAIL EARLY	ZIP	PLATE BLOCK	UN-USED	USED
	1973 POSTAL SERVICE EMPLOYEES								
1489-98	cpl., 10 Vars., att'd.	....	8.75	12.00	18.00(50)	....	....	8.75(20)	4.00
1489-93	cpl., 5 Vars., att'd.	....	....	....	....	....	4.50(10)	....	....
1494-98	cpl., 5 Vars., att'd.	....	....	....	....	....	4.50(10)	....	....
1489-98	cpl., set of singles	31.50	....	....	....	....	....	3.75	1.15
1489	8¢ Window Clerk	3.35	....	....	....	....	....	.40	.12
1490	8¢ Mail Pickup	3.35	....	....	....	....	....	.40	.12
1491	8¢ Conveyor Belt	3.35	....	....	....	....	....	.40	.12
1492	8¢ Sacking Parcels	3.35	....	....	....	....	....	.40	.12
1493	8¢ Mail Cancelling	3.35	....	....	....	....	....	.40	.12
1494	8¢ Manual Sorting	3.35	....	....	....	....	....	.40	.12
1495	8¢ Machine Sorting	3.35	....	....	....	....	....	.40	.12
1496	8¢ Loading Truck	3.35	....	....	....	....	....	.40	.12
1497	8¢ Letter Carrier	3.35	....	....	....	....	....	.40	.12
1498	8¢ Rural Delivery	3.35	....	....	....	....	....	.40	.12

1500   **1501**   **1502**

1499

1503

1504   **1505**   **1506**

1973 COMMEMORATIVES

1499	8¢ Harry S. Truman	1.75	3.25	12.00(32)	....	....	1.90	.40	.07
1500	6¢ Electronics	1.75	3.25	13.50(50)	1.95	1.35	1.40	.30	.18
1501	8¢ Electronics	1.75	3.25	18.00(50)	2.65	1.85	1.90	.40	.07
1502	15¢ Electronics	2.00	3.75	33.50(50)	4.75	3.25	3.50	.75	.80
1503	8¢ Lyndon B. Johnson	1.75	3.25	12.00(32)	....	....	5.25(12)	.40	.07

1973-74 RURAL AMERICA

1504	8¢ Angus Cattle	1.75	3.25	18.00(50)	2.65	1.85	1.90	.40	.07
1505	10¢ Chautauqua (1974)	1.75	3.25	20.00(50)	3.00	2.10	2.15	.45	.07
1506	10¢ Winter Wheat (1974)	1.75	3.25	20.00(50)	3.00	2.10	2.15	.45	.07

1507   **1508**   **1509,1519**   **1510,1520**   **1511**   **1518**

1973 CHRISTMAS

1507	8¢ Madonna	1.75	3.25	18.00(50)	1.85(4)	1.85	5.25(12)	.40	.06
1508	8¢ Christmas Tree	1.75	3.25	18.00(50)	1.85(4)	1.85	5.25(12)	.40	.06

SCOTT NO.	DESCRIPTION	FIRST DAY COVERS SING.	FIRST DAY COVERS PL.BLK.	MINT SHEET	MAIL EARLY	ZIP	PLATE BLOCK	UN- USED	USED

1973-74 REGULAR ISSUES

1509	10¢ Crossed Flags	1.75	3.25	40.00(100)	......	......	9.75(20)	.45	.06
1510	10¢ Jefferson Memorial	1.75	3.25	40.00(100)	3.00	2.10	2.15	.45	.06
1510a	10¢ precancelled	......	......	......	......	......	......	......	.45
1510b	10¢ b. pane of 5-Sl. VIII	2.50	......	......	......	......	......	2.50	......
1510c	10¢ b. pane of 8	3.00	......	......	......	......	......	3.75	......
1510d	10¢ b. pane of 6 (1974)	2.50	......	......	......	......	......	7.50	......
1511	10¢ Zip Code Theme (1974)	1.75	3.25	40.00(100)	3.00	2.10	4.00(8)	.45	.06

BOOKLET PANE SLOGANS

VI - Stamps in This Book....   VII - This Book Contains 25...   VIII - Paying Bills...

COIL STAMPS Perf. 10 Vertically

		LINE PR.					LINE PR.		
1518	6.3¢ Liberty Bell	1.75	2.75	......	......	......	1.10	.27	.30
1518a	6.3¢ precancelled	......	......	......	......	......	......	......	.40
1519	10¢ Crossed Flags	1.75	2.75	......	......	......	2.50	.55	.06
1520	10¢ Jefferson Memorial	1.75	2.75	......	......	......	1.25	.50	.06
1520a	10¢ precancelled	......	......	......	......	......	......	......	.35

1525

1527

1526

1528

1529

1974 COMMEMORATIVES

1505/52	(1505-06, 25-29, 38-52) 22 Vars ...	......	......	......	37.75(14)	28.75(15)	53.50(16)	9.50	1.75
1525	10¢ Veterans of Fgn. Wars	1.75	3.25	20.00(50)	3.00	2.10	2.15	.45	.07
1526	10¢ Robert Frost	1.75	3.25	20.00(50)	3.00	2.10	2.15	.45	.07
1527	10¢ Environment-Expo '74	1.75	3.25	16.00(40)	(combo)	2.10	6.00(12)	.45	.07
1528	10¢ Horse Racing	1.75	3.25	20.00(50)	2.10(4)	2.10	6.00(12)	.45	.07
1529	10¢ Skylab Project	1.75	3.25	20.00(50)	3.00	2.10	2.15	.45	.07

1530   **1531**   **1532**   **1533**

MAIL EARLY BLOCKS: Contain the inscription "Mail Early in the Day," a post office slogan designed to encourage their patrons to post their mail early in the morning. Mail Early Blocks are usually blocks of 6 since they come from the center of the sheet margin and six presents a balanced appearance.

SCOTT NO.	DESCRIPTION	FIRST DAY COVERS SING.	FIRST DAY COVERS PL.BLK.	MINT SHEET	MAIL EARLY	ZIP	PLATE BLOCK	UN-USED	USED

1534   1535   1536   1537

1974 UNIVERSAL POSTAL UNION

Scott No.	Description	Sing.	Pl.Blk.	Mint Sheet	Mail Early	Zip	Plate Block	Un-Used	Used
1530-37	8 Vars., att'd.	5.25	8.95(4)	14.50(32)	(combo)	3.00(6)	7.85(16)	3.60(8)	......
1530-37	cpl. set of singles	15.00	......	......	......	......	......	3.35	2.65
1530	10¢ Raphael	2.00	......	......	......	......	......	.45	.35
1531	10¢ Hokusai	2.00	......	......	......	......	......	.45	.35
1532	10¢ J.F. Peto	2.00	......	......	......	......	......	.45	.35
1533	10¢ J.E. Liotard	2.00	......	......	......	......	......	.45	.35
1534	10¢ G. Terborch	2.00	......	......	......	......	......	.45	.35
1535	10¢ J.B.S. Chardin	2.00	......	......	......	......	......	.45	.35
1536	10¢ T. Gainsborough	2.00	......	......	......	......	......	.45	.35
1537	10¢ F. deGoya	2.00	......	......	......	......	......	.45	.35

1538   1539   1540   1541

1974 COMMEMORATIVES

Scott No.	Description	Sing.	Pl.Blk.	Mint Sheet	Mail Early	Zip	Plate Block	Un-Used	Used
1538-41	Mineral Heritage 4 Vars., attd	4.75	6.75	19.00(48)	3.00	2.10	2.15	1.80	1.70
1538	10¢ Petrified Wood	3.00	......	......	......	......	......	.45	.12
1539	10¢ Tourmaline	3.00	......	......	......	......	......	.45	.12
1540	10¢ Amethyst	3.00	......	......	......	......	......	.45	.12
1541	10¢ Rhodochrosite	3.00	......	......	......	......	......	.45	.12

1542   1543   1544   1545   1546   1547

Scott No.	Description	Sing.	Pl.Blk.	Mint Sheet	Mail Early	Zip	Plate Block	Un-Used	Used
1542	10¢ Fort Harrod Bicent.	1.75	3.25	20.00(50)	3.00	2.10	2.15	.45	.07
1543-46	Continental COngress, 4 Vars., att'd.	3.00	4.50	20.00(50)	3.00	2.10	2.15	1.80	1.70
1543-46	10¢ Bicent. Emblem block	......	......	......	3.00	......	......	......	......
1543	10¢ Carpenter's Hall	1.75	......	......	......	......	......	.45	.10
1544	10¢ Quote-1st Congress	1.75	......	......	......	......	......	.45	.10
1545	10¢ Quote-Decl. of Indep.	1.75	......	......	......	......	......	.45	.10
1546	10¢ Independence Hall	1.75	......	......	......	......	......	.45	.10
1547	10¢ Energy Conservation	1.75	3.25	20.00(50)	3.00	2.10	2.15	.45	.07

SCOTT NO.	DESCRIPTION	FIRST DAY COVERS SING.	PL.BLK.	MINT SHEET	MAIL EARLY	ZIP	PLATE BLOCK	UN-USED	USED

1548

10

Retarded Children Can Be Helped

1549

| 1548 | 10¢ Sleepy Hollow | 1.75 | 3.25 | 20.00(50) | 3.00 | 2.10 | 2.15 | .45 | .07 |
| 1549 | 10¢ Retarded Children | 1.75 | 3.25 | 20.00(50) | 3.00 | 2.10 | 2.15 | .45 | .07 |

1550

1551

1552

1550	10¢ Christmas Angel	1.75	3.25	20.00(50)	3.00	2.10	5.00(10)	.45	.06
1551	10¢ Xmas-Currier & Ives	1.75	3.25	20.00(50)	2.10(4)	2.10	6.00(12)	.45	.06
1552	10¢ Xmas-Dove of Peace	1.75	3.25	20.50(50)	....	....	9.75(20)	.45	.07
1552	Same	....	....	....	....	....	6.00(12)		

1553

1554

1555

1556

1557

1558

1975 COMMEMORATIVES

1553-80	28 Vars., cpl.	....	....	....	45.00(17)	40.00(20)	87.50(20)	12.25	3.25
1553	10¢ Benjamin West-Arts	1.75	3.25	20.00(50)	3.00	2.10	5.00(10)	.45	.07
1554	10¢ Paul Dunbar-Arts	1.75	3.25	20.00(50)	3.00	2.10	5.00(10)	.45	.07
1555	10¢ D.W. Griffith-Arts	1.75	3.25	20.00(50)	3.00	2.10	2.15	.45	.07
1556	10¢ Pioneer 10	1.75	3.25	20.00(50)	3.00	2.10	2.15	.45	.07
1557	10¢ Mariner 10	1.75	3.25	20.00(50)	3.00	2.10	2.15	.45	.07
1558	10¢ Collective Bargaining	1.75	3.25	20.00(50)	3.00	2.10	4.00(8)	.45	.07

1559

1560

1561

1562

1975 CONTRIBUTORS TO THE CAUSE

1559	8¢ Sybil Ludington	1.85	3.75	18.00(50)	2.65	1.85	4.50(10)	.40	.25
1560	10¢ Salem Poor	1.85	3.75	20.00(50)	3.00	2.10	5.00(10)	.45	.07
1561	10¢ Haym Salomon	1.85	3.75	20.00(50)	3.00	2.10	5.00(10)	.45	.07
1562	18¢ Peter Francisco	1.95	4.25	36.00(50)	5.35	3.75	9.00(10)	.80	.90

1563   1564   1565   1566   1567   1568

SCOTT NO.	DESCRIPTION	FIRST DAY COVERS SING.	PL.BLK.	MINT SHEET	MAIL EARLY	ZIP	PLATE BLOCK	UN-USED	USED
1563	10¢ Lexington-Concord	1.75	3.25	16.00(40)	(combo)	2.10	6.00(12)	.45	.07
1564	10¢ Battle of Bunker Hill	1.75	3.25	16.00(40)	(combo)	2.10	6.00(12)	.45	.07
1565-68	Military Uniforms, 4 Vars. attd	3.25	4.50	20.00(50)	2.10(4)	2.10	6.00(12)	1.80	1.75
1565	10¢ Continental Army	2.00						.45	.10
1566	10¢ Continental Navy	2.00						.45	.10
1567	10¢ Continental Marine	2.00						.45	.10
1568	10¢ American Militia	2.00						.45	.10

1569

1570

1569-70	Apollo-Soyuz Mission, 2 Vars., att'd.	2.75	4.25	9.75(24)	(combo)	2.10	6.00(12)	.90	.80
1569	10¢ Docked	2.00						.45	.15
1570	10¢ Docking	2.00						.45	.15

1571   1572   1573   1574

1575   1576

1571	10¢ Int'l. Womens' Year	1.75	3.25	20.00(50)	3.00	2.10	3.00(6)	.45	.07
1572-75	Postal Service Bicent., 4 Vars., att'd.	2.75	4.25	20.00(50)	2.10(4)	2.10	6.00(12)	1.80	1.70
1572	10¢ Stagecoach & Trailer	1.75						.45	.12
1573	10¢ Locomotives	1.75						.45	.12
1574	10¢ Airplanes	1.75						.45	.12
1575	10¢ Satellite	1.75						.45	.12
1576	10¢ World Peace thru Law	1.75	3.25	20.00(50)	3.00	2.10	2.15	.45	.07

U.S. BICENTENNIAL: The U.S.P.S. issued stamps commemorating the 200th anniversary of the struggle for independence form 1775 through 1783. These include numbers: 1432, 1476-83, 1543-46, 1559-68, 1629-31, 1633-82, 1686-89, 1691-94, 1704, 1716-20, 1722, 1726, 1728-29, 1753, 1789, 1826, 1937-38, 1941, 2052 and C98.

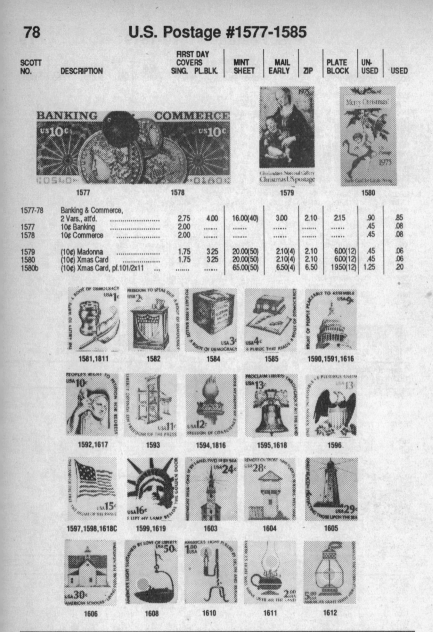

SCOTT NO.	DESCRIPTION	FIRST DAY COVERS SING.	PL.BLK.	MINT SHEET	MAIL EARLY	ZIP	PLATE BLOCK	UN-USED	USED
1577-78	Banking & Commerce, 2 Vars., att'd.	2.75	4.00	16.00(40)	3.00	2.10	2.15	.90	.85
1577	10¢ Banking	2.00	......	....	......	......	......	.45	.08
1578	10¢ Commerce	2.00	......	....	......	......	......	.45	.08
1579	(10¢) Madonna	1.75	3.25	20.00(50)	2.10(4)	2.10	6.00(12)	.45	.06
1580	(10¢) Xmas Card	1.75	3.25	20.00(50)	2.10(4)	2.10	6.00(12)	.45	.06
1580b	(10¢) Xmas Card, pf.101/2x11	......	......	65.00(50)	6.50(4)	6.50	19.50(12)	1.25	20

1975-81 AMERICANA ISSUE

SCOTT NO.	DESCRIPTION	FIRST DAY COVERS SING.	PL.BLK.	MINT SHEET	MAIL EARLY	ZIP	PLATE BLOCK	UN-USED	USED
1581-1612	(no 1590, 1590a, 1595 or 1598) 19 Vars., cpl.	......	......	....	140.00(18)	132.50(18)	157.50	29.75	6.85
1581	1¢ Inkwell & Quill (1977)	1.75	3.00	5.25(100)	.45	.30	33	.07	.06
1581a	1¢ precancelled	......	......	....	......	......	......	......	.07
1582	2¢ Speaker's Stand (1977)	1.75	3.00	9.75(100)	.70	.50	55	.11	.06
1582a	2¢ precancelled	......	......	....	......	......	......	......	.11
1584	3¢ Ballot Box (1977)	1.75	3.00	12.50(100)	1.00	.70	75	.15	.06
1584a	3¢ precancelled	......	......	....	......	......	......	......	.15
1585	4¢ Books & Eyeglasses (1977)	1.75	3.00	15.00(100)	1.20	.85	90	.18	.06
1585a	4¢ precancelled	......	......	....	......	......	......	......	.18

SCOTT NO.	DESCRIPTION	FIRST DAY COVERS SING.	FIRST DAY COVERS PL.BLK.	MINT SHEET	MAIL EARLY	ZIP	PLATE BLOCK	UN-USED	USED
1590	9¢ Capitol, from b. pane (1977) ...	17.50	......	......	......	......	......	1.10	.70
1590a	Same Pf. 10 (1977)	17.50	......	......	......	......	......	40.00	17.50
1590,1623	Attd. Pr., from b. pane	......	......	......	......	......	......	1.70	......
1590a,1623b	Attd. Pr., Pf. 10	......	......	......	......	......	......	43.50	......
1591	9¢ Capitol, grey paper	1.75	3.50	36.50(100)	2.65	1.85	1.95	.40	.06
1591a	9¢ precancelled	......	......	......	......	......	......	......	.40
1592	10¢ Justice (1977)	1.75	3.50	45.00(100)	3.25	2.25	2.50	.50	.06
1592a	10¢ precancelled	......	......	......	......	......	......	......	.55
1593	11¢ Printing Press	1.75	3.50	45.00(100)	3.25	2.25	2.50	.50	.06
1594	12¢ Torch (1981)	1.75	3.25	49.50(100)	3.50	2.50	3.50	.55	.07
1595	13¢ Liberty Bell from b. pane	1.75	......	......	......	......	......	.60	.06
1595a	13¢ booklet pane of 6	2.75	......	......	......	......	......	4.00	......
1595b	13¢ b. pane of 7 - VIII	3.25	......	......	......	......	......	4.75	......
1595c	13¢ booklet pane of 8	3.50	......	......	......	......	......	4.75	......
1595d	13¢ b. pane of 5 - IX (1976)	2.50	......	......	......	......	......	3.50	......

VIII - Paying Bills...   IX - Collect Stamps...

1596	13¢ Eagle & Shield	1.75	3.25	52.50(100)	2.50(4)	2.50	7.50(12)	.55	.06
1597	15¢ Fort McHenry Flag (1978) ...	1.75	3.25	60.00(100)	......	......	15.00(20)	.65	.06
1598	Same, from b. pane (1978)	1.75	......	......	......	......	......	.95	.07
1598a	15¢ b. pane of 8	4.00	......	......	......	......	......	7.50	......
1599	16¢ Statue of Liberty (1978)	1.75	3.50	76.50(100)	©4.10	4.10	4.25	.85	.20
1603	24¢ Old North Church	2.25	3.95	95.00(100)	6.50	4.50	4.75	1.00	.06
1604	28¢ Fort Nisqually (1978)	2.25	3.95	110.00(100)	©5.25	5.25	5.50	1.15	.06
1605	29¢ Lighthouse (1978)	2.50	4.25	120.00(100)	©5.75	5.75	6.75	1.25	.50
1606	30¢ School House (1979)	2.50	4.25	120.00(100)	©5.75	5.75	6.00	1.25	.07
1608	50¢ "Betty" Lamp (1979)	3.25	5.50	185.00(100)	©9.00	9.00	9.50	2.00	.08
1610	$1 Rush Lamp (1979)	4.75	10.00	215.00(100)	©11.00	11.00	12.50	2.25	.11
1611	$2 Kerosene Lamp (1978)	9.50	19.50	650.00(100)	©30.00	30.00	30.00	6.95	.80
1612	$5 Conductor's Lantern (1979) ...	22.50	50.00	1075.00(100)	©50.00	50.00	50.00	10.95	4.75

Copyright inscriptions replaced "Mail Early in the Day" inscriptions beginning in 1978; numbers 1599 and 1604-12 sheets all bear the Copyright inscription.

1613

1614

1615

1615C

1975-79 COIL STAMPS Perforated Vertically

SCOTT	DESCRIPTION	LINE PR.	LINE PR.				LINE PR.	LINE PR.	USED
1613-19	9 Varieties, cpl.	......	......	....	......	......	18.50	4.65	1.10
1613	3.1¢ Guitar (1979)	1.75	2.75	....	......	......	1.75	.20	.10
1613a	3.1¢ precancelled	......	......	....	......	......	......	......	.30
1614	7.7¢ Saxhorns (1976)	1.75	3.00	....	......	......	2.50	.45	.20
1614a	7.7¢ precancelled	......	......	....	......	......	......	......	.60
1615	7.9¢ Drum (1976)	1.76	2.75	....	......	......	2.15	.45	.20
1615a	7.9¢ precancelled	......	......	....	......	......	......	......	.55
1615C	8.4¢ Piano (1978)	1.75	3.50	....	......	......	4.50	.40	.18
1615Cd	8.4¢ precancelled	......	......	....	......	......	......	......	.50
1616	9¢ Capitol (1976)	1.75	2.75	....	......	......	1.85	.40	.10
1616b	9¢ precancelled	......	......	....	......	......	......	......	.50
1617	10¢ Justice (1977)	1.75	2.75	....	......	......	1.65	.45	.08
1617a	10¢ precancelled	......	......	....	......	......	......	......	.55
1618	13¢ Liberty Bell	2.00	3.25	....	......	......	2.50	.90	.07
1618a	13¢ precancelled	......	......	....	......	......	......	......	1.00
1619C	15¢ Fort McHenry (1978)	1.75	......	....	......	......	......	.80	.06
1619	16¢ Statue of Liberty (1978)	1.75	3.25	....	......	......	2.50	.80	.20

COIL LINE PAIRS: are two connected coil stamps with a line the same color as the stamps printed between the two stamps. This line usually appears every twenty to thirty stamps on a roll depending on the issue.

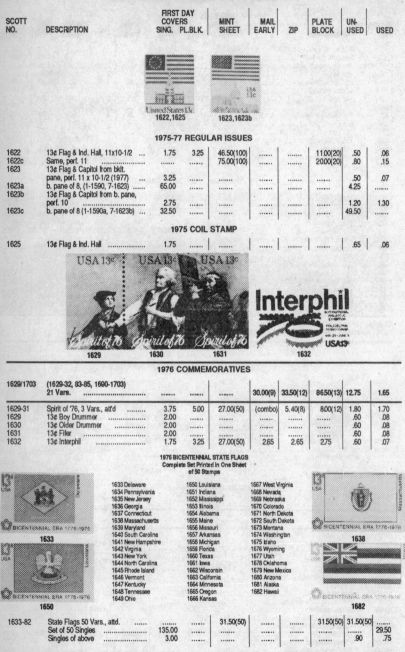

SCOTT NO.	DESCRIPTION	FIRST DAY COVERS SING.	FIRST DAY COVERS PL.BLK.	MINT SHEET	MAIL EARLY	ZIP	PLATE BLOCK	UN-USED	USED

1622, 1625   **1623, 1623b**

1975-77 REGULAR ISSUES

1622	13¢ Flag & Ind. Hall, 11x10-1/2 ...	1.75	3.25	46.50(100)	....	....	11.00(20)	.50	.06
1622c	Same, perf. 11	....	....	75.00(100)	....	....	20.00(20)	.80	.15
1623	13¢ Flag & Capitol from bklt.								
	pane, perf. 11 x 10-1/2 (1977) ...	3.25	....	....	....	....	....	.50	.07
1623a	b. pane of 8, (1-1590, 7-1623)	65.00	....	....	....	....	....	4.25	....
1623b	13¢ Flag & Capitol from b. pane,								
	perf. 10	2.75	....	....	....	....	....	1.20	1.30
1623c	b. pane of 8 (1-1590a, 7-1623b) ...	32.50	....	....	....	....	....	49.50	....

1975 COIL STAMP

| 1625 | 13¢ Flag & Ind. Hall .... | 1.75 | | | | | | .65 | .06 |

1629   **1630**   **1631**   **1632**

1976 COMMEMORATIVES

1629/1703	(1629-32, 83-85, 1690-1703) 21 Vars.	....	....	....	30.00(9)	33.50(12)	86.50(13)	12.75	1.65
1629-31	Spirit of '76, 3 Vars., att'd	3.75	5.00	27.00(50)	(combo)	5.40(8)	8.00(12)	1.80	1.70
1629	13¢ Boy Drummer	2.00	....	....	....	....	....	.60	.08
1630	13¢ Older Drummer	2.00	....	....	....	....	....	.60	.08
1631	13¢ Fifer	2.00	....	....	....	....	....	.60	.08
1632	13¢ Interphil	1.75	3.25	27.00(50)	2.65	2.65	2.75	.60	.07

1976 BICENTENNIAL STATE FLAGS
Complete Set Printed in One Sheet of 50 Stamps

1633

1633 Delaware	1650 Louisiana	1667 West Virginia
1634 Pennsylvania	1651 Indiana	1668 Nevada
1635 New Jersey	1652 Mississippi	1669 Nebraska
1636 Georgia	1653 Illinois	1670 Colorado
1637 Connecticut	1654 Alabama	1671 North Dakota
1638 Massachusetts	1655 Maine	1672 South Dakota
1639 Maryland	1656 Missouri	1673 Montana
1640 South Carolina	1657 Arkansas	1674 Washington
1641 New Hampshire	1658 Michigan	1675 Idaho
1642 Virginia	1659 Florida	1676 Wyoming
1643 New York	1660 Texas	1677 Utah
1644 North Carolina	1661 Iowa	1678 Oklahoma
1645 Rhode Island	1662 Wisconsin	1679 New Mexico
1646 Vermont	1663 California	1680 Arizona
1647 Kentucky	1664 Minnesota	1681 Alaska
1648 Tennessee	1665 Oregon	1682 Hawaii
1649 Ohio	1666 Kansas	

1638

1650   **1682**

1633-82	State Flags 50 Vars., attd.	....	....	31.50(50)	....	....	31.50(50)	31.50(50)	....
	Set of 50 Singles	135.00	....	....	....	....	....	....	29.50
	Singles of above	3.00	....	....	....	....	....	.90	.75

PLATE BLOCKS: are portions of a sheet of stamps adjacent to the number(s) indicating the printing plate number used to produce that sheet. Flat plate issues are usually collected in plate blocks of six (number opposite middle stamp) while rotary issues are normally corner blocks of four.

SCOTT NO.	DESCRIPTION	FIRST DAY COVERS SING.	FIRST DAY COVERS PL.BLK.	MINT SHEET	MAIL EARLY	ZIP	PLATE BLOCK	UN-USED	USED

1683   1684   1685

1683	13¢ Telephone	1.75	3.25	27.00(50)	3.90	2.65	2.75	.60	.07
1684	13¢ Aviation	1.75	3.25	27.00(50)	3.90	2.65	6.50(10)	.60	.07
1685	13¢ Chemistry	1.75	3.25	27.00(50)	2.65(4)	2.65	7.75(12)	.60	.07

1686   1687

1976 BICENTENNIAL SOUVENIR SHEETS

1686-89	4 Vars., cpl.	56.50						47.50	47.50
1686	65¢ Cornwallis Surrender	10.50						8.00	8.00
1686a-e	65¢ singles, each	3.50						1.75	1.75
1687	90¢ Independence	12.75						11.00	11.00
1687a-e	90¢ singles, each	3.75						2.50	2.50
1688	$1.20 Washington Crossing Delaware	16.50						14.00	14.00
1688a-e	$1.20 singles, each	4.25						3.25	3.25
1689	$1.55 Washington at Valley Forge	20.00						17.50	17.50
1689a-e	$1.55 singles, each	5.25						4.00	4.00

1690   1691   1692   1693   1694

1690	13¢ Benjamin Franklin	1.75	3.25	27.00(50)	3.90	2.65	2.75	.60	.07
1691-94	Declaration of Independence 4 Vars., att'd.	6.25	9.00	27.00(50)	(combo)	2.65	11.00(16)	2.40	2.25
1691	13¢ Delegation members	2.25						.60	.10
1692	13¢ Adams, etc.	2.25						.60	.10
1693	13¢ Jefferson, Franklin, etc.	2.25						.60	.10
1694	13¢ Hancock, Thomson, etc.	2.25						.60	.10

MINT SHEETS: From 1935 to date, we list prices for our standard size Mint Sheets in Fine, Never Hinged condition. The number of stamps in each sheet is noted in ( ).

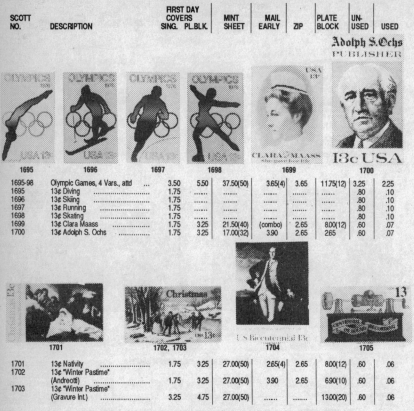

SCOTT NO.	DESCRIPTION	FIRST DAY COVERS SING.	PL.BLK.	MINT SHEET	MAIL EARLY	ZIP	PLATE BLOCK	UN-USED	USED
1695-98	Olympic Games, 4 Vars., attd ...	3.50	5.50	37.50(50)	3.65(4)	3.65	11.75(12)	3.25	2.25
1695	13¢ Diving	1.75	....	....	....	....	....	.80	.10
1696	13¢ Skiing	1.75	....	....	....	....	....	.80	.10
1697	13¢ Running	1.75	....	....	....	....	....	.80	.10
1698	13¢ Skating	1.75	....	....	....	....	....	.80	.10
1699	13¢ Clara Maass	1.75	3.25	21.50(40)	(combo)	2.65	8.00(12)	.60	.07
1700	13¢ Adolph S. Ochs	1.75	3.25	17.00(32)	3.90	2.65	2.65	.60	.07

1701	13¢ Nativity	1.75	3.25	27.00(50)	2.65(4)	2.65	8.00(12)	.60	.06
1702	13¢ "Winter Pastime" (Andreotti)	1.75	3.25	27.00(50)	3.90	2.65	6.90(10)	.60	.06
1703	13¢ "Winter Pastime" (Gravure Int.)	3.25	4.75	27.00(50)	....	....	13.00(20)	.60	.06

1702: Marginal Inscription 1/2 millimeters below design. Black lettering.
1703: Marginal Inscription 3/4 millimeters below design. Grey black lettering.

1977 COMMEMORATIVES

1704-30	27 Vars., cpl.	....	....	....	35.00(11)	43.50(16)	98.50(17)	15.50	2.00
1704	13¢ Princeton	1.75	3.25	21.50(40)	(combo)	2.65	6.90(10)	.60	.07
1705	13¢ Sound Recording	1.75	3.25	27.00(50)	3.90	2.65	2.75	.60	.07

Pueblo Art USA 13¢
1706

Pueblo Art USA 13¢
1707

Pueblo Art USA 13¢
1708

Pueblo Art USA 13¢
1709

1706-09	Pueblo Art 4 Vars., att'd	3.75	5.75	21.50(40)	(combo)	3.90(6)	6.90(10)	2.40	2.25
1706	13¢ Zia	1.75	....	....	....	....	....	.60	.09
1707	13¢ San Ildefonso	1.75	....	....	....	....	....	.60	.09
1708	13¢ Hopi	1.75	....	....	....	....	....	.60	.09
1709	13¢ Acoma	1.75	....	....	....	....	....	.60	.09

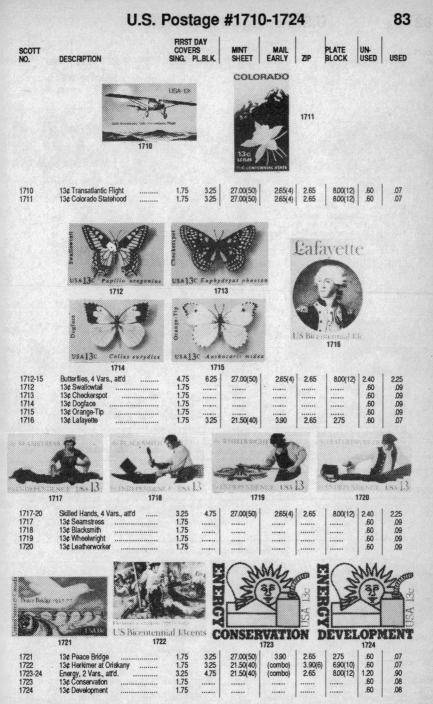

SCOTT NO.	DESCRIPTION	FIRST DAY COVERS SING.	PL.BLK.	MINT SHEET	MAIL EARLY	ZIP	PLATE BLOCK	UN-USED	USED
1710	13¢ Transatlantic Flight	....	1.75	3.25	27.00(50)	2.65(4)	2.65	8.00(12)	.60	.07
1711	13¢ Colorado Statehood	....	1.75	3.25	27.00(50)	2.65(4)	2.65	8.00(12)	.60	.07
1712-15	Butterflies, 4 Vars., att'd	....	4.75	6.25	27.00(50)	2.65(4)	2.65	8.00(12)	2.40	2.25
1712	13¢ Swallowtail	....	1.75	......	......	......	......	......	.60	.09
1713	13¢ Checkerspot	....	1.75	......	......	......	......	......	.60	.09
1714	13¢ Dogface	....	1.75	......	......	......	......	......	.60	.09
1715	13¢ Orange-Tip	....	1.75	......	......	......	......	......	.60	.09
1716	13¢ Lafayette	....	1.75	3.25	21.50(40)	3.90	2.65	2.75	.60	.07
1717-20	Skilled Hands, 4 Vars., att'd	......	3.25	4.75	27.00(50)	2.65(4)	2.65	8.00(12)	2.40	2.25
1717	13¢ Seamstress	....	1.75	......	......	......	......	......	.60	.09
1718	13¢ Blacksmith	....	1.75	......	......	......	......	......	.60	.09
1719	13¢ Wheelwright	....	1.75	......	......	......	......	......	.60	.09
1720	13¢ Leatherworker	....	1.75	......	......	......	......	......	.60	.09
1721	13¢ Peace Bridge	....	1.75	3.25	27.00(50)	3.90	2.65	2.75	.60	.07
1722	13¢ Herkimer at Oriskany	....	1.75	3.25	21.50(40)	(combo)	3.90(6)	6.90(10)	.60	.07
1723-24	Energy, 2 Vars., att'd.	....	3.25	4.75	21.50(40)	(combo)	2.65	8.00(12)	1.20	.90
1723	13¢ Conservation	....	1.75	......	......	......	......	......	.60	.08
1724	13¢ Development	....	1.75	......	......	......	......	......	.60	.08

VERY FINE QUALITY: From 1935 to date, add 20% to the Fine price. Minimum of 3¢ per stamp. For quality definitions, refer to pages 295-297.

SCOTT NO.	DESCRIPTION	FIRST DAY COVERS SING.	FIRST DAY COVERS PL.BLK.	MINT SHEET	MAIL EARLY	ZIP	PLATE BLOCK	UN-USED	USED

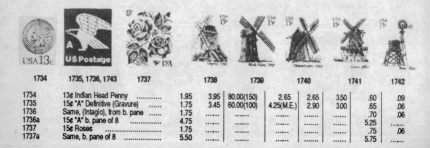

| | | 1725 | 1726 | | 1727 | | | 1728 | |

1725	13¢ Alta California	1.75	3.25	27.00(50)	3.90	2.65	2.75	.60	.07
1726	13¢ Articles of Confederation ...	1.75	3.25	27.00(50)	3.90	2.65	2.75	.60	.07
1727	13¢ Talking Pictures	1.75	3.25	27.00(50)	3.90	2.65	2.75	.60	.07
1728	13¢ Surrender at Saratoga	1.75	3.25	21.50(40)	(combo)	3.90(6)	6.90(10)	.60	.07

| | | 1729 | 1730 | 1731 | 1732 | | 1733 | | |

| 1729 | 13¢ Washington, Xmas | 2.50 | 4.25 | 53.50(100) | .... | .... | 13.50(20) | .60 | .06 |
| 1730 | 13¢ Rural Mailbox, Xmas | 2.50 | 4.25 | 53.50(100) | 3.90 | 2.65 | 6.90(10) | .60 | .06 |

SCOTT NO.	DESCRIPTION	FIRST DAY COVERS SING.	FIRST DAY COVERS PL.BLK.	MINT SHEET	COPY-RIGHT	ZIP	PLATE BLOCK	UN-USED	USED

1978 COMMEMORATIVES

1731/69	(1731-33, 44-56, 58-69) 28 Vars.	....	....	....	31.50(12)	42.50(16)	89.50(16)	17.00	2.25
1731	13¢ Carl Sandburg	1.75	3.25	27.00(50)	2.65	2.65	2.75	.60	.07
1732-33	Captain Cook, 2 Vars., att'd	2.50	....	27.00(50)	....	....	13.50(20)	1.20	.95
1732	13¢ Capt. Cook (Alaska)	1.75	3.25	....	2.65	2.65	2.75	.60	.08
1733	13¢ "Resolution" (Hawaii)	1.75	3.25	....	2.65	2.65	2.75	.60	.08

NOTE: The Plate Block set includes #1732 & 1733 P.B.'s of 4.

| | | 1734 | 1735, 1736, 1743 | 1737 | 1738 | 1739 | 1740 | 1741 | 1742 |

1734	13¢ Indian Head Penny	1.95	3.95	80.00(150)	2.65	2.65	3.50	.60	.09
1735	15¢ "A" Definitive (Gravure)	1.75	3.45	60.00(100)	4.25(M.E.)	2.90	3.00	.65	.06
1736	Same, (Intaglio), from b. pane	1.75	....	....	....	....	....	.70	.06
1736a	15¢ "A" b. pane of 8	4.75	....	....	....	....	....	5.25	....
1737	15¢ Roses	1.75	....	....	....	....	....	.75	.06
1737a	Same, b. pane of 8	5.50	....	....	....	....	....	5.75	....

SCOTT NO.	DESCRIPTION	FIRST DAY COVERS SING.	PL.BLK.	MINT SHEET	COPY-RIGHT	ZIP	PLATE BLOCK	UN-USED	USED
1738-42	Windmills Strip of 5, att'd. (1980)	3.75	......	......	......	......		4.00	......
1738	15¢ Virginia Windmill	1.75	......	......	......	......		.85	.07
1739	15¢ Rhode Island Windmill	1.75	......	......	......	......		.85	.07
1740	15¢ Massachusetts Windmill	1.75	......	......	......	......		.85	.07
1741	15¢ Illinois Windmill	1.75	......	......	......	......		.85	.07
1742	15¢ Texas Windmill	1.75	......	......	......	......		.85	.07
1742a	Same, b. pane of 10	6.50	......	......	......	......		7.75	......

1978 COIL STAMP

SCOTT NO.	DESCRIPTION	SING.	LINE PR.	MINT SHEET	COPY-RIGHT	ZIP	LINE PR.	UN-USED	USED
1743	15¢ "A" Definitive	1.75	2.75	......	......	......	1.80	.70	.06

1745

1746

1744

1747

1748

SCOTT NO.	DESCRIPTION	SING.	PL.BLK.	MINT SHEET	COPY-RIGHT	ZIP	PLATE BLOCK	UN-USED	USED
1744	13¢ Harriet Tubman	1.75	3.25	27.00(50)	2.65	2.65	8.00(12)	.60	.07
1745-48	Quilts, 4 Vars., att'd.	4.75	6.25	26.00(48)	(combo)	2.65	8.00(12)	2.40	2.25
1745	13¢ Flowers	2.50	......	......	......	......	......	.60	.09
1746	13¢ Stars	2.50	......	......	......	......	......	.60	.09
1747	13¢ Stripes	2.50	......	......	......	......	......	.60	.09
1748	13¢ Plaid	2.50	......	......	......	......	......	.60	.09

1749

1750

1751

1752

SCOTT NO.	DESCRIPTION	SING.	PL.BLK.	MINT SHEET	COPY-RIGHT	ZIP	PLATE BLOCK	UN-USED	USED
1749-52	American Dance, 4 Vars. attd	4.75	6.25	26.00(48)	(combo)	2.65	8.00(12)	2.40	2.00
1749	13¢ Ballet	2.00	......	......	......	......	......	.60	.09
1750	13¢ Theatre	2.00	......	......	......	......	......	.60	.09
1751	13¢ Folk	2.00	......	......	......	......	......	.60	.09
1752	13¢ Modern	2.00	......	......	......	......	......	.60	.09

1753

1754

1755

1756

SCOTT NO.	DESCRIPTION	FIRST DAY COVERS SING.	FIRST DAY COVERS PL.BLK.	MINT SHEET	COPY-RIGHT	ZIP	PLATE BLOCK	UN-USED	USED
1753	13¢ French Alliance	1.75	3.25	21.50(40)	2.65	2.65	2.75	.60	.07
1754	13¢ Dr. Papanicolaou	1.75	3.25	27.00(50)	2.65	2.65	2.75	.60	.12
1755	13¢ Jimmie Rodgers	1.75	3.25	27.00(50)	2.65	2.65	8.00(12)	.60	.12
1756	15¢ George M. Cohan	1.75	3.25	30.00(50)	2.95	2.95	8.50(12)	.65	.07

1757

Photography USA 15¢
1758

Viking missions to Mars
1759

1978 CAPEX SOUVENIR SHEET

SCOTT NO.	DESCRIPTION	FIRST DAY COVERS SING.	FIRST DAY COVERS PL.BLK.	MINT SHEET	COPY-RIGHT	ZIP	PLATE BLOCK	UN-USED	USED
1757	$1.04 CAPEX	5.25		26.00(6)	(combo)	4.50	4.50	4.25	3.95
1757a	13¢ Cardinal	1.75						.65	.50
1757b	13¢ Mallard	1.75						.65	.50
1757c	13¢ Canada Goose	1.75						.65	.50
1757d	13¢ Blue Jay	1.75						.65	.50
1757e	13¢ Moose	1.75						.65	.50
1757f	13¢ Chipmunk	1.75						.65	.50
1757g	13¢ Red Fox	1.75						.65	.50
1757h	13¢ Raccoon	1.75						.65	.50
1758	15¢ Photography	1.75	3.25	24.00(40)	(combo)	2.95	8.50(12)	.65	.07
1759	15¢ Viking Mission	1.75	3.25	30.00(50)	2.95	2.95	3.00	.65	.07

1760   1761   1762   1763   1768   1769

1764   1765   1766   1767

SCOTT NO.	DESCRIPTION	FIRST DAY COVERS SING.	FIRST DAY COVERS PL.BLK.	MINT SHEET	COPY-RIGHT	ZIP	PLATE BLOCK	UN-USED	USED
1760-63	American Owls, 4 Vars. att'd	4.75	6.25	32.50	3.20	3.20	3.25	2.80	2.50
1760	15¢ Great Gray	2.00						.70	.09
1761	15¢ Saw-Whet	2.00						.70	.09
1762	15¢ Barred Owl	2.00						.70	.09
1763	15¢ Great Horned	2.00						.70	.09

SCOTT NO.	DESCRIPTION	FIRST DAY COVERS SING.	FIRST DAY COVERS PL.BLK.	MINT SHEET	COPY-RIGHT	ZIP	PLATE BLOCK	UN-USED	USED
1764-67	Trees, 4 Vars., att'd.	3.75	5.50	27.00(40)	(combo)	3.20	9.50(12)	2.80	2.50
1764	15¢ Giant Sequoia	1.75	....	....	....	....	....	.70	.09
1765	15¢ Pine	1.75	....	....	....	....	....	.70	.09
1766	15¢ Oak	1.75	....	....	....	....	....	.70	.09
1767	15¢ Birch	1.75	....	....	....	....	....	.70	.09
1768	15¢ Madonna, Xmas	1.75	3.25	57.50(100)	2.95	2.95	8.50(12)	.65	.06
1769	15¢ Hobby Horse, Xmas	1.75	3.25	57.50(100)	2.95	2.95	8.50(12)	.65	.06

1770	1771	1772	1773	1774

1979 COMMEMORATIVES

SCOTT NO.	DESCRIPTION	FIRST DAY COVERS SING.	FIRST DAY COVERS PL.BLK.	MINT SHEET	COPY-RIGHT	ZIP	PLATE BLOCK	UN-USED	USED
1770/1802	(1770-94, 1799-1802) 29 Vars., cpl.	....	....	....	41.50(15)	45.75(16)	115.00(17)	18.50	2.45
1770	15¢ Robert F. Kennedy	1.75	3.25	28.50(48)	2.95	2.95	3.00	.65	.07
1771	15¢ Martin L. King Jr.	1.75	3.25	30.00(50)	2.95	2.95	8.50(12)	.65	.07
1772	15¢ Int'l. Year of the Child	1.75	3.25	30.00(50)	2.95	2.95	3.00	.65	.07
1773	15¢ John Steinbeck	1.75	3.25	30.00(50)	2.95	2.95	3.00	.65	.07
1774	15¢ Albert Einstein	1.75	3.25	30.00(500)	2.95	2.95	3.00	.65	.07

1775	1776	1779	1780	1783	1784

1777	1778	1781	1782	1785	1786

SCOTT NO.	DESCRIPTION	FIRST DAY COVERS SING.	FIRST DAY COVERS PL.BLK.	MINT SHEET	COPY-RIGHT	ZIP	PLATE BLOCK	UN-USED	USED
1775-78	Pennsylvania Toleware, 4 Vars., att'd.	3.75	5.50	27.00(40)	(combo)	4.50(6)	8.25(10)	2.80	2.50
1775	15¢ Coffee Pot	1.75	....	....	....	....	....	.70	.09
1776	15¢ Tea Caddy	1.75	....	....	....	....	....	.70	.09
1777	15¢ Sugar Bowl	1.75	....	....	....	....	....	.70	.09
1778	15¢ Coffee Pot	1.75	....	....	....	....	....	.70	.09
1779-82	Architecture, 4 Vars., att'd	3.75	5.50	33.50(48)	3.25	3.25	3.35	2.80	2.25
1779	15¢ Virginia Rotunda	1.75	....	....	....	....	....	.70	.09
1780	15¢ Baltimore Cathedral	1.75	....	....	....	....	....	.70	.09
1781	15¢ Boston State House	1.75	....	....	....	....	....	.70	.09
1782	15¢ Philadelphia Exchange	1.75	....	....	....	....	....	.70	.09
1783-86	Endangered Flora, 4 Vars., att'd	3.75	5.50	34.50(50)	3.20	3.20	9.50(12)	2.80	2.25
1783	15¢ Trillium	1.75	....	....	....	....	....	.70	.09
1784	15¢ Broadbean	1.75	....	....	....	....	....	.70	.09
1785	15¢ Wallflower	1.75	....	....	....	....	....	.70	.09
1786	15¢ Primrose	1.75	....	....	....	....	....	.70	.09

SCOTT NO.	DESCRIPTION	FIRST DAY COVERS SING.	PL.BLK.	MINT SHEET	COPY-RIGHT	ZIP	PLATE BLOCK	UN-USED	USED

1787   1788   1789,1789a,1789b   1790

1791   1792   1793   1794

1795   1796   1797   1798

1787	15¢ Guide Dog	1.75	3.25	30.00(50)	......	......	1450(20)	.65	.07
1788	15¢ Special Olympics	1.75	3.25	30.00(50)	2.95	2.95	750(10)	.65	.07
1789	15¢ John P. Jones, Pf. 11x12	1.75	3.25	36.50(50)	3.65	3.65	900(10)	.80	.07
1789a	Same, Pf. 11	1.75	3.25	30.00(50)	2.95	2.95	750(10)	.65	.07

NOTE: #1789a may be included in year date sets and special offers and not 1789.

1790	10¢ Summer Olympics, Javelin Thrower	1.75	3.25	21.50(50)	2.10	2.10	850(12)	.45	.25
1791-94	Summer Olympics, 4 Vars., att'd.	4.75	6.25	35.00(50)	3.50	3.50	1050(12)	3.00	2.75
1791	15¢ Runners	2.00	......	......	......	......	......	.75	.09
1792	15¢ Swimmers	2.00	......	......	......	......	......	.75	.09
1793	15¢ Rowers	2.00	......	......	......	......	......	.75	.09
1794	15¢ Equestrian	2.00	......	......	......	......	......	.75	.09

1980

1795-98	Winter Olympics, 4 Vars., att'd	4.75	6.25	39.50(50)	4.00	4.00	1200(12)	3.50	2.35
1795	15¢ Skater	2.00	......	......	......	......	......	.85	.09
1796	15¢ Downhill Skier	2.00	......	......	......	......	......	.85	.09
1797	15¢ Ski Jumper	2.00	......	......	......	......	......	.85	.09
1798	15¢ Hockey	2.00	......	......	......	......	......	.85	.09
1795a-98a	Same, Perf. 11, att'd.	......	......	95.00(50)	8.75	8.75	3250(12)	7.75	......
1795a	15¢ Skater	......	......	......	......	......	......	1.90	......
1796a	15¢ Downhill Skier	......	......	......	......	......	......	1.90	......
1797a	15¢ Ski Jumper	......	......	......	......	......	......	1.90	......
1798a	15¢ Hockey	......	......	......	......	......	......	1.90	......

1799   1800   1801   1802   1803   1804

1979 COMMEMORATIVES

1799	15¢ Xmas-Madonna	1.75	3.25	57.50(100)	2.95	2.95	850(12)	.65	.06
1800	15¢ Xmas-Santa Claus	1.75	3.25	57.50(100)	2.95	2.95	850(12)	.65	.06
1801	15¢ Will Rogers	1.75	3.25	30.00(50)	2.95	2.95	850(12)	.65	.07
1802	15¢ Vietnam Veterans	3.00	4.75	30.00(50)	2.95	2.95	750(10)	.65	.07

SCOTT NO.	DESCRIPTION	FIRST DAY COVERS SING.	FIRST DAY COVERS PL.BLK.	MINT SHEET	COPY-RIGHT	ZIP	PLATE BLOCK	UN-USED	USED
	1980 COMMEMORATIVES								
1795/1843	(1795-98, 1803-10, 1821-43) 35 Vars., cpl.	....	....	....	52.50(16)	56.50(17)	128.50(18)	23.50	2.90
1803	15¢ W.C. Fields	1.75	3.25	30.00(50)	2.95	2.95	8.50(12)	.65	.07
1804	15¢ Benjamin Banneker	1.75	3.25	30.00(50)	2.95	2.95	8.50(12)	.65	.07

| | 1805 | 1806 | 1807 | 1808 | 1809 | 1810 |

1805-10	6 Vars., att'd	5.75	....	37.50(60)	8.75(12)	8.75(12)	27.50(36)	4.00	....
1805-06	2 Vars., att'd	3.25	....	....	....	....	....	1.40	.90
1807-08	2 Vars., att'd	3.25	....	....	....	....	....	1.40	.90
1809-10	2 Vars., att'd	3.25	....	....	....	....	....	1.40	.90
1805	15¢ "Letters Preserve Memories"	2.00	....	....	....	....	....	.70	.12
1806	15¢ claret & multicolor	2.00	....	....	....	....	....	.70	.12
1807	15¢ "Letters Lift Spirits"	2.00	....	....	....	....	....	.70	.12
1808	15¢ green & multicolor	2.00	....	....	....	....	....	.70	.12
1809	15¢ "Letters Shape Opinions"	2.00	....	....	....	....	....	.70	.12
1810	15¢ red, white & blue	2.00	....	....	....	....	....	.70	.12

1813

1818,1819,1820

1980-81 Coil Stamps, Perf. 10 Vertically

		LINE PR.					LINE PR.		
1811	1¢ Inkwell & Quill	1.75	2.75	....	....	....	.65	.07	.06
1813	3.5¢ Two Violins	1.75	2.75	....	....	....	2.75	.17	.14
1813a	3.5¢ precancelled	....	....	....	....	....	....	....	.25
1816	12¢ Torch (1981)	1.75	2.95	....	....	....	3.35	.50	.30
1816a	12¢ precancelled	....	....	....	....	....	....	....	.65
1818	18¢ "B" definitive	3.00	4.50	70.00(100)	5.00(ME)	3.50	3.75	.75	.06
1819	18¢ "B" definitive, from b. pn.	2.00	....	....	....	....	....	1.00	.06
1819a	18¢ "B" b. pane of 8	6.25	....	....	....	....	....	7.95	....

1981 Coil Stamp Perf. Vertically

		LINE PR.					LINE PR.		
1820	18¢ "B" definitive	1.75	2.75	....	....	....	3.35	.95	.06

| 1821 | 1822 | 1823 | 1824 |

SCOTT NO.	DESCRIPTION	FIRST DAY COVERS SING.	PL.BLK.	MINT SHEET	COPY-RIGHT	ZIP	PLATE BLOCK	UN-USED	USED
1821	15¢ Frances Perkins	1.75	3.25	30.00(50)	2.95	2.95	3.00	.65	.07
1822	15¢ Dolley Madison	1.75	3.25	90.00(150)	2.95	2.95	3.95	.65	.07
1823	15¢ Emily Bissell	1.75	3.25	30.00(50)	2.95	2.95	3.00	.65	.07
1824	15¢ H. Keller & A. Sullivan	1.75	3.25	30.00(50)	2.95	2.95	3.00	.65	.07

1825   **1826**   **1827**   **1828**   **1829**   **1830**

1825	15¢ Veterans Administration	1.75	3.25	30.00(50)	2.95	2.95	3.00	.65	.07
1826	15¢ Gen. B. de Galvez	1.75	3.25	30.00(50)	2.95	2.95	3.00	.65	.07
1827-30	Coral Reefs, 4 Vars., att'd	4.75	6.25	32.50(50)	3.25	3.25	9.75(12)	2.80	2.25
1827	15¢ Brain Coral, Virgin Is.	2.00						.70	.09
1828	15¢ Elkhorn Coral, Florida	2.00						.70	.09
1829	15¢ Chalice Coral, Am. Samoa	2.00						.70	.09
1830	15¢ Finger Coral, Hawaii	2.00						.70	.09

1831   **1832**   **1833**

1831	15¢ Organized Labor	1.75	3.25	30.00(50)	2.95	2.95	8.50(12)	.65	.07
1832	15¢ Edith Wharton	1.75	3.25	30.00(50)	2.95	2.95	3.00	.65	.07
1833	15¢ Education	1.75	3.25	30.00(50)	2.95	2.95	4.35(6)	.65	.07

1834   **1835**   **1836**   **1837**

1834-37	American Folk Art, 4 Vars., att'd.	4.75	6.25	26.50(40)	(combo)	4.65(6)	7.25(10)	2.80	2.25
1834	15¢ Bella Bella Tribe	2.00						.70	.09
1835	15¢ Chilkat Tlingit Tribe	2.00						.70	.09
1836	15¢ Tlingit Tribe	2.00						.70	.09
1837	15¢ Bella Coola Tribe	2.00						.70	.09

1838   **1839**   **1840**   **1841**

SCOTT NO.	DESCRIPTION	FIRST DAY COVERS		MINT SHEET	COPY-RIGHT	ZIP	PLATE BLOCK	UN-USED	USED
		SING.	PL.BLK.						
1838-41	American Architecture, 4 Vars., att'd.	3.25	4.50	27.50(40)	3.35	3.35	3.50	3.00	2.25
1838	15¢ Smithsonian Inst.	1.75	....	....	....	....	....	.75	.09
1839	15¢ Trinity Church	1.75	....	....	....	....	....	.75	.09
1840	15¢ Penn. Academy	1.75	....	....	....	....	....	.75	.09
1841	15¢ Lyndhurst	1.75	....	....	....	....	....	.75	.09

1842

1843

1842	15¢ Madonna	1.75	3.25	30.00(50)	2.95	2.95	8.75(12)	.65	.06
1843	15¢ Xmas Wreath & Toy	1.75	3.25	30.00(50)	....	....	14.50(20)	.65	.06

1844

1845

1846

1847

1848

1849

1850

1851

1852

1853

1854

1855

1856

1857

1858

1859

1860

1861

1862

1863

1864

1865

1866

1867

1868

1869

1980-85 GREAT AMERICANS

1844-69	1¢-50¢, 26 Vars., cpl.	51.50	95.00	....	....	....	147.50	10.85	2.30
1844	1¢ Dorothea Dix (1983)	2.00	3.50	3.00(100)	....	....	1.25(20)	.06	.06
1845	2¢ Igor Stravinsky (1982)	2.00	3.50	5.50(100)	.35	.35	.50	.06	.06
1846	3¢ Henry Clay (1983)	2.00	3.50	10.75(100)	.60	.60	.75	.12	.07
1847	4¢ Carl Schultz (1983)	2.00	3.50	13.75(100)	.75	.75	.85	.15	.06
1848	5¢ Pearl Buck (1983)	2.00	3.50	18.50(100)	.95	.95	1.10	.20	.06
1849	6¢ W. Lippmann (1985)	2.00	3.50	11.75(100)	....	....	3.75(20)	.12	.07

SCOTT NO.	DESCRIPTION	FIRST DAY COVERS SING.	PL.BLK.	MINT SHEET	COPY-RIGHT	ZIP	PLATE BLOCK	UN-USED	USED
1850	7¢ A. Baldwin (1985)	2.00	3.50	13.50(100)	....	....	3.95(20)	.14	.06
1851	8¢ Henry Knox (1985)	2.00	3.50	15.00(100)	.85	.85	.95	.16	.16
1852	9¢ S. Thayer (1985)	2.00	3.50	17.00(100)	....	....	5.25(20)	.18	.15
1853	10¢ Richard Russell (1984)	2.00	3.50	19.00(100)	....	....	5.25(20)	.20	.07
1854	11¢ Partridge (1985)	2.00	3.50	21.00(100)	1.10	1.10	1.30	.22	.07
1855	13¢ Crazy Horse (1982)	2.00	3.50	45.00(100)	2.40	2.40	2.95	.50	.08
1856	14¢ Sinclair Lewis (1985)	2.00	3.50	26.75(100)	....	....	7.95(20)	.28	.08
1857	17¢ Rachel Carson (1981)	1.75	3.25	60.00(100)	3.00	3.00	3.25	.65	.07
1858	18¢ George Mason (1981)	1.75	3.25	65.00(100)	3.35	3.35	4.00	.70	.07
1859	19¢ Sequoyah	1.75	3.25	37.50(100)	1.85	1.85	2.95	.38	.22
1860	20¢ Ralph Bunche (1982)	2.00	3.50	75.00(100)	3.75	3.75	4.25	.80	.06
1861	20¢ Thomas Gallaudet (1983)	2.00	3.50	90.00(100)	4.75	4.75	5.95	1.00	.07
1862	20¢ Harry Truman (1984)	2.00	3.50	38.00(100)	....	....	12.50(20)	.40	.06
1863	22¢ J. Audubon (1985)	2.00	3.75	42.50(100)	....	....	13.50(20)	.45	.06
1864	30¢ Frank C. Laubach (1984)	2.25	4.75	57.50(100)	....	....	16.50(20)	.60	.12
1865	35¢ Charles Drew (1981)	2.65	5.25	67.50(100)	3.35	3.35	4.50	.70	.15
1866	37¢ Robert Millikan (1982)	2.65	5.50	72.50(100)	3.75	3.75	5.25	.75	.09
1867	39¢ Grenville Clark (1985)	2.65	5.00	77.50(100)	....	....	20.00(20)	.80	.10
1868	40¢ Lillian Gilbreth (1984)	2.65	6.00	77.50(100)	....	....	21.50(20)	.80	.14
1869	50¢ Chester Nimitz (1985)	2.75	5.00	95.00(100)	4.75	4.75	5.75	1.00	.14

USA 15c
Everett Dirksen

1874

Whitney Moore Young

Black Heritage USA 15c

1875

1981 COMMEMORATIVES

1874/1945	(1874-9, 1910-45) 42 Vars., cpl.	....	....	....	69.75(20)	76.50(21)	135.00(22)	33.50	3.65
1874	15¢ Everett Dirksen	1.75	3.25	30.00(50)	2.95	2.95	3.00	.65	.07
1875	15¢ Whitney M. Young	1.75	3.25	30.00(50)	2.95	2.95	3.00	.65	.07

Rose USA 18c

1876

Camellia USA 18c

1877

Dahlia USA 18c

1878

Lily USA 18c

1879

1876-79	Flowers, 4 Vars., att'd	2.75	4.00	36.00(48)	3.75	3.75	3.95	3.20	2.25
1876	18¢ Rose	1.75	....	....	....	....	....	.80	.09
1877	18¢ Camelia	1.75	....	....	....	....	....	.80	.09
1878	18¢ Dahlia	1.75	....	....	....	....	....	.80	.09
1879	18¢ Lily	1.75	....	....	....	....	....	.80	.09

1880, 1949

1881

1882

1883

1884

1885

1886

1887

1888

1889

SCOTT NO.	DESCRIPTION	FIRST DAY COVERS SING.	PL.BLK.	MINT SHEET	COPY-RIGHT	ZIP	PLATE BLOCK	UN-USED	USED

1981 WILDLIFE DEFINITIVES

1889a	Wildlife, b. pane of 10	7.75	....	....	....	....	....	10.75	....
1880-89	Wildlife, set of singles	16.50	....	....	....	....	....	....	.65
1880	18¢ Bighorned Sheep	1.75	....	....	....	....	....	1.10	.07
1881	18¢ Puma	1.75	....	....	....	....	....	1.10	.07
1882	18¢ Harbor Seal	1.75	....	....	....	....	....	1.10	.07
1883	18¢ Bison	1.75	....	....	....	....	....	1.10	.07
1884	18¢ Brown Bear	1.75	....	....	....	....	....	1.10	.07
1885	18¢ Polar Bear	1.75	....	....	....	....	....	1.10	.07
1886	18¢ Elk	1.75	....	....	....	....	....	1.10	.07
1887	18¢ Moose	1.75	....	....	....	....	....	1.10	.07
1888	18¢ White-tailed Deer	1.75	....	....	....	....	....	1.10	.07
1889	18¢ Pronghorned Antelope	1.75	....	....	....	....	....	1.10	.07

1890

1891

1892

1893

1894, 1895, 1896

1981 FLAG AND ANTHEM ISSUE

1890	18¢ "Waves of Grain"	1.75	3.50	72.50(100)	....	....	21.75(20)	.75	.06

1981 Coil Stamp Perf. 10 Vertically

SCOTT NO.	DESCRIPTION	FIRST DAY COVERS SING.	PL# STRIP 3	MINT SHEET	COPY-RIGHT	ZIP	PL# STRIP 3	UN-USED	USED
1891	18¢ "Shining Sea"	1.75	3.25	....	....	....	15.00	.80	.06

1981

1892	6¢ Stars, from b. pane	1.75	....	....	....	....	....	1.75	.18
1893	18¢ "Purple Mountains" from b. pane	1.75	....	....	....	....	....	.75	.12
1892-93	6¢ & 18¢ as above, attd pr.	....	....	....	....	....	....	2.65	....
1893a	6-1893, 2-1892 b. pane	5.25	....	....	....	....	....	7.00	....

SCOTT NO.	DESCRIPTION	SING.	PL. BLK.	MINT SHEET	COPY-RIGHT	ZIP	Pl. BLK.	UN-USED	USED
1894	20¢ Flag & Supreme Court	1.75	3.65	75.00(100)	....	....	18.50(20)	.80	.06

SCOTT NO.	DESCRIPTION	SING.	PL # STRIP 3	MINT SHEET	COPY-RIGHT	ZIP	PL # STRIP 3	UN-USED	USED
1895	20¢ Flag & Supreme Court	1.75	3.25	....	....	....	12.50	.85	.06

1981

1896	20¢ Flag & S.C., from b. pane	1.75	....	....	....	....	....	.80	.06
1896a	20¢ b. pane of 6	4.75	....	....	....	....	....	5.25	....
1896b	20¢ b. pane of 10	7.50	....	....	....	....	....	8.00	....

1897

1897A

1898

1898A

1899

1900

1901

1902

1903

SCOTT NO.	DESCRIPTION	FIRST DAY COVERS SING.	FIRST DAY COVERS PL.BLK.	MINT SHEET	COPY-RIGHT	ZIP	PLATE BLOCK	UN-USED	USED

1904   1905   1906   1907   1908

1981-84 Perf. 10 Vertically TRANSPORTATION COILS

SCOTT NO.	DESCRIPTION	FIRST DAY COVERS SING.	PL.BLK.	MINT SHEET	COPY-RIGHT	ZIP	PLATE BLOCK	PL # STRIP 3	UN-USED	USED
1897-1908	1¢-20¢, 14 Vars., cpl.	29.50	......	......	......	......		8650	4.25	1.20
1897	1¢ Omnibus (1983)	2.25	......	......	......	......		175	.06	.06
1897A	2¢ Locomotive (1982)	2.25	......	......	......	......		175	.06	.06
1898	3¢ Handcar (1983)	2.25	......	......	......	......		185	.07	.06
1898A	4¢ Stagecoach (1982)	2.25	......	......	......	......		425	.08	.06
1899	5¢ Motorcycle (1983)	2.25	......	......	......	......		325	.10	.07
1900	5.2¢ Sleigh (1983)	2.25	......	......	......	......		1500	.30	.10
1901	5.9¢ Bicycle (1982)	2.25	......	......	......	......		1500	.45	.15
1902	7.4¢ Baby Buggy (1984)	2.25	......	......	......	......		1500	.35	.15
1903	9.3¢ Mail Wagon	2.25	......	......	......	......		1850	.40	.15
1904	10.9¢ Hansom Cab (1982)	2.25	......	......	......	......		1975	.70	.13
1905	11¢ Caboose (1984)	2.25	......	......	......	......		875	.50	.08
1906	17¢ Electric Car	2.25	......	......	......	......		700	.35	.06
1907	18¢ Surrey	2.25	......	......	......	......		875	.75	.06
1908	20¢ Fire Pumper	2.25	......	......	......	......		775	.40	.06

NOTE: Plate # Strips of 3 have plate number under center stamp. Some issues also have lines between two of the stamps.

PRECANCELLED COILS
The following are for precancelled, unused, never hinged stamps. Stamps without gum sell for less.

SCOTT NO.	DESCRIPTION	PL # STRIP 3	UN-USED	SCOTT NO.	DESCRIPTION	PL # STRIP 3	UN-USED
1895e	20¢ Supreme Court	17.50	.90	1903a	9.3¢ Mail Wagon	7.50	.40
1898Ab	4¢ Stage coach	5.25	.15	1904a	10.9¢ Hansom Cab	27.50	.60
1900a	5.2¢ Sleigh	7.50	.40	1905a	11¢ Caboose	8.75	.70
1901a	5.9¢ Bicycle	26.75	.35	1906a	17¢ Electric Car	8.75	.85
1902a	7.4¢ Baby Buggy	7.50	.40				

SCOTT NO.	DESCRIPTION	FIRST DAY COVERS SING.	PL.BLK.	MINT SHEET	COPY-RIGHT	ZIP	PLATE BLOCK	UN-USED	USED

1909   1910   1911

1983 EXPRESS MAIL BOOKLET SINGLE

SCOTT NO.	DESCRIPTION	SING.	PL.BLK.	MINT SHEET	COPY-RIGHT	ZIP	PLATE BLOCK	UN-USED	USED
1909	$9.35 Eagle & Moon	49.95	......	......	......	......	......	37.50	17.50
1909a	$9.35 b. pane of 3	150.00	......	......	......	......	......	110.00	......

1981 COMMEMORATIVES

1910	18¢ American Red Cross	1.75	3.50	37.50(50)	3.65	3.65	3.75	.80	.07
1911	18¢ Savings & Loan Assoc.	1.75	3.50	37.50(50)	3.65	3.65	3.75	.80	.07

SCOTT NO.	DESCRIPTION	FIRST DAY COVERS SING.	PL.BLK.	MINT SHEET	COPY-RIGHT	ZIP	PLATE BLOCK	UN-USED	USED

1912 **1913** **1914** **1915**

1916 **1917** **1918** **1919**

1981 COMMEMORATIVES

SCOTT NO.	DESCRIPTION	SING.	PL.BLK.	MINT SHEET	COPY-RIGHT	ZIP	PLATE BLOCK	UN-USED	USED
1912-19	Space Achievement, 8 Vars., att'd.	8.75	9.50	36.50(48)	(combo)	7.35(8)	7.50(8)	6.75	4.75
1912-19	Same, set of singles	17.50	....	....	....	....	....		.90
1912	18¢ Exploring the Moon	2.25	....	....	....	....	....	.90	.12
1913	18¢ Releasing Boosters	2.25	....	....	....	....	....	.90	.12
1914	18¢ Cooling Electric Systems	2.25	....	....	....	....	....	.90	.12
1915	18¢ Understanding the Sun	2.25	....	....	....	....	....	.90	.12
1916	18¢ Probing the Planets	2.25	....	....	....	....	....	.90	.12
1917	18¢ Shuttle and Rockets	2.25	....	....	....	....	....	.90	.12
1918	18¢ Landing	2.25	....	....	....	....	....	.90	.12
1919	18¢ Comprehending Universe	2.25	....	....	....	....	....	.90	.12

1920 **1921** **1922** **1923** **1924**

SCOTT NO.	DESCRIPTION	SING.	PL.BLK.	MINT SHEET	COPY-RIGHT	ZIP	PLATE BLOCK	UN-USED	USED
1920	18¢ Professional Management	1.75	3.50	37.50(50)	3.65	3.65	3.75	.80	.07
1921-24	Wildlife Habitats, 4 Vars., att'd	3.50	4.75	37.50(50)	3.65	3.65	3.75	3.20	2.25
1921	18¢ Blue Heron	1.75	....	....	....	....	....	.80	.09
1922	18¢ Badger	1.75	....	....	....	....	....	.80	.09
1923	18¢ Grizzly Bear	1.75	....	....	....	....	....	.80	.09
1924	18¢ Ruffled-Grouse	1.75	....	....	....	....	....	.80	.09

1925 **1926** **1927**

SCOTT NO.	DESCRIPTION	SING.	PL.BLK.	MINT SHEET	COPY-RIGHT	ZIP	PLATE BLOCK	UN-USED	USED
1925	18¢ Disabled Persons	1.75	3.50	37.50(50)	3.65	3.65	3.75	.80	.07
1926	18¢ Edna St. Vincent Millay	1.75	3.50	37.50(50)	3.65	3.65	3.75	.80	.07
1927	18¢ Alcoholism	1.75	3.50	100.00(50)	....	....	59.50(20)	1.00	.07

SCOTT NO.	DESCRIPTION	FIRST DAY COVERS SING.	PL.BLK.	MINT SHEET	COPY-RIGHT	ZIP	PLATE BLOCK	UN-USED	USED

Architecture USA 18c   1928   Architecture USA 18c   1929   Architecture USA 18c   1930   Architecture USA 18c   1931

1928-31	American Architecture, 4 Vars., att'd.	3.50	4.50	36.75(40)	4.35	4.35	4.50	4.00	2.25
1928	18¢ New York Univ. Library	1.75	......	......	......	......	......	1.00	.09
1929	18¢ Biltmore House	1.75	......	......	......	......	......	1.00	.09
1930	18¢ Palace of the Arts	1.75	......	......	......	......	......	1.00	.09
1931	18¢ National Farmers Bank	1.75	......	......	......	......	......	1.00	.09

1932   1933   1934

1932	18¢ Babe Zaharias	1.75	3.50	37.50(50)	3.65	3.65	3.75	.80	.07
1933	18¢ Bobby Jones	1.75	3.50	37.50(50)	3.65	3.65	3.75	.80	.07
1934	18¢ Coming Through the Rye	1.75	3.50	37.50(50)	3.65	3.65	3.75	.80	.07

1935   1936   1937   1938

1935	18¢ James Hoban	1.75	3.50	37.50(50)	3.65	3.65	4.25	.80	.30
1936	20¢ James Hoban	2.25	3.75	37.50(50)	3.75	3.75	3.95	.80	.07
1937-38	18¢ Yorktown/Virginia Capes, 2 Vars., att'd.	2.75	3.75	37.50(50)	3.65	3.65	3.75	1.60	1.10
1937	18¢ Yorktown	2.15	......	......	......	......	......	.80	.08
1938	18¢ Virginia Capes	2.15	......	......	......	......	......	.80	.08

1939   1940   John Hanson   USA 20¢   1941

1939	(20¢) Madonna & Child	2.15	3.75	75.00(100)	3.75	3.75	3.95	.80	.06
1940	(20¢) Christmas Toy	2.15	3.75	37.50(50)	3.75	3.75	3.95	.80	.06
1941	20¢ John Hanson	2.15	3.75	37.50(50)	3.75	3.75	3.95	.80	.07

FIRST DAY COVERS: First Day Covers are envelopes cancelled on the "First Day of Issue" of the stamp used on the envelope. Usually they also contain a picture (cachet) on the left side designed to go with the theme of the stamp. From 1935 to 1944, prices listed are for cacheted, addressed covers. From 1945 to date, prices are for cacheted, unaddressed covers.

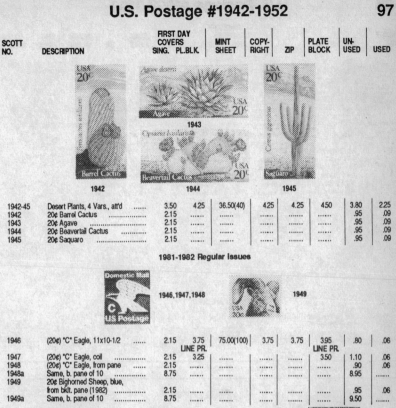

1943

1942   **1944**   **1945**

SCOTT NO.	DESCRIPTION	FIRST DAY COVERS SING.	PL.BLK.	MINT SHEET	COPY-RIGHT	ZIP	PLATE BLOCK	UN-USED	USED
1942-45	Desert Plants, 4 Vars., att'd	3.50	4.25	36.50(40)	4.25	4.25	4.50	3.80	2.25
1942	20¢ Barrel Cactus	2.15	......	......	......	......	......	.95	.09
1943	20¢ Agave	2.15	......	......	......	......	......	.95	.09
1944	20¢ Beavertail Cactus	2.15	......	......	......	......	......	.95	.09
1945	20¢ Saguaro	2.15	......	......	......	......	......	.95	.09

1981-1982 Regular Issues

1946, 1947, 1948

1949

Scott	Description	FDC SING.	PL.BLK.	MINT SHEET	COPY-RIGHT	ZIP	PLATE BLOCK	UN-USED	USED
1946	(20¢) "C" Eagle, 11x10-1/2	2.15	3.75	75.00(100)	3.75	3.75	3.95	.80	.06
			LINE PR.				LINE PR.		
1947	(20¢) "C" Eagle, coil	2.15	3.25	......	......	......	3.50	1.10	.06
1948	(20¢) "C" Eagle, from pane	2.15	......	......	......	......	......	.90	.06
1948a	Same, b. pane of 10	8.75	......	......	......	......	......	8.95	......
1949	20¢ Bighorned Sheep, blue, from bklt. pane (1982)	2.15	......	......	......	......	......	.95	.06
1949a	Same, b. pane of 10	8.75	......	......	......	......	......	9.50	......

1950   **1951**   **1952**

1982 COMMEMORATIVES

1950/2030	(1950-53, 2003-04, 06-30) 30 Vars.	SING.	PLATE BLOCK	MINT SHEET	COPY-RIGHT	ZIP	PLATE BLOCK	UN-USED	USED
		......	......	......	61.50(17)	61.50(17)	133.50(21)	24.50	2.25
1950	20¢ Franklin D. Roosevelt	2.15	3.75	36.00(48)	3.75	3.75	3.95	.80	.07
1951	20¢ LOVE, Perf. 11 x 10-1/2	2.25	4.00	42.50(50)	4.15	4.15	4.35	.90	.07
1951a	Same, Perf. 10			42.50(50)	4.15	4.15	4.35	.90	......

NOTE: Perforations will be mixed on Used #1951

| 1952 | 20¢ George Washington | 2.15 | 3.75 | 37.50(50) | 3.75 | 3.75 | 3.95 | .80 | .07 |

BOOKLET PANE SINGLES: Traditionally, booklet panes have been collected only as intact panes since, other than the straight edged sides, they were identical to sheet stamps. However, starting with the 1971 8¢ Eisenhower stamp, many issues differ from the comparative sheet stamp or may even be totally different issues (e.g. #1738-42 Windmills). These newer issues are now collected as booklet singles or panes — both methods being acceptable.

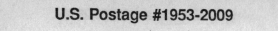

SCOTT NO.	DESCRIPTION	FIRST DAY COVERS SING. PL.BLK.		MINT SHEET	COPY- RIGHT	ZIP	PLATE BLOCK	UN- USED	USED

1982 STATE BIRDS AND FLOWERS

1953 Alabama	1970 Louisiana	1987 Ohio
1954 Alaska	1971 Maine	1988 Oklahoma
1955 Arizona	1972 Maryland	1989 Oregon
1956 Arkansas	1973 Massachusetts	1990 Pennsylvania
1957 California	1974 Michigan	1991 Rhode Island
1958 Colorado	1975 Minnesota	1992 South Carolina
1959 Connecticut	1976 Mississippi	1993 South Dakota
1960 Delaware	1977 Missouri	1994 Tennessee
1961 Florida	1978 Montana	1995 Texas
1962 Georgia	1979 Nebraska	1996 Utah
1963 Hawaii	1980 Nevada	1997 Vermont
1964 Idaho	1981 New Hampshire	1998 Virginia
1965 Illinois	1982 New Jersey	1999 Washington
1966 Indiana	1983 New Mexico	2000 West Virginia
1967 Iowa	1984 New York	2001 Wisconsin
1968 Kansas	1985 North Carolina	2002 Wyoming
1969 Kentucky	1986 North Dakota	

Alabama USA 20c — **1953**

Indiana USA 20c — **1966**

Massachusetts USA 20c — **1973**

Wyoming USA 20c — **2002**

Perf. 10-1/2 x 11

1953-2002	20¢, 50 Vars., att'd		....		36.50(50)	....	....	36.50(50)	36.50	....
	Set of Singles		97.50	....	....	....	....	....	....	17.50
	Singles of above		2.25	....	....	....	....	....	.85	.40
1953a-2002a	Same, perf. 11	....	....	....	47.50(50)	....	....	47.50(50)	47.50	....
	Singles of above		....	....	....	....	....	....	1.10	....

NOTE: Used singles will not be sorted by perf. sizes.

1982 USA THE NETHERLANDS — **2003**

Library of Congress USA 20c — **2004**

Wise shoppers stretch dollars — Consumer Education USA 20c — **2005**

2003	20¢ USA/Netherlands	....	2.15	3.75	37.50(50)	....	....	17.50(20)	.80	.07
2004	20¢ Library of Congress	....	2.15	3.75	37.50(50)	3.75	3.75	3.95	.80	.07

				PL # STRIP 3				PL # STRIP 3		
2005	20¢ Consumer Education, coil	......	2.15	9.25	....	....	....	59.50	1.15	.06

USA 20c Solar energy Knoxville World's Fair — **2006**

USA 20c Synthetic fuels Knoxville World's Fair — **2007**

20¢ Breeder reactor Knoxville World's Fair — **2008**

USA 20c Fossil fuels Knoxville World's Fair — **2009**

2006-09	World's Fair, 4 Vars., att'd	....	3.50	4.25	39.50(50)	4.15	4.15	4.25	3.40	2.10
2006	20¢ Solar Energy	....	2.15	....	....	....	....	....	.85	.09
2007	20¢ Synthetic Fuels	....	2.15	....	....	....	....	....	.85	.09
2008	20¢ Breeder Reactor	....	2.15	....	....	....	....	....	.85	.09
2009	20¢ Fossil Fuels	....	2.15	....	....	....	....	....	.85	.09

SE-TENANTS: Beginning with the 1964 Christmas issue (#1254-57), the United States has issued numerous Se-Tenant stamps covering a wide variety of subjects. Se-Tenants are issues whee two or more different stamp designs are produced on the same sheet in pair, strip or block form. Mint stamps are usually collected in attached blocks, etc. — Used are generally saved as single stamps. Our Se-Tenant sets follow in this collecting pattern.

SCOTT NO.	DESCRIPTION	FIRST DAY COVERS SING.	FIRST DAY COVERS PL.BLK.	MINT SHEET	COPY-RIGHT	ZIP	PLATE BLOCK	UN-USED	USED
2010	20¢ Horatio Alger	2.15	3.75	37.50(50)	3.75	3.75	3.95	.80	.07
2011	20¢ Aging Together	2.15	3.75	37.50(50)	3.75	3.75	3.95	.80	.07
2012	20¢ Barrymores	2.15	3.75	37.50(50)	3.75	3.75	3.95	.80	.07
2013	20¢ Dr. Mary Walker	2.15	3.75	37.50(50)	3.75	3.75	3.95	.80	.07
2014	20¢ Peace Garden	2.15	3.75	37.50(50)	3.75	3.75	3.95	.80	.07
2015	20¢ America's Libraries	2.15	3.75	37.50(50)	3.75	3.75	3.95	.80	.07
2016	20¢ Jackie Robinson	3.00	4.75	40.00(50)	4.00	4.00	4.15	.85	.07
2017	20¢ Touro Synagogue	2.25	4.25	42.50(50)	....	....	1950(20)	.90	.07
2018	20¢ Wolf Trap Farm	2.15	3.75	37.50(50)	3.75	3.75	3.95	.80	.07
2019-22	American Architecture. 4 Vars., att'd.	3.50	4.25	32.50(40)	4.00	4.00	4.25	3.40	2.25
2019	20¢ Falling Water Mill Run	2.15	....	....	....	....	....	.85	.09
2020	20¢ Illinois Inst. Tech.	2.15	....	....	....	....	....	.85	.09
2021	20¢ Gropius House	2.15	....	....	....	....	....	.85	.09
2022	20¢ Dulles Airport	2.15	....	....	....	....	....	.85	.09
2023	20¢ St. Francis of Assisi	2.15	3.75	37.50(50)	3.75	3.75	3.95	.80	.07
2024	20¢ Ponce de Leon	2.15	3.75	40.00(50)	....	....	1850(20)	.85	.07
2025	13¢ Kitten & Puppy Xmas	2.15	3.75	25.00(50)	2.50	2.50	260	.55	.12

MINT SHEETS: From 1935 to date, we list prices for our standard size Mint Sheets in Fine, Never Hinged condition.. The Number of stamps in each sheet is noted in ( ).

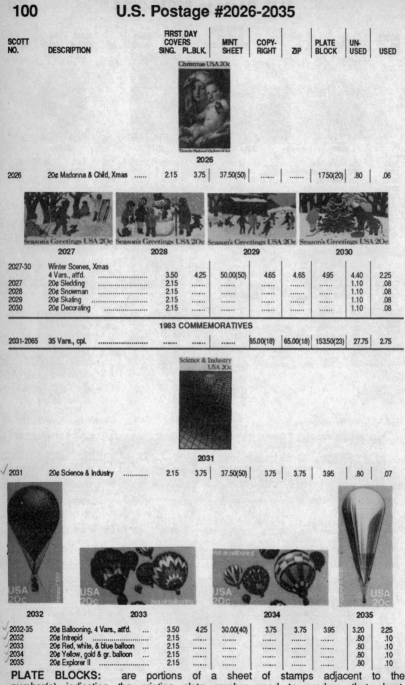

SCOTT NO.	DESCRIPTION	FIRST DAY COVERS SING.	PL.BLK.	MINT SHEET	COPY-RIGHT	ZIP	PLATE BLOCK	UN-USED	USED

2026

| 2026 | 20¢ Madonna & Child, Xmas | ...... | 2.15 | 3.75 | 37.50(50) | ...... | .... | 1750(20) | .80 | .06 |

2027   **2028**   **2029**   **2030**

2027-30	Winter Scenes, Xmas 4 Vars., att'd.	......	3.50	4.25	50.00(50)	4.65	4.65	4.95	4.40	2.25
2027	20¢ Sledding	......	2.15	......	......	......	......	......	1.10	.08
2028	20¢ Snowman	......	2.15	......	......	......	......	......	1.10	.08
2029	20¢ Skating	......	2.15	......	......	......	......	......	1.10	.08
2030	20¢ Decorating	......	2.15	......	......	......	......	......	1.10	.08

1983 COMMEMORATIVES

| 2031-2065 | 35 Vars., cpl. | ...... | ...... | ...... | ...... | 65.00(18) | 65.00(18) | 153.50(23) | 27.75 | 2.75 |

2031

| √ 2031 | 20¢ Science & Industry | ...... | 2.15 | 3.75 | 37.50(50) | 3.75 | 3.75 | 3.95 | .80 | .07 |

2032   **2033**   **2034**   **2035**

√ 2032-35	20¢ Ballooning, 4 Vars., att'd.	......	3.50	4.25	30.00(40)	3.75	3.75	3.95	3.20	2.25
√ 2032	20¢ Intrepid	......	2.15	......	......	......	......	......	.80	.10
√ 2033	20¢ Red, white, & blue balloon	......	2.15	......	......	......	......	......	.80	.10
√ 2034	20¢ Yellow, gold & gr. balloon	......	2.15	......	......	......	......	......	.80	.10
√ 2035	20¢ Explorer II	......	2.15	......	......	......	......	......	.80	.10

PLATE BLOCKS: are portions of a sheet of stamps adjacent to the number(s) indicating the printing plate number used to produce that sheet. Flat plate issues are usually collected in plate blocks of six (number opposite middle stamp) while rotary issues are normally corner blocks of four.

SCOTT NO.	DESCRIPTION	FIRST DAY COVERS SING.	PL.BLK.	MINT SHEET	COPY-RIGHT	ZIP	PLATE BLOCK	UN-USED	USED

2036　　**2037**　　**2038**　　**2039**

✓2036	20¢ USA/Sweden	2.15	3.75	37.50(50)	3.75	3.75	3.95	.80	.07
✓2037	20¢ Civilian Cons. Corps	2.15	3.75	37.50(50)	3.75	3.75	3.95	.80	.07
✓2038	20¢ Joseph Priestley	2.15	3.75	37.50(50)	3.75	3.75	3.95	.80	.07
✓2039	20¢ Volunteerism	2.15	3.75	37.50(50)	....	....	1750(20)	.80	.07

2040　　**2041**　　**2042**　　**2043**

✓2040	20¢ German Immigrants	2.15	3.75	37.50(50)	3.75	3.75	3.95	.80	.07
✓2041	20¢ Brooklyn Bridge	2.15	3.75	37.50(50)	3.75	3.75	3.95	.80	.07
✓2042	20¢ Tennessee Valley Auth.	2.15	3.75	37.50(50)	....	....	1750(20)	.80	.07
✓2043	20¢ Physical Fitness	2.15	3.75	37.50(50)	....	....	1750(20)	.80	.07

2044　　**2045**　　**2046**　　**2047**

✓2044	20¢ Scott Joplin	2.15	3.75	42.50(50)	4.00	4.00	4.15	.90	.07
✓2045	20¢ Medal of Honor	2.15	3.75	33.50(40)	4.00	4.00	4.15	.90	.07
✓2046	20¢ Babe Ruth	2.25	4.25	47.50(50)	4.50	4.50	4.65	1.00	.07
✓2047	20¢ Nathaniel Hawthorne	2.15	3.75	37.50(50)	3.75	3.75	3.95	.80	.07

2048　　**2049**　　**2050**　　**2051**

✓2048-51	13¢ Olympics, 4 Vars.	3.50	4.25	27.50(50)	2.75	2.75	2.85	2.40	1.75
✓2048	13¢ Discus	2.15	....	....	....	....	....	.60	.14
✓2049	13¢ High Jump	2.15	....	....	....	....	....	.60	.14
✓2050	13¢ Archery	2.15	....	....	....	....	....	.60	.14
✓2051	13¢ Boxing	2.15	....	....	....	....	....	.60	.14

2052　　**2053**　　**2054**

✓2052	20¢ Treaty of Paris	2.15	3.75	30.00(40)	3.75	3.75	3.95	.80	.07
✓2053	20¢ Civil Service	2.15	3.75	37.50(50)	....	....	1750(20)	.80	.07
✓2054	20¢ Metropolitan Opera	2.15	3.75	37.50(50)	3.75	3.75	3.95	.80	.07

SCOTT NO.	DESCRIPTION	FIRST DAY COVERS SING.	FIRST DAY COVERS PL.BLK.	MINT SHEET	COPY-RIGHT	ZIP	PLATE BLOCK	UN-USED	USED

	2055		2056		2057		2058		
2055-58	20¢ Inventors, 4 Vars., att'd	......	3.50	4.00	43.50(50)	4.25	4.25	4.50	3.80	2.25
2055	20¢ Charles Steinmetz		2.15	......	......	......	......	......	.95	.09
2056	20¢ Edwin Armstrong	....	2.15	......	......	......	......	......	.95	.09
2057	20¢ Nikola Tesla	....	2.15	......	......	......	......	......	.95	.09
2058	20¢ Phil T. Farnsworth		2.15	......	......	......	......	......	.95	.09

	2059		2060		2061		2062		
2059-62	20¢ Streetcars, 4 vars., att'd	...	3.50	4.00	46.50(50)	4.35	4.35	4.65	4.00	2.25
2059	20¢ First Streetcar		2.15	......	......	......	......	......	1.00	.09
2060	20¢ Electric Trolley		2.15	......	......	......	......	......	1.00	.09
2061	20¢ "Bobtail"		2.15	......	......	......	......	......	1.00	.09
2062	20¢ St. Charles Streetcar	....	2.15	......	......	......	......	......	1.00	.09

	2063		2064		2065		2066		
2063	20¢ Madonna	....	2.15	3.75	42.50(50)	4.15	4.15	4.25	.90	.06
2064	20¢ Santa Claus	....	2.15	3.75	42.50(50)	......	......	19.50(20)	.90	.06
2065	20¢ Martin Luther	....	2.15	3.75	36.00(50)	3.75	3.75	3.95	.80	.07

	1984 COMMEMORATIVES								
2066-2109	44 Varieities, cpl.	....	....	....	....	105.00(27)	110.00(28)	175.00(32)	35.00	3.20
2066	20¢ Alaska Statehood	....	2.15	3.75	36.00(50)	3.75	3.75	3.95	.80	.07

	2067		2068		2069		2070		
2067-70	Winter Olympics, 4 Vars., att'd	...	3.50	4.00	40.00(50)	4.00	4.00	4.25	3.40	2.25
2067	20¢ Ice Dancing	....	2.15	......	......	......	......	......	.85	.09
2068	20¢ Downhill Skiing	....	2.15	......	......	......	......	......	.85	.09
2069	20¢ Cross Country Skiing	....	2.15	......	......	......	......	......	.85	.09
2070	20¢ Hockey	....	2.15	......	......	......	......	......	.85	.09

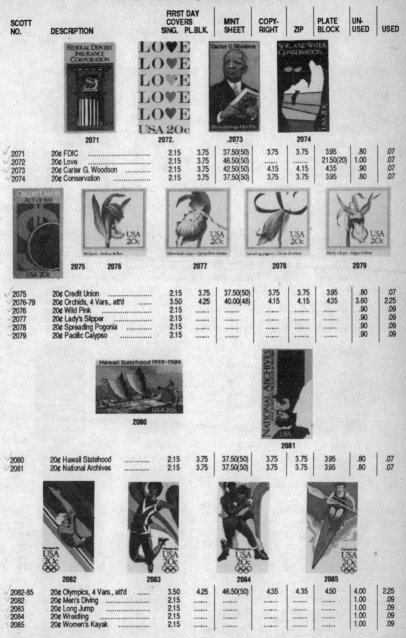

SCOTT NO.	DESCRIPTION	FIRST DAY COVERS SING.	FIRST DAY COVERS PL.BLK.	MINT SHEET	COPY-RIGHT	ZIP	PLATE BLOCK	UN-USED	USED
2071	20¢ FDIC	2.15	3.75	37.50(50)	3.75	3.75	3.95	.80	.07
2072	20¢ Love	2.15	3.75	46.50(50)	....	....	21.50(20)	1.00	.07
2073	20¢ Carter G. Woodson	2.15	3.75	42.50(50)	4.15	4.15	4.35	.90	.07
2074	20¢ Conservation	2.15	3.75	37.50(50)	3.75	3.75	3.95	.80	.07
2075	20¢ Credit Union	2.15	3.75	37.50(50)	3.75	3.75	3.95	.80	.07
2076-79	20¢ Orchids, 4 Vars., att'd	3.50	4.25	40.00(48)	4.15	4.15	4.35	3.60	2.25
2076	20¢ Wild Pink	2.15	....	....	....	....	....	.90	.09
2077	20¢ Lady's Slipper	2.15	....	....	....	....	....	.90	.09
2078	20¢ Spreading Pogonia	2.15	....	....	....	....	....	.90	.09
2079	20¢ Pacific Calypso	2.15	....	....	....	....	....	.90	.09
2080	20¢ Hawaii Statehood	....	2.15	3.75	37.50(50)	3.75	3.75	3.95	.80	.07
2081	20¢ National Archives	....	2.15	3.75	37.50(50)	3.75	3.75	3.95	.80	.07
2082-85	20¢ Olympics, 4 Vars., att'd	3.50	4.25	46.50(50)	4.35	4.35	4.50	4.00	2.25
2082	20¢ Men's Diving	2.15	....	....	....	....	....	1.00	.09
2083	20¢ Long Jump	2.15	....	....	....	....	....	1.00	.09
2084	20¢ Wrestling	2.15	....	....	....	....	....	1.00	.09
2085	20¢ Women's Kayak	2.15	....	....	....	....	....	1.00	.09

FIRST DAY COVERS: First Day Covers are envelopes cancelled on the "First Day of Issue" of the stamp used on the envelope. Usually they also contain a picture (cachet) on the left side designed to go with the theme of the stamp. From 1935 to 1944, prices listed are for cacheted, addressed covers. From 1945 to date, prices are for cacheted, unaddressed covers.

SCOTT NO.	DESCRIPTION	FIRST DAY COVERS SING.	FIRST DAY COVERS PL.BLK.	MINT SHEET	COPY-RIGHT	ZIP	PLATE BLOCK	UN-USED	USED

2086   **2087**   **2088**   **2089**

2086	20¢ Louisiana Exposition	....	2.15	3.75	30.00(40)	3.75	3.75	3.95	.80	.07
2087	20¢ Health Research	....	2.15	3.75	37.50(50)	3.75	3.75	3.95	.80	.07
2088	20¢ Douglas Fairbanks	....	2.15	3.75	37.50(50)	....	....	1750(20)	.80	.07
2089	20¢ Jim Thorpe	....	2.15	3.75	37.50(50)	3.75	3.75	3.95	.80	.07

2090   **2091**   **2092**   **2093**

2090	20¢ John McCormack	....	2.15	3.75	37.50(50)	3.75	3.75	3.95	.80	.07
2091	20¢ St. Lawrence Seaway	......	2.15	3.75	37.50(50)	3.75	3.75	3.95	.80	.07
2092	20¢ Preserving Wetlands	....	2.15	3.75	37.50(50)	3.75	3.75	3.95	.80	.07
2093	20¢ Roanoke Voyages	....	2.15	3.75	37.50(50)	3.75	3.75	3.95	.80	.07

2094   **2095**   **2096**   **2097**

2094	20¢ Herman Melville	....	2.15	3.75	37.50(50)	3.75	3.75	3.95	.80	.07
2095	20¢ Horace Moses	....	2.15	3.75	37.50(50)	3.75	3.75	1750(20)	.80	.07
2096	20¢ Smokey Bear	....	2.15	3.75	37.50(50)	3.75	3.75	3.95	.80	.07
2097	20¢ Roberto Clemente	....	2.15	3.75	42.50(50)	4.15	4.15	425	.90	.07

2098   **2099**   **2100**   **2101**

2098-2101	20¢ American Dogs, att'd	....	3.50	4.25	30.00(40)	3.75	3.75	3.95	3.20	2.25
2098	20¢ Beagle, Boston Terrier	....	2.15	....	....	....	....	....	.80	.09
2099	20¢ Chesapeake Bay Retriever, Cocker Spaniel		2.15	....	....	....	....	....	.80	.09
2100	20¢ Alaskan Malamute, Collie	...	2.15	....	....	....	....	....	.80	.09
2101	20¢ Black & Tan Coonhound, American Foxhound	....	2.15	....	....	....	....	....	.80	.09

MINT SHEETS: From 1935 to date, we list prices for our standard size Mint Sheets in Fine, Never Hinged condition. The number of stamps in each sheet is noted in ( ).

SCOTT NO.	DESCRIPTION	FIRST DAY COVERS SING.	PL.BLK.	MINT SHEET	COPY-RIGHT	ZIP	PLATE BLOCK	UN-USED	USED

2102 **2103** **2104** **2105**

2102	20¢ Crime Prevention	2.15	3.75	37.50(50)	3.75	3.75	3.95	.80	.07
2103	20¢ Hispanic Americans	2.15	3.75	30.00(40)	3.75	3.75	3.95	.80	.07
2104	20¢ Family Unity	2.15	3.75	37.50(50)	3.75	3.75	1750(20)	.80	.07
2105	20¢ Eleanor Roosevelt	2.15	3.75	30.00(40)	3.75	3.75	3.95	.80	.07

2106 **2107** **2108** **2109**

2106	20¢ Nation of Readers	2.15	3.75	37.50(50)	3.75	3.75	3.95	.80	.07
2107	20¢ Madonna & Child	2.15	3.75	37.50(50)	3.75	3.75	3.95	.80	.06
2108	20¢ Santa Claus	2.15	3.75	37.50(50)	3.75	3.75	3.95	.80	.06
2109	20¢ Vietnam Veterans	2.15	3.75	30.00(40)	(combo)	5.50(6)	3.95	.80	.07

2110 **2111, 2112, 2113** **2114, 2115** **2116**

1985 COMMEMORATIVES

| 2110/2166 | (2110, 2137-47, 52-66) 27 Vars. | .... | .... | .... | 57.50(17) | 57.50(17) | 8750(18) | 22.50 | 2.00 |
| 2110 | 22¢ Jerome Kern | 2.15 | 3.95 | 42.50(50) | 4.00 | 4.00 | 425 | .90 | .07 |

1985 REGULAR ISSUES

| 2111 | (22¢) "D" Eagle | 2.15 | 3.95 | 80.00(100) | .... | .... | 1975(20) | .85 | .06 |

			PL # STRIP 3				PL # STRIP 3		
2112	(22¢) "D" Eagle, coil	2.15	8.75	....	....	....	8.00	.90	.06
2113	(22¢) "D" Eagle from b. pane	2.15	....	....	....	....	....	1.00	.06
2113a	Same, b. pane of 10	8.75	....	....	....	....	....	9.75	....

			PL. BLK.				PL. BLK.		
2114	22¢ Flag over Capitol	2.15	3.95	42.50(100)	225	2.25	325	.45	.06

			PL # STRIP 3				PL # STRIP 3		
2115	22¢ Flag over Capitol, coil	2.15	9.50	....	....	....	750	.45	.06
2116	22¢ Flag over Capitol from booklet pane	2.15	....	....	....	....	....	.45	.07
2116a	Same, b. pane of 5	4.35	....	....	....	....	....	2.25	....

SCOTT NO.	DESCRIPTION	FIRST DAY COVERS SING.	PL.BLK.	MINT SHEET	COPY-RIGHT	ZIP	PLATE BLOCK	UN-USED	USED

2117   **2118**   **2119**   **2120**   **2121**

1985 SEASHELLS FROM BOOKLET PANE

Scott No.	Description	Sing.	PL.BLK.	Mint Sheet	Copyright	Zip	Plate Block	Unused	Used
2117-21	Strip of 5, att'd.	4.50	......	....	....	....	......	2.25	....
2117	22¢ Frilled Dogwinkle	2.15	......	....	....	....	......	.45	.07
2118	22¢ Reticulated Helmet	2.15	......	....	....	....	......	.45	.07
2119	22¢ New England Neptune	2.15	......	....	....	....	......	.45	.07
2120	22¢ Calico Scallop	2.15	......	....	....	....	......	.45	.07
2121	22¢ Lightning Whelk	2.15	......	....	....	....	......	.45	.07
2121a	22¢ Seashells, b. pane of 10	8.75	......	....	....	....	......	4.50	....

2122

1985 EXPRESS MAIL STAMP FROM BOOKLET PANE

Scott No.	Description	Sing.	PL.BLK.	Mint Sheet	Copyright	Zip	Plate Block	Unused	Used
2122	$10.75 Eagle & Moon	47.50	......	....	....	....	......	21.50	15.00
2122a	Same, b. pane of 3	150.00	......	....	....	....	......	63.75	....

2123   **2124**   **2125**   **2126**

2127   **2128**   **2129**   **2130**   **2131**

2132   **2133**   **2134**   **2135**   **2136**

VERY FINE QUALITY: From 1935 to date, add 20% to the Fine price. Minimum of 3¢ per stamp. For quality definitions, refer to pages vii — ix.

SCOTT NO.	DESCRIPTION	FIRST DAY COVERS SING.	FIRST DAY COVERS PL.BLK.	MINT SHEET	COPY-RIGHT	ZIP	PLATE BLOCK	UN-USED	USED

1985-87 TRANSPORTATION COILS
Perf. 10 Vertically

SCOTT NO.	DESCRIPTION	FIRST DAY COVERS SING.	PL. # STRIP 3				PL. # STRIP 3	UN-USED	USED
2123-36	3.4¢-25¢, 14 vars., cpl.	....	29.50	115.00	....	....	....	59.50	2.80	1.55
2123	3.4¢ School Bus	2.25	9.50	....	....	....	2.00	.08	.08
2124	4.9¢ Buckboard	2.25	9.50	....	....	....	2.25	.10	.09
2125	5.5¢ Star Route Truck(1986)	2.15	6.50	....	....	....	3.50	.11	.09
2126	6¢ Tricycle	2.25	9.50	....	....	....	3.75	.12	.10
2127	7.1¢ Tractor (1987)	2.15	6.50	....	....	....	5.25	.15	.11
2128	8.3¢ Ambulance	2.25	9.50	....	....	....	3.95	.17	.14
2129	8.5¢ Tow Truck (1987)	2.15	6.50	....	....	....	5.25	.17	.11
2130	10.1¢ Oil Wagon	2.25	9.50	....	....	....	5.50	.21	.15
2131	11¢ Stutz Bearcat	2.25	9.50	....	....	....	3.50	.22	.12
2132	12¢ Stanley Steamer	2.25	9.50	....	....	....	5.50	.24	.10
2133	12.5¢ Push Cart	2.25	9.50	....	....	....	5.75	.25	.20
2134	14¢ Iceboat	2.25	9.50	....	....	....	3.25	.28	.12
2135	17¢ Dog Sled (1986)	2.15	6.50	....	....	....	5.75	.35	.10
2136	25¢ Bread Wagon (1986)	2.15	6.50	....	....	....	7.50	.50	.10

PRECANCELLED COILS
The following prices are for precancelled, unused, never hinged stamps. Stamps without gum sell for less.

SCOTT NO.	DESCRIPTION	PL # STRIP 3	UN-USED	SCOTT NO.	DESCRIPTION	PL # STRIP 3	UN-USED
2123a	3.4¢ School Bus	2.50	.09	2128a	8.3 Ambulance	4.75	.20
2124a	4.9¢ Buckboard	4.75	.11	2129a	8.5¢ Tow Truck	5.50	.20
2125a	5.5¢ Star Route Truck	4.50	.12	2130a	10.1¢ Oil Wagon	6.75	.24
2126a	6¢ Tricycle	4.75	.13	2132a	12¢ Stanley Steamer	6.25	.27
2127a	7.1¢ Tractor	5.50	.17	2133a	12.5¢ Push Cart	8.75	.28

SCOTT NO.	DESCRIPTION	FIRST DAY COVERS SING.	FIRST DAY COVERS PL.BLK.	MINT SHEET	COPY-RIGHT	ZIP	PLATE BLOCK	UN-USED	USED

Broadbill Decoy
Folk Art USA 22
2138

Mallard Decoy
Folk Art USA 22
2139

2137

Winter Special Olympics
2142

Canvasback Decoy
Folk Art USA 22
2140

Redhead Decoy
Folk Art USA 22
2141

1985 COMMEMORATIVES

SCOTT NO.	DESCRIPTION	FIRST DAY COVERS SING.	FIRST DAY COVERS PL.BLK.	MINT SHEET	COPY-RIGHT	ZIP	PLATE BLOCK	UN-USED	USED
2137	22¢ Mary Bethune	2.15	3.95	40.00(50)	4.00	4.00	4.25	.85	.07
2138-41	Duck Decoys, 4 vars., attd	3.75	4.50	42.50(50)	4.25	4.25	4.50	3.60	2.25
2138	22¢ Broadbill	2.15	....	....	....	....	....	.90	.09
2139	22¢ Mallard	2.15	....	....	....	....	....	.90	.09
2140	22¢ Canvasback	2.15	....	....	....	....	....	.90	.09
2141	22¢ Redhead	2.15	....	....	....	....	....	.90	.09
2142	22¢ Winter Special Olympics	2.15	3.95	32.00(40)	4.00	4.00	4.25	.85	.07

SCOTT NO.	DESCRIPTION	FIRST DAY COVERS SING.	PL.BLK.	MINT SHEET	COPY-RIGHT	ZIP	PLATE BLOCK	UN-USED	USED

2143   **2144**   **2145**   **2146**

2143	22¢ "Love"	2.15	3.95	47.50(50)	4.50	4.50	475	1.00	.07
2144	22¢ Rural Electricity	2.15	3.95	40.00(50)	......	......	18.75(20)	.85	.07
2145	22¢ Ameripex '86	2.15	3.95	38.50(48)	4.00	4.00	425	.85	.07
2146	22¢ Abigail Adams	2.15	3.95	40.00(50)	4.00	4.00	425	.85	.07

2147   **2149**   **2150**

| 2147 | 22¢ Frederick Bartholdi | 2.15 | 3.95 | 40.00(50) | 4.00 | 4.00 | 425 | .85 | .07 |

1985 REGULAR ISSUE COILS

			PLATE # STRIP 3				PLATE # STRIP 3		
2149	18¢ G. Washington	2.15	5.75	......	......	......	595	.37	.15
2150	21.1¢ Envelope	2.15	5.75	......	......	......	675	.45	.15

PRECANCELLED COILS (unused with Gum)

| 2149a | 18¢ G. Washington | ...... | ...... | ...... | ...... | ...... | 675 | .40 | ...... |
| 2150a | 21.1¢ Envelopes | ...... | ...... | ...... | ...... | ...... | 795 | .50 | ...... |

2152   **2153**   **2154**

2152	22¢ Korean War Veterans	2.15	3.95	40.00(50)	4.00	4.00	425	.85	.07
2153	22¢ Social Security	2.15	3.95	40.00(50)	4.00	4.00	425	.85	.07
2154	22¢ World War I Veterans	2.15	3.95	40.00(50)	4.00	4.00	425	.85	.07

Quarter horse   Morgan   Saddlebred   Appaloosa

2155   **2156**   **2157**   **2158**

2155-58	American Horses, 4 vars., attd	3.75	4.50	35.00(40)	4.25	4.25	4.50	3.60	2.25
2155	22¢ Quarter Horse	2.15	......	......	......	......	......	.90	.09
2156	22¢ Morgan	2.15	......	......	......	......	......	.90	.09
2157	22¢ Saddlebred	2.15	......	......	......	......	......	.90	.09
2158	22¢ Appaloosa	2.15	......	......	......	......	......	.90	.09

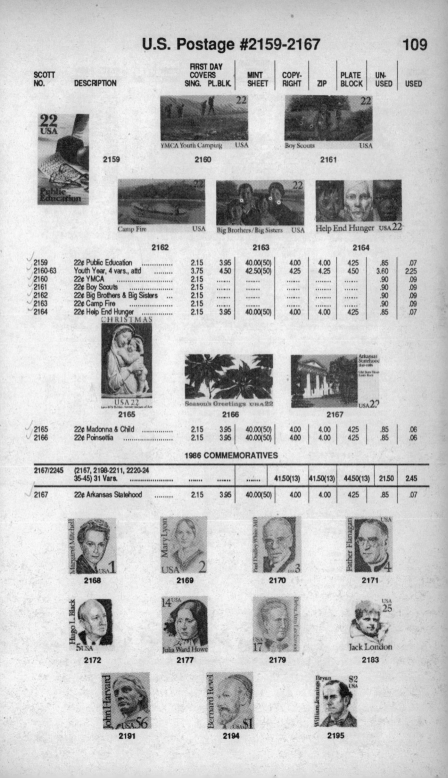

2159

2160 YMCA Youth Camping USA 22

2161 Boy Scouts USA 22

22 USA Public Education

2162 Camp Fire USA 22

2163 Big Brothers/Big Sisters USA 22

2164 Help End Hunger USA 22

Scott No.	Description	Sing.	Pl.Blk.	Mint Sheet	Copyright	Zip	Plate Block	Unused	Used
2159	22¢ Public Education	2.15	3.95	40.00(50)	4.00	4.00	425	.85	.07
2160-63	Youth Year, 4 vars., attd	3.75	4.50	42.50(50)	425	4.25	4.50	3.60	2.25
2160	22¢ YMCA	2.15						.90	.09
2161	22¢ Boy Scouts	2.15						.90	.09
2162	22¢ Big Brothers & Big Sisters	2.15						.90	.09
2163	22¢ Camp Fire	2.15						.90	.09
2164	22¢ Help End Hunger	2.15	3.95	40.00(50)	4.00	4.00	425	.85	.07

CHRISTMAS

2165 USA 22

2166 Season's Greetings USA 22

2167 Arkansas Statehood Old State House Little Rock 1836-1986 USA 22

Scott No.	Description	Sing.	Pl.Blk.	Mint Sheet	Copyright	Zip	Plate Block	Unused	Used
2165	22¢ Madonna & Child	2.15	3.95	40.00(50)	4.00	4.00	425	.85	.06
2166	22¢ Poinsettia	2.15	3.95	40.00(50)	4.00	4.00	425	.85	.06

1986 COMMEMORATIVES

Scott No.	Description	Sing.	Pl.Blk.	Mint Sheet	Copyright	Zip	Plate Block	Unused	Used
2167/2245	(2167, 2198-2211, 2220-24 35-45) 31 Vars.				41.50(13)	41.50(13)	44.50(13)	21.50	2.45
2167	22¢ Arkansas Statehood	2.15	3.95	40.00(50)	4.00	4.00	425	.85	.07

2168 Margaret Mitchell USA 1

2169 Mary Lyon USA 2

2170 Paul Dudley White USA 3

2171 Father Flanagan USA 4

2172 Hugo L. Black 5 USA

2177 14 USA Julia Ward Howe

2179 Bret Harte 17 USA

2183 USA 25 Jack London

2191 John Harvard USA $6

2194 Bernard Revel USA $1

2195 Bryan $2 USA William Jennings

SCOTT NO.	DESCRIPTION	FIRST DAY COVERS SING.	FIRST DAY COVERS PL.BLK.	MINT SHEET	COPY-RIGHT	ZIP	PLATE BLOCK	UN-USED	USED

1986-87 GREAT AMERICANS

2168	1¢ Margaret Mitchell	2.15	3.50	1.95(100)	.30	.30	35	.06	.07
2169	2¢ Mary Lyon (1987)	2.15	3.50	3.95(100)	.30	.30	35	.06	.07
2170	3¢ Dr. Paul D. White	2.15	3.50	5.95(100)	.35	.35	45	.07	.07
2171	4¢ Father Flanagan	2.15	3.50	7.95(100)	.45	.45	50	.08	.07
2172	5¢ Hugo L. Black	2.15	3.50	9.85(100)	.50	.50	65	.10	.07
2177	14¢ Julia Ward Howe (1987)	2.15	3.95	27.50(100)	1.35	1.35	150	.28	.10
2179	17¢ Belva Ann Lockwood	2.15	3.95	33.50(100)	1.75	1.75	225	.35	.08
2183	25¢ Jack London	2.25	4.25	48.75(100)	2.40	2.40	300	.50	.08
2191	56¢ J. Harvard	2.75	5.50	110.00(100)	5.50	5.50	650	1.15	.25
2194	$1 Dr. B. Revell	4.25	11.50	195.00(100)	9.50	9.50	1000	2.00	.30
2195	$2 William Jennings Bryan	7.50	19.50	375.00(100)	17.50	17.50	1950	3.95	.75
2196	$5 Bret Harte (1987)	17.50	47.50	965.00(100)	47.50	47.50	4875	9.95	4.50

2198	2199	2200	2201

1986 COMMEMORATIVES

2201a	Stamp Collecting booklet pane, 4 Vars., att'd.	5.25	......	......	......	......	......	3.35	2.50
2198	22¢ Cover & Handstamp	2.15	......	......	......	......	......	.85	.10
2199	22¢ Collector with Album	2.15	......	......	......	......	......	.85	.10
2200	22¢ No. 836 under magnifier	2.15	......	......	......	......	......	.85	.10
2201	22¢ President sheets	2.15	......	......	......	......	......	.85	.10

2202	2203	2204

2202	22¢ Love	2.15	3.95	21.75(50)	2.25	2.25	250	.45	.07
2203	22¢ Sojourner Truth	2.15	3.95	40.00(50)	4.00	4.00	425	.85	.07
2204	22¢ Texas Republic	2.15	3.95	40.00(50)	4.00	4.00	425	.85	.07

SCOTT NO.	DESCRIPTION	FIRST DAY COVERS SING.	FIRST DAY COVERS PL.BLK.	MINT SHEET	COPY-RIGHT	ZIP	PLATE BLOCK	UN-USED	USED

2205

2206

2207

2211

2208

2209

2210

2209a	22¢ Fish, 5 Vars., att'd	5.95	....	....	....	....	....	3.50	2.95
2205	22¢ Muskellunge	2.15	....	....	....	....	....	.70	.08
2206	22¢ Altantic Cod	2.15	....	....	....	....	....	.70	.08
2207	22¢ Largemouth Bass	2.15	....	....	....	....	....	.70	.08
2208	22¢ Bluefin Tuna	2.15	....	....	....	....	....	.70	.08
2209	22¢ Catfish	2.15	....	....	....	....	....	.70	.08
2210	22¢ Public Hospitals	2.15	3.95	32.50(50)	3.25	3.25	3.50	.70	.07
2211	22¢ Duke Ellington	2.15	3.95	32.50(50)	3.25	3.25	3.50	.70	.07

Presidents of
the United States: I

AMERIPEX 86
International
Stamp Show
Chicago, Illinois
May 22-June 1, 1986

2216

1986 PRESIDENTS MINIATURE SETS
Complete set printed on 4 miniature sheets of 9 stamps each.

2216a	Washington	2218a	Hayes
2216b	Adams	2218b	Garfield
2216c	Jefferson	2218c	Arthur
2216d	Madison	2218d	Cleveland
2216e	Monroe	2218e	B. Harrison
2216f	J.Q. Adams	2218f	McKinley
2216g	Jackson	2218g	T. Roosevelt
2216h	Van Buren	2218h	Taft
2216i	W.H. Harrison	2218i	Wilson
2217a	Tyler	2219a	Harding
2217b	Polk	2219b	Coolidge
2217c	Taylor	2219c	Hoover
2217d	Fillmore	2219d	F.D. Roosevelt
2217e	Pierce	2219e	White House
2217f	Buchanan	2219f	Truman
2217g	Lincoln	2219g	Eisenhower
2217h	A. Johnson	2219h	Kennedy
2217i	Grant	2219i	L.B. Johnson

1986 AMERIPEX '86 MINIATURE SHEETS

2216-19	22¢ 36 Vars., cpl. in 4 min. sht.	45.00	....	....	....	....	....	23.50	23.50
2216a-19i	Set of 36 singles	77.50	....	....	....	....	....	....	25.00
2216	22¢ Wash.-Harrison, 9 Vars.	11.95	....	....	....	....	....	5.95	5.95
2216a-i	22¢, any single	2.25	....	....	....	....	....	.80	.80
2217	22¢ Tyler-Grant, 9 Vars.	11.95	....	....	....	....	....	5.95	5.95
2217a-i	22¢, any single	2.25	....	....	....	....	....	.80	.80
2218	22¢ Hayes-Wilson, 9 Vars.	11.95	....	....	....	....	....	5.95	5.95
2218a-i	22¢, any single	2.25	....	....	....	....	....	.80	.80
2219	22¢ Harding-Johnson, 9 Vars.	11.95	....	....	....	....	....	5.95	5.95
2219a-i	22¢, any single	2.25	....	....	....	....	....	.80	.80

SCOTT NO.	DESCRIPTION	FIRST DAY COVERS SING.	PL.BLK.	MINT SHEET	COPY-RIGHT	ZIP	PLATE BLOCK	UN-USED	USED

2220

2221

Liberty 1886-1986

USA 22

2224

2222

2223

1986 COMMEMORATIVES

SCOTT NO.	DESCRIPTION	SING.	PL.BLK.	MINT SHEET	COPY-RIGHT	ZIP	PLATE BLOCK	UN-USED	USED
2220-23	Explorers, 4 Vars., att'd	3.75	4.50	32.50(50)	3.25	3.25	3.50	2.80	2.25
2220	22¢ Kane	2.15	......	......	......	......	......	.70	.09
2221	22¢ Greely	2.15	......	......	......	......	......	.70	.09
2222	22¢ Stefansson	2.15	......	......	......	......	......	.70	.09
2223	22¢ Peary, Henson	2.15	......	......	......	......	......	.70	.09
2224	22¢ Statue of Liberty	2.15	3.95	32.50(50)	3.25	3.25	3.50	.70	.07

Omnibus 1880s
1 USA

2225

Locomotive 1870s
2 USA

2226

Stagecoach 1890s
USA 4c

2228

1986-87 TRANSPORTATION COILS-Redrawn
Perf. 10 Vertically

SCOTT NO.	DESCRIPTION	SING.	PL.BLK.	PL # STRIP 3			PL # STRIP 3	UN-USED	USED
2225	1¢ Omnibus	2.15	6.50	......	......	1.85	.06	.06
2226	2¢ Locomotive (1987)	2.15	6.50	......	......	1.75	.06	.06
2228	4¢ Stagecoach	2.15	6.50	......	......	3.50	.08	.07

NOTE: #2225 — "¢" sign eliminated. #1897 has "1¢".
       #2226 — inscribed "2 USA". #1897A inscribed "USA 2¢".
       #2228 — "Stagecoach 1890's" is 17 mm. long.
       #1898A — "Stagecoach 1890's" is 19-1/2 mm. long.

SCOTT NO.	DESCRIPTION	FIRST DAY COVERS SING.	PL.BLK.	MINT SHEET	COPY-RIGHT	ZIP	PLATE BLOCK	UN-USED	USED

| 2235 | 2236 | 2237 | 2238 | 2239 |

2235-38	Navajo Art, 4 vars., attd.	3.75	4.50	32.50(50)	3.25	3.25	3.50	2.80	2.25
2235	22¢ Navajo Art	2.15	....	....	....	....	....	.70	.09
2236	22¢ Navajo Art	2.15	....	....	....	....	....	.70	.09
2237	22¢ Navajo Art	2.15	....	....	....	....	....	.70	.09
2238	22¢ Navajo Art	2.15	....	....	....	....	....	.70	.09
2239	22¢ T.S. Eliot	2.15	3.95	32.50(50)	3.25	3.25	3.50	.70	.07

| 2240 | 2241 | 2242 | 2243 | 2246 |

| 2244 | 2245 | 2247 | 2248 |

2240-43	Woodcarved Figurines, 4 vars., att'd.	3.75	4.50	32.50(50)	3.25	3.25	3.50	2.80	2.25
2240	22¢ Highlander Figure	2.15	....	....	....	....	....	.70	.09
2241	22¢ Ship Figurehead	2.15	....	....	....	....	....	.70	.09
2242	22¢ Nautical Figure	2.15	....	....	....	....	....	.70	.09
2243	22¢ Cigar Store Figure	2.15	....	....	....	....	....	.70	.09
2244	22¢ Madonna	2.15	3.95	65.00(100)	3.25	3.25	3.50	.70	.06
2245	22¢ Village Scene	2.15	3.95	65.00(100)	3.25	3.25	3.50	.70	.06

1987 COMMEMORATIVES

2246	22¢ Michigan Statehood	2.15	3.95	21.50(50)	2.25	2.25	2.50	.45	.07
2247	22¢ Pan American Games	2.15	3.95	21.50(50)	2.25	2.25	2.50	.45	.07
2248	22¢ LOVE	2.15	3.95	42.50(100)	2.25	2.25	2.50	.45	.06

SCOTT NO.	DESCRIPTION	FIRST DAY COVERS SING.	FIRST DAY COVERS PL.BLK.	MINT SHEET	COPY-RIGHT	ZIP	PLATE BLOCK	UN-USED	USED

2249   2250   2251   2259

1987 COMMEMORATIVES (continued)

SCOTT NO.	DESCRIPTION	SING.	PL.BLK.	MINT SHEET	COPY-RIGHT	ZIP	PLATE BLOCK	UN-USED	USED
✓2249	22¢ Jean Baptiste Pointe du Sable	2.15	3.95	21.50(50)	2.25	2.25	2.50	.45	.07
✓2250	22¢ Enrico Caruso	2.15	3.95	21.50(50)	2.25	2.25	2.50	.45	.07
✓2251	22¢ Girl Scouts	2.15	3.95	21.50(50)	2.25	2.25	2.50	.45	.07

1987 TRANSPORTATION COILS — Added Designs

		Plate # Strip 3					Plate # Strip 3		
✓2259	10¢ Canal Boat	2.15	6.50	....	......	......	5.25	.20	.06

2267   2270   2273

2268   2271   2272   2274   2269

1987 SPECIAL OCCASIONS BOOKLET PANE

SCOTT NO.	DESCRIPTION	SING.	PL.BLK.	MINT SHEET	COPY-RIGHT	ZIP	PLATE BLOCK	UN-USED	USED
✓2274a	Special Occasions bklt. Pane of 10, att'd.	6.75	......	......	......	......	......	4.25	......
✓2267	22¢ Congratulations!	2.15	......	......	......	......	......	.45	.07
✓2268	22¢ Get Well!	2.15	......	......	......	......	......	.50	.08
2269	22¢ Thank You!	2.15	......	......	......	......	......	.50	.08
✓2270	22¢ Love You, Dad!	2.15	......	......	......	......	......	.50	.08
2271	22¢ Best Wishes!	2.15	......	......	......	......	......	.50	.08
2272	22¢ Happy Birthday!	2.15	......	......	......	......	......	.45	.07
2273	22¢ Love You, Mother!	2.15	......	......	......	......	......	.50	.08
2274	22¢ Keep in Touch!	2.15	......	......	......	......	......	.50	.08

NOTE: #2274a contains 1 each of #2268-71, 2273-74 and 2 each of #2267 and 2272.

SCOTT NO.	DESCRIPTION	FIRST DAY COVERS SING.	FIRST DAY COVERS PL.BLK.	MINT SHEET	COPY-RIGHT	ZIP	PLATE BLOCK	UN-USED	USED

2275

2276

1987 COMMEMORATIVES (continued)

✓2275	22¢ United Way	2.15	3.95	21.50(50)	2.25	2.25	2.50	.45	.07

1987 REGULAR ISSUE

✓2276	22¢ Flag & Fireworks	2.15	3.95	42.50(100)	2.25	2.25	2.50	.45	.06

2286

2296

1987 AMERICAN WILDLIFE

2286 Barn Swallow
2287 Monarch Butterfly
2288 Bighorn Sheep
2289 Broad-tailed Hummingbird
2290 Cottontail
2291 Osprey
2292 Mountain Lion
2293 Luna Moth
2294 Mule Deer
2295 Gray Squirrel
2296 Armadillo
2297 Eastern Chipmunk
2298 Moose
2299 Black Bear
2300 Tiger Swallowtail
2301 Bobwhite
2302 Ringtail
2303 Red-winged Blackbird
2304 American Lobster
2305 Black-tailed Jack Rabbit
2306 Scarlet Tanager
2307 Woodchuck
2308 Roseate Spoonbill
2309 Bald Eagle
2310 Alaskan Brown Bear

2311 Iiwi
2312 Badger
2313 Pronghorn
2314 River Otter
2315 Ladybug
2316 Beaver
2317 White-tailed Deer
2318 Blue Jay
2319 Pika
2320 Bison
2321 Snowy Egret
2322 Gray Wolf
2323 Mountain Goat
2324 Deer Mouse
2325 Black-tailed Prairie Dog
2326 Box Turtle
2327 Wolverine
2328 American Elk
2329 California Sea Lion
2330 Mockingbird
2331 Raccoon
2332 Bobcat
2333 Black-footed Ferret
2334 Canada Goose
2335 Red Fox

2325

2335

✓2286-2335	22¢, 50 vars., att'd.	85.00	....	21.50(50)	....	....	21.50(50)	21.50	....
	Set of Singles	105.00	....	....	....	....	....	....	18.50
	Singles of above, each	2.25	....	....	....	....	....	.50	.40

| SCOTT NO. | DESCRIPTION | FIRST DAY COVERS SING. PL.BLK. | | MINT SHEET | COPY-RIGHT | ZIP | PLATE BLOCK | UN-USED | USED |

1987 COMMEMORATIVES (continued)

Scott No.	Description	FDC Sing.	FDC Pl.Blk.	Mint Sheet	Copyright	Zip	Plate Block	Unused	Used
....	22¢ Delaware Statehood	2.15	3.95	21.50(50)	225	2.25	250	.45	.07
....	22¢ Morocco	2.15	3.95	21.50(50)	225	2.25	250	.45	.07
....	22¢ William Faulkner	2.15	3.95	21.50(50)	225	2.25	250	.45	.07
....	Lacemaking, 4 vars., att'd.	3.75	4.50	....	225	2.25	250	1.80	1.75
....	22¢ Lace, Ruth Maxwell	2.15	....	....	....	....	....	.45	.09
....	22¢ Lace, Mary McPeek	2.15	....	....	....	....	....	.45	.09
....	22¢ Lace, Leslie K. Saari	2.15	....	....	....	....	....	.45	.09
....	22¢ Lace, Trenna Ruffner	2.15	....	....	....	....	....	.45	.09
....	22¢ Pennsylvania Statehood	2.15	3.95	21.50(50)	225	2.25	250	.45	.07
....	Drafting of Constitution booklet pane, 5 vars., att'd.	4.75	....	....	....	....	....	2.25	....
....	22¢ "The Bicentennial..."	2.15	....	....	....	....	....	.45	.10
....	22¢ "We the people..."	2.15	....	....	....	....	....	.45	.10
....	22¢ "Establish justice..."	2.15	....	....	....	....	....	.45	.10
....	22¢ "And secure..."	2.15	....	....	....	....	....	.45	.10
....	22¢ "Do ordain..."	2.15	....	....	....	....	....	.45	.10
....	22¢ New Jersey Statehood	2.15	3.95	21.50(50)	225	2.25	250	.45	.07
....	22¢ Signing of U.S. Constitution	2.15	3.95	21.50(50)	225	2.25	250	.45	.07
....	22¢ Certified Public Accountants	2.15	3.95	21.50(50)	225	2.25	250	.45	.07

SCOTT NO.	DESCRIPTION	PLATE BLOCK			UNUSED			USED	
		F/NH	F/OG	AVG/OG	F/NH	F/OG	AVG/OG	F	AVG

AIR MAIL STAMPS

C1-C3
Curtiss Jenny Biplane

C4
Airplane Propeller

C5
Badge of Air Service

C6
Airplane

C7-C9
Map of U.S. and Airplanes

1918

SCOTT NO.	DESCRIPTION	F/NH	F/OG	AVG/OG	F/NH	F/OG	AVG/OG	F	AVG
C1-3	6¢-24¢, 3 vars., cpl.	....	....	....	735.00	500.00	290.00	220.00	133.50
C1	6¢ orange	(6)1975.00	1575.00	950.00	160.00	125.00	75.00	57.50	35.00
C2	16¢ green	(6)4275.00	3375.00	2000.00	250.00	195.00	115.00	77.50	46.50
C3	24¢ carmine & blue	(12)4450.00	3500.00	2100.00	240.00	190.00	110.00	97.50	58.75

SCOTT NO.		CENTER LINE BLOCKS			ARROW BLOCKS		
		F/NH	F/OG	A/OG	F/NH	F/OG	A/OG
C1	6¢ orange	750.00	575.00	350.00	675.00	525.00	315.00
C2	16¢ green	1165.00	885.00	550.00	1075.00	825.00	495.00
C3	24¢ carmine & blue	1150.00	900.00	525.00	1025.00	800.00	475.00

SCOTT NO.	DESCRIPTION	PLATE BLOCK			UNUSED			USED	
		F/NH	F/OG	AVG/OG	F/NH	F/OG	AVG/OG	F	AVG

1923

C4-6	8¢-24¢, 3 vars., cpl.	....	....	....	625.00	485.00	295.00	200.00	120.00
C4	8¢ dark green	(6)1025.00	825.00	500.00	97.50	72.50	43.50	42.50	25.00
C5	16¢ dark blue	(6)6250.00	5000.00	3000.00	250.00	200.00	120.00	95.00	57.50
C6	24¢ carmine	(6)7000.00	5750.00	3500.00	300.00	240.00	145.00	75.00	45.00

1926-27

C7-9	10¢-20¢, 3 vars., cpl.	565.00	450.00	275.00	42.50	33.50	19.75	8.50	5.15
C7	10¢ dark blue	(6)125.00	100.00	60.00	7.75	6.25	3.75	.70	.45
C8	15¢ olive brown	(6)137.50	110.00	70.00	9.00	7.25	4.35	4.75	2.85
C9	20¢ yellow green (1927)	(6)325.00	260.00	160.00	27.50	21.75	13.00	3.50	2.10

C10
Lindbergh's Airplane "Spirit of St. Louis"

C11
Beacon and Rocky Mountains

C12, C16, C17, C19
Winged Globe

1927 LINDBERGH TRIBUTE ISSUE

C10	10¢ dark blue	(6)365.00	300.00	160.00	19.75	15.75	9.50	4.25	2.60
C10a	same, b. pane of 3	....	....	....	250.00	190.00	115.00	....	....

1928 BEACON

C11	5¢ carmine & blue	(6)125.00	100.00	65.00	10.00	8.00	5.25	1.00	.65
C11a	same, b. pane of 4	45.00	35.00	23.50	....	....	....	....	....

1930 Flat Plate Printing, Perf. 11

C12	5¢ violet	(6)500.00	425.00	260.00	19.75	15.75	10.50	.65	.45

VERY FINE QUALITY: To determine the Very Fine price, add the difference between the Fine and Average prices to the Fine quality price. For example: if the Fine price is $10.00 and the Average price is $6.00, the Very Fine price would be $14.00. From 1935 to date, add 20% to the Fine price to arrive at the Very Fine price.

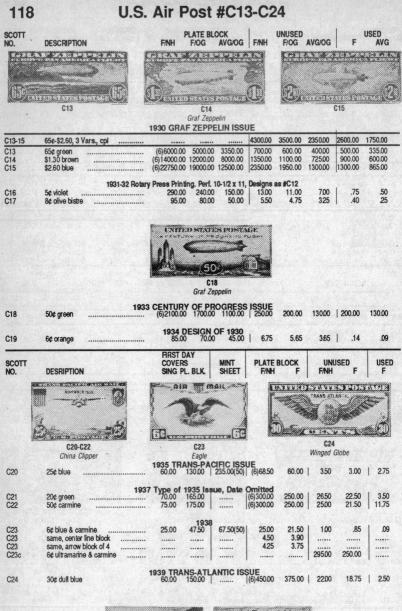

SCOTT NO.	DESCRIPTION	PLATE BLOCK F/NH	F/OG	AVG/OG	UNUSED F/NH	F/OG	AVG/OG	USED F	AVG

C13 — *Graf Zeppelin*
C14 — *Graf Zeppelin*
C15

1930 GRAF ZEPPELIN ISSUE

SCOTT NO.	DESCRIPTION	PLATE BLOCK F/NH	F/OG	AVG/OG	UNUSED F/NH	F/OG	AVG/OG	USED F	AVG
C13-15	65¢-$2.60, 3 Vars., cpl	....	....	....	4300.00	3500.00	2350.00	2600.00	1750.00
C13	65¢ green	(6)6000.00	5000.00	3350.00	700.00	600.00	400.00	500.00	335.00
C14	$1.30 brown	(6)14000.00	12000.00	8000.00	1350.00	1100.00	725.00	900.00	600.00
C15	$2.60 blue	(6)22750.00	19000.00	12500.00	2350.00	1950.00	1300.00	1300.00	865.00

1931-32 Rotary Press Printing. Perf. 10-1/2 x 11, Designs as #C12

| C16 | 5¢ violet | 290.00 | 240.00 | 150.00 | 13.00 | 11.00 | 7.00 | .75 | .50 |
| C17 | 8¢ olive bistre | 95.00 | 80.00 | 50.00 | 5.50 | 4.75 | 3.25 | .40 | .25 |

C18 — *Graf Zeppelin*

1933 CENTURY OF PROGRESS ISSUE

| C18 | 50¢ green | (6)2100.00 | 1700.00 | 1100.00 | 250.00 | 200.00 | 130.00 | 200.00 | 130.00 |

1934 DESIGN OF 1930

| C19 | 6¢ orange | 85.00 | 70.00 | 45.00 | 6.75 | 5.65 | 3.65 | .14 | .09 |

SCOTT NO.	DESRIPTION	FIRST DAY COVERS SING PL. BLK.	MINT SHEET	PLATE BLOCK F/NH	F	UNUSED F/NH	F	USED F

C20-C22 — *China Clipper*
C23 — *Eagle*
C24 — *Winged Globe*

1935 TRANS-PACIFIC ISSUE

| C20 | 25¢ blue | 60.00 130.00 | 235.00(50) | (6)68.50 | 60.00 | 3.50 | 3.00 | 2.75 |

1937 Type of 1935 Issue, Date Omitted

| C21 | 20¢ green | 70.00 165.00 | .... | (6)300.00 | 250.00 | 26.50 | 22.50 | 3.50 |
| C22 | 50¢ carmine | 75.00 175.00 | .... | (6)300.00 | 250.00 | 25.00 | 21.50 | 11.75 |

1938

C23	6¢ blue & carmine	25.00 47.50	67.50(50)	25.00	21.50	1.00	.85	.09
C23	same, center line block	....	....	4.50	3.90	....	....	....
C23	same, arrow block of 4	....	....	4.25	3.75	....	....	....
C23c	6¢ ultramarine & carmine	....	....	....	....	295.00	250.00	....

1939 TRANS-ATLANTIC ISSUE

| C24 | 30¢ dull blue | 60.00 150.00 | .... | (6)450.00 | 375.00 | 22.00 | 18.75 | 2.50 |

C25-C31

C32

NEVER HINGED: From 1893 to 1965, Unused OG or Unused prices are for stamps with original gum that have been hinged. If you desire Never Hinged stamps, order from the NH listings.

SCOTT NO.	DESCRIPTION	FIRST DAY COVERS SING	PL. BLK.	MINT SHEET	PLATE BLOCK F/NH	F	UNUSED F/NH	F	USED F
1941-44 TRANSPORT ISSUE									
C25-31	6¢-50¢, 7 vars., cpl.	....	....	....	310.00	277.50	50.00	45.75	8.75
C25	6¢ Transport Plane	5.50	8.75	14.50(50)	1.95	1.75	.30	.27	.07
C25a	same, b. pane of 3	15.00	....	....	....	....	8.50	7.75	....
C26	8¢ Transport Plane	5.50	8.75	18.75(50)	3.75	3.35	.40	.35	.07
C27	10¢ Transport Plane	6.50	15.00	170.00(50)	25.00	22.50	3.35	3.00	.20
C28	15¢ Transport Plane	8.00	17.50	300.00(50)	35.00	31.50	6.50	6.00	.45
C29	20¢ Transport Plane	9.75	22.50	265.00(50)	30.00	27.00	5.50	5.00	.45
C30	30¢ Transport Plane	16.50	35.00	300.00(50)	35.00	31.50	6.75	6.00	.45
C31	50¢ Transport Plane	40.00	85.00	1450.00(50)	195.00	175.00	30.00	27.50	7.50
1946									
C32	5¢ DC-4 Skymaster	2.00	3.25	10.00(50)	1.10	1.00	.22	.20	.07

C33, C37, C39, C41   C34   C35   C36

SCOTT NO.	DESCRIPTION	FIRST DAY COVERS SING	PL. BLK.	MINT SHEET	PLATE BLOCK F/NH	F	UNUSED F/NH	F	USED F
1947									
C33-36	5¢-25¢, 4 vars., cpl.	....	....	....	17.00	15.50	3.60	3.25	.32
C33	5¢ DC-4 Skymaster	2.00	3.25	20.00(100)	1.10	1.00	.22	.20	.07
C34	10¢ Pan American Bldg.	2.25	4.00	23.75(50)	3.25	3.00	.50	.45	.09
C35	15¢ New York Skyline	2.50	4.35	40.00(50)	3.75	3.35	.85	.75	.08
C36	25¢ Plane over Bridge	2.75	5.00	110.00(50)	10.00	9.00	2.25	2.00	.10

1948
Rotary Press Coil Perf. 10 Horiz.

SCOTT NO.	DESCRIPTION	LINE PR.			LINE PAIR				
C37	5¢ DC-4 Skymaster	2.35	3.85	....	18.00	16.50	2.00	1.80	2.25

C38   C40

SCOTT NO.	DESCRIPTION	PL. BLK.			PLATE BLOCK				
C38	5¢ New York Jubilee	2.00	4.75	33.75(100)	15.75	14.50	.22	.20	.20
1949									
C39	6¢ DC-4 Symaster (as #C33)	2.00	3.75	25.00(100)	1.25	1.15	.28	.25	.06
C39a	same, b. pane of 6	9.75	....	....	....	....	25.00	22.50	....
C40	6¢ Alexandria, Va.	2.00	3.75	12.50(50)	1.25	1.15	.28	.25	.20

Rotary Press Coil Perf. 10 Horiz.

SCOTT NO.	DESCRIPTION	LINE PR.			LINE PAIR				
C41	DC-4 Skymaster (as #C37)	2.00	3.25	....	27.50	25.00	6.85	6.35	.07

NOTE: Unused Air Mail coil pairs can be supplied at two times the single price.

C42   C43   C44

SCOTT NO.	DESRIPTION	FIRST DAY COVERS SING PL. BLK.		MINT SHEET	PLATE BLOCK F/NH	F	UNUSED F/NH	F	USED F
		1949 U.P.U. ISSUES							
C42-44	10¢-25¢, 3 vars., cpl.				23.50	21.50	235	2.10	2.50
C42	10¢ Post Office	2.25	3.75	26.50(50)	3.75	3.40	55	.50	.65
C43	15¢ Globe & Dove	2.75	5.00	33.75(50)	3.50	3.25	70	.65	.85
C44	25¢ Plane & Globe	3.25	6.75	70.00(50)	17.50	15.75	120	1.10	1.20

C45

C46

C47

		1949-58							
C45-51	7 Varieties, cpl.	....	....	....	....	....	2095	19.50	3.40
		1949							
C45	6¢ Wright Bros.	2.00	3.50	17.50(50)	1.60	1.45	38	.35	.18
		1952							
C46	80¢ Hawaii	21.75	57.50	925.00(50)	110.00	100.00	19.75	18.00	2.50
		1953							
C47	6¢ Powered Flight	2.00	3.50	12.50(50)	1.30	1.20	28	.25	.20

C48, C50

C49

C51, C52, C60, C61

		1954							
C48	4¢ Eagle	1.75	3.50	21.75(100)	4.75	4.35	20	.18	.14
		1957							
C49	8¢ Air Force	2.00	3.50	13.50(50)	1.60	1.45	28	.25	.15
		1958							
C50	5¢ Eagle	1.75	3.75	28.50(100)	4.00	3.65	28	.26	.35
C51	7¢ Silhouette of Jet, blue	1.75	3.00	31.50(100)	1.40	1.30	33	.30	.06
C51a	same, b. pane of 6	11.50	....	....	....	....	25.00	22.50	....

Rotary Press Coil Perf. 10 Horiz.

			LINE PR.			LINE PAIR			
C52	7¢ Silhouette of Jet, blue	....	1.75	3.00	....	37.50	35.00	5.00	4.50	.09

C53

C54

C55

C56

		1959 COMMEMORATIVES							
			PL. BLK.		PLATE BLOCK				
C53-56	4 Vars., cpl.	....	....	....	8.65	8.00	150	1.35	.95
C53	7¢ Alaska Statehood	2.00	3.25	15.00(50)	1.50	1.40	33	.30	.14
C54	7¢ Balloon Jupiter	2.00	3.25	18.50(50)	1.85	1.65	40	.36	.14
C55	7¢ Hawaii Statehood	2.00	3.25	15.00(50)	1.50	1.40	33	.30	.14
C56	10¢ Pan-Am Games	2.00	4.00	23.75(50)	4.25	3.95	50	.45	.60

C57,C62   C58   C59   C63

SCOTT NO.	DESCRIPTION	FIRST DAY COVERS SING	PL. BLK.	MINT SHEET	PLATE BLOCK F/NH	F	UNUSED F/NH	F	USED F
1959-1961 REGULAR ISSUES									
C57/63	(C57-60, 62-63) 6 Vars.	....	....	....	38.50	35.00	8.50	7.65	2.15
1959-60									
C57	10¢ Liberty Bell (1960)	2.00	5.75	200.00(50)	20.00	18.50	4.25	4.00	1.75
C58	15¢ Statue of Liberty	2.25	4.50	47.50(50)	4.50	4.00	1.00	.90	.10
C59	25¢ Abraham Lincoln (1960)	2.50	5.25	60.00(50)	5.75	5.25	1.25	1.15	.08
1960. Design of 1958									
C60	7¢ Jet Plane, carmine	1.75	3.50	32.75(100)	1.40	1.30	.33	.30	.06
C60a	same, b. pane of 6	12.75	....	....	....	....	29.50	27.00	....
Rotary Press Coil - Perf. 10 Horiz.									
		LINE PR.			**LINE PAIR**				
C61	7¢ Jet Plane, carmine	1.75	2.95	....	95.00	85.00	12.50	11.50	.45
1961									
		PL. BLK.			**PLATE BLOCK**				
C62	13¢ Liberty Bell	2.15	3.75	48.75(50)	4.75	4.35	1.00	.90	.18
C63	15¢ Statue re-drawn	2.15	3.75	40.00(50)	4.00	3.60	.85	.75	.08

C64,C65   C66   C67   C68   C69

SCOTT NO.	DESCRIPTION	FIRST DAY COVERS SING	PL. BLK.	MINT SHEET	PLATE BLOCK F/NH	F	UNUSED F/NH	F	USED F
1962-64									
C64/69	(C64, 66-69) 5 Vars.	....	....	....	23.00	21.00	3.60	3.25	2.00
1962									
C64	8¢ Plane & Capitol	1.75	3.50	30.00(100)	1.50	1.40	.33	.30	.06
C64b	same, b. pane of 5, Sl. 1	2.50	....	....	....	....	10.75	9.75	....
C64b	b. pane of 5, Sl. II(1963)	....	....	....	....	....	50.00	45.00	....
C64b	b. pane of 5, Sl. III(1964)	....	....	....	....	....	27.50	25.00	....
C64c	b. pane of 5, tagged, Slogan III (1964)	....	....	....	....	....	3.25	3.00	....

SLOGAN I Your Mailman Deserves Your Help...   SLOGAN II Use Zone Numbers...   SLOGAN III Always Use Zip Code...

SCOTT NO.	DESCRIPTION	FIRST DAY COVERS SING	PL. BLK.	MINT SHEET	PLATE BLOCK F/NH	F	UNUSED F/NH	F	USED F
Rotary Press Coil - Perf. 10 Horiz.									
		LINE PR.			**LINE PR.**				
C65	8¢ Plane & Capitol	1.75	3.00	....	6.50	6.00	.70	.65	.08
1963									
		PL. BLK.			**PLATE BLOCK**				
C66	15¢ Montgomery Blair	2.15	5.00	67.50(50)	8.95	8.25	1.50	1.35	1.45
C67	6¢ Bald Eagle	1.75	3.50	36.50(100)	5.75	5.35	.33	.30	.20
C68	8¢ Amelia Earhart	2.25	4.25	23.50(50)	2.95	2.65	.50	.45	.20
1964									
C69	8¢ Dr. Robert H. Goddard	2.50	4.75	52.50(50)	5.00	4.50	1.10	1.00	.20
C69	Zip Block	....	....	....	4.75	4.35	....	....	....

ZIP BLOCKS: are generally corner Blocks of Four that contain a drawing of "Mr. Zip" and the legend "USE ZIP CODE" or a similar design. They were introduced in 1964 and are still in use today.

| | | C70 | C71 | C72,C73 | C74 | | C75,C81 |

SCOTT NO.	DESCRIPTION	FIRST DAY COVERS SING.	PL.BLK.	MINT SHEET	MAIL EARLY	ZIP	PLATE BLOCK	UN-USED	USED
				1967-69					
C70/76	(C70-72, 74-76) 6 Vars.	....	....	....	....	26.50	31.00	5.25	1.00
				1967					
C70	8¢ Alaska Purchase	1.95	3.75	28.75(50)	....	2.75	4.75	.60	.27
C71	20¢ "Columbia" Jays	1.95	4.25	110.00(50)	....	9.75	10.00	2.25	.12
C72	10¢ 50-Stars	1.75	3.50	46.00(100)	6.50	5.25	2.50	.50	.06
C72b	same, b. pane of 8	3.95	....	....	....	....	....	5.75	....
C72c	same, b. pane of5, Sl. IV or V	190.00	....	....	....	....	....	8.95	....

SLOGAN IV - Mail Early in the Day　　　　**SLOGAN V - Use Zip Code.**

1968 Rotary Press Coil - Perf. 10 Vert.

SCOTT NO.	DESCRIPTION	FIRST DAY COVERS SING.	PL.BLK.	MINT SHEET	MAIL EARLY	ZIP	PLATE BLOCK	UN-USED	USED
			LINE PR.				LINE PR.		
C73	10¢ 50-Stars	1.75	3.00	....	....	....	4.50	.75	.08
			PL. BLK.				PL. BLK.		
C74	10¢ Air Mail Anniversary	2.50	4.75	31.75(50)	4.25	3.00	7.50	.60	.20
C75	20¢ "USA" & Plane	2.00	3.75	50.00(50)	7.25	5.00	5.50	1.10	.12
				1969					
C76	10¢ Man on the Moon	6.50	8.75	13.50(32)	3.00	2.10	2.25	.45	.30

| | FIRST MAN ON THE MOON C76 | C77 | C78,C82 | C79,C83 | C80 |

SCOTT NO.	DESCRIPTION	FIRST DAY COVERS SING.	PL.BLK.	MINT SHEET	MAIL EARLY	ZIP	PLATE BLOCK	UN-USED	USED
				1971-73					
C77-81	9¢-21¢, 5 Vars., cpl.	....	....	....	20.00	13.75	14.35	3.00	.70
C77	9¢ Delta Winged Plane	1.75	3.50	33.50(100)	2.30	1.60	1.65	.35	.35
C78	11¢ Silhouette of Plane	1.75	3.50	45.00(100)	3.25	2.25	2.35	.50	.06
C78b	same, precancelled	....	....	....	....	....	....	....	.80
C78a	11¢ b. pane of 4	3.25	....	....	....	....	....	2.25	....
C79	13¢ Letter (1973)	1.75	3.50	50.00(100)	3.50	2.40	2.50	.55	.06
C79b	same, precancelled	....	....	....	....	....	....	....	.60
C79a	13¢ b. pane of 5	3.25	....	....	....	....	....	2.95	....
C80	17¢ Liberty Head	2.25	4.50	47.50(50)	6.50	4.50	4.75	1.00	.17
C81	21¢ "USA" & Plane	2.25	4.50	37.50(50)	5.25	3.60	3.75	.80	.10

Rotary Press Coils Perf. 10 Vertically

SCOTT NO.	DESCRIPTION	FIRST DAY COVERS SING.	PL.BLK.	MINT SHEET	MAIL EARLY	ZIP	PLATE BLOCK	UN-USED	USED
			LINE PR.				LINE PR.		
C82	11¢ Silhouette of Jet	1.75	3.00	....	....	....	1.85	.60	.07
C83	13¢ Letter	1.75	3.00	....	....	....	2.25	.60	.08

SCOTT NO.	DESCRIPTION	FIRST DAY COVERS SING.	PL.BLK.	MINT SHEET	MAIL EARLY	ZIP	PLATE BLOCK	UN-USED	USED

C84   C85   C86   C87   C88   C89   C90

SCOTT NO.	DESCRIPTION	SING.	PL.BLK.	MINT SHEET	MAIL EARLY	ZIP	PLATE BLOCK	UN-USED	USED
	1972-76								
C84-90	7 Vars., cpl.	....	....	....	37.50	24.50	29.50	5.50	1.80
	1972								
C84	11¢ City of Refuge	1.75	3.25	22.50(50)	3.25	2.25	2.35	.50	.18
C85	11¢ Olympics	1.75	3.25	25.00(50)	3.60	2.50	6.25(10)	.55	.18
	1973								
C86	11¢ Electronics	1.75	3.25	22.50(50)	3.25	2.25	2.35	.50	.18
	1974								
C87	18¢ Statue of Liberty	1.75	3.75	47.50(50)	6.35	4.35	4.50	1.00	.95
C88	26¢ Mt. Rushmore	1.95	4.25	50.00(50)	6.50	4.50	4.75	1.10	.14
	1976								
C89	25¢ Plane & Globes	1.95	4.25	45.00(50)	6.50	4.50	4.75	1.00	.17
C90	31¢ Plane, Flag & Globes	1.95	4.50	55.00(50)	7.95	5.50	5.75	1.20	.09

C91   C92   C93   C94   C95   C96

SCOTT NO.	DESCRIPTION	SING.	PL.BLK.	MINT SHEET	MAIL EARLY	ZIP	COPY-RIGHT	UN-USED	USED
	1978-80								
C91-100	10 Vars., cpl.	....	....	....	50.00(7)	50.00(7)	100.00(7)	16.50	6.25
C91-92	2 Vars., att'd.	3.50	5.75	125.00(100)	6.75	6.75	7.00	3.00	2.00
C91	31¢ Wright Bros. & Plane	1.95	....	....	....	....	....	1.50	.20
C92	31¢ Wright Bros. & Shed	1.95	....	....	....	....	....	1.50	.20
	1979								
C93-94	2 Vars., att'd.	3.25	5.50	135.00(100)	7.25	7.25	7.50	3.00	2.40
C93	21¢ Chanute & Plane	1.95	....	....	....	....	....	1.50	.95
C94	21¢ Chanute & 2 Planes	1.95	....	....	....	....	....	1.50	.95
C95-96	2 Vars., att'd.	3.25	6.50	250.00(100)	13.00	13.00	15.00	5.50	3.00
C95	25¢ Post & Plane	1.95	....	....	....	....	....	2.75	1.25
C96	25¢ Plane & Post	1.95	....	....	....	....	....	2.75	1.25

SCOTT NO.	DESCRIPTION	FIRST DAY COVERS SING.	PL.BLK.	MINT SHEET	MAIL EARLY	ZIP	PLATE BLOCK	UN-USED	USED

C97 C98 C99 C100

| C97 | 31¢ High Jumper | 2.50 | 6.50 | 65.00(50) | 6.35 | 6.35 | 1975(12) | 1.40 | 1.00 |

1980

C98	40¢ Philip Mazzei	2.50	5.75	75.00(50)	7.00	7.00	2100(12)	1.60	.20
C99	28¢ Blanche S. Scott	1.95	4.50	57.50(50)	5.75	5.75	1650(12)	1.25	.30
C100	35¢ Glenn Curtiss	1.95	5.00	67.50(50)	6.50	6.50	1875(12)	1.40	.30

C101 C102 C103 C104

1983-85

| C101-16 | 16 Vars., cpl. | .... | .... | .... | 36.50(7) | 36.50(7) | 4250(7) | 19.75 | 7.15 |

1983

C101-104	4 Vars., att'd.	5.50	6.75	52.75(50)	5.25	5.25	5.50	4.50	4.75
C101	28¢ Womens Gymnastics	2.25	....	....	....	....	....	1.10	.70
C102	28¢ Hurdles	2.25	....	....	....	....	....	1.10	.70
C103	28¢ Womens Basketball	2.25	....	....	....	....	....	1.10	.70
C104	28¢ Soccer	2.25	....	....	....	....	....	1.10	.70

C105 C106 C107 C108

C105-08	4 Vars., att'd.	7.50	9.00	75.00(50)	7.25	7.25	750	6.50	6.75
C105	40¢ Shot Put	2.75	....	....	....	....	....	1.60	.40
C106	40¢ Mens Gymnastics	2.75	....	....	....	....	....	1.60	.40
C107	40¢ Womens Swimming	2.75	....	....	....	....	....	1.60	.40
C108	40¢ Weight-Lifting	2.75	....	....	....	....	....	1.60	.40

C109 C110 C111 C112

C109-12	35¢ Olympics, 4 vars., att'd	7.50	9.00	75.00(50)	7.25	7.25	750	6.50	6.75
C109	35¢ Fencing	2.50	....	....	....	....	....	1.60	.40
C110	35¢ Cycling	2.50	....	....	....	....	....	1.60	.40
C111	35¢ Volleyball	2.50	....	....	....	....	....	1.60	.40
C112	35¢ Pole Vault	2.50	....	....	....	....	....	1.60	.40

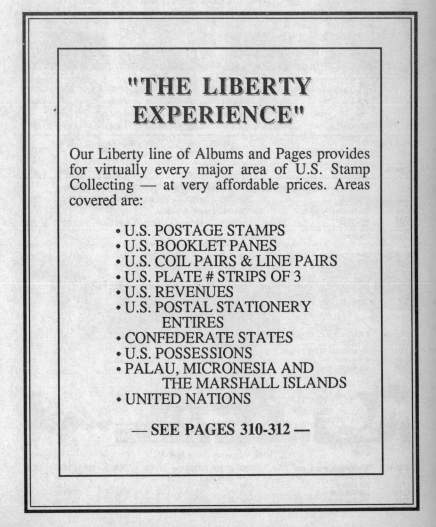

SCOTT NO.	DESCRIPTION	FIRST DAY COVERS SING.	PL.BLK.	MINT SHEET	MAIL EARLY	ZIP	PLATE BLOCK	UN-USED	USED
C113	33¢ Alfred Verville	2.50	5.00	33.75(50)	3.50	3.50	5.25	.70	.30
C114	39¢ Lawrence and Elmer								
	Sperry	2.65	5.65	38.75(50)	4.00	4.00	5.95	.80	.40
C115	44¢ Transpacific	2.80	6.75	42.50(50)	4.50	4.50	6.25	.90	.40
C116	44¢ Junipero Serra	2.80	6.75	67.50(50)	6.75	6.75	6.95	1.40	.40

SCOTT NO.	DESCRIPTION	PLATE BLOCK F/NH	F	AVG	UNUSED F/NH	F	AVG	USED F	AVG

AIR MAIL
SPECIAL DELIVERY
STAMPS

771,CE1,CE2

CE1	16¢ dark blue (1934)	....	(6)45.00	36.50	23.75	1.50	1.25	80	1.75	1.05
CE2	16¢ red & blue (1936)	....	23.75	19.75	13.50	1.15	.90	60	.50	.33
CE2	Same, center line block	....	5.50	4.65	3.15	......	......	......	......	......
CE2	Same, arrow block of 4	....	5.25	4.40	2.90	......	......	......	......	......

SCOTT NO.	DESCRIPTION	UNUSED O.G. F	AVG	UNUSED F	AVG	USED F	AVG

SPECIAL DELIVERY STAMPS

| E1 | E2,E3 | E4,E5 | E6,E8-11 |

1885 Inscribed "Secures Immediate Delivery at Special Delivery Office" Perf. 12

E1	10¢ blue	335.00	200.00	285.00	170.00	67.50	40.00

1888 Inscribed "Secures Immediate Delivery at any Post Office"

E2	10¢ blue	335.00	200.00	285.00	170.00	17.50	10.50

SCOTT NO.	DESCRIPTION	UNUSED NH F	AVG	UNUSED OG F	AVG	USED F	AVG

1893

E3	10¢ orange.........................	285.00	170.00	185.00	110.00	27.50	16.50

1894 Same type as preceding issue, but with line under "Ten Cents" Unwatermarked

E4	10¢ blue	1185.00	685.00	825.00	500.00	32.50	19.50

1895 Double Line Watermark

E5	10¢ blue	225.00	130.00	150.00	90.00	4.75	2.85

| E7 | E12,E13,E15-E18 | E14,E19 |

1902

E6	10¢ ultramarine	....	150.00	90.00	105.00	63.50	4.00	2.40

1908

E7	10¢ green...........................	125.00	70.00	90.00	55.00	67.50	40.00

1911 Single Line Watermark

E8	10¢ ultramarine	....	150.00	90.00	105.00	63.50	7.75	4.50

1914 Perf. 10

E9	10¢ ultramarine	....	300.00	170.00	225.00	135.00	10.75	6.50

1916 Unwatermarked Perf. 10

E10	10¢ pale ultra	....	550.00	300.00	375.00	225.00	38.75	23.00

1917 Perf. 11

E11	10¢ ultramarine	....	30.00	17.00	21.75	13.00	.65	.40
E11	Same, plate block of 6	...	350.00	200.00	250.00	150.00	......	......

SCOTT NO.	DESCRIPTION		PLATE BLOCK			UNUSED			USED	
		F/NH	F/OG	AVG/OG	F/NH	F/OG	AVG/OG		F	AVG

1922-25 Flat Plate Printing Perf. 11

SCOTT NO.	DESCRIPTION									
E12	10¢ deep ultra	(6)665.00	535.00	335.00	75.00	60.00	37.50		.25	.16
E13	15¢ deep orange (1925)	(6)395.00	325.00	210.00	47.50	38.75	25.00		1.65	1.00
E14	20¢ black (1925)	(6)90.00	75.00	50.00	5.75	4.75	3.00		4.25	2.75

SCOTT NO.	DESCRIPTION	FIRST DAY COVERS SING	PL. BLK.	MINT SHEET	PLATE BLOCK F/NH	F	UNUSED F/NH	F	USED F

1927-51 Rotary Press Printing Perf. 11 x 10-1/2

E15-19	10¢-20¢, 5 vars.	....	....	....	105.00	92.50	15.65	13.65	6.95
E15	10¢ gray violet	....	....	75.00(50)	13.50	11.50	1.50	1.25	.08
E16	15¢ orange (1931)	....	....	75.00(50)	8.95	7.50	1.50	1.25	.10
E17	13¢ blue (1944)	12.50	23.50	62.50(50)	8.25	7.25	1.30	1.15	.09
E18	17¢ yellow (1944)	17.50	30.00	395.00(50)	60.00	54.00	8.50	7.50	6.75
E19	20¢ black (1951)	7.00	10.75	170.00(50)	16.50	15.00	3.50	3.15	.10

E20, E21

E22, E23

1954-1957

E20	20¢ blue	3.25	5.50	57.50(50)	5.50	5.00	1.20	1.10	.09
E21	30¢ maroon (1957)	3.25	6.00	60.00(50)	6.00	5.50	1.25	1.15	.07

SCOTT NO.	DESCRIPTION	FIRST DAY COVERS SING.	PL.BLK.	MINT SHEET	MAIL EARLY	ZIP	PLATE BLOCK	UN-USED	USED

1969-1971

E22	45¢ red & blue	3.25	7.25	145.00(50)	19.50	13.50	15.00	2.95	.40
E23	60¢ blue & red (1971)	3.75	9.75	110.00(50)	15.75	10.75	11.50	2.50	.11

REGISTRATION STAMP

CERTIFIED MAIL STAMP

F1

FA1

SCOTT NO.	DESCRIPTION	UNUSED NH F	AVG	UNUSED OG F	AVG	USED F	AVG

1911 Registration

F1	10¢ ultramarine	175.00	100.00	125.00	75.00	9.25	5.50

SCOTT NO.	DESCRIPTION	FIRST DAY COVERS SING PL. BLK.		MINT SHEET	PLATE BLOCK F/NH	F	UNUSED F/NH	F	USED F

1955 Certified Mail

FA1	15¢ rose carmine	3.25	5.75	39.50(50)	11.75	10.75	.75	.65	.65

PLATE BLOCKS: are portions of a sheet of stamps adjacent to the number(s) indicating the printing plate number used to produce that sheet. Flat plate issues are usually collected in plate blocks of six (number opposite middle stamp) while rotary issues are normally corner blocks of four.

SCOTT NO.	DESCRIPTION	UNUSED O.G. F	AVG	UNUSED F	AVG	USED F	AVG

J1–J28

J29–J68

1879 Unwatermarked Perf. 12

SCOTT NO.	DESCRIPTION	UNUSED O.G. F	AVG	UNUSED F	AVG	USED F	AVG
J1	1¢ brown	30.00	18.00	25.00	15.00	8.00	4.75
J2	2¢ brown	220.00	135.00	185.00	110.00	7.50	4.50
J3	3¢ brown	23.75	14.50	20.00	12.00	3.75	2.25
J4	5¢ brown	300.00	180.00	250.00	150.00	28.50	17.00
J5	10¢ brown	400.00	240.00	350.00	210.00	11.50	6.95
J6	30¢ brown	180.00	105.00	150.00	90.00	27.50	16.50
J7	50¢ brown	285.00	165.00	235.00	140.00	47.50	28.50

1884-89

J15	1¢ red brown	38.50	23.50	32.50	19.75	4.15	2.50
J16	2¢ red brown	45.00	26.50	38.75	23.00	4.00	2.40
J17	3¢ red brown	565.00	335.00	475.00	285.00	100.00	60.00
J18	5¢ red brown	270.00	155.00	225.00	135.00	12.50	7.50
J19	10¢ red brown	215.00	127.50	185.00	110.00	7.00	4.25
J20	30¢ red brown	127.50	72.50	105.00	62.50	32.50	19.50
J21	50¢ red brown	1200.00	695.00	1000.00	600.00	150.00	90.00

1891-93

J22	1¢ bright claret	12.50	7.25	10.50	6.25	.75	.45
J23	2¢ bright claret	15.50	8.85	12.75	7.65	.70	.40
J24	3¢ bright claret	31.50	18.50	26.00	16.00	3.65	2.15
J25	5¢ bright claret	32.50	19.00	27.50	16.50	3.65	2.15
J26	10¢ bright claret	77.50	43.75	65.00	38.75	9.75	5.75
J27	30¢ bright claret	265.00	155.00	225.00	135.00	95.00	57.50
J28	50¢ bright claret	300.00	172.50	250.00	150.00	100.00	60.00

SCOTT NO.	DESCRIPTION	UNUSED NH F	AVG	UNUSED OG F	AVG	USED F	AVG

1894-95 Unwatermarked Perf. 12 (†)

J29	1¢ pale vermillion	850.00	500.00	550.00	335.00	100.00	60.00
J30	2¢ dark vermillion	365.00	210.00	230.00	140.00	40.00	23.75
J31	1¢ deep claret	28.75	16.50	18.50	11.00	4.50	2.70
J32	2¢ deep claret	23.50	13.50	15.00	9.00	3.00	1.80
J33	3¢ deep claret	120.00	67.50	75.00	45.00	21.50	12.85
J34	5¢ deep claret	130.00	75.00	82.50	49.50	28.50	17.00
J35	10¢ deep claret	120.00	67.50	77.50	45.00	16.50	10.00
J36	30¢ deep claret	315.00	180.00	200.00	120.00	55.00	33.50
J36b	30¢ rose	275.00	157.50	175.00	105.00	50.00	30.00
J37	50¢ deep claret	800.00	450.00	500.00	300.00	110.00	66.50

1895-97 Double Line Watermark Perf. 12 (†)

J38	1¢ deep claret	7.85	4.50	4.95	2.95	.50	.30
J39	2¢ deep claret	8.25	4.75	5.25	3.15	.30	.18
J40	3¢ deep claret	51.50	29.50	32.50	19.50	1.60	1.00
J41	5¢ deep claret	50.00	28.00	31.50	18.75	1.60	1.00
J42	10¢ deep claret	55.00	30.00	33.75	20.00	2.95	1.75
J43	30¢ deep claret	400.00	225.00	250.00	150.00	27.50	16.50
J44	50¢ deep claret	275.00	160.00	175.00	105.00	27.50	16.50

1910-12 Single Line Watermark Perf. 12

J45	1¢ deep claret	30.00	17.00	20.00	12.00	2.75	1.65
J46	2¢ deep claret	30.00	17.00	20.00	12.00	.27	.16
J47	3¢ deep claret	565.00	315.00	375.00	225.00	16.50	10.00
J48	5¢ deep claret	85.00	50.00	57.50	35.00	2.90	1.75
J49	10¢ deep claret	110.00	62.50	75.00	45.00	10.75	6.50
J50	50¢ deep claret	935.00	525.00	625.00	375.00	90.00	53.50

SCOTT NO.	DESCRIPTION	UNUSED NH F	AVG	UNUSED OG F	AVG	USED F	AVG

1914-15 Single Line Watermark Perf. 10

SCOTT NO.	DESCRIPTION	UNUSED NH F	AVG	UNUSED OG F	AVG	USED F	AVG
J52	1¢ carmine lake	60.00	33.50	39.75	23.75	8.50	5.25
J53	2¢ carmine lake	43.00	24.00	28.50	17.00	.32	.20
J54	3¢ carmine lake	600.00	335.00	400.00	240.00	15.00	9.00
J55	5¢ carmine lake	34.50	19.00	22.75	13.50	2.25	1.35
J56	10¢ carmine lake	56.50	31.50	37.50	22.50	1.65	1.00
J57	30¢ carmine lake	210.00	120.00	140.00	85.00	17.50	10.50
J58	50¢ carmine lake	....	....	....	....	400.00	240.00

1916 Unwatermarked Perf. 10

| J59 | 1¢ rose........................... | 1500.00 | 835.00 | 1000.00 | 600.00 | 165.00 | 100.00 |
| J60 | 2¢ rose........................... | 117.50 | 68.50 | 77.50 | 48.75 | 6.75 | 4.00 |

SCOTT NO.	DESCRIPTION	PLATE BLOCK F/NH	F/OG	AVG/OG	UNUSED F/NH	F/OG	AVG/OG	USED F	AVG

1917-23 Unwatermarked Perf. 11

SCOTT NO.	DESCRIPTION	PLATE BLOCK F/NH	F/OG	AVG/OG	UNUSED F/NH	F/OG	AVG/OG	USED F	AVG
J61	1¢ dull red	(6)60.00	45.00	27.50	5.75	4.25	2.60	.15	.09
J62	2¢ dull red	(6)55.00	40.00	25.00	4.75	3.50	2.10	.13	.08
J63	3¢ dull red	(6)150.00	110.00	67.50	15.00	11.00	6.75	.15	.09
J64	5¢ dull red	(6)150.00	110.00	67.50	15.00	11.00	6.75	.25	.15
J65	10¢ dull red	(6)200.00	150.00	90.00	19.75	14.75	9.50	.25	.15
J66	30¢ dull red	....	....	....	90.00	67.50	40.00	.60	.35
J67	50¢ dull red	....	....	....	110.00	80.00	52.50	.25	.15

1925

| J68 | 1/2¢ dull red .... | (6)16.50 | 12.50 | 7.50 | 1.10 | .85 | .50 | .18 | .11 |

J69-J76, J79-J86

J77, J78, J87

J88-J104

1930-31 Perf. 11

SCOTT NO.	DESCRIPTION	PLATE BLOCK F/NH	F/OG	AVG/OG	UNUSED F/NH	F/OG	AVG/OG	USED F	AVG
J69	1/2¢ carmine	(6)75.00	60.00	37.50	7.50	6.00	3.75	1.10	.70
J70	1¢ carmine	(6)57.50	42.75	26.50	5.50	4.15	2.60	.30	.18
J71	2¢ carmine	(6)90.00	70.00	45.00	8.50	6.75	4.35	.30	.18
J72	3¢ carmine	(6)475.00	375.00	235.00	47.50	37.50	23.50	1.95	1.25
J73	5¢ carmine	(6)435.00	335.00	215.00	45.00	35.00	22.50	2.50	1.60
J74	10¢ carmine	(6)825.00	625.00	400.00	90.00	70.00	45.00	.90	.55
J75	30¢ carmine	....	....	....	250.00	200.00	130.00	1.95	1.25
J76	50¢ carmine	....	....	....	250.00	200.00	130.00	.45	.30
J77	$1 scarlet	(6)500.00	400.00	260.00	57.50	45.00	28.75	.11	.07
J78	$5 scarlet	(6)775.00	600.00	375.00	85.00	67.50	41.50	.27	.17

1931-32 Rotary Press Printing Perf. 11 x 10-1/2

J79-86	1/2¢-50¢, 8 vars., cpl.	....	....	....	42.50	35.50	22.75	.85	.55
J79	1/2¢ carmine	50.00	41.50	26.00	2.25	1.80	1.15	.20	.14
J80	1¢ carmine	4.00	3.25	2.10	.22	.17	.11	.10	.07
J81	2¢ carmine	4.25	3.40	2.25	.30	.25	.16	.09	.06
J82	3¢ carmine	7.00	5.75	3.75	.55	.45	.30	.09	.06
J83	5¢ carmine	8.50	7.00	4.25	.80	.65	.40	.10	.07
J84	10¢ carmine	17.50	14.50	9.00	2.25	1.80	1.15	.09	.06
J85	30¢ carmine	100.00	82.50	51.50	18.75	15.75	10.00	.12	.08
J86	50¢ carmine	110.00	88.50	55.00	19.50	16.50	10.75	.12	.08

1956 Rotary Press Printing Perf. 10-1/2 x 11

| J87 | $1.00 scarlet .... | 475.00 | 425.00 | ...... | 87.50 | 77.50 | ...... | .25 | ...... |

NEVER HINGED: From 1893 to 1965, Unused OG or Unused prices are for stamps with original gum that have been hinged. If you desire Never Hinged stamps, order from the NH listings.

SCOTT NO.	DESCRIPTION	MINT SHEET	PLATE BLOCK F/NH	F	UNUSED F/NH	F	USED F
		1959					
J88-101	1/2¢-$5, 14 vars., cpl.	....	....	....	17.50	15.75	3.00
J88	1/2¢ red & black	600.00(100)	375.00	350.00	2.50	2.25	2.00
J89	1¢ red & black	3.00(100)	.60	.55	.07	.06	.07
J90	2¢ red & black	4.75(100)	.75	.70	.07	.06	.07
J91	3¢ red & black	6.75(100)	.85	.80	.08	.07	.07
J92	4¢ red & black	8.00(100)	1.25	1.15	.09	.08	.07
J93	5¢ red & black	10.00(100)	1.25	1.15	.11	.10	.07
J94	6¢ red & black	12.00(100)	1.40	1.30	.13	.12	.10
J95	7¢ red & black	14.00(100)	1.75	1.60	.15	.14	.12
J96	8¢ red & black	16.00(100)	2.00	1.80	.18	.16	.09
J97	10¢ red & black	20.00(100)	2.25	2.00	.22	.20	.06
J98	30¢ red & black	60.00(100)	5.75	5.25	.65	.60	.08
J99	50¢ red & black	100.00(100)	8.75	8.00	1.10	1.00	.07
J100	$1 red & black	195.00(100)	13.75	12.50	2.15	1.95	.07
J101	$5 red & black	975.00(100)	58.50	55.00	10.50	9.75	.20
		1978-1985					
J102	11¢ red & black	22.00(100)	3.50	....	.23	....	.25
J103	13¢ red & black	26.00(100)	3.75	....	.27	....	.35
J104	17¢ red & black (1985)	34.00(100)	5.75	....	.35	....	.35

SCOTT NO.	DESCRIPTION	UNUSED NH F	AVG	UNUSED OG F	AVG	USED F	AVG

OFFICES IN CHINA

SHANGHAI
2¢
CHINA

SHANGHAI
4Cts.
CHINA

	1919 K1-16: U.S. Postage 498-518 surcharged			1922 K17-18: U.S. Postage 498/528B with local surcharge			
		1919					
K1	2¢ on 1¢ green	32.75	18.75	23.50	14.00	26.50	16.00
K2	4¢ on 2¢ rose	32.75	18.75	23.50	14.00	26.50	16.00
K3	6¢ on 3¢ violet	66.50	37.50	47.50	28.50	57.50	35.00
K4	8¢ on 4¢ brown	77.50	45.00	55.00	33.50	60.00	36.50
K5	10¢ on 5¢ blue	85.00	47.50	60.00	36.50	70.00	42.50
K6	12¢ on 6¢ red orange	100.00	56.50	70.00	42.50	80.00	48.50
K7	14¢ on 7¢ black	110.00	65.00	75.00	45.00	90.00	55.00
K8	16¢ on 8¢ olive	85.00	48.75	60.00	36.50	70.00	42.50
K8a	16¢ on 8¢ olive green ...	77.50	45.00	55.00	33.50	65.00	39.50
K9	18¢ on 9¢ salmon red ...	95.00	53.50	67.50	40.00	72.50	43.75
K10	20¢ on 10¢ orange yellow	80.00	46.50	57.50	35.00	67.50	40.00
K11	24¢ on 12¢ brown carmine	95.00	53.50	67.50	40.00	75.00	45.00
K11a	24¢ on 12¢ claret brown	115.00	66.50	82.50	49.50	95.00	55.00
K12	30¢ on 15¢ gray	105.00	60.00	75.00	45.00	90.00	52.50
K13	40¢ on 20¢ ultramarine	170.00	97.50	120.00	72.50	140.00	85.00
K14	60¢ on 30¢ orange red ...	160.00	91.50	115.00	68.50	140.00	85.00
K15	$1 on 50¢ light violet ...	1050.00	600.00	750.00	450.00	625.00	375.00
K16	$2 on $1 violet brown ...	750.00	425.00	525.00	315.00	500.00	300.00
	1922 LOCAL ISSUES						
K17	2¢ on 1¢ green	140.00	80.00	100.00	60.00	85.00	51.50
K18	4¢ on 2¢ carmine	125.00	70.00	90.00	53.50	87.50	52.50

VERY FINE QUALITY: To determine the Very Fine price, add the difference between the Fine and Average prices to the Fine quality price. For example: if the Fine price is $10.00 and the Average price is $6.00, the Very Fine price would be $14.00. From 1935 to date, add 20% to the Fine price to arrive at the Very Fine price.

SCOTT NO.	DESCRIPTION	UNUSED O.G. F	AVG	UNUSED F	AVG	USED F	AVG

OFFICIAL STAMPS

O1-O9, O94, O95   O10-O14   O15-O24, O96-O103   O25-O34, O106, O107

Except for the Post Office Department, portraits for the various denominations are the same as on the regular issues of 1870-73

1873 Printed by the Continental Bank Note Co.
Thin hard paper

DEPARTMENT OF AGRICULTURE

Scott No.	Description	Unused O.G. F	AVG	Unused F	AVG	Used F	AVG
O1	1¢ yellow	70.00	42.50	57.50	35.00	35.00	21.00
O2	2¢ yellow	47.50	27.50	40.00	24.00	15.00	9.00
O3	3¢ yellow	40.00	24.00	33.50	20.00	4.25	2.50
O4	6¢ yellow	55.00	32.50	45.00	27.50	14.50	9.75
O5	10¢ yellow	120.00	72.50	100.00	60.00	53.50	32.50
O6	12¢ yellow	175.00	105.00	145.00	87.50	80.00	48.75
O7	15¢ yellow	120.00	72.50	100.00	60.00	53.50	32.50
O8	24¢ yellow	145.00	87.50	120.00	72.50	67.50	40.00
O9	30¢ yellow	200.00	120.00	165.00	100.00	95.00	56.50

EXECUTIVE DEPARTMENT

Scott No.	Description	Unused O.G. F	AVG	Unused F	AVG	Used F	AVG
O10	1¢ carmine	300.00	180.00	250.00	150.00	100.00	60.00
O11	2¢ carmine	190.00	120.00	160.00	97.50	77.50	46.50
O12	3¢ carmine	190.00	120.00	160.00	97.50	77.50	46.50
O13	6¢ carmine	335.00	200.00	280.00	170.00	160.00	97.50
O14	10¢ carmine	315.00	190.00	265.00	160.00	160.00	97.50

DEPARTMENT OF THE INTERIOR

Scott No.	Description	Unused O.G. F	AVG	Unused F	AVG	Used F	AVG
O15	1¢ vermillion	19.75	12.00	16.50	10.00	2.85	1.75
O16	2¢ vermillion	15.50	9.25	13.00	7.75	1.90	1.10
O17	3¢ vermillion	26.50	16.00	22.50	13.50	1.90	1.10
O18	6¢ vermillion	19.75	12.00	16.50	10.00	1.90	1.10
O19	10¢ vermillion	15.50	9.25	13.00	7.75	4.25	2.50
O20	12¢ vermillion	24.00	14.50	20.00	12.00	3.00	1.80
O21	15¢ vermillion	47.50	28.75	40.00	24.00	8.75	5.25
O22	24¢ vermillion	37.75	22.75	31.50	19.00	6.35	3.85
O23	30¢ vermillion	50.00	30.00	42.50	25.00	6.75	4.00
O24	90¢ vermillion	110.00	65.00	90.00	55.00	14.50	9.50

DEPARTMENT OF JUSTICE

Scott No.	Description	Unused O.G. F	AVG	Unused F	AVG	Used F	AVG
O25	1¢ purple	46.50	28.00	38.75	23.50	20.00	12.00
O26	2¢ purple	75.00	45.00	62.50	37.50	22.75	13.75
O27	3¢ purple	82.50	50.00	70.00	42.50	8.50	5.15
O28	6¢ purple	68.75	41.75	57.50	35.00	11.50	6.85
O29	10¢ purple	77.50	46.50	65.00	38.75	29.50	17.50
O30	12¢ purple	55.00	32.50	45.00	27.50	14.00	8.50
O31	15¢ purple	125.00	75.00	105.00	62.50	55.00	32.50
O32	24¢ purple	350.00	210.00	300.00	180.00	135.00	80.00
O33	30¢ purple	325.00	195.00	275.00	165.00	95.00	56.50
O34	90¢ purple	475.00	285.00	400.00	240.00	195.00	115.00

OFFICIAL STAMPS: From 1873 to 1879, Congress authorized the use of Official Stamps to prepay postage on government mail. Separate issues were produced for each department so that mailing costs could be assigned to that department's budget. Penalty envelopes replaced Official Stamps on May 1, 1879.

SCOTT NO.	DESCRIPTION	UNUSED O.G. F	AVG	UNUSED F	AVG	USED F	AVG

O35-O45   O47-O56, O108   O57-O67   O68-O71 *Seward*

NAVY DEPARTMENT

Scott No.	Description	Unused OG F	Unused OG AVG	Unused F	Unused AVG	Used F	Used AVG
O35	1¢ ultramarine	38.50	23.00	32.50	19.50	12.50	7.50
O36	2¢ ultramarine	26.00	15.50	21.75	13.00	10.00	6.00
O37	3¢ ultramarine	31.75	19.50	26.50	16.00	3.75	2.25
O38	6¢ ultramarine	26.00	15.50	21.75	13.00	5.75	3.50
O39	7¢ ultramarine	100.00	115.00	160.00	97.50	70.00	42.50
O40	10¢ ultramarine	37.50	24.00	31.50	20.00	13.00	7.75
O41	12¢ ultramarine	51.50	31.50	42.50	26.00	10.00	6.00
O42	15¢ ultramarine	90.00	53.75	75.00	45.00	27.50	16.50
O43	24¢ ultramarine	90.00	53.75	75.00	45.00	35.00	21.00
O44	30¢ ultramarine	75.00	45.00	62.50	37.50	15.00	9.00
O45	90¢ ultramarine	360.00	215.00	300.00	180.00	105.00	63.50

POST OFFICE DEPARTMENT

Scott No.	Description	Unused OG F	Unused OG AVG	Unused F	Unused AVG	Used F	Used AVG
O47	1¢ black	10.50	6.50	8.75	5.25	3.75	2.25
O48	2¢ black	10.25	6.25	8.50	5.15	3.00	1.80
O49	3¢ black	3.50	2.10	3.00	1.80	1.00	.60
O50	6¢ black	10.25	6.25	8.50	5.15	2.15	1.30
O51	10¢ black	45.00	27.00	37.50	22.50	21.75	13.00
O52	12¢ black	22.00	13.00	18.50	11.00	4.50	2.70
O53	15¢ black	26.50	16.00	22.50	13.50	7.50	4.50
O54	24¢ black	32.50	19.50	27.50	16.50	9.75	5.85
O55	30¢ black	32.50	19.50	27.50	16.50	8.75	5.25
O56	90¢ black	53.75	32.50	45.00	27.00	13.00	7.75

DEPARTMENT OF STATE

Scott No.	Description	Unused OG F	Unused OG AVG	Unused F	Unused AVG	Used F	Used AVG
O57	1¢ dark green	45.00	27.00	37.50	22.50	12.00	7.25
O58	2¢ dark green	100.00	60.00	85.00	51.50	31.50	19.00
O59	3¢ bright green	38.50	23.00	32.50	19.50	9.00	5.35
O60	6¢ bright green	37.50	22.50	31.50	19.00	9.00	5.35
O61	7¢ dark green	75.00	45.00	62.50	37.50	19.50	11.50
O62	10¢ dark green	45.00	27.00	37.50	22.5C	14.50	9.75
O63	12¢ dark green	92.50	55.00	77.50	46.50	31.50	19.00
O64	15¢ dark green	68.50	41.75	57.50	35.00	18.50	11.00
O65	24¢ dark green	190.00	115.00	160.00	97.50	90.00	55.00
O66	30¢ dark green	165.00	100.00	140.00	85.00	67.50	40.00
O67	90¢ dark green	385.00	230.00	325.00	195.00	140.00	85.00
O68	$2 green & black	675.00	400.00	565.00	340.00	285.00	170.00
O69	$5 green & black	5350.00	3250.00	4500.00	275.00	2250.00	1350.00
O70	$10 green & black	3250.00	1950.00	2750.00	1650.00	1500.00	900.00
O71	$20 green & black	2850.00	1700.00	2375.00	1450.00	1150.00	695.00

O72-O82, O109-O113   O83-O93, O114-O120

ORIGINAL GUM: Prior to 1893, the Unused price is for stamps either without gum or with partial gum. If you require full original gum, use the Unused OG column. Never Hinged quality is scarce on these issues — please write for specific quotations if NH is required.

SCOTT NO.	DESCRIPTION	UNUSED O.G. F	AVG	UNUSED F	AVG	USED F	AVG
		TREASURY DEPARTMENT					
O72	1¢ brown	15.00	9.00	12.50	7.50	2.25	1.35
O73	2¢ brown	23.00	14.00	19.50	11.75	2.25	1.35
O74	3¢ brown	12.75	7.75	10.75	6.50	1.25	.75
O75	6¢ brown	23.00	14.00	19.50	11.75	1.25	.75
O76	7¢ brown	46.50	26.75	38.75	23.50	12.50	7.50
O77	10¢ brown	46.50	26.75	38.75	23.50	4.50	2.75
O78	12¢ brown	45.00	27.00	37.50	22.50	2.00	1.20
O79	15¢ brown	45.00	27.00	37.50	22.50	4.00	2.40
O80	24¢ brown	210.00	125.00	175.00	105.00	60.00	36.50
O81	30¢ brown	65.00	37.50	52.50	31.50	4.00	2.40
O82	90¢ brown	70.00	42.00	60.00	36.00	3.75	2.25
		WAR DEPARTMENT					
O83	1¢ rose	65.00	38.50	55.00	32.50	3.95	2.35
O84	2¢ rose	62.50	37.50	52.50	31.50	6.00	3.60
O85	3¢ rose	56.50	34.50	47.50	28.50	1.35	.80
O86	6¢ rose	300.00	175.00	250.00	150.00	4.75	2.85
O87	7¢ rose	56.50	34.50	47.50	28.50	35.00	21.50
O88	10¢ rose	18.00	10.75	15.00	9.00	4.00	2.40
O89	12¢ rose	56.50	34.50	47.50	28.50	2.65	1.60
O90	15¢ rose	15.75	9.50	13.00	7.75	1.60	.95
O91	24¢ rose	15.75	9.50	13.00	7.75	2.25	1.35
O92	30¢ rose	18.00	10.75	15.00	9.00	2.00	1.20
O93	90¢ rose	45.00	27.00	38.50	23.00	11.50	7.00

1879 Printed by American Bank Note Co. Soft Porous Paper.

SCOTT NO.	DESCRIPTION	UNUSED O.G. F	AVG	UNUSED F	AVG	USED F	AVG
		DEPARTMENT OF AGRICULTURE					
O94	1¢ yellow	1675.00	1000.00	1400.00	850.00	....	....
O95	3¢ yellow	215.00	130.00	180.00	110.00	37.50	22.50
		DEPARTMENT OF INTERIOR					
O96	1¢ vermillion	155.00	92.50	130.00	77.50	70.00	42.50
O97	2¢ vermillion	3.35	2.10	2.85	1.75	1.00	.60
O98	3¢ vermillion	2.80	1.70	2.35	1.40	.85	.55
O99	6¢ vermillion	3.85	2.30	3.25	1.95	1.25	.75
O100	10¢ vermillion	35.00	21.00	29.50	17.50	19.50	11.50
O101	12¢ vermillion	65.00	37.50	52.50	31.50	37.50	22.50
O102	15¢ vermillion	180.00	105.00	150.00	90.00	85.00	52.50
O103	24¢ vermillion	1375.00	835.00	1150.00	700.00	....	....
		DEPARTMENT OF JUSTICE					
O106	3¢ bluish purple	53.50	32.50	45.00	27.00	19.50	11.75
O107	6¢ bluish purple	125.00	75.00	105.00	62.50	70.00	42.50
		POST OFFICE DEPARTMENT					
O108	3¢ black	10.50	6.00	8.50	5.15	1.70	1.05
		TREASURY DEPARTMENT					
O109	3¢ brown	30.00	17.50	25.00	15.00	3.25	1.95
O110	6¢ brown	62.50	37.50	51.50	31.00	19.50	11.75
O111	10¢ brown	82.50	50.00	70.00	42.50	17.50	10.50
O112	30¢ brown	925.00	550.00	775.00	465.00	150.00	90.00
O113	90¢ brown	925.00	550.00	775.00	465.00	150.00	90.00
		WAR DEPARTMENT					
O114	1¢ rose red	2.80	1.65	2.35	1.40	1.00	.60
O115	2¢ rose red	3.75	2.25	3.15	1.90	1.25	.75
O116	3¢ rose red	3.75	2.25	3.15	1.90	.80	.50
O117	6¢ rose red	3.60	2.10	3.00	1.80	.95	.60
O118	10¢ rose red	23.75	13.00	18.75	11.00	7.25	4.35
O119	12¢ rose red	19.00	11.00	15.75	9.50	2.25	1.35
O120	30¢ rose red	50.00	30.00	42.50	25.00	29.50	17.50

O121-O126   O127-O136   O138

1910-11
Double Line Watermark

SCOTT NO.	DESCRIPTION	UNUSED O.G. F	AVG	UNUSED F	AVG	USED F	AVG
O121	2¢ black	16.50	9.50	11.50	7.00	1.50	.90
O122	50¢ dark green	170.00	95.00	115.00	70.00	37.50	22.50
O123	$1 ultramarine	160.00	87.50	110.00	65.00	11.50	6.85

Single Line Watermark

O124	1¢ dark violet	7.25	4.25	5.25	3.15	1.30	.80
O125	2¢ black	50.00	28.00	35.00	21.00	4.25	2.60
O126	10¢ carmine	15.00	8.50	10.50	6.25	1.30	.80

SCOTT NO.	DESCRIPTION	FIRST DAY COVERS SING	PL. BLK.	MINT SHEET	COPY-RIGHT	PLATE BLOCK	UN-USED	USED
		1983-1985						
O127	1¢ Great Seal	2.00	3.50	3.00(100)	.35	.35	.06	....
O128	4¢ Great Seal	2.00	3.50	9.00(100)	.75	.95	.10	....
O129	13¢ Great Seal	2.00	3.50	28.75(100)	2.00	2.75	.30	....
O129A	14¢ Great Seal (1985)	2.00	....	29.50(100)	2.00	....	.30	....
O130	17¢ Great Seal	2.00	3.95	33.75(100)	2.15	3.00	.35	....
O132	$1.00 Great Seal	6.50	15.00	210.00(100)	11.75	12.50	2.25	....
O133	$5.00 Great Seal	16.50	55.00	975.00(100)	52.50	55.00	10.75	....
		PL. # ST. 3				**PLATE # STRIP 3**		
O135	20¢ Great Seal, coil	2.00	6.50	....	....	15.00	1.10	....
O136	22¢ Seal, coil (1985)	2.00	....	....	....	....	.50	....

1985 Non-Denominated Issues

SCOTT NO.	DESCRIPTION	FIRST DAY COVERS SING	PL. BLK.	MINT SHEET	COPY-RIGHT	PLATE BLOCK	UN-USED	USED
O138	(14¢) Great Seal	2.00	3.95	57.50(100)	2.75	3.25	.60	....
		PL. # ST. 3				**PLATE # STRIP 3**		
O139	(22¢) Great Seal	2.00	7.50	....	....	39.75	2.50	....

SCOTT NO.	DESCRIPTION	UNUSED O.G. F	AVG	UNUSED F	AVG	USED F	AVG

PARCEL POST STAMPS

PARCEL POST DUE STAMPS

SPECIAL HANDLING STAMPS

Q1-Q12 Various Designs   JQ1-JQ5   QE1-QE4

1912-13 Parcel Post — All Printed in Carmine Rose

SCOTT NO.	DESCRIPTION	UNUSED O.G. F	AVG	UNUSED F	AVG	USED F	AVG
Q1	1¢ P.O. Clerk	8.25	4.95	5.50	3.35	1.65	1.00
Q2	2¢ City Carrier	9.00	5.15	6.35	3.85	1.10	.65
Q3	3¢ Railway Clerk	21.00	12.00	15.00	9.00	15.00	9.00
Q4	4¢ Rural Carrier	62.50	35.00	43.50	26.00	3.50	2.10
Q5	5¢ Mail Train	70.00	38.75	47.50	28.50	3.00	1.80
Q6	10¢ Steamship	87.50	50.00	62.50	37.50	3.75	2.25
Q7	15¢ Auto Service	120.00	70.00	87.50	52.50	12.50	7.50
Q8	20¢ Airplane	250.00	140.00	175.00	105.00	25.00	15.00
Q9	25¢ Manufacturing	135.00	77.50	95.00	57.50	7.50	4.50
Q10	50¢ Dairying	450.00	260.00	325.00	195.00	57.50	35.00
Q11	75¢ Harvesting	150.00	87.50	110.00	65.00	47.50	28.75
Q12	$1 Fruit Growing	700.00	400.00	500.00	300.00	42.50	25.00

1912 Parcel Post Due

SCOTT NO.	DESCRIPTION	UNUSED O.G. F	AVG	UNUSED F	AVG	USED F	AVG
JQ1	1¢ dark green	23.50	13.50	16.50	10.00	5.50	3.35
JQ2	2¢ dark green	160.00	97.50	115.00	70.00	25.00	15.00
JQ3	5¢ dark green	24.75	14.00	17.50	10.50	6.25	3.75
JQ4	10¢ dark green	290.00	165.00	210.00	125.00	65.00	40.00
JQ5	25¢ dark green	150.00	90.00	110.00	67.50	6.50	4.00

1925-29 Special Handling

SCOTT NO.	DESCRIPTION	UNUSED O.G. F	AVG	UNUSED F	AVG	USED F	AVG
QE1	10¢ yellow green	3.15	1.95	2.50	1.60	1.95	1.25
QE2	15¢ yellow green	3.75	2.40	3.00	2.00	1.95	1.25
QE3	20¢ yellow green	4.95	3.10	3.95	2.60	2.75	1.75
QE4	25¢ yellow green	46.50	26.50	37.50	22.50	12.50	8.00
QE4a	25¢ deep green	53.50	33.75	42.50	28.50	9.75	6.25

PLATE BLOCKS

SCOTT NO.	UNUSED N.H. F	AVG	UNUSED O.G. F	AVG	SCOTT NO.	UNUSED N.H. F	AVG	UNUSED O.G. F	AVG
O121	(6)350.00	200.00	250.00	150.00	JQ1	(6)1050.00	600.00	750.00	450.00
O124	(6)210.00	120.00	150.00	90.00	JQ3	(6)1350.00	725.00	900.00	550.00
O126	(6)425.00	240.00	300.00	180.00	QE1	(6)40.00	25.00	31.50	21.00
Q1	(6)150.00	90.00	110.00	67.50	QE2	(6)60.00	37.50	47.50	31.75
Q2	(6)195.00	115.00	140.00	85.00	QE3	(6)60.00	37.50	47.50	31.75
Q3	(6)350.00	200.00	250.00	150.00	QE4	(6)465.00	300.00	375.00	250.00
Q4	(6)1500.00	885.00	1100.00	665.00	QE4a	(6)565.00	360.00	450.00	300.00
Q5	(6)1450.00	850.00	1050.00	635.00					

POSTAL NOTE STAMPS

PN1-P18
All values printed in black

SCOTT NO.	DESCRIPTION	PLATE BLOCK F/NH	F/OG	UNUSED F/NH	F/OG	USED F
PN1-18	1¢-90¢, 18 vars., cpl.	550.00	475.00	36.50	32.50	1.50

SCOTT NO.	DESCRIPTION	UNUSED ENTIRE	UNUSED CUT SQ.	USED CUT SQ.

ENVELOPES

SCOTT NO.	DESCRIPTION	UNUSED ENTIRE	UNUSED CUT SQ.	USED CUT SQ.
U44	24¢ green & red on buff	435.00	140.00	125.00
U45	40¢ red & black on buff	475.00	185.00	200.00

U1-U18
Washington

U19-W25, U28, U29
Franklin

U26-U33
Washington

U46-U49　　*Jackson*　　U50-W57

1863-64

1853-55

U1	3¢ red on white, die 1	800.00	160.00	9.75
U2	3¢ red on buff, die 1	550.00	57.50	4.75
U3	3¢ red on white, die 2	2000.00	500.00	27.50
U4	3¢ red on buff, die 2	975.00	165.00	9.25
U5	3¢ red on white, die 3	......	......	325.00
U6	3¢ red on buff, die 3	650.00	110.00	16.50
U7	3¢ red on white, die 4	3500.00	500.00	45.00
U8	3¢ red on buff, die 4	3250.00	900.00	65.00
U9	3¢ red on white, die 5	45.00	10.00	.80
U10	3¢ red on buff, die 5	35.00	6.00	.75
U11	6¢ red on white	165.00	87.50	40.00
U12	6¢ red on buff	150.00	65.00	40.00
U13	6¢ green on white	240.00	135.00	65.00
U14	6¢ green on buff	265.00	130.00	50.00
U15	10¢ green on white, die 1	210.00	90.00	33.50
U16	10¢ green on buff, die 1	140.00	50.00	27.50
U17	10¢ green on white, die 2	210.00	125.00	60.00
U18	10¢ green on buff, die 2	120.00	52.50	27.50

U46	2¢ black on buff, die 1	45.00	23.75	11.00
W47	2¢ black on dark manila, die 1	45.00	26.50	20.00
U48	2¢ black/dark manila, die 1	2200.00	950.00	......
U49	2¢ black on orange, die 2	1500.00	725.00	......
U50	2¢ black on orange, die 2	17.50	7.50	6.50
W51	2¢ black on buff, die 3	165.00	110.00	97.50
U52	2¢ black on buff, die 3	14.75	7.00	5.00
W53	2¢ black on dark manila, die 3	47.50	16.50	15.00
U54	2¢ black on buff, die 4	15.00	9.00	8.00
W55	2¢ black on buff, die 4	95.00	55.00	34.50
U56	2¢ black on orange, die 4	8.50	6.50	5.00
W57	2¢ black on light manila, die 4	14.00	7.50	7.50

1860-61

U19	1¢ blue on buff, die 1	42.50	18.00	8.00
W20	1¢ blue on buff, die 1	70.00	40.00	30.00
W21	1¢ blue on manila, die 1	52.50	25.00	22.50
U23	1¢ blue on orange, die 2	400.00	325.00	325.00
U24	1¢ blue on buff, die 3	240.00	140.00	70.00
U26	3¢ red on white	20.00	15.00	8.50
U27	3¢ red on buff	16.50	11.50	6.50
U28	3¢ + 1¢ red & blue on white	375.00	265.00	175.00
U29	3¢ + 1¢ red & blue on buff	325.00	180.00	150.00
U30	6¢ red on white	2400.00	1650.00	975.00
U31	6¢ red on buff	1900.00	120.00	750.00
U32	10¢ green on white	......	575.00	250.00
U33	10¢ green on buff	1775.00	575.00	145.00

U58-U65　　*Washington*　　U66-873

1864-65

U58	3¢ pink on white	5.25	3.00	.90
U59	3¢ pink on buff	5.25	2.35	.60
U60	3¢ brown on white	57.50	24.50	17.00
U61	3¢ brown on buff	57.50	22.50	15.00
U62	6¢ pink on white	57.50	27.50	18.00
U63	6¢ pink on buff	52.50	20.00	15.00
U64	6¢ purple on white	40.00	22.50	17.50
U65	6¢ purple on buff	45.00	22.50	15.00
U66	9¢ lemon on buff	435.00	210.00	160.00
U67	9¢ orange on buff	145.00	62.50	62.50
U68	12¢ brown on buff	375.00	195.00	165.00
U69	12¢ red brown on buff	90.00	65.00	45.00
U70	18¢ red on buff	155.00	60.00	45.00
U71	24¢ blue on buff	155.00	55.00	45.00
U72	30¢ green on buff	140.00	40.00	40.00
U73	40¢ rose on buff	180.00	50.00	120.00

U34-U39　　*Washington*　　U40-U45

1861

U34	3¢ pink on white	27.50	10.00	2.75
U35	3¢ pink on buff	27.50	10.00	2.75
U36	3¢ pink on blue (letter sheet)	130.00	47.50	25.00
U38	6¢ pink on white	120.00	85.00	75.00
U39	6¢ pink on buff	85.00	50.00	47.50
U40	10¢ yellow green on white	40.00	20.00	19.00
U41	10¢ yellow green on buff	42.50	18.50	16.00
U42	12¢ brown & red on buff	265.00	135.00	100.00
U43	20¢ blue & red on buff	325.00	120.00	120.00

U74-W77, U106-U1211
Franklin

U78-W81, U122-W158,
Jackson

U82-U84, U159-U169
Washington

SCOTT NO.	DESCRIPTION	UNUSED ENTIRE	UNUSED CUT SQ.	USED CUT SQ.

U172-U180
Taylor

U85-U87, U181-U184
Lincoln

U88, U185, U186
Stanton

U89-U92,
U187-U194
Jefferson

U93-U95,
U195-U197
Clay

U96-U98
U198-U200
Webster

U99-U101
U201-U203
Scott

U102-U104, U204-
U210, U336-U341
Hamilton

U105-U107, U211-
U217, U342-U347
Perry

1870-71 REAY ISSUE

SCOTT NO.	DESCRIPTION	UNUSED ENTIRE	UNUSED CUT SQ.	USED CUT SQ.
U74	1¢ blue on white	35.00	20.00	14.75
U74a	1¢ ultramarine on white	65.00	37.50	19.50
U75	1¢ blue on amber	37.50	18.00	13.75
U75a	1¢ ultramarine on amber	50.00	28.50	16.75
U76	1¢ blue on orange	18.75	9.75	8.25
W77	1¢ blue on manila	50.00	23.50	21.00
U78	2¢ brown on white	42.50	19.50	8.50
U79	2¢ brown on amber	23.50	10.00	5.50
U80	2¢ brown on orange	9.00	4.75	4.00
W81	2¢ brown on manila	23.50	11.50	11.50
U82	3¢ green on white	5.25	3.00	.55
U83	3¢ green on amber	7.25	3.25	1.35
U84	3¢ green on cream	12.75	6.50	2.25
U85	6¢ dark red on white	13.50	9.00	9.00
U86	6¢ dark red on amber	19.00	13.50	7.75
U87	6¢ dark red on cream	30.00	16.50	10.00
U88	7¢ vermillion on amber	42.50	21.75	90.00
U89	10¢ black on white	375.00	250.00	185.00
U90	10¢ olive black on amber	375.00	250.00	185.00
U91	10¢ brown on white	62.50	37.50	45.00
U92	10¢ brown on amber	77.50	55.00	42.50
U93	12¢ plum on white	185.00	62.50	45.00
U94	12¢ plum on amber	150.00	75.00	45.00
U95	12¢ plum on cream	250.00	150.00	115.00
U96	15¢ red orange on white	100.00	40.00	57.50
U97	15¢ red orange on amber	350.00	115.00	130.00
U98	15¢ red orange on cream	225.00	140.00	170.00
U99	24¢ purple on white	140.00	82.50	62.50
U100	24¢ purple on amber	285.00	120.00	185.00
U101	24¢ purple on cream	275.00	130.00	185.00
U102	30¢ black on white	180.00	47.50	60.00

SCOTT NO.	DESCRIPTION	UNUSED ENTIRE	UNUSED CUT SQ.	USED CUT SQ.
U103	30¢ black on amber	425.00	135.00	185.00
U104	30¢ black on cream	265.00	130.00	215.00
U105	90¢ carmine on white	165.00	115.00	160.00
U106	90¢ carmine on amber	750.00	210.00	265.00
U107	90¢ carmine on cream	750.00	210.00	265.00

1874-86 PLIMPTON ISSUE

SCOTT NO.	DESCRIPTION	UNUSED ENTIRE	UNUSED CUT SQ.	USED CUT SQ.
U108	1¢ dark blue on white, die 1	75.00	60.00	22.50
U109	1¢ dark blue on amber, die1	110.00	75.00	45.00
U110	1¢ dark blue on cream, die 1	......	475.00	....;
U111	1¢ dark blue on cream, die 1	22.50	10.50	8.00
U111a	1¢ dark blue on orange, die 1	14.00	12.00	6.75
W112	1¢ dark blue on manila, die 1	52.50	28.50	20.00
U113	1¢ light blue on white, die 2	1.10	.60	.30
U113a	1¢ dark blue on white, die 2	10.00	4.95	3.25
U114	1¢ light blue on amber, die 2	3.25	2.00	1.15
U115	1¢ blue on cream, die 2	3.25	2.00	1.30
U115a	1¢ dark blue on cream, die 2	12.00	10.50	3.25
U116	1¢ light blue on orange, die 2	.40	.30	.12
U116a	1¢ dark blue on orange, die 2	4.25	1.00	.60
U117	1¢ blue on blue, die 2	3.25	2.50	2.00
U118	1¢ blue on fawn, die 2	3.50	2.50	2.00
U119	1¢ blue on manila, die 2	3.25	2.50	1.75
W120	1¢ light blue on manila, die 2	.90	.60	.40
W120a	1¢ dark blue on manila, die 2	3.50	2.25	1.50
U121	1¢ blue on amber manila, die 2	5.00	4.00	4.00
U122	2¢ brown on white, die 1	80.00	60.00	22.50
U123	2¢ brown on amber, die 1	50.00	27.50	18.00
U124	2¢ brown on cream, die 1	......	375.00	......
U126	2¢ brown on manila, die 1	60.00	50.00	25.00
W127	2¢ vermillion on manila, die 1	900.00	725.00	215.00
U128	2¢ brown on white, die 2	50.00	27.50	13.50
U129	2¢ brown on amber, die 2	52.50	42.50	15.00
U131	2¢ brown on manila, die 2	9.25	7.25	6.25
U132	2¢ brown on white, die 3	65.00	47.50	15.00
U133	2¢ brown on amber, die 3	180.00	160.00	50.00
U134	2¢ brown on white, die 4	550.00	500.00	85.00
U135	2¢ brown on amber, die 4	300.00	240.00	67.50
U136	2¢ brown on orange, die 4	47.50	25.00	21.50
W137	2¢ brown on manila, die 4	50.00	42.50	25.00
U139	2¢ brown on white, die 4	37.50	32.50	27.50
U140	2¢ brown on amber, die 5	60.00	50.00	40.00
W141	2¢ brown on manila, die 5	25.00	20.00	18.00
U142	2¢ vermillion on white, die 5	4.00	3.25	1.65
U143	2¢ vermillion on amber, die 5	3.25	2.35	1.30
U144	2¢ vermillion on cream, die 5	6.25	4.35	3.65
U146	2¢ vermillion on blue, die 5	125.00	75.00	20.00
U147	2¢ vermillion on fawn die 5	5.25	3.75	3.00
W148	2¢ vermillion on manila, die 5	3.25	2.10	1.40
U149	2¢ vermillion on white, die 6	30.00	25.00	13.50
U150	2¢ vermillion on amber, die 6	25.00	14.00	10.00
U151	2¢ vermillion on blue, die 6	7.00	5.00	4.25
U152	2¢ vermillion on fawn, die 6	6.00	5.00	3.25
U153	2¢ vermillion on white, die 7	50.00	37.50	21.75
U154	2¢ vermillion on amber, die 7	175.00	150.00	50.00
W155	2¢ vermillion on manila, die 7	10.00	7.50	5.75
U156	2¢ vermillion on white, die 8	500.00	350.00	90.00
W158	2¢ vermillion on manila, die 8	95.00	55.00	45.00
U159	3¢ green on white, die 1	18.00	14.00	3.00
U160	3¢ green on amber, die 1	20.00	17.00	5.25
U161	3¢ green on cream, die 1	30.00	24.50	5.75
U163	3¢ green on white, die 2	1.00	.50	.12
U164	3¢ green on amber, die 2	1.50	.50	.25
U165	3¢ green on cream, die 2	6.25	3.50	2.25
U166	3¢ green on blue, die 2	7.00	4.00	2.75
U167	3¢ green on fawn, die 2	5.00	2.25	.95
U168	3¢ green on white, die 3	1700.00	375.00	32.50
U169	3¢ green on amber, die 3	230.00	140.00	75.00
U172	5¢ blue on white, die 1	8.50	5.00	4.50
U173	5¢ blue on amber, die 1	8.50	6.25	5.25
U174	5¢ blue on cream, die 1	80.00	65.00	30.00
U175	5¢ blue on blue, die 1	10.75	5.25	5.00
U176	5¢ blue on fawn, die 1	175.00	75.00	40.00
U177	5¢ blue on white, die 2	7.00	3.50	2.50
U178	5¢ blue on amber, die 2	2.75	3.50	2.50
U179	5¢ blue on blue, die 2	11.00	9.00	5.00
U180	5¢ blue on fawn, die 2	90.00	60.00	30.00
U181	6¢ red on white	6.00	2.35	1.85
U182	6¢ red on amber	10.00	3.25	3.00

SCOTT NO.	DESCRIPTION	UNUSED ENTIRE	UNUSED CUT SQ.	USED CUT SQ.
U183	6¢ red on cream	17.50	12.50	8.00
U184	6¢ red on fawn	17.50	11.75	7.00
U185	7¢ vermillion on white	......	700.00	......
U186	7¢ vermillion on amber	90.00	60.00	45.00
U187	10¢ brown on white, die 1	37.50	14.00	10.00
U188	10¢ brown on amber, die 1	65.00	42.50	25.00
U189	10¢ chocolate on white, die 2	4.75	3.00	2.00
U190	10¢ chocolate on amber, die 2	6.50	4.00	3.50
U191	10¢ brown on buff, die 2	6.00	4.50	4.00
U192	10¢ brown on blue, die 2	6.75	5.25	4.00
U193	10¢ brown on manila, die 2	9.00	5.25	4.50
U194	10¢ brown/amber manila, die 2	9.00	5.00	4.50
U195	12¢ plum on white	150.00	90.00	45.00
U196	12¢ plum on amber	200.00	135.00	110.00
U197	12¢ plum on cream	650.00	135.00	110.00
U198	15¢ orange on white	65.00	24.50	18.50
U199	15¢ orange on amber	130.00	75.00	60.00
U200	15¢ orange on cream	825.00	300.00	185.00
U201	24¢ purple on white	180.00	125.00	67.50
U202	24¢ purple on amber	165.00	125.00	65.00
U203	24¢ purple on cream	650.00	100.00	90.00
U204	30¢ black on white	52.50	40.00	19.00
U205	30¢ black on amber	77.50	40.00	35.00
U206	30¢ black on cream	675.00	285.00	190.00
U207	30¢ black on oriental buff	95.00	65.00	55.00
U208	30¢ black on blue	80.00	70.00	55.00
U209	30¢ black on manila	75.00	50.00	45.00
U210	30¢ black on amber manila	85.00	50.00	45.00
U211	90¢ carmine on white	87.50	75.00	45.00
U212	90¢ carmine on amber	140.00	87.50	140.00
U213	90¢ carmine on cream	1450.00	875.00	......
U214	90¢ carmine on oriental buff	210.00	140.00	165.00
U215	90¢ carmine on blue	180.00	125.00	150.00
U216	90¢ carmine on manila	145.00	80.00	140.00
U217	90¢ carmine on amber manila	165.00	75.00	115.00

U227-U230	U231-U429, U260-W292	U250-U259
	Washington	*Jackson*

1883 OCTOBER

U227	2¢ red on white	3.00	2.25	.80
U228	2¢ red on amber	4.00	2.50	.90
U229	2¢ red on blue	5.75	4.25	2.75
U230	2¢ red on fawn	5.25	3.75	1.35

1883 NOVEMBER
Four Wavy Lines in Oval

U231	2¢ red on white	3.75	1.40	.45
U232	2¢ red on amber	3.50	2.00	.85
U233	2¢ red on blue	6.00	2.75	1.75
U234	2¢ red on fawn	5.00	2.75	1.25
W235	2¢ red on manila	8.50	4.50	2.50

1884 JUNE

U236	2¢ red on white	5.75	2.85	1.35
U237	2¢ red on amber	9.00	6.25	3.00
U238	2¢ red on blue	12.00	8.50	5.00
U239	2¢ red on fawn	9.50	6.25	3.00
U240	2¢ red on white (3-1/2 links)	37.50	30.00	16.50
U241	2¢ red on amber (3-1/2 links)	600.00	500.00	240.00
U243	2¢ red on white (2 links)	50.00	40.00	27.50
U244	2¢ red on amber (2 links)	125.00	85.00	47.50
U245	2¢ red on blue (2 links)	265.00	210.00	80.00
U246	2¢ red on fawn (2 links)	250.00	185.00	80.00
U247	2¢ red on white (Round 0)	800.00	575.00	185.00
U249	2¢ red on fawn (Round 0)	525.00	400.00	185.00

1883-86

U250	4¢ green on white, die 1	3.00	1.50	1.50
U251	4¢ green on amber, die 1	3.50	1.95	1.20
U252	4¢ green on buff, die 1	7.25	3.25	3.00
U253	4¢ green on blue, die 1	7.00	3.50	2.35
U254	4¢ green on manila, die 1	8.25	5.25	3.00
U255	4¢ green/amber manila, die 1	18.50	12.00	6.25
U256	4¢ green on white, die 2	6.75	3.00	1.40
U257	4¢ green on amber, die 2	9.75	6.50	3.00
U258	4¢ green on manila, die 2	7.50	2.85	2.40
U259	4¢ green/amber manila, die 2	7.50	4.00	2.50

1884 MAY

U260	2¢ brown on white	7.50	5.75	1.75
U261	2¢ brown on amber	8.75	6.75	2.00
U262	2¢ brown on blue	9.50	7.50	3.25
U263	2¢ brown on fawn	7.00	5.75	3.00
W264	2¢ brown on manila	11.00	7.75	5.75

1884 JUNE

U265	2¢ brown on white	10.75	8.00	2.25
U266	2¢ brown on amber	43.75	37.50	13.50
U267	2¢ brown on blue	8.00	6.25	3.25
U268	2¢ brown on fawn	8.25	7.00	4.00
W269	2¢ brown on manila	14.50	12.00	8.00
U270	2¢ brown on white (2 links)	75.00	52.50	30.00
U271	2¢ brown on amber (2 links)	185.00	150.00	77.50
U273	2¢ brown on white (Round 0)	120.00	95.00	50.00
U274	2¢ brown on amber (Round 0)	120.00	95.00	50.00
U276	2¢ brown on fawn (Round 0)	795.00	550.00	325.00

U218-U221, U582
Pony Express Rider and Train

U222-U226
Garfield

Die 1. Single thick line under "POSTAGE"
Die 2. Two thin lines under "POSTAGE"

1876 CENTENNIAL ISSUE

U218	3¢ red on white, die 1	70.00	50.00	20.00
U219	3¢ green on white, die 1	60.00	40.00	12.00
U221	3¢ green on white, die 2	80.00	45.00	12.00

1882-86

U222	5¢ brown on white	2.50	2.00	.90
U223	5¢ brown on amber	5.50	2.50	1.40
U224	5¢ brown on oriental buff	75.00	70.00	37.50
U225	5¢ brown on blue	52.50	32.50	19.50
U226	5¢ brown on fawn	215.00	160.00	......

NOTE: For details on die or similar appearing varieties of envelopes, please refer to the Scott Specialized Catalogue.

SCOTT NO.	DESCRIPTION	UNUSED ENTIRE	UNUSED CUT SQ.	USED CUT SQ.
	1884-86			
	Two Wavy Lines in Oval			
U277	2¢ brown on white, die 1	.40	.18	.12
U277a	2¢ brown lake on white, die 1	18.00	15.00	7.00
U278	2¢ brown on amber, die 1	.65	.25	.12
U279	2¢ brown on buff, die 1	2.85	2.00	1.15
U280	2¢ brown on blue, die 1	1.60	1.00	.80
U281	2¢ brown on fawn, die 1	2.50	1.40	1.10
U282	2¢ brown on manila, die 1	7.00	5.75	2.35
W283	2¢ brown on manila, die 1	5.75	3.25	1.65
U284	2¢ brown/amber manila, die 1	5.50	3.95	2.25
U285	2¢ red on white, die 1	575.00	475.00	....
U286	2¢ red on blue, die 1	185.00	160.00	....
W287	2¢ red on manila, die 1	100.00	80.00	....
U288	2¢ brown on white, die 2	275.00	115.00	16.50
U289	2¢ brown on amber, die 2	11.50	6.75	5.75
U290	2¢ brown on blue, die 2	475.00	425.00	110.00
U291	2¢ brown on fawn, die 2	20.00	13.50	12.00
W292	2¢ brown on manila, die 2	17.50	15.00	11.75

U293
Grant

1886

U293	2¢ green on white	....	5.25	4.50
	Entire letter sheet	....	19.50	5.00

U294-U304, U352-W357
Franklin

U305-U323, 358-U370
Washington

U324-U329
Jackson

U330-U335, U377-U378
Grant

1887-94

U294	1¢ blue on white	.50	.30	.07
U295	1¢ dark blue on white	7.75	5.25	1.20

SCOTT NO.	DESCRIPTION	UNUSED ENTIRE	UNUSED CUT SQ.	USED CUT SQ.
U296	1¢ blue on amber	3.00	1.85	.60
U297	1¢ dark blue on amber	35.00	30.00	12.50
U300	1¢ blue on manila	.70	.30	.07
W301	1¢ blue on manila	.50	.18	.07
U302	1¢ dark blue on manila	20.00	16.00	5.25
W303	1¢ dark blue on manila	11.50	9.00	6.25
U304	1¢ blue on amber manila	4.25	2.50	1.60
U305	2¢ green on white, die 1	9.50	4.75	3.50
U306	2¢ green on amber, die 1	17.50	11.00	6.50
U307	2¢ green on buff, die 1	65.00	50.00	22.50
U308	2¢ green on blue, die 1	....	2000.00	450.00
U309	2¢ green on manila, die 1	3500.00	1100.00	275.00
U311	2¢ green on white, die 2	.30	.20	.07
U312	2¢ green on amber, die 2	.40	.27	.07
U313	2¢ green on buff, die 2	.55	.40	.10
U314	2¢ green on blue, die 2	.65	.40	.10
U315	2¢ green on manila, die 2	1.35	.60	.25
W316	2¢ green on manila, die 2	3.00	.90	.60
U317	2¢ green/amber manila, die 2	2.00	.55	.22
U318	2¢ green on white, die 3	90.00	70.00	8.00
U319	2¢ green on amber, die 3	115.00	100.00	12.50
U320	2¢ green on buff, die 3	130.00	120.00	18.00
U321	2¢ green on blue, die 3	140.00	130.00	26.75
U322	2¢ green on manila, die 3	125.00	100.00	42.50
U323	2¢ green/amber manila, die 3	265.00	235.00	62.50
U324	4¢ carmine on white	1.85	.85	.55
U325	4¢ carmine on amber	2.50	1.30	.60
U326	4¢ carmine on oriental buff	5.50	3.25	1.60
U327	4¢ carmine on blue	4.25	3.25	1.50
U328	4¢ carmine on manila	5.50	3.50	2.35
U329	4¢ carmine on amber manila	5.00	2.25	1.40
U330	5¢ blue on white, die 1	4.25	1.20	1.15
U331	5¢ blue on amber, die 1	5.00	1.90	1.15
U332	5¢ dark blue on buff, die 1	7.50	2.75	2.25
U333	5¢ dark blue on blue, die 1	5.75	3.25	2.75
U334	5¢ blue on white, die 2	6.50	4.50	4.00
U335	5¢ blue on amber, die 2	9.00	3.00	2.75
U336	30¢ brown on white	37.50	25.00	22.50
U337	30¢ brown on amber	37.50	23.50	22.50
U338	30¢ red on oriental buff	26.50	21.50	20.00
U339	30¢ red on blue	25.00	20.00	17.50
U340	30¢ red brown on manila	30.00	25.00	13.75
U341	30¢ red brown/amber manila	30.00	21.50	14.00
U342	90¢ purple on white	50.00	35.00	32.50
U343	90¢ purple on amber	60.00	35.00	32.50
U344	90¢ purple on oriental buff	60.00	45.00	37.50
U345	90¢ purple on blue	75.00	45.00	37.50
U346	90¢ purple on manila	75.00	40.00	37.50
U347	90¢ purple on amber manila	85.00	42.50	37.50

U348-U351
Columbus and Liberty, with Shield and Eagle

1893 COLUMBIAN ISSUE

U348	1¢ deep blue on white	2.95	1.50	.55
U349	2¢ violet on white	2.25	1.00	.25
U350	5¢ chocolate on white	17.50	7.00	4.50
U351	10¢ slate brown on white	75.00	40.00	17.50

SCOTT NO.	DESCRIPTION	UNUSED ENTIRE	UNUSED CUT SQ.	USED CUT SQ.
W384	1¢ green on manila	.95	.75	.22
U385	2¢ carmine on white	.45	.25	.07
U386	2¢ carmine on amber	1.95	.90	.12
U387	2¢ carmine on oriental buff	1.65	.95	.27
U388	2¢ carmine on blue	2.10	.85	.45
W389	2¢ carmine on manila	11.75	10.00	4.75
U390	4¢ chocolate on white	14.00	11.50	4.75
U391	4¢ chocolate on amber	14.00	11.50	5.00
W392	4¢ chocolate on manila	14.00	10.75	5.25
U393	5¢ blue on white	12.00	10.00	4.25
U394	5¢ blue on amber	14.50	11.00	5.25

1904 RECUT DIE

SCOTT NO.	DESCRIPTION	UNUSED ENTIRE	UNUSED CUT SQ.	USED CUT SQ.
U395	2¢ carmine on white	.60	.30	.10
U396	2¢ carmine on amber	6.25	5.75	.22
U397	2¢ carmine on oriental buff	4.75	4.00	.50
U398	2¢ carmine on blue	2.65	2.10	.55
W399	2¢ carmine on manila	13.00	9.00	4.75

U371-U373
Lincoln

U374-W376

1899

SCOTT NO.	DESCRIPTION	UNUSED ENTIRE	UNUSED CUT SQ.	USED CUT SQ.
U352	1¢ green on white	.55	.30	.22
U353	1¢ green on amber	4.50	2.85	.90
U354	1¢ green on oriental buff	7.75	6.75	1.65
U355	1¢ green on blue	7.75	6.75	1.65
U356	1¢ green on manila	2.10	.75	.35
W357	1¢ green on manila	2.65	.75	.35
U358	2¢ carmine on white, die 1	5.25	1.65	.70
U359	2¢ carmine on amber, die 1	18.50	13.50	6.75
U360	2¢ carmine on buff, die 1	14.00	12.00	5.75
U361	2¢ carmine on blue, die 1	42.50	37.50	16.50
U362	2¢ carmine on white, die 2	.35	.18	.07
U363	2¢ carmine on amber, die 2	1.25	.50	.07
U364	2¢ carmine on buff, die 2	1.25	.40	.12
U365	2¢ carmine on blue, die 2	2.00	.80	.40
W366	2¢ carmine on manila, die 2	3.25	2.65	.90
U367	2¢ carmine on white, die 3	4.75	2.15	.80
U368	2¢ carmine on amber, die 3	8.00	4.50	2.10
U369	2¢ carmine on buff, die 3	25.00	17.50	4.75
U370	2¢ carmine on blue, die 3	16.50	5.75	4.75
U371	4¢ brown on white, die 1	14.00	12.00	7.25
U372	4¢ brown on amber, die 1	18.00	12.00	7.25
U373	4¢ brown on white, die 2	3300.00	2800.00	275.00
U374	4¢ brown on white, die 3	12.00	6.25	4.00
U375	4¢ brown on amber, die 3	35.00	30.00	8.00
W376	4¢ brown on manila, die 3	10.75	9.25	5.25
U377	5¢ blue on white	8.00	7.00	2.65
U378	5¢ blue on amber	11.75	8.25	5.25

U400-W405, U416, U417
Franklin

U406-W415, U418, U419
Washington

1907-16

SCOTT NO.	DESCRIPTION	UNUSED ENTIRE	UNUSED CUT SQ.	USED CUT SQ.
U400	1¢ green on white	.30	.25	.07
U401	1¢ green on amber	.75	.45	.25
U402	1¢ green on oriental buff	1.00	.65	.25
U403	1¢ green on blue	2.50	2.15	.60
U404	1¢ green on manila	2.50	2.00	.80
W405	1¢ green on manila	.50	.40	.12
U406	2¢ brown red on white	.60	.30	.08
U407	2¢ brown red on amber	4.50	2.85	1.00
U408	2¢ brown red on oriental buff	4.50	3.50	1.10
U409	2¢ brown red on blue	4.00	2.50	.50
W410	2¢ brown red on manila	30.00	22.50	14.00
U411	2¢ carmine on white	.30	.12	.07
U412	2¢ carmine on amber	.35	.10	.08
U413	2¢ carmine on oriental buff	.35	.18	.12
U414	2¢ carmine on blue	.35	.12	.08
W415	2¢ carmine on manila	3.50	1.75	.90
U416	4¢ black on white	4.00	1.50	.50
U417	4¢ black on amber	5.00	2.85	1.85
U418	5¢ blue on white	5.50	3.25	1.60
U419	5¢ blue on amber	10.50	8.75	6.25

U379-W384
Franklin

U385-W389, U395-W399
Washington

U390-W392
Grant

U393, U394
Lincoln

1903

SCOTT NO.	DESCRIPTION	UNUSED ENTIRE	UNUSED CUT SQ.	USED CUT SQ.
U379	1¢ green on white	.70	.50	.08
U380	1¢ green on amber	10.00	7.25	1.75
U381	1¢ green on oriental buff	9.50	7.00	1.75
U382	1¢ green on blue	8.75	7.75	1.40
U383	1¢ green on manila	3.00	1.85	.70

U420-U428,
U440-U442
Franklin

U429-U439, U443-U445,
U481-U485, U529-U531
Washington

1916-32

SCOTT NO.	DESCRIPTION	UNUSED ENTIRE	UNUSED CUT SQ.	USED CUT SQ.
U420	1¢ green on white	.25	.08	.07
U421	1¢ green on amber	.50	.35	.30
U422	1¢ green on oriental buff	1.45	1.00	.90
U423	1¢ green on blue	.55	.35	.10
U424	1¢ green on manila	5.25	4.25	2.00

SCOTT NO.	DESCRIPTION	UNUSED ENTIRE	UNUSED CUT SQ.	USED CUT SQ.
W425	1¢ green on manila	.12	.10	.08
U426	1¢ green on brown (glazed)	30.00	17.00	9.00
W427	1¢ green on brown (glazed)	65.00	55.00	......
U428	1¢ green on brown (unglazed)	725	4.75	4.00
U429	2¢ carmine on white	25	.07	.07
U430	2¢ carmine on amber	.35	.15	.08
U431	2¢ carmine on oriental buff	3.00	.50	25
U432	2¢ carmine on blue	50	.12	.07
W433	2¢ carmine on manila	25	.14	.09
W434	2¢ carmine on brown (glazed)	85.00	70.00	37.50
W435	2¢ carmine/brown (unglazed)	70.00	60.00	35.00
U436	3¢ dark violet on white	30	.12	.07
U436f	3¢ purple on white (1932)	40	.12	.07
U436h	3¢ carmine on white (error)	20.00	15.00	15.00
U437	3¢ dark violet on amber	3.00	1.75	.50
U437a	3¢ purple on amber (1932)	55	.18	.07
U437g	3¢ carmine on amber (error)	250.00	200.00	140.00
U437h	3¢ black on amber (error)	130.00	100.00	......
U438	3¢ dark violet on buff	20.00	17.50	.80
U439	3¢ dark violet on blue	8.50	4.00	65
U439a	3¢ purple on blue (1932)	50	.22	.07
U439g	3¢ carmine on blue (error)	275.00	225.00	195.00
U440	4¢ black on white	2.00	.75	.40
U441	4¢ black on amber	3.25	1.75	65
U442	4¢ black on blue	3.50	1.75	.50
U443	5¢ blue on white	3.25	1.75	.60
U444	5¢ blue on amber	3.50	2.00	.90
U445	5¢ blue on blue	3.50	2.00	.90

1920-21 SURCHARGED

SCOTT NO.	DESCRIPTION	UNUSED ENTIRE	UNUSED CUT SQ.	USED CUT SQ.
U456	2¢ on 2¢ carmine on buff (U431)	160.00	135.00	......
U457	2¢ on 2¢ carmine on blue (U432)	160.00	140.00	......
U458	2¢ on 3¢ violet on white (U436)	.40	.18	.10
U459	2¢ on 3¢ violet on amber (U437)	235	1.50	.50
U460	2¢ on 3¢ violet on buff (U438)	3.00	2.00	60
U461	2¢ on 3¢ violet on blue (U439)	3.00	2.25	55
U462	2¢ on 4¢ chocolate on white (U390)	275.00	250.00	80.00
U463	2¢ on 4¢ chocolate on amber (U391)	275.00	250.00	52.50
U464	2¢ on 5¢ blue on white (U443)	575.00	475.00	......

Type 4 like Type 3, but bars 1-1/2mm. apart

SCOTT NO.	DESCRIPTION	UNUSED ENTIRE	UNUSED CUT SQ.	USED CUT SQ.
U465	2¢ on 1¢ green on white (U420)	700.00	575.00	......
U466A	2¢ on 2¢ carmine on white (U429)	185.00	140.00	......
U467	2¢ on 3¢ green on white, die (U163)	175.00	150.00	......
U468	2¢ on 3¢ violet on white (U436)	.70	.30	.18
U469	2¢ on 3¢ violet on amber (U437)	2.25	1.50	85
U470	2¢ on 3¢ violet on buff (U438)	4.00	3.25	1.60
U471	2¢ on 3¢ violet on blue (U439)	3.50	2.50	.80
U472	2¢ on 4¢ chocolate on white (U390)	16.50	8.00	4.75
U473	2¢ on 4¢ chocolate on amber (U391)	14.00	9.00	4.75
U474	2¢ on 1¢ on 3¢ violet on white (U436)	170.00	140.00	......
U475	2¢ on 1¢ on 3¢ violet on amber (U437)	150.00	135.00	......

Type 1

U446	2¢ on 3¢ violet on white (U436)	9.50	8.00	7.50

Type 2 | **Type 3**

Surcharge on Envelopes of 1916-21 Type 2

U447	2¢ on 3¢ violet on white, rose (U436)	525	4.25	4.25
U448	2¢ on 3¢ violet on white (U436)	1.80	1.50	1.25
U449	2¢ on 3¢ violet on amber(U437)	4.00	3.35	3.25
U450	2¢ on 3¢ violet on buff (U438)	11.75	9.50	8.75
U451	2¢ on 3¢ violet on blue (U439)	8.50	7.50	5.50

Surcharge on Envelopes of 1874-1921 Type 3 Bars 2mm. apart

U454	2¢ on 2¢ carmine on white (U429)	65.00	52.50	......
U455	2¢ on 2¢ carmine on amber (U430)	700.00	650.00	......

Type 5   Type 6   Type 7

Surcharge on Envelope of 1916-21 Type 5

U476	2¢ on 3¢ violet on amber (U437)	85.00	72.50	......

Surcharge on Envelope of 1916-21 Type 6

U477	2¢ on 3¢ violet on white (U436)	85.00	72.50	......
U478	2¢ on 3¢ violet on amber (U437)	160.00	130.00	......

Surcharge on Envelope of 1916-21 Type 7

U479	2¢ on 3¢ violet on white (black) (U436)	325.00	265.00	......

1925

U481	1-1/2¢ brown on white	60	.12	.08
U481b	1-1/2¢ purple on white (error) (1934)	67.50	60.00	......
U482	1-1/2¢ brown on amber	1.50	.85	25

SCOTT NO.	DESCRIPTION		UNUSED ENTIRE	UNUSED CUT SQ.	USED CUT SQ.
U483	1-1/2¢ brown on blue		1.50	1.20	.65
U484	1-1/2¢ brown on manila		8.50	4.25	2.00
W485	1-1/2¢ brown on manila		1.10	.70	.12

Type 8   Type 9

Surcharge on Envelopes of 1887 Type 8

SCOTT NO.	DESCRIPTION		UNUSED ENTIRE	UNUSED CUT SQ.	USED CUT SQ.
U486	1-1/2¢ on 2¢ green on white	(U311)	400.00	350.00	....
U487	1-1/2¢ on 2¢ green on amber	(U312)	625.00	575.00	....

Surcharge on Envelopes of 1899 Type 8

U488	1-1/2¢ on 1¢ green on white	(U352)	550.00	450.00	....
U489	1-1/2¢ on 1¢ green on amber	(U353)	55.00	50.00	35.00

Surcharge on Envelopes of 1907-10 Type 8

U490	1-1/2¢ on 1¢ green on white	(U400)	3.50	2.50	2.25
U491	1-1/2¢ on 1¢ green on amber	(U401)	6.00	3.25	1.50
U492	1-1/2¢ on 1¢ green on oriental buff	(U402)	135.00	110.00	37.50
U493	1-1/2¢ on 1¢ green on blue	(U403)	60.00	50.00	22.50
U494	1-1/2¢ on 1¢ green on manila	(U404)	210.00	185.00	65.00

Surcharge on Envelopes of 1916-21 Type 8

U495	1-1/2¢ on 1¢ green on white	(U420)	.50	.30	.20
U496	1-1/2¢ on 1¢ green on amber	(U421)	13.50	9.50	9.50
U497	1-1/2¢ on 1¢ green on buff	(U422)	4.25	2.75	1.60
U498	1-1/2¢ on 1¢ green on blue	(U423)	1.60	.85	.55
U499	1-1/2¢ on 1¢ green on manila	(U424)	12.50	7.50	4.75
U500	1-1/2¢ on 1¢ green on brown (unglazed)	(U428)	47.50	42.50	18.75
U501	1-1/2¢ on 1¢ green on brown (glazed)	(U426)	45.00	37.50	14.50
U502	1-1/2¢ on 2¢ carmine on white	(U429)	195.00	165.00	....
U503	1-1/2¢ on 2¢ carmine on buff	(U431)	210.00	180.00	....
U504	1-1/2¢ on 2¢ carmine on blue	(U432)	210.00	170.00	....

Surcharge on Envelopes of 1925 Type 8

U505	1-1/2¢ on 1-1/2¢ brown on white	(U481)	375.00	300.00	....
U506	1-1/2¢ on 1-1/2¢ brown on blue	(U483)	60.00	235.00	....

Surcharge on Envelope of 1899 Type 9

U508	1-1/2¢ on 1¢ green on amber	(U353)	50.00	40.00	....

Surcharge on Envelope of 1903 Type 9

U508A	1-1/2¢ on 1¢ green on white	(U379)	1100.00	900.00	....
U509	1-1/2¢ on 1¢ green on amber	(U380)	8.50	3.75	2.25
U509B	1-1/2¢ on 1¢ green on buff	(U381)	42.50	37.50	13.75

Surcharge on Envelopes of 1907-10 Type 9

U510	1-1/2¢ on 1¢ green on white	(U400)	2.25	1.50	.90
U511	1-1/2¢ on 1¢ green on amber	(U401)	105.00	95.00	40.00
U512	1-1/2¢ on 1¢ green on buff	(U402)	4.50	2.75	1.50
U513	1-1/2¢ on 1¢ green on blue	(U403)	4.50	2.75	1.65
U514	1-1/2¢ on 1¢ green on manila	(U404)	22.75	11.00	4.00
U515	1-1/2¢ on 1¢ green on white	(U420)	.50	.30	.18
U516	1-1/2¢ on 1¢ green on amber	(U421)	32.50	25.00	17.50
U517	1-1/2¢ on 1¢ green on buff	(U422)	3.25	2.75	.65
U518	1-1/2¢ on 1¢ green on blue	(U423)	3.25	2.75	.80
U519	1-1/2¢ on 1¢ green on manilia	(U424)	12.50	9.75	5.75
U520	1-1/2¢ on 2¢ carmine on white	(U429)	110.00	80.00	....
U521	1-1/2¢ on 1¢ green on white magenta surcharge	(U420)	3.50	2.75	1.65

U522   U523-U528

U522: Die 1. "E" of 'POSTAGE' has center bar shorter than top bar.

U522a: Die 2. "E" of "POSTAGE" has center and top bars same length.

U525: Die 1. "S" of "POSTAGE" even with "T."
U525a: Die 2. "S" of "POSTAGE" higher than "T."

1926 SESQUICENTENNIAL EXPOSITION

U522	2¢ carmine on white, die 1	3.50	2.25	.60
U522a	2¢ carmine on white, die 2	12.50	8.00	4.50

SCOTT NO.	DESCRIPTION	UNUSED ENTIRE	UNUSED CUT SQ.	USED CUT SQ.
1932 WASHINGTON BICENTENNIAL				
U523	1¢ olive green on white	2.75	2.25	.50
U524	1-1/2¢ dark brown on white	5.75	4.50	1.70
U525	2¢ carmine on white, die 1	1.10	.80	.07
U525a	2¢ carmine on white, die 2	110.00	80.00	11.00
U526	3¢ violet on white	4.50	4.00	.40
U527	4¢ black on white	47.50	35.00	14.00
U528	5¢ dark blue on white	7.50	5.25	3.00
1932 Designs of 1916-32				
U529	6¢ orange on white	10.00	5.75	2.25
U530	6¢ orange on amber	17.50	11.75	5.75
U531	6¢ orange on blue	16.75	11.50	5.75

SCOTT NO.	DESCRIPTION	FIRST DAY COVER	UNUSED ENTIRE	USED CUT SQ.

U532, U536
Franklin

U533, U534
Washington

U535
Washington

1950				
U532	1¢ green	2.50	7.00	1.50
U533	2¢ carmine	2.50	1.65	.10
U534	3¢ dark violet	2.50	.55	.12
1951-58				
U535	1-1/2¢ brown		5.75	2.75
U536	4¢ red violet	2.00	1.25	.08

U537, U538, U552, U556   U539, U540, U545, U553

Surcharges on Envelopes of 1916-32, 1950, 1965, 1971

1958				
U537	2¢ + 2¢(4¢) carmine (U429)		4.50	1.10
U538	2¢ + 2¢(4¢) carmine (U533)		1.25	.22
U539	3¢ + 1¢(4¢) purple, die 1 ....(U436a)		18.50	
U539a	3¢ + 1¢(4¢) purple, die 7 ....(U436e)		16.50	
U539b	3¢ + 1¢(4¢) purple, die 9 ....(U436f)		19.75	
U540	3¢ + 1¢(4¢) dark violet ......(U534)		.75	.10

U541
Franklin

U542
Washington

U544
Lincoln

SCOTT NO.	DESCRIPTION	FIRST DAY COVER	UNUSED ENTIRE	USED CUT SQ.

U543   U546

1960				
U541	1-1/2¢ turquoise	1.75	1.10	.60
U542	2-1/2¢ blue	1.75	1.35	.60
U543	4¢ Pony Express	2.00	.85	.18
1962				
U544	5¢ blue	1.75	1.50	.25
Surcharged on Envelope of 1958				
U545	4¢ + 1¢ red violet (U536)	......	2.25	.50
1964				
U546	5¢ N.Y. World's Fair	1.75	1.10	.25

U547, U548, U548A, U556   U549

U550   U551

1965-69				
U547	1-1/4¢ brown	1.75	1.50	.08
U548	1-4/10¢ brown (1968)	1.75	1.60	.08
U548A	1-6/10¢ orange (1969)	1.75	1.50	.10
U549	4¢ blue	1.75	1.65	.12
U550	5¢ purple	1.75	1.50	.07
U551	6¢ light green (1968)	1.75	1.40	.07
1968				
1958 Type Surcharges on Envelopes of 1965				
U552	4¢ + 2¢(6¢) blue (U549)	......	4.75	.50
U553	5¢ + 1¢(6¢) purple (U550)	......	3.50	1.75

U554   U555

1970				
U554	6¢ Moby Dick	1.75	.75	.08
1971				
U555	6¢ Conf. on Youth	1.75	1.00	.08

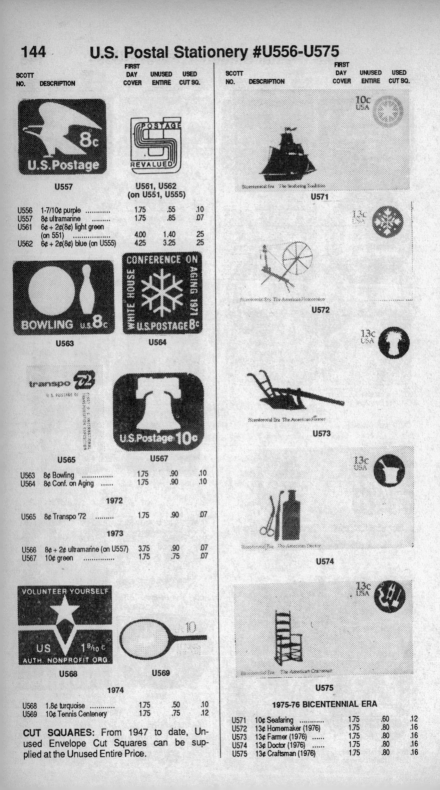

SCOTT NO.	DESCRIPTION	FIRST DAY COVER	UNUSED ENTIRE	USED CUT SQ.

U557

U561, U562 (on U551, U555)

U556	1-7/10¢ purple	1.75	.55	.10
U557	8¢ ultramarine	1.75	.85	.07
U561	6¢ + 2¢(8¢) light green (on 551)	4.00	1.40	25
U562	6¢ + 2¢(8¢) blue (on U555)	425	3.25	25

U563   **U564**

U563	8¢ Bowling	1.75	.90	.10
U564	8¢ Conf. on Aging	1.75	.90	.10

U565   **U567**

1972

U565	8¢ Transpo '72	1.75	.90	.07

1973

U566	8¢ + 2¢ ultramarine (on U557)	3.75	.90	.07
U567	10¢ green	1.75	.75	.07

U568   **U569**

1974

U568	1.8¢ turquoise	1.75	.50	.10
U569	10¢ Tennis Centenery	1.75	.75	.12

CUT SQUARES: From 1947 to date, Unused Envelope Cut Squares can be supplied at the Unused Entire Price.

SCOTT NO.	DESCRIPTION	FIRST DAY COVER	UNUSED ENTIRE	USED CUT SQ.

U571

U572

U573

U574

U575

1975-76 BICENTENNIAL ERA

U571	10¢ Seafaring	1.75	.60	.12
U572	13¢ Homemaker (1976)	1.75	.80	.16
U573	13¢ Farmer (1976)	1.75	.80	.16
U574	13¢ Doctor (1976)	1.75	.80	.16
U575	13¢ Craftsman (1976)	1.75	.80	.16

SCOTT NO.	DESCRIPTION	FIRST DAY COVER	UNUSED ENTIRE	USED CUT SQ.

U576

U577

U578

U579

U580

U581

1975

U576	13¢ orange, brown	1.75	.65	.16

1976-78

U577	2¢ red	1.75	.45	.07
U578	2.1¢ green (1977)	1.75	.45	.07
U579	2.7¢ green (1978)	1.75	.55	.07
U580	15¢ "A" orange (1978)	1.75	.80	.18
U581	15¢ red & white (1978)	1.75	.80	.18

1976

U582	13¢ Bicentennial (design of U218)	1.75	.75	.16

1977

U583	13¢ Golf	1.75	1.00	.16

U584

U585

U584	13¢ multicolored	1.75	.80	.16
U585	13¢ multicolored	1.75	.80	.16

U586, U588

U586

1978

U586	15¢ on 16¢ blue & white	1.75	.80	.18

Auto Racing

U587

U587	15¢ Auto Racing	1.75	.80	.18
U588	15¢ on 13¢ white, brown (U576)	1.75	.80	.18

U589

U590

1979

U589	3.1¢ blue & white	1.75	.35	.07

1980

U590	3.5¢ purple	1.75	.35	.10

U591

U592

U593

U594

1981-82

U591	5.9¢ brown (1982)	1.85	.40	.10
U592	(18¢) "B" purple & white	1.75	.90	22
U593	18¢ white & dark blue ...	1.75	.90	22
U594	(20¢) "C" burnt orange & white	2.00	1.00	.12

SCOTT NO.	DESCRIPTION	FIRST DAY COVER	UNUSED ENTIRE	USED CUT SQ.

U595

U596

1979

| U595 | 15¢ Veterinarians | 1.75 | .80 | .18 |
| U596 | 15¢ Moscow Olympics | 1.75 | 1.25 | .18 |

U597

U598   **U599**

1980

U597	15¢ Bicycle	1.75	.80	.18
U598	15¢ America's Cup	1.75	.80	.18
U599	15¢ Honeybee	1.75	.80	.18

U600

1981

| U600 | 18¢ Blinded Veterans | 1.75 | .90 | 22 |

SCOTT NO.	DESCRIPTION	FIRST DAY COVER	UNUSED ENTIRE	USED CUT SQ.

U601   **U602**

U603   **U604**

| U601 | 20¢ plum & white | 2.00 | .90 | .12 |

1982

| U602 | 20¢ black, blue & red | 2.00 | .90 | .12 |
| U603 | 20¢ Purple Heart | 2.00 | .90 | .12 |

1983

| U604 | 5.2¢ orange & white | 2.00 | .40 | .12 |

U605   **U606**

| U605 | 20¢ Paralyzed Veterans | 2.00 | .90 | .12 |

1984

| U606 | 20¢ Small Business | 2.00 | .90 | .12 |

U607   **U608**

1985

| U607 | (22¢) "D" | 2.15 | .90 | .15 |
| U608 | 22¢ Bison | 2.15 | .60 | .15 |

U609   **U610**

| U609 | 6¢ Old Ironsides | 2.15 | .30 | .12 |

1986

| U610 | 8.5¢ Mayflower | 2.15 | .30 | .15 |

SCOTT NO.	DESCRIPTION	UNUSED ENTIRE	UNUSED CUT SQ.	USED CUT SQ.

UC1

UC2-UC7

Airplane in Circle

Die 1. Vertical rudder not semi-circular, but slopes to the left. Tail projects into "G".
Die 2. Verical rudder is semi-circular. Tail only touches "G"
  Die 2a. "6" is 6-1/2mm. wide.
  Die 2b. "6" is 6mm. wide.
  Die 2c. "6" is 5-1/2mm. wide.
Die 3. Vertical rudder leans forward. "5" closer to "O" than to T" of "POSTAGE" and "E" has short center bar.

1929-44

SCOTT NO.	DESCRIPTION		UNUSED ENTIRE	UNUSED CUT SQ.	USED CUT SQ.
UC1	5¢ blue, die 1		6.50	4.50	1.75
UC2	5¢ blue, die 2		15.00	12.00	3.00
UC3	6¢ orange, die 2a		1.75	1.40	.18
UC3n	6¢, die 2a, no border		2.50	2.00	.50
UC4	6¢, die 2b, with border		62.50	40.00	11.75
UC4n	6¢, die 2b, no border		4.00	3.50	1.35
UC5	6¢, die 2c, no border		1.15	.90	.30
UC6	6¢ orange on white, die 3		2.00	.95	.30
UC6n	6¢, die 3, no border		2.50	1.75	.50
UC7	8¢ olive green		20.00	14.50	2.65

Envelopes
of
1916-32
surcharged

1945

UC8	6¢ on 2¢ carmine on white	(U429)	1.95	1.25	.50
UC9	6¢ on 2¢ carmine on white	(U525)	85.00	60.00	25.00

UC10-13 Surcharged:

REVALUED
5¢
P.O. DEPT.

UC14, UC15, UC18, UC26
DC-4 Skymaster

UC14: Die 1. Small projection below rudder is rounded.
UC15: Die 2. Small projection below rudder is sharp pointed.

1946

UC10	5¢ on 6¢, die 2a	(UC3n)	4.50	3.25	1.15
UC11	5¢ on 6¢, die 2b	(UC4n)	12.50	10.00	4.25

UC12	5¢ on 6¢, die 2c	(UC5)	1.25	.75	.45
UC13	5¢ on 6¢, die 3	(UC6n)	1.15	.95	.40

SCOTT NO.	DESCRIPTION	FIRST DAY COVER	UNUSED ENTIRE	USED CUT SQ.
UC14	5¢ carmine, die 1	3.25	1.25	.10
UC15	5¢ carmine, die 2	......	1.40	.18

UC16
DC-4 Skymaster

UC17
Washington and Franklin, Mail-carrying Vehicles

1947-55

UC16	10¢ red on blue, cut square		5.50	4.95
UC16	Entire "Air Letter" on face, 2-line inscription on back	6.75	8.25	......
UC16a	Entire, "Air Letter" on face, 4-line inscription on back		12.50	......
UC16c	Entire "Air Letter" and "Aerogramme" on face, 4-line inscription on back		65.00	......
UC16d	Entire "Air Letter" and "Aerogramme" on face, 3-line inscription on back		9.00	......

1947 CIPEX COMMEMORATIVE

UC17	5¢ carmine	3.50	.85	.30

1950 Design of 1946

UC18	6¢ carmine	1.75	.70	.10

REVALUED
6¢
P. O. DEPT.
ENVELOPE
of 1946
Surcharged

REVALUED
6¢
P.O. DEPT.
ENVELOPE
of 1946-47
Surcharged

1951 (Shaded Numeral)

UC19	6¢ on 5¢, die 1	(UC14)	1.60	.60
UC20	6¢ on 5¢, die 2	(UC15)	1.60	.60

1952 (Solid Numeral)

UC21	6¢ on 5¢, die 1	(UC14)	29.75	12.50
UC22	6¢ on 5¢, die 2	(UC15)	5.00	1.75
UC23	6¢ on 5¢	(UC17)	700.00	......

UC25

Surcharge on Envelopes of 1934 to 1956

UC27-UC31

1956 FIPEX COMMEMORATIVE

UC25	6¢ carmine	2.00	1.50	.30

1958 Design of 1946

UC26	7¢ blue	2.00	1.25	.25

SCOTT NO.	DESCRIPTION	FIRST DAY COVER	UNUSED ENTIRE	USED CUT SQ.
	1958			
UC27	6¢ & 1¢(7¢) orange, die 2a (UC3n)	......	240.00	......
UC28	6¢ & 1¢(7¢), die 2b (UC4n)	......	70.00	60.00
UC29	6¢ & 1¢(7¢) orange, die 2c (UC5)	......	40.00	37.50
UC30	6¢ & 1¢(7¢) carmine (UC18)	......	1.60	.35
UC31	6¢ & 1¢(7¢) carmine (UC25)	......	2.50	.50

UC32

UC33, UC34
1958-59

	1958			
UC32	10¢ blue & carmine Entire letter sheet, 2-line inscription on back (1959)	....	...... 8.00	1.50 ......
UC32a	Entire letter sheet, 3 line inscription on back	2.50	12.75	......

	1958			
UC33	7¢ blue	2.00	1.35	.15

	1960			
UC34	7¢ red	1.75	1.25	.15

UC35

UC36

	1961			
UC35	11¢ red & blue	4.50	3.50	1.75

	1962			
UC36	8¢ red	1.75	1.25	.10

UC37

UC38, UC39

	1965			
UC37	8¢ red	1.75	.80	.08
UC38	11¢ J.F. Kennedy	2.00	5.25	1.20

	1967			
UC39	13¢ J.F. Kennedy	2.00	5.00	.85

UC40

UC41 (on UC37)

	1968			
UC40	10¢ red	1.75	1.25	.08
UC41	8¢ & 2¢(10¢) red	13.50	1.50	.18

UC42

UC42	13¢ Human Rights Year	2.75	12.75	2.50

UC43
1971

UC43	11¢ red & blue	1.75	.90	.12

UC44

UC44	15¢ gray, red blue	1.75	2.75	1.00
UC44a	Aerogramme added	1.75	2.75	1.00

UC45 (on UC40)
1971 Revalued

UC45	10 & 1¢(11¢) red	8.95	3.25	.25

UC46

UC47
1973

UC46	15¢ Ballooning	1.75	1.25	.50
UC47	13¢ red	1.75	.65	.12

SCOTT NO.	DESCRIPTION	FIRST DAY COVER	UNUSED ENTIRE	USED CUT SQ.

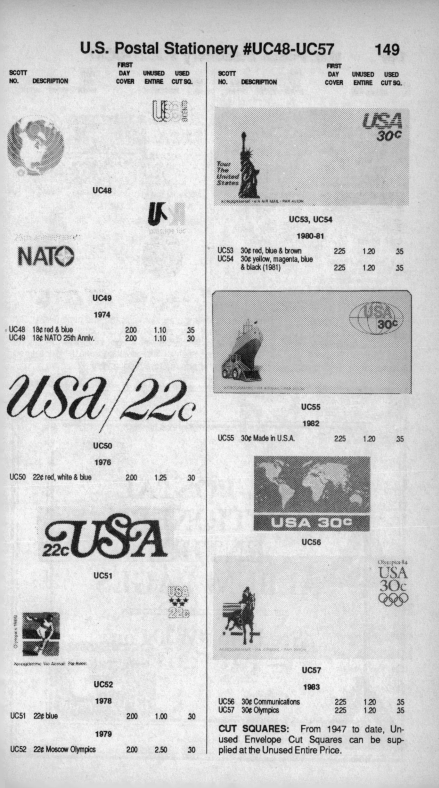

UC48

UC49

1974

SCOTT NO.	DESCRIPTION	FIRST DAY COVER	UNUSED ENTIRE	USED CUT SQ.
UC48	18¢ red & blue	2.00	1.10	35
UC49	18¢ NATO 25th Anniv.	2.00	1.10	30

UC50

1976

| UC50 | 22¢ red, white & blue | 2.00 | 1.25 | 30 |

UC51

UC52

1978

| UC51 | 22¢ blue | 2.00 | 1.00 | 30 |

1979

| UC52 | 22¢ Moscow Olympics | 2.00 | 2.50 | 30 |

UC53, UC54

1980-81

| UC53 | 30¢ red, blue & brown | 2.25 | 1.20 | 35 |
| UC54 | 30¢ yellow, magenta, blue & black (1981) | 2.25 | 1.20 | 35 |

UC55

1982

| UC55 | 30¢ Made in U.S.A. | 2.25 | 1.20 | 35 |

UC56

UC57

1983

| UC56 | 30¢ Communications | 2.25 | 1.20 | 35 |
| UC57 | 30¢ Olympics | 2.25 | 1.20 | 35 |

CUT SQUARES: From 1947 to date, Unused Envelope Cut Squares can be supplied at the Unused Entire Price.

SCOTT NO.	DESCRIPTION	FIRST DAY COVER	UNUSED ENTIRE	USED CUT SQ.

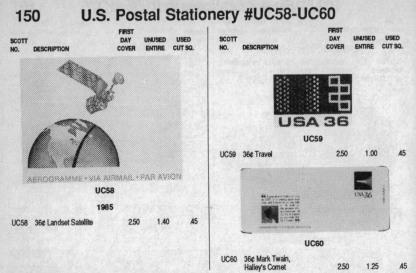

UC58

1985

SCOTT NO.	DESCRIPTION	FIRST DAY COVER	UNUSED ENTIRE	USED CUT SQ.
UC58	36¢ Landset Satellite	2.50	1.40	.45

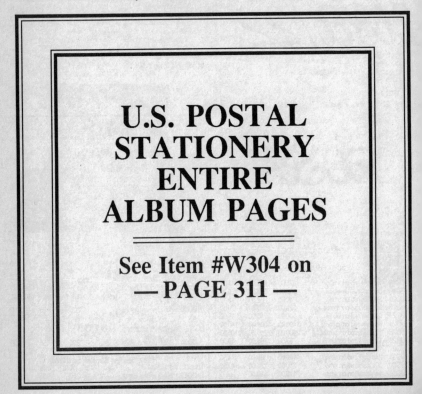

UC59

UC59	36¢ Travel	2.50	1.00	.45

UC60

UC60	36¢ Mark Twain, Halley's Comet	2.50	1.25	.45

FIRST DAY COVERS: First Day Covers are envelopes cancelled on the "First Day of Issue" of the stamp used on the envelope. Usually they also contain a picture (cachet) on the left side designed to go with the theme of the stamp. From 1935 to 1944, prices listed are for cacheted, addressed covers. From 1945 to date, prices are for cacheted, unaddressed covers.

SCOTT
NO.   DESCRIPTION

		UNUSED ENTIRE	UNUSED CUT SQ.	USED CUT SQ.

OFFICIAL ENVELOPES

NOTE: For details on similar appearing varieties please refer to the Scott specialized Catalogue

UO1-UO13   UO14-UO17

POST OFFICE DEPARTMENT

1873 SMALL NUMERALS

UO1	2¢ black on lemon	10.50	7.00	3.75
UO2	3¢ black on lemon	6.00	2.00	1.75
UO4	6¢ black on lemon	12.50	7.00	5.00

1874-79 LARGE NUMERALS

UO5	2¢ black on lemon	5.00	2.40	2.40
UO6	2¢ black on white	47.50	35.00	19.50
UO7	3¢ black on lemon	7.95	1.50	.28
UO8	3¢ black on white	500.00	400.00	425.00
UO9	3¢ black on amber	30.00	27.50	19.50
UO12	6¢ black on lemon	4.50	2.25	1.25
UO13	6¢ black on white	575.00	425.00	......

1877 POSTAL SERVICE

UO14	black on white	2.10	1.40	1.15
UO15	black on amber	90.00	17.50	9.00
UO16	blue on amber	70.00	17.00	11.00
UO17	blue on blue	4.50	2.25	3.00

UO18-UO69
Washington   ### UO70-UO72

Portraits for the various denominations are the same as on the regular issue of 1870-73

WAR DEPARTMENT

1873 REAY ISSUE

UO18	1¢ dark red on white	475.00	365.00	135.00
UO19	2¢ dark red on white	500.00	400.00	130.00
UO20	3¢ dark red on white	40.00	27.50	15.00
UO22	3¢ dark red on cream	325.00	250.00	70.00
UO23	6¢ dark red on white	140.00	110.00	35.00
UO24	6¢ dark red on cream	1400.00	1000.00	180.00
UO25	10¢ dark red on white	2300.00	1200.00	185.00
UO26	12¢ dark red on white	87.50	65.00	18.00
UO27	15¢ dark red on white	85.00	65.00	18.00
UO28	24¢ dark red on white	100.00	85.00	14.50
UO29	30¢ dark red on white	250.00	225.00	47.50
UO30	1¢ vermillion on white	175.00	110.00	......

SCOTT
NO.   DESCRIPTION

		UNUSED ENTIRE	UNUSED CUT SQ.	USED CUT SQ.
WO31	1¢ vermillion on manila	7.00	5.00	2.25
UO32	2¢ vermillion on white	2750.00	130.00	......
WO33	2¢ vermillion on manila	135.00	100.00	......
UO34	3¢ vermillion on white	85.00	40.00	14.50
UO35	3¢ vermillion on amber	150.00	47.50	......
UO36	3¢ vermillion on cream	12.50	4.00	2.00
UO37	6¢ vermillion on white	65.00	47.50	......
UO38	6¢ vermillion on cream	4000.00	185.00	......
UO39	10¢ vermillion on white	250.00	110.00	......
UO40	12¢ vermillion on white	135.00	80.00	......
UO41	15¢ vermillion on white	1400.00	115.00	......
UO42	24¢ vermillion on white	275.00	190.00	......
UO43	30¢ vermillion on white	400.00	275.00	......

1875 PLIMPTON ISSUE

UO44	1¢ red on white	77.50	67.50	50.00
UO45	1¢ red on amber	......	350.00	......
WO46	1¢ red on manila	2.40	.90	.55
UO47	2¢ red on white	57.50	50.00	......
UO48	2¢ red on amber	17.50	14.00	2.90
UO49	2¢ red on orange	30.00	27.50	5.75
WO50	2¢ red on manila	70.00	45.00	27.50
UO51	3¢ red on white	8.00	6.50	3.25
UO52	3¢ red on amber	6.25	4.75	3.00
UO53	3¢ red on cream	2.50	1.90	.95
UO54	3¢ red on blue	1.50	1.20	.45
UO55	3¢ red on fawn	1.70	.75	.60
UO56	6¢ red on white	45.00	19.00	9.25
UO57	6¢ red on amber	57.50	47.50	14.50
UO58	6¢ red on cream	100.00	70.00	40.00
UO59	10¢ red on white	90.00	75.00	40.00
UO60	10¢ red on amber	750.00	650.00	......
UO61	12¢ red on white	45.00	15.00	14.50
UO62	12¢ red on amber	450.00	400.00	......
UO63	12¢ red on cream	450.00	300.00	......
UO64	15¢ red on white	110.00	80.00	32.50
UO65	15¢ red on amber	475.00	425.00	......
UO66	15¢ red on cream	475.00	425.00	......
UO67	30¢ red on white	110.00	85.00	47.50
UO68	30¢ red on amber	675.00	600.00	......
UO69	30¢ red on cream	800.00	700.00	......

1911 POSTAL SAVINGS

UO70	1¢ green on white	50.00	45.00	5.25
UO71	1¢ green on oriental buff	140.00	110.00	35.00
UO72	2¢ carmine on white	6.25	4.25	.80

UO73   UO74

1983

SCOTT NO.	DESCRIPTION	FIRST DAY COVER	UNUSED ENTIRE	USED CUT SQ.
UO73	20¢ blue and white	2.25	1.25	1.10

1985

UO74	22¢ blue and white	2.25	.55	.50

1987 Design Similar to UO74

UO75	22¢ Savings Bond	2.50	.55	......

152 U.S. Postal Stationery #UX1-UX27

POSTAL CARDS

Prices Are For Entire Cards

MINT: As Issued, no printing or writing added.
UNUSED: Uncancelled, with printing or writing added.

UX1, UX3, UX65   UX4, UX5, UX7   UX6, UX13, UX16
    Liberty   Liberty   Liberty

1873

UX1	1¢ brown, large watermark	350.00	45.00	17.00
UX3	1¢ brown, small watermark	80.00	12.50	1.50

1875 Inscribed "Write the Address," etc.

UX4	1¢ black, watermarked	1400.00	575.00	200.00
UX5	1¢ black, unwatermarked	67.50	3.75	.40

1879

UX6	2¢ blue on buff	20.00	6.00	17.50

1881 Inscribed "Nothing but the Address." etc.

UX7	1¢ black on buff	60.00	3.50	.30

UX8   Jefferson   UX9

1885

UX8	1¢ brown on buff	35.00	5.00	.90

1886

UX9	1¢ black on buff	13.50	1.25	.50

UX10, UX11   UX12   UX14
   Grant   Jefferson

1891

UX10	1¢ black on buff	35.00	3.50	.60
UX11	1¢ blue on gray white	14.00	3.00	1.50

1894 Small Wreath and Name below

UX12	1¢ black on buff	35.00	1.15	.30

1897 Large wreath and name below

UX13	2¢ black on cream	135.00	45.00	65.00
UX14	1¢ black on buff	27.50	1.50	.30

UX15   UX18   UX19, UX20
John Adams   McKinley

1898

UX15	1¢ black on buff	37.50	6.00	12.00
UX16	2¢ black on buff	10.00	4.75	10.00

1902 Profile Background

UX18	1¢ black on buff	11.50	1.00	.40

1907

UX19	1¢ black on buff	35.00	1.25	.40

1908 Correspondence Space at Left

UX20	1¢ black on buff	45.00	5.00	3.25

UX21   UX22, UX24   UX23, UX26

UX25   UX27

1910 Background Shaded

UX21	1¢ blue on bluish	110.00	12.50	3.75

White Portrait Background

UX22	1¢ blue on bluish	15.00	.95	.30

1911

UX23	1¢ red on cream	9.75	1.85	5.00
UX24	1¢ red on cream	10.75	2.50	.30
UX25	2¢ red on cream	2.00	.25	8.00

1913

UX26	1¢ green on cream	9.50	1.25	5.00

1914

UX27	1¢ green on buff	.35	.20	.12

UX28, UX43   UX29, UX30   UX32, UX33

SCOTT NO.	DESCRIPTION	MINT	UNUSED	USED
	1917-18			
UX28	1¢ green on cream	.80	.40	.40
UX29	2¢ red on buff, die 1 ...	35.00	3.75	1.25
UX30	2¢ red on buff, die 2 ...	21.75	3.00	1.25

NOTE: On UX29 end of queue slopes sharply down to right while on UX30 it extends nearly horizontally.

	1920 UX29 & UX30 Revalued			
UX32	1¢ on 2¢ red, die 1	47.50	9.00	8.75
UX33	1¢ on 2¢ red, die 2	8.50	1.25	1.25

UX37	**UX38**	**UX39-42**

	1926			
UX37	3¢ red on yellow	3.75	.30	.30

SCOTT NO.	DESCRIPTION	FIRST DAY COVERS	MINT	USED
	1951			
UX38	2¢ rose	2.00	.55	.35

1952 UX27 & UX28 Surcharged by cancelling machine, light green

UX39	2¢ on 1¢ green	....	30.00	.75	.30
UX40	2¢ on 1¢ green	....	......	.95	.45

UX27 & UX28 Surcharge Typographed, dark green

UX41	2¢ on 1¢ green	....	......	4.00	1.85
UX42	2¢ on 1¢ green	....	......	6.95	2.50

	1952 Design of 1917			
UX43	2¢ rose	....	2.00	.40	25

UX44	**UX45, UY16**	**UX46, UY17**

1956 FIPEX COMMEMORATIVE

UX44	2¢ magenta & blue	1.75	.35	25

1956 INTERNATIONAL CARD

UX45	4¢ red & blue	1.75	1.75	.14

	1958			
UX46	3¢ purple	1.75	.60	25

As above, but with printed precancel lines

UX46c	3¢ purple	......	5.00	2.50

UX47	**UX48, UY18**

1958 UX38 Surcharged

UX47	2¢ + 1¢ carmine rose ...	......	165.00	195.00

Mint *UX47 has advertising

	1962-56			
UX48	4¢ red violet	......	1.75	.40	25
UX48at	4¢ luminescent (1966)	......	3.50	1.00	25

UX50

UX49, UX54, UX59, UY19, UY20

	1963			
UX49	7¢ Tourism	....	1.75	2.25	.60
UX50	4¢ Customs Service	...	1.75	.75	.60

UX51	**UX52**

UX51	4¢ Social Security	......	1.75	.75	25

	1965			
UX52	4¢ Coast Guard	....	1.75	.50	25

UX53	**UX56, UY21**

UX53	4¢ Census Bureau	......	1.75	.50	25

	1967 Design of UX49			
UX54	8¢ Tourism	....	1.75	2.25	.60

	1968			
UX55	5¢ emerald	....	1.75	.40	.18

UX56	**UX58, UY22**

UX57

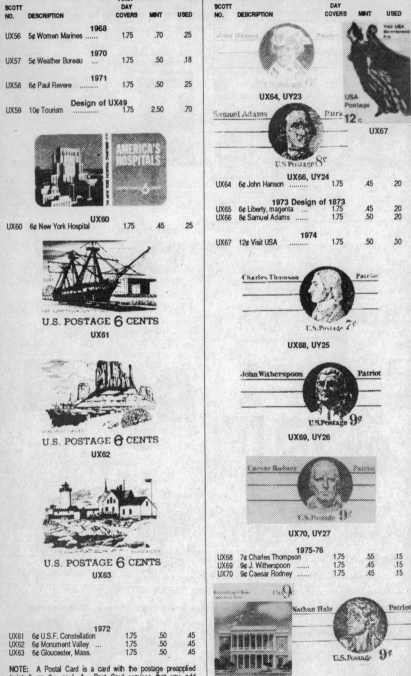

SCOTT NO.	DESCRIPTION	FIRST DAY COVERS	MINT	USED
	1968			
UX56	5¢ Women Marines	1.75	.70	25
	1970			
UX57	5¢ Weather Bureau ...	1.75	.50	.18
	1971			
UX58	6¢ Paul Revere	1.75	.50	25
	Design of UX49			
UX59	10¢ Tourism	1.75	2.50	.70

UX60

UX60	6¢ New York Hospital	1.75	.45	25

UX61

UX62

UX63

	1972			
UX61	6¢ U.S.F. Constellation	1.75	.50	45
UX62	6¢ Monument Valley ...	1.75	.50	45
UX63	6¢ Gloucester, Mass.	1.75	.50	45

NOTE: A Postal Card is a card with the postage preapplied (printed) on the card. A Post Card requires that you add postage stamps.

UX64, UY23

UX67

UX66, UY24

UX64	6¢ John Hanson	1.75	.45	20
	1973 Design of 1873			
UX65	6¢ Liberty, magenta ...	1.75	.45	20
UX66	8¢ Samuel Adams ...	1.75	.50	20
	1974			
UX67	12¢ Visit USA	1.75	.50	30

UX68, UY25

UX69, UY26

UX70, UY27

	1975-76			
UX68	7¢ Charles Thompson	1.75	.55	.15
UX69	9¢ J. Witherspoon	1.75	.45	.15
UX70	9¢ Caesar Rodney	1.75	.45	.15

UX71   **UX72, UY28**

SCOTT NO.	DESCRIPTION	FIRST DAY COVERS	MINT	USED
	1977			
UX71	9¢ Federal Court House	1.75	.45	.15
UX72	9¢ Nathan Hale	1.75	.45	.15

UX73

UX74,UX75, UY29,UY30

UX76

SCOTT NO.	DESCRIPTION	FIRST DAY COVERS	MINT	USED
	1978			
UX73	10¢ Music Hall	1.75	.50	.16
UX74	(10¢) John Hancock ...	1.75	.50	.15
UX75	10¢ John Hancock	1.75	.50	.15
UX76	14¢ "Eagle"	1.75	.60	.20

UX77

Molly Pitcher, Monmouth, 1778

| UX77 | 10¢ multicolored .... | 1.75 | .50 | .15 |

UX78

George Rogers Clark, Vincennes, 1779

USA 10c
UX79

Casimir Pulaski, Savannah, 1779

UX80

USA 10c
Historic Preservation
UX81

SCOTT NO.	DESCRIPTION	FIRST DAY COVERS	MINT	USED
	1979			
UX78	10¢ Fort Sackville	1.75	.55	.15
UX79	10¢ Casimir Pulaski ...	1.75	.55	.18
UX80	10¢ Moscow Olympics	1.75	.80	.30
UX81	10¢ Iolani Palace	1.75	.50	.15

UX82

Salt Lake Temple USA 10c
HISTORIC PRESERVATION
UX83

USA 10c
UX84

Landing of Rochambeau, 1780

USA 10c
UX85

Battle of Kings Mountain, 1780

UX86

Drake's Golden Hinde 1580

UX87

USA 10c · Battle of Cowpens, 1781

1980

UX82	14¢ Winter Olympics ...	1.75	.85	.30
UX83	10¢ Salt Lake Temple	1.75	.50	.15
UX84	10¢ Count Rochembeau	1.75	.50	.15
UX85	10¢ Kings Mountain ...	1.75	.50	.15
UX86	19¢ Sir Francis Drake	1.75	.95	20
UX87	10¢ Cowpens	1.75	.50	.10

UX88, UY31
UX89, UY32

UX90

USA 12c · Nathanael Greene, Eutaw Springs 1781

UX91

USA 12c · Lewis and Clark Expedition, 1806

UX92, UY33
UX93, UY34

UX94

USA 13c · "Swamp Fox" Francis Marion, 1782

1981

UX88	"B" (12¢) purple & white	1.75	.60	.15
UX89	12¢ Isiah Thomas	1.75	.55	.15
UX90	12¢ Eutaw Springs	1.75	.55	.15
UX91	12¢ Lewis & Clark	1.75	.55	.15
UX92	(13¢) Robert Morris ...	1.75	.60	.15
UX93	13¢ Robert Morris ...	1.75	.60	.15
UX94	13¢ Francis Marion ...	1.75	.60	.15

UX95

USA 13c · La Salle claims Louisiana, 1682

UX96

PHILADELPHIA · ACADEMY OF MUSIC · USA · 13¢

UX97

Old Post Office St. Louis Missouri · USA 13c · Historic Preservation

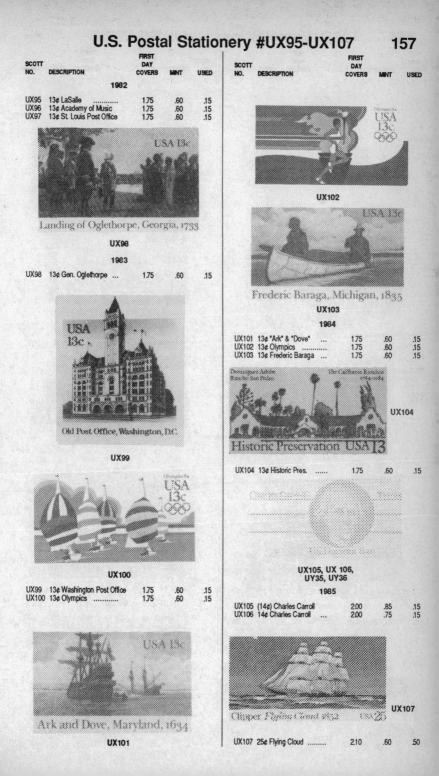

SCOTT NO.	DESCRIPTION	FIRST DAY COVERS	MINT	USED
1982				
UX95	13¢ LaSalle	1.75	.60	.15
UX96	13¢ Academy of Music	1.75	.60	.15
UX97	13¢ St. Louis Post Office	1.75	.60	.15

Landing of Oglethorpe, Georgia, 1733

UX98

1983				
UX98	13¢ Gen. Oglethorpe ...	1.75	.60	.15

Old Post Office, Washington, D.C.

UX99

UX100

UX99	13¢ Washington Post Office	1.75	.60	.15
UX100	13¢ Olympics	1.75	.60	.15

Ark and Dove, Maryland, 1634

UX101

UX102

Frederic Baraga, Michigan, 1835

UX103

SCOTT NO.	DESCRIPTION	FIRST DAY COVERS	MINT	USED
1984				
UX101	13¢ "Ark" & "Dove" ...	1.75	.60	.15
UX102	13¢ Olympics	1.75	.60	.15
UX103	13¢ Frederic Baraga ...	1.75	.60	.15

Historic Preservation USA 13

UX104

UX104	13¢ Historic Pres.	1.75	.60	.15

UX105, UX 106, UY35, UY36

1985				
UX105	(14¢) Charles Carroll	2.00	.85	.15
UX106	14¢ Charles Carroll ...	2.00	.75	.15

Clipper Flying Cloud 1852   USA 25

UX107

UX107	25¢ Flying Cloud	2.10	.60	.50

SCOTT NO.	DESCRIPTION	FIRST DAY COVERS	MINT	USED

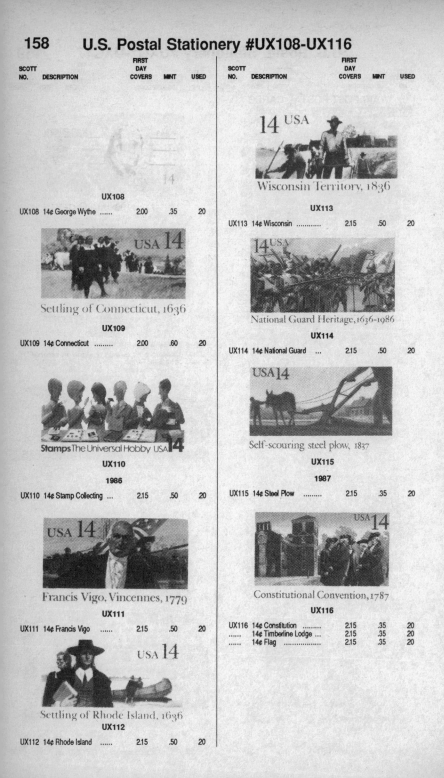

UX108

| UX108 | 14¢ George Wythe ...... | 2.00 | .35 | 20 |

Settling of Connecticut, 1636

UX109

| UX109 | 14¢ Connecticut .... | 2.00 | .60 | 20 |

Stamps The Universal Hobby USA **14**

UX110

1986

| UX110 | 14¢ Stamp Collecting ... | 2.15 | .50 | 20 |

Francis Vigo, Vincennes, 1779

UX111

| UX111 | 14¢ Francis Vigo ...... | 2.15 | .50 | 20 |

Settling of Rhode Island, 1636

UX112

| UX112 | 14¢ Rhode Island ...... | 2.15 | .50 | 20 |

14 USA

Wisconsin Territory, 1836

UX113

| UX113 | 14¢ Wisconsin .... | 2.15 | .50 | 20 |

National Guard Heritage, 1636-1986

UX114

| UX114 | 14¢ National Guard ... | 2.15 | .50 | 20 |

Self-scouring steel plow, 1837

UX115

1987

| UX115 | 14¢ Steel Plow .... | 2.15 | .35 | 20 |

Constitutional Convention, 1787

UX116

UX116	14¢ Constitution	2.15	.35	20
......	14¢ Timberline Lodge ...	2.15	.35	20
......	14¢ Flag	2.15	.35	20

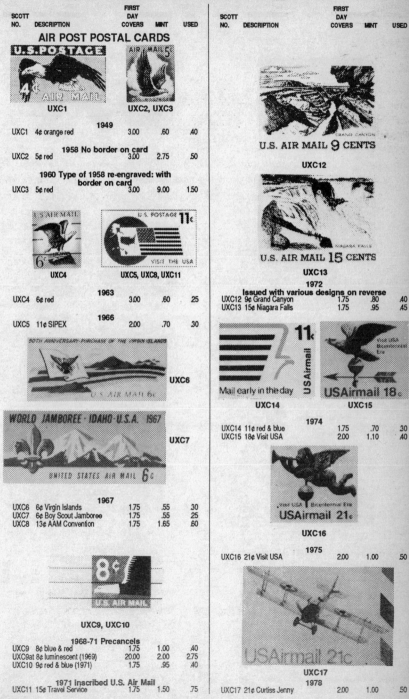

SCOTT NO.	DESCRIPTION	FIRST DAY COVERS	MINT	USED

AIR POST POSTAL CARDS

UXC1

UXC2, UXC3

1949

| UXC1 | 4¢ orange red | 3.00 | .60 | .40 |

1958 No border on card

| UXC2 | 5¢ red | 3.00 | 2.75 | .50 |

1960 Type of 1958 re-engraved: with border on card

| UXC3 | 5¢ red | 3.00 | 9.00 | 1.50 |

UXC4

UXC5, UXC8, UXC11

1963

| UXC4 | 6¢ red | 3.00 | .60 | .25 |

1966

| UXC5 | 11¢ SIPEX | 2.00 | .70 | .30 |

UXC6

UXC7

1967

UXC6	6¢ Virgin Islands	1.75	.55	.30
UXC7	6¢ Boy Scout Jamboree	1.75	.55	.25
UXC8	13¢ AAM Convention	1.75	1.65	.60

UXC9, UXC10

1968-71 Precancels

UXC9	8¢ blue & red	1.75	1.00	.40
UXC9a	t 8¢ luminescent (1969)	20.00	2.00	2.75
UXC10	9¢ red & blue (1971)	1.75	.95	.40

1971 Inscribed U.S. Air Mail

| UXC11 | 15¢ Travel Service | 1.75 | 1.50 | .75 |

UXC12

UXC13

1972

Issued with various designs on reverse

| UXC12 | 9¢ Grand Canyon | 1.75 | .80 | .40 |
| UXC13 | 15¢ Niagara Falls | 1.75 | .95 | .45 |

UXC14

UXC15

1974

| UXC14 | 11¢ red & blue | 1.75 | .70 | .30 |
| UXC15 | 18¢ Visit USA | 2.00 | 1.10 | .40 |

UXC16

1975

| UXC16 | 21¢ Visit USA | 2.00 | 1.00 | .50 |

UXC17

1978

| UXC17 | 21¢ Curtiss Jenny | 2.00 | 1.00 | .50 |

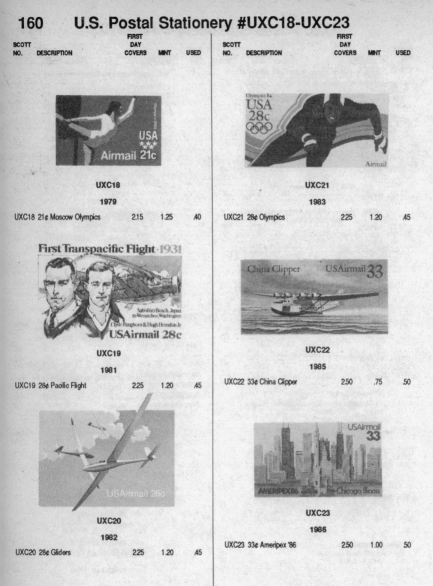

SCOTT NO.	DESCRIPTION	FIRST DAY COVERS	MINT	USED
	UXC18			
	1979			
UXC18	21¢ Moscow Olympics	2.15	1.25	.40
	UXC19			
	1981			
UXC19	28¢ Pacific Flight	2.25	1.20	.45
	UXC20			
	1982			
UXC20	28¢ Gliders	2.25	1.20	.45

SCOTT NO.	DESCRIPTION	FIRST DAY COVERS	MINT	USED
	UXC21			
	1983			
UXC21	28¢ Olympics	2.25	1.20	.45
	UXC22			
	1985			
UXC22	33¢ China Clipper	2.50	.75	.50
	UXC23			
	1986			
UXC23	33¢ Ameripex '86	2.50	1.00	.50

SCOTT
NO.   DESCRIPTION   MINT   UNUSED   USED

PAID REPLY CARDS: Consist of two halves — one of your message and one for the other party to use to reply. Our prices are for unfolded cards.

UY1m, UY3m   UY2m, UY11m   UY4m

UY1r, UY3r   UY2, UY11r   UY4r

1892 Card Framed

SCOTT NO.	DESCRIPTION		MINT	UNUSED	USED
UY1	1¢ + 1¢ unsevered		60.00	8.50	3.75
UY1m	1¢ black	(Message)	6.00	1.85	.95
UY1r	1¢ black	(Reply)	6.00	1.85	.95

1893

UY2	2¢ + 2¢ unsevered		25.00	8.00	12.50
UY2m	2¢ blue	(Message)	3.50	1.25	1.50
UY2r	2¢ blue	(Reply)	3.50	1.25	1.50

1898 Designs of 1892 Card Unframed

UY3	1¢ + 1¢ unsevered		110.00	12.50	7.25
UY3m	1¢ black	(Message)	12.50	2.75	1.60
UY3r	1¢ black	(Reply)	12.50	2.75	1.60

1904

UY4	1¢ + 1¢ unsevered		70.00	4.75	2.10
UY4m	1¢ black	(Message)	12.50	1.30	.50
UY4r	1¢ black	(Reply)	11.00	1.30	.50

UY5m, UY6m,   UY8m   UY12m
UY7m, UY13m

UY5r, UY6r,   UY8r   UY12r
UY7r, UY13r

1910

UY5	1¢ + 1¢ unsevered		100.00	22.50	6.50
UY5m	1¢ blue	(Message)	5.50	2.50	1.25
UY5r	1¢ blue	(Reply)	5.50	2.50	1.75

1911 Double Line Around Instructions

UY6	1¢ + 1¢ unsevered		105.00	30.00	19.75
UY6m	1¢ green	(Message)	20.00	10.00	2.50
UY6r	1¢ green	(Reply)	20.00	8.00	3.75

SCOTT
NO.   DESCRIPTION   MINT   UNUSED   USED

1915 Single Frame Line Around Instruction

UY7	1¢ + 1¢ unsevered		2.15	.40	.60
UY7m	1¢ green	(Message)	.60	.18	.25
UY7r	1¢ green	(Reply)	.60	.18	.25

1918

UY8	2¢ + 2¢ unsevered		110.00	20.00	30.00
UY8m	2¢ red	(Message)	15.00	6.00	4.00
UY8r	2¢ red	(Reply)	15.00	6.00	4.00

1920 UY8 Surcharged

UY9	1¢/2¢ + 1¢/2¢ unsevered		32.50	4.00	6.00
UY9m	1¢ on 2¢ red	(Message)	6.50	1.40	2.00
UY9r	1¢ on 2¢ red	(Reply)	6.50	1.40	2.25

1924 Designs of 1893

UY11	2¢ + 2¢ unsevered		3.25	1.25	1.35
UY11m	2¢ red	(Message)	1.00	.35	.40
UY11r	2¢ red	(Reply)	1.00	.35	.40

1926

UY12	3¢ + 3¢ unsevered		14.00	2.75	3.00
UY12m	3¢ red	(Message)	3.00	1.35	1.40
UY12r	3¢ red	(Reply)	3.00	1.35	1.40

SCOTT
NO.   DESCRIPTION   FIRST DAY COVERS   MINT   USED

1951 Design of 1910 Single Line Frame

UY13	2¢ + 2¢ unsevered		3.00	2.25	.65
UY13m	2¢ rose	(Message)	....	.65	.30
UY13r	2¢ rose	(Reply)	....	.65	.30

UY7 Surcharged by cancelling machine, light green

UY14	2¢/1¢ + 2¢/1¢ unsevered		....	2.25	.60
UY14m	2¢ on 1¢ green	(Message)	....	.60	.30
UY14r	2¢ on 1¢ green	(Reply)	....	.60	.30

1952 UY7 Surcharge Typographed, dark green

UY15	2¢/1¢ + 2¢/1¢ unsevered		....	130.00	40.00
UY15m	2¢ on 1¢ green	(Message)	....	20.00	6.00
UY15r	2¢ on 1¢ green	(Reply)	....	20.00	6.00

1956 Design of UX45

UY16	4¢ + 4¢ unsevered		1.75	2.00	.75
UY16m	4¢ red rose	(Message)	....	.85	.35
UY16r	4¢ red rose	(Reply)	....	.85	.35

1958 Design of UX46

UY17	3¢ + 3¢ purple, unsevered	1.75	7.50	.50

1962 Design of UX48

UY18	4¢ + 4¢ light purple, unsevered	2.25	6.00	1.00

1962 Design of UX49

UY19	7¢ + 7¢ unsevered		2.25	4.75	1.35
UY19m	7¢ blue & red	(Message)	....	1.75	.65
UY19r	7¢ blue & red	(Reply)	....	1.75	.65

1967 Design of UX54

UY20	8¢ + 8¢ unsevered		2.25	4.25	1.40
UY20m	8¢ blue & red	(Message)	....	1.50	.60
UY20r	8¢ blue & red	(Reply)	....	1.50	.60

1968 Design of UX55

UY21	5¢ + 5¢ emerald	2.25	2.75	.50

1971 Design of UX58

UY22	6¢ + 6¢ brown	2.00	1.50	.50

1972 Design of UX64

UY23	6¢ + 6¢ light blue	1.75	1.50	.50

SCOTT NO.	DESCRIPTION	FIRST DAY COVERS	MINT	USED
1973 Design of UX66				
UY24	8¢ + 8¢ orange	1.75	1.50	.50
1975				
UY25	7¢ + 7¢ design of UX68	1.75	1.50	.50
UY26	9¢ + 9¢ design of UX69	1.75	1.50	.50
1976				
UY27	9¢ + 9¢ design of UX70	1.75	1.50	.50
1977				
UY28	9¢ + 9¢ design of UX72	1.75	1.50	.50
1978				
UY29	(10¢ + 10¢) design of UX74	4.00	14.50	.60
UY30	10¢ + 10¢ design of UX75	1.75	1.50	.50
1981				
UY31	(12¢ + 12¢) "B" Eagle, design of UX88	1.75	1.50	.50
UY32	12¢ + 12¢ blue, design of UX89	1.75	1.50	.50
UY33	(13¢ + 13¢) orange, design of UX92	2.00	2.00	.50
UY34	13¢ + 13¢ orange, design of UX93	2.00	1.50	.50
1985				
UY35	(14¢ + 14¢) Carroll, design of UX105	2.35	1.50	.60
UY36	14¢ + 14¢ Carroll, design of UX106	2.35	1.25	.60
UY37	14¢ + 14¢ Wythe, design of UX108	2.35	.90	.60

OFFICIAL POSTAL CARDS

UZ1   UZ2, UZ3

SCOTT NO.	DESCRIPTION	FIRST DAY COVERS	MINT	USED
1913				
UZ1	1¢ black (Printed Address)	......	325.00	185.00
1983				
UZ2	13¢ blue	2.00	.65	.80
1985				
UZ3	14¢ blue	2.15	.35	.50

SCOTT NO.	DESCRIPTION	IMPERFORATE(a) F	AVG	PART. PERF.(b) F	AVG	PERFORATED(c) F	AVG

1863-71 FIRST ISSUE

When ordering from this issue be sure to indicate whether the "a", "b" or "c" variety is wanted. Example: R27c. Prices are for used singles.

	R1-R4	R5-R15	R16-R42	R43-R53	R54-R65	R66-R76

Scott No.	Description	Imperf F	Imperf AVG	Part Perf F	Part Perf AVG	Perf F	Perf AVG
R1	1¢ Express	57.50	37.50	42.50	25.00	1.25	.75
R2	1¢ Playing Cards	850.00	550.00	415.00	250.00	115.00	70.00
R3	1¢ Proprietary	575.00	375.00	115.00	70.00	.45	.27
R4	1¢ Telegraph	325.00	215.00	....	....	9.75	5.75
R5	2¢ Bank Check, blue	.90	.60	1.10	.65	.10	.06
R6	2¢ Bank Check, orange	....	....	90.00	55.00	.10	.06
R7	2¢ Certificate, blue	12.50	8.25	....	....	23.50	14.00
R8	2¢ Certificate, orange	....	....	....	....	23.50	14.00
R9	2¢ Express, blue	11.50	7.50	14.75	8.75	.30	.18
R10	2¢ Express, orange	....	....	....	....	7.25	4.35
R11	2¢ Playing Cards, blue	....	....	160.00	95.00	3.00	1.80
R12	2¢ Playing Cards, orange	....	....	28.75	17.00		
R13	2¢ Proprietary, blue	....	....	140.00	85.00	.45	.27
R14	2¢ Proprietary, orange	....	....	....	....	36.50	21.50
R15	2¢ U.S. Internal Revenue	....	....	....	....	.10	.06
R16	3¢ Foreign Exchange	....	....	160.00	95.00	3.00	1.80
R17	3¢ Playing Cards	....	....	....	....	115.00	70.00
R18	3¢ Proprietary	....	....	225.00	135.00	2.25	1.35
R19	3¢ Telegraph	55.00	37.50	20.00	18.00	2.75	1.65
R20	4¢ Inland Exchange	....	....	....	....	2.00	1.20
R21	4¢ Playing Cards	....	....	....	....	385.00	230.00
R22	4¢ Proprietary	....	....	200.00	120.00	3.00	1.80
R23	5¢ Agreement	....	....	....	....	.25	.15
R24	5¢ Certificate	3.00	2.00	10.00	6.00	.15	.09
R25	5¢ Express	4.25	2.80	4.75	2.85	.33	.20
R26	5¢ Foreign Exchange	....	....	....	....	.33	.20
R27	5¢ Inland Exchange	4.25	2.85	3.75	2.25	.20	.12
R28	5¢ Playing Cards	....	....	....	....	15.00	9.00
R29	5¢ Proprietary	....	....	....	....	19.50	11.75
R30	6¢ Inland Exchange	....	....	....	....	1.15	.70
R32	10¢ Bill of Lading	55.00	37.50	150.00	90.00	1.10	.65
R33	10¢ Certificate	110.00	70.00	115.00	70.00	.30	.18
R34	10¢ Contract, blue	....	....	110.00	70.00	.30	.18
R34e	10¢ Contract, ultramarine	....	....	300.00	185.00	.60	.35
R35	10¢ Foreign Exchange	....	....	....	....	3.75	2.25
R35e	10¢ Foreign Exchange, ultra	....	....	....	....	8.00	4.85
R36	10¢ Inland Exchange	140.00	90.00	3.75	2.25	.25	.15
R37	10¢ Power of Attorney	375.00	250.00	19.50	11.75	.40	.25
R38	10¢ Proprietary	....	....	....	....	16.00	9.75
R39	15¢ Foreign Exchange	....	....	....	....	15.00	9.00
R40	15¢ Inland Exchange	28.75	19.00	12.50	7.50	1.25	.75
R41	20¢ Foreign Exchange	47.50	31.50	....	....	37.50	22.50
R42	20¢ Inland Exchange	14.00	9.00	18.75	11.00	.40	.25

SCOTT NO.	DESCRIPTION	IMPERFORATE(a) F	AVG	PART. PERF.(b) F	AVG	PERFORATED(c) F	AVG
R43	25¢ Bond	97.50	62.50	5.85	3.50	2.00	1.20
R44	25¢ Certificate	6.00	3.95	5.75	3.50	.12	.07
R45	25¢ Entry of Goods	18.50	11.00	37.50	22.50	.60	.35
R46	25¢ Insurance	10.75	7.00	11.50	7.00	.30	.18
R47	25¢ Life Insurance	37.50	25.00	125.00	75.00	5.00	3.00
R48	25¢ Power of Attorney	5.75	3.75	18.00	10.75	.30	.18
R49	25¢ Protest	23.75	15.75	145.00	87.50	6.00	3.65
R50	25¢ Warehouse Receipt	40.00	26.00	145.00	87.50	25.00	15.00
R51	30¢ Foreign Exchange	70.00	45.00	350.00	210.00	42.50	25.00
R52	30¢ Inland Exchange	40.00	26.50	52.50	32.50	2.40	1.45
R53	40¢ Inland Exchange	500.00	225.00	4.25	2.50	2.50	1.50
R54	50¢ Conveyance, blue	13.00	8.50	1.25	.75	.15	.09
R54e	50¢ Conveyance, ultra	....	....	....	....	.25	.15
R55	50¢ Entry of Goods	....	....	12.50	7.50	.28	.17
R56	50¢ Foreign Exchange	42.50	27.50	36.50	21.50	5.00	3.00
R57	50¢ Lease	25.00	16.00	57.50	35.00	6.25	3.75
R58	50¢ Life Insurance	31.50	20.00	65.00	39.50	.80	.50
R59	50¢ Mortgage	11.50	7.50	1.75	1.05	.40	.25
R60	50¢ Original Process	3.15	2.10	....	....	.35	.20
R61	50¢ Passage Ticket	70.00	45.00	115.00	70.00	.65	.40
R62	50¢ Probate of Will	37.50	25.00	52.50	32.50	20.00	12.00
R63	50¢ Surety Bond, blue	150.00	100.00	2.65	1.60	.25	.15
R63e	50¢ Surety Bond, ultra	....	....	....	....	1.00	.60
R64	60¢ Inland Exchange	95.00	60.00	46.50	28.50	6.00	3.65
R65	70¢ Foreign Exchange	350.00	225.00	100.00	60.00	6.25	3.75
R66	$1 Conveyance	12.50	8.25	285.00	170.00	2.25	1.35
R67	$1 Entry of Goods	28.75	18.75	....	....	1.60	.95
R68	$1 Foreign Exchange	52.50	35.00	....	....	.75	.45
R69	$1 Inland Exchange	12.50	8.25	285.00	170.00	.55	.35
R70	$1 Lease	35.00	22.50	....	....	1.30	.80
R71	$1 Life Insurance	160.00	105.00	....	....	5.00	3.00
R72	$1 Manifest	65.00	42.50	....	....	23.50	14.00
R73	$1 Mortgage	25.00	15.00	....	....	145.00	85.00
R74	$1 Passage Ticket	180.00	115.00	....	....	145.00	85.00
R75	$1 Power of Attorney	75.00	47.50	....	....	1.75	1.05
R76	$1 Probate of Will	65.00	42.50	....	....	36.50	21.75

R77-R80   R81-R87   R88-R96   R97-R101

Washington

SCOTT NO.	DESCRIPTION	IMPERFORATE F	AVG	PART. PERF. F	AVG	PERFORATED F	AVG
R77	$1.30 Foreign Exchange	....	....	....	....	62.50	37.50
R78	$1.50 Inland Exchange	23.75	15.75	....	....	2.90	1.75
R79	$1.60 Foreign Exchange	750.00	485.00	....	....	97.50	58.50
R80	$1.90 Foreign Exchange	2000.00	1300.00	....	....	70.00	42.50
R81	$2 Conveyance	105.00	70.00	850.00	500.00	1.85	1.10
R82	$2 Mortgage	90.00	57.50	....	....	2.50	1.50
R83	$2 Probate of Will	....	....	....	....	47.50	28.50
R84	$2.50 Inland Exchange	1050.00	675.00	....	....	3.25	1.95
R85	$3 Charter Party	110.00	70.00	....	....	3.75	2.25
R86	$2 Manifest	110.00	70.00	....	....	25.00	15.00
R87	$3.50 Inland Exchange	1000.00	650.00	....	....	55.00	33.50

SCOTT NO.	DESCRIPTION	IMPERFORATE(a) F	AVG	PART. PERF.(b) F	AVG	PERFORATED(c) F	AVG

R102

R88	$5 Charter Party	265.00	175.00	....	....	4.75	2.85
R89	$5 Conveyance	37.50	25.00	....	....	3.75	2.25
R90	$5 Manifest	100.00	65.00	....	....	95.00	57.50
R91	$5 Mortgage	100.00	65.00	....	....	18.50	11.00
R92	$5 Probate of Will	450.00	285.00	....	....	17.50	10.50
R93	$10 Charter Party	425.00	275.00	....	....	23.75	14.00
R94	$10 Conveyance	85.00	55.00	....	....	60.00	36.50
R95	$10 Mortgage	400.00	265.00	....	....	25.00	15.00
R96	$10 Probate of Will	950.00	625.00	....	....	25.00	15.00
R97	$15 Mortgage, blue	1100.00	700.00	....	....	115.00	70.00
R97e	$15 Mortgage, ultramarine	....	....	....	....	180.00	110.00
R98	$20 Conveyance	55.00	35.00	....	....	30.00	18.00
R99	$20 Probate of Will	1100.00	700.00	....	....	1000.00	600.00
R100	$25 Mortgage	850.00	550.00	....	....	97.50	57.50
R101	$50 U.S. Internal Revenue	175.00	115.00	....	....	100.00	60.00
R102	$200 U.S. Int. Revenue	1150.00	750.00	....	....	675.00	400.00

1871 SECOND ISSUE

NOTE: The individual denominations vary in design from the illustrations shown which are more typical of their relative size.

R103, R104, R134, R135, R151

R105-R111
R136-R139

R112-R114

R115-R117
R142-R143

R118-R122, R144

R123-R126, R145-R147

R127, R128, R148, R149

R129-R131, R150

SCOTT NO.	DESCRIPTION	USED F	AVG
R103	1¢ blue and black	28.75	17.50
R104	2¢ blue and black	1.15	.70
R105	3¢ blue and black	13.75	8.00
R106	4¢ blue and black	55.00	33.50
R107	5¢ blue and black	1.25	.75
R108	6¢ blue and black	80.00	48.50
R109	10¢ blue and black	.90	.55
R110	15¢ blue and black	25.00	15.00
R111	20¢ blue and black	5.00	3.00
R112	25¢ blue and black	.65	.40
R113	30¢ blue and black	52.50	31.50
R114	40¢ blue and black	31.50	18.75
R115	50¢ blue and black	.65	.40
R116	60¢ blue and black	70.00	42.50
R117	70¢ blue and black	26.50	17.75
R118	$1 blue and black	3.00	1.80
R119	$1.30 blue and black	230.00	140.00
R120	$1.50 blue and black	12.50	7.50
R121	$1.60 blue and black	400.00	240.00

SCOTT NO.	DESCRIPTION	F	USED AVG
R122	$1.90 blue and black	140.00	85.00
R123	$2.00 blue and black	12.00	7.25
R124	$2.50 blue and black	21.75	13.00
R125	$3.00 blue and black	37.50	22.50
R126	$3.50 blue and black	115.00	70.00
R127	$5 blue and black	18.50	11.00
R128	$10 blue and black ...	115.00	70.00
R129	$20 blue and black ...	350.00	210.00
R130	$25 blue and black ...	350.00	210.00
R131	$50 blue and black ...	375.00	225.00

1871-72 THIRD ISSUE

SCOTT NO.	DESCRIPTION	F	USED AVG
R134	1¢ claret and black ...	23.50	14.00
R135	2¢ orange and black ...	.11	.07
R135b	2¢ orange and black (center inverted)	325.00	195.00
R136	4¢ brown and black ...	32.50	19.50
R137	5¢ orange and black ...	.30	.18
R138	6¢ orange and black ...	35.00	21.50

SCOTT NO.	DESCRIPTION	F	USED AVG
R139	15¢ brown and black	9.50	5.75
R140	30¢ orange and black	11.50	6.85
R141	40¢ brown and black	22.50	13.50
R142	60¢ orange and black	52.50	31.75
R143	70¢ green and black ...	31.75	19.50
R144	$1 green and black ...	1.35	.80
R145	$2 vermillion and black	21.00	12.50
R146	$2.50 claret and black	37.50	22.50
R147	$3 green and black ...	36.50	21.50
R148	$5 vermillion and black	18.75	11.00
R149	$10 green and black ...	110.00	67.50
R150	$20 orange and black	425.00	250.00

1874 on greenish paper

SCOTT NO.	DESCRIPTION	F	USED AVG
R151	2¢ orange and black ...	.11	.07
R151a	2¢ orange and black (center inverted)	375.00	225.00

R152
Liberty

R153

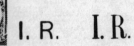

R154, R155

R161-R172

R173-R178, R182, R183

SCOTT NO.	DESCRIPTION	UNUSED F	AVG	USED F	AVG
	1875-78				
R152a	2¢ blue on blue silk paper	....	....	.11	.07
R152b	2¢ watermarked ("USIR") paper	....	....	.11	.07
R152c	2¢ watermarked, rouletted	....	....	37.50	22.50
	1898 Postage Stamps 279 & 267 Surcharged				
R153	1¢ green, small I.R.	1.25	.75	1.10	.65
R154	1¢ green, large I.R.	.20	.12	.15	.09
R155	2¢ carmine, large I.R.	.20	.12	.11	.07

DOCUMENTARY STAMPS
Newspaper Stamp PR121 Surcharged

SCOTT NO.	DESCRIPTION	UNUSED F	AVG	USED F	AVG
R159	$5 dark blue, red surcharge reading down....................	180.00	115.00	150.00	95.00
R160	$5 dark blue, red surcharge reading up....................	85.00	55.00	57.50	36.50
	1898 Battleships Inscribed "Documentary"				
R161	1/2¢ orange....................	2.00	1.20	6.00	3.65
R162	1/2¢ dark gray....................	.18	.11	.13	.08
R163	1¢ pale blue....................	.11	.07	.10	.06
R164	2¢ carmine....................	.14	.09	.10	.06
R165	3¢ dark blue....................	.85	.50	.15	.09
R166	4¢ pale rose....................	.35	.22	.13	.08
R167	5¢ lilac....................	.20	.12	.11	.07
R168	10¢ dark brown....................	.28	.17	.11	.07
R169	25¢ purple brown....................	.28	.17	.13	.06
R170	40¢ blue lilac ....(cut cancel 25)	37.50	22.50	1.25	.75
R171	50¢ slate violet	3.00	1.80	.17	.10
R172	80¢ bistre ....(cut cancel 15)	17.50	10.50	.40	.25
R173	$1 dark green....................	3.00	1.80	.13	.08
R174	$3 dark brown ....(cut cancel 18)	6.50	3.95	.30	.18

SCOTT NO.	DESCRIPTION	UNUSED F	AVG	USED F	AVG
R175	$5 orange red ....(cut cancel .25)	....	....	1.25	.75
R176	$10 black ....(cut cancel .70)	27.50	16.50	2.75	1.65
R177	$30 red ....(cut cancel 30.00)	140.00	85.00	85.00	50.00
R178	$50 gray brown ...(cut cancel 1.50)	55.00	33.50	3.00	1.80

R179, R225, R246, R248
Marshall

R180, R226, R249
Hamilton

R181, R224, R227, R247, R250
Madison

R195-R216

R217-R223

1899 Various Portraits Inscribed "Series of 1898"

SCOTT NO.	DESCRIPTION	UNUSED F	AVG	USED F	AVG
R179	$100 yellow brown & black (cut cancel 14.50)	57.50	35.00	29.50	17.50
R180	$500 carmine lake & black (cut cancel 200.00)	....	....	450.00	275.00
R181	$1000 green & black (cut cancel 110.00)	450.00	275.00	350.00	215.00

1900

R182	$1 carmine ....(cut cancel .15)	5.25	3.15	.55	.35
R183	$3 lake ....(cut cancel 8.75)	57.50	35.00	42.50	25.00

Designs of R173-78 surcharged

R184-R189

R190-R194

R228-239, R251-256, R260-263

R240-245 R257-259

R184	$1 gray ....(cut cancel .08)	3.00	1.80	.17	.10
R185	$2 gray ....(cut cancel .08)	2.75	1.65	.17	.10
R186	$3 gray ....(cut cancel 1.85)	25.00	15.00	12.75	7.75
R187	$5 gray ....(cut cancel .35)	15.00	9.00	4.75	2.85
R188	$10 gray ....(cut cancel 3.75)	40.00	24.00	11.50	7.00
R189	$50 gray ....(cut cancel 75.00)	550.00	335.00	350.00	215.00

1902

R190	$1 green ....(cut cancel .30)	5.75	3.50	2.50	1.50
R191	$2 green ....(cut cancel .25)	5.75	3.50	1.25	.75
R191a	$2 surcharged as R185	50.00	30.00	50.00	30.00
R192	$5 green ....(cut cancel 2.15)	32.50	19.50	13.50	8.00
R192a	$5 surcharge omitted	60.00	36.50	....	....
R193	$10 green ....(cut cancel 30.00)	230.00	140.00	150.00	90.00
R194	$50 green ....(cut cancel 250.00)	1100.00	650.00	725.00	435.00

1914 Inscribed "Series of 1914"
Single Line Watermark "USPS"

R195	1/2¢ rose....................	4.75	2.85	2.50	1.50
R196	1¢ rose....................	1.25	.75	.17	.11
R197	2¢ rose....................	1.25	.75	.15	.10
R198	3¢ rose....................	27.50	16.50	21.50	13.00
R199	4¢ rose....................	6.75	4.00	1.10	.70
R200	5¢ rose....................	2.40	1.50	.17	.11
R201	10¢ rose....................	2.00	1.25	.13	.08
R202	25¢ rose....................	12.00	7.50	.50	.32
R203	40¢ rose....................	7.00	4.35	.65	.40
R204	50¢ rose....................	3.00	1.85	.14	.09
R205	80¢ rose....................	40.00	25.00	7.00	4.25

SCOTT NO.	DESCRIPTION	UNUSED F	UNUSED AVG	USED F	USED AVG
	1914 Double Line Watermark "USIR"				
R206	1/2¢ rose..	1.30	.80	.55	.35
R207	1¢ rose..	.15	.10	.10	.06
R208	2¢ rose..	.20	.13	.10	.06
R209	3¢ rose..	1.30	.80	.25	.16
R210	4¢ rose..	2.50	1.60	.35	.22
R211	5¢ rose..	1.20	.75	.14	.09
R212	10¢ rose...	.40	.25	.11	.07
R213	25¢ rose...	3.75	2.35	.75	.50
R214	40¢ rose ....(cut cancel .60)	32.50	21.00	7.25	4.50
R215	50¢ rose...	7.50	4.65	.17	.11
R216	80¢ rose ....(cut cancel 1.25)	42.50	27.50	9.00	5.75
R217	$1 green ....(cut cancel .08)	9.50	6.00	.17	.11
R218	$2 carmine ....(cut cancel .09)	18.75	11.75	.20	.13
R219	$3 purple ....(cut cancel .25)	30.00	19.00	1.25	.80
R220	$5 blue ....(cut cancel .65)	25.00	16.00	1.75	1.10
R221	$10 orange ....(cut cancel 1.00)	47.50	30.00	5.00	3.25
R222	$30 vermillion ......(cut cancel 2.25)	97.50	60.00	11.00	6.95
R223	$50 violet ....(cut cancel 275.00)	975.00	625.00	650.00	415.00
	1914-15 Various Portraits Inscribed "Series of 1914" or "Series of 1915"				
R224	$60 brown ....(cut cancel 57.50)	....	....	115.00	75.00
R225	$100 green ....(cut cancel 18.50)	....	....	50.00	31.75
R226	$500 blue ....(cut cancel 250.00)	....	....	525.00	335.00
R227	$1000 orange ...(cut cancel 250.00)	....	....	525.00	335.00
	1917 Perf. 11				
R228	1¢ carmine rose	.15	.10	.11	.07
R229	2¢ carmine rose	.11	.07	.09	.06
R230	3¢ carmine rose	.30	.20	.22	.14
R231	4¢ carmine rose	.18	.11	.09	.06
R232	5¢ carmine rose	.20	.13	.09	.06
R233	8¢ carmine rose	1.85	1.20	.17	.11
R234	10¢ carmine rose	.20	.13	.09	.06
R235	20¢ carmine rose	.35	.22	.11	.07
R236	25¢ carmine rose	.75	.50	.11	.07
R237	40¢ carmine rose	1.25	.80	.13	.08
R238	50¢ carmine rose..............................	1.60	1.00	.11	.07
R239	80¢ carmine rose	3.65	2.30	.13	.08
	Same design as issue of 1914-15 Without dates.				
R240	$1 green..	4.35	2.75	.11	.07
R241	$2 rose...	9.50	5.95	.13	.08
R242	$3 violet ....(cut cancel .15)	21.50	13.50	.55	.35
R243	$4 yellow brown ....(cut can. .18)	12.50	8.00	1.10	.70
R244	$5 blue (cut can. .10) (perf. in 12)	9.50	5.95	.22	.14
R245	$10 orange ....(cut cancel .18)	17.50	11.00	.65	.40
	Types of 1899 Various Portraits Perf. 12				
R246	$30 vermillion, Grant (cut can. .70)	32.50	20.00	2.50	1.60
R247	$60 brown, Lincoln (cut can. 95)	35.00	22.50	7.25	4.65
R248	$100 green, Washington(c. can. .45)	25.00	16.00	.85	.55
R249	$500 blue., Hamilton (c. can. 10.00)	....	....	35.00	22.50
R249a	$500 Numerals in orange	....	....	87.50	55.00
R250	$1000 orange, Madison (Perf. In. 4.00)			12.50	7.75
	..................................(cut cancel 4.25)	100.00	62.50		
	1928-29 Perf. 10				
R251	1¢ carmine rose	2.15	1.35	1.25	.80
R252	2¢ carmine rose	.60	.38	.20	.13
R253	4¢ carmine rose	6.00	3.75	4.25	2.75
R254	5¢ carmine rose	1.15	.75	.40	.25
R255	10¢ carmine rose	1.75	1.10	1.10	.70
R256	20¢ carmine rose	6.00	3.75	4.75	3.00
R257	$1 green ....(cut cancel 6.50)	50.00	31.75	28.75	18.75
R258	$2 rose..	14.75	9.00	1.85	1.20
R259	$10 orange ....(cut cancel 22.50)	75.00	47.50	35.00	22.50
	1929-30 Perf. 11 x 10				
R260	2¢ carmine rose	2.85	1.85	2.50	1.60
R261	5¢ carmine rose	2.10	1.35	1.75	1.10
R262	10¢ carmine rose	8.25	5.75	7.00	4.50
R263	20¢ carmine rose	15.00	9.50	9.50	6.00

SCOTT NO.	DESCRIPTION	PLATE BLOCK F/NH	F	UNUSED F/NH	F	UNCUT	FINE USED CUT CANCEL	PERF INIT

R733, R734

1962 CENTENNIAL INTERNAL REVENUE Inscribed "Established 1862"

SCOTT NO.	DESCRIPTION	PLATE BLOCK F/NH	F	UNUSED F/NH	F	UNCUT	CUT CANCEL	PERF INIT
R733	10¢ blue & green	27.50	25.00	2.25	2.00	.30	.15	.12

1964 Without Inscription Date

R734	10¢ blue & green	50.00	45.00	5.00	4.50	.22	.10	.08

SCOTT NO.	DESCRIPTION	VIOLET PAPER(a) F	AVG	GREEN PAPER(b) F	AVG

RB1-2   RB3-7   RB11-12   RB13-19

PROPRIETARY STAMPS

1871-74 Perforated 12

SCOTT NO.	DESCRIPTION	VIOLET PAPER(a) F	AVG	GREEN PAPER(b) F	AVG
RB1	1¢ green & black...............	4.00	2.40	6.75	4.00
RB2	2¢ green & black	4.75	2.90	14.00	8.50
RB3	3¢ green & black	12.00	7.25	42.50	26.50
RB4	4¢ green & black	8.50	5.25	15.00	9.00
RB5	5¢ green & black	110.00	67.50	115.00	70.00
RB6	6¢ green & black	32.50	19.50	85.00	51.50
RB7	10¢ green & black	150.00	90.00	42.50	26.50
RB8	50¢ green & black (large)	650.00	400.00	1000.00	600.00

SCOTT NO.	DESCRIPTION	SILK PAPER(a) F	AVG	WMKD., PERF.(b) F	AVG	ROULETTE(c) F	AVG

1875-81 NATIONAL BANK NOTE

SCOTT NO.	DESCRIPTION	SILK PAPER(a) F	AVG	WMKD., PERF.(b) F	AVG	ROULETTE(c) F	AVG
RB11	1¢ green...........................	1.50	.90	.35	.20	36.50	21.50
RB12	2¢ brown..........................	1.85	1.10	1.25	.75	55.00	33.50
RB13	3¢ orange..........................	10.75	6.50	2.50	1.50	55.00	33.50
RB14	4¢ red brown	4.75	2.85	4.50	2.75	....	....
RB15	4¢ red..............................	....	....	3.75	2.25	55.00	33.50
RB16	5¢ black............................	95.00	57.50	85.00	52.50	....	....
RB17	6¢ violet blue	21.50	13.00	14.50	8.75	150.00	90.00
RB18	6¢ violet	....	....	22.50	13.50	185.00	110.00
RB19	10¢ blue	....	....	225.00	135.00	....	....

RB20-31   RB32-64   RB65-73

SCOTT NO.	DESCRIPTION	UNUSED F	AVG	USED F	AVG

1898 Battleship Inscribed "Proprietary"

SCOTT NO.	DESCRIPTION	UNUSED F	AVG	USED F	AVG
RB20	1/8¢ yellow green	.10	.06	.10	.06
RB21	1/4¢ brown..................................	.10	.06	.10	.06
RB22	3/8¢ deep orange	.15	.09	.12	.09
RB23	5/8¢ deep ultramarine	.15	.09	.14	.08

SCOTT NO.	DESCRIPTION	UNUSED F	AVG	USED F	AVG
RB24	1¢ dark green	.40	25	.20	.12
RB25	1-1/4¢ violet	.13	.08	.11	.07
RB26	1-7/8¢ dull blue	2.40	1.45	.80	.50
RB27	2¢ violet brown	.45	27	.25	.15
RB28	2-1/2¢ lake	.50	.30	.15	.09
RB29	3-3/4¢ olive gray	6.00	3.65	3.00	1.80
RB30	4¢ purple	2.40	1.45	.95	.55
RB31	5¢ brown orange	2.40	1.45	.95	.55

1914 Watermarked "USPS"

SCOTT NO.	DESCRIPTION	UNUSED F	AVG	USED F	AVG
RB32	1/8¢ black	.20	.12	.15	.09
RB33	1/4¢ black	1.25	.75	.90	.55
RB34	3/8¢ black	.20	.12	.15	.09
RB35	5/8¢ black	2.40	1.45	1.50	.90
RB36	1-1/4¢ black	1.85	1.10	.95	.55
RB37	1-7/8¢ black	24.50	14.75	14.50	8.75
RB38	2-1/2¢ black	3.25	1.95	2.40	1.45
RB39	3-1/8¢ black	75.00	45.00	53.50	32.50
RB40	3-3/4¢ black	24.50	14.75	14.50	8.75
RB41	4¢ black	40.00	24.00	27.50	16.50
RB43	5¢ black	90.00	55.00	60.00	36.50

1914 Watermarked "USIR"

SCOTT NO.	DESCRIPTION	UNUSED F	AVG	USED F	AVG
RB44	1/8¢ black	.15	.09	.14	.08
RB45	1/4¢ black	.15	.09	.14	.08
RB46	3/8¢ black	.60	.35	.35	.20
RB47	1/2¢ black	2.75	1.65	2.00	1.20
RB48	5/8¢ black	.13	.08	.12	.07
RB49	1¢ black	3.50	2.10	2.75	1.65
RB50	1-1/4¢ black	.35	22	.25	.15
RB51	1-1/2¢ black	3.00	1.85	2.25	1.35
RB52	1-7/8¢ black	.90	.55	.70	.45
RB53	2¢ black	5.00	3.00	4.00	2.40
RB54	2-1/2¢ black	1.20	.75	1.10	.65
RB55	3¢ black	3.75	2.25	3.00	1.80
RB56	3-1/8¢ black	4.25	2.50	3.00	1.80
RB57	3-3/4¢ black	8.75	5.25	7.50	4.50
RB58	4¢ black	.30	.18	.25	.15
RB59	4-3/8¢ black	11.00	6.65	7.50	4.50
RB60	5¢ black	2.75	1.65	2.50	1.50
RB61	6¢ black	47.50	28.50	36.50	21.75
RB62	8¢ black	13.50	8.00	11.00	6.50
RB63	10¢ black	9.00	5.50	7.50	4.50
RB64	20¢ black	17.50	10.50	13.50	8.00

1919 Offset Printing

SCOTT NO.	DESCRIPTION	UNUSED F	AVG	USED F	AVG
RB65	1¢ dark blue	.13	.08	.11	.07
RB66	2¢ dark blue	.15	.10	.11	.07
RB67	3¢ dark blue	.75	.50	.50	.33
RB68	4¢ dark blue	1.10	.70	.50	.33
RB69	5¢ dark blue	1.10	.70	.55	.35
RB70	8¢ dark blue	10.75	7.00	8.25	5.25
RB71	10¢ dark blue	2.25	1.40	1.50	.95
RB72	20¢ dark blue	3.75	2.40	2.75	1.75
RB73	40¢ dark blue	21.75	14.00	7.00	4.50

FUTURE DELIVERY STAMPS

FUTURE

DELIVERY

Type I

FUTURE

DELIVERY

Type II

Documentary
Stamps of 1917
Overprinted

1918-34 Perf. 11, Type I Overprint Lines 8mm. Apart

SCOTT NO.	DESCRIPTION		UNUSED F	AVG	USED F	AVG
RC1	2¢ carmine rose		.90	.60	.13	.08
RC2	3¢ carmine rose	(cut cancel12.50)	30.00	19.50	25.00	16.00
RC3	4¢ carmine rose		1.10	.70	.13	.08
RC3A	5¢ carmine rose		....	....	3.00	1.90
RC4	10¢ carmine rose		2.25	1.40	.13	.08
RC5	20¢ carmine rose		2.50	1.60	.13	.08

SCOTT NO.	DESCRIPTION		UNUSED F	AVG	USED F	AVG
RC6	25¢ carmine rose	...(cut cancel .10)	9.50	6.25	.50	.33
RC7	40¢ carmine rose	...(cut cancel .10)	7.00	4.50	.50	.33
RC8	50¢ carmine rose		2.40	1.60	.15	.10
RC9	80¢ carmine rose	...(cut cancel .85)	16.50	10.75	6.00	3.85
RC10	$1 green	...(cut cancel .07)	....	....	.20	.13
RC11	$2 rose	...(cut cancel .07)	....	....	.20	.13
RC12	$3 violet	...(cut cancel .15)	....	....	1.25	.80
RC13	$5 dark blue	...(cut cancel .10)	....	....	.30	.20
RC14	$10 orange	...(cut cancel .20)	....	....	.60	.40
RC15	$20 olive bistre	...(cut cancel .55)	....	....	3.65	2.35

Perforated 12

RC16	$30 vermillion	...(cut cancel 1.25)	....	....	3.35	2.15
RC17	$50 olive green	...(cut cancel .50)	....	....	1.10	.70
RC18	$60 brown	...(cut cancel .90)	....	....	1.75	1.10
RC19	$100 yellow grn.	(cut cancel 6.00)	....	....	24.50	16.00
RC20	$500 blue	...(cut cancel 4.25)	60.00	38.75	9.50	6.25
RC21	$1000 orange	......(cut cancel 1.75)	....	....	4.25	2.75
RC22	1¢ c. rose (lines 2mm., apart)	....	.45	.30	.13	.08
RC23	80¢ c. rose (lines 2mm. apart)(c.c. .25)		....	....	1.50	.95

1925-34 Perf. 11, Type II Overprint

RC25	$1 green	...............(cut cancel .08)	6.00	3.85	.60	.40
RC26	$10 orange	............(cut cancel 5.75)	....	....	12.00	7.75

STOCK TRANSFER STAMPS

STOCK

Documentary
Stamps of 1917
Overprinted

STOCK

TRANSFER

TRANSFER

Type I

Type II

1918-22 Perf. 11 Type I Overprint

RD1	1¢ carmine rose		.30	.20	.13	.08
RD2	2¢ carmine rose		.13	.08	.09	.06
RD3	4¢ carmine rose		.15	.10	.09	.06
RD4	5¢ carmine rose		.18	.12	.09	.06
RD5	10¢ carmine rose		.15	.10	.09	.06
RD6	20¢ carmine rose		.25	.16	.09	.06
RD7	25¢ carmine rose	(cut cancel .07)	.70	.45	.13	.08
RD8	40¢ carmine rose		.60	.40	.09	.06
RD9	50¢ carmine rose		.30	.20	.09	.06
RD10	80¢ carmine rose	(cut cancel .07)	.75	.50	.25	.16
RD11	$1 green (red ovpt.)	...(c.cancel .55)	30.00	19.50	7.50	4.75
RD12	$1 green (black ovpt.)		1.50	.95	.09	.06
RD13	$2 rose...............................		1.50	.95	.09	.06
RD14	$3 violet	...............(cut cancel .25)	5.25	3.35	.90	.60
RD15	$4 yellow brown	...(cut cancel .06)	3.75	2.50	.09	.06
RD16	$5 dark blue	............(cut cancel .06)	2.50	1.60	.09	.06
RD17	$10 orange	...............(cut cancel .07)	3.75	2.50	.15	.10
RD18	$20 olive bistre	...(cut cancel 3.50)	35.00	22.50	17.50	11.50

Perforated 12

RD19	$30 vermillion	...(cut cancel 1.20)	13.50	8.75	4.25	2.75
RD20	$50 olive green	(cut cancel 12.00)	70.00	45.00	35.00	35.00
RD21	$60 brown	...(cut cancel 6.00)	55.00	35.00	16.50	10.75
RD22	$100 green	............(cut cancel 1.75)	14.75	9.50	4.75	3.00
RD23	$500 blue	............(cut cancel 47.50)	....	....	110.00	70.00
RD24	$1000 orange	...(cut cancel 27.50)	....	....	77.50	50.00

1928. Perf. 10. Type I Overprint

RD25	2¢ carmine rose		.30	.20	.09	.06
RD26	4¢ carmine rose		.30	.20	.09	.06
RD27	10¢ carmine rose		.35	.23	.10	.07
RD28	20¢ carmine rose		.55	.35	.10	.07
RD29	50¢ carmine rose		1.00	.65	.13	.08
RD30	$1 green...............................		1.65	1.10	.09	.06
RD31	$2 carmine rose...............................		1.65	1.10	.09	.06
RD32	$10 orange	...............(cut cancel .07)	7.50	4.75	.20	.13

SCOTT NO.	DESCRIPTION	UNUSED		USED	
		F	AVG	F	AVG

1920-28 Perf. 11 Type II Overprint

RD33	2¢ carmine rose	2.65	1.75	.50	.33
RD34	10¢ carmine rose	.40	25	.09	.06
RD35	20¢ carmine rose	.45	.30	.09	.06
RD36	50¢ carmine rose	1.00	.65	.11	.07
RD37	$1 green ....(cut cancel .30)	12.00	7.85	5.50	3.50
RD38	$2 rose ....(cut cancel .30)	8.75	5.75	5.50	3.50

1920-28 Perf. 10 Type II Overprint

RD39	2¢ carmine rose	2.75	1.75	.30	.20
RD40	10¢ carmine rose	.75	.50	.09	.06
RD41	20¢ carmine rose	1.00	.65	.09	.06

SILVER TAX STAMPS

Documentary Stamps of 1917 Overprinted

SILVER TAX

1934-36

RG1	1¢ carmine rose	.75	.50	.35	.23
RG2	2¢ carmine rose	1.10	.70	.40	27
RG3	3¢ carmine rose	1.20	.80	.50	.32
RG4	4¢ carmine rose	1.20	.80	.60	.40
RG5	5¢ carmine rose	1.50	1.00	.90	.60
RG6	8¢ carmine rose	2.00	1.30	1.25	.80
RG7	10¢ carmine rose	2.00	1.30	1.25	.80
RG8	20¢ carmine rose	4.50	2.95	3.00	1.95
RG9	25¢ carmine rose	4.50	2.95	3.50	2.25
RG10	40¢ carmine rose	6.00	3.85	5.25	3.35
RG11	50¢ carmine rose	7.00	4.50	5.75	3.75
RG12	80¢ carmine rose	11.00	7.00	7.00	4.50
RG13	$1 green	11.00	7.00	8.25	5.50
RG14	$2 rose	14.50	9.50	12.00	8.00
RG15	$3 violet	30.00	19.50	25.00	16.00
RG16	$4 yellow brown	20.00	13.00	15.00	10.00
RG17	$5 dark blue	26.50	17.50	14.50	9.50
RG18	$10 orange	45.00	28.75	14.50	9.50
RG19	$30 vermillion ......(cut cancel 20.00)	....	....	35.00	22.50
RG20	$60 brown ....(cut cancel 30.00)	....	....	60.00	38.75
RG21	$100 green	105.00	70.00	35.00	22.50
RG22	$500 blue ....(cut cancel 110.00)	300.00	200.00	235.00	160.00
RG23	$1000 orange ......(cut cancel 70.00)	....	....	120.00	77.50
RG26	$100 green, 11mm. spacing	130.00	85.00	60.00	38.75
RG27	$1000 orange, 11mm. spacing	....	....	575.00	375.00

TOBACCO SALE TAX STAMPS

Documentary Stamps of 1917 Overprinted

TOBACCO SALE TAX

1934

RJ1	1¢ carmine rose	.40	25	.20	.13
RJ2	2¢ carmine rose	.45	.30	.25	.17
RJ3	5¢ carmine rose	1.40	.90	.45	.30
RJ4	10¢ carmine rose	1.75	1.15	.45	.30
RJ5	25¢ carmine rose	4.75	3.00	1.85	1.20
RJ6	50¢ carmine rose	4.75	3.00	1.85	1.20
RJ7	$1 green	8.00	3.00	1.85	1.20
RJ8	$2 rose	15.00	9.50	2.15	1.40
RJ9	$5 dark blue	17.50	11.00	4.75	3.00
RJ10	$10 orange	30.00	19.00	12.00	7.75
RJ11	$20 olive bistre	70.00	45.00	15.00	9.75

HUNTING PERMIT STAMPS

RW1

RW6

SCOTT NO.	DESCRIPTION	PLATE BLOCK			UNUSED			USED	
		F/NH	F/OG	AVG/OG	F/NH	F/OG	AVG/OG	F	AVG

1934-1938 Inscribed: DEPARTMENT OF AGRICULTURE

SCOTT NO.	DESCRIPTION	F/NH	F/OG	AVG/OG	F/NH	F/OG	AVG/OG	F	AVG
RW1	1934 $1 Mallards	....	....	....	550.00	365.00	215.00	100.00	60.00
RW2	1935 $1 Canvasbacks	....	....	....	625.00	415.00	250.00	200.00	120.00
RW3	1936 $1 Canada Geese	....	....	....	350.00	230.00	140.00	90.00	55.00
RW4	1937 $1 Scaup Ducks	2650.00	1800.00	1100.00	225.00	150.00	90.00	42.50	26.50
RW5	1938 $1 Pintail Drake	2750.00	1850.00	1150.00	240.00	160.00	100.00	42.50	26.50

1939-1958 Inscribed: DEPARTMENT OF INTERIOR

SCOTT NO.	DESCRIPTION	F/NH	F/OG	AVG/OG	F/NH	F/OG	AVG/OG	F	AVG
RW6	1939 $1 Green-Winged Teal	1800.00	1200.00	750.00	185.00	125.00	80.00	30.00	19.50
RW7	1940 $1 Black Mallards	1700.00	1100.00	700.00	180.00	120.00	75.00	30.00	19.50
RW8	1941 $1 Ruddy Ducks	1500.00	1000.00	625.00	180.00	120.00	75.00	30.00	19.50
RW9	1942 $1 Baldpates	1400.00	950.00	575.00	180.00	120.00	75.00	30.00	19.50
RW10	1943 $1 Wood Ducks	625.00	425.00	280.00	85.00	60.00	40.00	30.00	19.50
RW11	1944 $1 White Fronted Geese	625.00	425.00	280.00	85.00	60.00	40.00	25.00	16.50
RW12	1945 $1 Shoveller Ducks	400.00	300.00	200.00	55.00	40.00	27.00	20.00	13.00
RW13	1946 $1 Redhead Duck	400.00	300.00	200.00	55.00	40.00	27.00	13.75	9.00
RW14	1947 $1 Snow Geese	400.00	300.00	200.00	55.00	40.00	27.00	13.75	9.00
RW15	1948 $1 Buffleheads	400.00	300.00	200.00	55.00	40.00	27.00	13.75	9.00

RW18   RW24

SCOTT NO.	DESCRIPTION	F/NH	F/OG	AVG/OG	F/NH	F/OG	AVG/OG	F	AVG
RW16	1949 $2 Goldeneye Ducks	400.00	300.00	200.00	57.50	41.50	28.00	12.50	8.00
RW17	1950 $2 Trumpeter Swans	475.00	390.00	260.00	67.50	55.00	35.00	12.50	8.00
RW18	1951 $2 Gadwell Ducks	475.00	390.00	260.00	67.50	55.00	35.00	9.50	6.25
RW19	1952 $2 Harlequin Ducks	475.00	390.00	260.00	67.50	55.00	35.00	9.50	6.25
RW20	1953 $2 Blue-Winged Teal	475.00	390.00	260.00	67.50	55.00	35.00	9.50	6.25
RW21	1954 $2 Ring-Necked Ducks	500.00	400.00	270.00	70.00	56.50	36.50	9.50	6.25
RW22	1955 $2 Blue Geese	500.00	400.00	270.00	70.00	56.50	36.50	9.50	6.25
RW23	1956 $2 American Merganser	500.00	400.00	270.00	70.00	56.50	36.50	9.50	6.25
RW24	1957 $2 American Eider	500.00	400.00	270.00	70.00	56.50	36.50	9.50	6.25
RW25	1958 $2 Canada Geese	500.00	400.00	270.00	70.00	56.50	36.50	9.50	6.25

NOTES ON HUNTING PERMIT STAMPS
1. Unused stamps without gum (uncancelled) are priced at one-half gummed price.
2. The date printed on the stamp is one year later than the date of issue listed above.
3. #RW1-RW22 and RW31 are plate blocks of 6.

VERY FINE QUALITY: To determine the Very Fine price, add the difference between the Fine and Average prices to the Fine quality price. For example: if the Fine price is $10.00 and the Average price is $6.00, the Very Fine price would be $14.00. From 1935 to date, add 20% to the Fine price to arrive at the Very Fine price.

SCOTT NO.	DESCRIPTION	PLATE BLOCKS F/NH	F/OG	UNUSED F/NH	F/OG	USED F

RW26

MIGRATORY BIRD HUNTING STAMP
RW36

1959-1987

SCOTT NO.	DESCRIPTION	PLATE BLOCKS F/NH	F/OG	UNUSED F/NH	F/OG	USED F
RW26	1959 $3 Dog & Mallard	500.00	425.00	100.00	85.00	8.75
RW27	1960 $3 Redhead Ducks	550.00	460.00	110.00	90.00	8.75
RW28	1961 $3 Mallard Hen & Dklngs.	600.00	500.00	125.00	105.00	8.75
RW29	1962 $3 Pintail Drakes	675.00	575.00	140.00	120.00	8.75
RW30	1963 $3 Brant Landing Ducks	675.00	575.00	140.00	120.00	8.75
RW31	1964 $3 Hawaiian Nene Goose	3500.00	3000.00	135.00	115.00	8.75
RW32	1965 $3 Canvasback Drakes ...	650.00	550.00	135.00	115.00	8.75
RW33	1966 $3 Whistling Swans	650.00	550.00	135.00	115.00	8.75
RW34	1967 $3 Old Squaw Ducks	650.00	550.00	135.00	115.00	8.75
RW35	1968 $3 Hooded Mergansers ...	350.00	300.00	75.00	66.50	8.75
RW36	1969 $3 White-Winged Scoters	325.00	280.00	70.00	62.50	8.75
RW37	1970 $3 Ross' Goose	285.00	250.00	60.00	52.50	8.75
RW38	1971 $3 Three Cinnamon Teal	220.00	195.00	45.00	40.00	8.75
RW39	1972 $5 Emperor Geese	165.00	145.00	35.00	31.00	7.50
RW40	1973 $5 Steller's Eider	16500	145.00	35.00	31.00	7.50
RW41	1974 $5 Wood Ducks	120.00	110.00	25.00	22.50	7.50
RW42	1975 $5 Canvasbacks	120.00	110.00	25.00	22.50	7.50

RW46

U.S. DEPARTMENT OF THE INTERIOR
RW53

SCOTT NO.	DESCRIPTION	PLATE BLOCKS F/NH	F/OG	UNUSED F/NH	F/OG	USED F
RW43	1976 $5 Canada Geese	120.00	110.00	25.00	22.50	7.50
RW44	1977 $5 Pair of Ross' Geese ...	120.00	110.00	25.00	22.50	7.50
RW45	1978 $5 Hooded Merganser Drake	120.00	110.00	25.00	22.50	7.50
RW46	1979 $7.50 Green-Winged Teal	120.00	110.00	25.00	22.50	7.50
RW47	1980 $7.50 Mallards	120.00	110.00	25.00	22.50	7.50
RW48	1981 $7.50 Ruddy Ducks	120.00	110.00	25.00	22.50	7.50
RW49	1982 $7.50 Canvasbacks	120.00	110.00	25.00	22.50	7.50
RW50	1983 $7.50 Pintails	120.00	110.00	25.00	22.50	7.50
RW51	1984 $7.50 Wigeon	95.00	....	20.00	....	7.50
RW52	1985 $7.50 Cinnamon Teal	87.50	....	18.50	....	7.50
RW53	1986 $7.50 Fulvous Whistling	87.50	....	18.50	....	7.50
RW54	1987 $10.00 Redhead Ducks ...	97.50	....	20.00	....	8.75

SCOTT NO.	DESCRIPTION	UNUSED NH F	AVG	UNUSED OG F	AVG	USED F	AVG

CANAL ZONE

CANAL ZONE

1904
U.S. Stamp 300,
319, 304, 306-07
overprinted **PANAMA**

4	1¢ blue green	55.00	30.00	35.00	21.00	32.50	19.50
5	2¢ carmine	46.50	26.75	30.00	18.50	25.00	15.00
6	5¢ blue	170.00	100.00	110.00	67.50	87.50	52.50
7	8¢ violet black	300.00	165.00	195.00	115.00	150.00	90.00
8	10¢ pale red brown	300.00	165.00	195.00	115.00	150.00	90.00

1924-25 CANAL
U.S. Stamps 551-54,
557, 562, 564-66, 569-71
overprinted ZONE

Type 1 Flat Tops on Letters "A." Perf. 11

70	1/2¢ olive brown	2.25	1.20	1.50	.85	1.25	.75
71	1¢ deep green	3.75	2.10	2.50	1.50	1.00	.60
71e	same, b. pane of 6	210.00	120.00	140.00	85.00	....	....
72	1-1/2¢ yellow brown	4.95	2.75	3.35	1.95	2.00	1.20
73	2¢ carmine	18.50	10.50	12.50	7.50	2.25	1.35
73a	same, b. pane of 6	265.00	150.00	175.00	105.00	....	....
74	5¢ dark blue	42.75	25.00	28.50	17.50	12.50	7.50
75	10¢ orange	110.00	63.50	75.00	45.00	27.50	16.50
76	12¢ brown violet	82.50	48.50	55.00	33.50	38.75	23.00
77	14¢ dark blue	52.50	29.50	35.00	21.00	27.50	16.50
78	15¢ gray	130.00	75.00	85.00	52.50	42.50	25.00
79	30¢ olive brown	80.00	46.50	52.50	32.50	37.50	22.50
80	50¢ lilac	190.00	105.00	125.00	75.00	50.00	30.00
81	$1 violet brown	600.00	350.00	400.00	240.00	200.00	120.00

1925-28 CANAL
U.S. Stamps 554-55,
557, 564-66, 623, 567,
569-71, overprinted
ZONE

Type II Pointed Tops on Letters "A"

84	2¢ carmine	63.50	35.00	42.50	25.00	17.50	10.75
84d	same, b. pane of 6	300.00	170.00	200.00	120.00	....	....
85	3¢ violet	9.50	5.25	6.25	3.75	4.50	2.75
86	5¢ dark blue	9.50	5.25	6.25	3.75	3.25	1.95
87	10¢ orange	75.00	42.50	50.00	30.00	15.00	9.00
88	12¢ brown violet	56.50	31.50	37.50	22.50	25.00	15.00
89	14¢ dark blue	45.00	26.50	30.00	18.00	27.50	16.50
90	15¢ gray	14.75	8.00	9.75	5.75	5.75	3.50
91	17¢ black	9.50	5.25	6.25	3.75	5.75	3.50
92	20¢ carmine	15.00	8.50	10.00	6.00	6.75	4.00
93	30¢ olive brown	11.75	6.75	7.75	4.75	6.00	3.65
94	50¢ lilac	600.00	335.00	400.00	240.00	200.00	120.00
95	$1 violet brown	300.00	165.00	200.00	120.00	75.00	45.00

1926 Type II overprint on U.S. Stamp 627

| 96 | 2¢ carmine rose | 9.95 | 5.50 | 6.75 | 4.00 | 5.00 | 3.00 |

1927 Type II overprint on U.S. Stamps 583-84, 591
Rotary Press Printing, Perf. 10

97	2¢ carmine	90.00	51.50	60.00	36.50	15.75	9.50
98	3¢ violet	18.50	10.75	12.50	7.50	7.00	4.25
99	10¢ orange	29.50	16.50	19.50	11.75	11.75	7.00

VERY FINE QUALITY: To determine the Very Fine price, add the difference between the Fine and Average prices to the Fine quality price. For example: if the Fine price is $10.00 and the Average price is $6.00, the Very Fine price would be $14.00. From 1935 to date, add 20% to the Fine price to arrive at the Very Fine price.

SCOTT NO.	DESCRIPTION	PLATE BLOCK F/NH	F	AVG	UNUSED F/NH	F	AVG	USED F	AVG

1927-31
Type II overprint on U.S. Stamps 632, 634-35, 637, 642
Rotary Press Printing, Perf. 11 x 10-1/2

100	1¢ green	35.00	25.00	15.00	4.25	3.25	1.95	1.75	1.00
101	2¢ carmine	37.50	26.50	16.00	4.50	3.35	2.10	1.10	.65
101a	same, b. pane of 6	....	....	....	250.00	200.00	125.00	....	....
102	3¢ violet (1931)	160.00	115.00	70.00	7.50	5.50	3.35	4.50	2.75
103	5¢ dark blue	300.00	215.00	130.00	45.00	32.50	19.50	15.00	9.00
104	10¢ orange (1930)	280.00	200.00	120.00	35.00	25.00	15.00	17.50	10.50

105,160   106   107   108,161   109

110   111   112   113   114

1928-40 Builders Issue

105-14	1¢ to 50¢ cpl., 10 vars.	....	....	....	14.50	10.75	7.00	6.75	4.25
105	1¢ Gorgas	1.25(6)	.95	.60	.16	.12	.08	.13	.08
106	2¢ Goethals	3.50(6)	2.75	1.65	.32	.25	.16	.18	.11
106a	same, b. pane of 6	....	....	....	25.00	18.75	11.00	....	....
107	5¢ Gaillard Cut (1929)	20.00(6)	15.50	9.50	2.50	1.90	1.15	1.00	.60
108	10¢ Hodges (1932)	8.25(6)	6.25	3.85	.50	.37	.23	.25	.16
109	12¢ Galliard (1929)	16.50(6)	12.50	7.50	1.75	1.30	.80	1.00	.60
110	14¢ Sibert (1937)	18.50(6)	14.00	8.50	2.00	1.50	.95	1.35	.85
111	15¢ Smith (1932)	11.00(6)	8.75	5.50	.80	.60	.38	.65	.40
112	20¢ Rousseau (1932)	11.50(6)	9.00	5.75	1.30	1.00	.65	.35	.22
113	30¢ Williamson (1940)	16.50(6)	12.75	7.75	1.75	1.30	.90	1.10	.70
114	50¢ Blackburn (1929)	27.50(6)	21.50	13.50	3.65	2.75	1.75	1.10	.70

1933
Type II overprint on U.S. Stamps 720 & 695
Rotary Press Printing, Perf. 11 x 10-1/2

| 115 | 3¢ Washington | 26.50 | 20.00 | 12.50 | 3.75 | 3.00 | 1.85 | .50 | .30 |
| 116 | 14¢ Indian | 69.50 | 55.00 | 32.75 | 9.75 | 7.75 | 4.75 | 5.75 | 3.75 |

117,153

1934

| 117 | 3¢ Goethals | 3.00(6) | 2.40 | 1.50 | .25 | .20 | .13 | .12 | .08 |
| 117a | same, b. pane of 6 | .... | .... | .... | 75.00 | 55.00 | 35.00 | .... | .... |

PLATE BLOCKS: are portions of a sheet of stamps adjacent to the number(s) indicating the printing plate number used to produce that sheet. Flat plate issues are usually collected in plate blocks of six (number opposite middle stamp) while rotary issues are normally corner blocks of four.

SCOTT NO.	DESCRIPTION	PLATE BLOCKS F/NH	PLATE BLOCKS F/OG	UNUSED F/NH	UNUSED F/OG	USED F

1939 U.S. Stamps 803, 805 overprinted

| 118 | 1/2¢ red orange | 3.75 | 3.00 | .18 | .15 | .13 |
| 119 | 1-1/2¢ bistre brown | 4.50 | 3.75 | .22 | .18 | .18 |

122 Gaillard Cut — Before	123 After
124 Bas Obispo — Before	125 After
126 Gatun Locks — Before	127 After
128 Canal Channel — Before	129 After
130 Gamboa — Before	131 After
132 Pedro Miguel Locks — Before	133 After
134 Gatun Spillway — Before	135 After

120
Balboa — Before

121
Balboa — After

1939 25th ANNIVERSARY ISSUE

120-35	1¢-50¢ cpl., 16 vars.			225.00	190.00	115.00
120	1¢ yellow green	12.00(6)	10.00	.95	.80	.70
121	2¢ rose carmine	13.50(6)	10.75	1.25	1.05	.90
122	3¢ purple	12.00(6)	10.00	.95	.80	.40
123	5¢ dark blue	19.50(6)	16.00	1.95	1.65	1.65
124	6¢ red orange	45.00(6)	38.50	5.50	4.75	2.75
125	7¢ black	45.00(6)	38.50	5.50	4.75	2.75
126	8¢ green	62.50(6)	53.50	7.75	6.65	6.00
127	10¢ ultramarine	62.50(6)	53.50	7.75	6.65	4.50
128	11¢ blue green	140.00(6)	120.00	17.50	14.75	13.75
129	12¢ brown carmine	125.00(6)	105.00	15.00	12.75	11.75
130	14¢ dark violet	130.00(6)	110.00	16.00	13.50	11.75
131	15¢ olive green	200.00(6)	170.00	25.00	21.50	9.50
132	18¢ rose pink	185.00(6)	160.00	22.50	19.00	15.00
133	20¢ brown	225.00(6)	190.00	27.50	23.50	8.00
134	25¢ orange	365.00(6)	315.00	45.00	38.50	21.75
135	50¢ violet brown	400.00(6)	340.00	50.00	42.50	9.50

1946-49

136-40	1/2¢-25¢ cpl., 5 vars.			5.50	4.65	3.50
136	1/2¢ Major General Davis (1948)	5.25(6)	4.50	.65	.55	.35
137	1-1/2¢ Gov. Magoon (1948)	5.25(6)	4.50	.65	.55	.35
138	2¢ T. Roosevelt (1948)	1.60(6)	1.20	.18	.15	.14
139	5¢ Stevens	6.75(6)	5.25	.75	.60	.27
140	25¢ J.F. Wallace (1948)	30.00(6)	25.00	3.50	2.90	2.50

141 **142** **143** **144** **145**

1948 CANAL ZONE BIOLOGICAL AREA

141	10¢ Map & Coati-mundi	25.00(6)	21.50	3.25	2.85	1.95

1949 CALIFORNIA GOLD RUSH

142-45	3¢-18¢ cpl., 4 vars.			9.75	8.35	6.95
142	3¢ "Forty Niners"	8.75(6)	7.85	1.10	1.00	.55
143	6¢ Journey-Las Cruces	11.75(6)	10.50	1.10	1.00	.75
144	12¢ Las Cruces-Panama Trail	27.50(6)	23.75	3.35	2.85	2.35
145	18¢ Departure-San Francisco	35.00(6)	30.00	4.50	4.00	3.50

AVERAGE QUALITY: From 1935 to date, deduct 20% from the Fine price to determine the price for an Average quality stamp.

SCOTT NO.	DESCRIPTION	PLATE BLOCKS F/NH	F	UNUSED F/NH	F	USED F

C36   C37   C38   C39

C40   C41   C42-C53

1951-58

Scott No.	Description	PB F/NH	PB F	Unused F/NH	Unused F	Used F
146	10¢ West Indian Labor	47.50(6)	42.50	5.75	5.25	2.75
147	3¢ Panama Railroad (1955)	12.50(6)	11.00	1.50	1.35	1.10
148	3¢ Gorgas Hospital (1957)	7.50	6.50	1.10	1.00	.75
149	4¢ S.S. Ancon (1958)	6.75	6.00	1.00	.90	.65
150	5¢ T. Roosevelt (1958)	7.50	6.50	1.00	.90	.75

1960-62

151	4¢ Boy Scout Badge	7.00	6.25	1.10	1.00	.70
152	4¢ Administration Building	2.50	2.25	.50	.45	.35

LINE PAIR

153	3¢ G.W. Goethals, coil	2.10	1.90	.30	.27	.20
154	4¢ Admin. Building, coil	2.35	2.10	.40	.35	.25
155	5¢ J.F. Stevens, coil (1962)	2.50	2.25	.60	.55	.35

PLATE BLOCK

156	4¢ Girl Scout Badge (1962)	6.50	5.75	.85	.75	.60
157	4¢ Thatcher Ferry Bridge (1962)	7.50	6.75	.70	.65	.50

158   159   163   165

1968-78

158	6¢ Goethals Memorial	4.00	....	.65	....	.25
159	8¢ Fort San Lorenzo (1971)	5.50	....	.80	....	.30

LINE PAIR

160	1¢ W.C. Gorgas, coil (1975)	2.00	....	.18	....	.15
161	10¢ H.F. Hodges, coil (1975)	8.75	....	1.50	....	.80
162	25¢ J.F. Wallace, coil (1975)	45.00	....	6.75	....	4.00

PLATE BLOCK

163	13¢ Cascades Dredge (1976)	4.50	....	.90	....	.60
163a	same, b. pane of 4	....	....	4.50	....	....
164	5¢ J.F. Stevens (#117)					
	Rotary Press (1977)	5.00	....	1.00	....	.80
165	15¢ Locomotive (1978)	4.50	....	.90	....	.60

SCOTT NO.	DESCRIPTION	PLATE BLOCK F/NH	F	AVG	UNUSED F/NH	F	AVG	USED F	AVG

AIR MAIL STAMPS

105 & 106 Surcharged

AIR MAIL

1929-31   **25 CENTS 25**

C1	15¢ on 1¢ green, Type I	300.00(6)	200.00	120.00	25.00	16.50	10.00	10.00	6.00
C2	15¢ on 1¢ y. green, Type II (1931)	......	......	......	180.00	120.00	72.50	120.00	72.50
C3	25¢ on 2¢ carmine	190.00(6)	125.00	75.00	11.75	6.00	3.65	5.50	3.25

AIR MAIL

≡10 c

1929

C4	10¢ on 50¢ lilac	215.00(6)	150.00	90.00	22.50	15.00	9.00	12.75	7.75
C5	20¢ on 2¢ carmine	175.00(6)	120.00	72.50	15.00	10.00	6.00	3.25	1.95

C6-14   C15   C16   C17

C18   C19   C20

1931-49

C6-14	4¢-$1 cpl., 9 vars.	......	......	......	50.00	37.50	24.50	13.50	8.95
C6	4¢ Gaillard Cut, red violet (1949)	12.50(6)	8.50	5.75	1.75	1.30	.85	1.30	.85
C7	5¢ Same, yellow green	8.75(6)	6.50	4.25	1.20	.90	.55	.70	.45
C8	6¢ Same, yellow brown (1946)	12.50(6)	8.50	5.75	1.75	1.30	.85	.70	.45
C9	10¢ Same, orange	20.00(6)	15.00	10.00	2.00	1.50	1.00	.70	.45
C10	15¢ Same, blue	27.50(6)	21.00	12.50	2.75	2.10	1.25	.55	.35
C11	20¢ Same, red violet	40.00(6)	30.00	20.00	4.95	3.75	2.50	.55	.35
C12	30¢ Same, rose lake (1941)	67.50(6)	50.00	33.50	7.50	5.65	3.75	2.10	1.40
C13	40¢ Same, yellow	67.50(6)	50.00	33.50	7.50	5.65	3.75	2.10	1.40
C14	$1 Same, black	200.00(6)	150.00	100.00	23.50	17.50	11.50	5.00	3.35

SCOTT NO.	DESCRIPTION	PLATE BLOCKS F/NH	F/OG	UNUSED F/NH	F/OG	USED F

1939 25th ANNIVERSARY ISSUE

C15-20	5¢-$1 cpl., 6 vars.	......	......	160.00	125.00	105.00
C15	5¢ Plane over Sosa Hill	60.00(6)	47.50	7.75	6.25	5.75
C16	10¢ Map of Central America	75.00(6)	60.00	7.75	6.25	5.50
C17	15¢ Scene near Fort Amador	75.00(6)	60.00	7.75	6.25	2.35
C18	25¢ Clipper at Cristobal Harbor	300.00(6)	240.00	37.50	30.00	19.50
C19	30¢ Clipper over Gaillard Cut	250.00(6)	200.00	27.50	21.75	15.00
C20	$1 Clipper Alighting	600.00(6)	475.00	75.00	60.00	60.00

SCOTT NO.	DESCRIPTION	PLATE BLOCKS F/NH	F/OG	UNUSED F/NH	F/OG	USED F

C21-31, C34　　　C32　　　C33　　　C35

1951

C21-26	4¢-80¢ cpl., 6 vars.	....	....	45.00	40.00	16.75
C21	4¢ Globe & Wing, red violet ...	12.00(6)	11.00	1.50	1.35	.60
C22	6¢ Same, brown	10.00(6)	9.00	1.25	1.10	.50
C23	10¢ Same, red orange	15.00(6)	13.50	1.75	1.55	.75
C24	21¢ Same, blue	130.00(6)	115.00	16.50	15.00	6.75
C25	31¢ Same, cerise	120.00(6)	110.00	15.00	13.50	5.75
C26	80¢ Same, gray black	100.00(6)	90.00	12.50	11.00	2.75

1958

C27-31	5¢-35¢ cpl., 5 vars.	....	....	57.50	51.50	14.95
C27	5¢ Globe & Wing, y. green	13.50	12.0	2.75	2.50	1.35
C28	7¢ Same, olive	11.75	10.50	2.00	1.80	1.00
C29	15¢ Same, brown violet	72.50	65.00	12.50	11.00	3.50
C30	25¢ Same, orange yellow	160.00	140.00	27.50	25.00	4.75
C31	35¢ Same, dark blue	100.00	90.00	17.50	15.75	4.50

1961-63

C32	15¢ Emblem Caribbean School	25.00	22.50	3.50	3.15	2.25
C33	7¢ Anti-Malaria (1962)	7.75	7.00	1.30	1.20	1.00
C34	8¢ Globe & Wing, carmine (1963)	11.50	10.50	1.45	1.30	.65
C35	15¢ Alliance for Progress (1963)	30.00	27.00	3.25	2.85	1.95

C36　　　C37　　　C38　　　C39

C40　　　C41　　　C42-C53

1964, 50th ANNIVERSARY ISSUE

C36-41	6¢-80¢ cpl., 6 vars.	....	....	23.50	21.00	16.50
C36	6¢ Cristobal	5.75	5.15	.95	.85	.80
C37	8¢ Gatun Locks	6.50	5.85	1.10	1.00	.75
C38	15¢ Madden Dam	16.00	14.50	2.75	2.50	1.25
C39	20¢ Gaillard Cut	20.00	18.00	3.50	3.15	1.95
C40	30¢ Miraflores Locks	35.00	31.50	6.00	5.35	4.75
C41	80¢ Balboa	57.50	52.50	10.00	9.00	7.50

1965

C42-47	6¢-80¢ cpl., 6 vars.	....	....	12.75	....	6.25
C42	6¢ Gov. Seal, green & black	5.00	....	.80	....	.65
C43	8¢ Same, rose red & black	5.25	....	.85	....	.35
C44	15¢ Same, blue & black	5.25	....	.85	....	.65
C45	20¢ Same, lilac & black	8.25	....	1.65	....	.95
C46	30¢ Same, brown & black	11.50	....	2.25	....	1.00
C47	80¢ Same, yellow black	35.00	....	7.00	....	2.75

SCOTT NO.	DESCRIPTION	PLATE BLOCKS F/NH	F	UNUSED F/NH	F	USED F
		1968-76				
C48-53	10¢-35¢ cpl., 6 vars.	....	....	10.75	....	5.75
C48	10¢ Gov. Seal, salmon & black	3.75	....	.75	....	.50
C48a	same, b. pane of 4	....	....	7.50	....	....
C49	11¢ Seal, olive & black (1971)	4.25	....	.90	....	.60
C49a	same, b. pane of 4	....	....	6.25	....	....
C50	13¢ Seal, green & black (1974)	9.75	....	2.00	....	.95
C50a	same, b. pane of 4	....	....	10.00	....	....
C51	22¢ Seal, blue & black (1976)	12.50	....	2.25	....	1.15
C52	25¢ Seal, light olive & black	12.50	....	2.25	....	1.15
C53	35¢ Seal, salmon & black (1976)	15.00	....	3.00	....	1.50

AIR MAIL OFFICIAL STAMPS

C7-14 Overprinted
1941-42 Overprint 19 to 20-1/2mm. long

SCOTT NO.	DESCRIPTION	PLATE BLOCKS		UNUSED F/NH	F	USED F
CO1-7	5¢-$1 cpl., 7 vars.	....	....	250.00	185.00	70.00
CO1	5¢ Gaillard Cut, l. green (#C7)	....	....	10.75	8.00	3.50
CO2	10¢ Same, orange (#C9)	....	....	19.50	14.75	4.75
CO3	15¢ Same, blue (#C10)	....	....	26.50	20.00	6.50
CO4	20¢ Same, deep violet (#C11)	....	....	35.00	26.50	10.00
CO5	30¢ Same, rose lake (1942)(#C12)	....	....	42.50	31.75	10.00
CO6	40¢ Same, yellow (#C13)	....	....	52.50	38.75	16.50
CO7	$1 Same, black (#C14)	....	....	70.00	55.00	22.50

1947 Overprint 19 to 20-1/2mm. Long

CO14	6¢ yellow brown (#C8)	....	....	....	29.50	23.75	10.00

SCOTT NO.	DESCRIPTION	UNUSED NH F	AVG	UNUSED F	AVG	USED F	AVG

POSTAGE DUE STAMPS

1914
U.S. Postage Due Stamps
J45-46, 49 overprinted　　*CANAL ZONE*

J1	1¢ rose carmine	150.00	82.50	95.00	57.50	25.00	15.00
J2	2¢ rose carmine	395.00	250.00	250.00	150.00	95.00	55.00
J3	10¢ rose carmine	1100.00	600.00	700.00	425.00	95.00	55.00

1924 Type I overprint on U.S. Postage Due Stamps J61-62, 65

J12	1¢ carmine rose	225.00	125.00	150.00	90.00	45.00	27.50
J13	2¢ deep claret	140.00	77.50	95.00	57.50	22.50	13.50
J14	10¢ deep claret	525.00	295.00	350.00	215.00	87.50	52.50

1925
Canal Zone Stamps　　**POSTAGE**
71, 73, 75 overprinted　　**DUE**

J15	1¢ deep green	170.00	95.00	120.00	72.50	30.00	18.00
J16	2¢ carmine	47.50	26.50	33.75	20.00	12.50	7.50
J17	10¢ orange	80.00	45.00	57.50	35.00	18.75	11.00

1925 Type II overprint on U.S. Postage Due Stamps J61-62, 65

J18	1¢ deep claret	17.50	9.75	12.50	7.50	4.75	2.85
J19	2¢ deep claret	27.50	14.50	18.75	11.00	8.50	5.25
J20	10¢ deep claret	210.00	120.00	150.00	90.00	32.50	19.50

POSTAGE DUE

1929-30
107 surcharged　　≡ **-1-** ≡

J21	1¢ on 5¢ blue	6.75	3.75	5.00	3.00	2.75	1.65
J22	2¢ on 5¢ blue	12.75	8.00	9.50	5.75	4.00	2.50
J23	5¢ on 5¢ blue	12.75	8.00	9.50	5.75	4.75	3.00
J24	10¢ on 5¢ blue	12.75	8.00	9.50	5.75	4.75	3.00

SCOTT NO.	DESCRIPTION	UNUSED NH F	AVG	UNUSED OG F	AVG	USED F	AVG

J25-29

1932-41

SCOTT NO.	DESCRIPTION	UNUSED NH F	AVG	UNUSED OG F	AVG	USED F	AVG
J25-29	1¢-15¢ cpl., 5 vars.	7.00	4.50	5.25	3.50	5.00	3.00
J25	1¢ claret	.25	.16	.18	.12	.20	.14
J26	2¢ claret	.40	.25	.30	.20	.20	.13
J27	5¢ claret	.80	.50	.60	.40	.40	.25
J28	10¢ claret	3.15	2.15	2.35	1.75	2.50	1.60
J29	15¢ claret (1941)	2.75	1.70	2.10	1.40	1.80	1.10

SCOTT NO.	DESCRIPTION	UNUSED F/NH	F	USED F

OFFICIAL STAMPS

1941
105, 117, 107, 108, 111, 112,
114, 139 overprinted

OFFICIAL PANAMA CANAL

OFFICIAL PANAMA CANAL

"PANAMA" 10mm. Long

SCOTT NO.	DESCRIPTION	UNUSED F/NH	F	USED F
O1/9	1¢-50¢ (O1-2, 4-7, 9) 7 vars.	....	200.00	150.00	35.00
O1	1¢ yellow green (#105)		4.75	3.50	.85
O2	3¢ deep violet (#117)		8.75	6.50	1.50
O3	5¢ blue (#107)		....	....	52.50
O4	10¢ orange (#108)		13.50	10.00	3.75
O5	15¢ gray (#111)		26.50	20.00	4.25
O6	20¢ olive brown (#112)		29.50	22.50	5.00
O7	50¢ rose lilac (#114)		110.00	82.50	15.00

1947

| O9 | 5¢ deep blue (#139) | | 19.75 | 14.75 | 6.00 |

CANAL ZONE MINT POSTAL STATIONERY ENTIRES

SCOTT NO.	DESCRIPTION	MINT ENTIRE
	ENVELOPES	
U16	1934, 3¢ purple	2.15
U17	1958, 4¢ blue	2.40
U18	1969, 4¢ + 1¢ blue	2.40
U19	1969, 4¢ + 2¢ blue	4.50
U20	1971, 8¢ Gaillard Cut	1.40
U21	1974, 8¢ + 2¢ Gaillard Cut	1.95
U22	1976, 13¢ Gaillard Cut	1.15
U23	1978, 13¢ + 2¢ Gaillard Cut	1.25
	AIR MAIL ENVELOPES	
UC3	1949, 6¢ DC-4 Skymaster	7.50
UC4	1958, 7¢ DC-4 Skymaster	7.75
UC5	1963, 3¢ + 5¢ purple	10.00
UC6	1964, 8¢ Tail Assembly	3.50
UC7	1964, 4¢ + 4¢ blue	6.75
UC8	1966, 8¢ Tail Assembly	6.75
UC9	1968, 8¢ + 2¢ Tail Assembly	5.25
UC10	1968, 4¢ + 4¢ + 2¢ blue	3.75
UC11	1969, 10¢ Tail Assembly	6.95
UC12	1971, 4¢ + 5¢ + 2¢ blue	5.95
UC13	1971, 10¢ + 1¢ Tail Assembly	6.50
UC14	1971, 11¢ Tail Assembly	2.00
UC15	1974, 11¢ + 2¢ Tail Assembly	2.75
UC16	1975, 8¢ + 2¢ + 3¢ emerald	3.00

SCOTT NO.	DESCRIPTION	MINT ENTIRE
	POSTAL CARDS	
UX10	1935, 1¢ ov. print on U.S. #UX27	2.50
UX11	1952, 2¢ ov. print on U.S. #UX38	2.75
UX12	1958, 3¢ Ship in Lock	2.50
UX13	1963, 3¢ + 1¢ Ship in Lock	7.75
UX14	1964, 4¢ Ship in Canal	6.50
UX15	1965, 4¢ Ship in Lock	1.75
UX16	1968, 4¢ + 1¢ Ship in Lock	1.75
UX17	1969, 5¢ Ship in Lock	1.50
UX18	1971, 5¢ + 1¢ Ship in Lock	1.10
UX19	1974, 8¢ Ship in Lock	.90
UX20	1976, 8¢ + 1¢ Ship in Lock	.90
UX21	1978, 8¢ + 2¢ Ship in Lock	.90
	AIR MAIL POSTAL CARDS	
UXC1	1958, 5¢ Plane, Flag & Map	6.75
UXC2	1963, 5¢ + 1¢ Plane, Flag & Map	15.00
UXC3	1965, 4¢ + 2¢ Ship in Lock	6.75
UXC4	1968, 4¢ + 4¢ Ship in Lock	5.25
UXC5	1971, 5¢ + 4¢ Ship in Lock	1.10

SCOTT NO.	DESCRIPTION	UNUSED OG F	AVG	UNUSED F	AVG	USED F	AVG

CONFEDERATE STATES

6: Fine Print
7: Coarse Print

1, 4	2, 5	3	6, 7
Jefferson Davis	Thomas Jefferson	Andrew Jackson	Jefferson Davis

1861

Scott	Description	UNUSED OG F	AVG	UNUSED F	AVG	USED F	AVG
1	5¢ green	275.00	165.00	210.00	130.00	130.00	80.00
2	10¢ blue	350.00	210.00	265.00	165.00	225.00	140.00

1862

Scott	Description	UNUSED OG F	AVG	UNUSED F	AVG	USED F	AVG
3	2¢ green	875.00	500.00	650.00	400.00	800.00	495.00
4	5¢ blue	187.50	110.00	140.00	85.00	115.00	70.00
5	10¢ rose	1300.00	775.00	1000.00	625.00	700.00	430.00
6	5¢ blue, London print	18.00	10.50	13.50	8.25	18.75	11.50
7	5¢ blue, Local print	24.00	14.00	18.00	11.50	19.50	12.00

8	9	10, 11 (Die A)	12(Die B)	13	14
Andrew Jackson		Jefferson Davis		George Washington	John C. Calhoun

1863

Scott	Description	UNUSED OG F	AVG	UNUSED F	AVG	USED F	AVG
8	2¢ brown red	100.00	58.50	75.00	46.50	300.00	185.00
9	10¢ blue (TEN)	1175.00	675.00	875.00	535.00	700.00	430.00
10	10¢ blue (with frame line)	....	....	3500.00	2150.00	1800.00	1100.00
11	10¢ blue (no frame)	20.00	11.50	15.00	9.25	17.50	10.75
12	10¢ blue, filled corner	21.00	12.50	15.75	9.75	18.50	11.50
13	20¢ green	70.00	40.00	52.50	32.50	300.00	180.00

1862

Scott	Description	UNUSED OG F	AVG	UNUSED F	AVG	USED F	AVG
14	1¢ orange	200.00	120.00	150.00	95.00	....	....

SCOTT NO.	DESCRIPTION	UNUSED NH F	AVG	UNUSED OG F	AVG	USED F	AVG

CUBA

U.S. Administration

1899

U.S. Stamps of
267, 279, 279B,
268, 281, 282C surcharged

221	1¢ on 1¢ yellow green ...	7.50	4.25	5.00	3.00	.75	.45
222	2¢ on 2¢ carmine	7.50	4.25	5.00	3.00	.60	.35
223	2-1/2¢ on 2¢ red	5.25	2.90	3.50	2.10	.75	.45
224	3¢ on 3¢ purple	14.75	8.00	9.75	5.75	1.60	.95
225	5¢ on 5¢ blue..................	14.75	8.00	9.75	5.75	1.60	.95
226	10¢ on 10¢ brown	41.75	23.50	27.50	16.50	10.00	6.00

Republic under U.S. Military Rule
Watermarked US-C

		227	228	229		230	231

227	1¢ Columbus	5.25	2.95	3.50	2.10	.25	.15
228	2¢ Coconut Palms	5.25	2.95	3.50	2.10	.25	.15
229	3¢ Allegory "Cuba"	5.25	2.95	3.50	2.10	.35	.22
230	5¢ Ocean Liner	8.75	4.95	5.75	3.50	.40	.25
231	10¢ Cane Field	18.75	10.50	12.50	7.50	.90	.55

SPECIAL DELIVERY

1899 Surcharge of 1899 on U.S. E5

E1	10¢ on 10¢ blue	175.00	100.00	115.00	70.00	95.00	55.00

Republic under U.S. Military Rule
Watermarked US-C Inscribed "Immediate"

E2
Special Delivery Messenger

E2	10¢ orange..........................	80.00	45.00	52.50	31.50	13.75	8.00

POSTAGE DUE STAMPS

1899 Surcharge of 1899 on U.S. J38-39, J41-42

J1	1¢ on 1¢ deep claret	41.75	23.50	27.50	16.50	4.25	2.60
J2	2¢ on 2¢ deep claret	35.00	19.50	23.75	14.00	4.25	2.60
J3	5c on 5¢ deep claret	41.75	23.50	27.50	16.50	4.25	2.60
J4	10¢ on 10¢ deep claret ...	35.00	19.50	23.75	14.00	1.85	1.10

GUAM
1899

U.S. Stamps of 279,
267, 268, 272, 280-82C,
284, 275, 276 overprinted

GUAM

GUAM

1	1¢ deep green	50.00	28.50	33.50	20.00	37.50	22.50
2	2¢ carmine..........................	50.00	28.50	33.50	20.00	37.50	22.50
3	3¢ purple...........................	250.00	140.00	165.00	100.00	200.00	120.00
4	4¢ lilac brown	250.00	140.00	165.00	100.00	200.00	120.00
5	5¢ blue.................................	67.50	38.50	45.00	27.50	50.00	30.00
6	6¢ lake.................................	250.00	140.00	165.00	100.00	185.00	110.00
7	8¢ violet brown	240.00	135.00	160.00	95.00	200.00	120.00
8	10¢ brown (Type II)	105.00	60.00	70.00	42.50	85.00	51.50
10	15¢ olive green	250.00	140.00	165.00	100.00	200.00	120.00
11	50¢ orange..........................	435.00	240.00	285.00	170.00	325.00	195.00
12	$1 black (Type II)	750.00	425.00	500.00	300.00	575.00	350.00

SPECIAL DELIVERY

U.S. Stamp E5 overprint

E1	10¢ blue	275.00	150.00	185.00	110.00	225.00	135.00

SCOTT NO.	DESCRIPTION	UNUSED OG F	AVG	UNUSED F	AVG	USED F	AVG

23, 24

25, 26

1864 Laid Paper

| 23 | 1¢ black | 225.00 | 135.00 | 170.00 | 105.00 | .... | .... |
| 24 | 2¢ black | 225.00 | 135.00 | 170.00 | 105.00 | .... | .... |

1865 Wove Paper

| 25 | 1¢ blue | 230.00 | 140.00 | 175.00 | 110.00 | .... | .... |
| 26 | 2¢ blue | 185.00 | 120.00 | 145.00 | 97.50 | .... | .... |

27-29, 50, 51
King Kamehameha IV

30
Princess Kamamalu

31
King Kamehameha IV

32, 39, 52C
King Kamehameha V

33

34
Mataia Kekuanaoa

1861-63

| 27 | 2¢ car. rose, horiz. laid ppr. | 225.00 | 135.00 | 190.00 | 115.00 | 170.00 | 120.00 |
| 28 | 2¢ car. rose, vert. laid ppr. | 225.00 | 135.00 | 190.00 | 115.00 | 170.00 | 120.00 |

1869 Engraved

| 29 | 2¢ red, thin wove paper | 70.00 | 40.00 | 57.50 | 35.00 | .... | .... |

1864-71 Wove Paper

30	1¢ purple	10.75	6.35	9.00	5.50	7.25	4.35
31	2¢ vermillion	16.50	9.35	13.50	8.00	8.25	5.00
32	5¢ blue	70.00	40.00	57.50	35.00	21.75	13.00
33	6¢ green	24.00	14.00	20.00	12.00	7.00	4.25
34	18¢ rose	115.00	63.50	95.00	55.00	16.50	10.00

35, 38, 43
King David Kalakaua

36, 46
Prince William Pitt Leleiohoku

37, 42
Princess Likelike

40, 44, 45
King David Kalakaua

1875

| 35 | 2¢ brown | 8.50 | 5.00 | 7.00 | 4.25 | 2.75 | 1.65 |
| 36 | 12¢ black | 57.50 | 32.50 | 47.50 | 28.50 | 24.50 | 14.75 |

41
Queen Kapiolani

47
Statue of King Kamehameha I

48
King William Lunalilo

49
Queen Emma Kaleleonalani

52
Queen Liliuokalani

1882

37	1¢ blue	5.50	3.25	4.65	2.85	4.65	2.85
38	2¢ lilac rose	135.00	77.50	110.00	65.00	36.50	21.75
39	5¢ ultramarine	17.75	10.00	14.75	8.75	2.75	1.65
40	10¢ black	31.75	18.50	26.50	16.00	18.50	11.00
41	15¢ red brown	57.50	32.75	47.50	28.75	27.50	16.50

1883-86

42	1¢ green	3.15	1.85	2.65	1.60	1.90	1.10
43	2¢ rose	4.75	2.75	4.00	2.40	1.10	.65
44	10¢ red brown	24.00	14.00	20.00	12.00	7.75	4.65
45	10¢ vermillion	26.75	15.50	22.50	13.50	15.00	9.00
46	12¢ red lilac	85.00	48.75	70.00	42.50	36.50	21.50
47	25¢ dark violet	115.00	63.50	95.00	55.00	48.75	29.00

SCOTT NO.	DESCRIPTION	UNUSED OG F	AVG	UNUSED F	AVG	USED F	AVG
48	50¢ red..................	190.00	110.00	160.00	97.50	85.00	50.00
49	$1 rose red................	265.00	155.00	225.00	135.00	95.00	55.00

1890-91

52	2¢ dull violet	8.00	4.75	6.75	4.00	1.50	.90
52C	5¢ dark blue	157.50	95.00	130.00	80.00	90.00	55.00

1893 Provisional Government
Red Overprint

53	1¢ purple...........	5.25	3.00	4.35	2.60	3.85	2.30
54	1¢ blue.............	5.25	3.00	4.35	2.60	5.50	3.25
55	1¢ green............	2.10	1.20	1.75	1.05	2.25	1.35
56	2¢ brown............	6.85	4.00	5.75	3.50	11.50	7.00
57	2¢ dull violet	2.00	1.15	1.65	1.00	1.50	.90
58	5¢ dark blue	12.00	7.00	10.00	6.00	17.50	10.75
59	5¢ ultramarine	6.75	3.95	5.65	3.40	3.85	2.35
60	6¢ green............	13.00	7.75	11.00	6.75	17.50	10.75
61	10¢ black............	9.35	5.50	7.75	4.75	9.00	5.50
62	12¢ black............	10.50	6.25	8.75	5.25	10.00	6.00
63	12¢ red lilac..........	165.00	95.00	135.00	81.50	170.00	100.00
64	25¢ dark violet	28.50	16.00	23.75	14.00	22.50	13.50

Black Overprint

65	2¢ rose vermillion	67.50	38.75	56.50	33.75	55.00	33.50
66	2¢ rose.............	1.80	1.05	1.50	.90	2.00	1.20
67	10¢ vermillion	16.00	9.00	13.00	7.75	20.00	12.00
68	10¢ red brown	8.00	4.65	6.75	4.00	10.00	6.00
69	12¢ red lilac	315.00	185.00	265.00	160.00	285.00	170.00
70	15¢ red brown	23.50	13.50	19.50	11.50	28.75	17.50
71	18¢ dull rose	30.00	17.00	25.00	15.00	33.75	20.00
72	50¢ red.............	77.50	47.50	65.00	40.00	85.00	51.50
73	$1 rose red	130.00	77.50	110.00	67.50	140.00	85.00

74, 80
Coat of Arms

75, 81
View of Honolulu

76
Statue of King
Kamehameha I

77
Star and Palm

78
S.S. "Arawa"

79
Pres. S.B. Dole

82
Statue of King
Kamehameha I

O1-6
Lorrin A. Thurston

SCOTT NO.	DESCRIPTION	UNUSED NH F	AVG	UNUSED OG F	AVG	USED F	AVG

1894

74	1¢ yellow............	3.15	1.75	2.10	1.25	1.45	.85
75	2¢ brown............	3.40	1.90	2.25	1.35	.80	.50
76	5¢ rose lake	6.50	3.65	4.25	2.60	1.90	1.15
77	10¢ yellow green	8.25	4.75	5.50	3.35	5.25	3.25
78	12¢ blue	18.00	10.00	12.00	7.25	12.00	7.25
79	25¢ deep blue	18.00	10.00	12.00	7.25	12.00	7.25

1899

80	1¢ dark green	2.65	1.50	1.75	1.05	1.45	.85
81	2¢ rose.............	2.50	1.40	1.65	1.00	1.35	.80
82	5¢ blue.............	8.25	4.65	5.50	3.35	3.50	2.10

1896 OFFICIAL STAMPS

O1	2¢ green............	45.00	27.50	30.00	18.00	19.50	11.75
O2	5¢ black brown	45.00	27.50	30.00	18.00	19.50	11.75
O3	6¢ deep ultramarine	45.00	27.50	30.00	18.00	19.50	11.75
O4	10¢ rose............	45.00	27.50	30.00	18.00	19.50	11.75
O5	12¢ orange...........	45.00	27.50	30.00	18.00	19.50	11.75
O6	25¢ gray violet	45.00	27.50	30.00	18.00	19.50	11.75

MARSHALL ISLANDS

The Marshall Islands are a part of the U.S. administered Trust Territories of the Pacific formed in 1947. They were granted postal autonomy in 1984 on their way to independence.

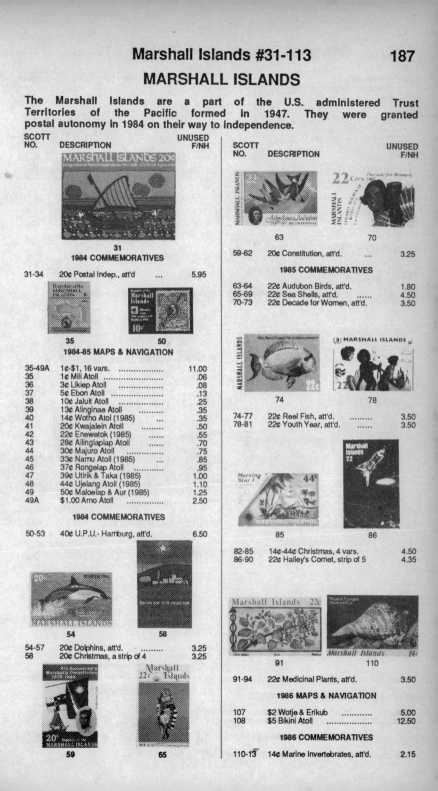

SCOTT NO.	DESCRIPTION	UNUSED F/NH

31

1984 COMMEMORATIVES

| 31-34 | 20¢ Postal Indep., att'd. ... | 5.95 |

35   50

1984-85 MAPS & NAVIGATION

35-49A	1¢-$1, 16 vars.	11.00
35	1¢ Mili Atoll	.06
36	3¢ Likiep Atoll	.08
37	5¢ Ebon Atoll	.13
38	10¢ Jaluit Atoll	.25
39	13¢ Alinginae Atoll	.35
40	14¢ Wotho Atol (1985) ...	.35
41	20¢ Kwajalein Atoll ...	.50
42	22¢ Enewetok (1985) ...	.55
43	28¢ Ailingiaplap Atoll	.70
44	30¢ Majuro Atoll	.75
45	33¢ Namu Atoll (1985) ...	.85
46	37¢ Rongelap Atoll	.95
47	39¢ Utirik & Taka (1985)	1.00
48	44¢ Ujelang Atoll (1985)	1.10
49	50¢ Maloelap & Aur (1985)	1.25
49A	$1.00 Arno Atoll	2.50

1984 COMMEMORATIVES

| 50-53 | 40¢ U.P.U.- Hamburg, att'd. | 6.50 |

54   58

| 54-57 | 20¢ Dolphins, att'd. .... | 3.25 |
| 58 | 20¢ Christmas, a strip of 4 | 3.25 |

59   65

SCOTT NO.	DESCRIPTION	UNUSED F/NH

63   70

| 59-62 | 20¢ Constitution, att'd. ... | 3.25 |

1985 COMMEMORATIVES

63-64	22¢ Audubon Birds, att'd.	1.80
65-69	22¢ Sea Shells, att'd.	4.50
70-73	22¢ Decade for Women, att'd.	3.50

74   78

| 74-77 | 22¢ Reel Fish, att'd. .... | 3.50 |
| 78-81 | 22¢ Youth Year, att'd. ...... | 3.50 |

85   86

| 82-85 | 14¢-44¢ Christmas, 4 vars. | 4.50 |
| 86-90 | 22¢ Halley's Comet, strip of 5 | 4.35 |

91   110

| 91-94 | 22¢ Medicinal Plants, att'd. | 3.50 |

1986 MAPS & NAVIGATION

| 107 | $2 Wotje & Erikub .... | 5.00 |
| 108 | $5 Bikini Atoll .... | 12.50 |

1986 COMMEMORATIVES

| 110-13 | 14¢ Marine Invertebrates, att'd. | 2.15 |

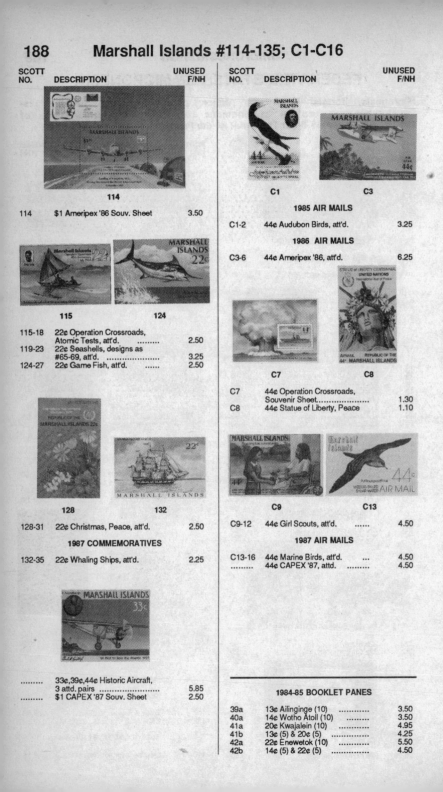

SCOTT NO.	DESCRIPTION	UNUSED F/NH

114

| 114 | $1 Ameripex '86 Souv. Sheet | 3.50 |

115   **124**

115-18	22¢ Operation Crossroads, Atomic Tests, att'd.	2.50
119-23	22¢ Seashells, designs as #65-69, att'd.	3.25
124-27	22¢ Game Fish, att'd.	2.50

128   **132**

| 128-31 | 22¢ Christmas, Peace, att'd. | 2.50 |

1987 COMMEMORATIVES

| 132-35 | 22¢ Whaling Ships, att'd. | 2.25 |

| .... | 33¢,39¢,44¢ Historic Aircraft, 3 attd. pairs .... | 5.85 |
| .... | $1 CAPEX '87 Souv. Sheet | 2.50 |

SCOTT NO.	DESCRIPTION	UNUSED F/NH

C1   **C3**

1985 AIR MAILS

| C1-2 | 44¢ Audubon Birds, att'd. | 3.25 |

1986 AIR MAILS

| C3-6 | 44¢ Ameripex '86, att'd. | 6.25 |

C7   **C8**

| C7 | 44¢ Operation Crossroads, Souvenir Sheet.................... | 1.30 |
| C8 | 44¢ Statue of Liberty, Peace | 1.10 |

C9   **C13**

| C9-12 | 44¢ Girl Scouts, att'd. ...... | 4.50 |

1987 AIR MAILS

| C13-16 | 44¢ Marine Birds, att'd. ... | 4.50 |
| .... | 44¢ CAPEX '87, attd. .... | 4.50 |

1984-85 BOOKLET PANES

39a	13¢ Ailinginge (10)	3.50
40a	14¢ Wotho Atoll (10)	3.50
41a	20¢ Kwajalein (10)	4.95
41b	13¢ (5) & 20¢ (5)	4.25
42a	22¢ Enewetok (10)	5.50
42b	14¢ (5) & 22¢ (5)	4.50

FEDERATED STATES OF MICRONESIA

Micronesia, formed from the major portion of the Caroline Islands, became postally autonomous in 1984. It forms part of the U.S. administered Trust Territories of the Pacific.

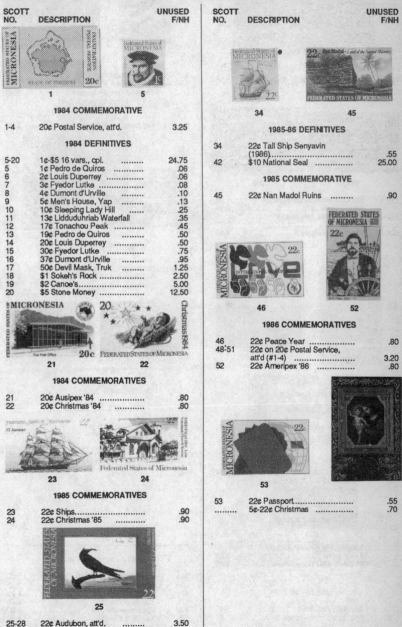

SCOTT NO.	DESCRIPTION	UNUSED F/NH

1 **5**

1984 COMMEMORATIVE

| 1-4 | 20¢ Postal Service, att'd. | 3.25 |

1984 DEFINITIVES

5-20	1¢-$5 16 vars., cpl.	24.75
5	1¢ Pedro de Quiros	.06
6	2¢ Louis Duperrey	.06
7	3¢ Fyedor Lutke	.08
8	4¢ Dumont d'Urville	.10
9	5¢ Men's House, Yap	.13
10	10¢ Sleeping Lady Hill	.25
11	13¢ Lidduduhriab Waterfall	.35
12	17¢ Tonachou Peak	.45
13	19¢ Pedro de Quiros	.50
14	20¢ Louis Duperrey	.50
15	30¢ Fyedor Lutke	.75
16	37¢ Dumont d'Urville	.95
17	50¢ Devil Mask, Truk	1.25
18	$1 Sokeh's Rock	2.50
19	$2 Canoe's	5.00
20	$5 Stone Money	12.50

21 **22**

1984 COMMEMORATIVES

| 21 | 20¢ Ausipex '84 | .80 |
| 22 | 20¢ Christmas '84 | .80 |

23 **24**

1985 COMMEMORATIVES

| 23 | 22¢ Ships | .90 |
| 24 | 22¢ Christmas '85 | .90 |

25

| 25-28 | 22¢ Audubon, att'd. | 3.50 |

SCOTT NO.	DESCRIPTION	UNUSED F/NH

34 **45**

1985-86 DEFINITIVES

| 34 | 22¢ Tall Ship Senyavin (1986) | .55 |
| 42 | $10 National Seal | 25.00 |

1985 COMMEMORATIVE

| 45 | 22¢ Nan Madol Ruins | .90 |

46 **52**

1986 COMMEMORATIVES

46	22¢ Peace Year	.80
48-51	22¢ on 20¢ Postal Service, att'd (#1-4)	3.20
52	22¢ Ameripex '86	.80

53

| 53 | 22¢ Passport | .55 |
| | 5¢-22¢ Christmas | .70 |

SCOTT NO.	DESCRIPTION	UNUSED F/NH

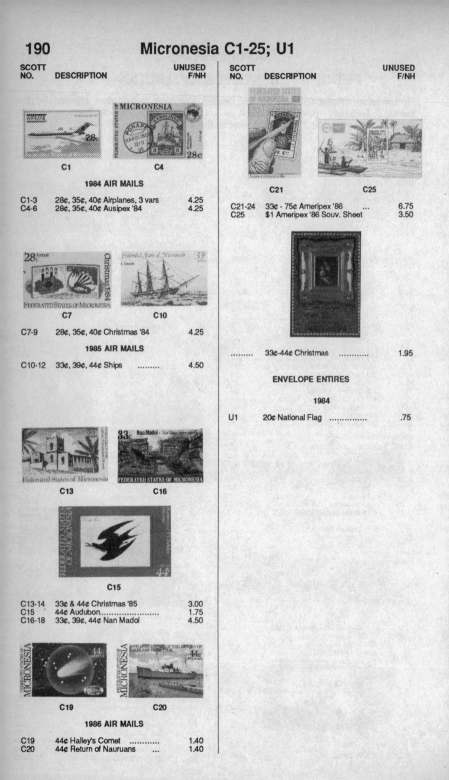

C1 C4

1984 AIR MAILS

| C1-3 | 28¢, 35¢, 40¢ Airplanes, 3 vars | 4.25 |
| C4-6 | 28¢, 35¢, 40¢ Ausipex '84 | 4.25 |

C7 C10

| C7-9 | 28¢, 35¢, 40¢ Christmas '84 | 4.25 |

1985 AIR MAILS

| C10-12 | 33¢, 39¢, 44¢ Ships .... | 4.50 |

C13 C16

C15

C13-14	33¢ & 44¢ Christmas '85	3.00
C15	44¢ Audubon......................	1.75
C16-18	33¢, 39¢, 44¢ Nan Madol	4.50

C19 C20

1986 AIR MAILS

| C19 | 44¢ Halley's Comet .... | 1.40 |
| C20 | 44¢ Return of Nauruans ... | 1.40 |

SCOTT NO.	DESCRIPTION	UNUSED F/NH

C21 C25

| C21-24 | 33¢ - 75¢ Ameripex '86 ... | 6.75 |
| C25 | $1 Ameripex '86 Souv. Sheet | 3.50 |

| .... | 33¢-44¢ Christmas .... | 1.95 |

ENVELOPE ENTIRES

1984

| U1 | 20¢ National Flag .... | .75 |

REPUBLIC OF PALAU

Palau is a Strategic Trust of the United States; a designation granted by the United Nations after World War II. It is the first Trust Territory to be granted postal independence, which became effective November 1, 1982. The first stamps were issued March 10, 1983.

SCOTT NO.	DESCRIPTION	UNUSED F/NH

1

5

1983 COMMEMORATIVES

| 1-4 | 20¢ Art and Preamble, att'd. | 5.95 |
| 5-8 | 20¢ Birds, att'd. | 3.25 |

9

24

1983-84 DEFINITIVES

9-21	1¢-$5, 13 vars., cpl.	24.50
9	1¢ Sea Fan	.06
10	3¢ Map Cowrie	.08
11	5¢ Jellyfish	.13
12	10¢ Hawksbill Turtle	.25
13	13¢ Giant Clam	.35
14	20¢ Parrotfish	.50
15	28¢ Chambered Nautilus	.70
16	30¢ Dappled Sea Cucumber	.75
17	37¢ Sea Urchin	.95
18	50¢ Starfish	1.25
19	$1 Squid	2.50
20	$2 Dugong (1984)	5.00
21	$5 Pink Sponge (1984)	12.50

1983 COMMEMORATIVES

| 24-27 | 20¢ Whales, att'd. | 3.25 |

28

29

| 28-32 | 20¢ Christmas, att'd. | 4.00 |

33

34

35

| 33-40 | 20¢ When Different Worlds Meet, att'd. | 6.50 |

41

51

1984 COMMEMORATIVES

| 41-50 | 20¢ Seashells, att'd. | 7.75 |
| 51-54 | 40¢ Explorer Ships, att'd. | 6.50 |

55

59

| 55-58 | 20¢ Fishing, att'd. | 3.25 |
| 59-62 | 20¢ Xmas, Flowers, att'd. | 3.25 |

63

67

1985 COMMEMORATIVES

| 63-66 | 22¢ Audubon-Birds, att'd. | 3.50 |
| 67-70 | 22¢ Canoes, att'd. | 3.50 |

75

1985-86 DEFINITIVES

75-81	14¢-44¢, 6 vars., cpl.	5.00
75	14¢ Trumpet Triton	.35
76	22¢ Parrotfish	.55
77	25¢ Damsel Fish	.65
79	33¢ Clownfish	.85
80	39¢ Sea Turtle	1.00
81	44¢ Sailfish	1.10
85	$10 Spinner Dolphins (1986)	25.00

SCOTT NO.	DESCRIPTION	UNUSED F/NH

SCOTT NO.	DESCRIPTION	UNUSED F/NH

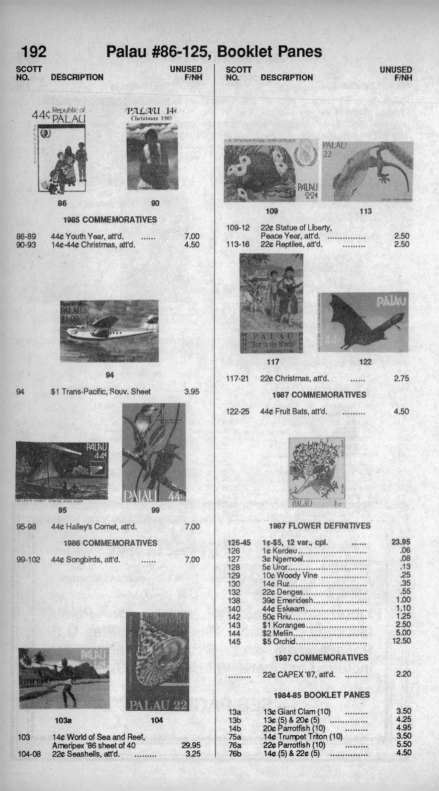

86

90

1985 COMMEMORATIVES

86-89	44¢ Youth Year, att'd.	7.00
90-93	14¢-44¢ Christmas, att'd.	4.50

94

94	$1 Trans-Pacific, Souv. Sheet	3.95

95

99

95-98	44¢ Halley's Comet, att'd.	7.00

1986 COMMEMORATIVES

99-102	44¢ Songbirds, att'd.	7.00

103a

104

103	14¢ World of Sea and Reef, Ameripex '86 sheet of 40	29.95
104-08	22¢ Seashells, att'd.	3.25

109

113

109-12	22¢ Statue of Liberty, Peace Year, att'd.	2.50
113-16	22¢ Reptiles, att'd.	2.50

117

122

117-21	22¢ Christmas, att'd.	2.75

1987 COMMEMORATIVES

122-25	44¢ Fruit Bats, att'd.	4.50

1987 FLOWER DEFINITIVES

126-45	1¢-$5, 12 var., cpl.	23.95
126	1¢ Kerdeu.............................	.06
127	3¢ Ngemoel.........................	.08
128	5¢ Uror.................................	.13
129	10¢ Woody Vine	.25
130	14¢ Ruz...............................	.35
132	22¢ Denges.........................	.55
138	39¢ Emeridesh.....................	1.00
140	44¢ Eskeam	1.10
142	50¢ Rriu...............................	1.25
143	$1 Koranges........................	2.50
144	$2 Meliin.............................	5.00
145	$5 Orchid.............................	12.50

1987 COMMEMORATIVES

....	22¢ CAPEX '87, att'd.	2.20

1984-85 BOOKLET PANES

13a	13¢ Giant Clam (10)	3.50
13b	13¢ (5) & 20¢ (5)	4.25
14b	20¢ Parrotfish (10)	4.95
75a	14¢ Trumpet Triton (10)	3.50
76a	22¢ Parrotfish (10)	5.50
76b	14¢ (5) & 22¢ (5)	4.50

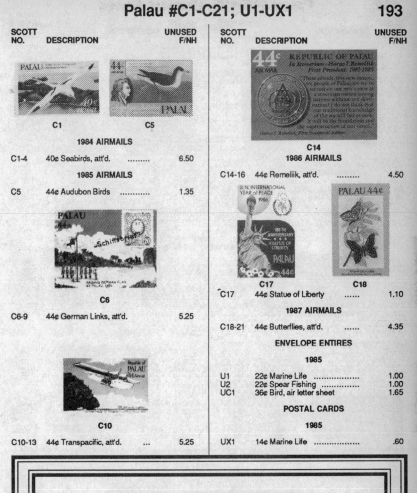

SCOTT NO.	DESCRIPTION	UNUSED F/NH

C1   **C5**

1984 AIRMAILS

| C1-4 | 40¢ Seabirds, att'd. | .... | 6.50 |

1985 AIRMAILS

| C5 | 44¢ Audubon Birds | .... | 1.35 |

C6

| C6-9 | 44¢ German Links, att'd. | | 5.25 |

C10

| C10-13 | 44¢ Transpacific, att'd. | ... | 5.25 |

SCOTT NO.	DESCRIPTION	UNUSED F/NH

C14

1986 AIRMAILS

| C14-16 | 44¢ Remeliik, att'd. | .... | 4.50 |

C17   **C18**

| C17 | 44¢ Statue of Liberty | ...... | 1.10 |

1987 AIRMAILS

| C18-21 | 44¢ Butterflies, att'd. | ...... | 4.35 |

ENVELOPE ENTIRES

1985

U1	22¢ Marine Life	....	1.00
U2	22¢ Spear Fishing	....	1.00
UC1	36¢ Bird, air letter sheet		1.65

POSTAL CARDS

1985

| UX1 | 14¢ Marine Life | .... | .60 |

SCOTT NO.	DESCRIPTION	UNUSED NH F	AVG	UNUSED OG F	AVG	USED F	AVG

PHILIPPINES

U.S. Stamps of various
issues overprinted

PHILIPPINES

1899
On 260. Unwatermarked

| 212 | 50¢ orange | 700.00 | 395.00 | 450.00 | 275.00 | 275.00 | 165.00 |

On 279, 279d, 267-68, 281, 282C, 283, 284, 275
Double Line Watermark

213	1¢ yellow green	6.50	3.65	4.25	2.60	1.10	.65
214	2¢ orange red	3.00	1.70	2.00	1.20	.85	.50
215	3¢ purple	11.50	6.50	7.50	4.50	2.15	1.30
216	5¢ blue	11.50	6.50	7.50	4.50	1.75	1.05
217	10¢ brown (Type I)	32.75	18.50	21.75	13.00	5.75	3.50
217A	10¢ orange brown (Type II)	435.00	240.00	285.00	170.00	57.50	35.00
218	15¢ olive green	56.50	31.50	37.50	22.50	10.00	6.00
219	50¢ orange	210.00	120.00	140.00	85.00	55.00	3.35

1901
On 280, 282, 272, 276-78

220	4¢ orange brown	37.50	21.00	25.00	15.00	6.75	4.00
221	6¢ lake	45.00	25.00	30.00	18.00	6.75	5.25
222	8¢ violet brown	49.00	27.50	32.50	19.50	9.00	5.50
223	$1 black (Type I)	800.00	450.00	525.00	325.00	300.00	180.00
223A	$1 black (Type II)	4250.00	2300.00	2750.00	1650.00	1350.00	825.00
224	$2 dark blue	1175.00	665.00	775.00	475.00	395.00	240.00
225	$5 dark green	....	....	1850.00	1100.00	1200.00	725.00

1903-04
On 300-313

226	1¢ blue green	7.50	4.25	5.00	3.00	.55	.35
227	2¢ carmine	12.50	7.15	8.25	5.75	2.15	1.30
228	3¢ bright violet	125.00	70.00	82.50	50.00	17.00	10.50
229	4¢ brown	130.00	75.00	87.50	52.50	27.50	16.50
230	5¢ blue	20.00	11.50	13.75	8.00	1.60	1.00
231	6¢ brownish lake	137.50	77.50	92.50	56.50	22.50	13.50
232	8¢ violet black	67.50	38.50	45.00	27.50	17.50	10.50
233	10¢ pale red brown	40.00	22.75	26.50	16.00	4.00	2.40
234	13¢ brown violet	57.50	32.75	38.75	23.50	19.50	11.50
235	15¢ olive green	97.50	56.50	65.00	40.00	15.00	9.00
236	50¢ orange	275.00	160.00	190.00	115.00	60.00	36.50
237	$1 black	1050.00	600.00	700.00	425.00	330.00	200.00
238	$2 dark blue	2775.00	1500.00	1850.00	1100.00	1100.00	675.00
239	$5 dark green	....	....	2250.00	1350.00	1450.00	875.00

On 319

| 240 | 2¢ carmine | 9.00 | 4.95 | 6.00 | 3.65 | 2.85 | 1.75 |

SPECIAL DELIVERY STAMPS
1901
U.S. E5 Surcharged

PHILIPPINES

| E1 | 10¢ dark blue | 190.00 | 105.00 | 125.00 | 75.00 | 140.00 | 85.00 |

POSTAGE DUE STAMPS
1899
U.S. J38-44
overprinted

PHILIPPINES

J1	1¢ deep claret	8.25	4.65	5.50	3.35	2.25	1.35
J2	2¢ deep claret	8.00	4.50	5.35	3.25	2.25	1.35
J3	5¢ deep claret	18.00	10.00	12.00	7.25	4.00	2.40
J4	10¢ deep claret	25.00	14.00	16.50	10.00	7.75	4.75
J5	50¢ deep claret	275.00	150.00	185.00	110.00	120.00	72.50

1901

| J6 | 3¢ deep claret | 25.00 | 14.00 | 16.50 | 10.00 | 11.50 | 7.00 |
| J7 | 30¢ deep claret | 375.00 | 210.00 | 250.00 | 150.00 | 105.00 | 65.00 |

SCOTT NO.	DESCRIPTION	UNUSED NH F	AVG	UNUSED OG F	AVG	USED F	AVG

PUERTO RICO

1899
U.S. Stamps 279-79B, 281,
272, 282C overprinted

PORTO RICO

210	1¢ yellow green	10.75	6.15	7.25	4.35	1.95	1.15
211	2¢ carmine	10.00	5.65	6.75	4.00	1.75	1.05
212	5¢ blue	14.75	8.00	9.75	5.75	2.75	1.65
213	8¢ violet brown	48.75	27.75	32.50	19.75	19.00	11.50
214	10¢ brown (i)	33.50	18.75	22.50	13.50	6.75	4.00

1900
U.S. 279, 279B overprinted

PUERTO RICO

215	1¢ yellow green	11.50	6.50	7.50	4.50	2.00	1.20
216	2¢ carmine	10.50	5.50	6.75	4.00	1.65	1.00

POSTAGE DUE STAMPS

1899

U.S. Postage Due Stamps
J38-39, J41 overprinted

PORTO RICO

J1	1¢ deep claret	35.00	21.00	23.50	14.00	9.00	5.50
J2	2¢ deep claret	25.00	14.00	16.50	10.00	8.00	4.85
J3	10¢ deep claret	250.00	140.00	165.00	100.00	62.50	37.50

The Ryukyu Islands were under U.S. administration from April 1, 1945 till May 15, 1972. Prior to the General Issues of 1948 several Provisional Stamps were used.

SCOTT NO.	DESCRIPTION	UNUSED F/NH	F

RYUKYU ISLANDS

1,1a,3,3a

2,2a,5,5a

4,4a,6,6a

7,7a

1949 Second Printing
White gum & paper; sharp colors; clean perfs.

Scott No.	Description	F/NH	F
1-7	5s to 1y, 7 vars., cpl.	22.50	20.00
1	5s Cycad	1.85	1.65
2	10s Lily	5.50	5.00
3	20s Cycad	3.75	3.35
4	30s Sailing Ship	2.25	2.00
5	40s Lily	1.95	1.75
6	50s Sailing Ship	4.25	3.75
7	1y Farmer	4.25	3.75

1948 First Printing
Thick yellow gum; gray paper; dull colors; rough perfs.

Scott No.	Description	F/NH	F
1a-7a	5s to 1y, 7 vars., cpl.	365.00	325.00
1a	5s Cycad	3.50	3.15
2a	10s Lily	1.75	1.60
3a	20s Cycad	1.75	1.60
4a	30s Sailing Ship	3.50	3.15
5a	40s Lily	47.50	42.50
6a	50s Sailing Ship	3.50	3.15
7a	1y Farmer	325.00	285.00

8   9   10

11   12   13

Scott No.	Description	F/NH	F
8-13	50s to 5y, 6 vars., cpl.	60.00	54.50
8	50s Tile Roof	.30	.27
9	1y Ryukyu Girl	3.75	3.35
10	2y Shun Castle	9.50	8.50
11	3y Dragon Head	27.50	25.00
12	4y Women at Beach	13.75	12.50
13	5y Seashells	8.50	7.65

NOTE: the 1950 printing of #8 is on toned paper and has yellowish gum. A 1958 printing exhibits white paper and colorless gum.

14

15

1951

Scott No.	Description	F/NH	F
14	3y Ryukyu University	55.00	50.00
15	3y Pine Tree	48.50	43.50

改訂

•

10 圓

16,16a-b,17

18

1952

Scott No.	Description	F/NH	F
16	10y/50s (no. 8) Type II	14.00	12.50
16a	Same, Type I	32.50	29.50
16b	Same, Type III	45.00	40.00
17	100y on 2y (No. 10)	1950.00	1750.00
18	3y Govt. of Ryukyu	100.00	90.00

Type 1 - Bars are narrow spaced; '10' normal
Type II - Bars are wide spaced; '10' normal
Type III - Bars are wide spaced; '10' wide spaced

SCOTT NO.	DESCRIPTION	UNUSED F/NH

19   20   21

1952-53

19-26	1y to 100y, 8 vars., cpl.	43.75
19	1y Mandanbashi Bridge	.35
20	2y Main Hall of Shun Castle	.45
21	3y Shurei Gate	.55
22	6y Stone Gate, Sognji Temple	2.75
23	10y Benzaiten do Temple	3.50
24	30y Altar at Shuri Castle	12.75
25	50y Tamaudun Shuri	11.75
26	100y Stone Bridge, Hosho Pond	14.50

27    28

29    30

1953

27	3y Reception at Shuri Castle	15.00
28	6y Perry and Fleet	1.40
29	4y Chofu Ota and Pencil	13.50

1954

30	4y Shigo Toma & Pen	15.00

31    32    33

1954-55

31	4y Pottery	1.00
32	15y Lacquerware (1955)	3.50
33	20y Textile Design (1955)	3.25

SCOTT NO.	DESCRIPTION	UNUSED F/NH

34    35

36    37    38

1955

34	4y Noguni Shrine & Sweet Potato Plant	14.75

1956

35	4y Stylized Trees	13.75
36	5y Willow Dance	1.00
37	8y Straw Hat Dance	2.35
38	14t Group Dance	2.75

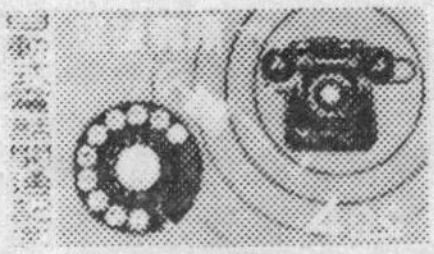

39    40

39	4y Dial Telephone	19.50
40	2y Garland, Bamboo & Plum	2.10

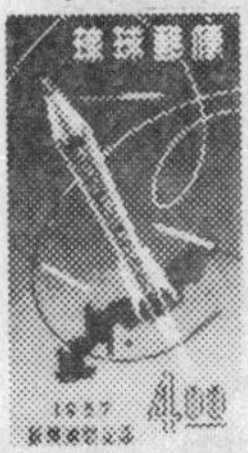

41    42

1957

41	4y Map & Pencil Rocket	.95
42	2y Phoenix	.25

43    44-53

SCOTT NO.	DESCRIPTION	UNUSED F/NH
	1958	
43	4y Ryukyu Stamps	1.00
44-53	1/2¢ to $1.00, 10 vars., cpl., ungummed	50.00
44	1/2¢ Yen, Symbol & Denom, orange	.60
45	1¢ Same, yellow green	1.00
46	2¢ Same, dark blue	1.40
47	3¢ Same, deep carmine	1.10
48	4¢ Same, bright bright green	1.35
49	5¢ Same, orange	3.50
50	10¢ Same, aquamarine	5.50
51	25¢ Same, bright violet blue	7.50
51a	25¢ Same, bright violet blue (with gum)	9.50
52	50¢ Same, gray	17.50
52a	50¢ Same, gray (with gum)	14.50
53	$1 Same, rose lilac	13.00

54

55

| 54 | 3¢ Gate of Courtesy | 1.75 |
| 55 | 1-1/2¢ Lion Dance | .27 |

56

57

1959

| 56 | 3¢ Mountains & Trees | 1.10 |
| 57 | 3¢ Yonaguni Moth | 1.60 |

58,76

59,77

60,78

61,79

62,80

63

SCOTT NO.	DESCRIPTION	UNUSED F/NH
58-62	1/2¢ to 17¢, 5 vars., cpl.	36.50
58	1/2¢ Hibiscus	.30
59	3¢ Moorish Idol	1.35
60	8¢ Seashell	9.95
61	13¢ Dead Leaf Butterfly	3.60
62	17¢ Jellyfish	22.50
63	1-1/2¢ Toy (Yakaji)	.80

64

65,81

1960

| 64 | 3¢ University Badge | 1.25 |

DANCES II

65-68	1¢-10¢, 4 vars., cpl.	5.50
65	1¢ Munsunu	1.40
66	2-1/2¢ Nutwabushi	2.40
67	5¢ Hatomabushi	.90
68	10¢ Hanafubushi	.95

72

| 72 | 3¢ Torch & Nago Bay | 7.50 |
| 73 | 8¢ Runners | 1.10 |

74

75

| 74 | 3¢ Egret & Sun | 7.50 |
| 75 | 1-1/2¢ Bull Fight | 2.15 |

1960-61 REDRAWN INSCRIPTION

76-80	1/2¢ to 17¢, 5 vars., cpl.	14.50
76	1/2¢ Hibiscus	.50
77	3¢ Moorish Idol	1.45
78	8¢ Seashell	1.45
79	13¢ Dead Leaf Butterfly	2.00
80	17¢ Jellyfish	9.50

SCOTT NO.	DESCRIPTION	UNUSED F/NH

84A   **85**

WITH "RYUKYUS" ADDED
1961-64

81-87	1¢ to $1.00, 8 vars., Dancers, cpl.	15.75
81	1¢ Munsuru	.25
82	2-1/2¢ Nufwabushi (1962)	.30
83	5¢ Hatomabushi (1962)	.55
84	10¢ Hanafubushi (1962)	1.15
84A	20¢ Shundun (1964)	1.75
85	25¢ Hanagasabushi (1962)	2.25
86	50¢ Nubui Kuduchi	4.25
87	$1 Kutubushi	6.75

88

90

89

92   **91**

1961

88	3¢ Pine Tree	2.15
89	3¢ Naha, Steamer & Sailboat	2.75
90	3¢ White Silver Temple	2.75
91	3¢ Books & Bird	1.85
92	1-1/2¢ Eagles & Rising Sun	3.25

SCOTT NO.	DESCRIPTION	UNUSED F/NH

93

95

94

97   **96**

1962

93	1-1/2¢ Steps, Trees & Building	.85
94	3¢ GRI Building	1.35
95	3¢ Malaria Eradication	.80
96	8¢ Eradication Emblem	1.65
97	3¢ Children's Day	1.85

98   **99**   **100**

98-102	1/2¢ to 17¢ vars., flowers, cpl.	2.95
98	1/2¢ Sea Hibiscus	.18
99	3¢ Indian Coral Tree	.40
100	8¢ Iju	.50
101	13¢ Touch-Me-Not	.75
102	17¢ Shell Flower	1.25

VERY FINE QUALITY: From 1935 to date, add 20% to the Fine price.
Minimum of 3¢ per stamp..

SCOTT NO.	DESCRIPTION	UNUSED F/NH

103

105

104

103	3¢ Earthware	4.75
104	3¢ Japanese Fencing	5.75
105	1-1/2¢ Bingata Cloth	1.35

106

107

108

109

1963

106	3¢ Stone Relief	1.35
107	1-1/2¢ Gooseneck Cactus	.12
108	3¢ Trees & Hills	1.35
109	3¢ Map of Okinawa	1.65

110

111

112

113

110	3¢ Hawks & Islands	1.35
111	3¢ Shioya Bridge	1.25
112	3¢ Lacquerqware Bowl	3.75
113	3¢ Map of Far East	1.15

SCOTT NO.	DESCRIPTION	UNUSED F/NH

114

116

117

115

114	15¢ Mamaomoto	1.30
115	3¢ Nakagusuku Castle Site	1.10
116	3¢ Human Rights	1.10
117	1-1/2¢ Dragon	.50

118

119

120, 120a

121

1964

118	3¢ Mothers Day	.65
119	3¢ Agricultural Census	.65
120	3¢ Minsah Oil, pink	.85
120a	Same, carmine	1.10
121	3¢ Girl Scout & Emblem	.50

122, 122a

123

122	3¢ Shuri Relay Station	1.10
122a	3¢ Same, Inverted "1"	37.50
123	8¢ Antenna & Map	1.65

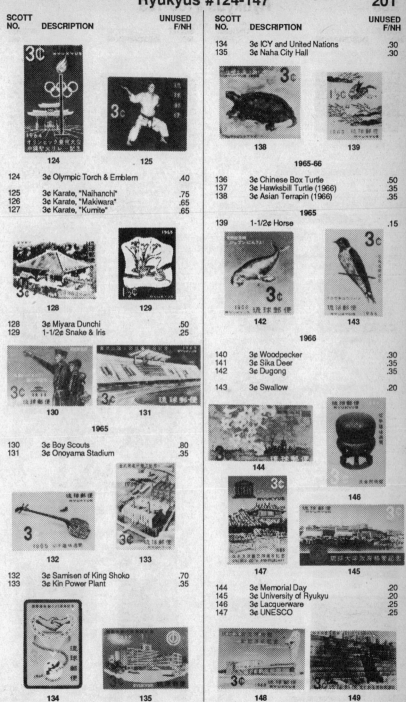

SCOTT NO.	DESCRIPTION	UNUSED F/NH
	124	
124	3¢ Olympic Torch & Emblem	.40
	125	
125	3¢ Karate, "Naihanchi"	.75
126	3¢ Karate, "Makiwara"	.65
127	3¢ Karate, "Kumite"	.65
	128 **129**	
128	3¢ Miyara Dunchi	.50
129	1-1/2¢ Snake & Iris	.25
	130 **131**	
	1965	
130	3¢ Boy Scouts	.80
131	3¢ Onoyama Stadium	.35
	132 **133**	
132	3¢ Samisen of King Shoko	.70
133	3¢ Kin Power Plant	.35
	134 **135**	

SCOTT NO.	DESCRIPTION	UNUSED F/NH
134	3¢ ICY and United Nations	.30
135	3¢ Naha City Hall	.30
	138 **139**	
	1965-66	
136	3¢ Chinese Box Turtle	.50
137	3¢ Hawksbill Turtle (1966)	.35
138	3¢ Asian Terrapin (1966)	.35
	1965	
139	1-1/2¢ Horse	.15
	142 **143**	
	1966	
140	3¢ Woodpecker	.30
141	3¢ Sika Deer	.35
142	3¢ Dugong	.35
143	3¢ Swallow	.20
	144	
	146	
	147 **145**	
144	3¢ Memorial Day	.20
145	3¢ University of Ryukyu	.20
146	3¢ Lacquerware	.25
147	3¢ UNESCO	.25
	148 **149**	

SCOTT NO.	DESCRIPTION	UNUSED F/NH
148	3¢ Government Museum	.20
149	3¢ Nakasone T. Genga's Tomb	.20

150   **151**

| 150 | 1-1/2¢ Ram in Iris Wreath | .15 |

1966-67

151-55	5 vars., Fish, cpl.	1.60
151	3¢ Clown Fish	.30
152	3¢ Young Boxfish (1967)	.30
153	3¢ Forceps Fish (1967)	.35
154	3¢ Spotted Triggerfish (1967)	.35
155	3¢ Saddleback Butterflyfish (1967)	.40

156   **157**

1966

| 156 | 3¢ Tsuboya Urn | .30 |

1967-68

157-61	5 vars., Seashells, cpl.	1.95
157	3¢ Episcopal Miter	.30
158	3¢ Venus Comb Murex	.30
159	3¢ Chiragra Spider	.35
160	3¢ Green Turban	.35
161	3¢ Euprotomus Bulla	.75

162   **165**

163

SCOTT NO.	DESCRIPTION	UNUSED F/NH

164   **166**

1967

162	3¢ Roofs & ITY Emblem	.25
163	3¢ Mobile TB Clinic	.25
164	3¢ Hoja Bridge, Enkoku Temple	.30
165	1-1/2¢ Monkey	.20
166	3¢ TV Tower & Map	.35

167   **169**

170

168   **171**

1968

167	3¢ Dr. Nakachi & Helper	.35
168	3¢ Pill Box	.55
169	3¢ Man, Library, Book & Map	.50
170	3¢ Mailmen's Uniforms & 1948 Stamp	.50
171	3¢ Main Gate-Enkaku Temple	.50

172   **173**

| 172 | 3¢ Old Man's Dance | .50 |

VERY FINE QUALITY: From 1935 to date, add 20% to the Fine price. Minimum of 3¢ per stamp.

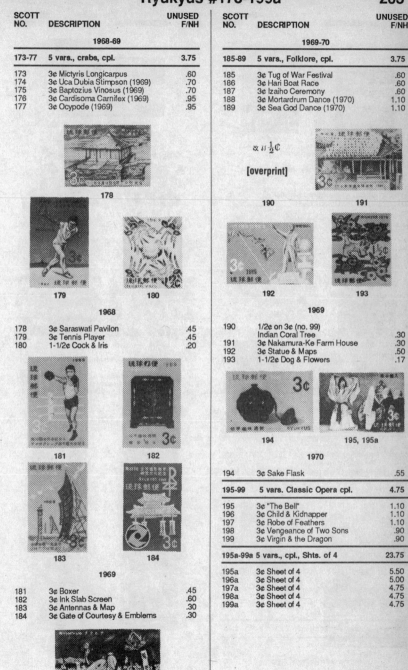

SCOTT NO.	DESCRIPTION	UNUSED F/NH
1968-69		
173-77	**5 vars., crabs, cpl.**	**3.75**
173	3¢ Mictyris Longicarpus	.60
174	3¢ Uca Dubia Stimpson (1969)	.70
175	3¢ Baptozius Vinosus (1969)	.70
176	3¢ Cardisoma Carnifex (1969)	.95
177	3¢ Ocypode (1969)	.95

178

179

180

1968

178	3¢ Saraswati Pavilion	.45
179	3¢ Tennis Player	.45
180	1-1/2¢ Cock & Iris	.20

181

182

183

184

1969

181	3¢ Boxer	.45
182	3¢ Ink Slab Screen	.60
183	3¢ Antennas & Map	.30
184	3¢ Gate of Courtesy & Emblems	.30

185

SCOTT NO.	DESCRIPTION	UNUSED F/NH
1969-70		
185-89	**5 vars., Folklore, cpl.**	**3.75**
185	3¢ Tug of War Festival	.60
186	3¢ Hari Boat Race	.60
187	3¢ Izaiho Ceremony	.60
188	3¢ Mortardrum Dance (1970)	1.10
189	3¢ Sea God Dance (1970)	1.10

$\frac{1}{2}$¢

[overprint]

190

191

192

193

1969

190	1/2¢ on 3¢ (no. 99) Indian Coral Tree	.30
191	3¢ Nakamura-Ke Farm House	.30
192	3¢ Statue & Maps	.50
193	1-1/2¢ Dog & Flowers	.17

194

195, 195a

1970

194	3¢ Sake Flask	.55
195-99	**5 vars. Classic Opera cpl.**	**4.75**
195	3¢ "The Bell"	1.10
196	3¢ Child & Kidnapper	1.10
197	3¢ Robe of Feathers	1.10
198	3¢ Vengeance of Two Sons	.90
199	3¢ Virgin & the Dragon	.90
195a-99a	**5 vars., cpl., Shts. of 4**	**23.75**
195a	3¢ Sheet of 4	5.50
196a	3¢ Sheet of 4	5.00
197a	3¢ Sheet of 4	4.75
198a	3¢ Sheet of 4	4.75
199a	3¢ Sheet of 4	4.75

SCOTT NO.	DESCRIPTION	UNUSED F/NH

200 **201**

| 200 | 3¢ Underwater Observatory | .45 |

1970-71 Portraits

201	3¢ Noboru Jahana	.65
202	3¢ Saion Guschichan Bunjaku	1.75
203	3¢ Choho Giwan (1971)	.80

204 **205**

206 **207**

1970

204	3¢ Map & People	.30
205	3¢ Great Cycad of Une	.35
206	3¢ Flag, Diet & Map	1.20
207	1-1/2¢ Boar & Cherry Blossoms	.17

212 **213**

1971

208-12	5 vars., Workers, cpl.	2.75
208	3¢ Low Hand Loom	.50
209	3¢ Filature	.50
210	3¢ Farmer with Raincoat & Hat	.50
211	3¢ Rice Huller	.90
212	3¢ Fishermen's Box & Scoop	.60
213	3¢ Water Carrier	.60

SCOTT NO.	DESCRIPTION	UNUSED F/NH

214

215 **216**

214	3¢ Old & New Naha	.35
215	2¢ Caesalpinia Pulchermima	.20
216	3¢ Madder	.20

217 **218**

1971-72 Government Parks

217	3¢ View from Mabuni Hill	.40
218	3¢ Mt. Arashi from Haneji Sea	.40
219	4¢ Yabuchi Is. from Yakena Port	.45

220 **222**

221 **223**

1971

220	4¢ Dancer	.20
221	4¢ Deva King	.30
222	2¢ Rat & Chrysanthemums	.20
223	4¢ Student Nurse	.35

SCOTT NO.	DESCRIPTION	UNUSED F/NH

224   226   228

225   227

1972

224	5¢ Birds & Seashore	.65
225	5¢ Coral Reef	.65
226	5¢ Sun Over Islands	.75
227	5¢ Dove & Flags	1.10
228	5¢ Antique Sake Pot	.90

AIR MAIL STAMPS

C1-3   C4-8

1950

C1	8y Dove & Map, bright blue	95.00
C2	12y Same, green	33.50
C3	16y Same, rose carmine	22.50

1951-54

C4-8	13y to 50y, 5 vars., cpl.	34.50
C4	13y Heavenly Maiden, blue	3.25
C5	18y Same, green	4.25
C6	30y Same, cerise	6.50
C7	40y Same, red violet (1954)	9.00
C8	50y Same, yell. orange (1954)	13.00

改訂 9¢

琉球郵便 15.00

C9-13   C14-18

1957

C9-13	15y tp 60y, 5 vars., cpl.	75.00
C9	15y Maiden Playing Flute, blue green	5.25
C10	20y Same, rose carmine	8.95
C11	35y Same, yellow green	16.50
C12	45y Same, reddish brown	20.00
C13	60y Same, gray	27.50

1959

C14-18	9¢ to 35¢, 5 vars., cpl.	51.50
C14	9¢ on 15y (no. C9)	3.25
C15	14¢ on 20y (no. C10)	4.25
C16	19¢ on 35y (no. C11)	8.75
C17	27¢ on 45y (no. C12)	16.00
C18	35¢ on 60y (no. C13)	21.75

改訂 ═══

[overprint]

9¢

C19-23   C24

1960

C19-23	9¢ to 35¢, 5 vars., cpl.	22.95
C19	9¢ on 4y (no. 31)	3.50
C20	14¢ on 5y (no. 36)	2.75
C21	19¢ on 15y (no. 32)	1.95
C22	27¢ on 14y (no. 38)	7.50
C23	35¢ on 20y (no. 33)	8.50

1961

C24-28	9¢ to 35¢, 5 vars., cpl.	6.25
C24	9¢ Heavenly Maiden	.55
C25	14¢ Maiden Playing Flute	.80
C26	19¢ Wind God	.95
C27	27¢ Wind God	2.40
C28	35¢ Maiden Over Tree Tops	1.95

C29   C30   E1

1963

| C29 | 5-1/2¢ Jet & Gate of Courtesy | .25 |
| C30 | 7¢ Jet Plane | .30 |

SPECIAL DELIVERY

1950

| E1 | 5y Dragon & Map | 31.75 |

UNITED NATIONS (NEW YORK)

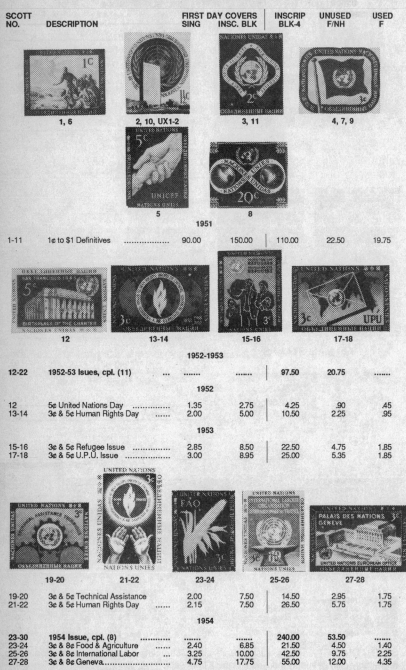

1, 6

2, 10, UX1-2

3, 11

4, 7, 9

5

8

1951

SCOTT NO.	DESCRIPTION	FIRST DAY COVERS SING	INSC. BLK	INSCRIP BLK-4	UNUSED F/NH	USED F
1-11	1¢ to $1 Definitives	90.00	150.00	110.00	22.50	19.75

12

13-14

15-16

17-18

1952-1953

12-22	**1952-53 Isues, cpl. (11)**	...	....	97.50	20.75	....
			1952			
12	5¢ United Nations Day	1.35	2.75	4.25	.90	.45
13-14	3¢ & 5¢ Human Rights Day	2.00	5.00	10.50	2.25	.95
			1953			
15-16	3¢ & 5¢ Refugee Issue	2.85	8.50	22.50	4.75	1.85
17-18	3¢ & 5¢ U.P.U. Issue	3.00	8.95	25.00	5.35	1.85

19-20

21-22

23-24

25-26

27-28

19-20	3¢ & 5¢ Technical Assistance	2.00	7.50	14.50	2.95	1.75
21-22	3¢ & 5¢ Human Rights Day	2.15	7.50	26.50	5.75	1.75
			1954			
23-30	**1954 Issue, cpl. (8)**	....	....	240.00	53.50	....
23-24	3¢ & 8¢ Food & Agriculture	2.40	6.85	21.50	4.50	1.40
25-26	3¢ & 8¢ International Labor	3.25	10.00	42.50	9.75	2.25
27-28	3¢ & 8¢ Geneva	4.75	17.75	55.00	12.00	4.35

SCOTT NO.	DESCRIPTION	FIRST DAY COVERS		INSCRIP BLK-4	UNUSED F/NH	USED F
		SING	INSC. BLK			

	29-30	**31-32**	**33-34**		**35-38**	
29-30	3¢ & 8¢ Human Rights Day	......	9.50	35.00	135.00	29.75	8.50

1955

31/40	1955 Issues, No #38 (9)	...	....	....	**140.00**	**30.00**	....
31-32	3¢ & 8¢ Int. Civil Aviation Org.		5.25	20.00	60.00	12.95	4.75
33-34	3¢ & 8¢ UNESCO		2.25	8.25	21.00	4.50	1.95
35-37	3¢ to 8¢ United Nations	....	3.25	11.75	50.00	10.75	2.75
38	Same, Souvenir Sheet	....	125.00			375.00	95.00
38 Var.	2nd Print, retouched	....	....			450.00	150.00

	39-40	**41-42**	**43-44**		**45-46**	
39-40	3¢ & 8¢ Human Rights Day	......	2.25	7.50	16.00	3.50	1.65

1956

41-48	1956 Issues, cpl. (8)	....	....	....	**34.00**	**7.50**	....
41-42	3¢ & 8¢ International Telecommunications	....	2.25	7.50	16.00	3.50	1.65
43-44	3¢ & 8¢ World Health Org.	......	2.25	7.50	16.00	3.50	1.65
45-46	3¢ & 8¢ United Nations Day	......	1.00	2.00	1.85	.40	.35

	47-48	**49-50**	**51-52 (No Halo)**	**53-54 (Halo)**	**55-56**	
47-48	3¢ & 8¢ Human Rights Day	......	1.00	2.00	1.60	.35	.30

1957

49-58	1957 Issues, cpl. (10)	......	....	....	**8.00**	**1.70**	....
49-50	3¢ & 8¢ Meteorological Org.	...	1.00	2.00	1.60	.35	.30
51-52	3¢ & 8¢ Emergency Force	....	1.00	2.00	1.60	.35	.30
53-54	Same, Re-engraved	....	....	....	3.25	.70	.50
55-56	3¢ & 8¢ Security Council		1.00	2.00	1.60	.35	.30

SETS ONLY: Prices listed are for complete sets as indicated. We regrettably cannot supply individual stamps from sets.

SCOTT NO.	DESCRIPTION	FIRST DAY COVERS SING	INSC. BLK	INSCRIP BLK-4	UNUSED F/NH	USED F

57-58   59-60   61-62   63-64   65-66

| 57-58 | 3¢ & 8¢ Human Rights Day | ...... | 1.00 | 2.00 | 1.60 | .35 | .30 |

1958

59-68	1958 Issues, cpl. (10)	......	......	......	7.65	1.70	......
59-60	3¢ & 8¢ Atomic Energy Agency		1.00	2.00	1.60	.35	.30
61-62	3¢ & 8¢ Central Hall	......	1.00	2.00	1.60	.35	.30
63-64	4¢ & 8¢ U.N. Seal	......	1.00	2.00	1.60	.35	.30
65-66	4¢ & 8¢ Econ. & Social Council		1.00	2.00	1.60	.35	.30

67-68   69-70   71-72   73-74   75-76

| 67-68 | 4¢ & 8¢ Human Rights Day | ...... | 1.00 | 2.00 | 1.60 | .35 | .30 |

1959

69-76	1959 Issues, cpl. (8)	......	......	......	8.00	1.80	......
69-70	4¢ & 8¢ Flushing Meadows	......	1.00	2.00	1.95	.45	.35
71-72	4¢ & 8¢ Economic Com. Europe		1.10	2.50	2.50	.55	.45
73-74	4¢ & 8¢ Trusteeship Council	...	1.00	2.00	1.95	.45	.35
75-76	4¢ & 8¢ World Refugee Year	...	1.00	2.00	1.95	.45	.35

77-78   79-80   81-82   83-85   86-87

1960

77/87	1960 Issues, No #85 (10)	......	......	......	8.50	1.90	......
77-78	4¢ & 8¢ Palais de Chaillot	......	1.00	2.00	1.80	.40	.35
79-80	4¢ & 8¢ Economic Comm. Asia		1.00	2.00	1.80	.40	.35
81-82	4¢ & 8¢ 5th World Forestry Con.		1.00	2.00	1.80	.40	.35
83-84	4¢ & 8¢ 15th Anniversary	......	1.00	2.00	1.80	.40	.35
85	Same, Souvenir Sheet	......	5.75			4.25	3.75
85var	Broken "V" variety	......	175.00			150.00	150.00
86-87	4¢ & 8¢ International Bank	......	1.00	2.00	1.80	.40	.35

FIRST DAY COVERS: Prices for United Nations First Day Covers are for cacheted, unaddressed covers with each variety in a set mounted on a separate cover. Complete sets mounted on one cover do exist and sell for a slightly lower price.

SCOTT NO.	DESCRIPTION	FIRST DAY COVERS SING	INSC. BLK	INSCRIP BLK-4	UNUSED F/NH	USED F

88-89   90-91   92   93-94

1961

88-99	1961 Issues, cpl. (12)	....	....	19.00	4.25	....
88-89	4¢ & 8¢ Int. Court of Justice ...	1.00	2.00	1.75	.40	.35
90-91	4¢ & 7¢ Int. Monetary Fund	1.00	2.00	1.75	.40	.35
92	30¢ Abstract Flags	.85	2.65	4.35	.95	.60
93-94	4¢ & 11¢ Economic Committee Latin America................................	1.15	2.50	5.50	1.25	.80

95-96   97-99   100-01   102-03

| 95-96 | 4¢ & 11¢ Economic Comm. Africa | 1.00 | 2.50 | 2.75 | .60 | .50 |
| 97-99 | 3¢, 4¢ & 13¢ Childrens Fund ... | 1.50 | 3.50 | 3.95 | .85 | .60 |

1962

100-13	1962 Issues, cpl. (14)	....	....	28.50	6.35	....
100-01	4¢ & 7¢ Housing & Community Development	1.00	2.50	2.30	.50	.45
102-03	4¢ & 11¢ Malaria Eradication	1.00	2.50	3.35	.70	.50

104   105   106   107

| 104-07 | 1¢ to 11¢ Definitives .... | 2.00 | 4.00 | 5.00 | 1.10 | .65 |

108-09   110-11   112-13   114-15   116-17

108-09	5¢ & 15¢ Memorial Issue	1.10	3.35	11.25	2.50	.75
110-11	4¢ & 11¢ Operation in the Congo	1.00	3.25	8.75	1.95	.75
112-13	4¢ & 11¢ Peace. Use of Out. Space	1.00	2.50	2.75	.60	.50

SCOTT NO.	DESCRIPTION	FIRST DAY COVERS SING	INSC. BLK	INSCRIP BLK-4	UNUSED F/NH	USED F
		1963				
114-22	1963 Issues, cpl. (9)	....	....	14.50	3.00	....
114-15	5¢ & 11¢ Science & Technology	1.00	2.50	2.75	.60	.50
116-17	5¢ & 11¢ Freedom From Hunger	1.00	2.50	2.75	.60	.50

118   **119-20**   **121-22**   **123-24**

SCOTT NO.	DESCRIPTION	SING	INSC. BLK	BLK-4	F/NH	F
118	25¢ UNTEA	1.20	3.00	4.00	.80	.60
119-20	5¢ & 11¢ General Assem. Bldg.	1.00	2.50	2.75	.60	.50
121-22	5¢ & 11¢ Human Rights	1.00	2.50	2.75	.60	.50
		1964				
123-36	1964 Issues, cpl. (14)	....	....	21.50	4.65	....
123-24	5¢ & 11¢ Maritime Org. (IMCO)	1.00	2.50	2.75	.60	.50

125, UX3   **126**   **127**   **128, U3-4**

SCOTT NO.	DESCRIPTION	SING	INSC. BLK	BLK-4	F/NH	F
125-28	2¢ to 50¢ Definitives	3.25	7.50	10.50	2.25	1.35

129-30   **131-32**   **133**   **134-36**

SCOTT NO.	DESCRIPTION	SING	INSC. BLK	BLK-4	F/NH	F
129-30	5¢ & 11¢ Trade & Development	1.00 50	2.25	.70	.50	.50 .55
131-32	5¢ & 11¢ Narcotics Control	1.00	2.50	2.50	.55	.50
133	5¢ Cessation of Nuclear Testing	.50	1.00	.70	.15	.14
134-36	4¢ to 11¢ Education for Progress	1.50	3.25	2.85	.60	.55

137-38   **139-40**   **141-42**   **143-45**

SCOTT NO.	DESCRIPTION	SING	INSC. BLK	BLK-4	F/NH	F
137/53	1965 Issues, No #145 or 150 (15)	....	....	23.00	4.95	....
137-38	5¢ & 11¢ U.N. Special Fund	1.00	2.35	2.30	.50	.45
139-40	5¢ & 11¢ U.N. Forces in Cyprus	1.00	2.35	2.30	.50	.45
141-42	5¢ & 11¢ I.T.U. Centenary	1.00	2.35	2.30	.50	.45
143-44	5¢ & 15¢ Int'l. Cooperation Year	1.00	2.50	2.65	.60	.50
145	Same, Souvenir Sheet	2.25	....	....	1.25	1.15

SCOTT NO.	DESCRIPTION	FIRST DAY COVERS SING	INSC. BLK	INSCRIP BLK-4	UNUSED F/NH	USED F

146   147   148   149   150

| 146-49 | 1¢ to 25¢ Definitive | .... | 3.75 | 9.75 | 12.00 | 2.50 | 1.85 |

1966

| 150 | $1 Definitive | .... | 3.95 | 12.50 | 17.50 | 3.85 | 2.75 |

151-53   154-55   156-57   158-69   160

1965

| 151-53 | 4¢ to 11¢ Population Trends | ... | 1.50 | 3.00 | 2.65 | .60 | .50 |

1966

150/63	1966 Issues, cpl. (11)	....	....	....	28.75	6.25	....
154-55	5¢ & 15¢ World Fed. (WFUNA)		1.00	2.50	2.85	.60	.45
156-57	5¢ & 11¢ World Health Org.	....	1.00	2.50	2.35	.50	.40
158-59	5¢ & 11¢ Coffee Agreement	...	1.00	2.50	2.85	.60	.45
160	15¢ Peacekeeping Observers	...	.60	1.85	2.10	.45	.40

161-63   164-65   166   167   168-69

| 161-63 | 4¢ to 11¢ UNICEF | .... | 1.50 | 3.00 | 2.75 | .60 | .50 |

1967

164/80	1967 Issues, No #179 (16)	....	....	....	20.00	4.25	....
164-65	5¢ & 11¢ Development	....	1.00	2.25	2.35	.50	.40
166-67	1-1/2¢ & 5¢ Definitives	....	1.00	1.75	1.15	.25	.20
168-69	5¢ & 11¢ Independence	....	1.00	2.25	2.35	.50	.40

170   171   173   174   172

| 170-74 | 4¢ to 15¢ Expo '67-Canada | ...... | 3.35 | 8.50 | 8.25 | 1.75 | 1.60 |

SCOTT NO.	DESCRIPTION	FIRST DAY COVERS SING	INSC. BLK	INSCRIP BLK-4	UNUSED F/NH	USED F

175-76

177-78

179

180

175-76	5¢ & 15¢ Int'l. Tourist Year ...	1.00	2.50	2.75	.60	.50
177-78	6¢ & 13¢ Towards Disarmament	1.00	2.50	3.25	.70	.50
179	36¢ Chagall Windows Souv. Sheet	1.40	....	....	1.10	1.00
180	6¢ Kiss of Peace	.50	1.00	.95	.20	.18

181-82　　183-84　　185-86　　187, U5　　188-89

181-91	1968 Issues, cpl. (11)	....	....	35.75	7.65	....
181-82	6¢ & 13¢ Secretariat	1.10	2.75	2.75	.60	.55
183-84	6¢ & 75¢ H. Starcke	7.75	23.50	23.50	5.00	4.75
185-86	6¢ & 13¢ Industrial Development	1.10	2.75	2.75	.60	.55
187	6¢ Definitive	.50	1.00	.95	.20	.18
188-89	6¢ & 20¢ Weather Watch	1.10	3.00	3.95	.85	.65

190-91　　192-93　　194-95　　196　　197-98

| 190-91 | 6¢ & 13¢ Int'l. Year—Human Rights | 1.20 | 3.25 | 3.50 | .75 | .65 |

1969

192-202	1969 Issues (11)	....	16.50	3.60	....	
192-93	6¢ & 13¢ Inst. Tng., Research	1.00	2.50	2.75	.60	.50
194-95	6¢ & 15¢ U.N. Building-Chile ...	1.00	2.75	3.25	.70	.60
196	13¢ Definitive	.75	2.00	2.10	.45	.40
197-98	6¢ & 13¢ Peace Through Int'l. Law	1.00	2.50	2.75	.60	.50

SETS ONLY: Prices listed are for complete sets as indicated. We regrettably cannot supply individual stamps from sets.

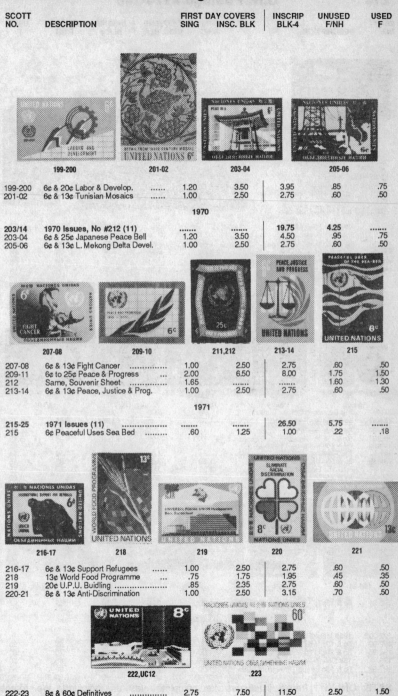

199-200 **201-02** **203-04** **205-06**

| 199-200 | 6¢ & 20¢ Labor & Develop. | .... | 1.20 | 3.50 | 3.95 | .85 | .75 |
| 201-02 | 6¢ & 13¢ Tunisian Mosaics | .... | 1.00 | 2.50 | 2.75 | .60 | .50 |

1970

203/14	1970 Issues, No #212 (11)	....	....	19.75	4.25	....
203-04	6¢ & 25¢ Japanese Peace Bell	1.20	3.50	4.50	.95	.75
205-06	6¢ & 13¢ L. Mekong Delta Devel.	1.00	2.50	2.75	.60	.50

207-08 **209-10** **211,212** **213-14** **215**

207-08	6¢ & 13¢ Fight Cancer	....	1.00	2.50	2.75	.60	.50
209-11	6¢ to 25¢ Peace & Progress	...	2.00	6.50	8.00	1.75	1.50
212	Same, Souvenir Sheet	....	1.65	....	....	1.60	1.30
213-14	6¢ & 13¢ Peace, Justice & Prog.	1.00	2.50	2.75	.60	.50

1971

| 215-25 | 1971 Issues (11) | .... | .... | .... | 26.50 | 5.75 | .... |
| 215 | 6¢ Peaceful Uses Sea Bed | .... | .60 | 1.25 | 1.00 | .22 | .18 |

216-17 **218** **219** **220** **221**

216-17	6¢ & 13¢ Support Refugees	....	1.00	2.50	2.75	.60	.50
218	13¢ World Food Programme	...	.75	1.75	1.95	.45	.35
219	20¢ U.P.U. Buidling	....	.85	2.35	2.75	.60	.50
220-21	8¢ & 13¢ Anti-Discrimination	1.00	2.50	3.15	.70	.50

222,UC12 **223**

| 222-23 | 8¢ & 60¢ Definitives | .... | 2.75 | 7.50 | 11.50 | 2.50 | 1.50 |

SCOTT NO.	DESCRIPTION	FIRST DAY COVERS SING	INSC. BLK	INSCRIP BLK-4	UNUSED F/NH	USED F

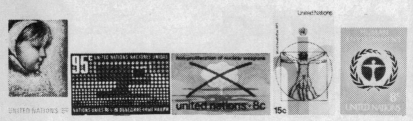

224-25	226	227	228	229-30

| 224-25 | 8¢ & 21¢ International School | 1.25 | 4.00 | 4.75 | 1.00 | .90 |

1972

226-33	1972 Issues, cpl. (8)	....	....	28.00	6.00	....
226	95¢ Definitive	3.25	10.75	14.50	3.15	2.50
227	8¢ Non-Proliferation	.65	1.35	1.40	.30	.20
228	15¢ World Health Org.	.75	2.00	2.35	.50	.40
229-30	8¢ & 15¢ Environment	1.00	3.00	3.50	.75	.65

231	232-33	234-35	236-37	238-39

| 231 | 21¢ Economic Comm. Europe | ... | .90 | 3.00 | 3.85 | .85 | .70 |
| 232-33 | 8¢ & 15¢ Art-Sert Ceiling | ...... | 1.10 | 3.25 | 3.85 | .85 | .75 |

1973

234-43	1973 Issues, cpl. (10)	......	....	20.50	4.50	....
234-35	8¢ & 15¢ Disarmament Decade	1.20	3.50	3.85	.85	.75
236-37	8¢ & 15¢ Drug Abuse	1.25	3.50	3.85	.85	.75
238-39	8¢ & 21¢ Volunteers Programme	1.50	4.50	5.25	1.15	1.00

240-41	242-43	244-45	246

| 240-41 | 8¢ & 15¢ Namibia | 1.30 | 3.50 | 4.25 | .95 | .75 |
| 242-43 | 8¢ & 21¢ Human Rights | 1.50 | 4.00 | 4.25 | .95 | .80 |

1974

244-55	1974 Issues, cpl. (12)	......	....	25.75	5.50	....
244-45	10¢ & 21¢ ILO Headquarters	...	1.50	4.50	5.75	1.25	.95
246	10¢ Universal Postal Union	......	.60	1.35	1.40	.30	.23

INSCRIPTION BLOCKS: Each corner of United Nations complete sheets contains the U.N. emblem plus the name of the issue in the selvedge. These are offered as Inscription Blocks of Four.

SCOTT NO.	DESCRIPTION	FIRST DAY COVERS SING	INSC. BLK	INSCRIP BLK-4	UNUSED F/NH	USED F

247-48   249   250, U6   251   252-53

Scott	Description	Sing	Insc. Blk	Blk-4	Unused	Used
247-48	10¢ & 18¢ Brazil Peace Mural	1.15	3.50	4.25	.95	.75
249-51	2¢ to 18¢ Definitives	1.50	3.75	4.60	1.00	.75
252-53	10¢ & 18¢ World Population Year	1.50	3.95	5.00	1.10	.85

254-55   256-57   258-59   260-62   263-64

Scott	Description	Sing	Insc. Blk	Blk-4	Unused	Used
254-55	10¢ & 26¢ Law of the Sea	1.50	4.75	6.00	1.25	1.10

1975

Scott	Description	Sing	Insc. Blk	Blk-4	Unused	Used
256/66	1975 Issues, No #262 (10)	....	....	26.50	5.65	....
256-57	10¢ & 26¢ Peaceful Use of Space	1.50	4.75	6.00	1.25	1.10
258-59	10¢ & 18¢ Int'l. Women's Year	1.35	4.00	5.00	1.10	.90
260-61	10¢ & 26¢ Anniversary	1.50	4.50	6.50	1.35	1.00
262	Same, Souvenir Sheet	2.15	....	....	2.15	1.85
263-64	10¢ & 18¢ Namibia	1.40	3.75	4.25	.95	.80

265-66   267   268   269   270   271

Scott	Description	Sing	Insc. Blk	Blk-4	Unused	Used
265-66	13¢ & 26¢ Peacekeeping	1.50	4.50	5.95	1.30	1.00

1976

Scott	Description	Sing	Insc. Blk	Blk-4	Unused	Used
267-80	1976 Issues, cpl. (14)	....	....	85.00	18.75	....
267-71	3¢ to 50¢ Definitives	4.50	13.50	16.00	3.50	3.00

272-73   274-75   276-77   278-79   280

SCOTT NO.	DESCRIPTION	FIRST DAY COVERS SING	FIRST DAY COVERS INSC. BLK	INSCRIP BLK-4	UNUSED F/NH	USED F
272-73	13¢ & 26¢ World Federation ...	1.75	5.75	6.25	1.35	1.25
274-75	13¢ & 31¢ Conference on Trade & Development	1.65	5.50	6.75	1.45	1.35
276-77	13¢ & 25¢ Conference on Human Settlements	1.50	5.25	6.00	1.50	1.25
278-79	13¢ & 31¢ Postal Admin.	11.75	40.00	52.50	11.50	9.75
280	13¢ World Food Council	.80	2.00	2.50	.55	.40

281-82

283-84

285-86

287-88

1977

281-90	Issues, cpl. (10)	......	......	33.50	7.15	......
281-82	13¢ & 31¢ WIPO	1.75	5.75	8.00	1.70	1.30
283-84	13¢ & 25¢ Water Conference ...	1.65	5.50	7.00	1.50	1.25
285-86	13¢ & 31¢ Security Council	1.75	5.75	8.25	1.75	1.35
287-88	13¢ & 25¢ Combat Racism	1.65	5.00	6.50	1.40	1.10

289-90   **291**   **292**   **293**

289-90	13¢ & 18¢ Atomic Energy	1.50	4.25	5.35	1.15	.90

1978

291-303	1978 Issues, cpl. (13)	......	......	56.50	11.95	......
291-93	1¢, 25¢ & $1 Definitives	5.50	16.50	23.50	4.95	3.75

294-95

296-97

298-99

300-01

294-95	13¢ & 31¢ Smallpox Eradication	1.65	5.75	8.50	1.85	1.35
296-97	13¢ & 18¢ Namibia	1.35	4.50	5.75	1.25	1.00
298-99	13¢ & 25¢ ICAO	1.65	5.25	6.75	1.50	1.20
300-01	13¢ & 18¢ General Assembly ...	1.30	4.50	5.75	1.25	1.00

302-03   **304**   **305**   **306**

307

SCOTT NO.	DESCRIPTION	FIRST DAY COVERS SING	INSC. BLK	INSCRIP BLK-4	UNUSED F/NH	USED F
302-03	13¢ & 31¢ TCDC	1.85	6.25	9.25	1.95	1.50

1979

304-15	**1979 Issues, cpl. (12)**	....	....	40.00	8.00	....
304-07	5¢, 14¢, 15¢ & 20¢ Defin.	....	2.75	7.25	9.50	2.00	1.50

308-09   **310-11**   **312-13**   **314-15**   **316-17**

308-09	15¢ & 20¢ UNDRO.......................	1.75	5.50	6.50	1.40	1.25
310-11	15¢ & 31¢ I.Y.C...........................	5.00	11.00	15.00	2.00	1.85
312-13	15¢ & 31¢ Namibia	1.90	5.95	8.00	1.75	1.35
314-15	15¢ & 20¢ Court of Justice	1.75	4.75	6.00	1.30	1.00

1980

316/42	**1980 Issues, No #324 (26)**	....	....	68.50	17.25	....
316-17	15¢ & 31¢ Economics	2.00	5.95	7.50	1.80	1.30

318-19   **320-21**   **322-23**   **341-42**

325

TURKEY	326 Luxembourg 331 Bangladesh 336 Salvador
	327 Fiji 332 Mali 337 Madagascar
	328 Vietnam 333 Yugoslavia 338 Cameroun
	329 Guinea 334 France 339 Rwanda
	330 Suriname 335 Venezuela 340 Hungary

318-19	15¢ & 20¢ Decade for Women	1.60	4.95	6.50	1.40	1.10
320-21	15¢ & 31¢ Peacekeeping	2.00	7.25	10.50	2.25	1.75
322-23	15¢ & 31¢ Anniversary	1.90	5.75	8.40	1.60	1.25
324	Same, Souvenir Sheet	1.75	....	....	1.75	1.40
325-40	1980 World Flags, 16 varieties	12.75	....	32.50	7.95	7.15
325-28	15¢ World Flags, 4 varieties ...	....	....	8.25	2.00	1.80
329-32	15¢ World Flags, 4 varieties ...	....	....	8.25	2.00	1.80
333-36	15¢ World Flags, 4 varieties ...	....	....	8.25	2.00	1.80
337-40	15¢ World Flags, 4 varieties ...	....	....	8.25	2.00	1.80
341-42	15¢ & 20¢ Economic and Social Council...	1.50	4.85	6.50	1.40	1.10

FIRST DAY COVERS: Prices for United Nations First Day Covers are for cacheted, unaddressed covers with each variety in a set mounted on a separate cover. Complete sets mounted on one cover do exist and sell for a slightly lower price.

SCOTT NO.	DESCRIPTION	FIRST DAY COVERS SING	INSC. BLK	INSCRIP BLK-4	UNUSED F/NH	USED F

343

344-45

346-47

348-49

366-67

350

351 Sri Lanka	356 Thailand	361 Egypt
352 Bolivia	357 Trinidad	362 United States
353 Equatorial Guinea	358 Ukraine	363 Singapore
354 Malta	359 Kuwait	364 Panama
355 Czechoslovakia	360 Sudan	365 Costa Rica

1981

Scott No.	Description	Sing	Insc. Blk	Inscrip Blk-4	Unused F/NH	Used F
343-67	1981 Issues, cpl. (25)	....	....	92.50	21.00	....
343	15¢ Palestinian People	1.00	2.50	2.75	.60	.50
344-45	20¢ & 35¢ Disabled Persons	2.35	6.75	10.75	2.25	1.50
346-47	20¢ & 31¢ Fresco	2.25	6.75	9.75	2.10	1.50
348-49	20¢ & 40¢ Sources of Energy	2.50	8.50	12.50	2.65	1.95
350-65	1981 World Flags, 16 varieties	17.50	....	52.50	12.50	12.50
350-53	20¢ World Flags, 4 vars.	....	....	13.50	3.25	3.25
354-57	20¢ World Flags, 4 vars.	....	....	13.50	3.25	3.25
358-61	20¢ World Flags, 4 vars.	....	....	13.50	3.25	3.25
362-65	20¢ World Flags, 4 vars.	....	....	13.50	3.25	3.25
366-67	18¢ & 28¢ Volunteers Program	2.25	6.75	9.50	2.00	1.50

368

369

370

371-72

373

390-91

374

375 Malaysia	380 Dominica	385 Burma
376 Seychelles	381 Solomon Is.	386 Cape Verde
377 Ireland	382 Philippines	387 Guyana
378 Mozambique	383 Swaziland	388 Belgium
379 Albania	384 Nicaragua	389 Nigeria

1982

Scott No.	Description	Sing	Insc. Blk	Inscrip Blk-4	Unused F/NH	Used F
368-91	1982 Issues, cpl. (24)	....	....	110.00	25.00	....
368-70	17¢, 28¢ & 40¢ Definitives	3.50	11.75	16.00	3.50	2.75
371-72	20¢ & 40¢ Human Environment	2.75	8.00	13.50	2.95	1.75
373	20¢ Space Exploration	1.25	3.25	4.00	.90	.65
374-89	World Flags, 16 vars.	19.50	....	75.00	17.50	17.50
374-77	20¢ World Flags, 4 vars.	....	....	20.00	4.50	4.50
378-81	20¢ World Flags, 4 vars.	....	....	20.00	4.50	4.50
382-85	20¢ World Flags, 4 vars.	....	....	20.00	4.50	4.50
386-89	20¢ World Flags, 4 vars.	....	....	20.00	4.50	4.50
390-91	20¢ & 28¢ Nature Conservation	2.50	7.00	9.50	2.00	1.50

392-93   394-95   396   397-98   415-16

399

400 Barbados	405 Jamaica	410 Canada
401 Nepal	406 Kenya	411 Somalia
402 Israel	407 China	412 Senegal
403 Malawi	408 Peru	413 Brazil
404 Byelorussia	409 Bulgaria	414 Sweden

1983

Scott No.	Description	SING	INSC. BLK	INSCRIP BLK-4	UNUSED F/NH	USED F
392-416	1983 Issues, cpl. (25)	....	....	120.00	27.50	....
392-93	20¢ & 40¢ World Comm. Year	2.75	8.75	11.00	2.40	1.95
394-95	20¢ & 37¢ Safety at Sea	2.50	8.50	12.75	2.75	1.95
396	20¢ World Food Program	1.25	3.50	3.00	1.00	.70
397-98	20¢ & 28¢ Trade & Development	2.50	7.00	9.25	1.95	1.50
399-414	World Flags, 16 vars.	19.50	....	75.00	17.50	17.50
399-402	20¢ World Flags, 4 vars.	....	....	20.00	4.50	4.50
403-06	20¢ World Flags, 4 vars.	....	....	20.00	4.50	4.50
407-10	20¢ World Flags, 4 vars.	....	....	20.00	4.50	4.50
411-14	20¢ World Flags, 4 vars.	....	....	20.00	4.50	4.50
415-16	20¢ & 40¢ Human Rights	3.50	11.75	16.00	3.50	2.75

417-18   419-20   421-22   423-24

426 Pakistan	431 Uruguay	436 Bahamas
427 Benin	432 Chile	437 Paraguay
428 Italy	433 Tanzania	438 Bhutan
429 Poland	434 Unit. Arab Emir.	439 Cent. African Rep.
430 Papua New Guinea	435 Ecuador	440 Australia

425

1984

Scott No.	Description	SING	INSC. BLK	INSCRIP BLK-4	UNUSED F/NH	USED F
417-42	1984 Issues, cpl. (26)	....	....	120.00	27.50	....
417-18	20¢ & 40¢ Population	2.75	8.00	10.75	2.25	1.75
419-20	20¢ & 40¢ Food Day	2.75	8.00	10.75	2.25	1.75
421-22	20¢ & 50¢ Heritage	2.95	9.00	12.50	2.75	2.00
423-24	20¢ & 50¢ Future for Refugees	2.95	9.00	12.50	2.75	2.00
425-40	1984 World Flags, 16 varieties	18.50	....	70.00	16.50	16.50
425-28	20¢ World Flags, 4 vars.	....	....	18.00	4.25	4.25
429-32	20¢ World Flags, 4 vars.	....	....	18.00	4.25	4.25
433-36	20¢ World Flags, 4 vars.	....	....	18.00	4.25	4.25
437-40	20¢ World Flags, 4 vars.	....	....	18.00	4.25	4.25
441-42	20¢ & 35¢ Youth Year	2.75	8.00	10.75	2.25	1.75

SCOTT NO.	DESCRIPTION	FIRST DAY COVERS SING	INSC. BLK	INSCRIP BLK-4	UNUSED F/NH	USED F

443

444

445

446

CRENADA

UNITED NATIONS 22¢

450

451 Germany-West	456 U.S.S.R.	461 Dominican Rep.
452 Saudi Arabia	457 India	462 Oman
453 Mexico	458 Liberia	463 Ghana
454 Uganda	459 Mauritius	464 Sierra Leone
455 Sao Tome and Principe	460 Chad	465 Finland

1985

SCOTT NO.	DESCRIPTION	SING	INSC. BLK	INSCRIP BLK-4	UNUSED F/NH	USED F
443/67	1985 Issues, No. #449 (24)	....	....	138.75	30.75	....
443	23¢ ILO-Turin Centre	1.75	4.00	4.25	.90	.75
444	50¢ U.N. University in Japan	2.50	7.75	9.50	1.95	1.75
445-46	22¢ & $3 Definitives	8.75	31.50	47.50	9.75	7.50
447-48	22¢ & 45¢ 40th Anniversary	3.75	10.50	12.50	2.75	2.25
449	Same, Souvenir Sheet	3.50	....	....	2.75	2.25
450-65	1985 World Flag, 16 varieties	19.50	....	62.50	14.95	14.95
450-53	22¢ World Flags, 4 vars.	....	....	16.00	3.85	3.85
454-57	22¢ World Flags, 4 vars.	....	....	16.00	3.85	3.85
458-61	22¢ World Flags, 4 vars.	....	....	16.00	3.85	3.85
462-65	22¢ World Flags, 4 vars.	....	....	16.00	3.85	3.85
466-67	22¢ & 33¢ Child Survival	2.75	8.00	10.50	2.25	1.75

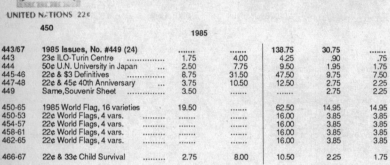

468

469

473

475

476

UNITED NATIONS 22¢

477

478 Lao People's Rep.	483 Jordan	488 Botswana
479 Burkina Faso	484 Zambia	489 Romania
480 Gambia	485 Iceland	490 Togo
481 Maldives	486 Antigua & Barbuda	491 Mauritania
482 Ethiopia	487 Angola	492 Colombia

1986

SCOTT NO.	DESCRIPTION	SING	INSC. BLK	INSCRIP BLK-4	UNUSED F/NH	USED F
468-92	1986 Issues (25)	....	....	58.75	15.50	....
468	22¢ African Crisis	1.75	3.50	3.25	.70	.60
469-72	22¢ Development, 4 vars., att'd	3.25	3.95	3.25	2.75	....
473-74	22¢ & 44¢ Philately	3.75	9.00	9.75	2.10	1.75
475-76	22¢ & 33¢ Peace Year	3.65	8.75	7.00	1.50	1.25
477-92	1986 World Flags, 16 vars.	23.75	....	37.50	8.95	8.95
477-80	22¢ World Flags, 4 vars.	....	....	9.75	2.35	2.35
481-84	22¢ World Flags, 4 vars.	....	....	9.75	2.35	2.35
485-88	22¢ World Flags, 4 vars.	....	....	9.75	2.35	2.35
489-92	22¢ World Flags, 4 vars.	....	....	9.75	2.35	2.35

SCOTT NO.	DESCRIPTION	FIRST DAY COVERS SING	INSC. BLK	INSCRIP BLK-4	UNUSED F/NH	USED F

493

494

495

1986

| 493 | 22¢ to 44¢ WFUNA Souvenir Sheet of 4.................................. | 4.25 | .... | .... | 3.50 | 3.50 |

1987

| 494 | 22¢ Trygve Lie .... | 1.75 | 3.75 | 2.50 | .55 | .50 |
| 495-96 | 22¢ & 44¢ Shelter Homeless ... | 3.75 | 8.50 | 8.00 | 1.65 | 1.50 |

497

1987 FLAGS

Comoros	Gabon	St. Lucia
Democratic	Zimbabwe	Bahrain
Yemen	Iraq	Haiti
Mongolia	Argentina	Afghanistan
Vanuatu	Congo	Greece
Japan	Niger	

497-98	22¢ & 33¢ Anti-Drug Campaign	3.65	7.75	6.50	1.40	1.30
499-514	1987 World Flags, 16 vars. ...	23.75	....	37.50	8.95	8.95
499-502	22¢ World Flags, 4 vars.	....	....	9.75	2.35	2.35
503-06	22¢ World Flags, 4 vars.	....	....	9.75	2.35	2.35
507-10	22¢ World Flags, 4 vars.	....	....	9.75	2.35	2.35
511-14	22¢ World Flags, 4 vars.	....	....	9.75	2.35	2.35

SCOTT NO.	DESCRIPTION	FIRST DAY COVERS SING	INSC. BLK	INSCRIP BLK-4	UNUSED F/NH	USED F

AIR MAIL ISSUE

C1-2, UC5   C3-C4, UC1-2   C5-6, UXC1, UXC3   C7, UC4

1951-1977

| C1-C23 | Airmails, cpl. (23) | .... | .... | .... | 79.50 | 16.95 | .... |

1951-59

| C1-4 | 6¢, 10¢, 15¢ & 20¢ | 28.75 | 55.00 | 29.75 | 6.25 | 5.75 |
| C5-7 | 4¢, 5¢ & 7¢ (1957-59) | 1.50 | 3.25 | 2.85 | .60 | .60 |

C8, UXC4   C9, UC6, UC8   C10   C11   C12

C13   C14   C15, UXC8   C16, UC10

C17, UXC10   C18   C19, UC11

C20, UXC11   C21   C22   C23

1963-77

C8-12	6¢, 8¢, 13¢, 15¢ & 25¢ (1963-64)	3.25	11.50	19.75	4.25	2.75
C13-14	10¢ & 20¢ (1968-69)	2.00	4.95	5.25	1.10	1.00
C15-18	9¢, 11¢, 17¢ & 21¢ (1972)	3.00	8.50	10.75	2.25	1.75
C19-21	13¢, 18¢ & 26¢ (1974)	3.25	7.75	9.25	1.95	1.50
C22-23	25¢ & 31¢ (1977)	2.95	6.95	6.75	1.40	1.35

ENVELOPES AND AIR LETTER SHEETS

U1-U2   UC3

SCOTT NO.	DESCRIPTION	FIRST DAY COVER	UNUSED ENTIRE
1953			
U1	3¢ blue	5.75	1.00
1958			
U2	4¢ ultramarine	1.10	1.15
1963			
U3	5¢ multicolored (design #128)	1.15	.40
1969			
U4	6¢ multicolored (design #128)	.95	.40
1973			
U5	8¢ multicolored (design #187)	.95	.40
1975			
U6	10¢ multicolored (design #250)	1.25	.50
1985			
U7	22¢ Strip Bouquet	1.50	.70

AIRMAILS

SCOTT NO.	DESCRIPTION	FIRST DAY COVER	UNUSED ENTIRE
1952			
UC1	10¢ blue, air letter (design #C3)	11.75	65.00
1954			
UC2	10¢ blue, white border aerogramme (design of #C3)		14.75
1958			
UC2a	10¢ blue, no border (design #C3)		12.75
1959			
UC3	7¢ blue	1.50	4.75
1960			
UC4	10¢ blue on blue, letter sheet (design of #C7)	1.25	1.20
1961			
UC5	11¢ blue on blue, letter sheet (design of #C1)	1.25	.65
1965			
UC5a	11¢ blue on green, letter sheet (design of #C1)		2.10
1963			
UC6	8¢ multicolored (design #C9)	1.25	.70

UC7

SCOTT NO.	DESCRIPTION	FIRST DAY COVER	UNUSED ENTIRE
1958			
UC7	13¢ shades-blue, letter sheet	1.20	.75
1969			
UC8	10¢ multicolored (design #C9)	1.20	.70

UC9

SCOTT NO.	DESCRIPTION	FIRST DAY COVER	UNUSED ENTIRE
1972			
UC9	15¢ shades-blue, letter sheet	1.20	.85
1973			
UC10	11¢ multicolored (design #C16)	1.20	.65
1975			
UC11	13¢ multicolored (design #C19)	1.30	.65
UC12	18¢ multicolored, aerogramme (design of #222)	1.30	.80

22¢   UNITED NATIONS

UC13

SCOTT NO.	DESCRIPTION	FIRST DAY COVER	UNUSED ENTIRE
1977			
UC13	22¢ multicolored, aerogramme	1.50	.95

1982

SCOTT NO.	DESCRIPTION	FIRST DAY COVER	UNUSED ENTIRE
UC14	30¢ gray, aerogramme	1.50	1.15

POSTAL CARDS

SCOTT NO.	DESCRIPTION	FIRST DAY COVER	UNUSED ENTIRE
	1952		
UX1	2¢ blue on buff (design of #2)	2.00	25
	1958		
UX2	3¢ light olive brown on buff (design of #2)	1.25	1.10
	1963		
UX3	4¢ multicolored (design of #125)	1.00	30

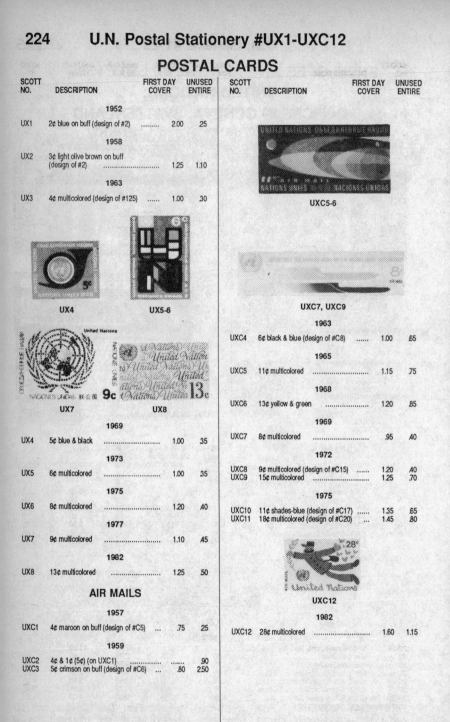

UX4

UX5-6

UX7

9c

UX8 **13c**

SCOTT NO.	DESCRIPTION	FIRST DAY COVER	UNUSED ENTIRE
	1969		
UX4	5¢ blue & black	1.00	35
	1973		
UX5	6¢ multicolored	1.00	35
	1975		
UX6	8¢ multicolored	1.20	40
	1977		
UX7	9¢ multicolored	1.10	45
	1982		
UX8	13¢ multicolored	1.25	50

AIR MAILS

SCOTT NO.	DESCRIPTION	FIRST DAY COVER	UNUSED ENTIRE
	1957		
UXC1	4¢ maroon on buff (design of #C5) ...	.75	25
	1959		
UXC2	4¢ & 1¢ (5¢) (on UXC1)	....	.90
UXC3	5¢ crimson on buff (design of #C6) ...	.80	2.50

UXC5-6

UXC7, UXC9

SCOTT NO.	DESCRIPTION	FIRST DAY COVER	UNUSED ENTIRE
	1963		
UXC4	6¢ black & blue (design of #C8)	1.00	.65
	1965		
UXC5	11¢ multicolored	1.15	.75
	1968		
UXC6	13¢ yellow & green	1.20	.85
	1969		
UXC7	8¢ multicolored	.95	.40
	1972		
UXC8	9¢ multicolored (design of #C15)	1.20	.40
UXC9	15¢ multicolored	1.25	.70
	1975		
UXC10	11¢ shades-blue (design of #C17)	1.35	.65
UXC11	18¢ multicolored (design of #C20) ...	1.45	.80

28¢

United Nations

UXC12

SCOTT NO.	DESCRIPTION	FIRST DAY COVER	UNUSED ENTIRE
	1982		
UXC12	28¢ multicolored	1.60	1.15

SCOTT NO.	DESCRIPTION	FIRST DAY COVERS SING	INSC. BLK	INSCRIP BLK-4	UNUSED F/NH	USED F

UNITED NATIONS;
OFFICES IN GENEVA, SWITZERLAND
Denominations in Swiss Currency

NOTE: Unless illustrated, designs can be assumed to be similar to the equivalent New York issues.

1 5 7 8 9 13

2 3 4 6

10 11 12 14

1969-70

1-14	5¢ to 10fr Definitives	....	55.00	110.00	110.00	22.75	16.50

1971

15-21	1971 Issues, cpl. (7)	....	....	....	45.00	9.50	....
15	30¢ Peaceful Uses Sea Bed	......	1.30	2.75	1.75	.35	.40
16	50¢ Support for Refugees	....	1.35	4.25	4.00	.85	.95
17	50¢ World Food Programme	...	1.65	4.75	4.75	1.00	1.10
18	75¢ U.P.U. Building	....	3.25	11.50	12.00	2.50	2.75
19-20	30¢ & 50¢ Anti-Discrimination		2.75	8.75	8.50	1.75	2.00
21	1, 10fr International School	...	4.50	16.00	16.75	3.50	3.75

22

1972

22-29	1972 Issues, cpl. (8)	....	....	....	72.50	15.00	....
22	40¢ Definitive	....	1.30	3.25	2.95	.60	.65
23	40¢ Non Proliferation	....	2.75	9.75	9.75	2.00	2.25
24	80¢ World Health Day	....	2.75	9.75	9.75	2.00	2.25
25-26	40¢ & 80¢ Environment	....	4.75	16.75	19.50	3.95	4.25
27	1, 10fr Economic Comm. Europe		4.00	14.00	15.75	3.25	3.50
28-29	40¢ & 80¢ Art-Sert Ceiling	...	4.75	16.75	19.00	4.00	4.25

FIRST DAY COVERS: Price for United Nations First Day Covers are for cacheted, unaddressed covers with each variety in a set mounted on a separate cover. Complete sets mounted on one cover do exist and sell for a slightly lower price.

SCOTT NO.	DESCRIPTION	FIRST DAY COVERS SING	INSC. BLK	INSCRIP BLK-4	UNUSED F/NH	USED F
		1973				
30-36	**1973, Issues, cpl. (7)**	....	....	53.50	11.25	....
30-31	60¢ & 1, 10fr Disarm. Decade	4.75	17.50	19.00	4.00	4.25
32	60¢ Drug Abuse...........................	2.00	6.75	7.75	1.60	1.75
33	80¢ Volunteers	2.25	7.50	8.50	1.75	1.90
34	60¢ Namibia	2.25	7.50	8.25	1.75	1.90
35-36	40¢ & 80¢ Human Rights	3.50	11.50	12.75	2.75	2.95
		1974				
37-45	**1974 Issues, cpl. (9)**	....	....	57.50	12.35	....
37-38	60¢ & 80¢ ILO Headquarters ...	3.50	11.50	12.75	2.75	3.00
39-40	30¢ & 60¢ U.P.U. Centenary	2.65	8.50	8.00	1.75	1.95
41-42	60¢ & 1fr Brazil Peace Mural	4.00	14.00	15.75	3.35	3.50
43-44	60¢ & 80¢ World Population Year	3.50	11.50	13.50	2.85	3.00
45	1, 30fr Law of the Sea	2.85	10.00	10.50	2.25	2.50
		1975				
46-56	**1975 Issues, No #52 (10)**	....	....	62.50	13.25	....
46-47	60¢ & 90¢ Peaceful Use of Space	3.75	13.00	14.00	3.00	3.25
48-49	60¢ & 90¢ Int'l. Women's Year	4.25	15.00	17.00	3.65	3.85
50-51	60¢ & 90¢ 30th Anniversary ...	2.75	9.75	10.75	2.25	2.50
52	Same, Souvenir Sheet	3.75	....	....	3.00	3.25
53-54	50¢ & 1, 30fr Namibia	3.35	12.00	13.50	2.75	3.00
55-56	60¢ & 70¢ Peacekeeping	2.75	9.75	10.50	2.25	2.50

61-62   65-66   67-68   69-70   71-72

		1976				
57-63	**1976 Issues, (7)**	....	....	97.50	20.75	....
57	90¢ World Federation	2.35	8.25	8.75	1.85	2.00
58	1, 10fr Conference - T. & D. ...	2.50	9.00	9.35	2.00	2.25
59-60	40¢ & 1, 50fr Human Settlement	3.50	12.75	14.85	3.15	3.25
61-62	80¢ & 1, 10fr Postal Admin. ...	14.00	52.50	63.50	13.50	13.00
63	70¢ World Food Council	1.80	6.25	6.50	1.40	1.50
		1977				
64-72	**1977 Issues, cpl. (9)**	....	....	55.00	11.75	....
64	80¢ WIPO...................................	1.95	6.95	7.00	1.50	1.65
65-66	80¢ & 1, 10fr Water Conference	3.75	12.50	12.50	2.65	2.85
67-68	80¢ & 1, 10fr Security Council	3.75	12.50	12.50	2.65	2.85
69-70	40¢ & 1, 10fr Combat Racism	2.95	10.00	10.50	2.25	2.40
71-72	80¢ & 1, 10fr Atomic Energy	4.25	14.00	15.75	3.35	3.50

73   74-75   77-78   79-80

		1978				
73-81	**1978 Issues, cpl. (9)**	....	....	53.75	11.50	....
73	35¢ Definitive	1.00	3.25	3.15	.70	.75
74-75	80¢ & 1, 10fr Smallpox Eradic.	3.75	13.00	14.00	3.00	3.25
76	80¢ Namibia..............................	2.00	7.00	7.00	1.50	1.75
77-78	70¢ & 80¢ ICAO.........................	3.25	11.50	11.75	2.50	2.75
79-80	70¢ & 1, 10fr General Assembly	4.00	12.75	13.85	2.95	3.15
81	80¢ TCDC..................................	2.00	7.00	6.95	1.50	1.75

SCOTT NO.	DESCRIPTION	FIRST DAY COVERS SING	INSC. BLK	INSCRIP BLK-4	UNUSED F/NH	USED F

82-83 84-85 87-88 90-91

1979

82-88	1979 Issues, cpl. (7)	....	....	61.50	12.95	....
82-83	80¢ & 1, 50fr UNDRO	4.75	17.00	18.75	3.95	4.25
84-85	80¢ & 1, 10fr I.Y.C.	6.00	18.75	21.50	4.50	4.75
86	1, 10fr Namibia	2.50	8.50	9.25	1.95	2.10
87-88	80¢ & 1, 10fr Court of Justice	4.25	14.50	15.75	3.35	3.50

1980

89/97	1980 Issues, No #95 (8)	...	....	42.50	9.25	....
89	80¢ Economics	2.25	7.95	7.95	1.75	1.95
90-91	40¢ & 70¢ Decade for Women	2.75	10.00	10.50	2.25	2.50
92	1, 10fr Peacekeeping	2.50	8.95	9.00	1.95	2.20

94 97 105-06 107 110

93-94	40¢ & 70¢ 35th Anniversary	...	2.75	9.25	9.00	1.95	2.20
95	Same, Souvenir Sheet	3.25			2.50	2.75
96-97	40¢ & 70¢ Econ. & Social Council	2.50	8.95	9.00	1.95	2.20

1981

98-104	1981 Issues, cpl. (7)	....	....	50.00	10.65	....
98	80¢ Palestinian People	2.00	7.00	75.00	1.60	1.75
99-100	40¢ & 1, 50fr Disabled People	4.25	15.00	16.50	3.50	3.75
101	80¢ Fresco	2.00	7.00	7.50	1.60	1.75
102	1, 10fr Sources of Energy	2.75	9.75	10.50	2.25	2.40
103-04	40¢ & 70¢ Volunteers Program	2.75	9.75	10.50	2.25	2.40

1982

105-12	1982 Issues, cpl. (8)	....	....	53.75	11.50	....
105-06	30¢ & 1fr Definitives	3.25	11.00	11.50	2.50	2.75
107-08	40¢ & 1, 20fr Human Environ.	3.65	12.75	13.75	3.00	3.25
109-10	80¢ & 1fr Space Exploration	4.00	13.75	14.75	3.25	3.50
111-12	40¢ & 1, 50fr Conservation	4.25	15.00	16.50	3.50	3.75

115 118 119-20 122-23 124-25

1983

113-20	1983 Issues, cpl. (8)	....	....	60.75	12.95	....
113	1, 20fr World Communications	2.75	10.00	10.95	2.35	2.50
114-15	40¢ & 80¢ Safety at Sea	2.95	10.75	11.50	2.50	2.65
116	1, 50fr World Food Program	3.65	13.50	13.85	2.95	3.25
117-18	80¢ & 1, 10fr Trade & Develop.	3.85	14.00	13.50	2.85	3.15
119-20	40¢ & 1, 20fr Human Rights	3.75	13.50	14.00	3.00	3.25

SCOTT NO.	DESCRIPTION	FIRST DAY COVERS SING	INSC. BLK	INSCRIP BLK-4	UNUSED F/NH	USED F
		1984				
121-28	**1984 Issues, cpl. (8)**	....	....	59.75	12.75	....
121	1, 20fr Population	2.75	10.00	10.50	2.25	2.50
122-23	50¢ & 80¢ Food Day	3.25	11.50	11.75	2.50	2.75
124-25	50¢ & 70¢ Heritage	2.75	10.00	10.50	2.25	2.50

126-27	128	130	133	134

| 126-27 | 35¢ & 1.50fr Future for Refugees | 5.00 | 18.50 | 19.75 | 4.25 | 4.50 |
| 128 | 1.20fr Youth Year | 2.75 | 10.00 | 10.50 | 2.25 | 2.50 |

		1985				
129/39	**1985 Issues, No #137 (10)**	....	....	100.00	21.50	....
129-30	80¢-1.20fr Turin Centre	5.25	18.75	21.50	4.50	4.75
131-32	50¢-80¢ U.N. University	3.35	11.50	12.50	2.65	2.85
133-34	20¢-1.20fr Definitives	4.25	15.00	16.50	3.50	3.75
135-36	50¢-70¢ 40th Anniversary	3.50	12.50	12.95	2.75	3.00
137	Same, Souvenir Sheet	3.25	....	....	2.65	2.95
138-39	50¢-4fr Child Survival	10.00	37.50	42.50	8.95	9.50

145	148	152	153

		1986				
140-49	**1986 Issues (10)**	....	....	41.50	10.95	
140	1.40fr Africa in Crisis	3.50	12.75	14.00	2.95	3.25
141-44	35¢ Development, 4 vars., att'd.	3.75	5.00	3.50	2.95	3.25
145	5¢ Definitive	1.50	2.50	.50	.10	.12
146-47	50¢ & 80¢ Philately	3.25	11.50	11.75	2.50	2.75
148-49	45¢ & 1.40fr Peace Year	3.75	13.00	14.00	3.00	3.25
150	35¢-70¢ WFUNA, Souv. Sheet	4.25	....	....	3.50	3.75

		1987				
151	1.40fr Trygve Lie	2.75	10.00	10.75	2.25	2.50
152-53	90¢-1.40fr Definitives	4.50	16.00	17.50	3.75	4.00
154-55	50¢-90¢ Shelter Homeless	3.00	10.00	10.75	2.25	2.50
156-57	70¢-1.20fr Anti-Drug Campaign	3.75	13.00	14.00	3.00	3.25

AIR LETTER SHEETS & POSTAL CARDS

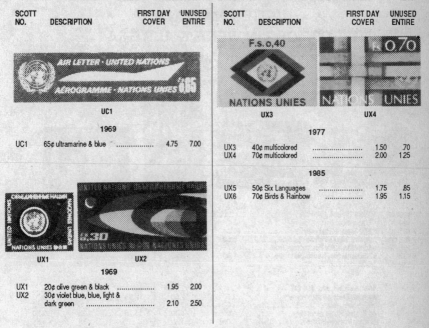

SCOTT NO.	DESCRIPTION	FIRST DAY COVER	UNUSED ENTIRE
UC1			
1969			
UC1	65¢ ultramarine & blue	4.75	7.00
UX1 **UX2**			
1969			
UX1	20¢ olive green & black	1.95	2.00
UX2	30¢ violet blue, blue, light & dark green	2.10	2.50

SCOTT NO.	DESCRIPTION	FIRST DAY COVER	UNUSED ENTIRE
UX3 **UX4**			
1977			
UX3	40¢ multicolored	1.50	.70
UX4	70¢ multicolored	2.00	1.25
1985			
UX5	50¢ Six Languages	1.75	.85
UX6	70¢ Birds & Rainbow	1.95	1.15

SCOTT NO.	DESCRIPTION	FIRST DAY COVERS SING	INSC. BLK	INSCRIP BLK-4	UNUSED F/NH	USED F

UNITED NATIONS:
OFFICES IN VIENNA, AUSTRIA
Denominations in Austrian Currency

NOTE: Unless illustrated, designs can be assumed to be similar to the equivalent New York or Geneva issue.

| 1 | 3 | 5 | 9-10 |

1979

Scott	Description	Sing	Insc. Blk	Inscrip Blk-4	Unused F/NH	Used F
1-8	1979 issues, cpl. (8)	....	....	110.00	10.75	....
1-6	50g to s10 Defintives	8.50	26.75	23.00	5.50	6.00
7	s4 International Economic Order	5.75	20.00	85.00	4.95	5.25
8	s2.50 Internat. Econ. Definitive	1.00	3.25	3.25	.70	.75

1980

9/16	1980 Issues, No #14 (7) ...	....	....	48.50	9.75	....
9-10	s4 & s6 Decade for Women	3.50	12.50	12.95	2.75	3.00
11	s6 Peacekeeping	2.00	7.75	9.25	1.95	2.10
12-13	s4 & s6 35th Anniversary	4.00	14.00	15.75	3.35	3.50
14	Same, Souvenir Sheet	4.65	....	....	3.85	4.25
15-16	s4 & s6 Econ. and Social Council	3.00	10.00	10.50	2.25	2.50

| 19 | 24 | 37-38 |

1981

17-23	1981 Issues, cpl. (7)	....	....	43.00	9.00	....
17	s4 Palestinian People	1.75	6.00	6.35	1.35	1.50
18-19	s4 & s6 Disabled Persons	3.00	10.00	10.65	2.25	2.50
20	s6 Fresco.............................	1.90	6.75	7.00	1.50	1.65
21	s7.50 Sources of Energy	2.25	7.50	7.75	1.65	1.75
22-23	s5 & s7 Volunteers Program ...	3.50	12.50	12.95	2.75	3.00

1982

24-29	1982 Issues, cpl. (6)	....	....	35.00	7.25	....
24	s3 Definitive	1.25	3.50	3.50	.75	.80
25-26	s5 & s7 Human Environment ...	3.75	13.50	13.95	3.00	3.25
27	s5 Space Exploration	1.75	6.00	6.50	1.35	1.50
28-29	s5 & s7 Nature Conservation ...	3.50	12.00	12.95	2.75	3.00

1983

30-38	1983 Issues, cpl. (9)	....	....	55.75	11.85	....
30	s4 World Comm.	1.35	4.50	4.50	.95	1.10
31-32	s4 & s6 Safety at Sea	3.15	10.50	10.50	2.25	2.50
33-34	s5 & s7 World Food Program ...	3.75	13.00	13.75	2.95	3.25
35-36	s4 & s8.50 Trade and Develop.	3.85	13.00	13.75	2.95	3.25
37-38	s5 & s7 Human Rights	4.25	14.00	15.75	3.35	3.65

SCOTT NO.	DESCRIPTION	FIRST DAY COVERS SING	INSC. BLK	INSCRIP BLK-4	UNUSED F/NH	USED F

40-41 42-43 44-45 46-47

1984

39-47	1984 Issues, cpl. (9)	....	....	75.00	15.95	....
39	s7 Population	2.50	9.00	9.15	1.95	2.25
40-41	s4.50 & s6 Food Day	4.00	14.00	15.00	3.25	3.50
42-43	s3.50 & s15 Heritage	6.25	22.50	23.50	4.95	5.50
44-45	s4.50 & s8.50 Future for Refugees	4.75	17.00	18.50	3.95	4.25
46-47	s3.50 & s6.50 Youth Year	3.50	12.50	12.95	2.75	3.00

50 64-65 72 73

48/56	1985 Issues, No #54 (8)	....	....	59.75	12.95	....
48	s7.50 I.L.O. Turin Centre	2.25	7.95	8.25	1.75	1.95
49	s8.50 U.N. University	2.50	9.00	9.75	2.10	2.25
50-51	s4.50 & s15 Definitives	5.00	18.00	19.75	4.25	4.50
52-53	s6.50 & s8.50 40th Anniv.	3.75	13.00	13.75	2.95	3.25
54	Same, Souvenir Sheet	3.50	....	....	2.95	3.25
55-56	s4-s6 Child Survival	3.50	12.00	12.50	2.75	3.00

1986

57-65	1986 Issues (9)	....	....	32.50	9.95	....
57	s8 Africa in Crisis	2.50	9.00	9.75	2.10	2.25
58-61	s4.50 Development, 4 Var., att.	5.00	6.00	5.25	4.25	4.50
62-63	s3.50 & s6.50 Philately	2.75	8.95	8.75	1.95	2.10
64-65	s5 & s6 Peace Year	3.25	10.50	10.00	2.25	2.50
66	s4 to s7 WFUNA, Souvenir Sheet	5.00	....	....	4.25	4.50

1987

67	s8 Tryqve Lie	2.00	7.00	7.50	1.60	1.75
68-69	s4 & s9.50 Shelter Homeless	3.50	11.75	12.50	2.65	2.85
70-71	s5 & s8 Anti-Drug Campaign	3.25	10.75	11.75	2.50	2.65
72-73	s2 & s 7 Definitives	4.50	16.00	17.50	3.65	3.95

AIR LETTER SHEETS & POSTAL CARDS

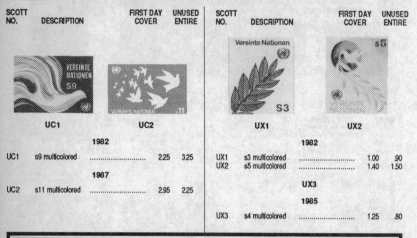

SCOTT NO.	DESCRIPTION	FIRST DAY COVER	UNUSED ENTIRE
	1982		
UC1	s9 multicolored	2.25	3.25
	1987		
UC2	s11 multicolored	2.95	2.25

SCOTT NO.	DESCRIPTION	FIRST DAY COVER	UNUSED ENTIRE
	1982		
UX1	s3 multicolored	1.00	.90
UX2	s5 multicolored	1.40	1.50
	UX3		
	1985		
UX3	s4 multicolored	1.25	.80

CANADA

| 1, 4, 12 | 2, 5, 10, 13 | 7 | 8, 11 | 9 |
| Beaver | Prince Albert | Jacques Cartier | | Queen Victoria |

SCOTT NO.	DESCRIPTION	UNUSED O.G. F	AVG	UNUSED F	AVG	USED F	AVG
1851 Laid paper, Imperforate							
1	3p red	....	....	....	....	750.00	450.00
2	6p grayish purple	....	....	....	....	900.00	550.00
1852-55 Wove paper							
4	3p red	....	....	1250.00	750.00	210.00	125.00
4d	3p red (thin paper)	....	....	....	....	225.00	135.00
5	6p slate gray	....	....	....	....	800.00	485.00
1855							
7	10p blue	....	....	....	....	750.00	450.00
1857							
8	1/2p rose	900.00	500.00	600.00	375.00	465.00	285.00
9	7-1/2p green	....	....	....	....	1950.00	1150.00
Very thick soft wove paper							
10	6p reddish purple	....	....	....	....	1950.00	1200.00
1858-59 Perf. 12							
11	1/2p rose	....	....	1350.00	750.00	775.00	465.00
12	3p red	....	....	2250.00	1350.00	450.00	275.00
13	6p brown violet	....	....	....	....	3500.00	2150.00

| 14 | 15 | 16, 17 | 18 | 19 | 20 |
| Queen Victoria | Beaver | Prince Albert | Queen Victoria | Jacques Cartier | Queen Victoria |

1859							
14	1¢ rose	315.00	175.00	225.00	135.00	37.50	25.00
15	5¢ vermillion	275.00	150.00	200.00	120.00	16.50	10.00
16	10¢ black brown	....	....	....	....	2000.00	1200.00
17	10¢ red lilac	685.00	375.00	485.00	295.00	56.50	33.50
18	12-1/2¢ yellow green	385.00	235.00	295.00	175.00	52.50	31.50
19	17¢ blue	685.00	375.00	485.00	295.00	80.00	65.00
1864							
20	2¢ rose	400.00	225.00	275.00	175.00	185.00	110.00

| 21 | 22, 23, 31 | 24, 32 | 25, 33 |

ORIGINAL GUM: Prior to 1897, the Unused price is for stamps either without gum or with partial gum. If you require full original gum, use the Unused OG column. Never Hinged quality is scarce on those issues. Please write for specific quotations if NH is required.

SCOTT NO.	DESCRIPTION	UNUSED O.G.		UNUSED		USED	
		F	AVG	F	AVG	F	AVG

26　　27　　28　　29, 30

Queen Victoria

1868-75 Wove paper, Perf. 12, unwkd.

21	1/2¢ black	59.50	33.50	47.50	28.50	42.50	25.00
22	1¢ brown red	435.00	250.00	350.00	210.00	57.50	35.00
23	1¢ orange	850.00	475.00	675.00	400.00	66.50	40.00
24	2¢ green	395.00	230.00	315.00	190.00	40.00	24.00
25	3¢ red	850.00	475.00	675.00	400.00	15.00	9.00
26	5¢ olive gr. (pf. 11-1/2x12)	850.00	475.00	675.00	400.00	95.00	56.50
27	6¢ brown	815.00	450.00	650.00	385.00	45.00	27.50
28	12-1/2¢ blue	415.00	240.00	335.00	200.00	45.00	27.50
29	15¢ gray violet	57.50	33.50	46.50	28.00	28.50	17.00
29b	15¢ red lilac	700.00	400.00	575.00	350.00	75.00	45.00
30	15¢ gray	55.00	31.50	43.50	26.50	27.50	16.50

1873-74 Wove paper. Perf. 11-1/2 x 12, unwkd.

21a	1/2¢ black	59.50	33.50	47.50	28.50	42.50	25.00
29a	15¢ gray violet	625.00	375.00	500.00	300.00	130.00	77.50
30a	15¢ gray	625.00	375.00	500.00	300.00	130.00	77.50

1868 Wove paper. Perf. 12 wmkd.

22a	1¢ brown red	1450.00	850.00	1150.00	700.00	175.00	105.00
24a	2¢ green	1450.00	850.00	1150.00	700.00	185.00	110.00
25a	3¢ red	....	....	1700.00	1000.00	165.00	100.00
27b	6¢ dark brown	....	....	....	....	550.00	335.00
28a	12-1/2¢ blue	1100.00	650.00	900.00	550.00	180.00	110.00
29c	15¢ gray violet	....	....	....	....	500.00	300.00

1868 Laid Paper

31	1¢ brown red	....	....	....	....	1600.00	950.00
33	3¢ bright red	....	....	....	....	325.00	195.00

34　　35　　36　　37, 41　　38, 42

39, 43　　44　　40, 45　　46, 47

Queen Victoria

1870-89 Perf. 12

34	1/2¢ black	7.75	4.50	6.50	3.95	6.50	3.95
35	1¢ yellow	25.00	15.00	21.00	12.75	.60	.35
35a	1¢ orange	77.50	46.50	65.00	40.00	7.00	4.25
36	2¢ green	33.50	20.00	27.50	16.50	.95	.55
36d	2¢ blue green	53.50	31.50	45.00	27.50	2.75	1.65
37	3¢ dull red	72.50	41.75	60.00	36.50	1.85	1.10
37c	3¢ orange red	66.50	38.50	55.00	33.50	1.40	.85
37d	3¢ copper red, pf. 12-1/2	....	....	....	....	475.00	285.00
38	5¢ slate green	260.00	150.00	215.00	130.00	14.00	8.50
39	6¢ yellow brown	190.00	110.00	160.00	95.00	16.50	10.00
40	10¢ rose lilac	360.00	210.00	300.00	180.00	52.75	31.50

SCOTT NO.	DESCRIPTION	UNUSED O.G. F	AVG	UNUSED F	AVG	USED F	AVG
		1873-79 Perf. 11-1/2 x 12					
35d	1¢ orange	140.00	80.00	115.00	70.00	10.50	6.35
36e	2¢ green	190.00	110.00	160.00	95.00	15.00	9.00
37e	3¢ red	167.50	100.00	140.00	85.00	9.25	5.65
38a	5¢ slate green	400.00	240.00	335.00	200.00	27.50	16.50
39b	6¢ yellow brown	400.00	240.00	335.00	200.00	27.50	16.50
40c	10¢ pale rose lilac	775.00	450.00	650.00	395.00	125.00	75.00
		1888-93 Perf. 12					
41	3¢ vermillion	18.75	11.00	16.00	9.75	.33	.20
41a	3¢ rose carmine	350.00	200.00	300.00	180.00	7.25	4.35
42	5¢ gray	41.50	25.00	35.00	21.50	3.85	2.30
43	6¢ red brown	43.00	26.50	36.50	22.50	9.00	5.50
43a	6¢ chocolate	60.00	34.50	50.00	30.00	15.00	8.50
44	8¢ gray	50.00	30.00	42.50	26.00	4.00	2.40
45	10¢ brown red	140.00	82.50	120.00	72.50	32.50	19.75
46	20¢ vermillion	210.00	125.00	175.00	105.00	45.00	27.50
47	50¢ deep blue	340.00	200.00	285.00	170.00	32.50	19.75

NOTE: For N.H. prior to 1897 please add 50% to the desired condition price.

SCOTT NO.	DESCRIPTION	UNUSED NH F	AVG	UNUSED OG F	AVG	USED F	AVG

50-65
Queen Victoria in 1837 & 1897

1897 JUBILEE ISSUE

50	1/2¢ black	117.50	67.50	82.50	50.00	82.50	50.00
51	1¢ orange	13.75	7.75	9.50	5.75	6.25	3.75
52	2¢ green	18.50	10.75	13.00	8.00	10.00	6.00
53	3¢ bright rose	13.50	7.25	9.00	5.50	1.75	1.05
54	5¢ deep blue	41.50	23.50	27.50	16.50	19.75	11.75
55	6¢ yellow brown	210.00	120.00	140.00	85.00	140.00	85.00
56	8¢ dark violet	52.50	30.00	35.00	21.50	35.00	21.50
57	10¢ brown violet	115.00	65.00	77.50	46.50	75.00	45.00
58	15¢ steel blue	195.00	110.00	130.00	80.00	130.00	80.00
59	20¢ vermillion	225.00	125.00	150.00	90.00	150.00	90.00
60	50¢ ultramarine	250.00	140.00	165.00	100.00	130.00	80.00
61	$1 lake	900.00	500.00	600.00	365.00	565.00	340.00
62	$2 dark purple	1700.00	950.00	1100.00	675.00	475.00	285.00
63	$3 yellow bistre	1875.00	1050.00	1250.00	750.00	875.00	525.00
64	$4 purple	1875.00	1050.00	1250.00	750.00	875.00	525.00
65	$5 olive green	1875.00	1050.00	1250.00	750.00	875.00	525.00

66-73 **74-84** **85-86**
Queen Victoria *Map Showing British Empire*

77: 2¢ Die I. Frame of four thin lines
77a: 2¢ Die II. Frame of thick line between two thin lines

1897-98 Maple Leaves

66	1/2¢ black	7.25	4.00	4.95	2.95	4.95	2.95
67	1¢ blue green	14.50	8.00	10.00	6.00	.75	.45
68	2¢ purple	18.50	10.00	12.50	7.50	1.30	.80
69	3¢ carmine (1898)	18.50	10.00	12.50	7.50	.33	.20

SCOTT NO.	DESCRIPTION	UNUSED NH F	AVG	UNUSED F	AVG	USED F	AVG
70	5¢ dark blue, bluish paper	100.00	57.50	65.00	40.00	4.50	2.75
71	6¢ brown............................	90.00	50.00	60.00	35.00	24.75	14.75
72	8¢ orange..........................	150.00	85.00	100.00	60.00	8.50	5.00
73	10¢ brown violet (1898)	250.00	135.00	165.00	100.00	67.50	40.00

1898-1902 Numerals

74	1/2¢ black	3.00	1.70	2.15	1.30	1.35	.85
75	1¢ gray green	18.00	10.00	12.50	7.50	.12	.08
76	2¢ purple (I)	16.00	9.00	11.00	6.75	.15	.09
77	2¢ carmine (I) (1899) ...	23.00	13.00	16.00	9.75	.12	.08
77a	2¢ carmine (II)	25.00	14.00	17.50	10.50	.35	.22
78	3¢ carmine........................	35.00	20.00	23.50	14.00	.35	.22
79	5¢ blue, bluish paper	135.00	70.00	87.50	52.50	.95	.55
80	6¢ brown...........................	140.00	80.00	90.00	53.50	30.00	18.00
81	7¢ olive yellow (1902) ...	80.00	45.00	55.00	32.50	12.50	7.50
82	8¢ orange..........................	175.00	95.00	115.00	70.00	16.50	10.00
83	10¢ brown violet	275.00	155.00	175.00	110.00	12.75	7.75
84	20¢ olive green (1900) ...	450.00	250.00	300.00	180.00	67.50	40.00

1898 IMPERIAL PENNY POSTAGE COMMEMORATIVE

85	2¢ black, lavender & carmine	33.50	18.00	22.50	13.50	6.25	3.75
86	2¢ black, blue & carmine	33.50	18.00	22.50	13.50	6.25	3.75

1899
69 & 78 surcharged

87	2¢ on 3¢ carmine	11.00	6.25	7.75	4.65	5.00	3.00
88	2¢ on 3¢ carmine	12.75	7.25	9.00	5.50	3.50	2.10

89-95
King Edward VII

1903-08

89	1¢ green............................	16.50	9.50	11.50	7.00	.13	.08
90	2¢ carmine........................	16.50	9.50	11.50	7.00	.10	.06
90a	2¢ carmine, imperf. pair	65.00	43.50	45.00	30.00	37.50	25.00
91	5¢ blue, bluish paper	90.00	50.00	60.00	36.50	2.25	1.35
92	7¢ olive bistre	82.50	46.50	54.50	32.75	2.40	1.45
93	10¢ brown lilac	165.00	90.00	110.00	65.00	5.25	3.25
94	20¢ olive green	375.00	210.00	250.00	150.00	20.00	12.00
95	50¢ purple (1908)	800.00	450.00	525.00	315.00	65.00	40.00

96
Princess and Prince of Wales

97
Jacques Cartier and Samuel Champlain

98
Queen Alexandra and King Edward

99
Champlain's Home in Quebec

100
Generals Montcalm and Wolfe

101
View of Quebec in 1700

102
Champlain's Departure for the West

103
Arrival of Cartier at Quebec

NEVER HINGED: From 1897 to 1949, Unused OG or Unused prices are for stamps with original gum that have been hinged. If you desire Never Hinged stamps, order from the NH listings.

SCOTT NO.	DESCRIPTION	UNUSED NH F	AVG	UNUSED F	AVG	USED F	AVG
	1908 QUEBEC TERCENTENARY ISSUE						
96-103	1/2¢-20¢ cpl., 8 vars.	665.00	380.00	435.00	270.00	365.00	220.00
96	1/2¢ black brown	5.75	3.35	4.25	2.50	4.50	2.70
97	1¢ blue green	11.50	6.25	8.00	4.75	4.50	2.70
98	2¢ carmine	16.00	9.50	11.00	7.00	1.10	.65
99	5¢ dark blue	70.00	40.00	47.50	27.50	36.50	21.50
100	7¢ olive green	90.00	50.00	61.50	36.50	39.75	23.75
101	10¢ dark violet	145.00	87.50	95.00	60.00	70.00	42.50
102	15¢ red orange	165.00	95.00	110.00	67.50	100.00	60.00
103	20¢ yellow brown	200.00	110.00	125.00	80.00	130.00	80.00

104-34, 136-38, 184
King George V

1912-25

104-22	1¢-$1 cpl., 18 vars.	775.00	450.00	550.00	330.00	35.50	21.50
104	1¢ green..........................	7.75	4.50	5.50	3.35	.10	.06
104a	same, booklet pane of 6	33.50	18.50	23.50	14.00	....	....
105	1¢ yellow (1922)	7.00	4.00	5.00	3.00	.17	.10
105a	same, booklet pane of 4	75.00	41.50	55.00	32.50	....	....
105b	same, booklet pane of 6	55.00	33.50	40.00	24.50	....	....
106	2¢ carmine	8.00	4.65	5.75	3.50	.10	.06
106a	same, booklet pane of 6	45.00	25.00	32.50	19.00	....	....
107	2¢ yellow green (1922)	7.35	4.25	5.25	3.15	.10	.06
107b	same, booklet pane of 4	95.00	51.50	67.50	40.00	....	....
107c	same, booklet pane of 6	550.00	325.00	400.00	250.00	....	....
108	3¢ brown (1918)	8.75	5.00	6.25	3.75	.10	.06
108a	same, booklet pane of 4	130.00	73.50	95.00	57.50	....	....
109	3¢ carmine (1923)	7.00	4.00	5.00	3.00	.10	.06
109a	same, booklet pane of 4	70.00	38.75	50.00	30.00	....	....
110	4¢ olive bistre (1922) ...	33.50	19.00	23.50	14.00	3.00	1.80
111	5¢ dark blue	105.00	62.50	75.00	45.00	.40	.25
112	5¢ violet (1922)	16.00	9.35	11.50	7.00	.50	.30
113	7¢ yellow ochre	23.00	13.50	16.50	10.00	2.00	1.20
114	7¢ red brown (1924)	23.50	14.00	16.75	10.50	7.00	4.25
115	8¢ blue (1925)	32.75	18.75	23.50	14.00	9.00	5.35
116	10¢ plum........................	167.50	96.50	120.00	72.50	1.40	.85
117	10¢ blue (1922)	41.50	23.50	29.50	17.50	1.40	.85
118	10¢ bistre brown (1925)	37.50	21.50	26.50	16.00	1.05	.65
119	20¢ olive green	75.00	42.50	52.50	31.50	1.15	.70
120	50¢ black brown (1925)	85.00	48.75	60.00	36.50	2.50	1.50
120a	50¢ black.........................	120.00	70.00	87.50	52.50	3.75	2.25
122	$1 orange (1923)	125.00	75.00	90.00	55.00	7.00	4.25
	1912 Coil Stamps Perf. 8 Horizontally						
123	1¢ green............................	75.00	42.50	55.00	30.00	36.50	21.50
124	2¢ carmine	75.00	42.50	55.00	30.00	36.50	21.50
	1912-24 Perf. 8 Vertically						
125-30	1¢-3¢ cpl., 6 vars.	127.50	73.50	91.50	55.00	16.50	9.95
125	1¢ dark green	12.50	7.25	9.00	5.50	.55	.35
126	1¢ yellow (1923)	10.00	5.65	7.50	4.50	6.25	3.75
126a	1¢ pair, imperf. between	50.00	31.50	37.50	25.00	....	....
127	2¢ carmine	20.00	12.00	15.00	9.00	.40	.25
128	2¢ green (1922)	12.00	7.00	8.75	5.25	.45	.27
128a	2¢ pair, imperf. between	50.00	31.50	37.50	25.00	....	....

SCOTT NO.	DESCRIPTION	UNUSED NH F	AVG	UNUSED F	AVG	USED F	AVG
129	3¢ brown (1918)	9.75	5.65	7.00	4.25	.55	.35
130	3¢ carmine (1924)	70.00	40.00	50.00	30.00	9.00	5.50
130a	3¢ pair, imperf. between	875.00	550.00	650.00	435.00	....	....

1915-24 Perf. 12 Horizontally

131	1¢ dark green	9.50	5.25	6.75	4.00	6.75	4.00
132	2¢ carmine	27.50	15.00	19.50	11.50	19.50	11.50
133	2¢ yellow green (1924)	120.00	70.00	87.50	52.50	87.50	52.50
134	3¢ brown (1921)	9.00	5.00	6.50	4.00	6.00	3.65

135
Quebec Conference of 1867

1917 CONFEDERATE ISSUE

135	3¢ brown....................	31.00	18.00	21.75	13.00	.45	.27

1924 Imperforate

136	1¢ yellow....................	65.00	40.00	50.00	33.50	55.00	36.50
137	2¢ green.....................	65.00	40.00	50.00	33.50	55.00	36.50
138	3¢ carmine..................	32.50	20.00	25.00	16.50	27.50	18.50

1926
109 Surcharged

139	2¢ on 3¢ carmine	85.00	48.75	60.00	36.50	60.00	36.50

109 Surcharged

140	2¢ on 3¢ carmine	32.50	18.50	23.50	14.00	23.50	14.00

141	142	143	144	145
Sir John MacDonald	The Quebec Conference of 1867	The Parliament Building at Ottawa	Sir Wilfred Laurier	Map of Canada

1927 CONFEDERATION ISSUE

141-45	1¢-12¢ cpl., 5 vars.	48.50	27.00	35.00	21.75	12.00	7.25
141	1¢ orange...........................	3.95	2.20	2.95	1.75	.60	.35
142	2¢ green.............................	2.20	1.25	1.65	1.00	.12	.08
143	3¢ brown carmine	13.00	7.35	9.50	5.75	5.00	3.00
144	5¢ violet	7.50	4.00	5.50	3.35	2.35	1.40
145	12¢ dark blue	24.50	14.00	18.00	11.50	4.65	2.75

146	147	148
Thomas McGee	Sir Wilfred Laurier and Sir John MacDonald	Robert Baldwin and L.H. Lafontaine

1927 HISTORICAL ISSUE

146-48	5¢-20¢ cpl., 3 vars.	43.75	25.50	32.75	20.00	11.50	6.85
146	5¢ violet	5.25	2.95	3.95	2.35	2.50	1.50
147	12¢ green..........................	14.00	7.95	10.50	6.35	4.35	2.60
148	20¢ brown carmine	27.50	15.95	19.75	12.50	5.00	3.00

SCOTT NO.	DESCRIPTION	UNUSED NH F	AVG	UNUSED F	AVG	USED F	AVG

George V

149-154,160,161

Mt. Hurd

155

156	**157**	**158**	**159**
Quebec Bridge	*Harvesting Wheat*	*Fishing Schooner "Bluenose"*	*The Parliament Building at Ottawa*

1928-29

SCOTT NO.	DESCRIPTION	UNUSED NH F	AVG	UNUSED F	AVG	USED F	AVG
149-59	1¢-$1 cpl., 11 vars. ...	850.00	485.00	635.00	385.00	145.00	88.50
149-55	1¢-10¢, 7 varieties ...	81.50	47.50	61.50	37.50	23.75	14.25
149	1¢ orange........................	2.85	1.65	2.25	1.35	.20	.12
149a	same, booklet pane of 6	31.75	18.75	23.50	14.50	....	....
150	2¢ green.........................	1.50	.85	1.15	.70	.10	.06
150a	same, booklet pane of 6	31.75	18.75	23.50	14.50	....	....
151	3¢ dark carmine	25.00	13.75	18.75	11.00	11.75	7.00
152	4¢ bistre (1929)	22.50	13.50	15.00	11.50	4.50	2.75
153	5¢ deep violet	7.00	4.15	5.50	3.35	2.00	1.20
153a	same, booklet pane of 6	165.00	105.00	130.00	80.00	....	....
154	8¢ blue...........................	15.75	9.00	11.75	7.00	5.50	3.25
155	10¢ green.........................	12.00	6.75	9.00	5.50	.95	.55
156	12¢ gray (1929)	18.50	10.75	14.00	8.50	5.75	3.50
157	20¢ dark carmine (1929)	40.00	22.50	30.00	18.00	9.00	5.50
158	50¢ dark blue (1929)	335.00	190.00	250.00	150.00	52.50	32.50
159	$1 olive green (1929) ...	425.00	240.00	315.00	190.00	60.00	36.50

1929 Coil Stamps. Perf. 8 Vertically

SCOTT NO.	DESCRIPTION	UNUSED NH F	AVG	UNUSED F	AVG	USED F	AVG
160	1¢ orange.........................	26.75	14.95	19.75	11.95	16.50	10.00
161	2¢ green...........................	18.00	9.95	13.50	7.95	2.35	1.40

162-172,178-183
King George V

2¢ Die I. Above "POSTAGE" faint crescent in ball of ornament. Top letter "P" has tiny dot of color.

2¢ Die II. Stronger and clearer crescent spot of color in "P" is larger.

173
Parliament Library at Ottawa

174	**175**	**176**	**177**
The Old Citadel at Quebec	*Harvesting Wheat on the Prairies*	*The Museum at Grand Pre, and Monument to Evangeline*	*Mt. Edith Cavell*

VERY FINE QUALITY: To determine the Very Fine price, add the difference between the Fine and Average prices to the Fine quality price. For example: if the Fine price is $10.00 and the Average price is $6.00, the Very Fine price would be $14.00. From 1935 to date, add 20% to the Fine price to arrive at the Very Fine price.

SCOTT NO.	DESCRIPTION	UNUSED NH F	UNUSED NH AVG	UNUSED F	UNUSED AVG	USED F	USED AVG
			1930-31				
162-77	1¢-$1 cpl., 16 vars. ...	550.00	325.00	450.00	270.00	63.50	37.75
162-72	1¢-8¢, 11 vars.	63.50	38.50	51.50	31.50	23.50	14.00
162	1¢ orange...........................	1.00	.60	.80	.50	.45	.27
163	1¢ deep green	1.55	.90	1.25	.75	.10	.06
163a	same, booklet pane of 4	200.00	120.00	160.00	100.00	....	....
163c	same, booklet pane of 6	56.50	32.50	45.00	27.50	....	....
164	2¢ dull green	1.25	.70	1.00	.60	.12	.07
164a	same, booklet pane of 6	55.00	31.00	43.50	26.00	....	....
165	2¢ deep red, die II	1.90	1.10	1.50	.90	.10	.06
165a	2¢ deep red, die I	1.45	.85	1.15	.70	.15	.09
165b	same, booklet pane of 6	28.50	16.50	22.50	13.50	....	....
166	2¢ dark brown, die II (1931)	1.15	.65	.90	.55	.10	.06
166a	same, booklet pane of 4	190.00	110.00	150.00	90.00	....	....
166b	2¢ dark brown, die I	5.95	3.40	4.85	2.85	3.85	2.30
166c	same, booklet pane of 6	50.00	29.50	40.00	24.50	....	....
167	3¢ deep red (1931)	2.25	1.30	1.75	1.10	.10	.06
167a	same, booklet pane of 4	50.00	29.50	40.00	24.50	....	....
168	4¢ yellow bistre	12.95	7.75	10.75	6.50	5.75	3.50
169	5¢ dull violet	7.50	4.50	6.25	3.75	4.25	2.60
170	5¢ dull blue	4.50	2.65	3.60	2.25	.15	.09
171	8¢ dark blue	24.50	14.25	19.50	11.75	9.50	5.75
172	8¢ red orange	8.35	4.95	6.85	4.15	3.75	2.25
173	10¢ olive green	11.50	6.95	9.95	5.95	.95	.55
174	12¢ gray black	16.50	9.50	13.00	8.00	5.00	3.00
175	20¢ brown red	37.50	23.50	31.50	18.95	.45	.28
176	50¢ dull blue	225.00	130.00	180.00	110.00	12.50	7.50
177	$1 dark olive green	225.00	130.00	180.00	110.00	23.50	14.00

Coil Pairs for Canada can be supplied at double the single price.

	1930-31 Coil Stamps Perf. 8-1/2 Vertically						
178-83	1¢-3¢ cpl., 6 vars. ...	65.00	37.75	51.75	31.50	19.50	11.50
178	1¢ orange...........................	13.50	7.75	10.75	6.50	9.50	5.75
179	1¢ deep green	7.50	4.35	6.00	3.65	4.25	2.50
180	2¢ dull green	6.50	3.75	5.25	3.15	3.00	1.80
181	2¢ deep red	15.75	9.00	12.50	7.50	2.50	1.50
182	2¢ dark brown (1931) ...	11.00	6.50	8.75	5.25	.55	.35
183	3¢ deep red (1931)	15.00	8.65	12.00	7.25	.45	.27

	1931 Design of 1912-25 Perf. 12 x 8						
184	3¢ carmine	4.00	2.35	3.25	1.95	2.25	1.35

190	**192**	**193**	**194**
Sir George Etienne Cartier	*King George V*	*Prince of Wales*	*Allegorical Figure of Britannia Surveying the British Empire*

	1931						
190	10¢ dark green	10.50	6.75	9.25	5.50	.12	.07

	1932						
	165 & 165a surcharged						
191	3¢ on 2¢ deep red, die II	1.35	.85	1.10	.70	.12	.07
191a	3¢ on 2¢ deep red, die I	2.50	1.45	2.00	1.20	1.50	.90

SCOTT NO.	DESCRIPTION	UNUSED NH		UNUSED		USED	
		F	AVG	F	AVG	F	AVG

1932 OTTAWA CONFERENCE ISSUE

192-94	3¢-13¢ cpl., 3 vars. ...	20.00	12.00	16.00	10.50	7.75	5.00
192	3¢ deep red....................	1.00	.60	.80	.50	.12	.08
193	5¢ dull blue	8.25	5.25	6.50	4.35	2.25	1.50
194	13¢ deep green	12.00	6.65	9.50	6.35	5.75	3.85

195-200, 205-207
King George V

201
The Old Citadel at Quebec

1932

195-201	1¢-13¢, 7 vars.	115.00	73.50	91.50	60.00	12.00	8.00
195	1¢ dark green	.95	.60	.75	.50	.10	.06
195a	same, booklet pane of 4	135.00	80.00	100.00	65.00	....	....
195b	same, booklet pane of 6	31.50	19.00	25.00	16.00	....	....
196	2¢ black brown	1.20	.70	.95	.60	.10	.06
196a	same, booklet pane of 4	135.00	80.00	100.00	65.00	....	....
196b	same, booklet pane of 6	31.50	19.00	25.00	16.00	....	....
197	3¢ deep red.....................	1.50	.95	1.25	.80	.10	.06
197a	same, booklet pane of 4	37.50	24.00	30.00	20.00	....	....
198	4¢ ochre.........................	40.00	25.75	32.50	21.75	5.50	3.65
199	5¢ dark blue	7.50	4.85	6.00	4.00	.14	.09
200	8¢ red orange	25.00	16.00	19.95	13.00	3.75	2.50
201	13¢ dull violet	46.50	28.00	35.00	23.50	3.00	2.00

202
Parliament Buildings at Ottawa

203

204
S.S. Royal William

1933-34 COMMEMORATIVES

202/10	(202-04, 208-10) cpl., 6 varieties	110.00	68.75	87.50	57.50	27.75	18.00

1933

202	5¢ Postal Union	12.00	7.65	9.75	6.50	2.95	1.95
203	20¢ Grain Exhibition	50.00	31.75	40.00	26.50	13.00	8.50
204	5¢ Trans-Atlantic Crossing	11.50	7.25	9.00	6.00	2.95	1.95

1933 Coil Stamps Perf. 8-1/2 Vertically

205	1¢ green.........................	22.50	15.00	18.00	12.50	1.95	1.30
206	2¢ black brown	22.50	15.00	18.00	12.00	.70	.45
207	3¢ deep red.....................	15.00	9.65	12.00	8.00	.27	.18

208

209

210

1934

208	3¢ Jacques Cartier	4.35	2.80	3.50	2.35	1.20	.80
209	10¢ Loyalists Monument	35.00	21.50	27.75	17.75	7.00	4.50
210	2¢ New Brunswick	2.50	1.55	2.00	1.30	2.10	1.40

SCOTT NO.	DESCRIPTION	PLATE BLOCKS F/NH	F	UNUSED F/NH	F	USED F

211

212

213

214

215

216

1935 SILVER JUBILEE ISSUE

SCOTT NO.	DESCRIPTION	PLATE BLOCKS F/NH	F	UNUSED F/NH	F	USED F
211-16	1¢-13¢ cpl., 6 vars.	....	....	30.00	26.00	12.75
211	1¢ Princess Elizabeth	5.50(6)	4.50	.55	.45	.28
212	2¢ Duke of York...............	11.00(6)	9.50	1.10	.95	.18
213	3¢ George & Mary......................	23.75(6)	20.00	2.65	2.25	.11
214	5¢ Prince of Wales	65.00(6)	55.00	7.35	6.25	3.25
215	10¢ Windsor Castle	72.50(6)	61.75	8.25	7.00	2.65
216	13¢ Royal Yacht	90.00(6)	77.50	11.50	10.00	6.75

217-22, 228-30
King George V

223

224

225

226

227

1935

SCOTT NO.	DESCRIPTION	PLATE BLOCKS F/NH	F	UNUSED F/NH	F	USED F
217-27	1¢-$1 cpl., 11 vars.	....	....	195.00	165.00	19.50
217-25	1¢-20¢, 9 vars.	....	....	60.00	50.00	4.65
217	1¢ green......................	4.50(6)	4.00	.45	.40	.15
217a	same, booklet pane of 4	....	....	90.00	77.50	....
217b	same, booklet pane of 6	....	....	35.00	30.00	....
218	2¢ brown......................	5.00(6)	4.25	.50	.45	.10
218a	same, booklet pane of 4	....	....	90.00	77.50	....
218b	same, booklet pane of 6	....	....	27.50	23.50	....
219	3¢ dark carmine	8.50(6)	7.50	.85	.75	.10
219a	same, booklet pane of 6	....	....	27.50	23.50	....
220	4¢ yellow........................	30.00(6)	25.75	3.75	3.25	.50
221	5¢ blue........................	30.00(6)	25.75	3.75	3.25	.15
222	8¢ deep orange	30.00(6)	25.75	3.75	3.25	2.25
223	10¢ Mounted Policeman	75.00(6)	65.00	9.50	8.25	.20
224	13¢ Conference of 1864	80.00(6)	70.00	10.50	9.00	.90
225	20¢ Niagara Falls	235.00(6)	195.00	30.00	24.75	.55
226	50¢ Parliament Building	350.00(6)	300.00	45.00	38.75	5.25
227	$1 Champlain Monument	750.00(6)	650.00	95.00	80.00	10.00

1935 Coil Stamps Perf. 8 Vertically

SCOTT NO.	DESCRIPTION	PLATE BLOCKS F/NH	F	UNUSED F/NH	F	USED F
228-30	1¢-3¢ coils, cpl., 3 vars.	....	....	41.50	35.00	2.75
228	1¢ green........................	....	....	15.75	13.50	1.80
229	2¢ brown........................	....	....	13.50	11.50	.75
230	3¢ dark carmine	....	....	13.50	11.50	.35

SCOTT NO.	DESCRIPTION	PLATE BLOCKS F/NH	F	UNUSED F/NH	F	USED F

231-236,238-240
King George VI

237

1937

231-36	1¢-8¢ cpl., 6 vars.	....	....	12.00	10.50	.75
231	1¢ green	3.00	2.65	.50	.45	.06
231a	same, booklet pane of 4	....	....	17.50	15.00	....
231b	same, booklet pane of 6	....	....	3.50	3.00	....
232	2¢ brown	3.75	3.25	.65	.55	.06
232a	same, booklet pane of 4	....	....	17.50	15.00	....
232b	same, booklet pane of 6	....	....	9.75	8.25	....
233	3¢ carmine	4.25	3.75	.80	.70	.06
233a	same, booklet pane of 4	....	....	4.00	3.50	....
234	4¢ yellow	21.75	18.50	3.75	3.25	.15
235	5¢ blue	18.50	16.50	3.35	2.85	.07
236	8¢ orange	21.75	18.50	3.75	3.25	.40
237	3¢ Coronation	2.00	1.70	.25	.22	.10

Coil Stamps Perf. 8 Vertically

238-40	1¢-3¢ coils, cpl., 3 vars.	....	....	9.75	8.25	1.40
238	1¢ green	....	....	1.90	1.65	1.00
239	2¢ brown	....	....	3.15	2.65	.32
240	3¢ carmine	....	....	5.00	4.25	.13

241   242   244   246   247   243   245   248

1938

241-45	10¢-$1 cpl., 5 vars.	....	....	195.00	160.00	13.50
241	10¢ Memorial Hall	33.50	28.50	6.75	5.75	.10
242	13¢ Halifax Harbor	68.50	58.50	13.75	11.75	.45
243	20¢ Fort Garry Gate	155.00	130.00	28.50	24.00	.35
244	50¢ Vancouver Harbor	225.00	190.00	37.50	32.50	5.00
245	$1 Chateau de Ramezay	675.00	575.00	120.00	95.00	8.00

1939 ROYAL VISIT

246-48	1¢-3¢ cpl., 3 vars.	5.50	4.65	.70	.60	.27
246	1¢ Princess Elizabeth & Margaret	1.85	1.60	.25	.22	.12
247	2¢ War Memorial	1.85	1.60	.25	.22	.09
248	3¢ King George VI & Queen Eliza.	2.00	1.75	.25	.22	.08

PLATE BLOCKS: are portions of a sheet of stamps adjacent to the number(s) indicating the printing plate number used to produce that sheet. Flat plate issues are usually collected in plate blocks of six (number opposite middle stamp) while rotary issues are normally corner blocks of four.

SCOTT NO.	DESCRIPTION	PLATE BLOCKS F/NH	F	UNUSED F/NH	F	USED F

249,255,263 278

250,254,264 267,279,281

251,252,265 266,280

King George VI

253

256

257

258,259

260

261

262

1942-43 WAR ISSUE

SCOTT NO.	DESCRIPTION	PLATE BLOCKS F/NH	F	UNUSED F/NH	F	USED F
249-62	1¢-$1 cpl., 14 vars.	....	....	170.00	146.50	15.00
249-60	1¢-20¢ 12 vars.	....	....	40.00	34.00	5.35
249	1¢ green	1.30	1.15	.28	.24	.06
249a	same, booklet pane of 4	....	....	8.00	6.85	....
249b	same, booklet pane of 6	....	....	2.75	2.35	....
249c	same, booklet pane of 3	....	....	1.65	1.40	....
250	2¢ brown	2.50	2.25	.50	.45	.06
250a	same, booklet pane of 4	....	....	8.00	6.85	....
250b	same, booklet pane of 6	....	....	7.00	6.00	....
251	3¢ dark carmine	2.50	2.25	.50	.45	.06
251a	same, booklet pane of 4	....	....	3.35	2.85	....
252	3¢ rose violet (1943)	2.25	2.00	.45	.40	.06
252a	same, booklet pane of 4	....	....	3.35	2.85	....
252b	same, booklet pane of 3	....	....	2.75	2.50	....
252c	same, booklet pane of 6	....	....	7.50	6.50	....
253	4¢ Grain Elevators	13.75	12.00	1.95	1.65	.55
254	4¢ dark carmine (1943)	2.50	2.25	.50	.45	.06
254a	same, booklet pane of 6	....	....	3.00	2.60	....
254b	same, booklet pane of 3	....	....	3.50	3.00	....
255	5¢ deep blue	7.50	6.50	1.50	1.30	.07
256	8¢ Farm Scene	14.00	12.00	2.80	2.40	.45
257	10¢ Parliament Buildings	29.00	25.00	5.75	5.00	.10
258	13¢ "Ram" Tank	35.00	30.00	7.35	6.25	3.75
259	14¢ "Ram" Tank (1943)	52.50	43.75	11.00	9.25	.28
260	20¢ Corvette	45.00	38.75	9.50	8.00	.22
261	50¢ Munitions Factory	175.00	150.00	37.50	32.50	2.10
262	$1 Destroyer	475.00	400.00	97.50	83.50	8.25

Coil Stamps Perf. 8 Vertically

SCOTT NO.	DESCRIPTION	PLATE BLOCKS F/NH	F	UNUSED F/NH	F	USED F
263-67	1¢-4¢ cpl., 5 vars.	....	....	....	12.50	10.50	3.00
263	1¢ green	....	....	1.15	1.00	.55
264	2¢ brown	....	....	1.65	1.40	1.15
265	3¢ dark carmine	....	....	1.65	1.40	.90
266	3¢ rose violet (1943)	....	....	3.25	2.75	.35
267	4¢ dark carmine (1943)	....	....	5.25	4.50	.20

268

269

270

271

VERY FINE QUALITY: From 1935 to date, add 20% to the Fine price. Minimum of 3¢ per stamp.

SCOTT NO.	DESCRIPTION	PLATE BLOCKS F/NH	F	UNUSED F/NH	F	USED F

272   273

1946 PEACE ISSUE

268-73	8¢-$1 cpl., 6 vars.	....	....	93.50	79.50	6.25
268	8¢ Farm Scene	8.50	7.50	1.70	1.50	.80
269	10¢ Great Bear Lake	9.50	8.25	1.80	1.60	.10
270	14¢ Hydro-Electric Power Station	22.50	18.50	4.50	3.65	.20
271	20¢ Reaper & Harvester	26.00	22.00	5.00	4.25	.14
272	50¢ Lumber Industry	125.00	110.00	25.00	21.50	2.10
273	$1 New Train Ferry	315.00	285.00	60.00	51.50	3.25

274   275   276   277

1947-49 COMMEMORATIVES

274/83	(274-77, 82-83) cpl., 6 vars.	6.25	5.75	1.25	1.10	.55
274	4¢ Alexander G. Bell	1.10	1.00	.22	.20	.13
275	4¢ Canadian Citizen	1.10	1.00	.22	.20	.13

1948

276	4¢ Princess Elizabeth	1.10	1.00	.22	.20	.08
277	4¢ Parliament Building	1.10	1.00	.22	.20	.07

1948 Designs of 1942-43
Coil Stamps Perf. 9-1/2 Vertically

278-81	1¢-4¢ cpl., 4 vars.	....	....	38.50	32.50	15.50
278	1¢ green	....	....	4.00	3.35	2.40
279	2¢ brown	....	....	15.00	12.50	8.75
280	3¢ rose violet	....	....	8.75	7.50	2.40
281	4¢ dark carmine	....	....	11.75	10.00	2.75

282   283

1949

282	4¢ Cabot's "Matthew"	1.10	1.00	.22	.20	.08
283	4¢ Founding of Halifax	1.10	1.00	.22	.20	.10

COMMEMORATIVES: Commemorative stamps are special issues released to honor or recognize persons, organizations, historical events or landmarks. They are usually issued in the current first class denomination to supplement regular issues.

SCOTT NO.	DESCRIPTION	PLATE BLOCK F/NH	UNUSED F/NH	USED F

284,289,
295,297

285,290,298
305,309

286,291,
296,299

287,292,300,
306,310

288,293

King George VI

1949 (with "Postes-Postage")

SCOTT NO.	DESCRIPTION	PLATE BLOCK F/NH	UNUSED F/NH	USED F
284-88	1¢-5¢ cpl., 5 vars.	13.50	2.70	.35
284	1¢ green	.80	.14	.06
284a	booklet pane of 3	......	.55	......
285	2¢ sepia	1.65	.33	.07
286	3¢ rose violet	1.90	.38	.06
286a	booklet pane of 3	......	1.30	......
286b	booklet pane of 4	......	1.65	......
287	4¢ dark carmine	2.90	.60	.07
287a	booklet pane of 3	......	11.75	......
287b	booklet pane of 6	......	13.75	......
288	5¢ deep blue	6.75	1.40	.13

1950 TYPE OF 1949
(without "Postes-Postage")

SCOTT NO.	DESCRIPTION	PLATE BLOCK F/NH	UNUSED F/NH	USED F
289-93	1¢-5¢ cpl., 5 vars.	16.75	2.75	1.70
289	1¢ green	.65	.13	.08
290	2¢ sepia	3.25	.35	.18
291	3¢ rose violet	1.35	.25	.07
292	4¢ dark carmine	1.70	.35	.07
293	5¢ deep blue	10.50	1.80	1.35

294

301

294	50¢ Oil Wells, Alberta	95.00	19.50	1.60

Coil Stamps Perf. 9-1/2 Vertically

295-300	1¢-4¢ cpl., 6 vars.	......	23.50	5.00

(without "Postes-Postage")

295	1¢ green	......	.65	.40
296	3¢ rose violet	......	1.00	.80

(with "Postes-Postage")

297	1¢ green	......	.50	.30
298	2¢ sepia	......	3.00	2.50
299	3¢ rose violet	......	1.75	.25
300	4¢ dark carmine	......	17.50	1.10
301	10¢ Fur Resources	4.75	1.00	.08

302

303

304

1951

302	$1 Fishing	525.00	110.00	14.50

1951-52 COMMEMORATIVES

303/19	(303-04, 11-15, 17-19) cpl., 10 varieties	38.50	8.00	3.15
303	3¢ Sir Robert L. Borden	1.50	.33	.12
304	4¢ William L. M. King	1.65	.35	.12

(with "Postes-Postage")

305	2¢ olive green	1.10	.22	.06
306	4¢ orange vermillion	1.55	.33	.06
306a	booklet pane of 3	......	2.65	......
306b	booklet pane of 6	......	2.75	......

Coil Stamps Perf. 9-1/2 Vertically

309	2¢ olive green	......	1.50	.80
310	4¢ orange vermillion	......	2.50	.95

311

312

313

314

1951 "CAPEX" Exhibition

311	4¢ Trains of 1851 & 1951	3.75	.80	.14
312	5¢ Steamships	12.50	2.65	1.95
313	7¢ Stagecoach & Plane	7.75	1.55	.40
314	15¢ "Three Pence Beaver"	7.75	1.55	.35

315

316

317

318

319

315	4¢ Royal Visit	1.25	.25	.08

1952

316	20¢ Paper Production	9.25	1.90	.07
317	4¢ Red Cross	1.25	.25	.07
318	3¢ J.J.C. Abbott	1.35	.27	.07
319	4¢ A. Mackenzie	1.70	.35	.07

SCOTT NO.	DESCRIPTION	PLATE BLOCK F/NH	UNUSED F/NH	USED F

320

321

1952-53

| 320 | 7¢ Canada Goose | 2.40 | .50 | .07 |
| 321 | $1 Indian House & Totem Pole (1953) | 120.00 | 25.00 | .95 |

322

323

324

1953-54 COMMEMORATIVES

322/50	(322-24, 30, 35-3⁹, 49-50) cpl., 8 varieties	12.00	2.45	.60
322	2¢ Polar Bear	.95	.20	.10
323	3¢ Moose	1.25	.24	.08
324	4¢ Bighorn Sheep	1.50	.30	.08

325-329,331-333

330

1953

325-29	1¢-5¢ cpl., 5 vars.	5.15	1.05	.30
325	1¢ violet brown	.50	.10	.07
325a	booklet pane of 3	....	.65	....
326	2¢ green	.70	.14	.07
327	3¢ carmine rose	1.00	.20	.06
327a	booklet pane of 3	....	1.60	....
327b	booklet pane of 4	....	1.90	....
328	4¢ violet	1.40	.28	.06
328a	booklet pane of 3	....	1.80	....
328b	booklet pane of 6	....	2.50	....
329	5¢ ultramarine	1.85	.40	.07
330	4¢ Queen Elizabeth II	1.25	.25	.08

Coil Stamps Perf. 9-1/2 Vertically

331-33	2¢-4¢ cpl., 3 vars.	....	7.50	4.50
331	2¢ green	....	1.75	1.30
332	3¢ carmine rose	....	1.85	1.20
333	4¢ violet	....	4.25	2.25

SCOTT NO.	DESCRIPTION	PLATE BLOCK F/NH	UNUSED F/NH	USED F

334

335

336

337-342,345-348

343

| 334 | 50¢ Textile Industry | 35.00 | 7.50 | .27 |

1954

335	4¢ Walrus	1.95	.40	.08
336	5¢ Beaver	1.95	.40	.07
336a	booklet pane of 5	....	2.65	....
337-43	1¢-15¢ cpl., 7 vars.	14.50	3.00	.45
337	1¢ violet brown	.45	.09	.06
337a	booklet pane of 5	....	.75	....
338	2¢ green	.70	.14	.06
338a	miniature pane of 25	....	5.00	....
338a	sealed pack of 2	....	10.00	....
339	3¢ carmine rose	1.00	.22	.06
340	4¢ violet	1.35	.28	.06
340a	booklet pane of 5	....	1.85	....
340b	booklet pane of 6	....	6.75	....
341	5¢ bright blue	1.65	.33	.06
341a	booklet pane of 5	....	2.25	....
341b	miniature pane of 20	....	8.75	....
342	6¢ orange	2.50	.50	.11
343	15¢ Gannet	7.50	1.60	.10

Coil Stamps Perf. 9-1/2 Vertically

345-48	2¢-4¢ cpl., 3 vars.	....	4.95	.70
345	2¢ green	....	.65	.23
347	4¢ violet	....	1.75	.28
348	5¢ bright blue	....	2.75	.23

349

350

351

| 349 | 4¢ J.S.D. Thompson | 1.90 | .40 | .08 |
| 350 | 5¢ M. Bowell | 1.90 | .40 | .08 |

1955

| 351 | 10¢ Eskimo in Kayak | 2.40 | .50 | .07 |

352

353

SCOTT NO.	DESCRIPTION	PLATE BLOCK F/NH	UNUSED F/NH	USED F
1955-56 COMMEMORATIVES				
352/64	(352-61, 64) cpl., 11 varieties	21.50	4.50	1.00
352	4¢ Musk Ox	1.90	.40	.07
353	5¢ Whooping Cranes	2.15	.45	.08

355

357

354

356

358

1955

354	5¢ Int'l. Civil Aviation Org.	2.15	.45	.14
355	5¢ Alberta-Saskatchewan	2.15	.45	.15
356	5¢ Boy Scout Jamboree	2.15	.45	.10
357	4¢ R.B. Bennett	1.90	.40	.08
358	5¢ C. Tupper	2.15	.45	.08

359

360

361

362

363

364

1956

359	5¢ Hockey Players	1.90	.40	.10
360	4¢ Caribou	2.15	.45	.08
361	5¢ Mountain Goat	2.15	.45	.07
362	20¢ Paper Industry	10.50	2.25	.08
363	25¢ Chemical Industry	11.50	2.40	.09
364	5¢ Fire Prevention	1.65	.35	.08

365

366

367

368

1957 COMMEMORATIVES

365-74	cpl., 10 varieties	27.50(7)	7.50	4.00
365-68	Recreation, att'd.	2.75	2.25	2.00
365	5¢ Fishing	....	.55	27
366	5¢ Swimming	....	.55	27
367	5¢ Hunting	....	.55	27
368	5¢ Skiing	....	.55	27

369

370

371

372

373

374

369	5¢ Loon	1.60	.35	.08
370	5¢ D. Thompson, Explorer	1.60	.35	.10
371	5¢ Parliament Building	1.60	.35	.08
372	15¢ Posthorn & Globe	18.50	3.95	2.65
373	5¢ Coal Miner	1.40	.30	.10
374	5¢ Royal Visit	1.40	.30	.10

375

376

377

378

1958 COMMEMORATIVES

375-82	cpl., 8 varieties	....	2.65	.85
375	5¢ Newspaper	....	.35	.16
376	5¢ Int'l. Geophysical Year	....	.35	.13
377	5¢ Miner Panning Gold	2.50	.35	.13
378	5¢ La Verendrye, Explorer	1.75	.35	.10

SE-TENANTS: Se-Tenants are issues where two or more different stamp designs are produced on the same sheet in pair, strip or block form. Mint sheets are usually collected in attached blocks, etc. — Used are generally saved as single stamps. Our Se-Tenant sets follow in this collecting pattern.

SCOTT NO.	DESCRIPTION	PLATE BLOCK F/NH	UNUSED F/NH	USED F

379

380

381

382

379	5¢ S. deChamplain	3.95	.35	.10
380	5¢ National Health	1.75	.35	.09
381	5¢ Petroleum Industry	1.75	.35	.09
382	5¢ Speaker's Chair & Mace	1.75	.35	.10

383

384

385

386

389

387

388

1959 COMMEMORATIVES

383-88 cpl., 6 vars.		12.50	2.00	A5
383	5¢ Old & Modern Planes	1.75	.35	.09
384	5¢ NATO Anniversary	1.75	.35	.09
385	5¢ Woman Tending Tree	1.65	.35	.09
386	5¢ Royal Tour	1.65	.35	.09
387	5¢ St. Lawrence Seaway	4.75	.35	.09
388	5¢ Plains of Abraham	1.65	.35	.08

1960-62 COMMEMORATIVES

389-400 cpl., 12 vars.		18.50	3.95	.95
389	5¢ Girl Guides Emblem	1.60	.35	.08

SCOTT NO.	DESCRIPTION	PLATE BLOCK F/NH	UNUSED F/NH	USED F

390

391

392

390	5¢ Battle of Long Sault	1.60	.35	.08
	1961			
391	5¢ Earth Mover	1.60	.35	.08
392	5¢ E.P. Johnson	1.60	.35	.08

393

395

396

394

397

393	5¢ A. Meighen	1.60	.35	.08
394	5¢ Colombo Plan	1.60	.35	.08
395	5¢ Natural Resources	1.60	.35	.08
	1962			
396	5¢ Education	1.60	.35	.08
397	5¢ Red River Settlement	1.60	.35	.09

398

399

400

401-09

398	5¢ Jean Talon	1.60	.35	.08
399	5¢ Victoria, B.C.	1.60	.35	.09
400	5¢ Trans-Canada	1.60	.35	.09

PLATE BLOCKS: are portions of a sheet of stamps adjacent to the number(s) indicating the printing plate number used to produce that sheet. Flat plate issues are usually collected in plate blocks of six (number opposite middle stamp) while rotary issues are normally corner blocks of four.

SCOTT NO.	DESCRIPTION	PLATE BLOCK F/NH	UNUSED F/NH	USED F
	1962-63			
401-05	1¢-5¢ cpl., 5 vars.	7.50	.90	.28
401	1¢ deep brown ('63)	.45	.09	.06
401a	booklet pane of 5	......	4.25	......
402	2¢ green (1963)	3.75	.14	.06
402a	miniature pane of 25	......	6.50	......
402a	same, sealed pack of 2	......	13.00	......
403	3¢ purple (1963)	.90	.18	.06
404	4¢ carmine (1963)	1.25	.23	.06
404a	booklet pane of 5	......	4.50	......
404b	miniature pane of 25	......	9.50	......
405	5¢ violet blue	1.60	.30	.06
405a	booklet pane of 5	......	5.00	......
405b	miniature pane of 20	......	10.75	......

1963-64 Coil Stamps, Perf. 9-1/2 Horiz.

406-09	2¢-5¢ cpl., 4 vars.	......	14.50	4.50
406	2¢ green	......	4.25	1.85
407	3¢ purple (1964)	......	2.75	1.15
408	4¢ carmine	......	3.75	1.15
409	5¢ violet blue	......	4.50	.55

410 / 411 / 412 / 413

1963-64 COMMEMORATIVES

410/35	(410, 12-13, 16-17, 31-35) 10 varieties	13.85	3.00	.75
410	5¢ Sir Casimir S. Gzowski	1.60	.35	.08
411	$1 Export Trade	140.00	30.00	3.35
412	5¢ Sir M. Frobisher, Explorer	1.60	.35	.08
413	5¢ First Mail Routes	1.60	.35	.08

414,430,436 / 415

416 / 417

SCOTT NO.	DESCRIPTION	PLATE BLOCK F/NH	UNUSED F/NH	USED F
	1963-64			
414	7¢ Jet Takeoff (1964)	2.95	.65	.55
415	15¢ Canada Geese	21.50	4.75	20
	1964			
416	5¢ World Peace	1.60	.35	.08
417	5¢ Canadian Unity	1.40	.30	.09

418 — Ontario & White Trillium
429A — Canada & Maple Leaf

COATS OF ARMS & FLORAL EMBLEMS

419 Quebec & White Garden Lily
420 Nova Scotia & Mayflower
421 New Brunswick & Purple Violet (1965)
422 Manitoba & Prairie Crocus (1965)
423 British Columbia & Dogwood (1965)
424 Prince Edward Island & Lady's Slipper (1965)
425 Saskatchewan & Prairie Lily (1966)
426 Alberta & Wild Rose (1966)
427 Newfoundland & Pitcher Plant (1966)
428 Yukon & Fireweed (1966)
429 Northwest Territories & Mountain Avens (1966)

	1964-66			
418-29A	cpl., 13 varieties	17.95	3.70	2.00
418	5¢ red brown, buff & green	1.40	.30	20
419	5¢ green, yellow & orange	1.40	.30	.15
420	5¢ blue, pink & green	1.40	.30	.15
421	5¢ carmine, green & violet	1.40	.30	.15
422	5¢ brown, lilac & green	2.10	.30	.15
423	5¢ lilac, green & bistre	1.40	.30	.15
424	5¢ pink, green & purple	1.40	.30	.15
425	5¢ sepia, orange & green	1.40	.30	20
426	5¢ green, yellow & carmine	1.40	.30	.15
427	5¢ black, green & red	1.40	.30	.15
428	5¢ blue, red & green	1.40	.30	20
429	5¢ olive, yellow & green	1.40	.30	20
429A	5¢ blue & red (1966)	1.40	.30	.15

1964 Surcharged on 414

430	8¢ on 7¢ Jet Takeoff	2.10	.45	.45

431 / 432

434,435

433

437

SCOTT NO.	DESCRIPTION	PLATE BLOCK F/NH	UNUSED F/NH	USED F
431	5¢ Charlottetown Conference	1.60	.35	.08
432	5¢ Quebec Conference	1.40	.30	.08
433	5¢ Queen Elizabeth's Visit	1.40	.30	.08
434	3¢ Christmas	1.00	.22	.06
434a	miniature pane of 25	....	9.75	....
434a	same, sealed pack of 2	....	19.50	....
435	5¢ Christmas	1.40	.30	.07

Jet type of 1964

436	8¢ Jet Takeoff	2.50	.50	.30

1965 COMMEMORATIVES

437-44	8 Varieties	10.25	2.25	.70
437	5¢ I.C.Y.	1.40	.30	.09

438   **439**

440

441   **442**

438	5¢ Sir Wilfred Grenfell	1.40	.30	.09
439	5¢ National Flag	1.40	.30	.09
440	5¢ Winston Churchill	1.40	.30	.09
441	5¢ Inter-Parliamentary	1.40	.30	.12
442	5¢ Ottawa, National Capitol	1.40	.30	.12

443,444   **445**

446

443	3¢ Christmas	1.10	.23	.07
443a	miniature pane of 25	....	6.50	....
443a	same, sealed pack of 2	....	13.00	....
444	5¢ Christmas	1.40	.30	.07

1966 COMMEMORATIVES

445-52	8 varieties	10.00	2.20	.60
445	5¢ Alouette II Satellite	1.40	.30	.10
446	5¢ LaSalle Arrival	1.40	.30	.08

447   **448**

SCOTT NO.	DESCRIPTION	PLATE BLOCK F/NH	UNUSED F/NH	USED F
447	5¢ Highway Safety	1.40	.30	.09
448	5¢ London Conference	1.40	.30	.08

449

450   **451,452**   **453**

449	5¢ Atomic Reactor	1.40	.30	.08
450	5¢ Parliamentary Library	1.40	.30	.09
451	3¢ Christmas	.95	.20	.07
451a	miniature pane of 25	....	4.50	....
451a	same, sealed pack of 2	....	9.00	....
452	5¢ Christmas	1.40	.30	.07

1967 COMMEMORATIVES

453/77	(453, 69-77) cpl., 10 vars	13.00	2.75	.75
453	5¢ National Centennial	1.40	.30	.07

454   **455**   **456,466**

457,467   **458,468**   **459-460F,468A-B,543,549**

461   **465B**

Regional Views & Art Designs
1967-72 Perf. 12 except as noted.

454-65B	1¢-$1 cpl., 14 vars.	140.00	26.50	2.00
454-64	1¢-20¢ 11 varieties	30.00	4.25	.90
454	1¢ brown	1.00	.09	.06
454a	booklet pane of 5	....	.75	....
454b	bklt. pane, 1¢ (1), 6c (4)	....	2.25	....
454c	bklt. pane, 1c (5), 3c (4)	....	2.25	....

SCOTT NO.	DESCRIPTION	PLATE BLOCK F/NH	UNUSED F/NH	USED F

NOTE - #454d, 454e, 456a, 457d, 458d, 460g and 460h are Booklet Singles.

SCOTT NO.	DESCRIPTION	PLATE BLOCK F/NH	UNUSED F/NH	USED F
454d	1¢ perf. 10 (1968)	....	.30	25
454e	1¢ 12-1/2 x 12 (1969)	....	.50	.17
455	2¢ green	1.50	.12	.07
455a	bklt. pane, 2c (4), 3c (4)	....	2.50	....
456	3¢ dull purple	1.50	.13	.07
456a	3¢ 12-1/2 x 12 (1971)	....	1.15	.60
457	4¢ carmine rose	2.35	.20	.06
457a	booklet pane of 6	....	1.85	....
457b	miniature pane of 25	....	25.00	....
457c	booklet pane of 25	....	9.50	....
457d	4¢ perf. 10 (1968)	....	.70	.30
458	5¢ blue	1.10	.18	.06
458a	booklet pane of 5	....	6.75	....
458b	miniature pane of 20	....	40.00	....
458c	booklet pane of 20	....	9.50	....
458d	5¢ perf. 10 (1968)	....	.70	.30
459	6¢ orange, pf. 10 (1968)	4.75	.50	.07
459a	booklet pane of 25	....	11.00	....
459b	6¢ orange 12-1/2 x 12 ('69)	4.25	.55	.07
460	6¢ black, 12-1/2 x 12 (1970)	2.75	.35	.06
460b	b. pane of 25, 12-1/2 x 12	....	20.00	....
460g	6¢ black, perf. 10	....	1.50	.60
460a	b. pane of 25, perf. 10	....	25.00	....
460c	6¢ black, 12-1/2 x 12 (1970)	3.75	.45	.06
460d	b. pane of 4, 12-1/2 x 12	....	6.00	....
460h	6¢ black, perf. 10	....	2.10	1.00
460e	b. pane of 4, perf. 10	....	9.00	....
460f	6¢ black, pf. 12 (1973)	2.75	.45	.12

460, 460 a, b & g: Original Die. Weak shading lines around 6.
460 c, d, e & h: Reworked Plate. Lines strengthened, darker.
460f: Original Die. Strong shading lines, similar to 468B, but Perf. 12 x 12.

SCOTT NO.	DESCRIPTION	PLATE BLOCK	UNUSED	USED
461	8¢ "Alaska Highway"	3.00	.50	25
462	10¢ "The Jack Pine"	2.75	.50	.07
463	15¢ "Bylot Island"	4.75	.90	.12
464	20¢ "The Ferry, Quebec"	5.00	.95	.09
465	25¢ "The Solemn Land"	11.00	2.25	.10
465A	50¢ "Summer Stores"	30.00	6.25	.13
465B	$1 "Imp. Wildcat No. 3"	75.00	15.00	.90

1967-70 Coil Stamps

466-68B	3¢-6¢ cpl., 5 vars.	....	7.35	3.50

Perf. 9-1/2 Horizontally

466	3¢ dull purple	....	2.50	1.50
467	4¢ carmine rose	....	1.50	.90
468	5¢ blue	....	2.65	1.15

Perf. 10 Horizontally

468A	6¢ orange (1969)	....	.55	.09
468B	6¢ black (1970)	....	.55	.09

NOTE: See #543-50 for similar issues.

469   470

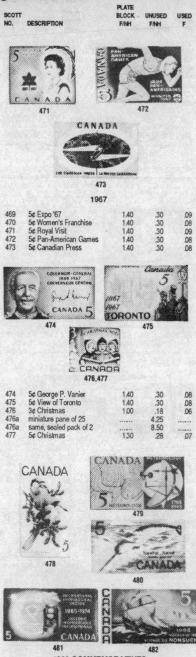

471   472

473

1967

SCOTT NO.	DESCRIPTION	PLATE BLOCK F/NH	UNUSED F/NH	USED F
469	5¢ Expo '67	1.40	.30	.09
470	5¢ Women's Franchise	1.40	.30	.08
471	5¢ Royal Visit	1.40	.30	.09
472	5¢ Pan-American Games	1.40	.30	.08
473	5¢ Canadian Press	1.40	.30	.08

474   475

476,477

474	5¢ George P. Vanier	1.40	.30	.08
475	5¢ View of Toronto	1.40	.30	.08
476	3¢ Christmas	1.00	.18	.06
476a	miniature pane of 25	....	4.25	....
476a	same, sealed pack of 2	....	8.50	....
477	5¢ Christmas	1.30	.28	.07

478   479

480

481   482

1968 COMMEMORATIVES

478-89	cpl., 12 varieties	32.50	6.35	2.75
478	5¢ Gray Jays	5.50	.65	.10

SCOTT NO.	DESCRIPTION	PLATE BLOCK F/NH	UNUSED F/NH	USED F
479	5¢ Weathermap & Instruments	1.40	.30	.09
480	5¢ Narwhal	1.40	.30	.09
481	5¢ Int'l. Hydro. Decade	1.40	.30	.09
482	5¢ Voyage of "Nonsuch"	1.60	.35	.16

483

484

485

486

483	5¢ Lacrosse Players	1.40	.30	.16
484	5¢ G. Brown, Politician	1.40	.30	.16
485	5¢ H. Bourassa, Journalist	1.40	.30	.09
486	15¢ W.W.I Armistice	14.50	2.95	1.70

NOTE: Beginning with #478, some issues show a printer's inscription with no actual plate number.

487

488

489

490

491

492

493

SCOTT NO.	DESCRIPTION	PLATE BLOCK F/NH	UNUSED F/NH	USED F
487	5¢ J. McCrae	1.60	.35	.10
488	5¢ Eskimo Family	1.25	.25	.06
488a	booklet pane of 10	......	4.00	......
489	6¢ Mother & Child	1.40	.30	.07

1969 COMMEMORATIVES

490-504 cpl., 15 varieties	78.50	16.50	9.85
490	6¢ Game of Curling	1.35	.30	.15
491	6¢ V. Massey	1.35	.30	.07
492	50¢ A. deSuzor-Cote, Artist	32.50	6.75	3.75
493	6¢ I.L.O.	1.60	.35	.11

494

495   **496**   **500**

501   **502, 503**

497   **498**

499   **504**

494	15¢ Vickers Vimy Over Atlantic	15.00	3.25	2.50
495	6¢ Sir W. Osler	1.50	.33	.11
496	6¢ White Throated Sparrow	1.90	.40	.09
497	10¢ Ipswich Sparrow	4.75	.95	.60
498	25¢ Hermit Thrush	14.00	2.95	2.50
499	6¢ Map of Prince Edward Island	1.60	.35	.15
500	6¢ Canada Games	1.35	.30	.09
501	6¢ Sir Isaac Brock	1.35	.30	.07

SCOTT NO.	DESCRIPTION	PLATE BLOCK F/NH	UNUSED F/NH	USED F
502	5¢ Children of Various Races	1.20	.25	.06
502a	booklet pane of 10	....	3.50	....
503	6¢ Children of Various Races	1.35	.30	.06
504	6¢ Stephen Leacock	1.60	.35	.11

505

506

507

1970 COMMEMORATIVES

SCOTT NO.	DESCRIPTION	PLATE BLOCK F/NH	UNUSED F/NH	USED F
505/31	(505-18, 31) 15 vars.	48.50	19.50	15.50
505	6¢ Manitoba Cent.	1.35	.30	.08
506	6¢ N.W. Territory Centenary	1.35	.30	.08
507	6¢ International Biological	1.35	.30	.11

508

509

510

511

508-11	Expo '70 att'd.	17.50	14.50	....
508	25¢ Emblems	....	3.25	3.25
509	25¢ Dogwood	....	3.25	3.25
510	25¢ Lily	....	3.25	3.25
511	25¢ Trillium	....	3.25	3.25

512

513-514

515

516

517

518

512	6¢ H. Kelsey-Explorer	1.35	.30	.11
513	10¢ 25th U.N. Anniversary	5.75	1.20	.75
514	15¢ 25th U.N. Anniversary	8.25	1.75	1.65
515	6¢ L. Riel-Metis Leader	1.35	.30	.09
516	6¢ Sir A. Mackenzie-Explorer	1.35	.30	.08
517	6¢ Sir O. Mowat Confederation Father	1.35	.30	.10
518	6¢ Isle of Spruce	1.35	.30	.08

519

524

529

530

529

530

519-30	5¢-15¢ cpl., 12 vars.	22.50	7.00	2.60
519-23	5¢ Christmas, att'd.	6.25(10)	2.40	....
519	5¢ Santa Claus	....	.50	.12
520	5¢ Sleigh	....	.50	.12
521	5¢ Nativity	....	.50	.12
522	5¢ Skiing	....	.50	.12
523	5¢ Snowman & Tree	....	.50	.12
524-28	6¢ Christmas, att'd.	7.25(10)	2.90	....
524	6¢ Christ Child	....	.60	.12
525	6¢ Tree & Children	....	.60	.12
526	6¢ Toy Store	....	.60	.12
527	6¢ Santa Claus	....	.60	.12
528	6¢ Church	....	.60	.12

Note: We cannot supply blocks or pairs of the 5¢ & 6¢ Christmas designs in varying combinations of designs.

529	10¢ Christ Child	3.10	.65	.30
530	15¢ Snowmobile & Trees	6.75	1.40	1.25

531

532

531	6¢ Sir Donald A. Smith	1.35	.30	.08

SCOTT NO.	DESCRIPTION	PLATE BLOCK F/NH	UNUSED F/NH	USED F
	1971 COMMEMORATIVES			
532/58	(532-42, 52-58) cpl. 18 varieties	42.95	8.50	5.00
532	6¢ E. Carr-Painter & Winter	1.35	.30	.08

534

533   **535**   **539**

533	6¢ Discovery of Insulin	1.35	.30	.08
534	6¢ Sir E. Rutherford-Physicist	1.35	.30	.08
535-38	6¢-7¢ Maple Leaves	6.25	1.35	.37
535	6¢ Maple Seeds	1.60	.35	.10
536	6¢ Summer Leaf	1.60	.35	.10
537	7¢ Autumn Leaf	1.60	.35	.10
538	7¢ Winter Leaf	1.60	.35	.10
539	6¢ L. Papineau-Polit. Reform	1.35	.30	.17

540   **541**

542   **543, 549**   **544, 550**

540	6¢ Copper Mine Expedition	1.35	.30	.17
541	15¢ Radio Canada Int'l.	12.00	2.50	2.25
542	6¢ Census Centennial	1.35	.30	.10
	1971			
543	7¢ Trans. & Communication	5.00	.45	.06
543a	b. pane, 7c (3), 3c (1), 1c (1)	......	4.50	......
543b	b. pane, 7c (12), 3c (4), 1c (4)	......	9.75	......
544	8¢ Parliamentary Library	3.75	.45	.06
544a	b. pane, 8c (2), 6c (1), 1c (3)	......	2.50	......
544b	b. pane, 8c (11), 6c (1), 1c (6)	......	7.50	......
544c	b. pane, 8c (5), 6c (1), 1c (4)	......	3.00	......
	1971 Coil Stamps Perf. 10 Horizontally			
549	7¢ Trans. & Communication	......	.65	.15
550	8¢ Parliamentary Library	......	.55	.09

552   **553**

552	7¢ B.C. Centennial	1.35	.30	.08
553	7¢ Paul Kane	4.00	.60	.12

554-55   **556-57**

554-57	6¢-15¢ Christmas	10.15	2.15	1.70
554	6¢ Snowflake, blue	1.20	.25	.06
555	7¢ Same, green	1.35	.30	.06
556	10¢ Same, red & silver	2.50	.55	.50
557	15¢ Same, red, blue & silver	5.25	1.10	1.10

558   **559**

558	7¢ P. Laporte	3.25	.33	.10

560   **561**

	1972 COMMEMORATIVES			
559/610	(559-61, 82-85, 606-10) 12 varieties	71.50(9)	16.95	15.25
559	8¢ Figure Skating	1.50	.33	.08
560	8¢ W.H.O. - Heart Disease	1.90	.42	.10
561	8¢ Frontenac & Ft. St. Louis	1.50	.33	.09

VERY FINE QUALITY: From 1935 to date, add 20% to the Fine price. Minimum of 3¢ per stamp.

SCOTT NO.	DESCRIPTION	PLATE BLOCK F/NH	UNUSED F/NH	USED F

Canada 8   **Canada 8**

562   566

Canada 8   **Canada 8**   **Canada 8**

564   568   572

Canada 8   **Canada 8**

570   574

1972-76 INDIAN PEOPLES OF CANADA

SCOTT NO.	DESCRIPTION	PLATE BLOCK F/NH	UNUSED F/NH	USED F
562-81	cpl., 20 varieties	18.95	8.00	2.70
562-63	Plains, att'd.	2.35	1.00	.90
562	8¢ Buffalo Chase	......	.50	.15
563	8¢ Indian Artifacts	......	.50	.15
564-65	Plains, att'd.	2.35	1.00	.90
564	8¢ Thunderbird Symbolism	......	.50	.15
565	8¢ Sun Dance Costume	......	.50	.15
566-67	Algonkians, att'd. (1973)	2.35	1.00	.90
566	8¢ Algonkian Artifacts	......	.50	.15
567	8¢ Algonkian Indians	......	.50	.15
568-69	Algonkians, att'd. (1973)	2.10	.90	.80
568	8¢ Thunderbird Symbolism	......	.45	.15
569	8¢ Costume	......	.45	.15
570-71	Pacific, att'd. (1974)	2.10	.90	.75
570	8¢ Nootka Sound House	......	.45	.13
571	8¢ Artifacts	......	.45	.13
572-73	Pacific, att'd. (1974)	2.10	.90	.75
572	8¢ Chief in Chilkat Blanket	......	.45	.13
573	8¢ Thunderbird-Kwakiuti	......	.45	.13
574-75	Subarctic, att'd. (1975)	1.65	.70	.65
574	8¢ Canoe & Artifacts	......	.35	.13
575	8¢ Dance-Kutcha-Kutchin	......	.35	.13

Canada 8   **Canada 10**   **Canada 10**

576   580   581

Canada 10   **Canada 10**

578   579

SCOTT NO.	DESCRIPTION	PLATE BLOCK F/NH	UNUSED F/NH	USED F
576-77	Subarctic, att'd. (1975)	1.65	.70	.65
576	8¢ Kutchin Costume	......	.35	.13
577	8¢ Ojibwa Thunderbird	......	.35	.13
578-79	Iroquois, att'd. (1976)	1.65	.70	.60
578	10¢ Masks	......	.35	.15
579	10¢ Camp	......	.35	.15
580-81	Iroquois, att'd. (1976)	1.65	.70	.60
580	10¢ Iroquois Thunderbird	......	.35	.15
581	10¢ Man & Woman	......	.35	.15

15 Canada   **Canada 15**

582   583

1972 EARTH SCIENCES

SCOTT NO.	DESCRIPTION	PLATE BLOCK F/NH	UNUSED F/NH	USED F
582-85	Sciences, att'd.	57.50(16)	14.00	......
582	15¢ Geology	......	3.50	3.50
583	15¢ Geography	......	3.50	3.50
584	15¢ Photogrammetry	......	3.50	3.50
585	15¢ Cartography	......	3.50	3.50

NOTE: Plate Block Price is for a miniature pane of 16 Stamps.

Canada 1   Canada 2   Canada 7   Canada 8

586   587   592   593,593b,593A 604,605

1973-76 DEFINITIVE ISSUE PERF. 12 X 12-1/2

SCOTT NO.	DESCRIPTION	PLATE BLOCK F/NH	UNUSED F/NH	USED F
586-93A	1¢-10¢, 9 varieties	7.75	1.60	.65
586	1¢ Sir J. MacDonald	.30	.06	.06
586a	b. pane, 1c (3), 6c (1), 8c (2)	......	.65	......
586b	b. pane, 1c (6), 6c (1), 8c (11)	......	2.65	......
586c	b. pane, 1c (2), 2c (4), 8c (4)	......	1.85	......
587	2¢ Sir W. Laurier	.40	.08	.06
588	3¢ Sir R.L. Borden	.55	.11	.09
589	4¢ W.L. Mackenzie King	.75	.15	.08
590	5¢ R.B. Bennett	1.00	.20	.08
591	6¢ L.B. Pearson	.95	.20	.07
592	7¢ L. St. Laurent (1974)	1.20	.25	.10
593	8¢ Queen Elizabeth	1.30	.27	.06
593b	8¢ Same, (pf. 13 x 13-1/2) (1976)	6.75	1.10	.75
593A	10¢ Queen Elizabeth (pf. 13 x 13-1/2) (1976)	1.70	.35	.08
593c	10¢ Same, pf. 12 x 12-1/2 booklet single	......	.45	.20

SCOTT NO.	DESCRIPTION	PLATE BLOCK F/NH	UNUSED F/NH	USED F

594, 594a, 594B   **599, 599a, 600**

1972-73 Photogravure & Engraved Perf. 12-1/2 x 12

594-99	10¢-$1, 6 varieties	37.50	7.85	1.15
594	10¢ Forests	1.65	.35	.09
595	15¢ Mountain Sheep	2.40	.50	.14
596	20¢ Prairie Mosaic	3.25	.70	.09
597	25¢ Polar Bears	4.00	.85	.09
598	50¢ Seashore	7.75	1.65	.12
599	$1 Vancouver Skyline (1973)	20.00	4.25	.70

NOTE: #594-97 exist with 2 types of phosphor tagging. Prices above are for Ottawa tagged. Winnipeg tagged are listed on page 2.

1976-77 Perf. 13

594a-99a	10¢-$1, 6 varieties	43.50	9.35	1.15
594a	10¢ Forests	2.35	.50	.08
595a	15¢ Mountain Sheep	2.85	.60	.25
596a	20¢ Prairie Mosaic	4.25	.90	.12
597a	25¢ Polar Bears	4.75	1.00	.11
598a	50¢ Seashore	13.00	2.85	.18
599a	$1 Vancouver Skyline (1977)	18.75	3.95	.50

1972 Lithographed & Engraved Perf. 11

600	$1 Vancouver Skyline	40.00	8.50	2.50
601	$2 Quebec Buildings	31.50	6.75	3.25

1974-76 Coil Stamps

604	8¢ Queen Elizabeth	....	.35	.07
605	10¢ Queen Elizabeth (1976)	....	.35	.09

606, 607   **608, 609**

1972

606-09	6¢-15¢ Christmas	11.00	2.35	1.70
606	6¢ 5 Candles	1.30	.27	.07
607	8¢ Same	1.60	.33	.07
608	10¢ 6 Candles	3.00	.65	.55
609	15¢ Same	5.50	1.20	1.10

610   **611**

610	8¢ C. Krieghoff-Painter	1.90	.40	.12

1973 COMMEMORATIVES

611-28	18 vars., cpl.	44.50	9.35	5.85
611	8¢ Monsignor De Laval	1.70	.35	.09

612   **614**

613

612	8¢ G.A. French & Map	1.70	.35	.09
613	10¢ Spectrograph	2.75	.60	.45
614	15¢ "Musical Ride"	4.75	1.00	.90

615   **616**

617   **618**

615	8¢ J. Mance-Nurse	1.70	.35	.09
616	8¢ J. Howe	1.70	.35	.09
617	15¢ "Mist Fantasy"-Painting	4.75	1.00	.80
618	8¢ P.E.I. Confederation	1.70	.35	.09

619   **620, 621**

619	8¢ Scottish Settlers	1.70	.35	.09
620	8¢ Royal Visit	1.70	.35	.17
621	15¢ Same	4.75	1.00	.85

SCOTT NO.	DESCRIPTION	PLATE BLOCK F/NH	UNUSED F/NH	USED F

622

623, 624

622	8¢ Nellie McClung	1.70	.35	.09
623	8¢ 21st Olympic Games	1.70	.35	.13
624	15¢ Same	4.75	1.00	.75

625

627

625-28	6¢ to 15¢ Christmas	9.50	2.00	1.45
625	6¢ Skate	1.20	.25	.07
626	8¢ Bird Ornament	1.70	.35	.07
627	10¢ Santa Claus	2.15	.45	.45
628	15¢ Shepherd	4.75	1.00	.90

629

633

1974 COMMEMORATIVES

| 629-55 | cpl., 27 varieties | 29.50(16) | 11.25 | 6.50 |

629-32	Summer Olympics, att'd.	2.10	1.80	1.80
629	8¢ Children Diving	....	.45	.17
630	8¢ Jogging	....	.45	.17
631	8¢ Bicycling	....	.45	.17
632	8¢ Hiking	....	.45	.17
633	8¢ Winnipeg Centennial	1.40	.30	.08

634

635

SCOTT NO.	DESCRIPTION	PLATE BLOCK F/NH	UNUSED F/NH	USED F
634-39	Postal Carriers, att'd.	3.50(6)	3.00	....
634	8¢ Postal Clerk & Client	....	.50	.42
635	8¢ Mail Pick-up	....	.50	.42
636	8¢ Mail Handler	....	.50	.42
637	8¢ Sorting Mail	....	.50	.42
638	8¢ Letter Carrier	....	.50	.42
639	8¢ Rural Delivery	....	.50	.42

640

641

642

643

644

648, 649

640	8¢ Agriculture Symbol	1.35	.30	.09
641	8¢ Antique to Modern Phones	1.35	.30	.09
642	8¢ World Cycling Championship	1.35	.30	.09
643	8¢ Mennonite Settlers	1.35	.30	.09
644-47	Winter Olympics, att'd.	2.10	1.80	1.70
644	8¢ Snowshoeing	....	.45	.18
645	8¢ Skiing	....	.45	.18
646	8¢ Skating	....	.45	.18
647	8¢ Curling	....	.45	.18
648	8¢ U.P.U. Cent.	1.35	.30	.09
649	15¢ Same	5.25	1.10	.95

650

651

650-53	6¢ to 15¢ Christmas	7.95	1.70	1.30
650	6¢ Nativity	1.15	.25	.07
651	8¢ Skaters in Hull	1.35	.30	.07
652	10¢ The Ice Cone	2.10	.45	.45
653	15¢ Laurentian Village	3.50	.75	.75

SCOTT NO.	DESCRIPTION	PLATE BLOCK F/NH	UNUSED F/NH	USED F

654

655

656

657

| 654 | 8¢ G. Marconi-Radio Inventor | 1.35 | .30 | .09 |
| 655 | 8¢ W.H. Merrit & Welland Canal | 1.35 | .30 | .09 |

1975 COMMEMORATIVES

656-680 cpl., 25 varieties		105.00(18)	25.50	17.75
656	$1 "The Sprinter"	23.75	4.95	3.75
657	$2 "The Plunger"	47.50	10.00	7.25

658

659

658-59	Writers, att'd.	1.35	.60	.50
658	8¢ L.M. Montgomery-Author	....	.30	.11
659	8¢ L. Hemon-Author	....	.30	.11

660

661

| 660 | 8¢ M. Bourgeoys-Educator | 1.35 | .30 | .11 |
| 661 | 8¢ A. Desjardins-Credit Union | 1.35 | .30 | .11 |

VERY FINE QUALITY: From 1935 to date, add 20% to the Fine price. Minimum of 3¢ per stamp.

662

664

662-63	Religious, att'd.	1.35	.60	.50
662	8¢ J. Cook & Church	....	.30	.18
663	8¢ S. Chown & Church	....	.30	.18
664	20¢ Pole Vaulter	4.15	.85	.75
665	25¢ Marathon Runner	5.25	1.10	.90
666	50¢ Hurdler	10.00	2.15	1.75

667

670

668

669

667	8¢ Calgary Centenary	1.35	.30	.08
668	8¢ Int'l. Women's Year	1.35	.30	.08
669	8¢ "Justice"	1.35	.30	.08
670-73	Ships, att'd.	3.50	3.00	2.35
670	8¢ W.D. Lawrence	....	.75	.40
671	8¢ Beaver	....	.75	.40
672	8¢ Neptune	....	.75	.40
673	8¢ Quadra	....	.75	.40

674

679

674-79	6¢ to 15¢ Christmas	7.00(4)	1.95	1.40
674-75	Xmas, att'd.	1.10	.45	.40
674	6¢ Santa Claus	....	.23	.10
675	6¢ Skater	....	.23	.10
676-77	Xmas, att'd.	1.15	.50	.40
676	8¢ Child	....	.25	.10
677	8¢ Family & Tree	....	.25	.10
678	10¢ Gift	1.60	.35	.35
679	15¢ Trees	3.25	.70	.70

SCOTT NO.	DESCRIPTION	PLATE BLOCK F/NH	UNUSED F/NH	USED F

680

681

| 680 | 8¢ Horn & Crest | 1.35 | .30 | .09 |

1976 COMMEMORATIVES

681-703 cpl., 23 varieties	130.00(18)	29.50	21.50

681	8¢ Olympic Flame	1.15	.25	.08
682	20¢ Opening Ceremony	3.50	.75	.70
683	25¢ Receiving Medals	4.65	1.00	1.00

684

685

687

684	20¢ Communication Arts	7.50	1.60	.90
685	25¢ Handicraft Tools	9.50	1.95	1.10
686	50¢ Performing Arts	15.00	3.25	1.95
687	$1 Notre Dame & Tower	23.50	5.00	3.50
688	$2 Olympic Stadium	47.50	10.00	7.50

689

690

691

689	20¢ Olympic Winter Games	5.25	1.15	.85
690	20¢ "Habitat"	3.50	.75	.75
691	10¢ Benjamin Franklin	1.85	.40	.25

692

693

692-93	Military College, att'd.	1.35	.60	.55
692	8¢ Color Parade	....	.30	.18
693	8¢ Wing Parade	....	.30	.18

694

695

696

697

694	20¢ Olympic-Phys. Disabled	3.50	.75	.75
695-96	Authors, att'd.	1.35	.60	.55
695	8¢ R.W. Service-Author	....	.30	.12
696	8¢ G. Guevremont-Author	....	.30	.12
697	8¢ Nativity Window	1.10	.23	.08
698	10¢ Same	1.25	.28	.07
699	20¢ Same	2.75	.60	.60

700

704

700-03	Inland Vessels, att'd.	2.10	1.80	2.25
700	10¢ Northcote	....	.45	.45
701	10¢ Chicora	....	.45	.45
702	10¢ Passport	....	.45	.45
703	10¢ Athabasca	....	.45	.45

1977 COMMEMORATIVES

704/51	(704, 732-51) cpl., 21 varieties	26.75(14)	8.35	5.15
704	25¢ Silver Jubilee	4.75	1.00	.80

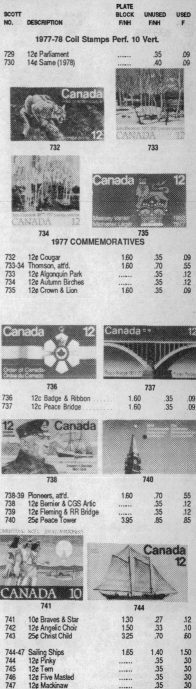

SCOTT NO.	DESCRIPTION	PLATE BLOCK F/NH	UNUSED F/NH	USED F

705,781,781a   713,713a,716,716a   714,715,729,730
789,789a,791,792   790,797,800,806

1977-79 Definitives
Perf. 12 x 12½

SCOTT NO.	DESCRIPTION	PLATE BLOCK F/NH	UNUSED F/NH	USED F
705-27	1¢ to $2 cpl., 22 vars.	93.50	19.75	5.50
705	1¢ Bottle Gentian	.35	.07	.06
707	2¢ West. Columbine	.45	.09	.06
708	3¢ Canada Lily	.50	.10	.08
709	4¢ Hepatica	.65	.13	.09
710	5¢ Shooting Star	.85	.17	.09
711	10¢ Lady 's Slipper	1.20	.25	.08
711a	10¢ Same, pf. 13 (1978)	1.40	.30	.09
712	12¢ Jewelweed, pf. 13 x 13-1/2 (1978)	1.85	.40	.14
713	12¢ Queen Elizabeth II, pf. 13 x 13-1/2	1.65	.35	.06
713a	12¢ Same, pf. 12 x 12-1/2	....	.35	.25
714	12¢ Parliament, pf. 13	1.65	.35	.06
715	14¢ Same, pf. 13 (1978)	1.65	.35	.06
716	14¢ Queen Elizabeth II, pf. 13 x 13-1/2	1.65	.35	.06
716a	14¢ Same, pf. 12 x 12-1/2	....	.40	20
716b	booklet pane of 25		8.00	

Note: 713a, 716a are from booklet panes. 713a will have one or more straight edges, 716a may or may not have straight edges.

717   723,723A

726

Perf. 13-1/2

717	15¢ Trembling Aspen	3.00	.65	.14
718	20¢ Douglas Fir	2.35	.50	.10
719	25¢ Sugar Maple	3.00	.65	.13
720	30¢ Oak Leaf	3.75	.80	.30
721	35¢ White Pine (1979)	4.00	.85	.40
723	50¢ Main Street (1978)	8.50	1.75	.35
723A	50¢ Same, 1978 Lic. Plate	7.00	1.50	25
724	75¢ Row Houses (1978)	9.50	2.00	.65
725	80¢ Maritime (1978)	10.00	2.10	.70
726	$1 Fundy Park (1979)	12.00	2.50	.55
727	$2 Kluane Park (1979)	23.00	4.75	1.40

1977-78 Coil Stamps Perf. 10 Vert.

729	12¢ Parliament	....	.35	.09
730	14¢ Same (1978)	....	.40	.09

732   733

734   735

1977 COMMEMORATIVES

732	12¢ Cougar	1.60	.35	.09
733-34	Thomson, att'd.	1.60	.70	.55
733	12¢ Algonquin Park	....	.35	.12
734	12¢ Autumn Birches	....	.35	.12
735	12¢ Crown & Lion	1.60	.35	.09

736   737

736	12c Badge & Ribbon	1.60	.35	.09
737	12c Peace Bridge	1.60	.35	.09

738   740

738-39	Pioneers, att'd.	1.60	.70	.55
738	12¢ Bernier & CGS Artic	....	.35	.12
739	12¢ Fleming & RR Bridge	....	.35	.12
740	25¢ Peace Tower	3.95	.85	.85

741   744

741	10¢ Braves & Star	1.30	.27	.12
742	10¢ Angelic Choir	1.50	.33	.10
743	25¢ Christ Child	3.25	.70	.60
744-47	Sailing Ships	1.65	1.40	1.50
744	12¢ Pinky	....	.35	.30
745	12¢ Tern	....	.35	.30
746	12¢ Five Masted	....	.35	.30
747	12¢ Mackinaw	....	.35	.30

SCOTT NO.	DESCRIPTION	PLATE BLOCK F/NH	UNUSED F/NH	USED F

748

750

748-49	Inuit, att'd.	1.60	.70	.65
748	12¢ Hunting Seal	....	.35	.18
749	12¢ Fishing	....	.35	.18
750-51	Inuit, att'd.	1.60	.70	.65
750	12¢ Disguised Archer	....	.35	.18
751	12¢ Hunters of Old	....	.35	.18

752

753

756a

1978 COMMEMORATIVES

752/79 (no 756a) 28 vars.		50.00(19)	14.50	7.85
752	12¢ Peregrine Falcon	1.60	.35	.12
753	12¢ CAPEX Victoria	1.60	.35	.09
754	14¢ CAPEX Cartier	1.85	.40	.15
755	30¢ CAPEX Victoria	4.00	.85	.80
756	$1.25 CAPEX Albert	15.00	3.25	1.75
756a	$1.69 CAPEX Sheet of 3	....	4.25	4.25

757

762

757	14¢ Games Symbol	1.60	.35	.10
758	30¢ Badminton Players	3.75	.80	.50
759-60	Comm. Games, att'd.	1.60	.70	.60
759	14¢ Stadium	....	.35	.14
760	14¢ Runners	....	.35	.14
761-62	Comm. Games, att'd.	3.75	1.60	1.60
761	30¢ Edmonton	....	.80	.50
762	30¢ Bowls	....	.80	.50

SCOTT NO.	DESCRIPTION	PLATE BLOCK F/NH	UNUSED F/NH	USED F

763

764

763-64	Captain Cook, att'd.	1.60	.70	.60
763	14¢ Captain Cook	....	.35	.14
764	14¢ Nootka Sound	....	.35	.14

765

767

768

769

765-66	Resources, att'd.	1.60	.70	.60
765	14¢ Miners	....	.35	.15
766	14¢ Tar Sands	....	.35	.15
767	14¢ CNE 100th Anniversary	1.60	.35	.13
768	14¢ Mere d'Youville	1.60	.35	.13
769-70	Inuit, att'd.	1.60	.70	.60
769	14¢ Woman Walking	....	.35	.18
770	14¢ Migration	....	.35	.18
771-72	Inuit, att'd.	1.60	.70	.60
771	14¢ Plane over Village	....	.35	.18
772	14¢ Dog Team & Sled	....	.35	.18

773

774

780

776

777

773	12¢ Mary & Child w/pea	1.55	.33	.12
774	14¢ Mary & Child w/apple	1.60	.35	.13
775	30¢ Mary & Child w/goldfinch	3.75	.80	.55

SCOTT NO.	DESCRIPTION	PLATE BLOCK F/NH	UNUSED F/NH	USED F
776-79	Ice Vessels, att'd.	1.85	1.60	1.60
776	14¢ Robinson	....	.40	.27
777	14¢ St. Roch	....	.40	.27
778	14¢ Northern Light	....	.40	.27
779	14¢ Labrador	....	.40	.27

1979 COMMEMORATIVES

780/846	(780, 813-20, 33-46) cpl., 23 varieties	35.00(16)	12.25	4.50
780	14¢ Quebec Winter Carnival	1.60	.35	.14

Types of #705-16

787

1977-83 Definitives Perf. 13 x 13-1/2

781-92	1¢-32¢ cpl., 11 vars.	16.50	3.40	.80
781	1¢ Gentian (1979)	.30	.06	.06
781a	1¢ Same, perf. 12 x 12-1/2	....	.10	.10
781b	b. pane, 1c (2-781a), 12c (4-713a)	....	1.35	....
782	2¢ Western Columbine (1979)	.35	.07	.06
782b	2¢ Same, perf. 12 x 12-1/2 (1978)	....	.10	.10
782a	b. pane, 2c (4-782b), 12c (4-713a)	....	1.35	....
783	3¢ Canada Lily (1979)	.45	.09	.07
784	4¢ Hepatica (1979)	.50	.10	.07
785	5¢ Shooting Star (1979)	.70	.15	.07
786	10¢ Lady's Slipper (1979)	1.20	.25	.08
787	15¢ Violet (1979)	1.85	.40	.14
789	17¢ Queen Elizabeth II (1979)	2.15	.45	.06
789a	17¢ Same, 12 x 12-1/2 ('79)	....	.50	.14
789b	booklet pane of 25	....	10.00	....
790	17¢ Parliament Bldg. (1979)	2.15	.45	.07
791	30¢ Queen Elizabeth II (1982)	3.65	.75	.09
792	32¢ Queen Elizabeth (1983)	3.85	.80	.06

NOTE: 781a, 782b, 797 & 800 are from booklet panes and will have one or more straight edges. 789a may or may nor have straight edges.

1979 Perf. 12 x 12-1/2

797	1¢ Parliament Building	....	.35	.35
797a	b. pane, 1c (1-797), 5c (3-800), 17c (2-789a)	....	1.50	....
800	5¢ Parliament Bldg.	....	.17	.12

1979 Coil Stamps Perf. 10 Vert.

806	17¢ Parli. Bldg., slate green	....	.55	.07

813

814

817   818

815   819

1979

813	17¢ Turtle	2.35	.50	.12
814	35¢ Whale	5.60	1.20	.60
815-16	Postal Code, att'd.	2.15	.90	.70
815	17¢ Woman's Finger	....	.45	.12
816	17¢ Man's Finger	....	.45	.12
817-18	Writers, att'd.	2.15	.90	.70
817	17¢ "Fruits of the Earth"	....	.45	.12
818	17¢ "The Golden Vessel"	....	.45	.12
819-20	Colonels, att'd.	2.15	.90	.70
819	17¢ Charles de Salaberry	....	.45	.12
820	17¢ John By	....	.45	.12

821 Ontario

PROVINCIAL FLAGS
822 Quebec
823 Nova Scotia
824 New Brunswick
825 Manitoba
826 British Columbia

827 Prince Edward Island
828 Saskatchewan
829 Alberta
830 Newfoundland
831 Northern Territories

832 Yukon Territory

832a	Sheet of 12 Vars., att'd.	....	4.95	....
821-32	Set of Singles	....	....	3.50
Any	17¢ Single	....	.50	.30

833   834

833	17¢ Canoe-Kayak	2.35	.50	.11
834	17¢ Field Hockey	2.35	.50	.11

SCOTT NO.	DESCRIPTION	PLATE BLOCK F/NH	UNUSED F/NH	USED F

835

837

835-36	Inuit, att'd.	2.15	.90	.70
835	17¢ Summer Tent	....	.45	.15
836	17¢ Igloo	....	.45	.15
837-38	Inuit, att'd.	2.15	.90	.70
837	17¢ The Dance	....	.45	.15
838	17¢ Soapstone Figures	....	.45	.15

839

840

841

842

839	15¢ Wooden Train	2.15	.45	.10
840	17¢ Horse Pull Toy	2.35	.50	.10
841	35¢ Knitted Doll	4.50	.95	.45
842	17¢ I.Y.C.	2.15	.45	.11

843

845

843-44	Flying Boats, att'd.	2.35	1.00	.70
843	17¢ Curtiss HS2L	....	.50	.11
844	17¢ Canadian CL215	....	.50	.11
845-46	Flying Boats, att'd.	4.75	2.00	1.75
845	35¢ Vickers Vedette	....	1.00	.65
846	35¢ Consolidated Canso	....	1.00	.65

847

848

1980 COMMEMORATIVES

847-77	cpl., 31 varieties	61.50(23)	18.00	7.00
847	17¢ Arctic Islands map	2.15	.45	.11
848	35¢ Olympic Skiing	4.65	1.00	.70

SCOTT NO.	DESCRIPTION	PLATE BLOCK F/NH	UNUSED F/NH	USED F

849

851

853

854

849-50	Artists, att'd.	2.35	1.00	.70
849	17¢ School Trustees	....	.50	.13
850	17¢ Inspiration	....	.50	.13
851-52	Artists, att'd.	4.35	1.90	1.75
851	35¢ Parliament Bldgs.	....	.95	.50
852	35¢ Sunrise on the Saguenay	....	.95	.50
853	17¢ Atlantic Whitefish	2.50	.55	.11
854	17¢ Greater Prairie Chicken	2.50	.55	.11

855

856

857

859

855	17¢ Gardening	2.15	.45	.11
856	17¢ Rehabilitation	2.15	.45	.11
857-58	"O Canada", att'd.	2.15	.90	.60
857	17¢ Bars of Music	....	.45	.12
858	17¢ 3 Musicians	....	.45	.12
859	17¢ John Diefenbaker	2.15	.45	.11

860

862

SCOTT NO.	DESCRIPTION	PLATE BLOCK F/NH	UNUSED F/NH	USED F

863 864

860-61	Musicians, att'd.	2.15	.90	.60
860	17¢ Emma Albani	....	.45	.12
861	17¢ Healey Willan	....	.45	.12
862	17¢ Ned Hanlan	2.15	.45	.11
863	17¢ Saskatchewan	2.15	.45	.11
864	17¢ Alberta	2.15	.45	.11

865 866

865	35¢ Uranium Resources	4.50	.95	.50
866-67	Inuit, att'd.	2.15	.90	.60
866	17¢ Sedna	....	.45	.13
867	17¢ Sun	....	.45	.13

868 870

868-69	Inuit, att'd.	4.50	1.90	1.75
868	35¢ Bird Spirit	....	.95	.50
869	35¢ Shaman	....	.95	.50
870	15¢ Xmas	1.90	.40	.10
871	17¢ Xmas	2.15	.45	.10
872	35¢ Xmas	4.50	.95	.50

873 875

877 878

873-74	Aircraft	2.35	1.00	.65
873	17¢ Avro Canada CF-100	....	.50	.12
874	17¢ Avro Lancaster	....	.50	.12

SCOTT NO.	DESCRIPTION	PLATE BLOCK F/NH	UNUSED F/NH	USED F
875-76	Aircraft, att'd.	4.65	2.00	1.75
875	35¢ Curtiss JN-4	....	1.00	.55
876	35¢ Hawker Hurricane	....	1.00	.55
877	17¢ Dr. Lachapelle	2.15	.45	.11

1981 COMMEMORATIVES

878-906 cpl., 29 vars.		48.50(19)	15.00	6.00
878	17¢ Antique Instrument	2.15	.45	.11

879 880

883 884

879-82	Feminists, att'd.	2.50	2.20	2.00
879	17¢ Emily Stowe	....	.55	.25
880	17¢ Louisa McKinney	....	.55	.25
881	17¢ Idola Saint-Jean	....	.55	.25
882	17¢ Henrietta Edwards	....	.55	.25
883	17¢ Marmot	2.35	.50	.11
884	35¢ Bison	5.40	1.15	.60

885 887

888 889

885-86	Women, att'd.	2.15	.90	.65
885	17¢ Kateri Tekakwitha	....	.45	.13
886	17¢ Marie de l'Incarnation	....	.45	.13
887	17¢ "At Baie St. Paul"	2.15	.45	.12
888	17¢ Self-Portrait	2.15	.45	.12
889	35¢ Untitled No. 6	4.50	.95	.65

SCOTT NO.	DESCRIPTION	PLATE BLOCK F/NH	UNUSED F/NH	USED F

890

894

SCOTT NO.	DESCRIPTION	PLATE BLOCK F/NH	UNUSED F/NH	USED F
890-93	Canada Day, att'd.	4.50(8)	2.00	1.70
890	17¢ Canada in 1867	......	.50	.25
891	17¢ Canada in 1873	......	.50	.25
892	17¢ Canada in 1905	......	.50	.25
893	17¢ Canada since 1949	......	.50	.25
894-95	Botanists, att'd.	2.15	.90	.60
894	17¢ Frere Marie Victorin	......	.45	.12
895	17¢ John Macoun	......	.45	.12

896

897

898

899

896	17¢ Montreal Rose	2.15	.45	.11
897	17¢ Niagara-on-the-Lake	2.15	.45	.11
898	17¢ Acadians	2.15	.45	.11
899	17¢ Aaron Mosher	2.15	.45	.11

900

901

900	15¢ Christmas Tree in 1781	1.85	.40	.10
901	15¢ Christmas Tree in 1881	1.85	.40	.10
902	15¢ Christmas Tree in 1981	1.85	.40	.10

903

905

SCOTT NO.	DESCRIPTION	PLATE BLOCK F/NH	UNUSED F/NH	USED F
903-04	Aircraft, att'd.	2.35	1.00	.65
903	17¢ Canadian Cl-41 Tutor	......	.50	.12
904	17¢ de Havilland Tiger Moth	......	.50	.12
905-06	Aircraft, att'd.	4.65	2.00	1.65
905	35¢ Avro Canada Jetliner	......	1.00	.60
906	35¢ de Haviland Canada Dash 7	......	1.00	.60

907, 908

909

| 907 | (30¢) "A" Maple Leaf | 3.75 | .80 | .12 |
| 908 | (30¢) "A" Maple Leaf, coil | ...... | 1.15 | .25 |

1982 COMMEMORATIVES

SCOTT NO.	DESCRIPTION	PLATE BLOCK F/NH	UNUSED F/NH	USED F
909/75	(909-16, 54, 67-75) 18 varieties, cpl.	69.50(16)	17.00	5.65
909	30¢ 1851 Beaver	3.75	.80	.18
910	30¢ 1908 Champlain	3.75	.80	.18
911	35¢ 1935 Mountie	4.15	.90	.55
912	35¢ 1928 Mt. Hurd	4.15	.90	.55
913	60¢ 1929 Bluenose	7.25	1.60	.85
913a	$1.90 Phil. Exhib. sheet of 5	......	5.75	......

914

915

916

914	30¢ Jules Leger	3.65	.80	.15
915	30¢ Terry Fox	3.65	.80	.15
916	30¢ Constitution	3.65	.80	.15

917   **923/951**   **925/952**

SCOTT NO.	DESCRIPTION	PLATE BLOCK F/NH	UNUSED F/NH	USED F

927

931

926

935

1982-85 Definitives

SCOTT NO.	DESCRIPTION	PLATE BLOCK F/NH	UNUSED F/NH	USED F
917-38	1¢-$5 cpl., 21 vars.	165.00	33.75	10.00
917-33	1¢-68¢, 17 vars.	61.50	12.00	3.25
917	1¢ Decoy	.30	.06	.06
918	2¢ Fishing Spear	.30	.06	.06
919	3¢ Stable Lantern	.35	.07	.06
920	5¢ Bucket	.60	.12	.06
921	10¢ Weathercock	1.10	.22	.07
922	20¢ Ice Skates	2.25	.45	.15
923	30¢ Maple Leaf, blue & red, pf. 13 x 13-1/2	3.75	.75	.11
923b	Same, pf. 12 x 12-1/2	....	.80	.20
923a	booklet pane of 20	....	12.50	....
924	32¢ Maple Leaf, red on tan, pf. 13 x 13-1/2 (1983)	3.95	.80	.07
924b	Same, pf. 12 x 12-1/2	....	.80	.20
924a	booklet pane of 25	....	16.50	....
925	34¢ Parliament, multicolored, pf. 13 x 13-1/2 (1985)	3.65	.75	.07
925b	Same, pf. 12 x 12-1/2	....	.80	.20
925a	booklet pane of 25	....	17.50	....
926	34¢ Elizabeth II (1985)	3.65	.75	.07
927	37¢ Plow (1983)	4.75	.95	.35
928	39¢ Settle Bed (1985)	4.25	.85	.30
929	48¢ Cradle (1983)	6.25	1.25	.35
930	50¢ Sleigh (1985)	5.35	1.10	.30
931	60¢ Ontario Street	7.50	1.50	.45
932	64¢ Stove (1983)	8.00	1.60	.45
933	68¢ Spinning Wheel (1985)	7.50	1.50	.50
934	$1 Glacier Park (1984)	8.50	2.15	.80
935	$1.50 Waterton Lakes	19.50	3.95	.90
936	$2 Banff Park (1985)	20.00	4.25	1.75
938	$5 Point Pelee (1983)	60.00	12.50	3.75

1982-85 BOOKLET SINGLES

SCOTT NO.	DESCRIPTION	PLATE BLOCK F/NH	UNUSED F/NH	USED F
939-47	2¢-34¢ cpl., 8 vars.	....	3.15	.85
939	2¢ West Block (1985)	....	.06	.06
940	5¢ Maple Leaf	....	.15	.14
941	5¢ East Block (1985)	....	.15	.10
941A	8¢ Maple Leaf (1983)	....	.22	.10
942	10¢ Maple Leaf	....	.30	.10
945	30¢ Maple Leaf, red pf. 12 x 12-1/2	....	.80	.18
945a	bklt. pane, 2 #940, 1 #942, 1 #945	....	1.25	....
946	32¢ Maple Leaf, brown on white, pf. 12 x 12-1/2	....	.85	.10
946a	bklt. pane 2 #940, 1 #941A, 1 #946	....	1.25	....

SCOTT NO.	DESCRIPTION	PLATE BLOCK F/NH	UNUSED F/NH	USED F
947	34¢ Library, slate blue, pf. 12 x 12-1/2	....	.80	.10
947a	b. pane, 3 #939, 2 #941, 1 #947	....	1.10	....

1982-85 COILS

SCOTT NO.	DESCRIPTION	PLATE BLOCK F/NH	UNUSED F/NH	USED F
950-52	30¢-34¢ cpl., 3 vars.	....	2.50	.35
950	30¢ Maple Leaf	....	.95	.17
951	32¢ Maple Leaf	....	.85	.12
952	34¢ Parliament	....	.80	.08

954

1982

SCOTT NO.	DESCRIPTION	PLATE BLOCK F/NH	UNUSED F/NH	USED F
954	30¢ Salvation Army	3.85	.80	.15

956 Quebec
957 Newfoundland
958 Northwest Territories
959 Prince Edward Island
960 Nova Scotia
961 Saskatchewan
962 Ontario
963 New Brunswick
964 Alberta
965 British Columbia
966 Manitoba

955 Yukon Territories

SCOTT NO.	DESCRIPTION	PLATE BLOCK F/NH	UNUSED F/NH	USED F
966a	Sheet of 12 vars., att'd.	....	12.50	....
955-66	Set of Singles	....	....	6.50
Any	30¢ Single	....	1.10	.55

967

968

SCOTT NO.	DESCRIPTION	PLATE BLOCK F/NH	UNUSED F/NH	USED F
967	30¢ Regina	3.85	.80	.15
968	30¢ Henley Regatta	3.85	.80	.15

969

971

SCOTT NO.	DESCRIPTION	PLATE BLOCK F/NH	UNUSED F/NH	USED F
969-70	Aircraft, att'd.	3.85	1.60	1.35
969	30¢ Fairchild FC-2W1	....	.80	.16
970	30¢ de Haviland Canada Beaver	....	.80	.16
971-72	Aircraft, att'd.	7.75	3.20	2.50
971	60¢ Noorduyn Norseman	....	1.60	.65
972	60¢ Fokker Super Universal	....	1.60	.65

SCOTT NO.	DESCRIPTION	PLATE BLOCK F/NH	UNUSED F/NH	USED F

973

977

976

978

973	30¢ Joseph, Mary & Infant	3.85	.80	.15
974	35¢ Shepherds	4.25	.90	.30
975	60¢ Wise Men	7.75	1.60	.60

1983 COMMEMORATIVES

976/1008	(976-82, 93-1008) cpl., 23 varieties	111.50(20)	25.00	7.50
976	32¢ World Comm. Year	4.25	.85	.15
977	$2.00 Commonwealth Day	23.50	4.95	2.25
978-79	Poet/Author, att'd.	4.25	1.70	1.40
978	32¢ Laure Conan	....	.85	.18
979	32¢ E.J. Pratt	....	.85	.18

980

981

980	32¢ St. John Ambulance	4.25	.85	.15
981	32¢ University Games	4.25	.85	.15
982	64¢ University Games	8.25	1.70	.70

983 Ft. Henry

984 Ft. William
985 Ft. Rodd Hill
986 Ft. Wellington
986 Ft. Prince of Wales
988 Halifax Citadel
989 Ft. Chambly
990 Ft. No. 1 Pt. Lewis
991 Ft. at Coteau-du-Lac

992 Ft. Beausejour

992a	32¢ Forts, pane of 10	....	9.00	....
983-92	Set of Singles	....	....	4.75
Any	32¢ Single	....	.95	.50

993

994

995

996

997

998

993	32¢ Boy Scouts	4.25	.85	.15
994	32¢ Council of Churches	4.25	.85	.15
995	32¢ Humphrey Gilbert	4.25	.85	.15
996	32¢ Nickel	4.25	.85	.15
997	32¢ Josiah Hensen	4.25	.85	.15
998	32¢ Fr. Antoine Labelle	4.25	.85	.15

999

1003

999-1000	Steam Trains, att'd.	4.25	1.70	1.50
999	32¢ Toronto 4-4-0	....	.85	.18
1000	32¢ Dorchester 0-4-0	....	.85	.18
1001	37¢ Samsen 0-6-0	4.75	.95	.40
1002	64¢ Adam Brown 4-4-0	8.25	1.70	.70
1003	32¢ Law School	4.25	.85	.15

1004

1007

1004	32¢ City Church	4.25	.85	.15
1005	37¢ Family	4.75	.95	.40
1006	64¢ County Chapel	8.25	1.70	.70

SCOTT NO.	DESCRIPTION	PLATE BLOCK F/NH	UNUSED F/NH	USED F
1007-08	Army Regiment, att'd.	425	1.70	1.35
1007	32¢ Can. & Br. Reg.	....	.85	.18
1008	32¢ Winn. & Dragoons	....	.85	.18

1009

1010

1011

1012

1984 COMMEMORATIVES

1009/44 (1009-15, 28-39, 40-44) cpl., 24 varieties		95.00(20)	21.95	5.95
1009	32¢ Yellowknife	425	.85	.15
1010	32¢ Year of the Arts	425	.85	.15
1011	32¢ Cartier	425	.85	.15
1012	32¢ Tall Ships	425	.85	.15

1013

1014

1015

1013	32¢ Canadian Red Cross	425	.85	.15
1014	32¢ New Brunswick	425	.85	.15
1015	32¢ St. Lawrence Seaway	425	.85	.15

1016 New Brunswick

1017 British Columbia
1018 Yukon Territory
1019 Quebec
1020 Manitoba
1021 Alberta
1022 Prince Edward Island
1023 Saskatchewan
1024 Nova Scotia
1025 Northwest Territories
1026 Newfoundland
1027 Ontario

SCOTT NO.	DESCRIPTION	PLATE BLOCK F/NH	UNUSED F/NH	USED F
1027a	Sheet of 12 vars., att'd.	....	8.95	....
1016-27	Set of Singles	....	....	3.50
Any	32¢ Single	....	.95	.30

1028

1029

1030

1028	32¢ Loyalists	425	.85	.15
1029	32¢ Catholicism	425	.85	.15
1030	32¢ Papal Visit	425	.85	.15
1031	64¢ Papal Visit	8.25	1.70	.80

1032

1040

1036

1032-35	Lighthouses, att'd.	425	3.40	2.50
1032	32¢ Louisbourg	....	.85	25
1033	32¢ Fisgard	....	.85	25
1034	32¢ Ile Verte	....	.85	25
1035	32¢ Gibralter Point	....	.85	25
1036-37	Locomotives, att'd.	425	1.70	1.35
1036	32¢ Scotia 0-6-0	....	.85	.18
1037	32¢ Countess of Dufferin 4-4-0	....	.85	.18
1038	37¢ Grand Trunk 2-6-0	4.75	.95	.40
1039	64¢ Canadian Pacific 4-6-0	8.25	1.70	.65
1039a	Locomotive Souvenir Sheet	....	4.25	4.00
1040	32¢ Christmas	4.75	.85	.15
1041	37¢ Christmas	4.75	.95	.40
1042	64¢ Christmas	8.25	1.70	.65

1043

1044

1043	32¢ Royal Air Force	425	.85	.15
1044	32¢ Newspaper	425	.85	.15

SCOTT NO.	DESCRIPTION	PLATE BLOCK F/NH	UNUSED F/NH	USED F

1045   **1046**

1985 COMMEMORATIVES

1045/76	(1045-49, 60-66, 67-76) cpl., 24 varieties	75.00(16)	20.50	5.50
1045	32¢ Youth Year	4.25	.85	.18
1046	32¢ Canadian Astronaut	4.25	.85	.18

1047   **1049**

1047-48	Women, att'd.	4.25	1.70	1.25
1047	32¢ T. Casgrain	....	.85	20
1048	32¢ E. Murphy	....	.85	20
1049	32¢ G. Dumont	4.25	.85	.18

1050 Lower Ft. Gerry

1050 Lower Ft. Gerry
1051 Fort Anne
1052 Fort York
1053 Castle Hill
1054 Fort Whoop-Up
1055 Fort Erie
1056 Fort Welsh
1057 Fort Lennox
1058 York Redoubt

1059 Fort Frederick

1059a	34¢ Forts, pane of 10	....	8.75	....
	Any 34¢ Single	....	.90	35

1060   **1061**   **1062**

1060	34¢ Louis Herbert	4.35	.90	20
1061	34¢ Inter-Parliamentary	4.35	.90	20
1062	34¢ Girl Guides	4.35	.90	20

1063   **1067**

1063-66	Lighthouses, att'd.	4.35	3.60	2.75
1063	34¢ Sisters Islets	....	.90	25
1064	34¢ Pelee Passage	....	.90	25
1065	34¢ Rose Blanche	....	.90	25
1066	34¢ Haut-fond Prince	....	.90	25
1066b	Lighthouse Souvenir Sheet	....	3.75	3.35
1067	34¢ Christmas	4.35	.90	20
1068	39¢ Christmas	5.25	1.10	30
1069	68¢ Christmas	8.75	1.80	60
1070	32¢ Xmas, bklt. single	....	.85	25
1070a	booklet pane of 10	....	8.00	....

1071

1071-72	Locomotives, att'd.	4.35	1.80	1.50
1071	34¢ GT Class K2	....	.90	25
1072	34¢ CP Class P2a	....	.90	25
1073	39¢ CNoR Class 010a	5.25	1.10	30
1074	68¢ CGR CLass H4D	8.75	1.80	60

1075   **1076**

1075	34¢ Royal Navy	4.35	.90	20
1076	34¢ Montreal Museum	4.35	.90	20

1077

1986 COMMEMORATIVES

1077/1121	(1077-79, 90-1107, 1108-16, 17-21) cpl., 35 vars.	105.00	32.95	8.95
1077	34¢ Computer Map	4.35	.90	20

SCOTT NO.	DESCRIPTION	PLATE BLOCK F/NH	UNUSED F/NH	USED F

1078   **1084**

| 1078 | 34¢ Expo '86 | 4.35 | .90 | 20 |
| 1079 | 39¢ Expo '86 | 5.25 | 1.10 | 30 |

1986-87 DEFINITIVES

| 1084 | $5 La Mauisie | 55.00 | 12.50 | 4.50 |

926A   **938A**   **941B**

926A	36¢ Elizabeth II	3.75	.75	.07
926B	36¢ Parliament in Autumn, multicolor	3.75	.75	.07
......	same, booklet single, multicolor	......	.75	.15
......	booklet pane of 10	......	7.25	......
......	booklet pane of 25	......	18.00	......
......	Booklet pane, 2-1¢, 2-6¢ 1-36¢	......	1.10	......
938A	1¢ Parliament, bklt. sngl.	......	.10	.10
941B	6¢ Parliament, bklt single	......	.15	.15
948	36¢ Parliament in Autumn, violet, booklet single	......	.90	25
953	36¢ Parliament, red, coil	......	.75	.10

1080   **1081**   **1082**

1987 HERITAGE ARTIFACTS

1080	25¢ Butter Stamp	2.40	.50	.15
1081	42¢ Linen Chest	4.00	.85	.35
1082	55¢ Iron Kettle	5.25	1.10	40
1083	72¢ Hand-drawn Cart	6.95	1.45	.50

1986 COMMEMORATIVES

1090   **1092**

1090	34¢ Philippe Aubert de Gaspe	4.35	.90	20
1091	34¢ Molly Brant	4.35	.90	20
1092	34¢ Expo '86	4.35	.90	20
1093	68¢ Expo '86	8.50	1.80	.60

1094   **1095**

1094	34¢ Canadian Forces Postal Service	4.35	.90	20
1095-98	Birds, att'd.	4.35	3.60	2.75
1095	34¢ Great Blue Heron	......	.90	25
1096	34¢ Snow Goose	......	.90	25
1097	34¢ Great Horned Owl	......	.90	25
1098	34¢ Spruce Grouse	......	.90	25

1099   **1103**

1099-1102	Science & Technology, attd	4.35	3.60	2.75
1099	34¢ Rotary Snowplow	......	.90	25
1100	34¢ Canadian	......	.90	25
1101	34¢ Antigravity Flight Suit	......	.90	25
1102	34¢ Variable-pitch Propeller	......	.90	25
1103	34¢ CBC	4.35	.90	20

1104   **1108**

1104-07	Exploration, attd	4.35	3.60	2.75
1104	34¢ Vikings	......	.90	25
1105	34¢ Continent	......	.90	25
1106	34¢ John Cabot	......	.90	25
1107	34¢ Hudson Bay	......	.90	25
1107b	CAPEX Souv. Sheet	......	3.75	3.25

SCOTT NO.	DESCRIPTION	PLATE BLOCK F/NH	UNUSED F/NH	USED F
1108-09	Frontier Peace-makers, attd.	4.35	1.80	1.50
1108	34¢ J.F. MacDeod	....	.90	.25
1109	34¢ Crowfoot	....	.90	.25

1110

1111

1110	34¢ Peace Year	4.35	.90	.20
1111-12	Calgary, attd.	4.35	1.80	1.50
1111	34¢ Ice Hockey	....	.90	.25
1112	34¢ Biathlon	....	.90	.25

1113

1117

1113	34¢ X-mas Angels	4.35	.90	.20
1114	39¢ X-mas Angels	5.25	1.10	.30
1115	68¢ X-mas Angels	8.50	1.80	.60
1116	29¢ X-mas Angels, booklet singles	....	.75	.25
1116a	booklet pane of 10	....	7.25	....
1117	34¢ John Molson	4.35	.90	.20

1118

1118-19	Locomotives, attd	4.35	1.80	1.50
1118	34¢ CN-V1a	....	.90	.25
1119	34¢ CP-T1a	....	.90	.25
1120	39¢ CN-U2a	5.25	1.10	.30
1121	68¢ CP-H1c	8.50	1.80	.60

1122

1126

1987 COMMEMORATIVES

1122	34¢ CAPEX '87	3.95	.85	.20

SCOTT NO.	DESCRIPTION	PLATE BLOCK F/NH	UNUSED F/NH	USED F
1126-29	Exploration, attd	3.50	2.80	2.75
1126	34¢ Brule	....	.70	.25
1127	34¢ Radisson	....	.70	.25
1128	34¢ Joliet	....	.70	.25
1129	34¢ Wilderness	....	.70	.25

1130

1132

1130	36¢ Calgary Olympics	3.50	.75	.20
1131	42¢ Calgary Olympics	4.00	.85	.30
1132	36¢ Volunteers	3.50	.75	.20

1133

1133	36¢ Charter of Freedom	3.50	.75	.20
....	36¢ Engineering	3.50	.75	.20

1987 CAPEX EXHIBITION

....	36¢ Nelson-Miramichi: Post Office	3.50	.75	.20
....	42¢ Saint-Ours P.O.	4.00	.85	.30
....	72¢ Battleford P.O.	7.00	1.45	.60
....	CAPEX Souv. Sheet	....	3.75	3.75

SCOTT NO.	DESCRIPTION	PLATE BLOCK F/NH	UNUSED F/NH	USED F
	1987 COMMEMORATIVES (continued)			

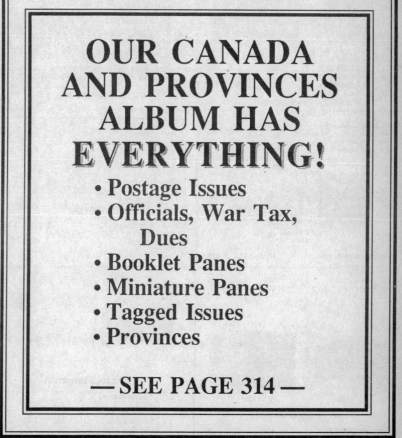

CANADA 36

SCOTT NO.	DESCRIPTION	PLATE BLOCK F/NH	UNUSED F/NH	USED F
......	36¢ Half-tone Engraving	......	.75	25
......	36¢ Underseas Telegraph	......	.75	25
......	Steamships, attd	3.50	1.50	1.40
......	36¢ Segwun	......	.75	25
......	36¢ Princess Marguarite	......	.75	25
......	Historic Shipwrecks, attd	3.50	3.00	2.90
......	36¢ San Juan	......	.75	25
......	36¢ Breadalbane	......	.75	25
......	36¢ Ericsson	......	.75	25
......	36¢ Hamilton/Scourge	......	.75	25
......	36¢ Air Canada	3.50	3.00	20
......	36¢ Quebec Summit	3.50	3.00	20

SCOTT NO.	DESCRIPTION	PLATE BLOCK F/NH	UNUSED F/NH	USED F
......	Science & Technology, attd.	3.50	3.00	2.90
......	36¢ AM Radio	......	.75	25
......	36¢ Newsprint Pulp	......	.75	25

SCOTT NO.	DESCRIPTION	BLANK CORNER BLOCKS F/NH	UNUSED F/NH	SCOTT NO.	DESCRIPTION	BLANK CORNER BLOCKS F/NH	UNUSED F/NH

CANADA PHOSPHOR TAGGED ISSUES

Overprinted with barely visible phosporescent ink.

TYPES OF TAGGING
I = Wide Side Bars
II = Wide Bar in Middle
III = Bar at Right or Left
IV = Narrow Bar in Middle
V = Narrow Side Bars

1962-63 Queen Elizabeth II

337-41p	1¢-5¢ Elizabeth	(5) 65.00	13.50
401-5p	1¢-5¢ Elizabeth	(5) 10.75	2.25
404pIV	4¢ carmine-IV	6.00	1.25
404pII	4¢ carmine-II	13.50	2.75
405q	5¢ Elizabeth, miniature pane of 20	....	47.50

1964-67

434-35p	3¢-5¢ 1964 Xmas	(2) 14.00	2.75
434q	3¢ miniature pane of 25	....	15.00
434q	same, sealed pack of 2	....	30.00
443-44p	3¢-5¢ 1965 Xmas	(2) 3.75	.75
443q	3¢ miniature pane of 25	....	10.00
443q	same, sealed pack of 2	....	20.00
451-52p	3¢-5¢ 1966 Xmas	(2) 4.35	.90
451q	3¢ miniature pane of 25	....	6.75
451q	same, sealed pack of 2	....	13.50
453p	5¢ Centennial	3.00	.60

1967-72 Queen Elizabeth II

454-58pI	1¢-5¢-I	(4) 10.00	1.50
454-58pII	1¢-5¢-II	(4) 12.50	1.65
454-57pV	1¢-5¢-V	(4) 7.75	.95
454ep	1¢ book sing.-V	....	.25
457p	4¢ carmine-III	3.50	.65
458q	5¢ miniature pane of 20	....	65.00
459p	6¢ orange, pf. 10-I	7.75	.70
459bp	6¢ orange, perf. 12-1/2 x 12-I	6.50	.90
460p	6¢ black, pf. 12-1/2 x 12-I	3.50	.50
460cp	6¢ black, pf. 12-1/2 x 12-II	4.25	.60
460gp	6¢ black, booklet sing. pf. 10-V	....	.75
460fpII	6¢ black, pf. 12-II	3.50	.55
460fpV	6¢ black, pf. 12-V	3.25	.50

1967 Views

462-65pI	10¢-25¢-I	(4) 47.50	9.50
462-63pV	10¢-15¢-V	(2) 13.50	2.75

1967-69

476-77p	3¢-5¢ 1967 Xmas	(2) 3.75	.70
476q	3¢ miniature pane of 25	....	4.75
476q	same, sealed pack of 2	....	9.50
488-89p	5¢-6¢ 1968 Xmas	(2) 3.95	.75
488q	5¢ booklet pane of 10	....	5.00
502-3p	5¢-6¢ 1969 Xmas	(2) 3.85	.75
502q	5¢ booklet pane of 10	....	4.75

1970-71

505p	6¢ Manitoba	1.95	.35
508-11p	25¢ Expo '70	(4) 19.75	17.50
513-14p	10¢-15¢ U.N.	(2) 18.75	3.75
519-30p	5¢-15¢ Xmas	(12) 25.00	8.00
541p	15¢ Radio Canada	19.50	3.75

1971 Queen Elizabeth II

543-44p	7¢-8¢-I	(2) 9.75	1.10
544q	b. pane, 8c (2), 6c (1), 1c (3)	....	2.75
544r	b. pane, 8c (11), 6c (1), 1c (6)	....	8.25
544s	b. pane, 8c (5), 6c (1), 1c (4)	....	3.50
544pV	8¢ slate-V	4.75	.65
550p	8¢ slate, coil		.65

1971-72

554-57p	6¢-15¢ Xmas	(4) 13.75	2.75
560p	8¢ World Health Day	4.25	.90
561p	8¢ Frontenac	4.50	.95
562-63p	8¢ Indians	(2) 3.75	1.40
564-65p	8¢ Indians	(2) 3.75	1.40
582-85p	15¢ Sciences	(4) 62.50	15.00

1972 Pictorials

594-97	10¢-25¢-V	(4) 11.30	2.40
594-97pI	10¢-25¢-I	(4) 38.75	7.75

1972

606-09p	6¢-15¢ Xmas-V	(4) 13.50	2.75
606-09pI	6¢-15¢ Xmas-I	(4) 18.50	3.75
610p	8¢ Krieghoff	4.00	.45

SCOTT NO.	DESCRIPTION	PLATE BLOCK F/NH	UNUSED F/NH	USED F

SEMI-POSTAL STAMPS

B1-3   B4

SCOTT NO.	DESCRIPTION	PLATE BLOCK F/NH	UNUSED F/NH	USED F

1974-76

| B1-12 | Olympics, 12 Vars. | 36.00 | 7.75 | 7.75 |

1974

B1-3	Emblems, 3 vars.	9.25	2.00	2.00
B1	8¢ + 2¢ Olympic Emblem	2.10	.45	.45
B2	10¢ + 5¢ Same	3.25	.70	.70
B3	15¢ + 5¢ Same	4.15	.90	.90

1975

B4-6	Water Sports, 3 vars.	9.25	2.00	2.00
B4	8¢ + 2¢ Swimming	2.10	.45	.45
B5	10¢ + 5¢ Rowing	3.25	.70	.70
B6	15¢ + 5¢ Sailing	4.15	.90	.90

B7   B10

B7-9	Combat Sports, 3 vars.	9.25	2.00	2.00
B7	8¢ + 2¢ Fencing	2.10	.45	.45
B8	10¢ + 5¢ Boxing	3.25	.70	.70
B9	15¢ + 5¢ Judo	4.15	.90	.90

1976

B10-12	Team Sports, 3 vars.	9.25	2.00	2.00
B10	8¢ + 2¢ Basketball	2.10	.45	.45
B11	10¢ + 5¢ Gymnastics	3.25	.70	.70
B12	20¢ + 5¢ Soccer	4.15	.90	.90

SCOTT NO.	DESCRIPTION	UNUSED NH		UNUSED OG		USED	
		F	AVG	F	AVG	F	AVG

AIR POST STAMPS

C1   C2   C3   C4

1928

| C1 | 5¢ brown olive .... | 12.00 | 6.75 | 8.50 | 5.00 | 3.75 | 2.25 |

1930

| C2 | 5¢ olive brown .... | 55.00 | 32.50 | 40.00 | 25.00 | 22.50 | 13.50 |

1932

| C3 | 6¢ on 5¢ brown olive ...... | 8.00 | 4.75 | 6.00 | 3.75 | 2.95 | 1.75 |
| C4 | 6¢ on 5¢ olive brown ...... | 18.00 | 10.50 | 13.50 | 8.50 | 10.75 | 6.50 |

SCOTT NO.	DESCRIPTION	PLATE BLOCKS F/NH	F	UNUSED F/NH	F	USED F

C5   C6   C7,8   C9

1935

| C5 | 6¢ red brown .... | 15.75 | 13.00 | 2.75 | 2.25 | 1.20 |

1938

| C6 | 6¢ blue... | 16.50 | 13.35 | 3.50 | 2.85 | .25 |

SCOTT NO.	DESCRIPTION	PLATE BLOCKS F/NH	F	UNUSED F/NH	F	USED F
		1942-43				
C7	6¢ deep blue.............................	21.00	18.50	4.25	3.75	1.00
C8	7¢ deep blue (1943)	4.00	3.50	.85	.75	.11
		1946				
C9	7¢ deep blue.............................	4.00	3.50	.85	.75	.10
C9a	same, booklet pane of 14	....	....	3.50	3.00	....

AIR POST SPECIAL DELIVERY

CE1, CE2   CE3, CE4

SCOTT NO.	DESCRIPTION	F/NH	F	F/NH	F	USED F
CE1-4	16¢-17¢ cpl., 4 vars.	87.50	80.00	18.50	16.50	16.50
		1942-43				
CE1	16¢ ultramarine	13.50	11.50	2.75	2.35	2.35
CE2	17¢ ultramarine (1943)	16.00	14.75	3.50	3.15	3.15
		1946				
CE3	17¢ ultramarine (Circumflex " ")	30.00	27.00	6.25	5.50	5.50
		1947				
CE4	17¢ ultramarine (Grave " ")	32.50	30.00	6.75	6.25	6.25

SCOTT NO.	DESCRIPTION	UNUSED NH F	AVG	UNUSED F	AVG	USED F	AVG

SPECIAL DELIVERY STAMPS

E1   E2   E3   E4

		1898					
E1	10¢ blue green	72.50	38.50	46.50	27.50	6.75	4.00
		1922					
E2	20¢ carmine	87.50	51.50	63.50	38.00	7.50	4.50
		1927					
E3	20¢ orange........................	12.00	6.75	8.50	5.00	7.50	4.50
		1930					
E4	20¢ henna brown	70.00	42.00	52.50	33.50	14.50	9.50

VERY FINE QUALITY: To determine the Very Fine price, add the difference between the Fine and Average prices to the Fine quality price. For example: if the Fine price is $10.00 and the Average price is $6.00, the Very Fine price would be $14.00. From 1935 to date, add 20% to the Fine price to arrive at the Very Fine price.

SCOTT NO.	DESCRIPTION	UNUSED NH F	AVG	UNUSED F	AVG	USED F	AVG

E5   E6   E7,E8   E9

1933

SCOTT NO.	DESCRIPTION	UNUSED NH F	AVG	UNUSED F	AVG	USED F	AVG
E5	20¢ henna brown	52.50	33.50	40.00	26.50	18.75	12.50

SCOTT NO.	DESCRIPTION	PLATE BLOCKS F/NH	F	UNUSED F/NH	F	USED F

1935

E6	20¢ dark carmine	85.00	72.50	10.75	8.75	6.50

1938-39

E7	10¢ dark green (1939)	37.50	32.50	7.50	6.50	3.15
E8	20¢ dark carmine	300.00	250.00	42.50	37.50	37.50
E9	10¢ on 20¢ carmine (#E8) (1939)	55.00	47.50	7.50	6.50	6.00

E10   E11

1942

E10	10¢ green...................................	17.00	15.00	3.50	3.15	1.45

1946

E11	10¢ green...................................	12.50	11.00	2.50	2.25	.90

SCOTT NO.	DESCRIPTION	UNUSED NH F	AVG	UNUSED F	AVG	USED F	AVG

WAR TAX STAMPS

MR1,MR2   MR3-MR7

2¢ + 1¢ Die I. Below large letter "T" there is a clear horizontal line of color.
DIE II. Right side of line is replaced by two short lines and five dots.

1915

MR1	1¢ green............................	8.00	4.50	5.25	3.15	.12	.07
MR2	2¢ carmine	8.00	4.50	5.25	3.15	.17	.10

1916 Perf. 12

MR3	2¢ + 1¢ carmine (I)	....	10.50	6.00	7.00	4.25	.13	.08
MR3a	2¢ + 1¢ carmine (II)	......	100.00	55.00	67.50	40.00	2.50	1.50
MR4	2¢ + 1¢ brown (II)	....	6.50	3.65	4.25	2.60	.13	.08
MR4a	2¢ + 1¢ brown (I)	....	28.50	150.00	190.00	110.00	6.50	3.95

Perf. 12 x 8

MR5	2¢ + 1¢ carmine	37.50	21.00	25.00	15.00	18.50	11.00

Coil Stamps Perf. 8 Vertically

MR6	2¢ + 1¢ carmine	87.50	50.00	57.50	35.00	3.75	2.25
MR7	2¢ + 1¢ brown (II)	12.75	7.35	8.50	5.25	.65	.40
MR7a	2¢ + 1¢ brown (I)	95.00	55.00	65.00	39.50	4.25	2.60

SCOTT NO.	DESCRIPTION	UNUSED O.G. F	AVG	UNUSED F	AVG	USED F	AVG

REGISTRATION STAMPS

F1-F3

1875-88 Perf. 12

SCOTT NO.	DESCRIPTION	UNUSED O.G. F	AVG	UNUSED F	AVG	USED F	AVG
F1	2¢ orange	55.00	32.50	45.00	27.50	3.00	1.80
F1a	2¢ vermillion	65.00	38.50	52.50	31.75	7.50	4.50
F1b	2¢ rose carmine	105.00	60.00	85.00	50.00	47.50	28.50
F1d	2¢ orange, pf. 12 x 11-1/2	215.00	135.00	180.00	110.00	32.50	19.50
F2	5¢ green	66.50	38.50	55.00	33.50	3.00	1.80
F2d	5¢ green, pf. 12 x 11-1/2	385.00	225.00	325.00	195.00	70.00	42.50
F3	8¢ blue	385.00	225.00	325.00	195.00	250.00	150.00

SCOTT NO.	DESCRIPTION	UNUSED NH F	AVG	UNUSED F	AVG	USED F	AVG

POSTAGE DUE STAMPS

J1-J5　　　　**J6-J10**　　　　**J11-J14**

1906-28

SCOTT NO.	DESCRIPTION	UNUSED NH F	AVG	UNUSED F	AVG	USED F	AVG
J1	1¢ violet	7.50	4.25	5.50	3.35	2.85	1.70
J2	2¢ violet	10.50	5.85	7.75	4.65	.70	.45
J3	4¢ violet (1928)	40.00	22.50	30.00	17.50	13.50	8.00
J4	5¢ violet	10.00	5.75	7.50	4.75	1.25	.75
J5	10¢ violet (1928)	30.00	17.50	22.50	15.50	8.75	5.25

1930-32

J6	1¢ dark violet	9.50	5.50	7.25	4.35	3.25	1.95
J7	2¢ dark violet	6.25	3.60	4.75	2.85	.70	.45
J8	4¢ dark violet	12.50	7.25	9.50	5.75	2.75	1.65
J9	5¢ dark violet	11.75	6.75	9.00	5.35	4.00	2.40
J10	10¢ dark violet	65.00	40.00	47.50	29.50	7.50	4.50

1933-34

J11	1¢ dark violet (1934)	9.75	5.50	8.00	4.85	5.00	3.25
J12	2¢ dark violet	3.95	2.25	3.25	1.95	.85	.55
J13	4¢ dark violet	9.85	6.00	8.25	5.25	4.75	3.00
J14	10¢ dark violet	15.50	9.75	13.00	8.25	4.00	2.50

SCOTT NO.	DESCRIPTION	PLATE BLOCKS F/NH	F	UNUSED F/NH	F	USED F

J15-J20　　　　**J21-J40**

1935-65

SCOTT NO.	DESCRIPTION	PLATE BLOCKS F/NH	F	UNUSED F/NH	F	USED F
J15-20	1¢-10¢ cpl., 7 vars.	40.00	36.50	5.50	4.95	3.35
J15	1¢ dark violet	1.15	1.00	.18	.15	.10
J16	2¢ dark violet	1.15	1.00	.18	.15	.10
J16B	3¢ dark violet (1965)	18.50	16.75	2.25	2.00	1.40
J17	4¢ dark violet	1.85	1.65	.30	.27	.09
J18	5¢ dark violet (1948)	2.75	2.50	.45	.40	.25
J19	6¢ dark violet (1957)	15.00	13.50	2.15	1.95	1.50
J20	10¢ dark violet	2.00	1.80	.33	.30	.09

POSTAGE DUES

1967 Perf. 12
Regular Size Design 20mm x 17mm

SCOTT NO.	DESCRIPTION	PLATE BLOCK F/NH	UNUSED F/NH	USED F
J21-27	1¢-10¢ cpl., 7 vars.	25.00	5.00	5.00
J21	1¢ carmine rose	2.00	.35	.35
J22	2¢ carmine rose	2.00	.35	.35
J23	3¢ carmine rose	2.00	.35	.35
J24	4¢ carmine rose	2.95	.60	.60
J25	5¢ carmine rose	12.00	2.50	2.50
J26	6¢ carmine rose	2.75	.55	.55
J27	10¢ carmine rose	2.75	.55	.55

1969-74 Perf. 12 (White or Yellow Gum)
Modular Size Design 20mm x 15-3/4mm

SCOTT NO.	DESCRIPTION	PLATE BLOCK F/NH	UNUSED F/NH	USED F
J28/37	(J28-31, 33-37) 9 vars.	10.00	2.00	1.85
J28	1¢ carmine rose ('70)	.60	.12	.12
J29	2¢ carmine rose ('72)	.75	.15	.13
J30	3¢ carmine rose ('74)	.75	.15	.13
J31	4¢ carmine rose ('69)	.80	.15	.15
J32a	5¢ carmine rose ('69)	140.00	28.50	28.50
J33	6¢ carmine rose ('72)	1.00	.20	.18
J34	8¢ carmine rose ('72)	1.30	.27	.24
J35	10¢ carmine rose ('69)	1.25	.25	.22
J36	12¢ carmine rose ('69)	1.75	.35	.30
J37	16¢ carmine rose ('74)	2.50	.50	.45

1977-78
Perf. 12-1/2 x 12

SCOTT NO.	DESCRIPTION	PLATE BLOCK F/NH	UNUSED F/NH	USED F
J28a-40	1¢-50¢ cpl., 9 vars.	23.00	4.65	4.25
J28a	1¢ carmie rose	.55	.11	.08
J31a	4¢ carmine rose	.65	.12	.12
J32	5¢ carmine rose	.65	.12	.12
J34a	8¢ carmine rose (1978)	2.25	.45	.30
J35a	10¢ carmine rose	1.35	.27	.25
J36a	12¢ carmine rose	7.50	1.50	1.35
J38	20¢ carmine rose	2.40	.50	.45
J39	24¢ carmine rose	2.65	.55	.50
J40	50¢ carmine rose	6.25	1.30	1.25

OFFICIAL STAMPS

1949-50
249, 250, 252, 254, 269-273
overprinted O.H.M.S.

SCOTT NO.	DESCRIPTION	PLATE BLOCK F/NH	UNUSED F/NH	USED F
O1-10	1¢-$1 cpl., 9 vars.	....	335.00	245.00
O1-8	1¢-20¢, 7 varieties	....	55.00	23.00
O1	1¢ green	12.50	2.50	2.25
O2	2¢ brown	120.00	17.50	14.50
O3	3¢ rose violet	11.50	2.25	1.30
O4	4¢ dark carmine	20.00	4.25	.65
O6	10¢ olive	27.50	5.50	.65
O7	14¢ black brown	35.00	7.25	2.15
O8	20¢ slate black	90.00	18.75	2.75
O9	50¢ dark blue green	1200.00	225.00	175.00
O10	$1 red violet	385.00	70.00	57.50

1950 294 overprinted O.H.M.S.

SCOTT NO.	DESCRIPTION	PLATE BLOCK F/NH	UNUSED F/NH	USED F
O11	50¢ dull green	190.00	40.00	22.50

1950 284-88 overprinted O.H.M.S.

SCOTT NO.	DESCRIPTION	PLATE BLOCK F/NH	UNUSED F/NH	USED F
O12-15A	1¢-5¢ cpl., 5 vars.	32.50	6.00	3.15
O12	1¢ green	3.50	.35	.32
O13	2¢ sepia	4.75	1.00	.85
O14	3¢ rose violet	6.50	1.30	.50
O15	4¢ dark carmine	6.50	1.30	.15
O15A	5¢ deep blue	12.75	2.35	1.50

1950 284-88, 269-71, 294, 273 overprinted G

SCOTT NO.	DESCRIPTION	PLATE BLOCK F/NH	UNUSED F/NH	USED F
O16-25	1¢-$1 cpl., 10 vars.	....	185.00	95.00
O16-24	1¢-50¢, 9 varieties	....	57.50	10.00
O16	1¢ green	1.85	.28	.15
O17	2¢ sepia	7.00	1.30	.80
O18	3¢ rose violet	6.50	1.30	.15
O19	4¢ dark carmine	7.00	1.40	.12
O20	5¢ deep blue	14.00	1.65	.90
O21	10¢ olive	18.50	3.75	.45
O22	14¢ black brown	50.00	10.50	1.85
O23	20¢ slate black	110.00	23.75	1.10
O24	50¢ dull green	77.50	16.00	5.00
O25	$1 red violet	575.00	135.00	90.00

1950-51 301, 302 overprinted G

SCOTT NO.	DESCRIPTION	PLATE BLOCK F/NH	UNUSED F/NH	USED F
O26	10¢ black brown	7.75	1.65	.20
O27	$1 bright ultramarine (1951)	560.00	115.00	80.00

1951-53 305-06, 316, 320-21 overprinted G

SCOTT NO.	DESCRIPTION	PLATE BLOCK F/NH	UNUSED F/NH	USED F
O28	2¢ olive green	2.65	.55	.12
O29	4¢ orange vermillion (1952)	4.50	.85	.11
O30	20¢ gray (1952)	13.50	2.75	.15
O31	7¢ blue (1952)	20.00	4.25	.95
O32	$1 gray (1953)	95.00	20.00	9.50

1953 325-29, 334 overprinted G

SCOTT NO.	DESCRIPTION	PLATE BLOCK F/NH	UNUSED F/NH	USED F
O33-37	1¢-5¢ cpl., 5 vars.	10.00	2.15	.45
O33	1¢ violet brown	1.50	.30	.11
O34	2¢ green	1.75	.38	.11
O35	3¢ carmine	1.75	.38	.08
O36	4¢ violet	2.85	.60	.07
O37	5¢ ultramarine	2.85	.60	.10
O38	50¢ light green	31.50	6.50	1.15

1955 351 overprinted G

SCOTT NO.	DESCRIPTION	PLATE BLOCK F/NH	UNUSED F/NH	USED F
O39	10¢ violet brown	4.65	1.00	.12

1955-56 337, 338, 340, 341, 362 overprinted G

SCOTT NO.	DESCRIPTION	PLATE BLOCK F/NH	UNUSED F/NH	USED F
O40-45	1¢-20¢ cpl., 5 vars.	25.00	5.25	.65
O40	1¢ violet brown (1956)	1.95	.40	.28
O41	2¢ green (1956)	2.25	.45	.10
O43	4¢ violet (1956)	7.25	1.50	.11
O44	5¢ bright blue	3.25	.65	.08
O45	20¢ green (1956)	11.75	2.50	.14

1963 401, 402, 404, 405 overprinted G

SCOTT NO.	DESCRIPTION	PLATE BLOCK F/NH	UNUSED F/NH	USED F
O46-49	1¢-5¢ cpl., 4 vars.	14.75	3.00	2.85
O46	1¢ deep brown	4.15	.85	.80
O47	2¢ green	4.15	.85	.80
O48	4¢ carmine	4.50	.95	.90
O49	5¢ violet blue	2.65	.55	.50

1949-50 AIR POST OFFICIAL STAMPS

SCOTT NO.	DESCRIPTION	PLATE BLOCK F/NH	UNUSED F/NH	USED F
CO1	7¢ blue, O.H.M.S. (C9)	55.00	11.50	5.75
CO2	7¢ blue, G (C9)	125.00	26.75	21.75

1950 SPECIAL DELIVERY OFFICIAL STAMPS

SCOTT NO.	DESCRIPTION	PLATE BLOCK F/NH	UNUSED F/NH	USED F
EO1	10¢ green, O.H.M.S. (E11)	120.00	26.50	24.00
EO2	10¢ green, G (E11)	215.00	45.00	41.50

SCOTT NO.	DESCRIPTION	UNUSED O.G. F	AVG	UNUSED F	AVG	USED F	AVG

1,2　　　　3,5　　　　4,6

Queen Victoria

1860 Perf. 14

| 2 | 2-1/2p dull rose .... | 400.00 | 235.00 | 275.00 | 165.00 | 175.00 | 105.00 |

VANCOUVER ISLAND

1865 Imperforate

| 4 | 10¢ blue .... | .... | .... | 1350.00 | 800.00 | 750.00 | 450.00 |

Perf. 14

| 5 | 5¢ rose............................ | 350.00 | 200.00 | 235.00 | 140.00 | 155.00 | 95.00 |
| 6 | 10¢ blue .... | 350.00 | 200.00 | 235.00 | 140.00 | 155.00 | 95.00 |

7　　　　　8-18

Seal

BRITISH COLUMBIA

1865

| 7 | 3p blue............................. | 120.00 | 72.50 | 85.00 | 51.50 | 82.50 | 50.00 |

New Values Surcharged on 1865 design
1867-69 Perf. 14

8	2¢ brown..........................	120.00	70.00	87.50	52.50	90.00	54.00
9	5¢ bright red	155.00	90.00	110.00	66.50	110.00	66.50
10	10¢ lilac rose	1400.00	800.00	1000.00	600.00	....	....
11	25¢ orange.......................	175.00	100.00	125.00	75.00	125.00	75.00
12	50¢ violet	600.00	365.00	425.00	250.00	....	....
13	$1 green...........................	875.00	500.00	625.00	375.00	....	....

1869 Perf. 12-1/2

14	5¢ bright red	925.00	535.00	675.00	400.00	675.00	400.00
15	10¢ lilac rose	665.00	385.00	475.00	275.00	425.00	250.00
16	25¢ orange.......................	600.00	335.00	425.00	250.00	365.00	225.00
17	50¢ violet	700.00	400.00	500.00	300.00	385.00	235.00
18	$1 green...........................	900.00	525.00	650.00	390.00	740.00	445.00

NEWFOUNDLAND

SCOTT NO.	DESCRIPTION	UNUSED O.G. F	AVG	UNUSED F	AVG	USED F	AVG

1,5,12A,15A,16,19 2,11,17 3,11A 4,12,18 6,13,20

7,14,21 8,22 9,10,15,23

1857 Imperforate, Thick Paper

Scott	Description	F	AVG	F	AVG	F	AVG
1	1p brown violet	100.00	57.50	70.00	42.50	130.00	80.00
2	2p scarlet vermillion	....	....	....	....	5500.00	3350.00
3	3p green	525.00	300.00	375.00	225.00	375.00	225.00
4	4p scarlet vermillion	....	....	....	....	3000.00	1800.00
5	5p brown violet	315.00	180.00	225.00	135.00	250.00	150.00
7	6-1/2 scarlet vermillion	2700.00	1500.00	1900.00	1150.00	2000.00	1200.00
8	8p scarlet vermillion	400.00	230.00	285.00	170.00	400.00	240.00

1860 Thin Paper

Scott	Description	F	AVG	F	AVG	F	AVG
11	2p orange	425.00	235.00	295.00	175.00	325.00	195.00
11A	3p green	87.50	50.00	62.50	37.50	85.00	51.50
12	4p orange	....	....	2500.00	1500.00	825.00	500.00
12A	5p violet brown	97.50	56.50	70.00	42.50	120.00	72.50
13	6p orange	....	....	2950.00	1975.00	575.00	350.00

1861-62 Thin Paper

Scott	Description	F	AVG	F	AVG	F	AVG
15A	1p violet brown	175.00	100.00	125.00	75.00	250.00	150.00
17	2p rose	210.00	120.00	150.00	90.00	175.00	105.00
18	4p rose	52.50	30.00	37.50	22.50	52.50	31.75
19	5p reddish brown	56.50	32.50	40.00	24.00	60.00	36.50
20	6p rose	25.00	14.00	17.50	10.50	45.00	27.50
21	6-1/2p rose	90.00	52.50	65.00	39.50	165.00	100.00

24,38
Codfish

25,26,40
Seal

27
Prince Albert

28,29
Queen Victoria

30
Fishing Ship

31
Queen Victoria

1865-94 Perf. 12 Yellow Paper

Scott	Description	F	AVG	F	AVG	F	AVG
24	2¢ green	65.00	38.50	52.50	31.50	27.50	16.50
24a	2¢ green (white paper)	53.50	30.00	42.50	25.00	21.00	12.75
25	5¢ brown	450.00	260.00	365.00	215.00	230.00	140.00
26	5¢ black (1868)	215.00	120.00	170.00	100.00	95.00	56.50
27	10¢ black	230.00	130.00	185.00	110.00	70.00	42.50
27a	10¢ black (white paper)	145.00	85.00	115.00	70.00	40.00	24.00
28	12¢ pale red brown	325.00	180.00	250.00	150.00	100.00	60.00
28a	12¢ pale red brn. (white ppr.)	43.50	25.00	35.00	21.00	35.00	21.00
29	12¢ brown (1894)	35.00	21.00	28.75	17.50	28.75	17.50
30	13¢ orange	95.00	53.50	75.00	45.00	60.00	36.50
31	24¢ blue	29.50	17.00	23.50	14.00	23.50	14.00

SCOTT NO.	DESCRIPTION	UNUSED O.G.		UNUSED		USED	
		F	AVG	F	AVG	F	AVG

32,32A,37
Prince of Wales

33-36,39
Queen Victoria

1868-94

32	1¢ violet	40.00	23.00	32.50	19.50	24.00	14.50
32A	1¢ brn. lilac, re-eng. (1871)	52.50	30.00	41.50	25.00	31.50	19.00
33	3¢ vermillion (1970)	270.00	155.00	215.00	130.00	100.00	60.00
34	3¢ blue (1973)	210.00	120.00	165.00	100.00	11.00	6.75
35	6¢ dull rose (1870)	12.50	7.25	10.00	6.00	10.00	6.00
36	6¢ carmine lake (1894)	17.50	11.00	15.00	8.75	10.50	6.25

1876-79 Rouletted

37	1¢ brown lilac (1877) ...	65.00	38.75	52.50	32.50	25.00	15.00
38	2¢ green (1879)	80.00	45.00	62.50	37.50	25.00	15.00
39	3¢ blue (1877)	200.00	120.00	160.00	100.00	9.00	5.50
40	5¢ blue..............................	125.00	70.00	100.00	60.00	9.00	5.50

41-45
Prince of Wales

46-48
Codfish

49-52
Queen Victoria

53-55
Seal

1880-96 Perf. 12

41	1¢ violet brown	13.00	7.75	11.00	6.75	9.25	5.50
42	1¢ gray brown	13.00	7.75	11.00	6.75	9.25	5.50
43	1¢ brown (Reissue) (1896)	31.75	18.00	26.50	16.00	26.50	16.00
44	1¢ deep green (1887)	6.50	3.65	5.25	3.15	3.50	2.10
45	1¢ green (Reissue) (1897)	8.75	5.00	7.25	4.35	6.50	3.95
46	2¢ yellow green	13.00	7.75	11.00	6.75	11.00	6.75
47	2¢ green (Reissue) (1896)	25.75	15.00	21.50	13.00	17.50	10.50
48	2¢ red orange (1887)	13.00	7.75	11.00	6.75	6.00	3.65
49	3¢ blue..............................	15.00	8.50	12.50	7.50	3.75	2.25
51	3¢ umber brown (1887) ...	14.50	8.25	12.00	7.25	3.75	2.25
52	3¢ violet brn. (Reissue) (1896)	37.50	22.00	31.50	19.00	31.50	19.00
53	5¢ pale blue	160.00	90.00	135.00	80.00	7.25	4.35
54	5¢ dark blue (1887)	78.50	46.50	65.00	40.00	7.25	4.35
55	5¢ bright blue (1894) ...	19.75	11.50	16.50	10.00	5.75	3.50

56-58
Newfoundland Dog

59
Schooner

60
Queen Victoria

1887-96

56	1/2¢ rose red	6.35	3.75	5.25	3.25	4.65	2.80
57	1/2¢ orange red (1896)	28.00	16.00	23.50	14.00	19.50	11.50
58	1/2¢ black (1894)	5.75	3.35	4.85	2.90	4.85	2.90
59	10¢ black..........................	56.50	33.50	47.50	28.50	37.50	22.50

1890

60	3¢ slate..............................	12.00	7.00	10.00	6.00	.75	.45

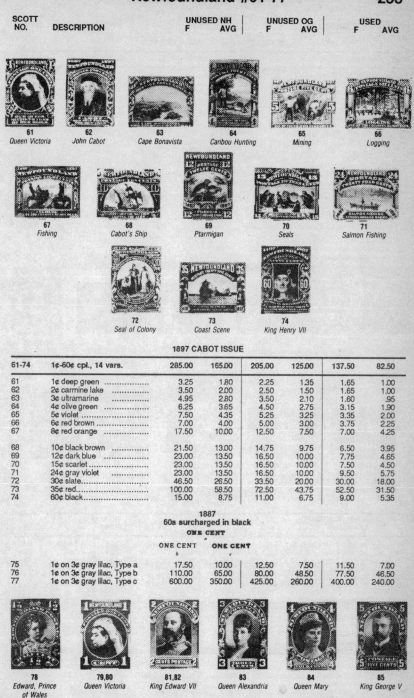

61 Queen Victoria
62 John Cabot
63 Cape Bonavista
64 Caribou Hunting
65 Mining
56 Logging

67 Fishing
68 Cabot's Ship
69 Ptarmigan
70 Seals
71 Salmon Fishing

72 Seal of Colony
73 Coast Scene
74 King Henry VII

1897 CABOT ISSUE

Scott No.	Description	Unused NH F	Unused NH AVG	Unused OG F	Unused OG AVG	Used F	Used AVG
61-74	1¢-60¢ cpl., 14 vars.	285.00	165.00	205.00	125.00	137.50	82.50
61	1¢ deep green	3.25	1.80	2.25	1.35	1.65	1.00
62	2¢ carmine lake	3.50	2.00	2.50	1.50	1.65	1.00
63	3¢ ultramarine	4.95	2.80	3.50	2.10	1.60	.95
64	4¢ olive green	6.25	3.65	4.50	2.75	3.15	1.90
65	5¢ violet	7.50	4.35	5.25	3.25	3.35	2.00
66	6¢ red brown	7.00	4.00	5.00	3.00	3.75	2.25
67	8¢ red orange	17.50	10.00	12.50	7.50	7.00	4.25
68	10¢ black brown	21.50	13.00	14.75	9.75	6.50	3.95
69	12¢ dark blue	23.00	13.50	16.50	10.00	7.75	4.65
70	15¢ scarlet	23.00	13.50	16.50	10.00	7.50	4.50
71	24¢ gray violet	23.00	13.50	16.50	10.00	9.50	5.75
72	30¢ slate	46.50	26.50	33.50	20.00	30.00	18.00
73	35¢ red	100.00	58.50	72.50	43.75	52.50	31.50
74	60¢ black	15.00	8.75	11.00	6.75	9.00	5.35

1887
60a surcharged in black

ONE CENT
a

ONE CENT
b

ONE CENT
c

Scott No.	Description	Unused NH F	Unused NH AVG	Unused OG F	Unused OG AVG	Used F	Used AVG
75	1¢ on 3¢ gray lilac, Type a	17.50	10.00	12.50	7.50	11.50	7.00
76	1¢ on 3¢ gray lilac, Type b	110.00	65.00	80.00	48.50	77.50	46.50
77	1¢ on 3¢ gray lilac, Type c	600.00	350.00	425.00	260.00	400.00	240.00

78 Edward, Prince of Wales
79,80 Queen Victoria
81,82 King Edward VII
83 Queen Alexandria
84 Queen Mary
85 King George V

SCOTT NO.	DESCRIPTION	UNUSED NH		UNUSED		USED	
		F	AVG	F	AVG	F	AVG

1897-1901 ROYAL FAMILY ISSUE

78-85	1/2¢-5¢ cpl., 8 vars.	88.75	51.50	63.50	38.50	16.00	9.50
78	1/2¢ olive green	4.00	2.30	2.85	1.75	2.85	1.70
79	1¢ carmine rose	5.65	3.25	4.00	2.40	3.00	1.80
80	1¢ yellow green (1898)	3.50	2.00	2.50	1.50	.22	.14
81	2¢ orange........................	6.00	3.50	4.25	2.60	2.85	1.70
82	2¢ vermillion (1898)	11.00	6.50	8.00	4.85	.60	.37
83	3¢ orange (1898)	12.50	7.50	8.50	5.00	.50	.30
84	4¢ violet (1901)	25.00	14.00	17.75	10.75	4.50	2.75
85	5¢ blue (1899)	30.00	17.50	21.50	13.00	2.50	1.50

86
Map of Newfoundland
1908

86	2¢ rose carmine	26.50	14.75	18.75	11.00	1.75	1.00

87
King James I

88
Arms of the London & Bristol Company

89
John Guy

90
Guy's Ship, the "Endeavor"

91
View of the Town of Cupids

92,92A,98
Lord Bacon

#92 Type I. "Z" of "COLONIZATION" is reversed.
#92A Type II. "Z" is normal.

93,99
View of Mosquito Bay

94,100
Logging Camp

95,101
Paper Mills

96,102
King Edward VII

97,103
King Goerge V

1910 JOHN GUY ISSUE
Lithographed Perf. 12

87-97	(87-91, 92A, 93-97) 11 varieties	340.00	190.00	250.00	150.00	240.00	142.50
87	1¢ deep green, perf. 12 x 11	2.30	1.30	1.75	1.05	1.00	.60
87a	1¢ deep green	5.00	2.80	3.75	2.25	2.15	1.30
87b	1¢ deep green, perf. 12 x 14	3.65	2.10	2.75	1.65	1.80	1.10
88	2¢ carmine........................	7.50	5.00	6.50	3.25	.80	.50
88a	2¢ carmine, perf. 12 x 14	5.35	3.00	4.00	2.40	.80	.50
88c	2¢ carm., perf. 12 x 11-1/2	185.00	105.00	135.00	80.00	95.00	56.50
89	3¢ brown olive	12.00	7.00	9.00	5.50	9.00	5.50
90	4¢ dull violet	18.50	10.50	13.75	8.25	10.75	6.50
91	5¢ ultramar., perf. 14 x 12	14.00	7.75	10.00	5.75	3.50	2.10
91a	5¢ ultramarine	14.00	7.95	10.50	6.35	3.85	2.30
92	6¢ claret (I)	95.00	55.00	70.00	42.50	60.00	36.50
92A	6¢ claret (II)	28.75	16.50	21.50	13.00	21.50	13.00
93	8¢ pale brown	50.00	28.00	37.50	22.50	37.50	22.50
94	9¢ olive green	50.00	28.00	37.50	22.50	37.50	22.50
95	10¢ violet black	58.50	32.50	43.50	26.00	43.50	26.00
96	12¢ lilac brown	56.75	31.50	42.50	25.00	42.50	25.00
97	15¢ gray black	58.50	32.50	43.50	26.00	43.50	26.00

SCOTT NO.	DESCRIPTION	UNUSED NH F	AVG	UNUSED F	AVG	USED F	AVG

1911 Engraved Perf.14

98-103	6¢-15¢ cpl., 6 vars. ...	360.00	200.00	270.00	160.00	270.00	160.00
98	6¢ brown violet	23.50	13.00	17.50	10.50	17.50	10.50
99	8¢ bistre brown	58.50	32.50	43.50	26.00	43.50	26.00
100	9¢ olive green	46.50	26.50	35.00	21.00	35.00	21.00
101	10¢ violet black	100.00	56.50	75.00	45.00	75.00	45.00
102	12¢ red brown	73.50	41.50	55.00	33.50	55.00	33.50
103	15¢ slate brown	73.50	41.50	55.00	33.50	55.00	33.50

104	105	106	107	108	109
Queen Mary	King George	Prince of Wales	Prince Albert	Princess Mary	Prince Henry

110	111	112	113	114
Prince George	Prince John	Queen Alexandria	Duke of Connaught	Seal of Colony

1911 ROYAL FAMILY ISSUE

104-14	1¢-15¢ cpl., 11 vars.	385.00	220.00	290.00	175.00	195.00	162.50
104	1¢ yellow green	3.00	1.70	2.25	1.35	.22	.14
105	2¢ carmine	3.00	1.70	2.25	1.35	.22	.14
106	3¢ red brown	30.00	16.75	22.50	13.50	19.50	11.75
107	4¢ violet	25.00	14.75	18.50	11.00	15.00	9.00
108	5¢ ultramarine	11.75	6.65	8.75	5.25	1.65	1.00
109	6¢ black........................	23.50	13.00	17.50	10.50	17.50	10.50
110	8¢ blue (paper colored)	77.50	43.75	57.50	35.00	57.50	35.00
110a	8¢ blue (paper colored)	87.50	49.75	65.00	39.75	65.00	39.75
111	9¢ blue violet	29.00	16.50	21.75	13.00	21.75	13.00
112	10¢ dark green	40.00	22.50	30.00	18.00	30.00	18.00
113	12¢ plum........................	40.00	22.50	30.00	18.00	30.00	18.00
114	15¢ magenta	36.50	21.00	27.50	16.50	27.50	16.50

115,117,118,120,122,124-126   116,119,121,123

1919 TRAIL OF THE CARIBOU ISSUE

115-26	1¢-36¢ cpl., 12 vars.	215.00	125.00	175.00	105.00	145.00	86.50
115	1¢ green........................	2.00	1.15	1.60	.95	.30	.18
116	2¢ scarlet	2.40	1.40	1.90	1.15	.45	.27
117	3¢ red brown	2.75	1.60	2.25	1.35	.25	.15
118	4¢ violet	4.35	2.50	3.50	2.10	1.25	.75
119	5¢ ultramarine	5.00	2.85	4.00	2.40	1.25	.75
120	6¢ gray.........................	28.50	16.00	22.50	13.50	19.50	11.75
121	8¢ magenta.....................	20.00	11.75	16.00	9.75	13.50	8.25
122	10¢ dark green	12.00	6.95	9.50	5.75	3.25	1.95
123	12¢ orange.....................	45.00	26.00	36.50	21.75	31.50	19.00
124	15¢ dark blue	31.50	18.00	25.00	15.00	23.00	14.00
125	24¢ bistre	39.50	23.00	31.50	19.00	29.50	17.50
126	36¢ olive green	35.00	20.00	28.50	17.00	27.50	16.50

SCOTT NO.	DESCRIPTION	UNUSED NH F	AVG	UNUSED F	AVG	USED F	AVG

1920

	72 *surcharged*	**TWO CENTS**		70 & 73 *surcharged*		**THREE CENTS**	
127	2¢ on 30¢ slate	8.00	4.50	6.00	3.65	6.00	3.65

Bars 10-1/2mm apart

| 128 | 3¢ on 15¢ scarlet .... | 265.00 | 150.00 | 200.00 | 120.00 | 200.00 | 120.00 |

Bars 13-1/2mm apart

| 129 | 3¢ on 15¢ scarlet .... | 15.00 | 8.25 | 11.00 | 6.65 | 10.50 | 6.35 |
| 130 | 3¢ on 35¢ red .... | 12.75 | 7.25 | 9.75 | 5.75 | 9.75 | 5.75 |

131   132   133   134   135   136

137   138   139   140   141

142   143   144

1923-24 PICTORIAL ISSUE

131-44	1¢-24¢ cpl., 14 vars.	148.00	83.75	117.50	71.50	110.00	65.00
131	1¢ gray green	3.15	1.80	2.50	1.50	.25	.15
132	2¢ carmine	2.10	1.20	1.65	1.00	.23	.14
133	3¢ brown.............................	2.75	1.65	2.25	1.50	.20	.12
134	4¢ brown violet	2.80	1.60	2.25	1.35	1.85	1.10
135	5¢ ultramarine	4.35	2.50	3.50	2.10	2.00	1.20
136	6¢ gray black	5.35	3.00	4.25	2.50	4.25	2.50
137	8¢ dull violet	4.65	2.65	3.75	2.25	3.50	2.10
138	9¢ slate green	31.50	18.00	25.00	15.00	25.00	15.00
139	10¢ dark violet	5.00	2.85	4.00	2.40	2.10	1.25
140	11¢ olive green	8.25	4.75	6.50	3.95	6.50	3.95
141	12¢ lake	8.50	4.95	6.75	4.10	6.75	4.10
142	15¢ deep blue	10.50	6.00	8.25	5.00	7.75	4.65
143	20¢ red brown (1924) ...	9.50	5.35	7.50	4.50	6.50	3.85
144	24¢ black brown (1924)	59.50	33.00	47.50	28.50	-47.50	28.50

145,163,172
Map of
Newfoundland

146,164,173
S.S. Caribou

147,165,174
Queen Mary and
King George

148,166,175
Prince of Wales

149,167,176
Express Train

150,168,177
Newfoundland Hotel
St. John's

SCOTT NO.	DESCRIPTION	UNUSED NH F	AVG	UNUSED F	AVG	USED F	AVG

151,178
Town of
Heart's Content

152,155
Cabot Tower,
St. John's

153,169,179
War Memorial
St. John's

154,158
Post Office,
St. John's

156,170,180
First Airplane to Cross
Atlantic Non-Stop

157,171,181
House of Parliament,
St. John's

159,182
Grand Falls,
Labrador

1928 TOURIST PUBLICITY ISSUE
Unwatermarked, Thin paper, dull colors

Scott	Description	NH F	NH AVG	Unused F	Unused AVG	Used F	Used AVG
145-59	1¢-30¢ cpl., 15 vars.	99.50	57.50	82.50	49.75	71.50	42.75
145	1¢ deep green	1.60	.95	1.30	.80	.70	.45
146	2¢ deep carmine	2.10	1.20	1.75	1.05	.65	.40
147	3¢ brown	2.70	1.55	2.25	1.35	.40	.25
148	4¢ lilac rose	3.40	2.10	2.85	1.70	1.95	1.15
149	5¢ slate green	6.50	3.75	5.25	3.25	3.75	2.25
150	6¢ ultramarine	5.15	3.00	4.25	2.60	3.50	2.10
151	8¢ light red brown	6.00	3.50	5.00	3.00	4.50	2.70
152	9¢ myrtle green	7.50	4.25	6.25	3.75	5.75	3.50
153	10¢ dark violet	7.25	4.10	6.00	3.60	5.00	3.00
154	12¢ brown carmine	5.75	3.35	4.75	2.85	4.00	2.40
155	14¢ red brown	7.50	4.25	6.25	3.75	5.00	3.00
156	15¢ dark blue	8.65	5.00	7.25	4.35	7.00	4.15
157	20¢ gray black	6.95	4.00	5.75	3.50	5.00	3.00
158	28¢ gray green	25.75	15.00	21.50	13.00	21.50	13.00
159	30¢ olive brown	7.50	4.25	6.25	3.75	6.25	3.75

1929
136 surcharged in red

Scott	Description	NH F	NH AVG	Unused F	Unused AVG	Used F	Used AVG
160	3¢ on 6¢ gray black	4.00	2.30	3.35	2.00	3.35	2.00

1929-31 Tourist Publicity Issue
Types of 1928 re-engraved
Unwatermarked, Thicker paper, brighter colors

Scott	Description	NH F	NH AVG	Unused F	Unused AVG	Used F	Used AVG
163-71	1¢-20¢ cpl., 9 vars.	121.50	70.00	100.00	60.00	61.50	37.00
163	1¢ green	1.90	1.10	1.60	.95	.50	.30
164	2¢ deep carmine	2.00	1.15	1.65	1.00	.25	.15
165	3¢ deep red brown	2.40	1.40	2.00	1.20	.20	.12
166	4¢ magenta	3.30	1.90	2.75	1.65	1.20	.75
167	5¢ slate green	3.90	2.25	3.25	1.95	1.20	.75
168	6¢ ultramarine	10.50	6.00	8.75	5.25	8.75	5.25
169	10¢ dark violet	4.50	2.60	3.75	2.25	1.90	1.15
170	15¢ deep blue (1930)	36.00	21.00	30.00	18.00	26.50	16.00
171	20¢ gray black (1931)	63.50	36.75	52.50	31.75	24.00	14.50

1931 Tourist Publicity Issue
Types of 1928 re-engraved, watermarked, coat of arms
Thicker paper, brighter colors.

Scott	Description	NH F	NH AVG	Unused F	Unused AVG	Used F	Used AVG
172-82	1¢-30¢ cpl., 11 vars.	200.00	115.00	165.00	100.00	125.00	75.00
172	1¢ green	2.40	1.40	2.00	1.20	1.00	.60
173	2¢ red	4.00	2.30	3.35	2.00	1.35	.85
174	3¢ red brown	3.60	2.10	3.00	1.80	1.00	.60

SCOTT NO.	DESCRIPTION	UNUSED NH F	AVG	UNUSED F	AVG	USED F	AVG
175	4¢ rose	5.25	3.00	4.35	2.60	1.70	1.00
176	5¢ greenish gray	11.50	6.75	9.50	5.75	7.50	4.50
177	6¢ ultramarine	24.00	13.75	20.00	12.00	18.75	11.00
178	8¢ light red brown	24.00	13.75	20.00	12.00	18.75	11.00
179	10¢ dark violet	13.00	7.50	10.75	6.50	7.75	4.65
180	15¢ deep blue	42.00	24.50	35.00	21.00	33.50	20.00
181	20¢ gray black	43.75	26.00	36.50	22.00	13.00	8.00
182	30¢ olive brown	36.00	21.00	30.00	18.00	28.75	17.00

183,184,253
Codfish

185,186
King George

187
Queen Mary

188,189
Prince of Wales

190,191,257
Caribou

192
Princess Elizabeth

5c. Die I. Antlers equal in height.
Die II. Antlers under "T" higher.

193,260
Salmon

194,261
Newfoundland Dog

195,262
Northern Seal

196,263
Trans-Atlantic Beacon

197,265
Sealing Fleet

198,199,266
Fishing Fleet

208
The Duchess of York

209,259
Corner Brook Paper Mills

210,264
Loading Iron Ore,
Bell Island

1932-37 RESOURCES ISSUE Perf. 13-1/2

Scott No.	Description						
183-99	1¢-48¢ cpl., 17 vars.	87.50	54.50	72.50	46.75	50.00	32.85
183	1¢ green	1.90	1.15	1.60	1.00	.45	.28
184	1¢ gray black	.32	.21	.27	.18	.11	.07
185	2¢ rose	1.65	.95	1.40	.85	.23	.15
186	2¢ green	1.40	.90	1.20	.80	.11	.07
187	3¢ orange brown	1.20	.75	1.00	.65	.18	.12
188	4¢ deep violet	5.65	3.40	4.75	3.00	1.65	1.10
189	4¢ rose lake	.70	.45	.60	.40	.15	.10
190	5¢ violet brown	6.25	4.00	5.25	3.50	1.00	.65
191	5¢ deep violet (II)	1.10	.65	.95	.60	.11	.07
191a	5¢ deep violet (I)	10.75	6.85	9.00	6.00	.75	.50
192	6¢ dull blue	13.00	8.00	11.00	7.00	10.00	6.50
193	10¢ olive black	1.60	1.00	1.35	.90	.75	.50
194	14¢ black	3.50	2.20	2.95	1.95	2.50	1.60
195	15¢ magenta	3.50	2.20	2.95	1.95	2.50	1.60
196	20¢ gray green	3.35	2.15	2.85	1.90	.95	.60
197	25¢ gray	3.85	2.45	3.25	2.15	2.00	1.30
198	30¢ ultramarine	30.00	18.50	25.00	16.00	25.00	16.00
199	48¢ red brown (1937)	13.00	7.75	10.75	6.75	4.75	3.15

1932 Perf. 13-1/2

Scott No.	Description						
208-10	7¢-24¢ cpl., 3 vars.	7.85	4.95	6.50	4.35	5.25	3.50
208	7¢ red brown	1.85	1.15	1.50	1.00	1.30	.85
209	8¢ orange red	1.95	1.20	1.65	1.10	1.25	.80
210	24¢ light blue	4.50	2.90	3.75	2.50	3.25	2.10

SCOTT NO.	DESCRIPTION	UNUSED NH		UNUSED		USED	
		F	AVG	F	AVG	F	AVG

211 *Plane & Dog Sled*

1933 LAND & SEA OVERPRINT

| 211 | 15¢ brown | 9.50 | 6.00 | 8.00 | 5.25 | 8.00 | 5.25 |

212 *Sir Humphrey Gilbert*

213 *Compton Castle, Devon*

214 *The Gilbert Arms*

215 *Eton College*

216 *Token to Gilbert from Queen Elizabeth*

217 *Gilbert Commissioned by Queen Elizabeth*

218 *Gilbert's Fleet Leaving Plymouth*

219 *The Fleet Arriving at St. John's*

220 *Annexation of Newfoundland*

221 *Coat of Arms of England*

222 *Gilbert on the "Squirrel"*

223 *1624 Map of Newfoundland*

224 *Queen Elizabeth I*

225 *Gilbert Statue at Truro*

1933 SIR HUMPHREY GILBERT ISSUE

212-25	1¢-32¢ cpl., 14 vars.	167.50	105.00	137.50	90.00	125.00	82.50
212	1¢ gray black	1.30	.80	1.10	.70	.75	.50
213	2¢ green	1.55	.95	1.30	.85	.75	.50
214	3¢ yellow brown	2.15	1.40	1.80	1.20	1.35	.90
215	4¢ carmine	2.15	1.40	1.80	1.20	.50	.32
216	5¢ dull violet	2.70	1.80	2.25	1.50	1.30	.85
217	7¢ blue	20.00	12.50	15.00	10.00	12.50	8.25
218	8¢ orange red	10.00	6.50	8.50	5.65	8.50	5.65
219	9¢ ultramarine	11.50	7.25	9.50	6.25	9.50	6.25
220	10¢ red brown	10.75	6.85	9.00	6.00	5.75	3.85
221	14¢ black	22.75	14.00	19.00	12.50	19.00	12.50
222	15¢ claret	21.50	13.50	18.00	12.00	18.00	12.00
223	20¢ deep green	12.50	8.00	10.50	7.00	7.50	5.00
224	24¢ violet brown	29.50	18.50	24.50	16.00	22.50	15.00
225	32¢ gray	29.50	18.50	24.50	16.00	22.50	15.00

SCOTT NO.	DESCRIPTION	UNUSED F/NH	F	USED F

226-229

230-232

1935 SILVER JUBILEE

SCOTT NO.	DESCRIPTION	F/NH	F	F
226-29	4¢-24¢ cpl. 4 vars.	13.50	11.50	10.85
226	4¢ bright rose	1.40	1.20	1.10
227	5¢ violet	1.40	1.20	1.10
228	7¢ dark blue	3.25	2.75	2.75
229	24¢ olive green	8.00	6.85	6.85

1937 CORONATION ISSUE

SCOTT NO.	DESCRIPTION	F/NH	F	F
230-32	2¢-5¢ cpl., 3 vars.	2.40	2.10	1.90
230	2¢ deep green	.70	.60	.55
231	4¢ carmine rose	.70	.60	.50
232	5¢ dark violet	1.10	.95	.95

233

234

3c DIE I: Fine Impression
DIE II: Coarse Impression

1937 LONG CORONATION ISSUE

SCOTT NO.	DESCRIPTION	F/NH	F	F
233-43	11 varieties	33.50	28.50	25.00
233	1¢ Codfish	.50	.45	.25
234	3¢ Map, Die I	2.10	1.80	.75
234a	3¢ Same, Die II	1.75	1.50	.50
235	7¢ Caribou	2.35	2.00	1.80
236	8¢ Paper Mills	2.35	2.00	1.80
237	10¢ Salmon	4.50	3.85	3.50
238	14¢ Newfoundland Dog	3.35	2.85	2.85
239	15¢ Northern Seal	4.00	3.40	3.30
240	20¢ Cape Race	3.15	2.65	2.30
241	24¢ Bell Island	4.00	3.40	3.35
242	25¢ Sealing Fleet	4.25	3.65	3.15
243	48¢ Fishing Fleet	4.50	3.85	3.85

245,254
King George VI

246,255
Queen Elizabeth

247,256
Princess Elizabeth

248,258
Queen Mary

1938 ROYAL FAMILY Perf. 13-1/2

SCOTT NO.	DESCRIPTION	F/NH	F	F
245-48	2¢-7¢ cpl., 4 vars.	7.25	6.25	1.65
245	2¢ green	1.85	1.60	.14
246	3¢ dark carmine	1.85	1.60	.16
247	4¢ light blue	2.35	2.00	.14
248	7¢ dark ultramarine	1.65	1.40	1.35

249

252

249	5¢ violet blue	1.10	1.00	1.00

249 SURCHARGED

250	2¢ on 5¢ violet blue	1.50	1.35	1.10
251	4¢ on 5¢ violet blue	1.25	1.15	.90

1941 GRENFELL ISSUE

252	5¢ dull blue	.45	.40	.35

1941-44 RESOURCES ISSUE
Designs of 1931-38, Perf. 12-1/2

SCOTT NO.	DESCRIPTION	F/NH	F	F
253-66	14 varieties	18.00	16.25	11.50
253	1¢ dark gray	.28	.25	.09
254	2¢ deep green	.33	.30	.08
255	3¢ rose carmine	.38	.35	.08
256	4¢ blue	.75	.65	.08
257	5¢ violet	.80	.70	.10
258	7¢ violet blue (1942)	1.20	1.10	1.00
259	8¢ red	.95	.85	.70
260	10¢ brownish black	1.00	.90	.60
261	14¢ black	1.85	1.65	1.30
262	15¢ rose violet	2.00	1.80	1.40
263	20¢ green	1.85	1.65	1.30
264	24¢ deep blue	2.35	2.10	1.70
265	25¢ slate	2.35	2.10	1.70
266	48¢ red brown (1944)	3.00	2.70	1.85

267

268

269

270

1943-47

267	30¢ Memorial University	1.35	1.25	1.10
268	2¢ on 30¢ Univ. (1946)	.35	.30	.30
269	4¢ Elizabeth (1947)	.35	.30	.10
270	5¢ Cabot (1947)	.35	.30	.20

SCOTT NO.	DESCRIPTION	UNUSED NH F	AVG	UNUSED F	AVG	USED F	AVG

AIR POST STAMPS

C2   C3

1919

C2	$1 on 15¢ scarlet	315.00	175.00	235.00	140.00	235.00	140.00
C2a	Same, w/o comma after "post"	380. 00	215.00	285.00	170.00	285.00	170.00

1921

C3	35¢ red............................	220.00	125.00	165.00	100.00	165.00	100.00
C3a	Same, w/ period after "1921"	275.00	160.00	200.00	125.00	200.00	125.00

C6,C9
Airplane and Dog Team

C7,C10
First Transatlantic Airmail

C8,C11
Routes of Historic Transatlantic Flights

1931 Unwatermarked

C6	15¢ brown	13.50	7.50	10.00	6.00	10.00	6.00
C7	50¢ green..........................	28.75	16.50	21.50	13.00	21.50	13.00
C8	$1 blue..............................	95.00	53.50	70.00	42.50	70.00	42.50

Watermarked Coat of Arms

C9	15¢ brown	10.50	5.95	7.75	4.75	7.75	4.75
C10	50¢ green..........................	46.50	26.50	35.00	21.00	35.00	21.00
C11	$1 blue..............................	120.00	68.50	90.00	55.00	85.00	52.50

C12   C13   C18   C19

1932 TRANS-ATLANTIC FLIGHT

C12	$1.50 on $1 blue	565.00	325.00	450.00	275.00	450.00	275.00

1933 LABRADOR ISSUE

C13-17	5¢-75¢ cpl., 5 vars.	210.00	120.00	175.00	105.00	175.00	105.00
C13	5¢ "Put to Flight"	15.75	9.25	13.00	8.00	13.00	8.00
C14	10¢ "Land of Heart's Delight"	22.50	12.75	18.75	11.00	18.75	11.00
C15	30¢ "Spotting the Herd"	42.50	25.00	35.00	21.50	35.00	21.50
C16	60¢ "News from Home" ...	65.00	38.50	55.00	33.50	55.00	33.50
C17	75¢ "Labrador, Land of Gold"	75.00	42.50	62.50	37.50	62.50	37.50

1933 BALBO FLIGHT ISSUE

C18	$4.50 on 75¢ bistre	800.00	460.00	675.00	400.00	675.00	400.00

1943

C19	7¢ St. John's	.55	....	.50	....	.27	....

VERY FINE QUALITY: To determine the Very Fine price, add the difference between the Fine and Average prices to the Fine quality price. For example: if the Fine price is $10.00 and the Average price is $6.00, the Very Fine price would be $14.00. From 1935 to date, add 20% to the Fine price to arrive at the Very Fine price.

SCOTT NO.	DESCRIPTION	UNUSED F/NH	F	USED F
	POSTAGE DUE STAMPS			

J1-J7

1939 Unwatermarked, perf. 10-1/2 x 10

SCOTT NO.	DESCRIPTION	UNUSED F/NH	F	USED F
J1	1¢ yellow green	225	1.95	1.95
J2	2¢ vermillion	325	2.80	2.80
J3	3¢ ultramarine	425	3.65	3.65
J4	4¢ yellow orange	525	4.50	4.50

SCOTT NO.	DESCRIPTION	UNUSED F/NH	F	USED F
J5	5¢ pale brown	3.85	3.25	3.25
J6	10¢ dark violet	3.85	3.25	3.25
	1946-49 **Unwatermarked, perf. 11**			
J1a	1¢ yellow green	4.25	3.75	3.75
	Unwatermarked, perf. 11 x 9			
J2a	2¢ vermilion	4.25	3.75	3.75
J3a	3¢ ultramarine	5.00	4.50	4.50
J4a	4¢ yellow orange	6.75	6.00	6.00
	Watermarked, perf. 11			
J7	10¢ dark violet	8.50	7.50	7.50

NEW BRUNSWICK

SCOTT NO.	DESCRIPTION	UNUSED O.G. F	AVG	UNUSED F	AVG	USED F	AVG

Crown of Great Britain Surrounded by Heraldic Flowers of the United Kingdom

1-4

1851 PENCE ISSUE, Imperforate

		UNUSED O.G. F	AVG	UNUSED F	AVG	USED F	AVG
1	3p red	1500.00	900.00	1050.00	650.00	335.00	200.00
2	6p olive yellow	....	....	2750.00	1650.00	625.00	375.00
3	1sh bright red violet	....	....	....	....	2500.00	1500.00
4	1sh dull violet	....	....	....	....	2500.00	1500.00

6　7　8　9　10　11

1860-63 CENTS ISSUE

		UNUSED O.G. F	AVG	UNUSED F	AVG	USED F	AVG
6	1¢ Locomotive	22.50	13.50	18.50	11.00	20.00	11.00
7	2¢ Queen Victoria, org. (1863)	11.00	6.25	8.75	5.25	9.50	5.75
8	5¢ same, yellow green	11.50	6.65	9.00	5.50	9.50	5.75
9	10¢ same, vermillion	26.75	16.00	22.50	13.50	22.50	13.50
10	12-1/2¢ Ships	50.00	28.75	40.00	24.00	40.00	24.00
11	17¢ Prince of Wales	41.50	24.00	32.50	20.00	32.50	20.00

ORIGINAL GUM: Prior to 1893, the Unused price is for stamps either without gum or with partial gum. If you require full original gum, use the Unused OG column. Never Hinged quality is scarce on these issues — please write for specific quotations if NH is required.

SCOTT NO.	DESCRIPTION	UNUSED O.G. F	AVG	UNUSED F	AVG	USED F	AVG

NOVA SCOTIA

1

2-7

*Royal Crown and Heraldic
Flowers of the United Kingdom*

1851-53 PENCE ISSUE
Imperf. Blue paper

No.	Description	O.G. F	O.G. AVG	Unused F	Unused AVG	Used F	Used AVG
1	1p Queen Victoria	1575.00	900.00	1100.00	675.00	375.00	225.00
2	3p blue	625.00	365.00	450.00	275.00	135.00	80.00
3	3p dark blue	850.00	475.00	600.00	360.00	150.00	90.00
4	6p yellow green	....	....	2400.00	1450.00	385.00	230.00
5	6p dark green	....	....	4750.00	2850.00	750.00	450.00
6	1sh reddish violet	....	....	....	....	3000.00	1800.00
7	1sh dull violet	....	....	....	....	3000.00	1800.00

8-10   11,12   13

Queen Victoria

1860-63 CENTS ISSUE
White or Yellowish paper, Perf. 12

No.	Description	O.G. F	O.G. AVG	Unused F	Unused AVG	Used F	Used AVG
8	1¢ black	6.25	3.65	5.00	3.00	5.50	3.35
9	2¢ lilac	9.65	5.50	7.75	4.65	7.50	4.50
10	5¢ blue	280.00	160.00	225.00	135.00	8.50	5.15
11	8-1/2¢ green	6.25	3.65	5.00	3.00	13.50	8.00
12	10¢ vermillion	9.35	5.25	7.50	4.50	7.75	4.65
13	12-1/2¢ black	31.50	18.00	25.00	15.00	23.50	14.00

SCOTT NO.	DESCRIPTION	UNUSED O.G. F	AVG	UNUSED F	AVG	USED F	AVG

PRINCE EDWARD ISLAND

1,5　　2,6　　3,7　　4　　8

Queen Victoria

1861 PENCE ISSUE, Perf. 9

1	2p rose	425.00	240.00	300.00	180.00	175.00	105.00
2	3p blue	750.00	425.00	525.00	315.00	325.00	195.00
3	6p yellow green	1050.00	565.00	750.00	450.00	435.00	260.00

1862-65 PENCE ISSUE, Perf. 11 to 12

4	1p yellow orange	26.75	17.50	21.50	13.00	22.50	13.50
5	2p rose	6.85	4.15	5.50	3.35	5.75	3.50
6	3p blue	8.75	5.00	7.00	4.25	8.50	5.25
7	6p green	68.50	40.00	55.00	33.50	55.00	33.50
8	9p violet	50.00	28.50	40.00	24.00	40.00	24.00

9　　10

Queen Victoria

1868 PENCE ISSUE

9	4p black	11.00	6.25	8.75	5.25	19.50	11.75

1870 PENCE ISSUE

10	4-1/2p brown	46.50	26.75	37.50	22.50	37.50	22.50

11　　12　　13　　14　　15　　16

Queen Victoria

1872 CENTS ISSUE

11	1¢ brown orange	6.00	3.50	5.00	3.00	8.75	5.25
12	2¢ ultramarine	13.50	7.75	11.00	6.75	26.50	16.00
13	3¢ rose	17.50	10.00	14.50	8.75	14.50	8.75
14	4¢ green	6.35	3.75	5.25	3.25	14.00	8.50
15	6¢ black	6.35	3.75	5.25	3.25	14.00	8.50
16	12¢ violet	6.35	3.75	5.25	3.25	17.50	10.50

QUALITY AND CONDITION DEFINITIONS

NEVER HINGED (NH)
This simply means that the stamps have never been hinged (Post Office or Mint condition). For 1847 through 1892, please send a want list. For 1893 through 1963, separate pricing columns are provided for Never Hinged. From 1964 to date, all stamps will be Never Hinged.

ORIGINAL GUM (OG)
From 1893 to date, unused stamps issued with gum will have full gum, although the stamp may have been hinged or have a hinge remnant. Prior to 1893, stamps normally will have partial gum or no gum — if you require full gum, use the approriate pricing columns.

AVERAGE (AVG)
The normal quality for earlier issues, generally acceptable to the majority of collectors. Perforations usually will touch or slightly cut into stamp design. Prices are listed for this grade until 1935. From 1935 to date, Average quality, when available, is priced at 25% below Fine. On these earlier issues, if you require better than Average quality, order the desired Fine quality.

Pre-1900 Average

Perfs will touch or slightly cut into the design.

Color should not be faded, but reasonable for the issue; slight oxidation or a light impression is acceptable.

Used copies may have moderately heavy cancellations as long as important features of the design are not obscured.

1900-1934 Average

Perfs may touch or slightly cut into the design.

Color should not be faded, but reasonable for the issue; slight oxidation or a light impression is acceptable.

Used copies may have moderately heavy cancellations as long as important features of the design are not obscured.

FINE (F)

Stamps of this quality will have perforations clear of the design, although designs may not be "well centered", that is, evenly positioned between the four edges. From 1935 to date, this is the quality provided at the prices given in the Fine column of our catalog. On some extremely poor-centered issues, perforations may touch the design on Fine quality. These are indicated by a "†" after the heading above the section. If you require well-centered stamps please order Very Fine.

Pre-1900 Fine

Perfs clear of the design (with the exception of a few varieties with difficult centering); the stamp need not be well-centered.

Good color, unfaded, and clean impression; no oxidizing.

Used copies from these years should have moderately light, readable, unsmeared cancellations.

1900-1940 Fine

Perfs clear of the design; on some normally poorly-centered issues, perfs may barely touch.

Unfaded, clean; good, clear impression.

Used copies must have a clean, readable cancellation.

1941 to date Fine

Perfs must be clear of design.

Unfaded, clean; good clear impression.

Used copies must have a clean, readable cancellation.

VERY FINE (VF)

Stamps of Very Fine quality are well centered. The difficulty of finding VF stamps, particularly on earlier issues, is reflected in the considerably higher retail price. Use the following pricing guidelines:

For 1847 to 1934, add the difference between the Average price and the Fine price to the Fine price to arrive at the Very Fine price.

For 1935 to date, add 20% to the Fine price. The minimum extra charge per item is 3¢. Note that all VF stamps from 1935 to 1963, and all Fine or better stamps from 1964 to date, will be Never Hinged.

Pre-1900 Very Fine

Perfs well clear of the design, or design reasonably well positioned with the margins or perforations.

Generally better color than usual; good, clear impressions.

Used copies must have light, unsmeared cancellations.

1900-1940 Very Fine

Perfs well clear of the design; well centered, but need not be *perfectly* centered.

Full color; neat, clear impression.

Used copies must have neat, clean, readable cancellations.

1941 to date Very Fine

Perfs well clear of the design; well centered, but need not be *perfectly* centered.

Full color; neat, clear impression.

Used copies must have neat, clean, readable cancellations.

The UNITED STATES
Stamp Identifier

SHOWS YOU HOW TO DISTINGUISH BETWEEN THE RARE AND COMMON UNITED STATES STAMPS THAT LOOK ALIKE

What does "Grill with points up" mean? "Single line watermark?" How can I tell whether my 15¢ "Landing of Columbus" stamp of 1869 is worth $1,150.00 (Type I) or $575.00 (Type II)?

At one time or another, every collector of United States stamps asks questions like these. For very often, it is a minute difference in design that determines not only whether a stamp is Type I, II, or III, but whether it is a great rarity or just another common variety. The different varieties of the 1¢ Franklin design of 1851-56, for example, range in price from $60.00 to $95,000.00. So it pays to know how to tell the correct types of your stamps! To enable you to do so easily and quickly is the purpose of this U.S. STAMP IDENTIFIER.

Other seemingly identical, but actually different United States stamps may be told apart by differ-ences in perforations, watermarks, grills or methods in printing. These terms are fully explained in the glossary at the back of this IDENT-IFIER. And charts are included which make it easy for you to quickly identify the most troublesome of U.S. stamps — the hard-to-classify regular issues of 1908 to 1932.

NOTE: The illustrations and catalog numbers used herein are from the Standard Postage Stamp Catalogue, by special permission of the publishers, Scott Publications, Inc.

FIRST UNITED STATES POSTAGE ISSUE OF 1847

1   2
Original Issue   *948 1947 "Cipex" Souvenir Sheet*   3   4
Reproductions of 1875

The first stamps of the United States Government the 5¢ and 10¢ designs shown to the left above were placed in use in July 1847, superseding the Postmasters' Provisionals then being used in several cities. In 1875, official reproductions (right above) were made from newly enrgraved printing plates.

In the original 5¢ design, the top edge of Franklin's shirt touches the circular frame about at a level with the top of the "F" of "FIVE", while in the 1875 reproduction it is on a level with the top of the figure "5."

In the original 10¢ design, the left edge of Washington's coat points to the "T" of "TEN," and the right edge points between the "T" and "S" of "CENTS." In the reproductions, the left and right outlines of the coat point to the right edge of "X" and to the center of "S" of "CENTS" respectively. Also, on the 1875 reprints, the eyes have a sleepy look and the line of the mouth is straighter.

The 1947 "Cipex" Souvenir Sheet, issued on the hundredth anniversary of United States stamps, features reproductions of the two original designs. Stamps cut out of the souvenir sheet are, of course, valid for postage. However, no difficulty in identification should be encountered since the 1947 reproductions are light blue (5¢) instead of the original red brown and brownish orange (10¢) instead of the original black.

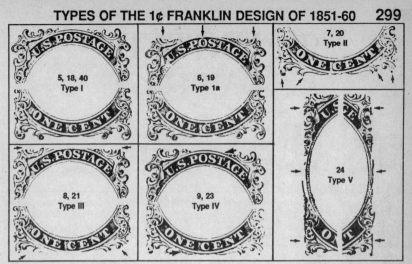

5, 18, 40
Type I

6, 19
Type 1a

7, 20
Type II

8, 21
Type III

9, 23
Type IV

24
Type V

TYPE I has the most complete design of the various types of this stamp. At the top and bottom there is an unbroken curved line running outside the bands reading "U.S. POSTAGE" and "ONE CENT." The scrolls at bottom are turned under, forming curls. The scrolls and outer line at top are complete.

TYPE Ia is like Type I at bottom but ornaments and curved line at top are partly cut away.

TYPE Ib (not illustrated) is like Type I at top but little curls at bottom are not quite so complete nor clear and scroll work is partly cut away.

TYPE II has the outside bottom line complete, but the little curls of the bottom scrolls, and the lower part of the plume ornaments are missing. Side ornaments are complete.

TYPE III has the outside lines at both top and bottom partly cut away in the middle. The side ornaments are complete.

TYPE IIIa (not illustrated) is similar to Type III with the outer line cut away at top or bottom, but not both. 8A, 22.

TYPE IV is similar to Type II but the curved lines at top or bottom (or both) have been recut in several different ways, and usually appear thicker than Type II.

TYPE V is similar to Type III but has the side ornaments partly cut away. Type V occurs only on perforated stamps.

TYPES OF 3¢ WASHINGTON DESIGN OF 1851-60

10, 11, 25, 41
Type I

26
Type II

26a
Type IIa

TYPE I has a frame line around the top, bottom and sides.
TYPE II has the frame line removed at top and bottom, while the side frame lines are continuous from top to bottom of the plate.

TYPE IIa is similar to Type II, but the side frame lines were recut individually, hence are broken between stamps.

TYPES OF THE 5¢ JEFFERSON DESIGN OF 1851-60

12, 27-29
Type I

30, 30A, 42
Type II

TYPE I is a complete design with projections (arrow) at the top and bottom as well as at the sides.

TYPE II has the projections at the top and bottom partly or completely cut away.

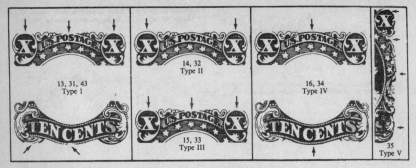

TYPE I has the "shells" at the lower corners practically complete, while the outer line below "TEN CENTS" is very nearly complete. At the top, the outer lines are broken above "U.S. POSTAGE" and above the "X" in each corner.

TYPE II has the design complete at the top, but the outer line at the bottom is broken in the middle and the "shells" are partially cut away.

TYPE III has both top and bottom outer lines partly cut away: that is similar to Type I at the top and Type II at the bottom.

TYPE IV has the outer lines at the top or bottom of the stamp, or at both places, recut to show more strongly and heavily.

TYPES I, II, and IV have complete ornaments at the sides and three small circles or pearls (arrow) at the outer edges of the bottom panel.

TYPE V has the side ornaments, including one or two of the small "pearls," partly cut away. The outside line over the "X" at the right top has also been partly cut away.

TYPES OF THE ISSUE OF 1861

Shortly after the outbreak of the Civil War in 1861, the Post Office denometized all stamps issued up to that time in order to prevent their use by the Confederacy. Two new sets of designs, consisting of six stamps shown above plus 24¢ and 30¢ denominations, were prepared by the American Bank Note Company. The first designs, except for the 10¢ and 24¢ values, were not regularly issued and are extremely rare and valuable. The second designs became the regular issue of 1861. The illustrations at the left below show the first (or un-issued) designs, which were all printed on thin, semi-transparent paper. The second (or regular) designs are shown at the right.

63 shows a small dash (arrow) under the top of the ornaments at the right of the figure "1" in the upper left hand corner of the stamp.

3¢ 1861 PINK (Scott's #64) — It is impossible to describe a "pink" in words, but it might be helpful to remember that this stamp is usually rather heavily inked, and has a tinge of blue or purple which makes it stand out from the various shades of rose to red brown sometimes mistaken for it.

64, 66 and 74 show a small ball (arrow) at each corner of the design. Also, the ornaments at the corner are larger than in A25a.

67, 75 and 76 have a leaflet (arrow) projecting from the scrolled ornament at each corner of the stamp.

58, 62B

58, 62B has no curved line below the row of stars and there is only one outer line of the ornaments above them.

68

68 has a heavy curved line below the row of stars (arrow), and the ornaments above the stars have a double outer line.

59   **69**

69 has an oval and scroll (arrow) in each corner of the design. **59** has no such design and the corners are rounded.

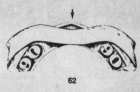

62

62 does not have the row of dashes or spot of color present in **72**.

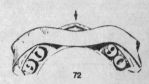

72

72 has a row of small dashes between the parallel lines of the angle at the top center of the stamp. There is also a spot of color (arrow) in the apex of the lower line of the single.

TYPES OF THE 15¢ "LANDING OF COLUMBUS" DESIGN OF 1869

118: Type I   **119: Type II**

118, TYPE I has the central picture without the frame line shown in Type II.
119, TYPE II has a frame line (arrows) around the central picture; also a diamond shaped ornament appears below the "T" of "POSTAGE."

129, TYPE III (not illustrated) is like Type I except that the fringe of brown shading lines which appears around the sides and bottom of the picture on Types I and II has been removed.

TYPES OF THE 1870-71 AND 1873 ISSUES

The stamps of the 1870-71 issue were printed by the National Bank Note Company. The similar issue of 1873 was printed by the Continental Bank Note Company. When Continental took over the plates previously used by National, they applied the so-called "secret marks" to the designs of the 1¢ through 15¢ denominations, by which the two issues, can be distinguished as shown below. The illustrations at the left show the original designs of 1870-71; those at the right show the secret marks applied to the issue of 1873.

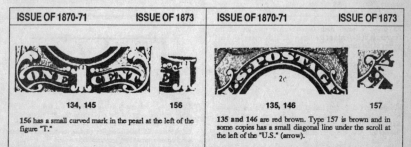

| ISSUE OF 1870-71 | ISSUE OF 1873 | ISSUE OF 1870-71 | ISSUE OF 1873 |

134, 145   **156**   **135, 146**   **157**

156 has a small curved mark in the pearl at the left of the figure "T."

135 and **146** are red brown. Type **157** is brown and in some copies has a small diagonal line under the scroll at the left of the "U.S." (arrow).

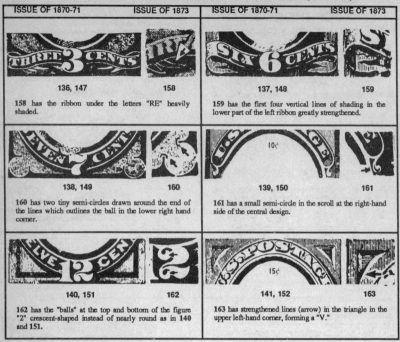

ISSUE OF 1870-71	ISSUE OF 1873	ISSUE OF 1870-71	ISSUE OF 1873

136, 147   **158**

158 has the ribbon under the letters "RE" heavily shaded.

137, 148   **159**

159 has the first four vertical lines of shading in the lower part of the left ribbon greatly strengthened.

138, 149   **160**

160 has two tiny semi-circles drawn around the end of the lines which outlines the ball in the lower right hand corner.

139, 150   **161**

161 has a small semi-circle in the scroll at the right-hand side of the central design.

140, 151   **162**

162 has the "balls" at the top and bottom of the figure "2" crescent-shaped instead of nearly round as in 140 and 151.

141, 152   **163**

163 has strengthened lines (arrow) in the triangle in the upper left-hand corner, forming a "V."

RE-ENGRAVED DESIGNS OF 1881-82

The 1¢, 3¢, 6¢ and 10¢ denominations of the 1873 & 1879 issues, shown above, were re-engraved in 1881-82. The new plates resulted in the four variations described below. The background shading lines in all four of these stamps appear stronger and more heavily inked than the earlier designs.

206

206 has strengthened vertical shading lines in the upper part of the stamp, making the background appear almost solid. Lines of shading have also been added to the curving ornaments in the upper corners.

208

208 has only three vertical lines between the edge of the panel and the outside left margin of the stamp. (In the preceding issues there were four such lines.)

207

207 has a solid shading line at the sides of the central oval (arrow) that is only about half the previous width. Also a short horizontal line has been cut below the "TS" of "CENTS."

209

209 has only four vertical lines between the left side of the oval and the edge of the shield. (In the preceding issues there were five such lines.) Also, the lines in the background have been made much heavier so that these stamps appear more heavily inked than previous issues.

TYPES OF THE REGULAR ISSUES OF 1890-98

Two varieties of the 1890-93 issue

1890-93. This issue, printed by the American Bank Note Company, consists of a 1¢, 2¢, 3¢, 4¢, 5¢, 6¢, 8¢, 10¢, 15¢, 30¢ and 90¢ denomination.

Two varieties of the 1894-98 issue

1894-98. This issue — and all subsequent regular United States issues — were printed by the Bureau of Engraving and Printing, Washington, D.C. In more recent years, starting in 1943, some commemorative issues were printed by private firms. The 1894-98 "Bureau" issue is similar in design to the issue of 1890 but triangles (arrows) were added to the upper corners of the stamps and there are some differences in denominations.

2¢ "CAP ON 2" VARIETY OF 1890

Cap on left "2"   *Cap on right "2"*

Plate defects in the printing of the 2¢ "Washington" stamp of 1890 accounts for the "Cap on left 2" and "Cap on both 2s" varieties illustrated above.

TYPES OF THE 2¢ WASHINGTON DESIGN OF 1894-98

The triangles in the upper right and left hand corners of the stamp determine the type.

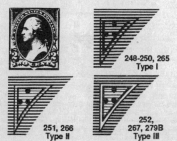

248-250, 265
Type I

251, 266
Type II

252,
267, 279B
Type III

TYPE I has horizontal lines of the same thickness within and without the triangle.

TYPE II has horizontal lines which cross the triangle but are thinner within it than without.

TYPE III has thin lines inside the triangle and these do not cross the double frame line of the triangle.

10¢ WEBSTER DESIGN OF 1898

282C
Type I

283
Type II

TYPE I has an unbroken, white curved line below the words "TEN CENTS."

In TYPE II the white line is broken by the ornaments at a point just below the "E" in "TEN" and the "T" in "CENTS" (arrows).

$1 PERRY DESIGN OF 1894-95

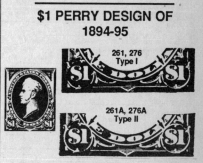

261, 276
Type I

261A, 276A
Type II

In Type I the circles around the "$1" are broken at the point where they meet the curved line below "ONE DOLLAR" (arrows).

Type II shows these circles complete.

2¢ COLUMBIAN "BROKEN HAT" VARIETY OF 1893

As a result of a plate defect, some stamps of the 2¢ Columbian design show a noticeable white notch or gash in the hat worn by the third figure to the left of Columbus. This "broken hat" variety is somewhat less common than the regular 2¢ design.

231   *Broken Hat variety, 231C*

4¢ COLUMBIAN BLUE ERROR — Collectors often mistake the many shades of the normal 4¢ ultramarine for the rare and valuable blue error. Actually, the "error" is not ultramarine at all, but a deep blue, similar to the deeper blue shades of the 1¢ Columbian.

Perforation	Watermark	Other Identifying Features	1¢	2¢	4¢	5¢	3¢ thru $1 denominations	8¢ thru $1 denominations
PERF. 12	USPS	White paper	331	332			333-42	422-23
		Bluish gray paper	357	358			359-66	
	USPS	White paper	374	375	405	406	376-82 407	414-21
COIL 12	USPS	Perf. Horizontal	348	349			350-51	
		Perf. Vertical	352	353			354-56	
	USPS	Perf. Horizontal	385	386				
		Perf. Vertical	387	388			389	
IMPERF.	USPS		343	344			345-47	
	USPS	Flat Plate	383	384	408	409		
		Rotary Press				459		
	Unwmkd.	Flat Plate			481	482-82 A	483-85	
		Offset			531	532-34B	535	
COIL 8½	USPS	Perf. Horizontal	390	391	410	411		
		Perf. Vertical	392	393	412	413	394-96	
PERF. 10	USPS							460
	USPS				424	425	426-30	431-40
	Unwmkd.	Flat Plate			462	463	464-69	470-78
		Rotary Press			543			
COIL 10	USPS	Perf. Horiz. Flat			441	442		
		Perf. Horiz. Rotary			448	449-50		
		Perf. Vert. Flat			443	444	445-47	
		Perf. Vert. Rotary			452	453-55	456-58	
	Unwmkd.	Perf. Horizontal			486	487-88	489	
		Perf. Vertical			490	491-92	493-96	497
PERF. 11	USPS			519				
	USPS					461		
	Unwmkd.	Flat Plate			498	499-500	501-07	508-18
		Rotary Press			*544-45	546		
		Offset			525	526-28B	529-30	
Perf. 12½	Unwmkd.	Offset			536			
11 x 10	Unwmkd.	Rotary			538	539-40	541	
10 x 11	Unwmkd.	Rotary			542			

⊄Design of #544 is 19 mm. wide x 22½ mm. high. #545 is 19½ to 20 mm. wide x 22 mm. high.

HOW TO USE THIS IDENTIFICATION CHART

Numbers referred to herein are from Scott's Standard Postage Stamp Catalog. To identify any stamp in this series, first check the type by comparing it with the illustrations at the top of the chart. Then check the perforations, and whether the stamp is single or double line watermarked or unwatermarked. With this information you can quickly find out the Standard Catalog number by checking down and across the chart. For example, a 1¢ Franklin, perf. 12, single line watermark, must be Scott's #374.

Size of Flat Plate Design

22mm

18½-19mm

Stamps printed by rotary press are always slightly wider or taller on issues prior to 1954. Measurements do not apply to booklet singles.

During the years 1912 through 1920, the 2¢ Washington design pictured below was issued and re-issued with slight variations which give rise to the many different types of this stamp. Certain of these types, as you will see by consulting a catalog of United States stamps, are far more valuable than others. The several variations in actual design are pictured and described below. For perforation, watermark and printing variations, see the handy indentification chart on the preceding page.

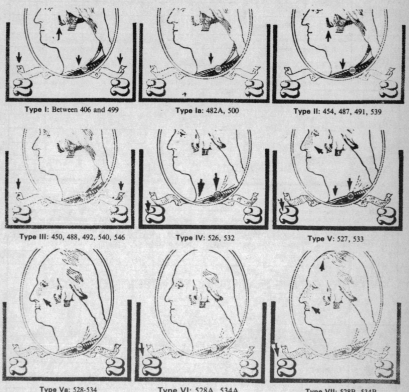

Type I: Between 406 and 499

Type Ia: 482A, 500

Type II: 454, 487, 491, 539

Type III: 450, 488, 492, 540, 546

Type IV: 526, 532

Type V: 527, 533

Type Va: 528-534

Type VI: 528A, 534A

Type VII: 528B, 534B

TYPE I — The ribbon at left above the figure "2" has one shading line in the first curve, while the ribbon at the right has one shading line in the second curve. Button of toga has a faint outline. Top line of toga, from button to front of throat, is very faint. Shading lines of the face, terminating in front of the ear, are not joined. Type I occurs on both flat and rotary press printings.

TYPE Ia — Similar to Type I except that all of the lines are stronger. Lines of the toga button are heavy. Occurs only on flat press printings.

TYPE II — Ribbons are shaded as in Type I. Toga button and shading lines to the left of it are heavy. The shading lines in front of the ear are joined and end in a strong vertically curved line (arrow). Occurs only on a rotary press printings.

TYPE III — Ribbons are shaded with two lines instead of one; otherwise similar to Type II. Occurs on rotary press printing only.

TYPE IV — Top line of toga is broken. Shading lines inside the toga button read "DID." The line of color in the left "2" is very thin and usually broken. Occurs on offset printings only.

TYPE V — Top line of toga is complete. Toga button has five vertical shaded lines. Line of color in the left "2" is very thin and usually broken. Nose shaded as shown in illustration. Occurs on offset printings only.

TYPE Va — Same as Type V except in shading dots of nose. Third row of dots from bottom has four dots instead of six. Also, the overall height of Type Va is 1/3 millimeter less than Type V. Occurs on offset printings only.

TYPE VI — Same as Type V except that the line of color in the left "2" is very heavy (arrow). Occurs on offset printing only.

TYPE VII — Line of color in left "2" is clear and continuous and heavier than in Types V or Va, but not as heavy as in Type VI. There are three rows of vertical dots (instead of two) in the shading of the upper lip, and additional dots have been added to the hair at the top of the head. Occurs on offset printings only.

Type I: Between 333 and 501

Type II: 484, 494, 502, 541

TYPE I. The top line of the toga is weak as are the top parts of the shading lines that join the toga line. The fifth shading line from the left (arrow) is partly cut away at the top. Also the line between the lip is thin. Occurs on flat and rotary press printings.

TYPE II. The top line of the toga is strong and the shading lines that join it are heavy and complete. The line between the lips is heavy. Occurs on flat and rotary press printings.

Type III: 529

Type IV: 530, 535

TYPE III. The top line of the toga is strong, but the fifth shading line from the left (arrow) is missing. The center line of the toga button consists of two short vertical lines with a dot between them. The "P" and "O" of "POSTAGE," are separated by a small line of color. Occurs on offset printings only.

TYPE IV. The shading lines of the toga are complete. The center line of the toga button consists of a single unbroken vertical line running through the dot in the center. The "P" and "O" of "POSTAGE" are joined. TYPE IV occurs only in offset printings.

TYPES OF THE 2¢ WASHINGTON DESIGN OF 1922-29

Type I has thin hair lines at top center of head.

Type II has three heavy hair lines (arrow) at top.

Type I: Between 554 and 634

Type II: 599A, 634A

ORIGINAL   REVISED   BOOKLET SINGLE

ORIGINAL has the vertical bar of the "¢" symbol pointing to the left part of the "E" of "POSTAGE." In the necktie area, there are complete downward sloping hatch lines which touch the right-hand side of the tie. (1288, 1305E)

REVISED has the vertical bar of the "¢" symbol pointing to the center of the "E" of "POSTAGE." In the tie, the downward sloping hatch lines are almost eliminated, while the lines angling upward do not touch the lower right-hand side of the tie. The third line from the bottom is very short, leaving a colorless spot. (1288d, 1305Ei)

BOOKLET SINGLE has the vertical bar of the "¢" symbol pointing more toward the "G" of "POSTAGE." The necktie is 4-1/2 millimeters long and is straightened down the center of the robe. The overall design size is smaller both vertically and horizontally. All copies have at least one straight edge. (1288B)

BOOKLET PANES are small sheets of stamps sold by the Post Office in booklet form. Most United States postage and airmail panes consist of a block of 6 stamps, or 5 stamps plus a label, that is straight-edged on all four sides but perforated between the stamps as illustrated. Booklet panes are usually collected unused, with the tab, or binding edge, attached.

Above: "sidewise coil".

Right: "endwise coil".

COIL STAMPS are stamps which come in long rolled strips, especially for use in vending machines, automatic affixing machines, etc. They have straight edges on two opposite sides and perforated edges on the other two sides. If the straight edges run up and down, the stamps are called "endwise coils"; if they run from side to side, they are called "sidewise coils." Coils are generally collected in singles, pairs or strips of four.

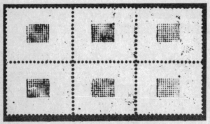

Block of six showing grill marks

GRILLS are raised impressions made in a stamp by pointed metal rollers, resembling the impressions made in a waffle by a waffle iron. The theory behind the grills used on the United States postage issues of 1867-71 was that the cancelling ink would soak into the broken fibers of the paper, thus preventing the stamp from being washed clean and used over again. If the grill impression is made from behind, so that the points show on the face of the stamp, the grill is said to be "points up." If done the opposite way, the grill is said to be "points down." Grills are further classified as "Grill A," "Grill B," etc., according to the type and size of the grill marks on the stamp. It should be remembered that a complete grill is not always found on any one stamp. Major varieties with grills are 79-101, 112-122 and 134-144.

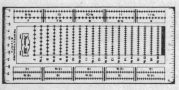

Perforation Gauge

PERFORATIONS around the edges of a stamp are measured by the number of perforation holes in a space of two centimeters, as "Perf. 11," "Perf. 12," etc. This sounds complicated but actually collectors use a simple measuring device called a perforation gauge which readily gives this information about any stamp. Where a stamp is identified by only one perforation number, it is perforated the same on all four sides; if two numbers are shown (e.g., 11 x 10-1/2), the first number indicates the top and bottom; the second the sides.

308

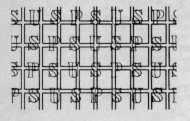

Double line watermark
PERIOD OF USE
Postage — 1895-1910

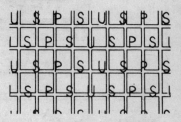

Single line watermark
PERIOD OF USE
Postage — 1910-1916

WATERMARKS are faint markings impressed into the paper during manufacture to help detect counterfeiting. Practically all United States postage stamps issued between the years 1895-1916 are watermarked "USPS" (United States Postal Service), either in single line or double line letters, as illustrated. Before 1895 and since 1916, all postage issues, except for Scott's #519 and some copies of the $1 "Presidential" — an error — are unwatermarked.

To see a watermark, place the stamp on a "watermark detector" and add a few drops of watermark fluid. The watermark — if there is one — will usually show clearly. From the illustrations it can be see that frequently only a part of a letter will appear.

HOW TO DISTINGUISH BETWEEN FLAT, ROTARY AND OFFSET PRINTINGS

FLAT PLATE means printed from flat metal plates or engravings.

ROTARY PRESS means printed from plates that are curved to fit around a cylinder. In the curving process, the designs of the stamp stretch slightly in the direction that the plate is curved, so that rotary press stamps issued prior to 1954 are always either slightly wider or slightly taller than the same designs printed from flat plates. Also, on rotary printings, one or more ridges have been forced into the paper to keep it from curling and these usually show across the back of the stamp. No such ridges are found in flat press stamps.

Left: *rotary press issue slightly taller than corresponding flat press design.*
Right: *rotary press stamp slightly wider than the stamp design printed from flat plates.*

OFFSET is a method of printing in which the plate transfers or "offsets" the design onto a rubber blanket which, in turn, transfers it to the paper. On stamps printed from flat press or rotary press plates (that is, engraved stamps), a relatively large amount of ink is deposited on the paper, giving the stamps a "rough" feeling. If you run a fingernail or metal edge lightly across the lines on such stamps, you can actually feel the ridges of ink. Offset stamps, on the other hand, have a smooth or "soapy" feeling. The ink lies down uniformly on the surface of the paper, and no ridges can be felt.

SPECIAL PRINTINGS are reprints, either from the original or from new engravings, of stamps previously issued. They are usually printed in limited quantities and for specific purposes, and can almost always be distinguished from the originals by differences in color perforations, gum, type of paper, etc. The largest single groups — the Special Printings of 1875 — consist of a complete set of all designs issued up to that date. They were prepared for display by the government at the Philadelphia Centennial Exposition of 1876. Another good example of a Special Printing is 1947 "CIPEX" souvenir sheet, shown at the front of this U.S. IDENTIFIER, which was printed as a souvenir of the Centenary International Philatelic Exposition held in New York in May, 1947.

NEW FOR 1987
'HERITAGE" VINYL
LOOSE-LEAF BINDERS

The New "Heritage" series of binders are a collector's delight: form and function combined! Each features sturdy, two post construction and ample capacity. The rich-looking virgin vinyl covers are solid in color with beautiful gold-tone lettering on the spine. A built-in label holder on the spine gives the option of organizing a collection however the collector wishes. All Harris album pages fit these binders.

F200	Standard Binder - 3-1/2" size, Grey & Gold	**$16.00**
F203	Statesman Binder - 2-1/2" size, Royal Blue & Gold	11.00
F208	Liberty Binder - 2-1/2" size, Azure Blue & Gold	10.00
F210	Masterwork Deluxe Binder - 3-1/2" size, Leather Brown & Gold	18.00
F222	Plate Block Binder - 3-1/2" size, Briarwood & Gold	16.00
F230	All-Purpose Binder - 2" size, Cherry Red & Gold	9.00
F260	Canada Binder - 2" size, Green & Gold	9.00
F262	Create-Your-Own Binder - 2" size, Green & Gold	9.00

"THE LIBERTY EXPERIENCE"

Our Liberty Albums offer comprehensive coverage of virtually every popular area of United States stamp collecting at a very affordable price. Compare price and quality! The "Liberty Experience" will win every time!

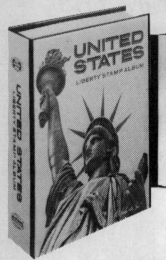

LIBERTY® UNITED STATES STAMP ALBUM $23.95

Includes United Nations Pages
Beautiful loose-leaf 100% illustrated

Without a doubt, the Harris Liberty is the most popular album for collectors of U.S. stamps. There are over 2,500 illustrations on pages that are printed on one side only on high quality white paper. Spaces are included for U.S. definitives, commemoratives, airmails, special delivery, postage dues and hunting permit stamps. This comprehensive album also includes spaces for Confederate States stamps, and the United Nations (complete). Rugged blue and green vinyl loose-leaf binder allows for maximum expansion. 256 sheets (512 pages). Update through September, 1986.

H108	U.S. Liberty Album	only **$23.95**
F108	U.S. Liberty Album, binder only	**10.00**

LIBERTY "HERITAGE" ALBUMS

VOLUME I — The same contents as our Liberty Album (H108) except that it is housed in our attractive "Heritage" Binder. The binder is 2-1/2" wide instead of 2" as in the H108 and has a label holder built into the spine.

H208	U.S. Liberty "Heritage" Album — Volume I	**$23.95**

THE "LIBERTY EXPERIENCE" CONTINUES!

VOLUME II — This special addition to the Heritage series contains U.S. Revenue stamps, U.S. Booklet Panes, Coil Pairs, Line Pairs and Plate # Strips of 3, U.S. Possessions and the Trust Territories. 160 sheets (320 pages). Updated through September, 1986. Housed in Liberty "Heritage" Binder.

H209 U.S. Liberty "Heritage" Album — Volume II $23.95

PAGES ONLY — The pages from H209 are offered separately so that collectors can use a regular Liberty Binder (F108) if they prefer.

W209 Liberty Volume II — Pages Only $15.95

TWO VOLUME SET

THE SET — Both volumes of the Liberty "Heritage" Album offered as a set in two Heritage Binders.

H207 Two Volume Liberty "Heritage" Album $45.00
F208 Heritage Liberty Expansion Binder 10.00

SPECIAL PAGES FOR YOUR
LIBERTY® ALBUM

W304 U.S. Postal Stationery Entires Innovative pages for all modern U.S. Entire Envelopes and Postal Cards, including virtually all issues from the 1930's to date. Includes Airletter Sheets and Postal Reply Cards. 144 sheets (288 pages) printed one side only $12.95

BLANK PAGES

Blank pages or convenient Speed-rille® pages with borders to match your U.S. albums. 64 sheets (128 pages) printed on both sides in each package; includes gummed titles.

W140 Speed-rille® extra pages $5.95
W141 Blank extra pages $5.95

PURCHASE RECORD PAGES

Keep an accurate record of your stamp purchases including costs, date of purchase, where boughtm etc., plus record of current value. Can be kept in your album or stored separately for security or estate purposes. 60 pages per set, printed on both sides.

W180 US/BNA Purchase Record Album Pages $3.95

THE "LIBERTY EXPERIENCE" CONTINUES!

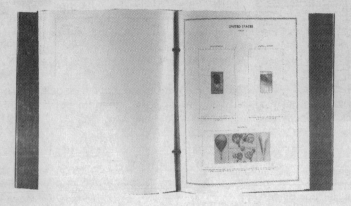

U.S. PLATE BLOCK ALBUM

This generous two-volume album houses your plate block collection in style. Volume A (480 pages printed one side only) includes commemoratives, air post, air post special delivery, special handling and certified mail 1901-1963 as well as regular postage and special delivery 1922-1963. Volume B (nearly 500 pages printed one side only) includes commemoratives, regular postage, air post and special delivery 1964 to present. Both volumes 100% illustrated; includes 1986 Supplement. Housed in new Liberty Heritage Binders (F208).

H219	U.S. Plate Block album, Volume A and B complete	....	$69.95
H220	U.S. Plate Block album, Volume A	....	36.95
H221	U.S. Plate Block album, Volume B	....	36.95
F208	Liberty Expansion Binder	....	10.00

NOTE: Binders for the above Plate Block Album are the same as used for the Liberty "Heritage" Album, forming a matching set.

"HERITAGE" PLATE BLOCK ALBUM
— A SINGLE-VOLUME ALBUM —

Brand-new single volume Plate Block album that contains everything included in both H120 and H121. Housed in our "Heritage" Plate Block binder (F222) which is 3-1/2" wide and contains plenty of room for the 480 sheets (960 pages). Heavy-duty Briarwood & Gold Binder.

| H222 | Heritage Plate Block Album | .... | $65.00 |
| F222 | Heritage Plate Block expansion binder | .... | 16.00 |

INDEPENDENCE® U.S. ALBUM

Contains the same information as the popular Liberty® Album, except that it doesn't have a U.N. section. Pages are printed both sides to make an excellent, low-priced album. Colorful vinyl binder. Expandable; loose-leaf. 208 pages (104 sheets).

H117   Independence Album $15.95
F117   Independence expansion binder, 1-1/4" size 8.00

FREEDOM II® U.S. ALBUM

Ideal for the young, beginning collector — an economical, softbound album with the same basic contents as the popular Independence® Album. Colorful cover. 208 pages (104 sheets) printed on both sides; cannot be expanded.

H170   Freedom II Album   .... only $7.95

FIRST DAY COVER
ALBUM $29.95

Handsome and durable loose-leaf album for all your covers

Luxurious leather-look album with gold-stamped title displays first day covers in clear vinyl pages. Two pockets per page; each 20-page album holds 80 covers back-to-back. Durable two-post loose-leaf binder makes it simple to add extra pages as your collection grows.

H139   Harris First Day Cover Album (U.S. and Foreign covers)   ...$29.95
W139   20 extra pages, 4" deep vinyl pockets 15.00
F139   First Day Cover Binder 17.00

CANADA & PROVINCES ALBUM

When your U.S. collection has nowhere to go, LOOK NORTH!

If you're at the point where only the rarest, costliest issues can advance your U.S. collection, or if you simply want a change, consider Canada. Canada offers the opportunity for 90% completion at an investment lower than the U.S. or many European countries. Canada's striking designs are considered by many to be superior to the United States', and it is acclaimed for its strict adherence to its own history and heritage for stamp subjects.

The handsome, comprehensive and fully illustrated Harris Canada Album offers over 400 artistically arranged pages of identifying photos, each framed and captioned. Important information such as color, perforation variety and paper type provided when necessary.

Includes all Canada issues from 1851 to date, including British Columbia & Vancouver Island, New Brunswick, Newfoundland and Prince Edward Island. Definitive and Commemorative Postage, Semi-Postals, Air Post, Air Post Special Delivery, miniature panes and phosphor tagged issues. Only great rarities excluded.

Sturdy loose-leaf binder with washable vinyl cover lets you expand or create specialty sections. New -issue supplements published yearly.

H160	Harris Canada Album	$29.95
W140	64 Matching Speed-rille® pages	5.95
W141	64 Matching Blank pages	5.95
F160	Canada expansion binder, 1-3/4" size	12.00

THE NEW STANDARD FOR THE INDUSTRY—
MASTERWORK DELUXE!

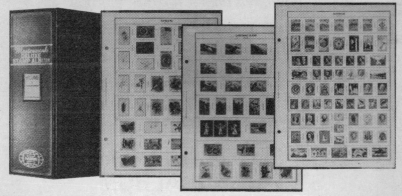

Our major project for 1987 is the introduction of our new "Masterwork Deluxe" Album — a massive four-volume 3700 page worldwide album containing space for more than 175,000 stamps with at least 100,000 illustrations.

The Masterwork Deluxe Album divides naturally into the Americas, Europe, U.S.S.R., Asia, Africa, and Oceania, or it can be divided between British and Non-British issues. That provides maximum flexibility and growth opportunity, all at an affordable price.

This album system holds the stamps that collectors might wish to acquire today, with particular emphasis on issues of the last 15-20 years. Each present-day country ends on a left-hand page so that supplements can be added in proper order. Each country is complete through the 1986 supplement contents and can be updated annually with the Harris Master Supplement.

Binders are handsome leather-brown vinyl over sturdy board with screwpost construction. Spine width is 3-1/2" with special label holder to permit personalized labeling.

H211	**Masterwork Deluxe Volume I** The Americas & Oceania	**$75.00**
H212	**Masterwork Deluxe Volume II** Europe (except U.S.S.R.)	**75.00**
H213	**Masterwork Deluxe Volume III** U.S.S.R. and Asia	**75.00**
H214	**Masterwork Deluxe Volume IV** Africa (Available 10/87)	**75.00**
H210	**The Complete Four-Volume Masterwork Deluxe Album** (H211, H212, H213, H214) (Avaiable 10/87)	**275.00**
F210	**Masterwork Deluxe expansion binder**	**18.00**

WORLDWIDE STAMPS ALBUMS

All albums have pages for U.S. stamps

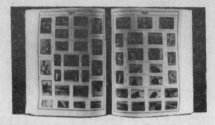

TWO-VOLUME "HERITAGE" STANDARD® ALBUM

This giant two-volume album covers all stamp-issuing countries. Space for 90,000 stamps; nearly 50,000 illustrations! Includes Worldwide Stamp Identifier and Collector's Dictionary, as well as geographical information and other helpful features. Housed in two "Heritage" Standard Binders. Almost 1800 pages printed on both sides.

H200	Two-Volume Standard® Album, complete	.... $95.00
F200	Standard® Expansion Binder - 3-1/2" size	.... 18.00

STATESMAN® ALBUM

Our most popular loose-leaf album! Covers all stamp-issuing countries, with space for more than 25,000 stamps. Includes interesting historical and geographical information. Vinyl loose-leaf binder. 560 pages (280 sheets) printed on both sides.

H103	Statesman® Album	.... $32.95
F103	Statesman® Expansion Binder - 2-1/2" size	.... 12.00

STATESMAN "HERITAGE" ALBUM

Same pages as the regular Statesman Album (H103) housed in the new "Heritage" Statesman binder.

H203	Statesman "Heritage" Album	.... $31.95
F203	Statesman "Heritage" Expansion Binder	.... 11.00

ALL-PURPOSE VINYL BINDER

Durable vinyl screw-post binder accommodates extra pages, Speed-rille® pages and all Harris supplements.

F130	All-Purpose Binder	.... $8.00

WORLDWIDE STAMP ALBUMS

TRAVELER® ALBUM

This excellent starter album has space for 10,000 stamps from the most popular countries. New headings feature the philatelic history of each stamp-issuing country. Brightly-colored loose-leaf chipboard binder. 272 pages (136 sheets) printed on both sides.

H175	Traveler® Album	$15.95
F175	Traveler® (chipboard) Expansion Binder	8.00

ADVENTURER II® ALBUM

Start a child collecting with this inexpensive softbound version of the Traveler® Album. Includes educational philatelic histories. Cannot be updated with supplements. 272 pages (136 sheets) printed both sides.

H171	Adventurer II® Album	$7.95

BLANK PAGES FOR WORLDWIDE ALBUMS

Speed-rille® Album Pages. Faint guide lines help you make neat, attractive arrangements without a lot of measuring. Use them to expand your album or create your own specialty pages. 128 pages (64 sheets) each package, printed on both sides with borders to match your worldwide albums. Includes 850 dry-gummed titles.

W150	Speed-rille® Worldwide Album Pages	$5.95

Blank Album Pages. Bordered blank pages to fit your loose-leaf worldwide albums. 128 pages (64 sheets) printed on both sides in each package. Includes 850 dry-gummed titles.

W151	Blank Worldwide Pages	$5.95

PURCHASE RECORD PAGES

Keep an accurate record of your purchases and current values on these special pages designed to fit into your worldwide album. 60 pages per set printed both sides.

W181	Worldwide Purchase Record Pages	$3.95

HARRIS SUPPLEMENTS

U.S. LIBERTY SUPPLEMENTS

NOTE: Can also be used in the Harris Independence Album. Includes United Nations Stamps.

X108Y	1986 Liberty	....	$3.95
X108X	1985 Liberty	....	2.95
X108W	1984 Liberty	....	2.95
X108U	1983 Liberty	....	2.95

U.S. PLATE BLOCK SUPPLEMENTS

X109Y	1986 Plate Block	....	$2.95
X109X	1985 Plate Block	....	3.95
X109W	1984 Plate Block	....	3.95
X109U	1983 Plate Block	....	3.95

U.S. CLASSIC SUPPLEMENTS

X113Y	1986 Classic	....	$3.95
X113X	1985 Classic	....	3.95
X113W	1984 Classic	....	3.95
X113U	1983 Classic	....	3.95

Please note: Supplements published in January of each year. Our 1986 supplements include issues released up to September 30, 1986. Supplements prior to those listed are out of print.

WORLDWIDE SUPPLEMENTS

X100Y	1986 Master	....	$6.95
X100X	1985 Master	....	5.95
X100W	1984 Master	....	5.95
X100U	1983 Master	....	5.95

CANADA SUPPLEMENTS

X160Y	1986 Canada	....	$1.95
X160X	1985 Canada	....	2.95
X160W	1984 Canada	....	2.95
X160U	1983 Canada	....	2.95

UNITED NATIONS SUPPLEMENTS

Purchase Liberty Supplements for later issues.

X165W	1984 U.N.	....	$2.95
X165U	1983 U.N.	....	2.95

STAMP COLLECTING KITS

UNITED STATES LIBERTY® KIT

The highlight of this exceptional kit is the comprehensive Liberty® U.S. Stamp Album. The fun starts right away with 100 different U.S. postage stamps, a magnifier, 600 stamp hinges, tongs. perforation gauge, PLUS U.S. State Flags and Presidential Portrait seals and a 22" x 34" U.S. Stamp Map. All in a handsome gift box.

L108   Liberty Kit (complete, gift-boxed) $37.95

INDEPENDENCE KIT

Everything you'll need to start a U.S. collection — the expandable but economical Independence® Album, 100 different U.S. postage stamps, a magnifier, 300 stamp hinges and U.S. State Flag and Presidential Portrait seals. Attractively gift-boxed.

L174   Independence Kit (complete, gift-boxed) $21.95

STATESMAN® KIT

We started with the popular Statesman® Album. Then we added all the essentials for starting or expanding your worldwide collection. The Statesman® Kit includes 300 different worldwide stamps, Flags of the World and U.S. President seals, 600 stamp hinges, stamp tongs, magnifier, and a 22" x 34" World Stamp Map.

L103   Statesman® Kit $43.95

TRAVELER® KIT

Our economical loose-leaf album kit, built around the Traveler® Album, with 300 different worldwide stamps, 200 Flags of the World seals, 300 stamp hinges, and a magnifier. An excellent starter kit.

L175   Traveler® Kit $21.95

STAMP COLLECTING ACCESSORIES

W152 **GLASSINE INTERLEAVES,** 100 transparent sheets protect stamps in albums **$5.95**

29001 **HOW TO COLLECT STAMPS GUIDE,** 1987 edition includes everything you need to know about stamp collecting, 224 pages softbound **$2.95**

Y720 **FLAGS OF THE WORLD,** 200 different orinted in true colors, perforated and gummed **$1.59**

Y723 **U.S. STATE FLAGS,** flags of all 50 states in beautiful color, perforated and gummed .... **.99¢**

Y724 **U.S. PRESIDENTS,** Washington thorugh Reagan in full color, perforated and gummed .... **.99¢**

Y801 **POCKET STOCK BOOK,** 5 tag stock pages w/ pockets, 4-1/4" x 7-1/4" **$2.75**

Y802 **HANDY STOCK BOOK,** 10 tag stock pages with pockets, 6" x 9" **$5.00**

H140 **MINT SHEET ALBUM,** cardboard covered book holds 96 sheets back-to-back in glassine pocket pages **$7.95**

Y738 **STAMP HINGES,** each package contains 2,000 pre-gummed hinges **$2.49**

Y781 **STAMP TONGS,** high-quality tongs for handling stamps safely **$2.25**

Y783 **PERFORATION GAUGE,** sturdy metal gauge measures perforations from 7 to 16-1/2" **$1.95**

Y753 **FOLDING MAGNIFIER,** 1-3/4" lens with 3x magnification folds into its vinyl handle for convenient carrying **$2.95**

THE SCOTT INTERNATIONAL ALBUM
The finest album the philatelic world has ever known!

If you're a serious worldwide collector there is only one album for you. The comprehensive one: Scott's International. It's the ultimate worldwide album. The Scott International is a full philatelic library with over 13,000 spacious pages for almost 200,000 world issues. Every space is illustrated or identifies each stamp and pages are chemically neutralized to protect your stamp treasures from deterioration. Start with one or more jumbo binder ($15.95 each) and purchase exactly the pages you want, when you want them. The full library is separated into 24 parts. You purchase pages separately, so you can start wherever you want and build your own album set. For the sophisticated collector there is no other choice. The International is the most treasured album in the world of stamp collecting. See next page for listing of pages.

SCOTT INTERNATIONAL BINDERS

Hinged post construction, blue reinforced binding, silver lettering. Each jumbo binder holds 400 pages.

F200Y	Scott International Binder, each	**$15.95**
F201Y	International Slipcase	15.95

SCOTT CATALOGS

Scott Worldwide catalogs list stamps of the entire world in four convenient volumes. The Scott numbers and identification of stamps are used everywhere and a Scott catalog is needed by every serious collector. Prices are given for both unused and used stamps. We ship the latest issue when you order.

Y865	Volume 1: United States, United Nations, and British Commonwealth of Nations	**$27.50**
Y866	Volume 2: Countries of the World, A-F	27.50
Y867	Volume 3: Countries of the World, G-O	27.50
Y869	Volume 4: Countries of the World, P-Z	27.50
Y686	Scott U.S. Specialized Catalog, Latest Edition	27.50

SCOTT INTERNATIONAL ALBUM PAGES

(When a part has an "A" and a "B" section, both sections are required to cover the time period stated in the listing.)

W200Z-1	Part 1A, 1840-1940, pages only	$89.95
W200Z-2	Part 1B, 1840, 1940, pages only	89.95
W200A-1	Part 2A, 1940-1949, pages only	89.95
W200A-2	Part 2B, 1940-1949, pages only	89.95
W200B-1	Part 3A, 1949-55, pages only	89.95
W200B-2	Part 3B, 1949-55, pages only	89.95
W200C-1	Part 4A, 1956-60, pages only	89.95
W200C-2	Part 4B, 1956-60, pages only	89.95
W200D	Part 5, 1960-1963, pages only	39.95
W200D-1	Part 5A, 1963-1965, pages only	39.95
W200E	Part 6, 1965-66, pages only	39.95
W200E-1	Part 6A, 1966-1968, pages only	39.95
W200F-1	Part 7A, 1968-1971, pages only	89.95
W200F-2	Part 7B, 1968-1971, pages only	89.95
W200G-1	Part 8A, 1971-73, pages only	89.95
W200G-2	Part 8B, 1971-73, pages only	89.95
W200H	Part 9, 1973-74, pages only	89.95
W200J	Part 10, 1074-75, pages only	89.95
W200K	Part 11, 1975-1976, pages only	89.95
W200L	Part 12, 1976-77, pages only	89.95
W200M	Part 13, 1977-1978, pages only	39.95
W200N	Part 14, 1978, pages only	34.95
W200P	Part 15, 1979, pages only	34.95
W200R	Part 16, 1980, pages only	34.95
W200S	Part 17, 1981, pages only	34.95
W200T	Part 18, 1982, pages only	39.95
W200U	Part 19, 1983, pages only	49.95
W200V	Part 20, 1984, pages only	49.95

SCOTT SPECIALTY ALBUMS

(Includes binder — through 1985)

H900	Great Britain	$69.95
H901	British Europe (Cyprus, Gibraltar, Malta)	56.95
H902	Canada	44.95
H903	France	89.95
H904	Germany, 1868-1949	55.95
H905	Germany, 1949-1985	78.95
H906	Japan	94.95
H907	Scandinavia, 1855-1965	67.95
H908	Scandinavia, 1966 to date	67.95
H909	Vatican	67.95
H910	Ireland	49.95
H911	Channel Islands	55.00
H912	Australia & Dependencies	77.50
H913	New Zealand	77.50
H914	Austria	67.50
H915	Germany, East	67.50
H916	Greece	55.00
H917	Luxembourg	55.00
H918	Monaco & Fr. Andorra	67.50
H919	Israel	49.95

APPLICATION FOR HARRIS CREDIT PLAN

Fill out and sign: Please read important information on back. Include $15 down payment if you are sending an order with your application. New members must be 18 or older.

Rank _____

Time In Service _____

Pay Grade _____

Name of Commanding Officer _____

IMPORTANT: Form must be completely filled out in order to be considered for membership.

Name _____ Date _____

Address _____ S.S. # _____

City _____ State _____ Zip _____

Phone # _____

Employer Name _____ Phone # _____

Address _____ Position _____

City _____ State _____ Zip _____

Date of Birth _____ # of Dependents _____

★ ★

If Response is None, Please Indicate None

Name of Bank _____

Type of Account _____ Account # _____

Address of Bank _____

City _____ State _____ Zip _____

	Exp. Date	Acct. #	Bank Name and Address
VISA			
MasterCard			
American Express			
Diners Club			

Name & Address of Landlord or Mortgage Bank _____

_____ Account # _____

Bank with Installment Loan _____

_____ Account # _____

List 2 places where you presently have charge accounts:

Name & Address _____

_____ Account # _____

Name & Address _____

_____ Account # _____

Please mail this application to:
H.E. HARRIS & CO., INC., BOX 7082, PORTSMOUTH, NH 03801
**Be sure to read, sign and return the agreement
on reverse side.**

H.E. HARRIS & CO., INC.
CREDIT PLAN AGREEMENT

1. In consideration of H.E. HARRIS & CO., INC. extending credit to me under its Harris Credit plan, I agree to the following terms and conditions: I can avoid incurring a FINANCE CHARGE by paying the New Balance in full provided that such payment is received within 28 days of the Closing Date shown on the Periodic Statement. If I do not timely pay the entire New Balance a FINANCE CHARGE will be computed monthly on the Previous Balance after applying payments and credits (Adjusted Balance Method). No FINANCE CHARGE will be added for a billing period in which there was no Previous Balance or during which payments or credits equal or exceed the Preious Balance. I may at any time pay the total amount owing (New Balance) on the account. Each month I have the option of paying the New Balance, 1/8 of the New Balance or any amount in-between. Minimum monthly payment will be no less than $15.00. Each payment received by H.E. Harris & Co., Inc. shall be applied to merchandise and services as follows: First to unpaid FINANCE CHARGE, then to any unpaid Previous Balance and then to new purchases.

2. I may pay the Minimum Payment Due shown on the periodic statement. If I avail myself of this option, I will incur and pay a FINANCE CHARGE. The FINANCE CHARGE is applied to the Previous Month's Balance after deducting payments, credits and returns (Adjusted Balance Method). The FINANCE CHARGE is determined by multiplying the appropriate Periodic Rate by the balance subject to FINANCE CHARGE shown in the table below.

	MONTHLY PERIODIC RATE	ANNUAL PERCENTAGE RATE
All states, U.S. territories and Canada	.75%	9.00%

3. If I default in making any required payment in full when due, H.E. Harris & Co., Inc. may declare the unpaid New Balance immediately due and may charge collection costs and attorney's fees to the extent permitted by law.

4. Subsequent purchases may be added to my account from time to time provided my account is in good standing.

5. I understand and agree that this Credit Agreement and the disclosures herein is not a commitment by H.E. Harris & Co., Inc. to extend credit.

6. On all first purchases on new accounts a minimum down payment of $15.00, with approved credit, will be required.

7. H.E. Harris & Co., Inc. is authorized to investigate my credit record and verify my credit, and to report to proper persons and bureaus my performance of this Agreement.

8. H.E. Harris & Co., Inc. reserves the right to change generally for all customers, from time to time, the terms of this Agreement in accordance with applicable law and on notice to me by postage prepaid of such change or changes.

9. I, the buyer, have read this Agreement and agree to its terms and conditions acknowledge receipt of a copy thereof.

10. A copy of your rights under the Federal Truth in Lending Act will be mailed to you upon acceptance into the Harris Credit Plan.

H.E. HARRIS & CO., INC.
By

| Signature | Seller's Approval |

H.E. HARRIS & CO., INC.
CREDIT PLAN AGREEMENT
CUSTOMER COPY

1. In consideration of H.E. HARRIS & CO., INC. extending credit to me under its Harris Credit plan, I agree to the following terms and conditions: I can avoid incurring a FINANCE CHARGE by paying the New Balance in full provided that such payment is received within 28 days of the Closing Date shown on the Periodic Statement. If I do not timely pay the entire New Balance a FINANCE CHARGE will be computed monthly on the Previous Balance after applying payments and credits (Adjusted Balance Method). No FINANCE CHARGE will be added for a billing period in which there was no Previous Balance or during which payments or credits equal or exceed the Preious Balance. I may at any time pay the total amount owing (New Balance) on the account. Each month I have the option of paying the New Balance, 1/8 of the New Balance or any amount in-between. Minimum monthly payment will be no less than $15.00. Each payment received by H.E. Harris & Co., Inc. shall be applied to merchandise and services as follows: First to unpaid FINANCE CHARGE, then to any unpaid Previous Balance and then to new purchases.

2. I may pay the Minimum Payment Due shown on the periodic statement. If I avail myself of this option, I will incur and pay a FINANCE CHARGE. The FINANCE CHARGE is applied to the Previous Month's Balance after deducting payments, credits and returns (Adjusted Balance Method). The FINANCE CHARGE is determined by multiplying the appropriate Periodic Rate by the balance subject to FINANCE CHARGE shown in the table below.

	MONTHLY PERIODIC RATE	ANNUAL PERCENTAGE RATE
All states, U.S. territories and Canada	.75%	9.00%

3. If I default in making any required payment in full when due, H.E. Harris & Co., Inc. may declare the unpaid New Balance immediately due and may charge collection costs and attorney's fees to the extent permitted by law.

4. Subsequent purchases may be added to my account from time to time provided my account is in good standing.

5. I understand and agree that this Credit Agreement and the disclosures herein is not a commitment by H.E. Harris & Co., Inc. to extend credit.

6. On all first purchases on new accounts a minimum down payment of $15.00, with approved credit, will be required.

7. H.E. Harris & Co., Inc. is authorized to investigate my credit record and verify my credit, and to report to proper persons and bureaus my performance of this Agreement.

8. H.E. Harris & Co., Inc. reserves the right to change generally for all customers, from time to time, the terms of this Agreement in accordance with applicable law and on notice to me by postage prepaid of such change or changes.

9. I, the buyer, have read this Agreement and agree to its terms and conditions acknowledge receipt of a copy thereof.

10. A copy of your rights under the Federal Truth in Lending Act will be mailed to you upon acceptance into the Harris Credit Plan.

HOW TO WRITE YOUR ORDER

Please use the Order Blank

1. Print name and address information complete-including Zip code.
2. Specify quantity, country, description of items, catalog number, and choice of condition.
3. Check whether stamp is used or unused.
4. Fill in retail price on each item.
5. Figure postage, handling, and insurance from chart on this page.
6. Make payment in U.S. funds to H.E. Harris & Co., Inc. Canada residents should write "U.S." after numerical dollar amount on check, or purchase money order in U.S. funds. If paying in Canadian funds, add 40% to total order.

Example:

Qty	Country & Catalog Number also specify single, plate block, etc.	Condition	Unused	Used	H.E.H. Price	Leave Blank
1	U.S. 651	FINE		✓	.95	
1	U.S. 660	F, NH	✓		6.50	
1	U.S. 743 Pl. Block	F, NH	✓		19.75	
1	Canada 141	F, NH	✓		3.95	
1	H108 Liberty Album				23.95	
TOTAL ALL PAGES					55.10	
INSURANCE, POSTAGE AND HANDLING					2.50	
TOTAL AMOUNT					57.60	

30-DAY MONEY-BACK GUARANTEE. All stamps, albums and supplied are sold by Harris on a 30-day money-back guarantee. You must be pleased or you may return any item for credit or refund. (Please enclose original order and indicate replacement or refund.)

NOTE ON CONDITION. When ordering from this catalog, specify the condition and list the price from the appropriate column in this catalog.

INSURANCE, POSTAGE AND HANDLING CHART
Charges include delivery, insurance, and handling. They defray only part of the guaranteed charges-we absorb the rest. Delivery of your order is guaranteed.

Stamp/Covers Only	**$1.75**
Mixed Stamps/Covers and Supplies	3.00
All Canadian Orders	5.00

**All Canada Customs Duties must be paid by the customer.
Actual postage and handling to all foreign countries
will be billed.**

H.E. HARRIS & CO., INC.
Box 7082, Portsmouth, NH 03801
MINIMUM CASH ORDER — $5.00 CHARGE — $15.00   Date
Prices in this edition are effective through August 31, 1988

Harris Credit Plan or Credit Card Number

Charge my purchase to:
- ☐ MasterCard
- ☐ VISA
- ☐ Chargex
- ☐ Amer. Exp.
- ☐ HCP

INTERBANK NO.:   EXP. DATE: Month   Year

USB88

Signature _____

Name _____
(Please Print or Type)

Street _____

City/State/Zip _____

Phone (in case of question about order) (   ) _____
Moved since your last order? If so please give your old address:

Street _____

City/State/Zip _____

All adjustment inquiries must be accompanied by this order blank.

Qty.	Country & Cat. No. also specify sing., pl. blk., etc.	Cond.	Unused	Used	H.E.H. Price	Leave Blank
TOTAL ALL PAGES						
Insurance, Postage and Handling (see Chart — preceding page)						
TOTAL AMOUNT						
Canadian Resident Paying in Canadian Funds must add 40% (See note/Terms and information)						
TOTAL ENCLOSED						

Order Blank, Page 2.

Qty.	Country & Cat. No. also specify sing., pl. blk., etc.	Cond.	Unused	Used	H.E.H. Price	Leave Blank
		TOTAL OF THIS PAGE				

CHARGE YOUR ORDER Read and sign credit agreement on preceding pages and attach to order with $15.00 down payment.

Box 7082, Portsmouth, NH 03801

MINIMUM CASH ORDER — $5.00 CHARGE — $15.00 Date

Prices in this edition are effective through August 31, 1988

Harris Credit Plan or Credit Card Number

INTERBANK NO.:

EXP. DATE: | Month | Year

Charge my purchase to:
- ☐ MasterCard
- ☐ VISA
- ☐ Chargex
- ☐ Amer. Exp.
- ☐ HCP

USB88

Signature _____

Name _____
(Please Print or Type)

Street _____

City/State/Zip _____

Phone (in case of question about order) ( ) _____
Moved since your last order? If so please give your old address:

Street _____

City/State/Zip _____

All adjustment inquiries must be accompanied by this order blank.

Qty.	Country & Cat. No. also specify sing., pl. blk., etc.	Cond.	Unused	Used	H.E.H. Price	Leave Blank
TOTAL ALL PAGES						
Insurance, Postage and Handling (see Chart — preceding page)						
TOTAL AMOUNT						
Canadian Resident Paying in Canadian Funds must add 40% (See note/Terms and information)						
TOTAL ENCLOSED						

Order Blank, Page 2.

Qty.	Country & Cat. No. also specify sing., pl. blk., etc.	Cond.	Unused	Used	H.E.H. Price	Leave Blank
TOTAL OF THIS PAGE						

CHARGE YOUR ORDER   Read and sign credit agreement on preceding pages and attach to order with $15.00 down payment.